INDIGENOUS LANGUAGES AND

THE PROMISE OF ARCHIVES

**New Visions in Native American
and Indigenous Studies**

SERIES EDITORS

Margaret D. Jacobs
Robert J. Miller

Indigenous Languages and the Promise of Archives

EDITED BY ADRIANNA LINK,
ABIGAIL SHELTON, AND PATRICK SPERO

CO-PUBLISHED BY THE UNIVERSITY OF NEBRASKA
PRESS AND THE AMERICAN PHILOSOPHICAL SOCIETY

© 2021 by the Board of Regents of the University of Nebraska

All rights reserved

Library of Congress Cataloging-in-Publication Data
Names: Translating across Time and Space: Endangered Languages, Cultural Revitalization, and the Work of History (Symposium), (2016: Philadelphia, Pa.) | Link, Adrianna, editor. | Shelton, Abigail, editor. | Spero, Patrick, editor. | Center for Native American and Indigenous Research sponsoring body. | American Philosophical Society sponsoring body.
Title: Indigenous languages and the promise of archives / edited by Adrianna Link, Abigail Shelton, and Patrick Spero. Description: [Lincoln]: Co-published by the University of Nebraska Press and the American Philosophical Society, 2021. | Series: New visions in Native American and indigenous studies | Papers presented at the symposium, Translating across Time and Space: Endangered Languages, Cultural Revitalization, and the Work of History, hosted by the Center for Native American and Indigenous Research (CNAIR) at the American Philosophical Society in Philadelphia, from October 13-15, 2016. | Includes bibliographical references and index. | Summary: "Explores new applications of the American Philosophical Society's Library materials as twenty-first century scholars seek to partner on collaborative projects, often through the application of digital technologies, that assist ongoing efforts at cultural and linguistic revitalization movements within Native communities"— Provided by publisher.
Identifiers: LCCN 2020040354
ISBN 9781496224330 (hardback)
ISBN 9781496224620 (paperback)
ISBN 9781496225184 (epub)
ISBN 9781496225191 (mobi)
ISBN 9781496225207 (pdf)
Subjects: LCSH: Indians of North America—Languages—Congresses. | Language revival—United States—Congresses. | Language revival—Canada—Congresses. | Indians of North America—Archives—Congresses. | Indians of North America—Library resources—Congresses.
Classification: LCC PM206 .T73 2016 | DDC 497—dc23
LC record available at https://lccn.loc.gov/2020040354

Set in Merope by Laura Buis.

CONTENTS

List of Illustrations   ix

Preface by Brian Carpenter   xi

Acknowledgments   xvii

Introduction: Collaborative Research and Language Revitalization: Toward a Relational Ontology across Time and Space   1
Regna Darnell

Part 1. Decolonizing Archives   25
Commentary by Robert J. Miller

1. Decolonial Futures of Sharing: "Protecting Our Voice," Intellectual Property, and Penobscot Nation Language Materials   31
Jane Anderson and James E. Francis Sr.

2. The Legacy of Hunter-Gatherers at the American Philosophical Society: Frank G. Speck, James M. Crawford, and Revitalizing the Yuchi Language   63
Richard A. Grounds

3. Supporting Researchers of Indigenous Vernacular Archives   99
Lisa Conathan

Part 2. Revitalization Tools   121
Commentary by Bethany Wiggin

4. Locally Contingent and Community-Dependent: Tools and Technologies for Indigenous Language Mobilization   125
Jennifer Carpenter, Annie Guerin, Michelle Kaczmarek, Gerry Lawson, Kim Lawson, Lisa P. Nathan, Mark Turin

5. Translating American Indian Sign Language from the 1800s to the Present Day   156
Jeffrey Davis

Part 3. Power and Language   189
Commentary by Diana E. Marsh

6. "The Indian Republic of Letters": Scholarly Networks and Indigenous Knowledge in Philology   197
Sean P. Harvey

7. Literacy, Cross-Cultural Interaction, and Colonialism: The Making of a Nineteenth-Century Nez Perce Mission Primer   227
Anne Keary

8. Across Space and Time: Letters from the Dakota People, 1838–1878   285
Gwen N. Westerman and Glenn M. Wasicuna

Part 4. Landscape and Language   305
Commentary by Michael Silverstein

9. *Cúz̓lhkan Sqwéqwel* ('I Am Going to Tell a Story'): Revitalizing Stories to Strengthen Fish, Water, and the Upper St'át'imc Salish Language   309
Sarah Carmen Moritz

10. No Time Like the Present: Living American Indian
    Languages, Landscapes, and Histories   349
    Bernard C. Perley, Margaret Ann Noodin, and Cary Miller

    Part 5. Creative Collaborations   375
    Commentary by Regna Darnell

11. "Going Over" and Coming Back: Reclaiming the *Cherokee
    Singing Book* for Contemporary Language Revitalization   379
    Sara Snyder Hopkins

12. Teaching Wailaki: Archives, Interpretation, and
    Collaboration   399
    Kayla Begay, Justin Spence, and Cheryl Tuttle

    Part 6. Transforming Collecting   425
    Commentary by Jennifer R. O'Neal

13. Museums and the Revitalization of Endangered Languages
    and Knowledge   429
    Gwyneira Isaac

14. *Shriniinlii* ('Fix It'): The Grease Mechanics of Translating
    Gwich'in   461
    Craig Mishler and Kenneth Frank

    Conclusion: The Power of Words, Relationships,
    and Archives   479
    Mary S. Linn

    Contributors   491

    Index   503

ILLUSTRATIONS

Figures

1. Andrew No Wife, syllabary practice with commentary (detail), undated (ca. 1880) — 104
2. Micmac Catholic Prayers (detail), undated (ca. 1825) — 116
3. Language mobilization nexus — 146
4. APS historical and literary report to George Izard, May 6, 1825 — 190
5. Chipeway (Chippewa) spellings for the schools, Canada Missionary Society, 1828 — 192
6. Letters in Dakota translated by Ella C. Deloria from Indians at the mission schools — 193
7. Lapwai mission school notebook, ca.1842 — 248
8. Detail of a Dakota song stick — 288
9. Pond alphabet — 289
10. Wanmdi Okiya's letter to Mato Ḣota (Gideon Pond), 1849 — 290

11.	Map of 1863 Dakota removal from Minnesota	292
12.	Transcribed and translated letter of Wanmdi Okiya, 1849	295
13.	Gwenis washed ashore at Anderson Lake, Seton Portage, Tsal'álh	313
14.	Watching for Gwenis at Anderson Lake shore	316
15.	Sacred winter fire for the Gwenis season	325
16.	Title page of *Pixem muta7 I7was*	330
17.	Example page from *Pixem muta7 I7was*	331
18.	*Lillooet Pictographs* by James Teit	332
19.	*Lillooet Pictographs* bear paws inspiration	333
20.	Collaborative installation *Experiencing Native North America*	351
21.	GRASAC visit, 2012	437
22.	Wauja visit, 2016	440
23.	Wanapum visit, 2015, Patrick Wyena and Clayton Buck	442
24.	Vadzaih Tth'an Oozhri': caribou bone names	473

Tables

1.	Historical and contemporary documentation of American Indian Sign Language	176
2.	Documentary linguistic fieldwork of the PISL variety	178
3.	Selected terms from the *Cherokee Singing Book*	394
4.	Transcriptional correspondences in Wailaki documentation	408

PREFACE

Brian Carpenter

The American Philosophical Society (APS), located in Philadelphia, resides in the broader region of Lenapehoking, the homelands of past, present, and future generations of the Lenape people. Since its founding in 1743, the APS has benefited from its occupation of this Lenape land. One of the main ways it has done so is in availing itself of the area's long-standing use as a meeting ground and place of exchange for people from many Native nations. This tradition began long before the arrival of European settlers, continued through the early colonial periods (when the APS got started), and continues to this day in gatherings such as the one that brought together the chapters in this volume.

On October 13–15, 2016, the Center for Native American and Indigenous Research (CNAIR) at the APS hosted Translating across Time and Space: Endangered Languages, Cultural Revitalization, and the Work of History, a symposium that drew together university- and Indigenous community-based scholars in multiple areas of expertise, including Indigenous-language speakers, activists, and teachers, from throughout North America. The symposium's themes centered on the reclamation, preservation, and restoration of Indigenous languages, both historically and in the present day; practices surrounding translation and translators over the last five centuries; the work of language and cultural revitalization; and models for collaboration in all of these areas. The symposium coincided with the APS Museum's 2016 exhibition, *Gathering Voices: Thomas Jefferson and Native America*, which told the history of the study of Indigenous languages of North America through manuscripts, images, and audio from the APS Library.

The APS served as a fitting venue for the conversations that animated this symposium, given its key role in that history, as a site and symbol of settler-colonial intellectual power, and its present-day initiatives in decolonizing its practices through establishing equitable relationships with the Indigenous communities that now constitute the majority of researchers utilizing the Indigenous archival materials it houses.[1] The APS Library is the oldest and one of the largest repositories in North America of materials on the languages, cultures, histories, and continuing presence of Indigenous people of the Americas. Its activities in this area first emerged from the interests of Thomas Jefferson, president of the APS from 1797 to 1815, who created printed lists of words he surmised would be universal to all languages and sent them to military officers, diplomats, and missionaries he knew would interact with Native people. By comparing these lists, he hoped to intuit historical "affinities" among Native nations—in part for purposes of military intelligence—from which he developed federal Indian policies that enabled war and genocide over the coming decades. One of his main successors at the APS, the linguist Peter Stephen Du Ponceau, encouraged Jefferson and others to give manuscripts of this kind to the APS Library, making Du Ponceau the first archivist of documents in Indigenous languages in the United States. As a result the APS became the main repository and research center in North America for information on Indigenous languages of the Americas. After Du Ponceau's death in 1844, a century passed at the APS with little activity in this area, until the collections were next transformed in 1945 by the acquisition of the papers of the influential anthropologist Franz Boas, along with much of the main linguistic and ethnographic manuscripts of many of his contemporaries and students. The collections have continued to grow since then, with the addition of papers by more generations of anthropologists, ethnographers, linguists, and other researchers, as well as materials produced from fieldwork sponsored by APS. The collections now consist of about 1,900 linear feet of manuscripts, photographs, and audiovisual materials relating to over 650 Indigenous cultures of the Americas, dating from 1553 to 2019.

Settler-colonial expansion, carried out especially through the sustained processes of land theft and resource extraction, generated the presumption of imminent Indigenous disappearance. This presumption motivated—and, in many cases, directly enabled—researchers to document Indigenous languages. The decisions to house this information permanently in an archive often were made separately, and by different people, but with the related rationale that its value as an object of study could be retained over time for researchers active in the ongoing development of Euro-American academic disciplines. Counter to these expectations, Native communities have been using these materials at the APS and other archival institutions for decades, despite formidable barriers to access, including the remoteness of these repositories from the communities where the knowledge originated.

The APS established the CNAIR in 2014 as a division of the library, devoted to assisting people in finding its extensive archival materials and utilizing them in innovative ways that honor Indigenous knowledge, cultivate scholarship, and strengthen languages and knowledge traditions. This work was made possible by the vision of CNAIR's late founding director, Timothy Powell, who emphasized the importance of understanding Native communities not merely as subject matter, but as core constituencies of the library and as intellectual authorities on the knowledge residing within it.

A key part of the development of CNAIR was the writing and formal adoption of the APS's "Protocols for the Treatment of Indigenous Materials," created by the library's Native American Advisory Board.[2] Through guidance from Indigenous community authorities, these protocols provide guidelines for the identification and protection of culturally sensitive information, as well as for the way the APS can and should consult with and establish relationships with these communities. Since 2008 CNAIR has shared digitized materials with over 150 Indigenous communities and currently maintains ongoing relationships with about 60 Indigenous communities throughout the continent.

These developments are not at all unique to the APS, but indicate a broader — and still quite incomplete — shift in the archival profession, as well as in memory institutions and related academic disciplines. Institutions such as the APS participating in this broader shift should not get credit for coming to these insights independently, as these initiatives in fact reflect an overdue response to a need that has long been expressed by Native communities.

In considering the insights of the scholars in this volume, we should also recognize the agency in archival material themselves, as well as the caretakers of that knowledge who communicated it. The promise and power of archives lies in the fact that the materials that comprise them are not passive, regardless of what we may propose that we ought to do to them or for them. These materials, whatever their documentary form, were created with an original intention (or intentions) about what they were meant to document, and suppositions about what preserving them in an archival setting would signify over time. The subsequent life they have had in an archive might be one in which they have experienced good company or solitude, prestige or neglect, safety or duress, hospitality or confinement, or many other ambivalent combinations of conditions. Nonetheless, in their archival setting, they also garner a power — one we often see them exert — to communicate messages that not only differ from what they were originally thought to convey, but that often directly subvert those original suppositions. We can look at the iconic examples of Jefferson's word lists and Boas's notebooks, recorded in part to chronicle disappearances that were presumed to be imminent and final. As records now used by those same Indigenous communities, they demonstrate instead the perseverance and continuity of those Indigenous intellectual traditions in the midst of the ongoing pressure of settler colonialism. Moreover, in our work as archivists, we frequently witness these communities exercising the authority of their expertise by critiquing the archival record, such as noting gaps and shortcomings in the understanding of the outside researcher who did not convey the context or import of the knowledge that was communicated to them. As many descendants of these knowledge keepers have attested, this knowledge was also communicated through these unwitting outsiders to future generations of kin who could understand it and use it properly.

Archives, like the materials that reside in them, are not passive entities. However, their agency is different from that of their residents, whose messages they cannot ultimately control, even if they fancy that they should make the attempt. As an archive with materials in over five hundred Indigenous languages, the APS Library is a place where a lot of talking is happening in and among the rows and rows of archival boxes. Rather than thinking solely in terms of people trying to find knowledge in the archives, we should also see another kind of activity: that the knowledge in the archives itself is trying to find the people it needs.

NOTES

1. For a fuller treatment of the scope and outcome of these initiatives, see Brian Carpenter, "Archival Initiatives for the Indigenous Collections at the American Philosophical Society," *Society of American Archivists Case Studies on Access Policies for Native American Archival Materials*, 2019, https://www2.archivists.org/sites/all/files/Case_1_Archival_Initiatives_for_Indiginous_Collections.pdf; and Timothy B. Powell, "Digital Knowledge Sharing: Forging Partnerships between Scholars, Archives, and Indigenous Communities," *Museum Anthropology Review* 10, no. 2 (2016): 66–90.
2. "The American Philosophical Society: Protocols for the Treatment of Indigenous Materials," *Proceedings of the American Philosophical Society* 158, no. 4 (2014): 411–20.

BIBLIOGRAPHY

"The American Philosophical Society: Protocols for the Treatment of Indigenous Materials." *Proceedings of the American Philosophical Society* 158, no. 4 (2014): 411–20.

Carpenter, Brian. "Archival Initiatives for the Indigenous Collections at the American Philosophical Society." *Society of American Archivists Case Studies on Access Policies for Native American Archival Materials*, 2019, https://www2.archivists.org/sites/all/files/Case_1_Archival_Initiatives_for_Indiginous_Collections.pdf (accessed August 24, 2020).

Powell, Timothy B. "Digital Knowledge Sharing: Forging Partnerships between Scholars, Archives, and Indigenous Communities." *Museum Anthropology Review* 10, no. 2 (2016): 66–90.

ACKNOWLEDGMENTS

The chapters in this volume first took shape as part of an international conference on the topic of endangered Native American and Indigenous languages held at the American Philosophical Society in Philadelphia, Pennsylvania, October 13–15, 2016. This conference, Translating Across Time and Space: Endangered Languages, Cultural Revitalization, and the Work of History, brought together scholars, archivists, librarians, knowledge keepers, Elders, and community leaders from across the United States and Canada to discuss the ways technology can help archives, scholars, and Indigenous communities preserve and revitalize endangered languages and cultural practices.

We are grateful to the conference organizers and committee members (especially Elizabeth Ellis and Bethany Wiggin), and to all who participated in the event for generating the rich discussions that make up the core of this publication. We additionally thank the Wolf Humanities Center at the University of Pennsylvania, and its director, James English, for partnering with the Society to host the proceedings. We also acknowledge the APS's facilities staff, including Nikolai Goripow, Donna Stumm, Jeremy Schoenrock, Todd Schoenrock, and Christina Schoenrock, for their work in ensuring a smooth conference experience.

The work is also indebted to the curatorial team responsible for the Society's 2016 exhibition *Gathering Voices: Thomas Jefferson and Native*

America. Led by APS museum director emerita Merrill Mason, this team consisted of Andrew W. Mellon Foundation postdoctoral curatorial fellows Lynette Regouby and Diana E. Marsh, who, with invaluable support from Mary Grace Wahl, associate director for collections and exhibitions, and exhibition advisors Margaret Bruchac (Abenaki) and Richard W. Hill Sr. (Tuscarora), researched and developed exhibition content that helped inspire the conference's themes.

Many APS staff members also assisted with this project, including Brenna Holland, assistant to the librarian; Mary McDonald, director of APS Publications; Bayard Miller, head of digital scholarship; and Joseph DiLullo, reference and digital services specialist. The editors are likewise appreciative of Matthew Bokovoy, Heather Stauffer, and Ann Baker at the University of Nebraska Press, who helped push the volume through during its final stages of development.

In acknowledging the contributions of APS staff, this volume would have been impossible without the efforts of Timothy Powell and Brian Carpenter. Under the tenure of librarian Martin Levitt and with the support of grants from the Getty Foundation and the Andrew W. Mellon Foundation, they worked to digitize and share photographs, audio recordings, and other cultural and linguistic materials housed within the APS Library in collaboration with the communities from which they originated—what we now call "digital knowledge sharing." Building on this work, in 2014 the library created the Center for Native American and Indigenous Research (CNAIR) to assist people in discovering and utilizing the library's archival materials related to the languages and traditions of over 650 different cultures throughout the Americas. Now an endowed center, thanks to generous support from donors and the National Endowment of the Humanities, CNAIR staff continue to find innovative ways to honor Indigenous knowledge, cultivate scholarship, and strengthen languages and cultural traditions. May this volume serve as a testament to the lasting impact of CNAIR and its continued work in building relations.

INDIGENOUS LANGUAGES AND

THE PROMISE OF ARCHIVES

Introduction

Collaborative Research and Language Revitalization:
Toward a Relational Ontology across Time and Space

Regna Darnell

The obligation to consider the world and one's place within it in terms of seven generations from the speaker—or actor, as the Anishinaabeg idiom puts it—is a rich metaphor widely deployed by Indigenous communities across Turtle Island. It firmly situates the present as evolving in continuity with a past that has ongoing consequences and continuously merges into the future. The present is an arbitrary snapshot with a fleeting existence in time, meaningful only when the consequences of present action are framed in reflexive terms across the expanding temporal reaches of personal, community, and global history. Human persons have a unique moral responsibility and accountability to live in harmony with (and, sometimes, to speak for as well as with) "all my relations" across the space of their territories. Each being or species is enjoined to act in accordance with its particular nature—that is, the world is structured spatially as well as temporally in terms of obligations and responsibilities extending from interpersonal behaviour to community sovereignty. This convergence is achieved by extending the metaphors of kinship, in sharp contrast to the entitlement taken for granted by the majority culture of the nation-state to unilaterally impose forms of governance, ownership, and law. Kinship crosses lines of species as well as of culture, ethnicity, race, gender, and other shibboleths that divide potential communities of fruitful interchange. From an Indigenous perspective, kinship is about the possibilities—indeed, necessities—of effective communication guided by ongoing relationships of respect and negotiation of conflict to produce agreement about the best way to move forward in a spirit of consensus. In Indigenous thought acts of agreement are arrived at through resolution of conflict.

This volume emerged from a conference held at the American Philosophical Society (APS) in 2016 that posed the all too rarely asked question of what Native American and Indigenous research would look like if initially considered, as it is above, from the multiple and complex standpoints of the communities whose very survival is entailed by the decisions we make together. Archives are called upon to cede at least some of their authority as "experts" and learn to listen to unfamiliar and often uncomfortable perspectives arising from a very different, community-based expertise.

The APS has long historical precedent for a central role in this reimagining of Indigenous-settler relations. To be sure, when Benjamin Franklin established the APS in 1743 "for the pursuit of useful knowledge," or when Thomas Jefferson amassed the world's largest collection of "Indian" vocabularies extant at the turn of the nineteenth century, they could not have envisioned—and would doubtless have been dismayed by—the forms of radical change considered by the contributors to this volume, who are situated in another time and place. Nonetheless, that early work laid a solid foundation on which contemporary scholars and Indigenous communities continue to build, modifying its legacy irreversibly in the process. Continuity and revolution move into the future hand in hand.

The APS is far from the only institution to have followed such a path. Collaborative work on Indigenous language revitalization is sprouting up in many places and with many variations. Institutions discussed in the following chapters include the Beinecke Library at Yale University, the University of British Columbia, the Smithsonian Institution, the Minnesota Historical Society, the American Museum of Natural History, the Milwaukee Indian Community School, and the California-based Breath of Life workshops. This list is arbitrary in the sense that conference organizers selected projects whose abstracts best corresponded with the APS vision of the intersections of language revitalization programs, collaboration with Indigenous communities, and the changing role of archives and the documents they hold. In the preface to this volume, Brian Carpenter describes the emergence of this perspective at the APS, as does Gwyneira Isaac, in chapter 13, for the Smithsonian Institution's National Museum of Natural History. Isaac reviews the history of the Museum's collecting and research priorities to illustrate changing relationships of potential users to "the same" material objects. Discrete context and interpretative framework render them different as a result of the relationships they encapsulate. Historicism is needed to avoid distortion of the stories the objects tell over time and the implications for contemporary use.

A critical mass of evidence presented in these chapters suggests that such work is growing rapidly in importance and visibility across Indian country and that the diversity of perspectives exemplified in this volume could serve and perhaps is already serving as a model for others. Archives, libraries, and museums are highly motivated to pursue collaborative projects with Indigenous communities, because funding institutions increasingly insist on prior consent and ongoing participation, as opposed to nominal inclusion at the end of the research. Increasingly, institutions apply their own protocols for the handling of relations with Indigenous communities; many have come to view themselves less as owners than as stewards of Indigenous materials. Such emerging goals, of course, require balancing with the legitimate interests of longer-established non-Indigenous publics and targeting collaborative educational programs. This volume reflects sharing of the experiences of seeking such balance on the part of many institutions and communities.

Ample evidence attests that programs imposed from the top down do not work. In the first chapter Jane Anderson and James E. Francis Sr. describe the fate of Penobscot tapes recorded by linguist Frank Siebert and duly returned to the community only to be shelved as family property, kept separate from everyday life and unable to mitigate the accelerating rate of language loss in the community. The response was totally different when an oral approach to the same textual materials drew upon the revival aspirations of some community members to reinstate the oral transmission of significant knowledge through revitalizing their traditional language. Rather than feel guilty over having lost their language, speakers could now take pride in their status as language learners, accepting that this is an ongoing process as they grew into roles requiring greater fluency throughout the life cycle. This is the traditional age-graded mode of learning and acquiring knowledge: it applies the principles of Indigenous pedagogies to strengthen the resolve of those who work toward language revitalization.

The variability of the projects designed to "reawaken" heritage languages responds to widely differing local agendas for their urgent preservation. On the surface this diversity may appear somewhat haphazard, but, when participants come together, they recognize a common cause that enables them to share experiences arising from similar historical factors as well as common cultural traditions. Each local context reflects unique ways of tying language to land, and the studies presented here are exemplary of a much wider field. They span the geographic range of North America: Penobscot, Mi'kmaw, Maliceet, Oneida, and Anishinaabemowin (Ojibwe) in the Northeast; Cherokee and Yuchi in the Southeast; Nimiipuu (Nez Perce), Menominee, Dakota, and Plains sign language in the interior; Hopi in the Southwest; Diidxaza (Zapotec) in Mexico; Heiltsuk (Bella Bella), Upper St'at'imc (Salish), and Gwich'in in the West.[1]

Each of these languages claims communities and individuals that identify with them and aspire to speak them, or to speak them again. They suffer degrees of endangerment ranging from declining use among young people, accelerating loss of the last generation of first-language speakers, and "reawakening" of languages long pronounced "extinct" by outsiders but understood as merely "sleeping" by the communities and individuals themselves. We must make no mistake: *all Indigenous communities have suffered protracted trauma and loss that cannot be measured in quantitative terms.* Although the challenges of this contemporary reality are particular to each community, each situation is crucially important to speakers and their descendants and thus holds equal significance in the collective project.

The studies brought together here represent the collaborative language revitalization work of community members, local scholars, and both local and national institutions. They range from single-scholar enterprises to large collaborative teams that draw on emerging technologies to enhance both the programs and the collaborations that sustain them. Many of the contributors are themselves Indigenous, reflecting a gathering momentum of building internal capacity to pursue community goals in locally appropriate ways. Richard A. Grounds (Yuchi) describes how his own work is rooted in his community; Bernard C. Perley, Margaret Ann Noodin, and Cary Miller are themselves Indigenous academics; James E. Francis Sr. (Penobscot), Glenn M. Wasicuna (Dakota), Craig Mishler (Gwch'in); Kayla Begay and Cheryl Tuttle (Wailaki), Jennifer Carpenter, Gerry Lawson, and Kim Lawson (Heiltsuk), and Annie Guerin (Musqueam) collaborate with scholars to interpret and translate older materials, as well as render them accessible. Scholars working on collaborative projects under the direction and priorities of communities include Sarah Carmen Moritz (Upper St'at'imc), Lisa Conathan (Cherokee, Mi'kmaw), Anne Keary (Nimiipuu), Sarah Snyder Hopkins (Cherokee), and Gwyneira Isaac (Hopi, Diidxasa, Wauja, Wanapumin, Anishinaabeg).

The volume sets out a cross-cutting agenda of intersecting variables that operate across time and space; the uniqueness of the collective project consists precisely in these juxtapositions. We call for mindful communication across customary silos of institution, disciplinary training, community identity, and local political alignment on the place of language revitalization in envisioned futures. By putting these variables into conversation with one another, the sum of the contributions belies any simple understanding of what is at stake or an arrival at any single approach that will apply in all cases.

The variability is far from random and lessons can be drawn from one case to another (see Darnell commentary in part 5)—a point to which we will return. Features are shared across cases in recombinant forms that do not fall into simple types; each combination is unique. Learning from the experience of others requires adapting their experience to one's own context and building a collaborative network that includes institutions with resources to support goals of linguistic and cultural revitalization as a route to language sovereignty. Because the language "belongs to" the speakers and their descendants, they claim jurisdiction over both language and its capacity to serve as a systematic mode of thought expressing the cultural heritage encoded in it as an ongoing resource for communities moving into their future.

Decolonization in the Context of Language Revitalization

The opening chapter by Anderson and Francis frames the task of language revitalization as decolonization, a general label for the dramatic societal changes required in both private and public spheres in pursuit of social equity and historical redress. Systemic discrimination and marginalization continue to operate at all levels of contemporary neocolonial or postcolonial society, often below the level of consciousness. The greatest challenge for Indigenous people may well be the burden of "double consciousness" (a term adopted from pioneer African American sociologist W. E. B. Du Bois), whereby marginalized individuals and communities view themselves through the demeaning eyes of others.[2] The hierarchical categorizing habits of colonialism must be unlearned by both colonizer and colonized.

Turning from decolonization as a theoretical construct to its emergence from grassroots experience, Richard A. Grounds describes in chapter 2 his personal journey to decolonize language revitalization in his Yuchi community in terms of the community's evolving understanding of the role the language plays in contemporary identity. In line with the seven generations admonition to responsibility cited above, he identifies the urgency and lost opportunity he felt twenty-five years ago while working with the last generation of Elders raised by their monolingual grandparents. At that time, many community members were hesitant to speak the language because they felt unequipped to handle the "powerful things" encoded in it. After many years of searching for records of the language in institutions and private hands, Grounds found himself working archivally with linguistic codes that were devoid of authority because they were isolated from the contemporary Yuchi community. Today there is an acute awareness of what can still be recovered, and active collaboration is underway to develop pedagogical materials.

Grounds provides a powerful analysis of the contrast between colonial agendas and the priorities of descendant communities. On the one hand, he castigates scholars of prior generations, including Thomas Jefferson's duplicitous collection of information intended to facilitate alienation of Native lands and Franz Boas's unwavering commitment to the salvage paradigm of the vanishing Indian. On the other hand, he contends that the resulting documents can be decoupled from the "salvage linguicide" of their "racist moorings." Community collaboration enables new ways of thinking about the uses of materials in the archives, and it would be counterproductive not to bring all available resources to bear on the task at hand.

The Canadian national imaginary is somewhat different; Indigenous issues are closer to the surface of public life. Canada's recent Truth and Reconciliation Commission (2015) acknowledges an urgent national crisis to repair the broken relationship between Native and non-Native people (see chapters 4 and 9). Activism is never far from the surface, and national research institutions such as Canada's Social Sciences and Humanities Research Council facilitate collaborations through its funding priorities and mandatory ethical protocols. Anthropologist Michael Asch argues persuasively that we are all treaty people, "here to stay" and bound by the treaties to live in a civil, orderly fashion with the First People who welcomed settlers to share their land and taught them how to live well alongside their hosts.[3] For Indigenous people, in contrast, the primary issue is healing; they are already well aware of injustices suffered and their ongoing consequences.[4]

Decolonization is the overarching theoretical framework of the volume, but the contributors address it in very particular ways, rendering its abstract workings intelligible through language revitalization programs in specific communities and tracing the relationships of these programs and the state-of-the-art technologies on which they are based to other Indigenous communities and to their settler neighbors. The shared relational and collaborative standpoint supports the efforts of all these individuals and communities to change the circumstances within which they operate and to move beyond the ongoing consequences of shared colonial histories. Transformative action is needed to challenge practices deeply embedded in capitalism and its institutions, and the urgency of language revitalization projects must be seen in this context. *Language is more than itself*: it stands in for the need to respond creatively and contextually in local terms, to adopt what Audra Simpson calls "an active refusal of the colonial order of things."[5]

The success of any project contains conditions of possibility. It requires language documentation available from a variety of sources, each of which can be assessed for its partial contribution to the intended goals. None of the existing resources can be taken at face value, but assessment of convergent evidence from multiple sources uses the strengths and weaknesses of each source to balance others and to fill gaps in the cumulative record. This can be done by activating knowledge still residing within the contemporary community as well as by making informed inferences from the comparison of prior records and by analogy from closely related languages. A linguistic purist, whether Indigenous or not, might argue that the language can never be brought back in precisely the same form that it was spoken in some idealized golden age in the past. This is of course true, but it does not invalidate the contemporary product. All languages change over time; distinct dialects develop as speech communities are divided by migration, colonial history, or environmental change. To freeze "the language" in some hypothetical form is effectively to declare it dead.

The difficulties of assessing past materials are myriad. The grammatical structures of most traditional languages of Turtle Island are agglutinative or polysynthetic—that is, fluent speakers produce nuanced verbal constructions that would require whole phrases or sentences in English. To consider each newly attested form as a separate "word" entails distorting the combinatorial capacities of these languages when they are spoken well. The expert speaker, usually one whose skills have been honed over a lifetime, marks personal pronouns, tense or modality (the latter being more common and focusing attention on the state of becoming, of action that is fluid and emergent), and location (on land and thus in space) within the verb. An adequate translation must be both linguistic and cultural.[6]

Language has a peculiar status in relation to the discipline of anthropology; it has been subject to far less critique than cultural anthropology or archaeology. Although there is considerable difference of opinion within communities, some members of many communities are willing—indeed eager—to collaborate with archives, museums, and libraries, despite their status as colonial institutions. The Association of Tribal Archives, Libraries and Museums (ATALM), arising from Indigenous initiative, draws together Indigenous and non-Indigenous scholars based in tribal archives, libraries, and museums. The Great Lakes Research Alliance for the Study of Aboriginal Arts and Cultures (GRASAC), a research network established by Ruth Phillips in 2012, links multiple partners, as does the California-based Breath of Life language revitalization workshops organized by Leanne Hinton. Growing resources enhance potential communication and innovation for particular projects.

This volume as a whole emphasizes the necessity for bold experiments that take action now on behalf of further generations. The proviso is always in place, however, that "some" members of every community are in strong support, while others are not. The views of those who do not see language revitalization as realistic or as a priority must be respected. Decision-making based on consensus allows space for variability and for each individual's autonomy to decide on what it means to be Indigenous at the present time.

Early in the development of the APS protocols for ethical collaborative relationships (see Miller commentary in part 1, and the preface by Carpenter), one community signed a memorandum of understanding, adding a codicil expressing their belief that, although its wording contradicted their own sense of sovereignty, they were signing because they wanted to pursue the relationship even though the terms were not entirely to their liking.[7] Compromise is often the key to successful collaboration. Not every situation of language loss lends itself to revitalization agendas; other urgent priorities may take precedence in a particular community (e.g., treaty negotiations, land rights, sovereignty, environmental protection). But, surprisingly frequently, language is the primary site of contestation and revitalization. Language stands for all that has been lost through colonial policies of genocide and assimilation, with residential schools punishing children for speaking their language and separating them from their families and communities. Contemporary activists for language revitalization believe that their language expresses an inalienable tie between personal and community identity and the particular land that constitutes the traditional territory. The underlying concepts cannot be expressed directly in English. Miscommunication abounds, with frustration on all sides.

The language belongs to the community. Consequently, many such programs are open only to tribal members and language teachers. Priorities often have to be set because resources are scarce and must be rationed for maximal effect. Other communities have the internal capacity to be more open to the additional commitment of sharing their knowledge in the interests of enhanced cross-cultural communication. Museum and exhibit partnerships illustrate the potentials (see chapters 10 and 13, and Marsh commentary in part 3).

The Projects

The particular projects are the sine qua non of testing the productivity of collaboration across long-established barriers of institutional cultures holding seemingly incommensurable positions. Chapters were selected to exemplify the myriad challenges attending successful mobilization of language programs through community-level collaboration. Because they are locally grounded, these projects are highly diverse in their details. Limitations and failures are as instructive as the nascent successes. All are immersed in a process whose end point cannot yet be known. Nonetheless, variables recur in the experience of various projects that attest to the potentials for transportable knowledge, for learning from one another's experience (see Darnell commentary in part 5). In a parallel vein, Jennifer R. O'Neal (commentary in part 6) highlights the extensive existing collections and research that preserve "Indigenous history and ways of knowing and thereby leave space for communities to tell their stories for future generations in the way they want them told" as a product of the collaborative language revitalization projects.

Recovering Voices

Telling stories as they are meant to be told by Indigenous users of archives entails hearing familiar words differently, often nonliterally. Indigenous cultural and spiritual knowledge is protected by its holders from inappropriate and potentially dangerous access to powerful forces. Metaphor is also a mode of explanation for those prepared to adapt literal meanings to other circumstances where their relevance is applicable; Bethany Wiggin identifies an "everyday tactic" available to the disenfranchised to preserve the standpoint at the basis of contemporary identity. Sometimes the writers of the documents encode their understandings in metaphoric terms; in other cases, contemporary Indigenous users call upon the metaphorical richness of their traditional knowledge to render older materials accessible and generative. Many chapters in this volume illustrate the depth of the gulf between Western and Indigenous ways of seeing. All remain optimistic that listeners can learn to see and hear differently to voices of revitalization, even in translation.

Missionaries have often been the source of documents that require contextualization for contemporary use by multiple audiences that may hold conflicting purposes. In chapter 7 Anne Keary describes a Nimiipuu (Nez Perce) language primer superficially created to "share stories to create relationships." Missionaries worked collaboratively on pedagogical materials to teach the language at the local level, intending this as an interim measure to facilitate conversion. Their overall commentary, however, subverted local pride in the language by undermining the local rationale for participation—that is, to preserve the traditional way of life. By relying on the Trickster cycle of Coyote stories, the community was able to link the traditional and the Christian religions. The missionary commentary on these narratives, however, framed them as untrue and therefore emblematic of the limitations of Nimiipuu thought. That "a Coyote is just a Coyote" may have been a position intelligible to those who funded missionary research, but it was deeply offensive to the Nimiipuu community. Contemporary Elders assisted by a linguist are now excavating this material in order to decolonize its layers of evangelical ideology and reinstate the authority of the local knowledge intended by the creators of this material.

In chapter 11 Sara Snyder Hopkins describes a parallel endeavor for missionary Samuel Wooster's Cherokee singing book in which the 1846 text, whether consciously or not, envisioned a two-stage process of adopting traditional Cherokee words while simultaneously incorporating layers of meaning that would gradually supersede the Cherokee worldview.

Power-laden ideological asymmetries reflected the cross-purposes of missionary interpretation and translation. Contemporary Cherokee Elders, however, reclaim the conceptual world of music and sound from the archive. Elder and academic Tom Belt emphasizes the incommensurability of the binary choice the missionaries posed between Christianity and traditional religion and contrasts it to the Cherokee acceptance of plural systems of thought that legitimately vary across contexts and individuals within the Cherokee community. He explains that when medicine men use polyvalent linguistics signs, they are comfortable with pragmatic slippage: "the jagged edges of meaning" implicit in a living language. In Belt's theory of Cherokee sound, metaphors bridge ontological worlds. Sound is water which is liquid and flexible enough to carry plural meanings; the concept of *covenant* evokes a belt, his own name, that can lead to the solidifying and connecting of relations, hence to effective cross-cultural communication. Sounds have life: they seek balance and recognize each other. He teaches this system of musical thought as it manifests in art classes, a medicine garden, and field schools, employing the language through everyday living rather than formal language classes. The relationships implicit in Belt's approach would have startled the missionary who saw the communication as a one-way process in which the Cherokee would inevitably yield to Christian ways of thinking (see also Harvey, chapter 6, and the preface by Carpenter).

In contrast to Snyder Hopkins's collaborative teaching and research in the Cherokee community for many years, Lisa Conathan approaches Cherokee language revitalization as an outsider scholar enhancing the potentials inherent in its "vernacular literacy" (since the invention of the Cherokee syllabary by Sequoiah around 1820). Because Cherokee language is still in active use, the Beinecke Library developed an open corpus with access controlled by the Cherokee collaborators. Multiple genres are represented, and Cherokee concerns for the secrecy of highly sensitive medical and magical formulae are often implicitly protected in archived documents by "arcane word play"; the encoded knowledge is not intelligible to those without the prior esoteric knowledge to interpret it. Interests of preservation and access often appear to be in conflict, and the transfer of control over access to the Cherokee themselves has been a gradual process. Curators at the Beinecke acknowledge their lack of expertise to manage such materials; a result of the collaboration, therefore, they have learned much about the meaning of the documents in their stewardship. Similar negotiations of relationship are taking place in many institutions today. The growth of tribal museums in part through repatriation and reclamation of "belongings" removed from communities also contributes to a new sense of collaboration on a more balanced and symmetrical basis.

Conathan contrasts the Cherokee situation to that of Mi'kmaw hieroglyphics that come to the Beinecke as a small, closed, esoteric set of materials for Catholic worship. A digitally enabled closed corpus allows for precise and detailed analysis. Each collaboration has its own parameters, to which institutional practices must adapt differently, depending on the circumstances and the objectives of their community partners in revisiting the archived materials. As Brian Carpenter notes in the preface, Indigenous partners are increasingly the primary constituency of the contemporary archive.

Varied documents can be deployed to recover voice for contemporary revitalization agendas. In chapter 8 Gwen A. Westerman and Glenn M. Wasicuna examine Dakota letters written from prison after the Sioux uprising of 1862 and subsequent removal, to explore how images of this group of people, including their self-images, have changed over time. The letters provide a rare glimpse of the standpoint of the Dakota—who are most often represented in the academic literature through the eyes of missionaries and government agents—speaking in their own words to an audience sharing their cultural world. The question of sincerity or good faith was taken for granted by Indigenous parties to the treaties and sometimes by treaty commissioners, even though the latter were likely to be overruled by their political superiors.[8] In the Nimiipuu case, treaty interpreters failed to translate much of what was said during the negotiations, a process Diana E. Marsh (see commentary in part 3) characterizes as "epistemicide." Until quite recently, only the written record has been considered authoritative. Language revitalization—recovering information from oral history—has been vital to acknowledging the knowledge encoded in the stories and teachings that are passed down through generations. The current Nimiipuu project is grounded on traditional territory, with an advisory board of speakers, language teachers, and a digital archaeologist: a critical mass of expertise producing a first-person narrative accessible to nonspeakers within the community. Wasicuna's fluency in multiple registers in both Nimiipuu and English enables him to provide both a text in colloquial English and a linguistic analysis.

Gwyneira Isaac, in chapter 13, situates the natural history context of collecting at the Smithsonian Institution within a contemporary pedagogical context at the National Museum of Natural History. The work of her Smithsonian colleague Gabriela Perez-Baez on Diidxaza (Zapotec) provides a rich database of botanical specimens that function as "critical stimuli" to recover and generate Zapotec knowledge, which rests on different classificatory principles and is intended for different uses than the standard Linnean system. For example, the architecture of the tree provides a classificatory principle inaccessible to collectors without access to traditional knowledge. The project is an activist one, its "analytic outputs" geared to sensitizing local children to loss of biodiversity, and the "convergent history" of the museum's salvage paradigm intersects with new critical research traditions. This critique allows older materials to bring their encoded knowledge forward into the present in ways accessible to the communities of their origin.

There is an implicit plurality in the museum's project, in that the Zapotec constitute a multisited audience for the recuperation of plant knowledge that cannot be adequately explored in a single research site. In this context, Bethany Wiggin (see commentary in part 2) emphasizes the "reparative" potential of the museum as a site for an ethical redefinition of relations between collections and the descendants of their providers. She argues that translation offers the possibility to create an "equivalence" of status of plural knowledges. Weak parties to power relations are often best poised to lead in ethical transformation.

Drawing on the collections of the Smithsonian Institution, Isaac's oral history project on Hopi pottery documents the physical experience of potting to engage younger generations of learners with the materials and the processes of traditional weaving. In the conference version of this chapter, Isaac describes how Hopi potters from First Mesa think with traditional conceptual frames and bring them into present-day practice. Pottery actively nurtures the whole person because it is "cosmologically charged." These potters practice the traditional Hopi protocol of "paying back" to underwrite outreach to non-Indigenous audiences through establishing reciprocal relations; they place traditional Hopi theories and practices about pottery, design, aesthetics, ethics, and the social value of shared work into a potential shared space, inviting Indigenous and non-Indigenous people to learn together. Isaac argues that the project transcends locality by using the resources of the national museum to enhance the field of communication beyond the local in an open-ended collaboration.

A different set of pragmatic metaphors is employed by Craig Mishler and Kenneth Frank in chapter 14 to convey the endangered way of life within the migration area of the Porcupine Caribou Herd for Alaskan and Yukon Elders. Bilingual texts present traditional stories about the intersection of human and caribou relations over time. Through "slow reflexive" translation aimed at conveying verbal art consistent with Gwich'in word mechanics and way of life alongside these "intelligent animals," Mishler's base metaphor for translation is that of "tools and grease mechanics." Traditional knowledge is balanced with his personal experience of living on the land. Mishler often consults his wife and finds that she has a different reading of the same traditional material; it is impossible to judge whether her view is an individual variation or more broadly characteristic of Gwich'in women. Working as a team, Mishler and Frank apply a "fix-it" approach to adjusting translation until it works in both languages for each of them. The pedagogical lessons are in the details—for example, body parts of the caribou were initially awkward in translation because they worked from naturalistic anatomical diagrams. But the Gwich-in do not understand caribou anatomy in natural science terms; rather, they meet and deal respectfully with flesh and blood of the recently living prey. A reconstituted anatomical diagram more accurately reflects the Gwich'in conception.

Transforming Relationships

Although most of the chapters primarily address particular projects, generalizations emerge, primarily from overlaps and contrasts. Many authors also attend to theoretical context and the role that Indigenous languages of the Americas have played in the American national imaginary and in the way the New World has been perceived by the Old. Contemporary interest in indigeneity extends beyond the Americas, and former colonial subjects around the globe are eager to explore the implications of linguistic revitalization in both old and new homelands.

The Enlightenment project of comparative linguistics was designed as an entrée to classifying the presumed unilinear evolution of complex societies on the assumption that such complexity would be reflected directly in so-called primitive languages. Such outdated theories are less important today than acknowledging the imperialist assumptions that drove scholarly networks on both sides of the Atlantic. In the period of most intensive collection, Peter S. Du Ponceau was the European face of the APS and solidified its reputation in Britain, Germany, and Russia. The universalist impetus of the language work spurred by Catherine the Great depended on American colleagues for information on Native languages; in chapter 6 Sean P. Harvey weaves a fascinating narrative of their jockeying for relative prestige. Du Ponceau, the APS's armchair linguistic philosopher, deployed information from missionaries, traders, and government officials to support his claim for peer status with European scholars. Retired Moravian missionary John Heckewelder aspired to a similar reputation as an independent scholar, but remained subordinate to Du Ponceau because of the latter's access to European correspondents. Similarly, the colonial hierarchy of authoritative knowledge marginalized gentleman-intellectual-turned–Indian agent Henry Rowe Schoolcraft and virtually ignored the knowledge implicit in the information he obtained from his Ojibwe wife, Jane Johnston Schoolcraft, based on her insider expertise. Authorship at this time and in this institutional context was the prerogative of relative cosmopolitan status as measured by European standards; it was indeed Harvey's "republic of letters."

Fast-forwarding several generations, Harvey turns to Franz Boas, who collaborated extensively with language speakers. In some—although not all—instances, Boas attributed authorship to George Hunt, his long-time collaborator among the Kwakwaka'wakw. Neither of them could have done their work without the other, and their roles were distinct. The potlatch ceremony was illegal under the infamous Potlatch Law that applied from 1885 to 1954, but both men were determined to record the event for future generations, each for his own reasons. Although Boas came out strongly against the universalist hierarchy of the older evolutionary paradigm, his own salvage paradigm retained the imperative to record languages and cultures of the "vanishing savage" in the face of manifest destiny. The founding generation of the APS would also have embraced this position, though their agenda had more to do with settler access to Indian land than with the ostensible scientific purposes.

Each position is deeply grounded in its own time and place. In our own time it is patently obvious that "they" are still here, and recognition of the fact that Indigenous people have a legitimate claim to control over the study of their own languages and cultures is growing. To jettison the material amassed by Boas and his students along with the then-unquestioned hierarchical and patriarchal assumptions of the late nineteenth and early twentieth centuries would, however, be counterproductive; such documentation can be and is being repurposed to contemporary ends. Although Boas's own audience was academic, Michael Silverstein argues that Boas's commitment to the importance of a permanent record of the knowledge that was available in his time remains an enduring legacy in developing "local practical consciousness" for multiple contemporary audiences. Regardless of intended audience, most early Boasians believed their work to be a calling, an obligation to record major forms of human expression before they were lost. "Language" means something quite different to linguists, anthropologists, and Indigenous communities envisioning "reimmersive uses in creative projects focused on heritage" (see commentary in part 4).

What I have called the "Americanist Tradition" established by Boas set precedents for the symbolic understanding of culture, accessible through spontaneous texts recorded in the traditional language (rather than elicited forms alone); language and culture cannot be separated.[9] These precedents continue to guide anthropological and linguistic work, although emerging new standards for collaboration and Indigenous control have built on them in ways that Boas and his contemporaries did not—indeed, could not—have imagined in their time and place. For example, the Franz Boas Papers Project,[10] in which the APS is a formal partner, is governed by an Indigenous advisory council mandated to oversee community control over culturally sensitive material, to return archive materials to descendant communities through digital knowledge sharing, and to build capacity in the descendant communities.[11] This structure emerges directly from the efforts of the APS and its Native American Advisory Council, on which I serve (see the preface by Carpenter, and Miller commentary in part 1) to devise more equitable protocols that transfer decision-making power over access and dissemination to the communities and honor their mechanisms for evaluation of relevant and ethically appropriate research. For this author the design also drew on protocols devised locally through long-term collaboration with Walpole Island First Nation (Three Fires Confederacy of the Anishinaabeg, Potawatomi, and Odawa).

Transforming the Archives

Employing this revisionist approach to updating and repurposing archival materials, in chapter 9 Sarah Carmen Moritz explores the value of Franz Boas's professional correspondence at the APS not only for contextualizing the linguistic and ethnographic texts, but also for revealing the networks and relationships underlying the assembly of such a record in order to better evaluate their reliability and validity. Authority still travels in the grooves explored by Harvey, and it still requires mindful reflexive strategies to counteract it. Moritz draws on Indigenous "metaphorical and metonymic lore" that embeds the language in a rich relational social ontology. For the Upper St'at'imc, the stories told in the language tie together and strengthen the fish, the water, and the inextricable bond between the people and the land; the "laws of the land" provide protocols that govern contemporary actions and decisions about desirable futures in a rapidly changing environment.

Rainer Hatoum provides an elegant example of the need for meticulous examination of these old records based on original documents now held in archives and still largely inaccessible to community members. He compares the field notes (meticulously deciphered from Boas's idiosyncratic shorthand system) to the published version of "the Kwakiutl potlatch."[12] Boas moved from the particulars of a single potlatch that he sponsored and George Hunt organized in 1894 as an occasion to pass hereditary titles to his son David to a generic account that omits many of the details of participants, locations on land, and names and titles held and transmitted. These details, however, are the most significant information for the contemporary community in its aspirations to revitalize potlatch institutions and the system of hereditary titles on which it is based. This kind of meticulous scholarship in the original field notes and letters facilitates new uses of existing archival materials.

Revitalization Tools

Technology has made possible a sharing of materials and experiences across Indigenous communities, often facilitated by collaboration of scholars and institutions as well by networks of community leaders and language teachers. In chapter 4 Mark Turin and his coauthors review the rapidly evolving state of available technologies, the technoscape of contemporary language research, first in relation to Turin's own work with Heiltsuk (Bella Bella), undertaken with community initiative and stewardship, and, by extension, offer a model that can be adapted elsewhere. The project aims to balance external metrics transferable in principle to the study of other colonial languages with the locally contingent knowledge of the Heilsuk. Interestingly, the chapter contends that much of what needs to be done is not "research" in the conventional understanding of that term; as such, it is not easy to obtain financial support to build human capacity within a community, never mind the research infrastructure to support a language revitalization program on a long-term basis. The Indigenous research funding priorities of Canada's Social Sciences and Humanities Research Council encourage experimentation, but have not provided a mechanism for ongoing operational funding.

In chapter 5 Jeffrey Davis reports a decades-long study of Plains Indian Sign Language (PISL) as distinct from American Sign Language (ASL) and reflective of what he believes to be precontact forms of communication among unrelated people meeting in the same territory to exploit similar resources. It is another powerful example of the distinction between local knowledge and global application, as people grounded in particular land-based traditions come into contact and adapt what is relevant in the storied and shared experience of others. The global remains anchored in the autonomy of its local constituents.

The implicit assumption that a single case is inherently limited in its generalizability is belied by Mark Turin's exemplar of digital knowledge sharing at its most productive. Turin and his coauthors emphasize that trickle-down approaches to systemic injustice are ineffective in "Indigenizing colonial thinking." Nonetheless, the question is still not posed from the standpoint of how Indigenous communities, as creators of the linguistic and cultural materials under consideration, perceive their own needs. We still do not have the needed flexibility to negotiate "epistemological and ontological boundaries." Turin identifies a significant information gap in the evaluation of language revitalization programs that might facilitate the sharing of effective (and not so effective) strategies; the comparative dimension of such a project would, of course, require a third party outside the perspective of any given local program. He cites an array of promising possibilities now available for comparison across languages and language families, and he simultaneously emphasizes the inevitable time lag. The technoscape is changing so rapidly that no published review can possibly be definitive or up-to-date; consequently, the direct and fluid communication customary in Indigenous relational protocols is—and will likely remain—maximally effective across programs and language specialists.

Multimedia Experiments

Technology also offers new forms of communication for the multimedia expression of Indigenous art, poetry, and storytelling, and the mutual enrichment of traditions. Bernard C. Perley (Maliceet), Margaret Ann Noodin (Anishinaabeg), and Cary Miller (Anishinaabeg), three Indigenous academics located in Milwaukee, Wisconsin, designed an interactive exhibit for symbolic expression of the commonalities across their traditions, alternating interior spaces of Indigenous experience with exterior spaces of colonial incursion.[13] "Living languages, landscapes, and histories" come together in an installation piece titled *Experiencing Native North America*. Perley shares a personal metaphor linking theories of fractal causality to the "unfolding fiddleheads of cause and effect": drawing on his experience of a salient plant resource of his Maliceet home territory enables deep emotional comparison of patterns applicable to other natural environments in the place where he now lives and works.

What the late Vine Deloria Jr. called "experiential history" (see chapter 4) also speaks to the viewer's emotions rather than solely to the intellect by creating "an immersive epistemic space" for teaching alternative ways of seeing and being. "Parallel experiences" coexist, balancing exterior colonial pressures with internal interconnectedness. The pedagogical effect for viewers comes through expressing trauma and exploding "prevalent historical myths . . . of benign empire." Decolonization acquires a human face. Without the technological breakthroughs used in the exhibit and in its dissemination to a variety of audiences, such a project would be limited to local effects, if it could indeed be conceived at all.

Conclusion

The themes that recur in the ground-up methodologies of Indigenous language revitalization, as well as collaborative research and practice, can be summarized by the Canadian government's statement of the principles of ownership, control, and possession (OCAP), a simple mnemonic to maintain focus on Indigenous priorities and provide guidelines for information use. *Ownership* by Indigenous communities or organizations ensures their control of use and mitigates against research that returns nothing to the community. *Access* to research-generated information collected for the communities and their members benefits the communities and generates internal capacity. *Possession* of research data in addition to interpretations placed on it by scholars, institutional users, policy makers, and the general public facilitates the much-needed work of reconciliation between Indigenous and non-Indigenous populations. The OCAP principles, taken together, balance the structural inequalities of power that plague language revitalization agendas and hinder decolonization.

Moreover, the knowledge from single projects does not stand alone. Communities and institutions alike are developing mechanisms to share their experience and adapt it to local conditions. Such dissemination and circulation of enriched information is a critical by-product of the collaborative methodologies developed at the local level. Theory, method, and practice intertwine in the shared experience of collaboration across communities, researchers, academic disciplines, and supporting institutions. As allies, they add its particular strengths and balance the limitations of understanding and relevance that are lost when it stands alone.

Language revitalization is a critical site for decolonializing work because its expertise necessarily resides with speakers and their communities. Without Indigenous collaboration, little meaningful new research can be done. Quantitative methodologies that rely heavily on statistics mask Indigenous relational ontologies that render information culturally appropriate and reveal the meaning of otherwise illogical practices. Spiritual and emotional resonances are inseparable from their physical embodiment. Positivist science too often claims its purely cognitive or rational ontology to be objective and universal, thereby justifying dismissal of alternative ways of knowing as unintelligible and thus meaningless. *The archives now being accessed by the projects described in this volume offer a remedy.* Archives have maintained materials in a state of stasis, waiting for users to reawaken their potential. That awakening is now well underway. It has enriched archives by teaching those who come in contact with linguistic and cultural materials to respect and learn from community agendas, and to perceive these documents from the standpoint of their creators and their descendants.

NOTES

1. Additional languages were discussed at the conference or discussed in more detail than in the revised versions selected for this volume. Contributors whose chapters were not included: Kelly Wisecup, Sin Hay Kin Jack, Elizabeth Ellis, Angie Bain, Mandy N'zinek Jimmie, Jenny Davis, Christopher Cox, L. G. Donovan, Sergio Romero, Gabriela Perez-Baez, Rosalyn LaPier, Mary Linn, and the late Timothy Powell.
2. See Baker, *From Savage to Negro*; and Baker, *Anthropology and the Racial Politics of Culture*.
3. See Asch, *On Being Here to Stay*; and, Asch, Borrows, and Tully, *Resurgence and Reconciliation*.
4. As this volume goes to press, naming the systemic intergenerational atrocities as "genocide" in the Final Report of the National Inquiry on Murdered and Missing Indigenous Women and Girls has been met with considerable backlash

from a Canadian public prepared to acknowledge past failures of social justice but not to embrace an ongoing colonial legacy of "slow cultural genocide" that contradicts the complacency of the national imaginary, despite congruence of the evidence with international definitions.
5. Simpson, "On Ethnographic Refusal."
6. Darnell, Smith, and Westman, *Land, Language, Locatives*.
7. Personal communication, Timothy Powell to Regna Darnell, August 8, 2012.
8. Asch, *On Being Here to Stay*.
9. Darnell, *Invisible Genealogies*.
10. Franz Boas Documentary Edition, Social Sciences and Humanities Research Council Partnership Grant, 2012–20.
11. Darnell, "Anthropological Legacy of 'Useful Knowledge.'"
12. Hatoum, "I Wrote all My Notes in Shorthand."
13. I cite this to Perley et al. (chapter 10) as Indigenous artist, corresponding author, conference presenter, and public voice in the formation and exegesis of the exhibit.

BIBLIOGRAPHY

Asch, Michael. *On Being Here to Stay: Treaties and Aboriginal Rights in Canada*. Toronto: University of Toronto Press, 2014.

Asch, Michael, John Borrows, and James Tully, eds. *Resurgence and Reconciliation*. Toronto: University of Toronto Press, 2018.

Association of Tribal Archives, Libraries, and Museums. Accessed August 20, 2020. www.atalm.org.

Baker, Lee D. *Anthropology and the Racial Politics of Culture*. Durham NC: Duke University Press, 2010.

——— . *From Savage to Negro: Anthropology and the Construction of Race, 1896–1954*. Berkeley: University of California Press, 1998.

Basso, Keith. *Wisdom Sits in Places*. Albuquerque: University of New Mexico Press, 1996.

Darnell, Regna. "An Anthropological Legacy of 'Useful Knowledge': The APS Archives and the Future of Americanist Anthropology." *Proceedings of the American Philosophical Society* 142, no. 1 (2018): 1–14.

——— . *Invisible Genealogies: A History of Americanist Anthropology*. Lincoln: University of Nebraska Press, 2001.

——— . "Reconciliation, Resurgence, and Revitalization: Collaborative Research Protocols with Contemporary First Nations Communities." In *Resurgence and Reconciliation*, edited by Michael Asch, John Borrows, and James Tully, 229–44. Toronto: University of Toronto Press, 2018.

Darnell, Regna, Joshua Smith, and Clint Westman, eds. *Land, Language, Locatives*. Forthcoming.

Government of Canada. OCAP Principles. Accessed August 20, 2020. http://fnigc.ca/ocapr.html.

Hatoum, Rainer. "'I Wrote All My Notes in Shorthand': A First Glance into the Treasure Chest of Franz Boas's Shorthand Field Notes." In *Local Knowledge, Global Stage*, edited by Regna Darnell and Frederic Gleach, 221–72. Lincoln: University of Nebraksa Press, 2016.

Phillips, Ruth. *Toward the Indigenization of Canadian Museums*. Montreal: McGill-Queen's University Press, 2012.

Simpson, Audra. "On Ethnographic Refusal: Indigeneity, 'Voice,' and Colonial Citizenship." *Junctures* 9 (2007): 67–80.

Tedlock, Dennis. *The Spoken Word and the Work of Interpretation*. Philadelphia: University of Pennsylvania Press, 1983.

Tedlock, Dennis, and Bruce Mannheim, eds. *The Dialectic Emergence of Culture*. Champaign: University of Illinois Press, 1995.

Truth and Reconciliation Commission. *Final Report: Canada's Residential Schools*. Montreal: McGill Queen's University Press, 2015.

PART 1

Decolonizing Archives

Commentary by Robert J. Miller

In chapter 2 Richard A. Grounds lays out a strong case for the negative impacts that colonial and ethnocentric thinking and methods have played in the study, collection, and ownership of language materials gathered from Indigenous people in general, and the Yuchi people in particular. Prompted by Thomas Jefferson, the president of the American Philosophical Society (APS) for seventeen years, the APS began focusing on collecting American Indian language materials. Grounds states that Jefferson instigated the APS's creation of the Historical and Literary Committee under Peter S. Du Ponceau and thereafter developed the world's largest collection of American Indian language manuscripts. He also states that the APS reasserted its dominance in the field by acquiring materials from Franz Boas and some of his students. Grounds alleges that the legacy of "hunter-gatherer" language collectors—here the students of Boas whose Yuchi materials are held by the APS—"elevates the collectors above the communities." He argues that language collection was based on colonial assumptions about the inevitable extinction of Native people. Grounds echoes concerns that Vine Deloria Jr. stated long ago about anthropologists: "The fundamental thesis of the anthropologist is that people are objects for observation, people are then considered objects for experimentation, for manipulation, and for eventual extinction. The anthropologist thus furnishes the justification for treating Indian people like so many chessmen available for anyone to play with."[1]

Jane Anderson and James E. Francis Sr., director of the Penobscot Nation Cultural and Historic Preservation Department, describe that nation's ongoing efforts to revive its language. In addition, they make similar points as Grounds about the colonial interpretive framing of language and the power imbalances between colonizers and the colonized. They focus most closely, however, on how intellectual property laws around the world, and in particular in the United States, leave Indigenous people asking repeatedly who owns materials that were gathered from Native people and what kinds of permissions Natives have to obtain from collectors and archives in order to access and use their own historic cultural knowledge and tools. The authors highlight the impact of intellectual property law on the Penobscot Nation and the Penobscot materials held by the APS and other archives. These laws, they contend, "bind Native communities to institutions that hold and own such important collections of cultural materials." Their chapter also reminds me of a comment by Vine Deloria Jr.: "The implications of the anthropologist [linguist?] . . . should be clear for the Indian. . . . We should not be objects of observation for those who do nothing to help us."[2]

I am not an archivist or a language researcher. I have no specific expertise with which to debate the extent of colonialism and ethnocentrism in the field of linguistic research and archival collection and management. But I do have one question as a layperson in this field, and Grounds, Anderson, and Francis all recognize this as well: Even if these materials were collected in the wrong way, for the wrong reasons, and intellectual property law actually prolongs those abuses today, aren't we all thankful that these materials were collected, archived, and preserved? As these authors amply demonstrate, the Yuchi and Penobscot materials at the APS are being put to excellent use and are helping these nations to study and revitalize their languages and their cultures.

Led by then–APS librarian Martin Levitt and a staff that included Daythal Kendall and Timothy Powell, the APS has worked since at least 2006 to digitize its Native American collections to make them more widely available, to become more sensitive and responsive to American Indian concerns, and to handle and share its Native American holdings on a more equal basis with Indian nations, and Native people and scholars. Over a four-year period Levitt and the APS convened the Native American Advisory Board to consider and debate some of the issues and concerns identified by Grounds, Anderson, and Francis, as well as by many others; the board then drafted and finalized the groundbreaking APS "Protocols for the Treatment of Indigenous Materials" in 2014.[3] The APS now follows these protocols in handling its Native American collections, consults and negotiates with Indian nations and religious and traditional leaders, enters into written agreements with tribal nations, shares its materials widely, and works with tribes and Native scholars in defining and providing extra protections for culturally sensitive materials. But, as Anderson and Francis correctly point out, the APS is still sometimes restricted by legal rights and intellectual property law in what it can do. Maybe amendments to federal copyright law should be proposed?

The APS also created its Center for Native American and Indigenous Research (CNAIR) in 2014 and received an NEH challenge grant to endow it. The current APS librarian, Patrick Spero, has strongly supported these endeavors and worked to create a program for American Indian scholars to visit the APS. The initial grant to commence the Native American Scholars Initiative was donated by the Andrew W. Mellon Foundation in late 2016; the program will support research in Native American studies for the next five years. American Indian scholars, tribal college faculty, and researchers who work closely with American Indian communities will be granted internships and fellowships to work at the APS.

Moreover, in chapter 3 Lisa Conathan teaches us much about the challenges archives face in making their collections more available and more valuable for Indian nations, communities, and cultures, and for Native and non-Native scholars. She describes the efforts of the Beinecke Library at Yale University to work more closely with Native communities and scholars and to create modern-day applications for two disparate collections. She relates how the library went through its own learning curve on how best to use two different sets of materials: rare Mi'kmaw hieroglyph writing, primarily created in the sixteenth century in the context of Catholic worship, which only a few people can work with at the present time; and Cherokee syllabary from the early twentieth century. The materials created different challenges because the Cherokee body of language materials is large and represents a writing system still in use today, while the Mi'kmaw hieroglyphic manuscripts represent a closed corpus and an esoteric system that is not well known today.

The Cherokee materials had been with the library since 1979, but were not cataloged until 2013. The trend of using archival materials to help modern-day Native communities combat language loss led the Beinecke to digitize its Cherokee collection and open it to community comment and interpretation, as well as to support classroom and researcher use. In doing so the library engaged in research and consultation to tap into the remote expertise of research communities and scholars and to promote the collection to Cherokee language teachers. The library engaged in outreach to get its materials to Cherokee country and funded Cherokee language scholars to visit the collection and help the library catalog it.

The Beinecke staff lacked the expertise necessary to describe these materials, to find specific manuscripts, and to answer questions about them. Thus, visiting Cherokee scholars assisted the library with reviewing the materials and consulting on the best way to promulgate them. Ultimately the scholars and staff created a finding aid in 2015, and the library was ready to make nonsensitive materials accessible online. Today the library continues to work with the Cherokee community, making these materials available digitally to Cherokee-speaking individuals as well as to university and tribal language programs.

In contrast, we can perceive some of the unique issues created by dissimilar language materials in what the Beinecke has planned to do with the Mi'kmaw materials: in this case it is not planning on creating a machine-readable text, because there are so few scholars of this language. However, the library is hopeful that, just by holding the materials and publicizing them, it might open an entirely new arena of linguistic research and help create new scholars of the language.

These chapters, and the endeavors mentioned above, raise important questions, point to promising research and archival methods and projects, and demonstrate the potential for archives to get their collections off the shelves and to become "living things" again. In the process, archives and their collections can assist American Indian nations and communities in their modern-day efforts to revitalize their languages and cultures.

NOTES

1. Deloria, *Custer Died for Your Sins*, 81.
2. Deloria, *Custer Died for Your Sins*, 94.
3. The complete protocols have been published as part of the APS *Proceedings* and are available online at https://www.amphilsoc.org/sites/default/files/2017-11/attachments/aps%20protocols.pdf (accessed August 20, 2020).

BIBLIOGRAPHY

Deloria, Vine, Jr. *Custer Died for Your Sins: An Indian Manifesto*. New York: Macmillan, 1969.

CHAPTER 1

Decolonial Futures of Sharing

"Protecting Our Voice," Intellectual Property, and Penobscot Nation Language Materials

Jane Anderson and James E. Francis Sr.

What kind of legal and social orders need to fragment in order to create the possibility for decolonial futures?[1] Are such futures even possible, and can they ever be really free from the colonial mentalities of rule and technologies of governing of which we are deeply—and uncomfortably—still enmeshed? As a range of activists and scholars across multiple contexts have observed, we are embedded in a predicament that emerges from current modern liberalism.[2] Of this predicament Wendy Brown asks, "What reactive political formations [can] emerge ... in an era of profound political disorientation?"[3] Alyosha Goldstein refines this line of questioning by asking which of the available elements and conjunctures for addressing the colonial present are most salient and significant. By this he means to point to how the "current moment is shaped by the fraught historical accumulation and shifting disposition of colonial processes, relations and practices."[4] This disorientation is prompting a critical rethinking of some of the core assumptions embedded within our conceptual, legal and political interpretations of the world; as a result, there is perhaps a different kind of awareness of the intertwining of history, politics, and the multiple forms of colonial exclusion that are still lived and carried in minds and bodies, in processes and practices, ingrained within the very infrastructures of key institutions.[5]

A key element of the decolonial project is the development of options for overcoming the colonial conditioning of the present. Decolonial thinking requires a double movement: both of identifying continued sites of power imbalance brought about through colonial regimes of organization, *and* developing practices that can transform thinking, knowing, and moving away from this interpretive framing. In this chapter we offer thoughts on this double movement. From our collaborative standpoint, decoloniality needs to be understood as an epistemic and political project of scale.[6] The experience of the Penobscot Nation in Maine illustrates the extent of the challenges within this kind of project, especially what it takes to resist and recast the legacies of legal exclusion from the archive, the relationships between these exclusions and the dispossession of lands and languages, and the ongoing assertions of non-Native control and possession over representations of Native cultures.

This chapter examines the discrete problem of colonial *legal* practices embedded within cultural institutions like museums, libraries, and archives. It follows the thinking of scholars Amy Lonetree and Robin Boast, who seek to move beyond the metaphor of the "contact zone" to explain the operation of the settler-colonial archive in the present.[7] This involves looking more deeply into the infrastructure of the archive that maintains and distributes settler-colonial instrumentality.[8] We are interested in asking about the possibility for developing decolonial futures for sharing collections of Native American cultural materials assembled through uneven and unequal research practices. Collections of such materials have not been not neutrally produced and assembled.[9] They are foundationally implicated in settler-colonial property and capitalist endeavors, especially in the efforts to control, subordinate, and disenfranchise Indigenous people.[10] The intents, the productions, and the exchanges that mark these collections trace a settler-colonial logic of inquiry and privilege. In this chapter collections of language materials are our primary focus, because they remain a key site of concern within the Penobscot Nation and also aptly illustrate the ongoing settler-colonial property relations that are foundational to any kind of collections of Native American cultural materials and their ongoing institutionalization.

To decolonize these collections and the institutions that hold them is to start by acknowledging their production and function within the settler-colonial project and then to actively tease out the indices of settler-colonial power that continue to organize them and their various relationships in the present. Tracing these indices is not a straightforward task; rather, it must move simultaneously forward and backward. Locating power in the present can be a useful tool for identifying where it installed itself in the past. Identifications of property and ownership in these collections and the continued exercise of possession is one place to start thinking about how to reorganize relationships between communities and institutions, and the relationships of property that bind Native communities to institutions that hold and own such important collections of cultural materials is one of this chapter's primary themes.

The decolonial future offers itself as an ambition, a place that we strive toward, that we commit ourselves to trying to achieve. But some things can never be undone, and some things should never be forgotten. The coloniality in and of our present remains thick and heavy; its patterns of order and organization are so deeply inscribed into thought, memory, and action. Settler colonialism has produced habits and traditions that are hard to identify, hard to shed, and hard to think beyond; a specific consciousness is needed to maneuver around the settler-colonial privilege that exerts itself within the archive. Here we seek to identify certain legal threads knitted tightly into institutional logics of operation and governance that continue to affect engagement with communities. The decolonial project demands attention to the ongoing hidden exertions of settler-colonial legal power.[11]

The chapter is divided into two sections that loosely follow the three-year grant awarded to the Penobscot Nation in 2012 by the Administration for Native Americans (ANA). Titled "'Recovering Our Voices': Language Immersion Project," this grant focused on stabilizing, protecting, and enhancing Penobscot as a spoken language of the Penobscot people. As Penobscot language collections are largely held outside the Penobscot community in collecting institutions such as the American Philosophical Society (APS), the University of Maine, and the Library of Congress, one important element of this project was to address the intellectual property and, more specifically, the copyright issues affecting Penobscot control over them. From a Penobscot perspective, understanding and resolving these legal issues remain critical to the preservation and revitalization of the Penobscot language. Moreover, finding ways to negotiate around them are central to the capacity for Penobscot to assert their rights to make decisions about how these materials are accessed and circulated into the future. The first section begins with James's experience within the Penobscot community, especially some of the key struggles with bringing the language back, alongside the motivations and achievements of the grant. The second section makes visible the relationships between copyright and settler colonialism and examines the specific complications of copyright ownership that affect the capacity for the Penobscot Nation to protect and control Penobscot language as an integral cultural source for future generations. The chapter concludes with examples of how the Penobscot Nation is maneuvering around copyright law, specifically in developing strategies for negotiating with institutions to recognize the Penobscot Nation as the appropriate cultural authority over these materials and developing training and educational workshops for other tribes to do their own work in this area.

Bringing Penobscot Back to the Ear

In southern New England, when I was three years old, my mom took me, my older brother, and my younger sister back to her home on the Penobscot Indian Reservation, on Indian Island, Maine. We moved into my grandmother Beatrice's house, where my mom had grown up. My mom was the second youngest of her siblings, with three sisters and five brothers. Beatrice was a strong Penobscot woman, completely blind in one eye and legally blind in the other, and she worked from home as a basket maker, spending much of her time braiding bundles of fragrant sweetgrass, winding the rope around a well-worn chair. The process amazed me, as did the speed of her fingers; the braids seemed to magically appear from her fingertips. The blades of grass made a whipping sound as they cut through the air.

Many people came by Beatrice's Oak Hill house: local basket makers to trade baskets for bundles of her sweet grass, as well as women from the neighborhood to play cards. It was during these visits that Beatrice would speak the language. She never shared the lyrical tongue with me or my siblings, and she did not teach it to her own nine children. Beatrice, who spoke it fluently, was trilingual, knowing Penobscot, Passamaquoddy, and English. She spoke with ease as she and her friends conversed and played cards.

I used to call myself a second-generation nonspeaker, but today I consider myself a student of the language. As a young adult returning home from the Air Force, I longed to learn it, but Beatrice died the same year I came home. I felt that something was missing; if I didn't speak the language, then what kind of Penobscot was I? Over time I realized that I wasn't alone, that this guilt around language loss has haunted the community for decades.

Beatrice made a conscious choice not to teach her children to speak the language. With each of them attending a school on Indian Island that was run by the Catholic Church and staffed by the Sisters of Mercy, speaking it could be harmful to them; stories of the language being beaten out of children are common in the community. So, out of love, Beatrice didn't teach it to her children or grandchildren, and she wasn't alone—many families didn't. The story of language loss in our community is rooted in historical trauma, and much healing needs to take place.

When I was growing up, the tribe had a language-preservation program headed by Frank Siebert, a retired pathologist with an interest in the Penobscot language that began when he was a boy visiting Old Town, Maine.[12] From the 1970s onward on behalf of the tribe he wrote and received many grants to help preserve the language.[13] I would often visit him in his office in the rear of the community building. He was not very personable and oftentimes grumpy. He had two staff people: Carol Dana, who is our language master today, and Pauleena MacDougall, who was employed at the University of Maine and has just recently retired. Carol is a tribal member; Pauleena, who is not, was an employee of the tribe and a graduate student working on her PhD at the same time.

One specific language-related project that I remember clearly as a youth was the Susie Dana tapes. Every household on the reservation received a long box containing about twenty-five cassette tapes with

Elder Susie Dana speaking in Penobscot. We never played the cassettes; my mom put the box up on the top shelf of the closet, where I am sure they still remain today, part of the family archive. When I became the director of the Cultural and Historic Preservation Department for the tribe, I recognized that the language didn't need to be preserved in the closet; it needed to be revitalized and spoken.

Seibert's other major project was to create a Penobscot dictionary. This was a major undertaking, for our language was spoken only; previous attempts to document it were inconsistent and often confusing. Seibert sought to standardize the language by creating the Penobscot alphabet, based on the International Phonetic Alphabet. This was far from simple, and Seibert was also impatient and had an authoritarian attitude; as a result, very few people learned the language. During this time many fluent speakers died.

When the dictionary was made available, it wasn't copyrighted immediately. It took Watie Akins, an Elder in the community, to do that work, and it was eventually copyrighted to the Penobscot Nation, in the early 2000s.[14] While this original dictionary wasn't the answer to getting people speaking the language, the dictionary was now the intellectual property of the Penobscot Nation. This mattered because the nation controlled how it could be shared and for what purposes.

The above-mentioned, complicated alphabet was the major hurdle to getting people to use the dictionary as a learning aid. It is is based on the Latin alphabet and comprised of letters that you would see in the English alphabet, but it also contains other letters, because it was designed as a way to record oral languages like ours. The addition of a *schwa*, which looks like a lowercase "e" spun 180 degrees, an alpha, and "k"s with superscript "w"s, made the alphabet daunting and the words unrecognizable and even harder to pronounce. Writing the language down further distanced it from the Penobscot people, which is why some linguists talk about how writing down oral languages could be understood as a further act of colonialism.[15] It made our language unrecognizable to us. In addition there are letters that do correspond to English but don't necessarily sound like the letters in English. For example, the letter "t" sounds like a "d," and the letter "p" sounds like a "b." So, for us to learn the language, we had to learn a brand-new alphabet from the colonized system, adding another colonial technology to the one we were taught in the Western school system, which had also deliberately forbidden our speaking our language. The only way back to it was first through the colonial English alphabet and then through this daunting phonetic system that few understood. This difficulty added to the problem of speaking and teaching the language and brought no healing to the community.

In addition to the Susie Dana tapes, we all got a dictionary, but it was hard to use. If you wanted to look up a word it was nearly impossible. Seibert decided to alphabetize the language according to Penobscot words using the newly designed alphabet—for example, if you wanted to look up the Penobscot word for "beaver," you would have to know the Penobscot word in the first place. And, even if you did know the word, the complication of the alphabet added to the problem. "Beaver," which is pronounced da-mar-quay in Penobscot, would be hard to find. Without knowledge of the structure of the alphabet, you would search under "d," when the word actually starts with "t" in Penobscot. This kind of complication frustrated many would-be learners in the community. Also, not everyone in the community is on board with learning the language. Many of the Elders feel they are too old, and others want to honor the decision of their parents not to teach them the language. For those who do want to learn, however, we are on the path of revitalization.

It became clear each time the community lost an Elder speaker that we needed to act quickly or think differently about language learning. For those Elders who do speak, many don't want the responsibility of teaching, because it can be an impossible burden. As a result we were running out of options. What we did have was the dictionary and the work Siebert had done. The tribal administration felt the dictionary project was important enough to employ Seibert to create it. So we turned to this document as the core of our revitalization project.

In 2011 we applied for an Administration for Native Americans (ANA) grant for revitalizing the language. We had three major goals: first, to speak all the words that were in the dictionary and record them; second, to republish the Penobscot dictionary with an English-to-Penobscot index; and, third, to protect this cultural source for future generations.

Recording the words and digitizing them is called "bringing Penobscot back to the ear," which I will address soon, but first let's see some of the challenges and some of the beauty of the original Penobscot Dictionary.

First, it is clear why Seibert alphabetized the dictionary in the way he did. The translation between English and Penobscot requires an entirely different worldview, an entirely different way of thinking, which would in turn require an altogether different order and organization. Often a word in English is actually a larger phrase in Penobscot, which are often descriptions—for example, the word for birch bark canoe is *ah gwee den* and means "that which floats lightly." The Penobscot phrase tells you something about how my ancestors viewed that craft and its inherent relationships to the environment. The only recourse to get back to these phrases, which are really situated and convey a certain kind of place, is to create a dictionary that would have an index that would allow a learner to search through phrases.

Another unfortunate design of the original dictionary was the lack of decoding. If you found *ah gwee den*, you would only see written "birch bark canoe." The whole concept of "that which floats lightly" would have been omitted, as such phrases often were, especially in words that are nouns. This is highly unfortunate, and it indicates the stretch of colonization and its affect on language and its meaning. Siebert didn't care to show how Penobscot people saw the world; that didn't matter to him, and it was not what he was focused on. He was interested in words and their literal, not conceptual, translation. As a result, this important information didn't make it into the dictionary, but Dr. Siebert's notes do contain a great deal of it, which he received this from fluent Penobscot speakers as he was conducting his research. This information is an important component to healing around language loss and to cultural growth. An Elder once told me, "To know the language you must understand the culture, and to understand the culture you must understand the language." When I first heard this it seemed like a catch-22, a double bind that never gets resolved, and something that could not help us, since we didn't have the language. Were we locked out of our own culture? However, the dictionary itself became a key to unlock some of the elements of this paradoxical situation.

Because Siebert alphabetized the dictionary according to Penobscot words, a student of the language will find what I call "cultural clusters." For example, the word for sturgeon, a large fish indigenous to the Penobscot River, is labeled as "sturgeon" in the dictionary, but, if you look at the words adjacent to it, a cultural worldview starts to appear. The common theme is based on the concept of "throwing something out of the water." This points to how Penobscot ancestors saw this fish, and to a unique attribute that would define it. A very deliberate and careful decoding can take place within the text of the dictionary and the notes of Dr. Seibert, where clues offer us insight into the construction of the language and hence the Penobscot cultural worldview. This reworking and rethinking of the language is the road to decolonization at the linguistic level: a project of undoing, unlearning, and reassembling.

"Bringing Penobscot back to the ear" was conceived as a necessary part of the ANA grant from an activity done by a young language apprentice many years ago. He visited people in the community and compiled Penobscot words that were being used on a daily basis. We were amazed to find dozens upon dozens of words interwoven in our daily speech. The sounds of the language were still vibrant; the ability to speak the sound was still present. So, within the same ANA grant to record all the Penobscot words in a digital forum, we thought it was important to bring these recorded sounds to the people, to (re)make it part of the everyday within the community.

Bringing the recorded audio to the ear was done in a couple of ways. First, it was important to revive the sounds of the Elders who had passed and fill the air with the language again. Installing seven televisions throughout common areas within the community achieved this: we programmed them with language lessons, sounds, and videos and used them to advertise our language classes, which were open to tribal members and apprentices.

Through the grant we supported fifteen apprentices, who were chosen because of where they worked. We had the teachers from the school, day care staff, a computer technology person, members of the Penobscot intellectual property committee, youth program staff, and a member of the Elders committee. The model was to have language learning trickle down to kids in day care, students in school, youth in afterschool programs, and some Elders. The apprentices were equipped with iPads programmed with language lessons developed for the Apple platform. In addition, online lessons were being developed in conjunction with a digital language database.

Getting people to attend classes on a regular basis has always been a challenge. Our strategy was to try and ensure that people could learn the language in the comfort of their own homes. We had to meet them where they are —in front of screens. The development of digitized language learning, an online database, and instructional videos has enabled us to deliver language learning content to learnings on their schedule, in their homes and at their pace.

The third strand of the ANA grant was to protect our language and to wrestle control of it out of non-Penobscot hands. Jane had been working with the tribe since 2010 on other intellectual property issues, which is how we met and began collaborating. Together our work is focused on unraveling the legal frameworks that have trapped our language as non-Penobscot institutional property. This work is for Penobscot people, but it is also about helping other communities do this same work for themselves. As we are thick within the digital age, it is clear that protecting our language material is vitally important. But, because of a range of historical factors (some of which I have already mentioned), our community does not have control over our language. We lost that control when it was written down and copyrighted by the researchers (predominately Seibert, but also earlier researchers like Frank Speck and Mary Haas) who were following their own agendas. If we knew then what we know now about copyright and the ownership of knowledge—for instance, who owns the documentation of our community when it is produced—this would not have happened. But no one in our community really knew or thought about this. Through processes of documentation, Penobscot language became something that could be possessed, that could become the property of others. Given the guilt around language learning that continues to permeate our community, it is imperative that we listen to the voices that are concerned about this and establish policies that respect and honor a vision that works to break this settler-colonial legal hold.

The Penobscot Nation's Cultural and Historic Preservation Committee has now established policies around language and language learning that address some of these issues. In these policies and at this stage, language learning is for Penobscot people only. This was enacted because of the discomfort of learning with nontribal members in the room—a legacy of the way Frank Siebert alienated people that tried to learn the language, and part of the historical trauma of language loss in our community that has led to shame that so many of us don't speak our language. In this policy we also decided that, despite its cumbersomeness, the Penobscot alphabet, as it was created by Siebert, will continue to be used. There is just no other way to begin and to continue. We do recognize the important work that Siebert did, even if it was not necessarily how we would have done it. Finally—and this is the ongoing work that we are doing—the Penobscot dictionary and all of Siebert's documentation, including recordings of speakers and field notes, all produced on behalf of the tribe, need to be protected from inappropriate circulation and use. This material must be returned to us and the Penobscot Nation recognized as the legitimate cultural authority over it in every archive and library where it is held.

We are using the Penobscot dictionary to help us revive our language and shape the language program in the future; it, along with Siebert's field notes, are the primary resources left for us. The Penobscot Nation felt it was important enough to hire Seibert and preserve our language. Our language needs to be taken out of the box, out of the archive, down from the closet. We need to take what was preserved, put it into motion, and reenergize it in our bodies, in our minds, and on our lands and our waters. The Penobscot Dictionary and its associated notes have become vitally important to our cultural identity, as well as to the possibilities for our language revitalization. It is the core of our linguistic future, and in a digital era we are poised to have a vibrant language again in our community.

I began this narrative speaking about my grandmother Beatrice and how she never taught her children to speak. However, her youngest daughter, Gayle, and her oldest daughter, Lorraine, are our most dedicated apprentices. Lorraine, who is eighty years old, is our star student.

She comes to every class with her iPad in hand, using it to record the class or herself practicing the words, watch language videos, access the online database, do lesson plans, and create lessons for herself. One day someone asked her why, at her age, she was so passionate about learning the language. She smiled and said, "I want to be able to speak to my mother and all of our ancestors in our language on the other side."

Protecting Our Voice

The problem of the possession and ownership of Native American cultural materials remains unresolved for many Indigenous communities, who are working with institutions over the digitization and the "return" of collections, and for whom questions of ownership, control and use repeatedly arise. The extensive projects attuned to developing local digital archives and portals to connect communities back to their belongings are rapidly increasing, and while there is complexity and nuance within these projects, all of them at some point have to grapple with the question of who legally owns these collections, what kind of permissions need to be secured from collectors, authors, and owners, and how communities can use and repurpose this material within their own contexts for their own needs.[16]

As explained above, the third strand woven into the ANA language grant concerned its future protection as a treasured part of Penobscot culture. Here it was the ongoing figure of property embedded in Penobscot language collections that the Penobscot Nation was seeking to explicitly address. This part of the grant required lengthy legal research into past practices of non-Penobscot individuals who had worked on the language, tracking down their archives and identifying the periods of copyright protection for all the materials. The grant also asked for the development of tribal policy and infrastructure to counter these historical and legally produced problems in order that they be recast and remedied. While the specific requirements of the grant have been met, much of this work negotiating with institutions and building community infrastructure around research and intellectual property continues. We are also using these experiences to inform training and education to support this work in other tribal contexts, as the Penobscot Nation is not unique in having these settler-colonial legal exclusions from institutions that hold Native materials.[17]

Many of the current problems with copyright have their beginning in the uneven and unequal research practices that made Indigenous groups, cultures, and languages subjects of and for research inquiry. The property that was produced in these encounters continues to influence and affect the relationships that communities have with institutions. Researchers, hobbyists, and others who worked in communities (e.g., missionaries and Indian agents), most of whom were not directly employed by the tribe, became the legal rights holders over any documentation that they made in these engagements. This was the case for all the researchers who worked in the Penobscot Nation, including Haas, Speck, and Siebert, and it rested on the assumption that one kind of originating knowledge-making activity was taking place and that that activity came with specific legal rights.[18]

As anthropologists of property have detailed, property organizes people in relationship to each other. In doing so it generates social relationships that can stretch across time. Yet the productions of property can be haphazard and have unpredictable effects and futures.[19] An important direction for thinking about relationships formed through the concept of property is how they are also formed through racialized and gendered ontologies, ideologies, and categories.[20] Aileen Morton-Robinson has recently examined relationships between whiteness, property, and Indigenous sovereignty.[21] She provides a close study for how property and possession are central for the relational operations of whiteness.[22] A key argument for Moreton-Robinson is that whiteness is not defined through Indigenous difference, but through the *possession* of Indigenous people and lands. Her critical work is dense with potential and, in particular, offers an invitation for further thinking about settler colonialism, property, and academic disciplines. This would necessitate a closer analysis of the relationships between settler colonialism and intellectual property as the key legal, social, and economic site for the possession and control of Indigenous knowledge.

Copyright and Colonialism

In the significant literature tracking the emergence of copyright in British and American contexts, only a very small portion has attended to the inherent relationships to colonialism in this body of law.[23] Most of the recent focus comes by way of attention to the consequences of intellectual property and copyright in non-European contexts, namely Africa, Asia, and, to a lesser extent, South America. Much of this literature points to the biases and privileges built into the laws themselves that facilitate inequity in a range of areas, including economic development, access to medicines, and trade. The consequences of intellectual property within these contexts have been wide reaching and significant; Madhavi Sunder argues that intellectual property laws foundationally now affect "human capacity to live a good life."[24]

Intellectual property law in Europe, particularly in Britain, began its development at the same time as our current conceptions of "real" property emerged.[25] The arguments of John Locke functioned as founding principles for copyright as well as real property, due to their reworking by the British jurist William Blackstone, at one time the most cited legal theorist in the early American republic.[26] The right of the individual to possess the products of his labor is a central principle for the granting of a copyright, the presumption here being that land and also knowledge is no one's until it is activated by deliberate acts of "discovery" and intelligible forms of labor. *Terra nullius* ('no one's land') and *gnaritus nullius* ('no one's knowledge') are activated, claimed, and made into property through the same gendered and racialized principles of labor and possession. While much scholarship has been devoted to understanding the role of property law in colonial ambitions in the dispossession of Indigenous lands, much less attention has been paid to the role of copyright law in the dispossession of Indigenous knowledges. If we take seriously the contention made by Moreton-Robinson that whiteness is fundamentally about Indigenous possession, then attention to copyright as a strategy in the possession of Indigenous knowledge must follow.

Copyright is an international framework of legal protection with surprisingly minimal variations across jurisdictions. This is because, from at least 1886, international conventions and agreements were entered into that maintained alignments between copyright development within countries.[27] Many countries that were once under colonial governance maintain those original intellectual property laws. For instance, Australia,

Canada, New Zealand, and South Africa enshrine early English ideas of copyright; now-independent countries in Africa formerly under British, German, or French rule embody the copyright frameworks of those countries, and so forth. Other countries that did not have explicit forms of copyright now do so as signatories to one of the biggest multilateral trade agreements made in 1994: the Agreement on Trade-Related Aspects of Intellectual Property Rights negotiated at the Uruguay Round of the General Agreement on Trades and Tariffs.[28]

Accounts of the intricate making of Indigenous culture into forms of intellectual property—through the strategy of copyright ownership, for instance—has not yet been told. This is surprising, given how much material is caught up in the folds of copyright, how implicated anthropologists and linguists are in this colonial project, how long copyright can last, how complicated it is to unravel, and what kinds of negotiations Indigenous people must now enter into in order to access and use this material. According to current law, copyright rests with researchers or other third parties because they were the ones writing things down, taking photographs, and making recordings of largely oral "traditional" (and therefore not original) cultures. In fixing the intangible spoken words and language into tangible representations, the general conditions for copyright protection—especially as most of this material was unpublished—were automatically met. These representations of Native culture became researcher or institutional (depending on who was being employed by whom) intellectual property. In the initial call from Thomas Jefferson in 1797 to document Native languages, heralding the "arrival of the modern preservationist paradigm," the long history of settler-colonial control of Indigenous knowledges, including languages, began.[29] Indeed, in the United States this protection is extensive and can extend for several generations.[30] Once the term for copyright protection ends, these previously protected works enter into a space called the "public domain." But the movement from copyright protection to the public domain does not provide Indigenous people with any relief; with public domain status, anybody can use previously copyrighted material. Indigenous people have no special rights to regain control over their culture and languages.

It is important to recognize that the initial motivation for language documentation was not developed to assist communities. It was conducted within a military and capitalist context of domination and later extended through the salvage paradigm for future research. This is a legacy that matters, especially if we acknowledge the inherent relationships between the original framing of these kinds of projects by, for example, Thomas Jefferson and John Wesley Powell, which inevitably also informed Frank Siebert's ad hoc teachers and mentors Edward Sapir and Frank Speck. The original intentions for documentation affected the techniques of documentation and, consequently, the conditions of ownership of this newly produced property. This continues to be of critical importance to Native American communities trying to access their language materials embedded within researcher collections or buried in books of field notes. To understand the dimensions and consequences of this dilemma, as well as how the Penobscot Nation has decided to proceed, we need to engage with the particularities of copyright law.

Some researchers who now hold copyright to various forms of language documentation were not necessarily aware of their legal rights in the course of their research; it was just a by-product. However, many were aware and understood exactly what rights they had, how these rights could be exerted and how copyright protected their possession and its future circulation.[31] For example, the copyright notice ©, required for copyright protection following the first federal Copyright Act in 1909, was consistently used by Edward Curtis on his photographs post-1909. While Curtis had distinct commercial interests in the photographs he made of Native Americans, it is reasonable to assume that he had knowledge of his copyright rights. Along with his photographs Curtis also accumulated over ten thousand recordings of songs and speech in more than eighty different community languages to which he, his descendants, or his estate retain copyright ownership, unless these materials have entered the public domain. From an Indigenous perspective there is a legitimate sense of inequity that the law vested property rights in the people who came uninvited onto tribal lands, asking questions and holding new technological equipment, not with those who held the knowledge in the first place and generously shared it. Copyright law, like real property law, was developed to support European ideas of property and was effectively used as a means for dispossession within settler-colonial contexts. As part of the settler-colonial legal apparatus, copyright set in place a series of hierarchies and relationships of power, many of which are only now being uncovered and almost all of which are still in place, operating in myriad hidden ways.[32]

Any decolonial future for museums and archives must come to terms with this area of property law and the networks of power, obligation, and expectation that have necessarily been generated through it. This means recognizing the unique nature of the problems that arise for communities as they encounter collections still under copyright, and the significant labor involved in making clear exactly what kinds of rights exist and need to be addressed at an institutional and at a community level. This takes time, but it can be done. The haphazard nature of copyright protection—the fact that different kinds of material (e.g., photographs, sound recordings, manuscripts) have different periods of protection—means special kinds of arrangements and alternative strategies that elevate Indigenous concerns above those of the standard public that the museum tends to assume, needs to be made. Agreements like memorandums of understanding between tribes and institutions are one option.[33] These draw on the potential of settler-colonial law to recast itself.[34] Realistically it is unlikely than new legislation will be developed to deal with this complexity for Indigenous collections. Moreover, there is only minimal political interest in making any amendments to already existing copyright legislation (though there is also clear resistance from multiple sectors to this as well).[35] For example, in the most recent amendment to the U.S. Copyright Act—the Music Modernization Act 2018—Indigenous interests were not taken into account at all, even though this legislation will greatly affect the circulation of pre-1972 Native sound recordings without community permission or knowledge.[36] As a result policy innovation and action takes place at a local level as each tribal authority works out how best to proceed and do their own legal research in order to know what exactly they are dealing with in the archive and what they need to put in place as tribal legal codes or policy.

Within the ANA grant, the Penobscot Nation directly took on the problem of copyright ownership. To really make the point about the long colonial reach of copyright ownership, let's take the documentation of Penobscot language made by Siebert and now housed at the APS as our point of departure. To begin, we need to consider the function and operation of copyright law as they relate to the various forms that language documentation can take.

What Is Copyright?

There are a variety of scholars who note how "property talk" reinscribes the power of this body of law. We are especially sensitive to this problematic because understanding these kinds of collections as property has extreme limits.[37] But, for tribes working with institutions to secure and even return their cultural heritage materials, there is a constant need to navigate around the institutional conceptualization of these materials as property. Thus we don't seek to reinscribe the power of property here, but to unravel what is at stake and how to begin to imagine strategies around it. In the ANA grant the Penobscot Nation wanted to develop culturally appropriate strategies for the future management of its cultural heritage as a valuable cultural element for future generations. To do this the Penobscot Tribal Council wanted to know *exactly* what kinds of property law were functioning to trap Penobscot cultural heritage and bind it to the institutions with which the Penobscot Nation would have to negotiate.

Since 1976 in the United States, copyright protection is automatic and persists from the time the work is created *in a fixed form*. The copyright in the work of authorship automatically becomes the property of the author who created the work; there is no need for registration. Only the author or those deriving their rights through the author can rightfully claim copyright. Prior to 1976 the U.S. Copyright Act of 1909 governed definitions of works as well as rights for reproduction and duplication. Under this act copyright protection attached to original works and only existed when those works were, first, published and, second, had a notice of copyright affixed. Thus, state copyright law (which preceded the 1909 act) governed protection for unpublished works, but published works, whether they contained a notice of copyright or not, were governed exclusively by federal law. If no notice of copyright was affixed to a work and the work was published, the 1909 act provided no copyright protection and the work became part of the "public domain."

The complication here in determining copyright for Native American material is that significant documentation occurred prior to 1976 as well as to 1909. Early sound technology, which facilitated an altogether different rendering of language and sound, was not protected by copyright until 1976. In some cases documentation made by a researcher falls across the period of the two copyright statutes of 1909 and 1976; consequently, different periods of protection are offered. For instance, Siebert started documenting the Penobscot language in the 1930s, and he left unpublished papers and field notes, as well as cylinder recordings made between 1935 and 1938. Siebert also made significant documentation of the Penobscot language from 1976 until his death in 1998. All this later material falls under the 1976 copyright statute; we will return to what this means for determining periods of protection.

Language and Copyright

Traditionally language has been considered to be a common resource not protected by property law or copyright. However, the ways in which language can been documented, and that language is not ever just "language" but is expressed in narratives, songs, and laws, means that language has become protected by copyright. Moreover, the written documentation of language — either as word slips, dictionaries, or lexicons, for instance — are protected by copyright as literary works. Sound recordings that capture oral narratives in a Native language are also protected. It is important to emphasize that copyright is largely disinterested in the content of a copyrighted work; for protection, it only matters that the work be original and made into its tangible form by the "author." It is this ambivalence to the actual content of a copyright work and the intensive research engagement with Native American communities, particularly over Native languages, that have made it possible for non-Native people to become legal rights holders over the documentation of Native languages. What makes this a particularly difficult and sensitive situation is that, in many instances, this documentation is now integral for the revitalization of Native languages and the rebuilding of communities of Native-language speakers. As James explained above, the loss of Native languages is experienced within communities as an ongoing historical trauma produced through settler colonialism. The settler-colonial twist is that now communities need to get permissions for copying and reproducing their own languages from researchers, many of whom were complicit in the settler-colonial project, or, at the very least, in the ideologies of salvage and documentation that propelled these research practices.

The Penobscot (Siebert) Language Collection

To provide some clear examples of exactly what kind of complexities of copyright might exist around a language collection, we want to look briefly at the current copyright conditions of the Siebert collection.[38] Since this is one of the most valuable and extensive collections of Penobscot language documentation, the Penobscot Nation has had to navigate a complex copyright framework, including different periods of protection for different kinds of documentation. This is not unusual for collections of tribal language materials; however, having now conducted this legal archival research, the Penobscot Nation is much clearer about what rights exist and for how long, what material now needs to be part of explicit agreements, and how to begin making plans for the next generation, when the bulk of this material enters into the public domain and can be used by anyone—a problem that presents another range of concerns. Knowing exactly how the law is functioning and how it will continue to affect Penobscot efforts at language revitalization contributes to Penobscot capacity to exercise sovereignty, control, and cultural authority over these collections.

According to the APS catalog and finding aid, the Siebert collection (measured as forty-one linear feet of shelf space) holds the most material relating to the Penobscot Nation.[39] This is in terms of both language materials and materials documenting cultural heritage at the Penobscot Nation from 1929 up to Siebert's death in 1998. These materials consist of:

Public lectures;
Letters and communications between Siebert and others;
Miscellaneous notes and field notes in notebooks (over a hundred);

Published materials;
Unpublished language documentation, including loose-leaf notes;
Handwritten notes and typed drafts for individual entries for the Penobscot Dictionary;
Collected texts and narratives of the Penobscot Nation;
Published articles (and their drafts);
Over eight hundred sketches and silver gelatin prints (1932–46 and 1985–94);
Sound recordings (1930s, 1950s, 1960s, 1970s, 1980s);
Penobscot language master cards.

Of all this, the published material is the easiest to deal with, as it has relatively clear periods of protection, at least for material produced post-1976. This is seventy years after the death of the author, making it available for any use with no permission from the Penobscot Nation in 2068. The lectures, letters, and field notes will all have various periods of protection, depending upon the date of their creation. If this is unknown—as is the case for a lot of this material—the earliest that it can be assumed to be in the public domain will also be 2068.

Some of the most valuable material from a Penobscot perspective falls into the "unpublished" category. This is a peculiar category, because the time period for copyright protection begins at the moment of publication. Unpublished works are therefore in a precopyright stasis—ostensibly protected, but for an unknown period. Unpublished material pre-1909, protected initially by state law, was brought into federal jurisdiction in the 1976 Copyright Act and will enter the public domain seventy years after the death of the author. Again, for Siebert, this will be 2068. Unpublished material post-1976 is protected automatically upon its creation and also protected for seventy years after the death of the author. After doing the research on the types of material in the Siebert collection and its periods of protection, it is clear that the bulk of it remains protected for another forty-nine years. Upon Siebert's death copyright in this collection was transferred to the APS by Siebert's heirs.[40] So it is the APS that now holds copyright and control over this material until 2068. This is an incredibly long period of time for the Penobscot Nation to have to negotiate access and control over culturally vital materials, especially with rapidly changing digital environments; the inequity is pronounced. The reach of settler-colonial control is long, and its effect is powerful.

It is worth asking why the Penobscot Nation—or any other tribe—just use their cultural heritage materials regardless: Who would police this use? And, more pressingly, wouldn't principles of sovereign immunity within Federal Indian Law offer some protections against suit, as least for federally recognized tribes? This relationship between copyright and sovereign immunity needs much closer examination and could provide one kind of strategy, but it would not work for all tribes, especially those that are not federally recognized.[41] Why wouldn't using these materials constitute an exception under the copyright exception of "fair use"? Couldn't Penobscot use of their own language materials be considered fair use? And, yes, like any copyright user, there are Penobscot uses that fall under this exception, but Penobscot are not just any user, and the publishing of this material online or making any new works, for instance, all require permissions and licenses from the copyright holder—in this instance, the APS. An additional problem is that none of this has been tested in court, and it is difficult and unwise to speculate about how a court would understand and interpret this issue. Breaches for copyright infringement incur costs and fines. Usually descendants of the copyright holders patrol these borders of infringement, as they feel particularly responsible for protecting the property of their author-relation. Institutions that hold these collections and are now the copyright holders could behave differently, though: they could enact policy that relinquishes control, at least of the copyright, for the communities whose material it really is. This would be the decolonial move that many communities are waiting for—that releases materials for them, but not necessarily into the public domain. Could an institution that promotes themselves as supporting Native interests answer this call and acknowledge that the colonial exclusions in the collections continues to affect present community revitalization and knowledge transmission? Could they make a deliberate move to unravel and reroute the legal power relations embedded in these collections? They can, and the decolonial imperative of the moment requires that they do.

Protecting Penobscot Voice

Let us conclude by returning to the reason the Penobscot Nation wrote the element "Protecting Penobscot Voice" into the ANA grant to start with. At the same time that the Penobscot Nation was developing the grant and refocusing attention on revitalization efforts in the community, a group of non-Penobscot scholars at the University of Maine, with the APS as a partner, wrote and submitted a grant to the National Science Foundation to digitize the Penobscot Dictionary. No one contacted the Penobscot Nation about this project, and it wasn't until the grant was rejected because of lack of community engagement that the researchers got in touch with the Penobscot Nation. That a project like this could be imagined, and a grant application written, without including the Penobscot Nation as a key partner, authority, and integral collaborator illustrates the habits of the settler-colonial research continuum and highlights the endemic exclusion of Native participation in projects that derive and utilize these unique cultural materials. That these kinds of research practices continue without critical reflection is exactly what the Penobscot Nation is concerned about. When research projects engage Native people as legitimate authorities and as collaborators on equal terms, different kinds of projects emerge, and these also tend to be more closely attentive to Native interests and needs. In 2012, when this grant application was written, this approach should have been the standard ethical research practice.

With the push to collaborate coming from the funding agency, both the University of Maine and the APS reached out to the Penobscot Nation, and the project turned into one from which the Penobscot people could also benefit. As a result, Penobscot entered into two agreements around access to the language materials. This saw the return to the community for the first time of select digitized language materials from the APS Penobscot (Siebert) collection.

The experience for Penobscot of getting to this stage of collaboration, however, was concerning. It was clear that Penobscot materials were and are still considered to be raw resources for researchers, as evidenced by the APS and the University of Maine applying for a grant to work with these materials, with no Penobscot involvement or consent. As Penobscot have no legal control over the use of these collections because of copyright, institutions perpetuate these exclusions by having no or very limited checks or procedures in place to make sure researchers engage with a community as the source community when using its cultural materials. This is a significant institutional failing. Institutions alert all users to copyright clearances and permissions for collections, but very few deal with the significant gaps in the law for the people and communities whose collections they hold but who are not legal rights holders, and very few have created policy to redirect settler-colonial research practices. Prejudices and mistakes continue in the practices and are also embedded within the archive itself, in the metadata and the way an institution structures the social use of these materials. There needs to be a different commitment to correcting mistakes in the documentation and shedding light on the complexity of culture hidden within the documentation—for example, like the cultural clusters found within verbs and phrases in the dictionary that link language to place and reveal the always already existing Penobscot worldview and clearly indicate who should have the authority to govern the decision to use these materials. There needs to be a different permission process that recognizes that Indigenous communities have rights and authority over these collections, and that they are not the same user-publics that the archive, library and museum has traditionally served.

The Penobscot Nation remains the legitimate cultural authority of all Penobscot language materials. The Penobscot Nation sees the decolonial future as an opportunity to collaborate in order to correct historical mistakes in meaning and understanding. The Penobscot voice remains strong, and the project is to regain control so that Penobscot can continue to share knowledge on Penobscot terms and in ways that reflect and respect always existing protocols and responsibilities of use.

Conclusion: The Penobscot Collections Project

The work that we have been doing together for the last nine years has required the interweaving of Penobscot pasts, presents, and futures. Like land, language is one of the most important and vital cultural elements, and revitalizing it requires bringing it back to the community and back to the ear. It also requires an interrogation of the settler-colonial histories of its written production, acquisition, and possession by non-Native people. It requires finding our language collections held in multiple institutions. It is about having them returned. It is also about understanding *exactly* how legal ownership of Penobscot language became possible, and how long it remains trapped by that body of law. This has meant developing new strategies and frameworks that can help institutions develop culturally appropriate processes to incorporate our perspectives and voice. We have found that one of the most effective (though still difficult) forms for doing this has been through direct nation-to-institution agreements. Penobscot language materials have specific conditions for their access and use. The decolonial project demands from all participants their respect for Penobscot sovereignty as well as Penobscot cultural authority. It asks for new relationships and practices to be developed, as the old ones are imbricated with settler-colonial ideologies and power relations and therefore cannot work for all of us equally or equitably.

From the ANA project we have established a firm base that is allowing us to develop a new project that brings language as well as other collections back to a Penobscot context. The newly developed Penobscot Nation Collections Project focuses on identifying and locating Penobscot tangible and intangible cultural heritage materials in U.S. and Canadian museums, archives, and libraries. Penobscot material is held in over thirty-five U.S. institutions alone. The aim of this project is to connect these collections to the Penobscot Nation and to reanimate them according to Penobscot perspectives and values. The Penobscot Nation is working with the content management system Mukurtu CMS to organize and import digital catalog records from the databases of collecting institutions.[42] The goal is to reconnect to histories and to culture: to reanimate the archive with Penobscot voices, on Penobscot terms, in Penobscot contexts. But return of collection does not bring legal ownership; therefore, where possible, we also continue to work on strategies for legal control over these materials.

The Penobscot Nation has developed our own set of traditional knowledge (TK) labels through the Local Contexts project.[43] We are working with institutions like the Library of Congress, the Abbe Museum, and the University of Maine to incorporate our TK labels into the already existing catalogs for these institutions. Even if we cannot legally claim material, we hold a central and unique position in educating people about it, including where it comes from and how it should be accessed, used, and circulated. The TK labels allow for the expression of our laws and protocols for the use of these materials into the digital infrastructures and the metadata of these collections. They also enable us to bring our names, our concepts of sharing, and the networks of circulation and possession into the catalog and the metadata. This is particularly important for researchers, who have not been properly educated about Penobscot history and may not have even considered that Penobscot people remain (the only) tribal authorities over Penobscot knowledge and language and must be consulted.

The return to thinking in and through our language is taking place even in the most complicated of circumstances that directly engage law and colonization. There are many kinds of decolonization required; communities have their own work to do here. What we need institutions like the APS to do is to participate in meaningful ways in a future decolonial ambition: where significant burdens and exclusions brought though ongoing settler-colonial encounters and laws that have made culture into property are radically shifted to Indigenous authority, autonomy, and sovereignty. Indigenous communities never ceded the copyright of their culture to researchers or institutions. The institutional decolonial imperative must acknowledge this settler-colonial appropriation that is embedded within institutional infrastructures, and it must work for a foundational change in the authority and control of these collections.

NOTES

1. Lonetree, *Decolonizing Museums*; Smith, *Decolonizing Methodologies*; Barker, *Native Acts*; Bruyneel, *Third Space of Sovereignty*; Mignolo, *Darker Side of Modernity*.
2. Butler, *Giving an Account of Oneself*; Byrd, *Transit of Empire*; Appadurai, *Future as Cultural Fact*; Comaroff and Comaroff, *Millennial Capitalism and the Culture of Neoliberalism*; Comaroff and Comaroff, *Theory from the South*.
3. Brown, *Politics Out of History*, 6.
4. Goldstein, "Introduction."
5. Byrd, *Transit of Empire*; Tuck and McKenzie, *Place in Research*; Nakata, *Disciplining the Savages*; Barker, *Critically Sovereign*; Barker, *Sovereignty Matters*; Simpson,

Mohawk Interruptus; Lonetree, *Decolonizing Museums*; Atalay, *Community-Based Archaeology*; Christen and Anderson, "Toward Slow Archives."
6. Smith, *Decolonizing Methodologies*; Morana, Dussel, and Jauregui, *Coloniality at Large*; Waziyatawin and Yellow Bird, *For Indigenous Minds Only*; Mihesuah and Wilson, *Indigenizing the Academy*; Mignolo, *Local Histories/Global Designs*; Lugones, "Hetersexualism and the Colonial/Modern Gender System."
7. Clifford, *Routes*; Lonetree, *Decolonizing Museums*; Boast, "Neocolonial Collaboration."
8. Anderson, "Anxieties of Authorship in the Colonial Archive."
9. Christen and Anderson, "Toward Slow Archives."
10. Anderson and Christen, "Decolonizing Attribution."
11. Simpson, *Mohawk Interruptus*.
12. Prins and Walker, "Preface," 70–71; Anderson, "Negotiating Who Owns Penobscot Culture."
13. National Endowment for the Humanities, Chairman's Grant: Planning Phase of Penobscot Dictionary (RT-0154-79-0736); National Science Foundation, Planning Phase of Penobscot Dictionary Project (RT 0154790736); National Science Foundation, Penobscot Lexicon (BNS #7924805); National Endowment for the Humanities, Research and Preparation of Penobscot Dictionary Project (RT 00154-79-0736).
14. The Penobscot Nation became the joint copyright holders in the Penobscot Dictionary through negotiation in 2006.
15. Bradley and Devlin-Glass, "Affect and Narrative Encoding."
16. Christen, "Does Information Really Want to Be Free?"; Christen, "Tribal Archives, Traditional Knowledge."
17. In 2018 the Penobscot Nation and Local Contexts received an IMLS Native American Enhancement Grant to deliver training to other tribes on intellectual property, governance, and decision-making. This training draws upon the work that Penobscot has undertaken over the last ten years and reflects the Penobscot Nation's commitment to supporting other tribes do this work. See https://www.imls.gov/grants/awarded/ng-03-18-0183-18 (accessed July 28, 2018).
18. Strathern, "Divided Origins and the Arithmetic of Ownership," 137.
19. Strathern, *Property, Substance, and Effect*; Verdery and Humphrey; *Property in Question*; Hayden, *When Nature Goes Public*; Myers, "Burning the Truck and Holding the Country"; Mauer and Schwab, *Accelerated Possession*.
20. Harris, "Whiteness as Property"; Bhandar, *Colonial Lives of Property*.
21. Moreton-Robinson, *White Possessive*.
22. For complementary work, see Harris, "Whiteness as Property"; and Best, *Fugitive's Properties*.

23. Bently, "Copyright, Translations, and Relations"; Bowrey and Anderson, "Politics of Global Information Sharing"; Wirten, "Colonial Copyright, Postcolonial Publics"; Boateng, *That Copyright Thing Doesn't Work Here*; Sunder, *From Goods to a Good Life*; Anderson and Christen, "Decolonizing Attribution."
24. Sunder, *From Goods to a Good Life*, 12.
25. In legal philosophy, especially in English common law traditions, the phrasing "real property" refers to land, including anything grown upon, affixed to, and built upon the land. Thus, real property marks a distinction between personal property and moveable property. "Intellectual property," as a more recent legal phrase, allows for the grouping of areas of distinct law (e.g., copyright, patents, designs) understood to transform into property something that was previously intangible — for instance, knowledge and culture.
26. Benton, *Law and Colonial Cultures*.
27. See the 1886 Berne Convention for the Protection of Literary and Artistic Works.
28. Drahos and Braithwaite, *Information Feudalism*; Drahos, "Universality of Intellectual Property Rights."
29. Hochman, *Savage Preservation*, 3.
30. The 2018 Music Modernization Act changes this for sound recordings. As a result, all recordings created before 1956 are now slated to enter the public domain earlier than the previous 2067 date. Copyright for the earliest sound recordings will now expire as early as 2022.
31. See the work of Trevor Reed on the Laura Boulton music collections. See also Reed, "Who Owns Our Ancestors Voices?"
32. Anderson and Christen, "Decolonizing Attribution."
33. See the May 10, 2018, memorandum of understanding between the Penobscot Nation and the University of Maine as an example: https://umaine.edu/nativeamericanprograms/wp-content/uploads/sites/320/2018/05/Penobscot-Nation-umaine-mou.pdf (accessed July 29, 2019).
34. Langton and Longbottom, *Community Futures, Legal Architecture*; Langton, Mazel, Palmer, Shain, and Tehan, *Settling with Indigenous People*; Langton and Palmer, "Modern Agreement Making."
35. Anderson, "Options for the Future Protection of GRTKTCES."
36. Brewer, "Is a New Copyright Law a Colonization of Knowledge?," *High Country News*, March 5, 2019, https://www.hcn.org/articles/tribal-affairs-is-a-new-copyright-law-a-colonization-of-knowledge.
37. Carpenter and Riley, "Owning Red," Brown, *Who Owns Native Culture?*
38. The problem of the researcher being named as the author is another part of the copyright continuum that excludes Indigenous people and community names. This is addressed at length in Anderson and Christen, "Decolonizing Attribution."

39. See the APS Frank Siebert Finding Aid, http://www.amphilsoc.org/collections/view?docId=ead/Mss.Ms.Coll.97-ead.xml (acccessed May 20, 2017).
40. This is discussed in Anderson, "Negotiating Who Owns Penobscot Culture."
41. This option is being researched more closely with Jason Schultz, professor of law at New York University.
42. For Mukurtu CMS, see www.mukurtu.org (accessed May 20, 2017).
43. For Local Contexts, see www.localcontexts.org (accessed May 20, 2017).

BIBLIOGRAPHY

Anderson, Jane. "Options for the Future Protection of GRTKTCES: The Traditional Knowledge License and Labels Initiative." *Journal of the World Intellectual Property Organization* 4, no. 1 (2012): 73–82.

———. "Anxieties of Authorship in the Colonial Archive." In *Media Authorship*, edited by Cynthia Chris and David A. Gerstner, 229–46. New York: Routledge, 2013.

———. "Negotiating Who Owns Penobscot Culture." *Anthropology Quarterly* 91, no. 1 (2018): 265–302.

Anderson, Jane, and Kim Christen. "Decolonizing Attribution: Traditions of Exclusion." *Journal of Radical Librarianship* 5 (2019): 113–52.

Appadurai, Arjun. *The Future as Cultural Fact: Essays on the Global Condition*. London: Verso, 2013.

Atalay, Sonya. *Community-Based Archaeology: Research With, By, and for Indigenous Communities*. Berkeley: University of California Press, 2012.

Barker, Joanne. *Sovereignty Matters: Locations of Contestation and Possibility in Indigenous Struggles for Self-Determination*. Lincoln: University of Nebraska, 2005.

———. *Native Acts: Law, Recognition, and Cultural Authenticity*. Durham NC: Duke University Press, 2011.

Barker, Joanne, ed. *Critically Sovereign: Indigenous Gender, Sexuality, and Feminist Studies*. Durham NC: Duke University Press, 2017.

Bently, Lionel. "Copyright, Translations, and Relations between Britain and India in the Nineteenth and Early Twentieth Centuries." *Chicago Kent Law Review* 82 (2007): 1181–240.

Benton, Lauren. *Law and Colonial Cultures: Legal Regimes in World History, 1400–1900*. New York: Cambridge University Press, 2002.

Best, Stephen. *The Fugitive's Properties: Law and the Poetics of Dispossession*. Chicago: University of Chicago Press, 2004.

Boast, Robin. "Neocolonial Collaboration: Museum as Contact Zone Revisited." *Museum Anthropology*, 34, no. 1 (2010): 56–70.

Boateng, Boatema. *That Copyright Thing Doesn't Work Here: Adinkre and Kente Cloth and Intellectual Property in Ghana*. Minneapolis: University of Minnesota Press, 2011.

Bowrey, Kathy, and Jane Anderson. "The Politics of Global Information Sharing: Whose Cultural Agendas Are Being Advanced?" *Social and Legal Studies* 18 (2009): 479.-504.

Bradley, John, and F. Devlin-Glass. "Affect and Narrative Encoding: The Problematics of Representing and Teaching Yanyuwa Narratives in Cyberspace." In *Teaching Literature at a Distance: Open, Online and Blended Learning*, edited by T. Kayalis and A. Natsina, 183–94. London: Continuum, 2010.

Brown, Michael F. *Who Owns Native Culture?* Cambridge MA: Harvard University Press, 2003.

Brown, Wendy. *Politics Out of History*. Princeton NJ: Princeton University Press, 2001.

Bruyneel, Kevin. *The Third Space of Sovereignty: The Postcolonial Politics of U.S.-Indigenous Relations*. Minneapolis: University of Minnesota Press, 2007.

Butler, Judith. *Giving an Account of Oneself*. New York: Fordham University Press, 2005.

Byrd, Jodi. *Transit of Empire: Indigenous Critiques of Colonialism*. Minneapolis: University of Minnesota Press, 2011.

Carpenter, Kristen, and Angela Riley. "Owning Red: A Theory of Indian Appropriation." *Texas Law Review* 94 (2016): 859–931.

Christen, Kim. "Does Information Really Want to Be Free? Indigenous Knowledge Systems and the Question of Openness." *International Journal of Communication* 6 (2012): 2870–93.

———. "Tribal Archives, Traditional Knowledge, and Local Contexts: Why the 's' Matters." *Journal of Western Archives* 6, no. 1 (2015): 1–19.

Christen, Kim, and Jane Anderson. "Toward Slow Archives." *Archival Science* 19 (2019): 87–116.

Clifford, James. *Routes: Travel and Translation in the Late Twentieth Century*. Cambridge MA: Harvard University Press. 1997.

Comaroff, Jean, and John Comaroff, eds. *Millennial Capitalism and the Culture of Neoliberalism*. Durham NC: Duke University Press, 2001.

———. *Theory from the South: Or How Euro America Is Evolving Toward Africa*. Boulder CO: Paradigm, 2012.

Drahos, Peter, with John Braithwaite. *Information Feudalism: Who Owns the Knowledge Economy?* London: Earthscan, 2002.

———. "The Universality of Intellectual Property Rights: Origins and Development." Paper presented at World Intellectual Property Organization, 2005. https://www.wipo.int/edocs/mdocs/tk/en/wipo_unhchr_ip_pnl_98/wipo_unhchr_ip_pnl_98_1.pdf, accessed July 28, 2019.

Goldstein, Alyosha. "Introduction: Toward a Genealogy of the U.S. Colonial Present." In *Formations of United States Colonialism*, edited by Alyosha Goldstein, 1–30. Durham NC: Duke University Press, 2015.

Harris, Cheryl. "Whiteness as Property." *Harvard Law Review* 106, no. 8 (1993): 1707–91.

Hayden, Cori. *When Nature Goes Public: The Making and Unmaking of Bioprospecting in Mexico*. Princeton NJ: Princeton University Press, 2003.

Hochman, Brian. *Savage Preservation: The Ethnographic Origins of Modern Media Technology*. Minneapolis: University of Minnesota Press, 2014.

Langton, Marcia, and Judy Longbottom, eds. *Community Futures, Legal Architecture: Foundations for Indigenous Peoples in the Global Mining Boom*. London: Routledge, 2012.

Langton, Marcia, and Lisa Palmer. "Modern Agreement Making and Indigenous People in Australia: Issues and Trends." *Australian Indigenous Law Reporter* 8, no. 1 (2003): 1–31.

Langton, Marcia, Odette Mazel, Lisa Palmer, Kathryn Shain, and Maureen Tehan, eds. *Settling with Indigenous People: Modern Treaty and Agreement-Making*. Annandale, AU: Federation, 2006.

Lonetree, Amy. *Decolonizing Museums: Representing Native America in National and Tribal Museums*. Chapel Hill NC: University of North Carolina Press, 2012.

Lugones, Maria. "Hetersexualism and the Colonial/Modern Gender System." *Hypatia* 22, no. 1 (2007): 186–209.

Mauer, Bill, and Gabriele Schwab, eds. *Accelerated Possession: Global Futures of Persons and Property and Personhood*. New York: Columbia University Press, 2006.

Mignolo, Walter. *Local Histories/Global Designs: Coloniality, Subaltern Knowledge, and Border Thinking*. Princeton NJ: Princeton University Press, 2000.

———. *The Darker Side of Modernity: Global Futures, Decolonial Options*. Durham NC: Duke University Press, 2011.

Mihesuah, Devon, and Angela Wilson, eds. *Indigenizing the Academy: Transforming Scholarship and Empowering Communities*. Lincoln: University of Nebraska Press, 2004.

Morana, Mabel, Enrique Dussel, and Carlos A. Jauregui, eds. *Coloniality at Large: Latin America and the Postcolonial Debates*. Durham NC: Duke University Press, 2008.

Moreton-Robinson, Aileen. *The White Possessive: Property, Power, and Indigenous Sovereignty*. Minneapolis: University of Minnesota Press, 2015.

Myers, Fred. "Burning the Truck and Holding the Country: Pintupi Forms of Property and Identity." In *We Are Here: Politics of Aboriginal Land Tenure*, edited by Edwin N. Wilmsen, 15–42. Berkeley: University of California Press, 1989.

Nakata, Martin. *Disciplining the Savages: Savaging the Disciplines*. Canberra: Aboriginal Studies Press, 2007.

Prins, Harald, and Willard Walker. "Preface." *Maine History: Specia Issue in Honor of Dr. Frank T. Siebert Jr.* 37, no. 3 (1998): 70–71.

Reed, Trevor. "Who Owns Our Ancestors' Voices? Tribal Claims to Pre-1972 Sound Recordings." *Columbia Journal of Law and the Arts* 40 (2016): 275–310.

Simpson, Audra. *Mohawk Interruptus: Political Life across the Borders of Settler States.* Durham NC: Duke University Press, 2014.
Smith, Linda Tuhiwai. *Decolonizing Methodologies: Research and Indigenous Peoples.* London: Zed, 1999.
Strathern, Marilyn. *Property, Substance, and Effect: Anthropological Essays on Persons and Things.* London: Athlone, 1999.
——— . "Divided Origins and the Arithmetic of Ownership." In *Accelerating Possession: Global Futures of Persons and Property and Personhood,* edited by Bill Mauer and Gabriele Schwab, 135–62. New York: Columbia University Press, 2006.
Sunder, Madhavi. *From Goods to a Good Life: Intellectual Property and Global Justice.* New Haven CT: Yale University Press, 2012.
Tuck, Eve, and Marcia McKenzie. *Place in Research: Theory, Methodology and Methods.* Abingdon, UK: Routledge. 2015.
Verdery, Katherine, and Caroline Humphrey, eds. *Property in Question: Value Transformation in the Global Economy.* Oxford: Bloomsbury Academic, 2004.
Waziyatawin, and Michael Yellow Bird. *For Indigenous Minds Only: A Decolonization Handbook.* Santa Fe NM: School of Advanced Research, 2012.
Wirten, Eva Hemmungs. "Colonial Copyright, Postcolonial Publics: The Berne Convention and the 1967 Stockholm Conference Revisited." *Scripted* 7 (2010): 532–50.

CHAPTER 2

The Legacy of Hunter-Gatherers at the American Philosophical Society

Frank G. Speck, James M. Crawford, and
Revitalizing the Yuchi Language

Richard A. Grounds

My reference in the title of this chapter to "hunter-gatherers" in relation to Franz Boas's students and the business of collecting Native American-language materials is a rather blunt attempt at leveling the playing field—or, at least registering that the (language) field is completely uneven. When the institutions that grow out of a colonial system of "civilization" are generally understood to represent fairness, the voice of reason, and notions such as scientific detachment, it becomes difficult to shape a critique from an Indigenous perspective that does not sound shrill, unreasonable, and overly judgmental. By naming Boas's students in the title rather than those gifted Yuchi Elders who are the bearers of our unique cultural expressions—who have worked to keep alive the gift of their language in the face of relentless cultural genocide—I would seem to continue the common discourse that elevates the collectors above the communities. By deploying a seemingly anachronistic referent to scholarly endeavors in terms of hunter-gatherers it might appear that I am unfairly invoking a much earlier time frame, when the colonial machinery was fresh, running in high gear, and eating up raw Indigenous resources. But, of course, that is the point. In my view, the legacy of scholarly hunter-gatherers has extended over time to today in almost pristine colonial form.

These colonial origins represent an important part of the picture for understanding the ongoing challenges in effectively engaging Indigenous communities today. The language collections developed under the colonial regime were not intended for Indigenous use during the first two centuries of gathering. And, indeed, full use of these collections remains extremely difficult for Indigenous–community scholars trying to utilize these archived resources.

The growing attention to the colonial legacy of linguistics is an important recent development as modeled by the work of Wesley Y. Leonard.[1] In another example recent discussion of the work of Franz Boas and his students at the turn of the twentieth century that focused on collecting language materials in trilogies with a set of texts, a dictionary, and a grammar is increasingly recognizing that the Boasian project was mired in colonial processes. However, these connections often are characterized in overly abstract or muted terms. Daisy Rosenblum and Andrea Berez-Kroeker, for example, comment that "such Boasian trilogies originated in a moment of salvage ethnography, born of the presumptive nostalgia assigned to Native communities imagined to be in the process of disappearing."[2] This depiction is insightful, but I think it is important to push for a closer examination of this "moment of salvage ethnography," since this moment lasted for decades and actually corresponds directly to a planned cultural genocide. The direct assault on Indigenous languages and communities through boarding schools and other measures of cultural suppression was carried out by the government and by churches for generations. My intention here is to balance the discussion and offer an Indigenous critical perspective on how we arrived in the predicament we are now trying to address as a common project in a unifying way among all stakeholders.

The observations offered here about the colonial situation that shapes the intersection between linguistics and Indigenous communities may seem unnecessarily abrasive unless one considers the larger context of anthropological studies. If we were to take a sweeping view of the four-field model of American anthropology, as early promulgated by Franz Boas—archeology, physical anthropology, cultural anthropology, and linguistics—it would appear that the discipline of linguistics has been exposed to the least level of core-critique and self-critique regarding the colonial nature of its historical and present work. The historical work in linguistics has been characterized by Josheph Errington in *Linguistics in a Colonial World* (2008) as both advancing scientific inquiry while also remaining deeply imbedded in larger projects of colonial power:

> Knowingly or not, willingly or not, colonial linguists carried out projects of physical and symbolic violence, some of them counting clearly as what Philo called "unspeakable evils." But they were also, knowingly or not, reducing to writing some of the evidence of a unity underlying linguistic and human diversity.... Always and everywhere, the work of linguistics in a colonial world was grounded in this enabling and conflicted condition, and the contradiction it presented for the work of power and knowledge.[3]

The remarks I offer here are presented in a spirit of cooperation as an effort to add to the conversation and to promote continuing forward progress in relations between colonial institutions and Indigenous communities even as promising programs and positive developments are slowly beginning to emerge. And it may be worth clarifying that this discussion does not impugn the good will and beneficial service of staff members at these institutions, since this analysis is focused on the systemic problems and not the individual players.

Speaking from an Indigenous perspective, our original languages are understood to be living and powerful; that is why the languages are essential for conducting our ceremonies. They are also critical to our identity and crucial to our cultural well-being as Indigenous nations. Some recognition of the power of Indigenous languages—at least in political, social, and military terms, though not, perhaps, in a spiritual sense—underlies the historical assault on Indigenous languages.

That assault was sustained in a massive, expensive, and programmatic way for over a century. Indigenous languages were perceived as real threats that required an extensive nationwide effort of active, planned suppression—a linguicide. It is a deep historical irony that Indigenous languages were powerfully deployed during World War I and World War II in support of U.S. military operations at the same time that these languages were heavily targeted for annihilation. The code talkers themselves were, of course, subjected to the pervasive colonial injunction that proscribed Native speech in most domains and said that the only significant value to be attributed to Indigenous languages was in terms of their usefulness for purposes of the state. With few exceptions the World War II generation, born in the 1920s, were the last cohort to speak their languages fluently. Almost none of them succeeded in transmitting the gift of their language to their children as a way to bypass the internalized colonization inculcated during those dark days of aggressive language suppression that sought to relegate Indigenous languages to the past. Trying to overcome the enforced language inertia among the "greatest generation" of Native language Elders and getting them fully engaged has been among the great challenges and rewards for community-based language programs.

It is the rich understandings of the power of our original languages that marks a fundamental cleavage between Indigenous approaches to language revitalization and the perspective underlying the mechanics of academic archival procedures. The archival system, by contrast, was set up and maintained under a regime of intellectual colonialism, and, as such, it serves its purpose rather well by making its resources available for scholarly research to institutionally supported academics. Like worlds out of phase, this great divide between Indigenous and academic perspectives seems to affect everything from how materials are acquired and the purposes for which they are used to patterns for storage and issues of access. In this chapter I want to address the challenges for Indigenous communities in working with archived materials framed against the colonial background that has given rise to the current challenges. This examination of these dysfunctional dynamics will be given with reference to the historical and present case of the Yuchi language and community.

Indigenous Perspectives on Languages and Recording

When I began twenty-five years ago actively trying to revitalize the language of my grandmother, there were probably more than thirty living first-language speakers of Yuchi. Although this may sound like a significantly sized group with whom to work, they were, of course, all part of the same cohort. As with three-quarters of Indian country, the last speakers of the language were limited to the World War II generation; they were, with few exceptions, born in the 1920s. In most cases these last speakers were themselves throwbacks, having been raised by their grandparents' generation. This meant that they were reared by monolingual adults, thereby receiving the full dose of cultural, historical, medicinal, and ceremonial knowledge that was carried within their family line and came packaged with the language. Since Yuchi stands as a language isolate, there were not other members of a common language family that might have offered help with figuring out grammatical patterns or reclaiming missing lexical items. Furthermore, many of the speakers with whom I had immediate access were somewhat out of practice in using the fullness of the language, since they had not been able to speak it on a daily basis for half a century.

All of this meant that finding any existing audio recordings from previous Yuchi speakers could be an enormous boost to the effort to bring back the fullness of the language to the Yuchi community. There were numerous dead ends in my search for existing recordings that had been generated by the Yuchi community—a search that continues to the present day. Over time some recordings of earlier language classes and Yuchi-language events had been randomly stolen from self-storage units, some were put in vulnerable storage situations during World War II, others had deteriorated due to poor heat and humidity control, and some had simply gone missing in the tumble of life.

The most extensive set of recordings that I kept hearing about had been produced by an old Yuchi-language preacher in the 1960s. It would be of great value to find dozens of recordings of old Yuchis in house meetings, giving testimonies and prayers, and communicating in the language. I went to great lengths to track down these elusive recordings. Eventually I was able to learn from a surviving sibling of the preacher that the large cache of recordings were, in fact, not to be found—they had been buried in the ground.

The tapes had been interred by one of the surviving members of this traditional family, who felt that these expressions of the language were not being handled in a proper way. This meant that the ancient understanding of proper ways of handling powerful and sacred things had been followed. Since language is living and powerful, it must be cared for appropriately. If this could not be done, it should be put away. This is the same rationale followed by Indigenous communities for a number of the old medicine bundles. If there was not enough specialized knowledge to care for them properly, then they were considered too powerful and dangerous to keep around in a casual manner. The burial of the tapes might, at first, appear to be a lost opportunity. But realizing the reason for the burial was the most important lesson to be learned, further underscoring the traditional understanding of the power of language. This type of burial process is parallel to the reburials being carried out by many Native American nations under the Native American Graves Protection and Repatriation Act (NAGPRA), which recognizes the priority of the living community over the demands of academic inquiry. And it stands in contrast to the archival process in which the maintenance of the gathered materials is more important than the cultural needs of the surviving Indigenous communities. We stand in need of direct legal protections for the cultural patrimony that is the gift of our languages.

Twenty years ago we spent months in negotiation within the Yuchi community, talking with fluent Elders led by the ceremonial ground chief, Jim Brown, in order to work out an agreement with older speakers for recording their voices as they spoke the Yuchi language. In the end their recordings were only to be used within the Yuchi community, specifically for teaching knowledge of the language to younger community members. However, there are other communities, such as the traditional Shawnee, who will not allow their language to be recorded even for teaching purposes, and for most Indigenous-language communities, including the Yuchi, there are language domains of restricted access that require special qualifications. In short, since language is powerful and sacred, it matters how language is handled and may result in limitations on how the traditional language is passed on to future generations.[4]

This depiction of the deep understanding of language as powerful is commonly found among Indigenous nations and stands in stark contrast to the development of archival institutions growing out of the complications of colonial expansion. In the colonial gaze, arising from a different epistemology, Indigenous languages may be viewed as a set of codes that are devoid of power. The rise of these academic institutions rests heavily on the contrasting Enlightenment conception that all knowledge is to be universally accessible to qualified scholars (as represented by the preferred production of scholarly work using the Latin language, going back to the fifteenth century).[5] The ongoing colonial irony is that these archives are largely inaccessible to Native "scholars" who are students of their own languages and cultures.

The sketch offered here of the colonial context for Indigenous-language revitalization work is intended to provide a useful frame for understanding the development of archival institutions and the resulting challenges for Indigenous communities in accessing and working with those institutions in the ongoing process of repurposing the legacy of hunter-gatherers.

Archives as Manifestations of Colonial Heritage

In order to understand these challenges it is necessary to appreciate the colonial origins of the collection process for Native-language materials in terms of the motivations and the dynamics of collecting that relied directly on the colonial machinery of the state in all its harsh forms. All of these extractive processes derived from a worldview built on colonial domination that required justification through the physical and intellectual subjugation of Indigenous Peoples.

The American Philosophical Society (APS) was the principal institution that took the lead in developing philological research into Native American languages beginning in the late eighteenth century. The APS, having been formed before the establishment of the U.S. government, became the central organizing place both for collecting and housing language materials as interest in Indigenous languages among colonial powers began to emerge. During George Washington's presidential tenure, Catherine II of Russia was making written requests to his office for lists of "Indian vocabularies," and Thomas Jefferson had already begun his own collection activities before 1780 and was actively promoting the project to others.[6] Jefferson then served as president of the APS from 1797 to 1814, during which he also served as president of the United States (1801–9). Jefferson was calling for a comparative study of Native languages as had already been voiced in his *Notes on the State of Virginia* (1783). Jefferson had collected around fifty vocabulary lists over a period of thirty years as an official of the nation state—that is, he was able to compile these lists because delegations of Indigenous nations who were being hammered on the anvil of genocidal American colonialism were compelled to make their way to the Capitol in the city of Washington, in the district named after Columbus. He had also been able to use various military officers and government agents to procure additions to the collection and had collated the majority of the material into a matched set of lists. However, the trunk containing them was broken into by thieves and dumped in the James River during his retirement to Monticello, in Virginia. A slave called Ned was punished for the action by burning (branding) his left hand and giving him thirty-nine lashes with a whip.[7]

While Jefferson's intellectual inquiries were able to produce a written record of such investigations, the collection of the data was profoundly intertwined with the colonial processes of the time. Its motivations derived from malevolent colonialism, and its effective implementation came from the brutal process of dispossession. Jefferson had used his position in the seat of colonial power to gather his language information from those who were considered to be disappearing people, carefully extracting his lists from leaders of beleaguered Native nations who were being battered by the cruel colonial actions that he helped orchestrate. The contrast in consequences across the colonial hierarchy could not be greater. Those held in slavery within the colonial system would be brutishly punished for scattering bits of paper on which words extorted from leaders of Indigenous nations had been inscribed. Yet colonial perpetrators represented by Jefferson who sundered entire Indigenous nations that spoke those very languages from which a few words had been extracted were to be lauded. Meanwhile, Indigenous Peoples, falling mostly outside the colonial structures, were meant to be swallowed up by the colonial leviathan with little concern about their real interests.

Jefferson was aware that this particular set of Native nations, then being decimated by the colonial steamroller, offered a unique and passing opportunity for documentation of their languages. As he wrote, with a twinge of colonial nostalgia, in reporting the loss of the language lists: "My opportunities were probably better than will ever occur again to any person having the same desire."⁸ By the winter of 1825 this pattern of collecting language lists from delegations of leaders of Indigenous nations traveling to the nation's capital garnered an early and extremely faulted set of Yuchi-language terms.⁹ The great motivation in these early days was clearly to gather language information for colonial comparative purposes since, of course, the nations who spoke these languages were already slated for destruction—pending the time when the military leverage could be mustered.

It was presumably by impetus from Jefferson that the APS formed the Historical and Literary Committee in 1815 under the leadership of Peter S. Du Ponceau that took on the charge of collecting manuscripts of Indigenous languages. The APS launched important publications on Indigenous languages by leading figures in philological inquiries and later linguistic studies throughout the nineteenth century, including such notables as Albert Gallatin, Daniel Brinton, David Zeisberger, John Heckewelder, and, later, Henry Schoolcraft and John Powell.¹⁰ Between 1780 and 1840 the APS developed the world's largest collection of Native American manuscript materials. It was later able to reestablish its preeminence in the field beginning with the acquisition of the Franz Boas collection of American Indian linguistics in 1945.¹¹

The belief in the inevitable disappearance of Indigenous nations was foundational to the colonial logics of dispossession. Much of the push for documenting Native languages also grew out of this notion. As Gallatin wrote in the introduction to his comparative philological study *Synopsis of Indian Tribes*, his inquiry was looking "to the means of subsistence of the Indians, to the causes of their gradual extinction."¹² Toward the end of the century, as Indigenous nations persisted, this notion of disappearance could take on more of a sense of cultural erasure, as John W. Powell wrote in 1881:

> Migrations and enforced removals placed tribes under conditions of strange environment where new customs and institutions were necessary, and in this condition civilization had a greater influence, and the progress of occupation by white men within the territory of the United States, at least, has reached such a stage that savagery and

barbarism have no room for their existence, and even customs and institutions must in a brief time be completely changed, *and what we are yet to learn of these people must be learned now.*[13]

This blatantly colonialist attitude still runs through almost all of the funding streams for Indigenous-language work to this day. It is easier to get funding to intellectually circumscribe a living language than it is to keep that language alive in its own Indigenous community.

The case of the Yuchi, traced over time, provides a telling thread of this notion of extinction, contrasting Indigenous realities with colonial longings. Beginning as early as 1821, the Florida Indian agent wrote in an official report of "some remains of ancient tribes, known by the names of Outchis, Chias, Canaake, but they consist of only few straggling families."[14] The year 1838 saw the published report of the "slaughter and almost total extinction of the Uchee tribe of Indians."[15] By the 1880s the expectation of extinction began to be articulated with pronouncements of finality as "Uchees" were designated as "in fact, an extinct nation, and their language is almost forgotten."[16] This curious use of American English to insist that an Indigenous nation could be extinct while at the same time admitting that they are still speaking their supposedly dying language is extraordinary. This illogical pattern of describing Native nations as extinct while acknowledging their existence eventually became so widespread within the logics of dispossession that it led to the oxymoronic redefinition of the word "extinct" in American dictionaries with special reference to Native Americans.[17]

The narrative of disappearance was to continue throughout the twentieth century, resulting in various authoritative reference publications that specifically declared the mistaken but convenient notion that Yuchi people were extinct. Barbara Leitch's *A Concise Dictionary of the Indian Tribes of North America* (1979) refers to Yuchis as "an extinct agricultural and hunting tribe," while Carl Waldman's *Encyclopedia of Native American Tribes* (1988) states that "the Yuchi eventually lost their tribal identity," and Paterek's *Encyclopedia of Native American Costume* (1994) says that "they seem to have disappeared from the records in the nineteenth century."[18]

The problem for the colonial project—especially in a nation-state where the foremost self-claim is that America is the preeminent land of justice and freedom—is the pesky persistence of the Indigenous nations themselves, since their existence calls into question the vision of the state. It would all be simpler if Indigenous nations would just disappear, in accordance with the colonial script. The need to resolve the historic "Indian problem" results in a kind of fictive ultimate solution: the repeated assertion that an Indigenous nation is "in fact, an extinct nation."

The reports of Yuchi demise, repeated for almost two full centuries, are belied by the counterhistorical success of the Yuchi community in maintaining the unbroken tradition of Yuchi ceremonial grounds and Yuchi language down to the present day. The anthropologist John R. Swanton has written of the Yuchis that "the only wonder is that, in the years of white contact and aggression, so much has remained... whereas the ethnology will undoubtedly lose its ancient character every year and finally pass out of existence."[19] It is now over a century since those words were written, and Yuchi ceremonial activities are gaining in strength and growing in participation even as I remark on these patterns of what might be called "intellectual erasure." To push back on these pervasive pressures, Mose Cahwee, the founding Elder for the Yuchi Language Project, would often say at Yuchi gatherings, "yUdjEhanAnô sôKAnAnô" (we Yuchi people, we are still here).

The presumed disappearance of Indigenous Peoples was a colonial-serving notion that began in earliest colonial times, growing out of the doctrine of discovery, and it later became crystallized in the set of conceptions known as "manifest destiny" that held sway during the greatest period of U.S. colonial aggression throughout the nineteenth century. Manifest destiny was an extreme conception that disavowed responsibility for the assault on Indigenous nations at the very time that the most genocidal actions were being aggressively pursued. As the so-called removal of what were then southwestern Native nations (in what became the states of Georgia, Alabama, and Florida) was being brutally executed, a clear articulation of manifest destiny as some deific operation strangely devoid of Euro-American agency was posted in a southern newspaper in 1836: "We gaze as upon a great drama, in which we are less actors than spectators, wherein the fortunes of millions have been guided, upon principles not yet developed to our understanding—full of obscure judgments, and incomprehensible dispensations of Providence, moving kingdoms and states as by the power of an unseen but irresistible and acknowledged DESTINY."[20]

While rationales of dispossession relied on the presumed disappearance of Indigenous Peoples, the importance of keeping a record of their passing languages for purposes of intellectual colonialism was to become a staple within the racist social hierarchy that the colonial structure relied upon in the nineteenth century. The coupling of the unacknowledged genocide of Indigenous Peoples with the collection of bits of their languages was clearly embraced and lauded from the early 1800s. The scattered fragments of language left behind by disappearing peoples, like so many shards, were to be collected as museum pieces to be preserved and studied by those Euro-American elites, who provided the rationales for the dirty work of displacing and decimating Indigenous populations.

In an 1848 discussion of "Uchees" and other southeastern nations, this sentiment was summed up in bald terms, since the "only vestiges" soon to be left of these disappearing peoples would be "the books of missionaries printed in their idioms, and vocabularies, unsatisfactory but invaluable to science. Too much honor and praise cannot be accorded to those enlightened men, who have devoted themselves to the preservation of these vestiges which are to become the fossil, organic remains of intellectual humanity."[21] Indeed, these linguistic curiosities served as the intellectual corollary to the physical collection of crania from Indigenous Peoples that filled phrenological cabinets during the nineteenth century.

These older colonialist rationales have demonstrated an extraordinary staying power, as they are tied to justifications for the sustained U.S. genocidal aggression against Indigenous Peoples. The present-day reliance on this same logic is seldom articulated in bare terms, but it still occasionally appears in a clear formulation. After a notice in the *Washington Post* about the demise of Native languages that featured Yuchi-language revitalization efforts, the syndicated columnist James J. Kilpatrick responded with an appeal to the older colonialist sentiments, stating that the loss of our language was only "a cause for cultural antiquarians" since it was merely "a specimen of linguistic paleontology": "Yuchi is a rare stamp, meant for a collector's album. Make some recordings. Let it go."[22]

The pervasive trope of Indigenous extinction continues from the colonial past with such profound saturation that it bleeds through to present-day representations of Indigenous-language revival even by those who are trying to support the effort. It is not surprising that Yuchi Elder k'asA Henry Washburn reported that the *National Geographic* photographer who showed up at his home to take photos for a story on the survival of Indigenous languages encouraged him to adopt a melancholy posture for the shoot. The sepia-tinged photo that appeared in the published article, showing our Elder small and alone, seemingly insignificant within the larger framing of the image,[23] clearly reflects both the title of the piece, "Vanishing Voices," and the process of colonial signification as identified by Charles H. Long.[24] Long argues that this type of colonial signifying, which can project the invisibility of the "other," is a power game that grows out of the construction of the social and symbolic order that developed with the colonial elaboration of the so-called New World and has been dominant for so long that it colors all that it purports to shed light upon and is especially evidenced in scholarly discourse about Indigenous and Black peoples. Within this larger context of colonial framing, our local efforts to promote positive images of Yuchi-language revitalization for the national magazine that would show the inspiring and active role of Elders in our community, whether in our tribal ceremonies or leading language classes, could easily be brushed aside by the on-site photographer. The intentionality of the morbid tone that would be displayed in the visual representation for the publication was further clarified by the photograph that was crafted and selected for display on the website gallery that accompanied the hard-copy article. The photograph shows two of our Yuchi Elders wearing traditional ribbon dresses literally standing in a graveyard surrounded by Yuchis past on the grounds of the historic Yuchi Methodist church, Pickett Chapel, outside Sapulpa, Oklahoma. A message of Yuchi demise could not be more compellingly presented. Like the ubiquitous image called *End of the Trail* of the slumped warrior on a broken-down pony that was created by James Earle Frasier a century ago to epitomize the demise of Indigenous nations, such symbolic representations have a significant impact on our Indigenous communities. They affect the attitudes of our youth toward the survival of our own culture and negatively influence the prospects for language revitalization as, indeed, one of the greatest challenges in strengthening our languages is to overcome the inertia of internalized colonization. The image of our Yuchi Elders was constructed in such a way that it covers over, and in effect buries, the life work of two full blood sisters, Joshephine Wildcat Bigler and Maxine Wildcat Barnett, who grew up with the gift of the Yuchi language and have spent the final decades of their lives working to teach the language to Yuchi youth. We are privileged at the Yuchi Language Project still to have the opportunity to work with the younger sister, Maxine Wildcat Barnett, now ninety-five years old, as she continues to share her original language and her passion for traditional stories, Yuchi songs, and little-known tribal history. Through the dedication of the Wildcat sisters working as Yuchi-language warriors and the efforts of other Elders, we have been able to grow twenty new speakers of Yuchi language who are empowered to carry the language and culture to future generations in defiance of the long-running colonial narrative of disappearance and silence.

American colonialism, as noted above, gave occasion for collecting Native language data as delegations visited the capital and also provided motivation for such work through rationales of dispossession predicated on Native extinction. But there was a darker side to American colonialism. The military structures for implementing the colonial goals were also to be utilized for the direct collecting of Native-language materials—that is, the action of physical genocide was intimately connected to the process of collecting language bits from those who were being directly decimated. The military operation would provide a primary mechanism for obtaining Indian vocabularies and other language information.

This process began with the actions of President Jefferson, who was the architect of colonial decimation of Indigenous nations through the collusion of colonial powers that promulgated the putative claims bound up in the Louisiana Purchase (1803). These paper claims to Indigenous lands were the legal machinations used by colonial actors seeking to implement the underlying doctrine of discovery. But the first step in making good these assertions was to survey the domains of Indigenous Peoples in order to facilitate the planning for the systematic depopulation and reoccupation of those lands. Jefferson gave the explicit charge to the Lewis and Clark expedition to collect Indian vocabularies and other language information in addition to the expected military reconnaissance for the War Department. In other words, in the planning for the coming flood of displacement, colonial authorities had the foresight to collect vocabularies prior to the genocidal deluge; these raw Native materials could then be used for their own purposes. This was an early expression of what might be considered salvage linguistics — or, perhaps more in keeping with the overall functioning of the broader colonial system, this amounted to a practice of salvage linguicide: purposefully collecting language bits at the same time, and often through the same processes, that the Indigenous Peoples were being genocided.

In Jefferson's charge to the party, all of this information was to be gathered in a duplicitous, hat-in-hand, manner: "In all your intercourse with the natives, treat them in the most friendly & conciliatory manner which their own conduct will admit; allay all jealousies as to the object of your journey, satisfy them of its innocence."[25] Jefferson's instructions demonstrate a clear recognition that this was merely the reconnaissance party collecting information during a time when the fledgling nation had not the military capacity to launch a massive assault. Carrying out the colonial theft of a third of the breadth of the continent would require a century of political, legal, economic, and military campaigns, ending with such punctuations as the slaughters on the Marias (1870) and at Wounded Knee (1890).

The continent-wide genocidal push continuing to the West Coast was marked by the emblematic capture of an unnamed Indigenous man in 1911 — a kind of coda to the long movement of sustained physical genocide that had begun three centuries before on the East Coast with the military actions of early English colonists against local Indigenous populations. The last Yana Yahi had lived his entire life in hiding in his own land: fifty years spent hiding from the genocide that wiped out his people and that had taken his immediate family members. He was the last speaker of his language. The anthropologists — led by one of Boas's students — had a special opportunity to study his language, as he was compelled to live in a museum, where he survived for only four years, but during that time of direct analysis they failed to even learn his name; he was simply referred to as "Ishi," which means "man" in his Yana Yahi language. He never trusted his captors with the power of his name. In the end his cautious reading of his precarious situation in the hands of his caretakers proved to be warranted. Shortly after his death his brain was removed and preserved for purposes of scientific analysis by his captor-custodians.

This reference to the direct personal assault on Ishi and his family is presented here as a cipher for understanding the ugly colonial assault on Native communities and cultures. For the loss of languages was not only a result of the frontal attack on the languages themselves through the boarding school system: a major factor stopping the intergenerational transmission of Indigenous languages was the larger pattern of physical genocide and associated terrors. According to the memory of California Indigenous survivors of the last wide-scale and publicly supported genocide in the United States, the final slave auctions in California were conducted in the 1920s.[26] Speakers of Indigenous languages in what had become the colonial state of California stopped passing their language to their children out of an experienced-based fear of genocide and enslavement.

In 1826 Albert Gallatin boosted his philological pursuits by enlisting the help of the secretary of war, James Barbour, to send out a circular to all Indian agents, superintendents, and missionaries to gather Indian vocabularies and simple grammatical information.[27] Gallatin also appealed successfully for additional language information to the territorial governor of Michigan, Lewis Cass, and to Thomas L. McKenney in the Office of Indian Affairs, which, during that time — given the bellicose actions of the United States against Indigenous Peoples — was logically housed within the War Department.[28] Indeed, it too was to become a common practice to involve the apparatus of the state (particularly the military officials and operations) to gather vocabularies and rudimentary linguistic data on Indigenous communities. The forces of government and federal funding were often drawn upon in the collection process and notably included government-sponsored expeditions throughout the nineteenth century, including, for example, the military-lead U.S. Exploring Expedition of 1838 to 1842, which collected 190 words in the Klamath language.[29] This was followed by another list of Klamath words from the topographical engineers exploring a railroad route to the Columbia River made under the secretary of war and reported to the U.S. Congress in 1857.[30] Additionally, extensive vocabulary and grammatical notes were included in the U.S. Geographical and Geological Survey of the Rocky Mountain Region for 1877.[31] The report of this last-mentioned survey describes the work of philologist Albert Gatschet, who gathered "certain statistics" in Oregon for his monumental Klamath dictionary and grammar, which was eventually published by the Department of the Interior as part of the reporting from the U.S. Geographical and Geological Survey of the Rocky Mountain Region.[32] The language material collected for Gatschet's project was being carried out almost immediately after the Modoc War had ended three years before, in 1873.

In looking at the business of collecting Native-language materials in its historical interplay with the U.S. government, we should not lose sight of the fact that all of these various collecting activities were being carried out in the context of incessant official military action against Indigenous Peoples throughout the nineteenth century. This meant that at times of open hostilities speakers were not accessible or that entire groups of Native speakers were under threat of being wiped out. For the language purposes of hunter-gatherers, the most beneficial outcome was when Native peoples were corralled into small reservation areas, where they became accessible to military and academic collectors (as in the case of Gatschet's collecting after the Modoc War, noted above). At times all of these factors converged—as shown, for example, in the Nineteenth Annual Report of the Bureau of American Ethnology at the close of the nineteenth century: "Owing to the fact that the Lipan were nearly exterminated a generation ago, and by reason of the isolation of the surviving remnants, doubt has been expressed as to their true affinity; but from vocabulary obtained by Mr. Mooney from members of this tribe associated with the Mescalero on their reservation, it is now known that they speak a well-defined Athapascan dialect." The Lipan Apache had been "nearly exterminated" by joint U.S. military action with the Mexican

Army in northern Mexico. Though it was perhaps more apparent at the time, present-day students, focusing on the linguistic work itself, may not always recognize the linkages of military operations to the production of extant linguistic materials collected by hunter-gatherers during the time period when Indigenous societies themselves were being targeted for direct decimation.

The motivation behind early philological work grew to a significant extent out of the construction of racialized hierarchies that were presumed to be reflected in the corresponding contrast between languages. As John Wesley Powell sounded the call for the study of the languages found in savagery in the First Annual Report of the Bureau of Ethnology, "Thus, by the study of the languages of tribes and the languages of nations, the methods and laws of development are discovered from the low condition represented by the most savage tribe to the highest condition existing in the speech of civilized man."[33] Likewise, racialized efforts to explain the origins of Indigenous Peoples appeared in disputes between advocates of monogenism and polygenism. As Sean Harvey writes about the underpinnings of "U.S. democratic colonialism" in *Native Tongues: Colonialism and Race from Encounter to the Reservation*:

> U.S. denial of Native sovereignty and claims to control Native peoples, land, and resources rested upon assertions about the deficiency of Native societies. . . . A flawed form of language as well as gender norms . . . figured prominently in notions of "savagery" or "barbarism." Scholars debated whether such traits were passing or permanent, and philology competed for influence with archaeology, ethnographic attention to customs and beliefs, and studies of skin color, hair, crania, and sexual reproduction.[34]

Thomas Jefferson was a seminal figure in working to answer these questions. He took the lead in using Native languages to address these issues while simultaneously acting as a founding figure in the repugnant practice of excavating Native burials. Jefferson's detailed reports on his early excavation of Native burials in his *Notes on the State of Virginia* earned him recognition as a founder of American archeology. These linguistic and archeological endeavors were parallel pursuits, designed to investigate the seemingly inexplicable origins of Native peoples. In both of these avenues of information gathering, genocidal processes were coupled with the collection activities of the perpetrating society in pursuit of pseudoscientific questions mired in racist ideologies that were demanded by the exigencies of colonial conquest. Moreover, the parsing of these questions by colonial powers relying on the military apparatus of the state wreaked violence on Indigenous communities.

In the case of the nineteenth-century cranial studies, there was a more raw linkage between direct decimation of Native peoples and the collection of Indian remains for scientific inquiries. In 1868 the assistant U.S. surgeon general sent out an official order to all army medical officers requesting submission of Native osteological remains to the Army Medical Museum that had been founded in 1862. These orders were repeated at least through the 1870s and yielded extensive results as the U.S. military routinely raided Native burial sites and preserved cranial and brain "specimens" from active battle sites, as exampled in the correspondence from surgeon B. E. Fryer of Fort Harker, Kansas, in 1869:

> I had already obtained for the Museum the skull of one of the Pawnees, killed in the fight you speak of, and would have had all had it not been that immediately after the engagement, the Indians lurked about their dead and watched them so closely, that the guide I sent out was unable to secure but one ... and it may be that if the remaining five (eight not seven were killed) are buried or have been hid near where the fight took place—about twenty miles from here—I can, after a time, obtain all—I shall certainly use every effort.[35]

Almost twenty years later, Franz Boas, who also played an important role in seeking to loosen ethnological studies from its racist moorings, provided three skulls from his tour of the Northwest Coast to the Army Medical Museum in exchange for ten dollars in 1887.[36]

I am raising the issue of these two parallel processes of data collection as linked to genocidal actions of the nation-state in order to clarify the nature of those colonial relations that precipitated the collection of Native materials that continue to be housed in archival institutions. The directives through the War Department for collecting primitive crania as well as the collecting of the language bits once carried within those skulls were related activities, both spurred by the same broad colonial impulse.

I am pointing to this problematic past as a corrective to our current elevation of scientific inquiry—and, especially, less controversial areas of study such as linguistics—as if it were nothing more than a value-neutral, objective process. As Rubem Alves reminds us in his poignant parable on the historic power imbalances between science and marginalized people, it is important for lambs, when inviting Professor Wolf to conference, always to inquire into the eating habits of colonial wolves.[37] It is critical to find out who benefits and whose young ends up getting eaten.

In short, the colonial origins of the collections in Native languages continue to have bearing on the challenges for Indigenous Peoples doing the work of revitalizing their languages. The actual materials that were collected were for purposes related to the colonial agenda and—though not entirely sequentially—were then used for various expressions of intellectual colonialism. Likewise, the manner of collecting was strongly connected to brutal colonial processes, and, to some extent, the important question of access to archives continues to reflect the economic impoverishment and educational limitations placed upon Indigenous Peoples—a status that was set by colonial inequalities that largely continue to the present day. The current funding structure for Indigenous-language work is perfectly continuous with the old colonial project, going back over two centuries.

The following remarks about the texture of the materials produced by Boas's students are set against this colonial background and point to the practical challenges for Indigenous communities trying to interface with archival resources. The mismatch of goals and the nature of the materials produced by linguists underscore some of the further challenges for community scholars.

Remarks on the Legacies of Boas's Students

Franz Boas and his students engaged in an elaborately conceived program of salvage ethnography that resulted in a great deal of sophisticated documentation of Native languages. The extensive development of what was to become an enormous body of materials, encompassing both detailed monographs and expansive comparative works, was not intended to be read by members of those communities who were having their languages carefully dissected and cataloged. This was part of an arcane intellectual activity with its own argot that took the language materials gathered from Indigenous communities to become grist in academic mills situated in intellectual capitals far from the small reservation islands left to Indigenous nations. It relied on fundamental colonial relations that had been in play for centuries, setting up a system that included a kind of profiteering on the plight of Indigenous Peoples. Raw Native materials were to be turned into objects of value within the Western intellectual tradition. Published grammars and dictionaries were to be displayed on the shelves of academic institutions like portraits of Indigenous languages fronze by the colonial gaze. Meanwhile, informants were to be left in relative poverty while those hunter-gatherers who were most successful in collecting and processing Indigenous raw materials for the economy of academe obtained higher ranks were rewarded with salary increases, having brought prestige to their home institutions, along with funding for future expeditions. While the outward expression of this intellectual colonialism has become less abrasive over time, the basic underlying dynamics of this system have changed little.

Yet the pursuit of the grand initiative shaped by Boas and his students meant that Yuchi would remain as a language of abiding academic interest, since it seemed to be a puzzling piece in the complicated mosaic of the North American language picture. The Yuchi language had long been noted for its distinctive characteristics. In the early nineteenth century Albert Gallatin asserted that "the Uchee language is the most guttural, uncouth, and difficult to express with our alphabet and orthography of any of the Indian languages within our knowledge."[38] By the late nineteenth century Albert Gatschet summed up the Yuchi language in sonorous Eurocentric tones:

> Not much is known of their language, but it might be easily obtained from the natives familiar with English. From what we know of it, it shows no radical affinity with any known American tongue, and its phonetics have often been noticed for their strangeness. They are

said to speak with an abundance of arrested sounds or voice-checks, from which they start again with a jerk of the voice. The accent often rests on the ultima (Powell's mscr. Vocabulary), and Ware ascribes to them, though wrongly, the Hottentot *click*.[39]

Frank G. Speck, one of Boas's earliest students, began his academic career working on Yuchi language. He came in 1904 to do his graduate research in prestatehood Oklahoma—the name, drawn from Choctaw language, is often conveniently glossed as meaning "home of the red people." In fact, over half of the fifty state names were derived from Indigenous Peoples or languages for the curious purpose of designating newly-formed Euro-American political entities.[40] Thus the name Oklahoma and its favored (mis)interpretation represents a common trope in the colonial displacement process by suppersessors who wanted to flaunt their recent claims to the original homes of Indigenous Peoples. The actual land that was referenced by this name of colonial appropriation had been taken over from the Indigenous Caddo, Wichita, Quapaw, and Osage nations in order to be doled out to other distant Indigenous Peoples by treaty agreements with the U.S. government. These Oklahoma lands were promised to remain in Native hands for "as long as water flows or grass grows upon the earth," in President Monroe's phraseology, which was also repeated by President Jackson. By the time Speck completed his last research trip among the Yuchis in 1908, the U.S. government had reneged on its promise, the Native-controlled State of Sequoya proposed in 1905 had been denied, and Oklahoma had become a state.

Unfortunately, Speck, despite his many gifts, was unable to comprehend the complexities of Yuchi grammatical forms, and his research was ultimately redirected to an ethnographic study that also reflected some of his work on the Yuchi language. Speck's publication on Yuchi ethnology was important, but it also left some inexplicable errors in his language references, the most glaring of which was his mistaken rendering of a term for one of the main ceremonial medicines used in Yuchi ceremonial grounds.[41]

For the Yuchi community the greatest challenge in attempts to utilize Speck's early linguistic work on Yuchi language is the scattered nature of his legacy, now housed in multiple archives, hundreds and some over a thousand miles away from the living Yuchi community. His handwritten notebooks containing unpublished stories in the Yuchi language are now back at the National Anthropological Archives in or near the nation's capitol. Meanwhile, the Speck correspondence, which includes later interaction with a young Ann Rolland, who was to become a leading member on our Yuchi Language Project Board, is located in the APS. And the early wax cylinder recordings of Yuchi that I first thought were most likely still at the University of Pennsylvania in Philadelphia turned out to be housed in the Archives of Traditional Music at Indiana University. Also, as if to illustrate the practices of the colonial hunter-gatherers, the Yuchi clothing and art items are now housed among the minerals and fauna at the American Museum of Natural History in New York City.

Two decades after Speck's forays into Yuchi country, because the unique Yuchi language had still not been properly documented, Boas's student, Günther Wagner, began coming out to the Yuchi community in Oklahoma in an effort to produce the Boasian triad of linguistic materials. He was able to develop a typescript for an unpublished English-Yuchi vocabulary list, provide a representative sketch of Yuchi grammar (1934), and record the largest body of Yuchi language materials to date, with his publication of *Yuchi Tales* (1931).[42] However, these important contributions remain flawed for their failure to represent the sound noted by the a-e ligature. This phonemic failure makes it difficult to ascertain the proper pronunciation and underlying meaning to be derived from his printed texts. The larger problem is that he relied on the most accessible "language informant," a Yuchi preacher named Maxey Simms (the grandfather of our Yuchi Language Project Board chair), who turned out to speak his own version of the Yuchi language that was quite different from native Yuchi speakers. Of course, none of these materials were produced with the idea that Yuchi community members would attempt to make use of them to strengthen their language revitalization efforts. Wagner's English-Yuchi vocabulary list is still used as a helpful reference tool in community-language work today. But, of course, the various authors of the published materials and manuscript materials on the Yuchi language have all used different writing systems, down to more recent master's and doctoral work.

From the perspective of the Yuchi community, the archived materials have been very safely guarded over many years, but they are not that easy to access, and they are not easy to decode. Even if the materials themselves can be made accessible to language learners, the plethora of writing patterns means that very few community members can effectively negotiate the variety of diverse writing systems in order to arrive at a fair representation of the spoken forms as used by the living Yuchi community.

By the 1970s sustained linguistic study of the Yuchi language was being done by James Crawford, who was preparing academic analyses while also attempting to add a more community-focused ethic as a supplement to his academic pursuits. His study of the language was carried out in a formalistic manner, but he did harbor intentions to produce a practical grammar and dictionary that could perhaps be used by Yuchi community members. Unfortunately, his extensive preparatory work was cut short by his untimely passing, and his Native-language files were submitted to the APS by his widow. The most promising legacy from Crawford's work on the Yuchi language is his Yuchi-language file slips, which number over eighty thousand pieces.

These extensive file slips, which are housed thirteen hundred miles away from the Yuchi community, have been a great lure to our local efforts to try to access and evaluate the contents of these over forty shoeboxes on the possible promise of extending our existing Yuchi-language vocabulary base. The episode around these extracted language materials offers a clear illustration of the built-in mismatch between the academic dissection of our language and the practical language needs of the living community. We spent an entire week of travel, using our meager funding and the time of an Elder and two staff, to drive to Philadelphia from Oklahoma—underscoring the heritage of the long-standing colonial arrangements where cultural booty is typically stored in old colonial seats of power far from traditional communities. We were trying to evaluate the contents of these voluminous file slips, which were not available for photocopying due to concerns over the potential impact of exposure to light on the long-term warehousing of these written bits of our language. Meanwhile, our small delegation was there attempting to breathe life into these old slips of paper with one of our most gifted first-language Yuchi Elders, k'asA Henry Washburn, a World War II navy veteran who had an amazing ability to speak both the men's and women's forms of the Yuchi language. In our effort to capture as much information as possible, we launched into a frantic push to take photographs (without flash) of as many of these individual file slips as possible during the limited hours of access. We were elated to find an extensive section covering words for cactus and other terms that present speakers were no longer using. As it turned out, we only ended up photographing an entire section of Yuki-language materials that had somehow been mistakenly filed in the Yuchi shoeboxes; presumably some graduate assistant had conflated the slip notes because of the similarity between the names Yuchi and Yuki. This meant that we lost a half-day of our feverish efforts due to this filing error. After ten days of travel and thousands of dollars, we were only able to net less than 10 percent of the file slips. Even then this was only the beginning of a longer process of printing and projecting the images, which would then require—as we were reminded by the Yuki incident—extensive input from our team of Elders in order to properly evaluate the accuracy and usefulness of the methodically collected documentation materials.

In summary, my understanding is that the limitations resulting from the colonialist legacy in developing archives of Native languages have been exceedingly difficult for Native language communities to overcome. These challenges include:

- The difficulty of access, given the location of old seats of colonial power and distance from community;
- The long-running assault on language communities, which has resulted in three-quarters of Indigenous languages now having first-language speakers only from the World War II generation. This means that they are now entering their nineties as the only ones who can fully vet the remaining records. The Yuchis, working to revitalize their heritage isolate language, are working with no safety net, since there are no comparative languages to aid in the process of vetting archived language materials;

The stasis of archival centers, which continue to cater to the academic community for whom the system was originally developed;

The fact that almost all funding for Native languages from all sources (both from within and beyond archives) is geared to support academics or formal academic processes;

The importance of acknowledging that the overall system of imbalances remains largely in place so that most language communities have few resources to redress the generations-long assault on their languages.

Fortunately, we are now starting to see the influence of positive developments, with new digital technology and programming such as the Center for Native American and Indigenous Research at the APS that will be able to ameliorate certain of these above listed challenges.[43] Current technological applications represent new prospects for bridging to Indigenous language communities. This is extremely important work for democratizing access to the extensive Native-language holdings, and we are appreciative of the potential benefits of the exchanges facilitated through the conference and present discourse represented in this volume. However, this new surge of access hardly applies to less well-funded archival institutions. Even for those archives that may have enough funding to digitize Native-language manuscript materials, forward progress will still require a clear vision and sustained commitment to make these materials more accessible to Indigenous communities by overturning these systemic challenges.

At the same time, the larger patterns of inequality and limited access for Indigenous community language programs remain firmly in place—the colonial heritage writ large in the social and economic fabric of the nation. Support for Indigenous community scholars is extremely limited. This seems to be especially prevalent among funder-driven financial support programs. The general pattern of documentation and academic analysis still predominates the language field. In 1992 Michael Krauss delivered his now (in)famous challenge to the linguistic community in a thematic volume of the journal *Language*: "Obviously we must do some serious rethinking of our priorities lest linguistics go down in history as the only science that presided obliviously over the disappearance of 90% of the very field to which it is dedicated."[44] Indigenous communities—who were not the intended recipients of collected language materials—continue to receive little practical or financial attention to their needs for successfully facing the practical challenges of creating a new generation of speakers. It has now been twenty years since Earl Shorris observed that "anthropologists and, until quite recently, most linguists have been content to embalm the dead, preparing languages for the file cabinet and the museum."[45] Indeed, the scholarly community is no longer content with the pattern of Native-language demise, but, in my view, very little has been accomplished toward changing that pattern, due to the lack of shift in the funding structure.

Perhaps surprisingly, there are millions of dollars being spent every year on Indigenous languages. However, the great majority of those funds continue to be restricted to documentation and linguistic research rather than going to direct language revitalization efforts that are being carried out at the community level. This entrenched pattern can be seen in spending at an international level, including in such programs as the Smithsonian/NSF/NEH Documenting Endangered Languages (2005) and the Volkswagen Stiftung in Germany (1998). The massive investment in documentation from the Hans Rausing Endangered Languages Project of the United Kingdom was launched with $30 million in 2005 and an additional $10 million in 2015.[46] The amount of funds going to salaries, academic research, and the costs of archiving are hundreds of times greater than the small amount of funds available to support community efforts to keep their languages alive.

In the scale of things, the maintenance of the overall archival structure remains heavily weighted toward servicing the academic community. I want to add to the growing argument calling for valuing and supporting community-based Indigenous-language work. As Daisy Rosenblum and Andrea Berez-Kroeker have remarked, "Twenty years after Himmelmann, we can see that the greatest value of good documentation is to today's descendants of the speakers themselves."[47] This means greater access to Native-language archival material and more funding support. The current funding imbalance reflects the prevailing perspective of colonial history where the more important project continues to be documentation of

Indigenous languages. While it may not be realistic to expect a reversal of the pattern of funding so that the majority of support would instead go to the Indigenous communities that actually carry those languages under study, we can at least call for an equitable rebalancing of the colonial inequation. The ethical demand is for a dollar-for-dollar match going to Indigenous communities. This would mean that whatever amounts are going to study our languages, an equal amount should then go to our communities to help provide resources to keep our languages alive. This would result in monies for language work being divided equally between academics and community-based language revitalization efforts.

As briefly sketched here, the colonial context is overbearing in stifling Native-language revitalization, especially as regards drawing on archival institutions. The exclusionary colonial structure is evidenced in the motives for having started the Native-language collections, the unsavory collection processes themselves, and the function of the collections (as measured by their usability for community members and their continued application primarily for academic projects), despite some growing effort to rethink documentation paradigms, and the access restrictions to many collections that are too often exclusionary for community scholars.[48] Additionally, the larger colonial framing has resulted in extreme economic disparities and challenging educational limitations that further compound the issues. For community language programs searching for funding, it is often difficult to develop winning proposals for grants that are putatively designed to support Indigenous-language work, since the process is almost wholly conceived only for the academic study of our languages. As a consequence funding proposals are often turned down with the explanation that the expected level of academic qualifications are not being met among the proposed staff who are community-based language scholars. A graduate degree for community-based staff may not be considered acceptable if it is not in linguistics, while a college degree specifically within the discipline of linguistics may not be deemed adequate. These patterns of rejecting proposals may prevail even though there is nothing in the description that requires these unstated academic qualifications. Notably, the boards overseeing these formal language grant opportunities are becoming more diverse, with growing numbers of members drawn from Indigenous nations. However, the pressure for community-based language programs to acquire expertise from the university system in order to have a realistic chance of winning these larger awards continues unabated rather than those Native board members pushing for a change in the stated and unstated rules of the game. The persistence of this pattern yet again demonstrates the ongoing vitality of colonial structures that continue to co-opt Indigenous scholars who have come up through the ranks of the academy.

On the whole the underlying system has changed little over time and continues to benefit the academic community that it was set up to serve. This can be seen in the case of junior scholars entering the field who are compelled to service the academic institutional demands of the discipline of linguistics. Instead of using the enormous amount of time absorbed from Elders and the significant funding from their years of dissertation research as an opportunity to directly support community language work, young scholars are required to pay the dole to the colonial intellectual project on the hope that it will somehow feed "down" to the level of community language needs. Only after the colonial priorities have been fully addressed may new scholars hope to find funding and institutional support in some indeterminate future where they might be able to offer practical support for community language revitalization.[49]

The pattern of deep-pocket funding going toward Native languages (e.g., Hans Rausing funding that focused on documentation and description) essentially replicates the old Jefferson project of trying to salvage pieces of these languages for academic analysis before they are crushed under the wheels of the colonial machinery. I am not sure how to express the strangeness of the two-centuries-long practice of language collecting within a colonial context that has brutally targeted Native peoples and their languages.[50] The drumming of the hunter-gatherers continues to be echoed in present-day calls to action within the linguistic fraternity (e.g., in the Smithsonian volume on languages in the *Handbook of North American Indians*: "Nearly all the [North American Indian] languages are destined to disappear by the middle of the twenty-first century [see introduction, table 2], which has made basic documentation a priority").[51]

The older colonial legacy is continued in the privileging of European notions of what constitutes legitimate use of resources and significant forms of inquiry. The net effect is the suppression of funding support for language revitalization work based within Native communities. The funding disparities between the large support for scholarly research about Native languages as opposed to the miniscule support for keeping alive the languages themselves is telling. It clearly shows that Indigenous knowledge is not to be valued at the same level as academic Western knowledge, even though it is derived from Indigenous sources. As a result the investment of support continues to be in the production and preservation of the records of Native languages rather than the living languages themselves. This is exactly backward. As we know, if investment is made to keep Indigenous languages alive across generations, then the documentation could always be done later. If communities are supported in producing a new generation of fully fluent and culturally competent speakers, then the dictionary project could as well be produced years from now sometime in "the middle of the twenty-first century."

Another indicator of long-standing colonial relations is reflected in the slow development of community-aware ethics for linguistic work and the old assumptions that collected language materials are legally considered the property of the researcher. There are many war stories in Native-language communities about the endless delays in delivering copies of materials recorded by linguists, dragging on for years, even decades. The problem is only compounded for smaller language communities who often do not have institutional review boards to protect community interests. What is needed is a legal structure parallel to NAGPRA that would protect our languages—because, indeed, the most important cultural patrimony of our Native American nations is our languages. The new legal structure would ensure that copies of all previous documentation was provided to language communities, and any new recordings would need to be provided at the time of production while all older recordings would be repatriated to Native-language communities. The key legal leverage—following the NAGPRA model—is that any future federal funding would be withheld from individual scholars or institutions who failed to comply.

The new regime could simply be called the Native American Languages Protection and Repatriation Act (or NALPRA).

We need a clearer understanding of the colonial heritage and resulting structures so we can redeploy resources and redirect funding to better support our Indigenous communities. We must move beyond the naïve reliance on the goodwill of individual players and allies among the many researchers, archivists, linguists, administrators, funders, and board members at specific institutions. We are still in need of sweeping systemic change that will provide a lifeline for our at-risk Indigenous-language communities.

Given the sacred place of our languages within Indigenous communities and the drag of colonialist history that has brought about the present crisis in Native language survival, aggressive action for change must be implemented. From establishing NALPRA to fairness in funding, to institutional access, we must work together to move beyond the shadow of the prevailing models inherited from hunter-gatherers of the past. The highest level of repurposing the archived Native-language materials is to empower the most urgent task of getting the language resources back to the original language communities who are the natural homes for Indigenous languages. Working together we can ensure a future where Indigenous Peoples carry forward the fullness of their ceremonial structures and traditional practices for their children and grandchildren.

Ôk'ajU k'aÔk'anEya TahA Ôk'âfATA (by working together we can move it forward).

KAdaTAl@hû (that should be enough).

NOTES

1. For example, see Leonard, "Producing Language Reclamation."
2. Rosenblum and Berez-Kroeker, "Reflections on Language Documentation," 341.
3. Errington, *Linguistics in a Colonial World*, viii.
4. See further comment on the implications of the understanding of Indigenous languages as powerful and sacred for the work of revitalization in Grounds, "Indigenous Perspectives and Language Habitats."
5. Gordin, "How Did Science Come to Speak Only English." Even the very writing of this present chapter may gain in academic acceptability the more it exhibits a Latin-based English lexicon.

6. Wissler, "American Indian and the American Philosophical Society."
7. Harvey, *Native Tongues*, 78–79.
8. Thomas Jefferson to Benjamin Smith Barton, September 21, 1809, APS.
9. Gallatin, "Synopsis of the Indian Tribes," 97.
10. Wissler, "American Indian and the American Philosophical Society."
11. Golla, "Records of American Indian Linguistics."
12. Gallatin, "Synopsis of the Indian Tribes," 7.
13. Emphasis added. Powell, "On Limitations," 76–77.
14. Peniere, "Extract of Letter to General Jackson."
15. Ransom, *Osceola; Or, Fact and Fiction*.
16. Lossing, *Lossing's New History of the United States*.
17. See *Webster's Third New International Dictionary*, 1961.
18. See discussion in Grounds, "Yuchi Travels."
19. Swanton, "Review of *Ethnology of the Yuchi Indians*," 521–22.
20. Capitals in original. *Floridian*, July 30, 1836.
21. W. B. Hodgson's introduction to Benjamin Hawkin's "Sketch of the Creek Country," *Collections of the Georgia Historical Society*, 1848.
22. "The Writer's Art," *Seattle Times*, August 22, 1999.
23. Rymer, "Vanishing Voices," 88–89.
24. Long, *Significations*
25. "Instructions for Meriwether Lewis."
26. Personal communication, Carter Blue Clark, June 20, 1995, confirming his remarks in public lecture.
27. The pattern of developing and distributing circulars that provided a standardized simple structure used for direct comparative efforts across languages became common practice throughout the nineteenth century. See summary of forms in Pilling, "Catalogue of Linguistic Manuscripts." A standardized vocabulary form was even used in the 1970s to tabulate Yuchi lexical terms by James Crawford.
28. Bieder, *Science Encounters the Indian*, 29–30.
29. Gatschet, *Klamath Indians of Southwestern Oregon*, xiii.
30. Gatschet, *Klamath Indians of Southwestern Oregon*, xv.
31. Powell, "Report of the Director" (1881), xii–xiii.
32. Powell, "Report of the Director" (1881), xiii.
33. Powell, "Report of the Director" (1881), xxiv.
34. Harvey, *Native Tongues*, 23.
35. Letter from B. E. Fryer to G. A. Otis, February 12, 1869, as cited in Bieder, *Science Encounters the Indian*, 38.
36. Letters from Franz Boas to John Billings, April 6, April 23, and May 6, 1887, cited in Bieder, *Science Encounters the Indian*, 39.

37. Alves, "On the Eating Habits of Science."
38. Gallatin, "Synopsis of the Indian Tribes," 97.
39. Gatschet, *Klamath Indians of Southwestern Oregon*, 18.
40. For discussion of colonial implications of Native-derived state names, see Grounds, "Hermeneutics of American Place-Names."
41. Speck, "Ethnology of the Yuchi Indians."
42. On a personal note, the preface recognizes support for the Yuchi language research with a double connection to my family. Surprisingly, Wagner acknowledges both my Yuchi aunt's father-in-law, Noah Gregory, as well as my grandfather's brother, Charles Grounds, from the Seminole side of my family.
43. These technological developments can have increased benefits for Indigenous communities when accompanied by activist archivists such as Brian Carpenter at the APS, who identifies the Indigenous recipients for archived materials: "It is precisely these people [community leaders and members] who are the primary constituency, core experts, and research public for these manuscripts." As quoted in Carpenter, "Kwakwaka'wakw Manuscripts of George Hunt."
44. Krauss, "World's Languages in Crisis," 10.
45. Shorris, "Last Word," 38.
46. Gibbs, "Saving Dying Languages," 83.
47. Rosenblum and Berez-Kroeker, "Reflections on Language Documentation," 341.
48. Leonard, "Producing Language Reclamation"; Rosenblum and Berez-Kroeker, "Reflections on Language Documentation."
49. As an example, the formal grammar produced on the Yuchi language—and chaired by a prominent linguist renowned for actively supporting Indigenous-language revitalization work—ended up producing a grammar of Yuchi for a dissertation project that no Yuchi community member can actually decode. See Linn, "Grammar of Euchee (Yuchi)." Those working desperately to revitalize the Yuchi language and investing their lives in honoring the words of their Elders are forced to take a back seat and wait for the possible future time when the formal grammar may eventually be transposed into some more accessible form for community use.
50. Again, it is not individual players but the overall system that is at issue.
51. Mithun, "Description of the Native Languages of North America."

BIBLIOGRAPHY

Alves, Rubem. "On the Eating Habits of Science." In *Faith and Science in an Unjust World*, vol. 1, edited by Roger L. Shinn, 41–43. Geneva: World Council of Churches, 1980.

Bieder, Robert. *Science Encounters the Indian, 1820–1880: The Early Years of American Ethnology*. Norman: University of Oklahoma Press, 1989.

——. "A Brief Historical Survey of the Expropriation of American Indian Remains." Paper for Native American Rights Fund, 1990, Boulder, Colorado.

Carpenter, Brian. "The Kwakwaka'wakw Manuscripts of George Hunt." CNAIR Stories, American Philosophical Society, https://www.amphilsoc.org/blog/canir-stories-kwakwakawakw-manusscripts-george-hunt (accessed April 2, 2019).

Errington, Joseph. *Linguistics in a Colonial World: A Story of Language, Meaning, and Power*. Oxford: Blackwell, 2008.

Gallatin, Albert. "A Synopsis of the Indian Tribes Within the United States East of the Rocky Mountains, and in the British and Russian Possessions in North America." *Archaeologia Americana* 2, (1836): 1–422.

Gatschet, Albert S. *A Migration Legend of the Creek Indians, With a Linguistic, Historic, and Ethnographic Introduction*. Philadelphia: D. G. Brinton, 1884.

——— . *The Klamath Indians of Southwestern Oregon*. Contributions to North American Ethnology, vol. 2. Department of the Interior, U.S. Geographical and Geological Survey of the Rocky Mountain Region. Washington: Government Printing Office, 1890.

Gibbs, W. Wayt. "Saving Dying Languages." *Scientific American*, 287 (August 2002): 78-85.

Golla, Victor. "The Records of American Indian Linguistics." In *Preserving the Anthropological Record*, edited by Sydel Silverman and Nancy J. Parezo, 143–57. New York: Wenner-Gren Foundation, 1995.

Gordin, Michael D. "How Did Science Come to Speak Only English." Aeon, February 4, 2015, https://aeon.co/essays/how-did-science-come-to-speak-only-english.

Grounds, Richard A. "Indigenous Perspectives and Language Habitats." Paper for International Expert Group Meeting on Indigenous Languages, United Nations, Permanent Forum on Indigenous Issues, January 19–21, 2016, United Nations Headquarters, New York City. https://www.un.org/development/desa/indigenouspeoples/meetings-and-workshops/8109-2.html (accessed August 31, 2020).

——— . "Tallahassee, Osceola, and the Hermeneutics of American Place-Names." *Journal of the American Academy of Religion* 69 (2001): 287–322.

——— . "Yuchi Travels: Up and Down the Academic 'Road to Disappearance.'" In *Native Voices: American Indian Identity and Resistance*, edited by Richard A. Grounds, David E. Wilkins, and George E. Tinker, 290–317. Lawrence: University Press of Kansas, 2003.

Harvey, Sean P. *Native Tongues: Colonialism and Race from Encounter to the Reservation*. Cambridge MA: Harvard University Press, 2015.

"Instructions for Meriwether Lewis." June 20, 1803, Thomas Jefferson Papers, Library of Congress, Washington DC. https://founders.archives.gov/documents/Jefferson/01-40-02-0136-0005 (accessed August 31, 2020).

Krauss, Michael. "The World's Languages in Crisis." *Language* 68 (1992): 4–10.

Leitch, Barbara A. *A Concise Dictionary of Indian Tribes of North America*. Algonac MI: Reference, 1979.

Leonard, Wesley Y. "Producing Language Reclamation by Decolonising 'Language.'" In *Language Documentation and Description*, edited by Wesley Y. Leonard and Haley De Korne, 15–36. Vol. 14. London: EL, 2017.

—— . "Reflections on (De)Colonialism in Language Documentation." In *Reflections on Language Documentation 20 Years after Himmelmann 1998*, edited by Bradley McDonnell, Andrea L. Berez-Krocker, and Gary Holton, 55–65. Language Documentation and Conservation Special Publication no. 15. Honolulu: University of Hawaii Press, 2018.

Linn, Mary S. "A Grammar of Euchee (Yuchi)." PhD diss., University of Kansas, 2001.

Long, Charles H. *Significations: Signs, Symbols, and Images in the Interpretation of Religion*. Philadelphia: Fortress, 1986.

Lossing, Benson J. *Lossing's New History of the United States, from the Discovery of the American Continent to the Present Time*. New York: Gay Brothers, 1881.

Mithun, Marianne. "The Description of the Native Languages of North America: Boas and After." In *Languages*, edited by Ives Goddard, 43–63. Vol 17. *Handbook of North American Indians*, edited by William C. Sturtevant. Washington DC: Smithsonian Institution, 1996.

Paterek, Josephine. *Encyclopedia of American Indian Costume*. Santa Barbara CA: ABC-CLIO, 1994.

Peniere, J. A. "Extract of Letter to General Jackson" (July 15, 1821). In *Letter from the Secretary of War, to the Chairman of the Committee on Indian Affairs*, n.p. Washington DC: Gales & Seaton, 1823.

Pilling, James C. "Catalogue of Linguistic Manuscripts in the Library of the Bureau of Ethnology." In *First Annual Report of the Bureau of Ethnology to the Secretary of the Smithsonian Institution, 1879–80*, n.p. Washington DC: Government Printing Office, 1881.

Powell, John Wesley. "On Limitations to the Use of Some Anthropologic Data." *First Annual Report of the Bureau of Ethnology to the Secretary of the Smithsonian Institution, 1879–80*, n.p. Washington DC: Government Printing Office, 1881.

—— . "Report of the Director." *First Annual Report of the Bureau of Ethnology to the Secretary of the Smithsonian Institution, 1879–80*, n.p. Washington DC: Government Printing Office, 1881.

—— . "Report of the Director." *Nineteenth Annual Report of the Bureau of American Ethnology to the Secretary of the Smithsonian Institution, 1897–98*, n.p. Washington DC: Government Printing Office, 1900.

Ransom, James Birchett. *Osceola; Or, Fact and Fiction: A Tale of the Seminole War, By a Southerner*. New York: Harper & Brothers, 1838.

Rosenblum, Daisy, and Andrea L. Berez-Kroeker. "Reflections on Language Documentation in North America." In *Reflections on Language Documentation 20 Years after Himmelmann 1998*, edited by Bradley McDonnell, Andrea L. Berez-Krocker, and Gary Holton, 340–53. Language Documentation and Conservation Special Publication no. 15. Honolulu: University of Hawaii Press, 2018.

Rymer, Russ. "Vanishing Voices." *National Geographic* 222 (July 2012): 60–93.

Shorris, Earl. "The Last Word: Can the World's Small Languages be Saved?" *Harper's Magazine*, August 2000, 35–43.

Speck, Frank G. "Ethnology of the Yuchi Indians." University of Pennsylvania, Anthropological Publications of the University Museum. Vol. 1. Philadelphia: University Museum, 1909.

Swanton, John R. Review of *Ethnology of the Yuchi Indians*, by Frank G. Speck. *American Anthropologist*, n.s. 1 (1909): 520–22.

Waldman, Carl. *Encyclopedia of Native American Tribes*. New York: Facts on File, 1988.

Wagner, Günter. *Yuchi Tales*. Publications of the American Ethnological Society. Vol. 13. Edited by Franz Boas. New York: G. E. Stechert, 1931.

——— . "Yuchi." In *Handbook of American Indian Languages*, 296–384. Vol. 3. New York: Columbia University Press, 1934.

Wissler, Clark. "The American Indian and the American Philosophical Society." *Proceedings of the American Philosophical Society* 86, no. 1 (1942): 189–204.

CHAPTER 3

Supporting Researchers of Indigenous Vernacular Archives

Lisa Conathan

The Beinecke Rare Book and Manuscript Library at Yale University, like many of its peer institutions, holds broad and deep collections documenting Native languages of North America, the legacy of decades of ethnographic and missionary collecting and documentation.[1] Among these holdings are manuscripts in Native scripts such as the Algonquian syllabary, Cherokee syllabary, and Mi'kmaw hieroglyphs, as well as voluminous print and manuscript sources that use orthographies based on a modified Latin alphabet. These collections have traditionally been kept in custodianship by archives, as documentation of Native life and culture, to support scholarly, governmental, or religious study. Modern library practices allow us to reassert the role of artifacts of vernacular literacy in the context of contemporary Native culture, affirming their utility, value, and currency.

This chapter contextualizes Beinecke's Cherokee and Mi'kmaw holdings and describes outreach efforts to cultivate research communities who interact with the manuscripts in a digitally-enabled environment. A public transcription platform (Transcribe@Yale), which debuted in 2016 with Cherokee manuscripts as its initial project, allows librarians to improve intellectual and virtual access to extraordinary manuscripts in the Cherokee and Mi'kmaw languages by engaging students, scholars, speakers, and language learners in their interpretation. The platform is one product of years of preparation, research, and contributions from library staff, Cherokee scholars, visiting consultants, a Beinecke fellow, and technologists. Library outreach efforts promote the study of two unique scripts (Cherokee syllabary and Mi'kmaw hieroglyphs), invigorating the study of paleography and textual analysis based on these vital, yet not easily accessible, corpora.

Cherokee and Mi'kmaw scripts have elements in common: they were codified and documented in the context of contact with European writing; they are nonalphabetic writing systems and therefore seem difficult and exotic to those of us most comfortable with ABCs; and their use and transmission are powerful symbols of autonomy and distinctiveness. The two corpora of manuscripts, however, differ starkly. The Cherokee corpus is relatively large and represents a writing system still in active use. It is therefore an open corpus, with new literature being created today. Mi'kmaw hieroglyphic manuscripts constitute a closed corpus, representing an esoteric writing system that is not well known or commonly used today. The Cherokee syllabary was adopted widely and used for diverse vernacular genres in the nineteenth and twentieth centuries, while the Mi'kmaw manuscripts on paper were chiefly created in the specific context of Catholic worship. The nineteenth-century promulgation of the Cherokee syllabary is well known, while the sixteenth-century codification and earlier roots of the Mi'kmaw hieroglyphs in the petroglyph tradition are not well represented in scholarly literature.

Kilpatrick Collection of Cherokee Manuscripts

The Kilpatrick Collection of Cherokee Manuscripts has resided in the Beinecke Library since 1979. This collection, documenting a unique tradition of Indigenous literacy among twentieth-century Cherokees in Oklahoma, was uncataloged until 2013, and library records reflect no research use between the time of acquisition and cataloging. In concert with current initiatives to promote the use of primary sources in Native American language education, as well as reflecting a broader trend of bringing historical documentation to bear on efforts to counteract contemporary decline in language usage, Beinecke is undertaking deliberate outreach to support use of this collection. In order to enable new educational and scholarly use and to enhance archival description, Beinecke is cultivating a user-centered approach to the collection by digitizing portions to make them available for community-sourced transcription. These portions are available online through Beinecke Digital Collections, and to transcribe through Transcribe@Yale. Based on feedback from Cherokee users and potential users, Beinecke strives to improve the user experience of Cherokee community interaction with digitized collections and facsimiles in order to maximize their local utility. These efforts have included the provision of images to be reproduced in facsimile in an exhibit by the United Keetoowah Band.

Opening the Kilpatrick Collection of Cherokee manuscripts to community discussion, interpretation, and transcription has supported classroom and research use of a collection that has been on Beinecke's shelves with little disturbance since 1979. In order to responsibly open the collection, however, the library had to conduct its own research and seek consultation to respectfully prepare the collection for public engagement. This cultural and technical mediation that undergirds the deceptively simple act of community sourcing has allowed us to tap into remote expertise, recruit remote research communities, and promote the collection to Cherokee language teachers.

Efforts to provide digital access to the collection began in 2012, with several goals: to understand the cultural resonance of the collection, including the sensitive nature of medical formulae; to increase intellectual access to the collection by creating representations in Yale's online library catalog; to improve researchers' ability to discover and access the collection by publishing digital representations; and to create machine-readable text to facilitate searching and analysis of Cherokee manuscripts that present many challenges to even the most skilled reader.

Creating machine-readable text also enhances readability by human eyes that may be unaccustomed to the diverse and sometimes archaic handwriting documented in the Kilpatrick manuscripts. Optical character recognition cannot be applied effectively to manuscript material in Cherokee because the total corpus is too small and variable to support the machine learning necessary to develop a successful algorithm. The texts must therefore be transcribed by hand. This type of meticulous editorial work, traditionally carried out by individual scholars or small groups of editors working on a scholarly research project or documentary edition, is increasingly being carried out in public. Community transcription projects benefit from the interest of diverse individuals and the satisfaction gained from contributing to a group endeavor. Successful community transcription programs are being developed in a diverse array of institutions, including the Smithsonian's Transcription Center, which highlights projects ranging from fifteenth-century Latin manuscripts to astronomy ledger books, and University of Iowa's DIY History site, built on an Omeka platform, which served as inspiration and source code for Transcribe@Yale. The task of transcribing Cherokee manuscripts presents several particular challenges, however, due to the language's unique writing system, the small population of fluent speakers, and the unique, sometimes esoteric, content of the texts.

Cherokee is a thriving language in the context of Native North America, with numbers of speakers counted in the hundreds rather than counted on fingers. Cherokees in Oklahoma and North Carolina have active education programs to instruct children and adults in Cherokee language, and Northeastern State University in Oklahoma offers undergraduate degrees in Cherokee cultural studies and Cherokee education. Cherokee is still, however, an endangered language. Its use is subject to a contraction of domains, as English is the dominant language in many contexts in the Cherokee Nation, the United Keetoowah Band, and the Eastern Band of Cherokee Indians. Along with a contraction of usage comes a contraction of vocabulary, grammar, and functionality, as the language is used in fewer daily situations, and with fewer regular interlocutors. This contraction of language knowledge among speakers creates challenges to reading and interpreting manuscripts, but it also increases the reward of engaging with language of an earlier generation.

Cherokee has a unique writing system that uses eighty-five characters to represent syllables. The system was created by the Cherokee cultural leader and silversmith Sequoyah around 1820 and was rapidly adopted, in order to promote Native literacy among nineteenth-century Cherokees. Sequoyah hoped that his invention would help Cherokees preserve their heritage, traditions, and religion, and the system provided a mechanism for communication among dispersed people during a time when families and communities were disrupted due to the forced relocations of the 1830s. Use of the Sequoyan syllabary was and remains a powerful symbol of Cherokee singularity, independence, and control over cultural and historical discourse.

After the syllabary came into use, Cherokee print culture developed rapidly, with backing from New England missionary organizations. Type was first cast in 1828 in New England. The *Cherokee Phoenix*, the first Native American newspaper, was first published in 1828 in New Echota, Georgia, as a bilingual publication. It remained in print only until 1835, when the press was confiscated by Georgia militia troops and some of the type was dumped in the well of Elias Boudinot, a prominent Cherokee leader.[2] The publication was revived later and survives today in print and online. In 1835 a second printing press was established in what is now Oklahoma. The *Cherokee Messenger*, a Baptist missionary publication, was the first periodical of any kind to be published in Indian Territory, debuting in August 1844 with a translation of the book of Genesis into Cherokee; it also included articles on Cherokee linguistic analysis. The *Advocate*, which first came out a month later in September 1844, was a competing periodical published by the Cherokee Nation that included commentary on tribal affairs, government, and social issues.

Literacy in the Sequoyan syllabary survived the Trail of Tears, the rupture of families caused by forced removals, the social and political upheaval of the 1840s, and the Civil War. Among historical documentation of Native North America, the robust corpus of Cherokee print and manuscript resources creative by native speakers of the language is singular. Large collections of Cherokee manuscripts are held by the American Philosophical Society (APS), the Smithsonian Institution, the Gilcrease Museum, the University of Oklahoma, and the Beinecke Library at Yale. The Kilpatrick Collection of Cherokee Manuscripts, which was acquired by Beinecke between 1979 and 1983, contains voluminous and diverse documentation of Cherokee language and culture from the late nineteenth century through the mid-twentieth century. Among the genres is practice writing that documents the cultivation of literacy among Cherokees, such as one manuscript by the scribe "Andrew No Wife," who

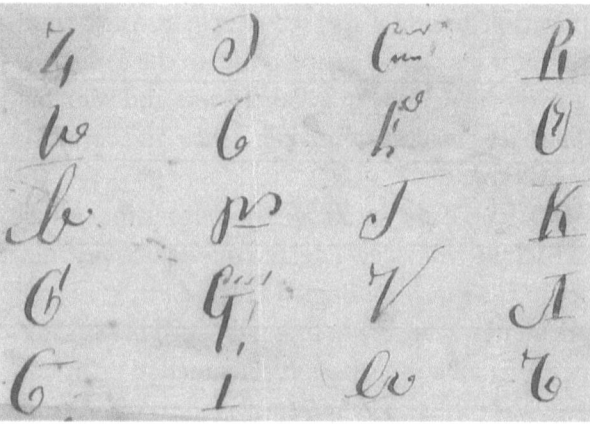

Fig. 1. Andrew No Wife, syllabary practice with commentary (detail), undated (ca. 1880). Kilpatrick Collection of Cherokee Manuscripts, Yale Collection of Western Americana, Beinecke Rare Book and Manuscript Library.

laid out the syllabary with commentary in approximately 1880 (see fig. 1). Other manuscripts include numerous funeral notices from the 1920s and 1930s and personal letters such as one from Jackson Standingdeer to his brother in 1936. Extensive notes and meeting minutes document the activity of Christian churches in Oklahoma in the 1930s, and a few manuscripts relate to the Keetoowah Society during the same period. The various nature of the contents reflects the pervasiveness of use the syllabary and of Native-language literacy among the authors. Collections of autograph manuscripts in Native American languages—that is, by Native authors in their own languages—are extraordinarily rare, and this is among the most diverse anywhere, in any North American language.

Jack Kilpatrick and Anna Gritts Kilpatrick, a Cherokee husband-and-wife team, set out to collect Cherokee language manuscripts in Oklahoma in the mid-twentieth century. Jack Kilpatrick was a composer and musicologist by training and was chair of the music department at Southern Methodist University. Anna Gritts was related to Uwedasat Sawali, a Cherokee shaman and Christian minister featured prominently in the Kilpatricks' studies, and her family connections assisted the Kilpatricks in pursuing their documentary collecting.[3] The Kilpatricks were motivated by a sense of impending loss due to language endangerment, and by a recognition that very little of a century of Cherokee literary output had been preserved in libraries or archives. They were practicing a vein of "salvage ethnography" that dominated early twentieth-century anthropology, pioneered by Franz Boas and practiced by other ethnomusicologists. Their mission was acutely personal, however, as they were collecting documentation in their home community and Native culture. In the preface to one of their publications, they lamented that, prior to World War II, "one might have obtained manuscripts in syllabary by the truckload," whereas by the mid-1960s "the average Cherokee cabin is likely to be as devoid of a single scrap of Sequoyan as it is of a copy of Catullus."[4]

The hyperbolic observation of the Kilpatricks echoes Frans Olbrechts's introduction to James Mooney's publication of the Cherokee "Swimmer" manuscript, in which Olbrechts sets the tone for his presentation of medical formulae by listing Cherokee manuscripts destroyed, lost, or mislaid, leading up to the disappearance of the original Swimmer autograph manuscript, which had been in Mooney's possession when he prepared its 1891 publication. The original manuscript had, according to Mooney, been in Cherokee syllabary, though when collaborating with the author to prepare it for publication in the Bureau of American Ethnology *Bulletin* he transliterated it into a Latin-based phonetic orthography.[5] Olbrechts's 1932 introduction recounts his effort to reconstruct certain aspects of Mooney's editorial intent, while restoring Olbrechts's understanding of aboriginal authenticity in others. In order to verify the texts, he asked a Cherokee consultant to revert the transliterated text to syllabary and then compared the reconstituted text to an illustration of the original text sourced from the Swimmer author Ayv'ini. Olbrecht's presentation of the texts, though, uses his own phonetic transcription, based on the oral performance of a 1930s medicine man reading the reconstituted syllabary text. The convoluted textual history of the Swimmer manuscript speaks to the American ethnographic context in which Cherokee texts have been published, analyzed, interpreted, and Latinized. The audience for the 1891 and 1932 publications were ethnographers, a category assumed to be mutually exclusive with Cherokee people. Presentation and discussion of the text in its original syllabary form was incompatible with scholarly analysis, and preservation of the authenticity of this text was never part of Mooney's nor Olbrechts's agenda.[6]

The Kilpatricks also reworked the manuscripts they collected in their many publications, which included English translations, and, in some cases, Latin transliterations, of a selection of manuscripts in their possession. The original manuscripts appeared as illustrations in occasional facsimile reproductions. They translated and commented on eighty-one short personal and legal texts in a 1965 monograph.[7] That same year they produced a volume of poetic translations of romantic love incantations, *Walk in Your Soul*.[8] One reviewer frames the presentation in translation and transliteration as a respectful way of distancing the publication from the effectiveness of the texts: "Perhaps out of deference to the large Cherokee-speaking population of Oklahoma, the authors have presented these texts in a poetic English. . . . To have reproduced these texts in the Sequoyah syllabary, or in transcription with literal interlinear translation as some scholars might demand, would certainly have created a panic among nubile Cherokees and consternation among their parents, for indiscriminate use of this medicine is a serious matter."[9] Preliminary research has identified thirty-seven original texts among Beinecke's holdings that correspond to those published in the Kilpatricks' volumes. Hundreds, however, remain unidentified, and undoubtedly additional correlations will be found.

The Beinecke Library acquired the Kilpatrick collection from Alan Kilpatrick, son of Jack and Anna, in several groups between 1979 and 1983. Without local staff expertise to catalog or even identify the individual manuscripts, the material was largely unused between then and 2013, when library staff created a library catalog record and began outreach efforts to identify Cherokee community members who could assist in assessing and interpreting the collection, and in promoting its use.

Challenges to Access

Access to the extraordinarily rich documentation in the Kilpatrick Collection has been hampered by several factors. First and foremost, its geographic location is remote from Cherokee communities in North Carolina and Oklahoma. Many individuals are aware of the Kilpatricks' work, the relationships they had with local Cherokee medicine men, and the collection they accumulated, as well as its eventual transfer to Yale. But no Cherokee researcher had traveled to consult the material before recent efforts to promote it, and no Yale representative had brought the material to Cherokee country.

In addition to the geographic barrier, intellectual barriers have created challenges to access. Beinecke staff lacks the expertise necessary to describe the material, find specific manuscripts, or answer questions about the contents. The collection came to Beinecke accompanied by documentation, but, as is common, the lists and descriptions covered only portions of the collection and did not always provide enough information to distinguish one item from another within the collection.

Even knowledge of Cherokee language is not sufficient to describe, transcribe, transliterate, or translate the manuscripts. Contemporary Cherokee people may not have been exposed to a wide range of handwriting styles, or to some of the language in the manuscripts. Most modern handwritten Cherokee is modeled on the print form of the syllabary.[10] In the late nineteenth and early twentieth centuries, however, it appears that handwriting styles were more varied, as is evident in the Kilpatrick Collection. In addition to personal handwriting variation, the genre of text influences the legibility and layout of the manuscripts. Some texts, such as obituary notices, were posted in public spaces and typically were written clearly in order to be read by a public audience. Others, such as notes or personal letters, were intended for a more closely defined, familiar audience and may be more difficult to interpret. Medical and magical documents in the collection were often intentionally obscure, written privately and making use of abbreviations or circumlocutions. In the words of Alan Kilpatrick, "They are secretive documents written in a highly specialized vocabulary, replete with arcane forms of wordplay, meant to baffle and confuse the uninitiated, the layman."[11] Each of the Cherokee researchers whom the author has observed read the manuscripts has remarked on the variation in handwriting, which makes the documents challenging to read.

The language of the texts may also be unfamiliar to today's fluent Cherokee speakers and language learners. Since use of the Cherokee language has generally contracted over the past century, the texts document vocabulary, usage, and grammar that may not be widely used or known today. This is, of course, exciting to scholars and students of the language, who are uncovering previously undocumented vocabulary, syntactic constructions, and dialect variants, but it presents challenges to the use and interpretation of the texts, especially in a classroom environment or in the support of emerging language learners. The newly created description of the manuscripts and tools that enable online interaction are designed to help bridge this gap between the manuscripts and potential researchers' experience and exposure to unfamiliar handwriting.

Another major barrier is the sensitive nature of a large portion of the collection. The Kilpatricks' collecting focused heavily on medical and magical formulae, including love magic, incantations to cure injury or illness, protective charms, and purification rites traditionally used by shamans or medicine men. This textual genre has been featured in the ethnographic literature since James Mooney's seminal publication in 1891 of "The Sacred Formulas of the Cherokees," in the seventh annual report of the Bureau of American Ethnology. Besides "sacred," Mooney uses the terminology "medicinal prescriptions" to describe the contents of these publications.

The Kilpatricks continued Mooney's line of research, publishing a monograph on Cherokee magic in 1967 and a "Notebook of a Cherokee Shaman" in 1970, both after Jack Kilpatrick's death. Each of these publications included Latin transliterations of Cherokee-language formulae, along with translations into English and commentary. Jack and Anna Kilpatrick's son Alan also published a book on the topic in 1997. His monograph *The Night Has a Naked Soul: Witchcraft and Sorcery among the Western Cherokee* similarly included Latin transliterations and English translations of formulae. None of these publications included Cherokee language in syllabary, aside from the occasional facsimile illustration.

Despite a substantial history of scholarly research on these formulae, as well as significant current interest, their publication remains controversial. The use of formulae in a Cherokee context is mediated by cultural protocols and requires extensive preparation and instruction in their use. Misuse or disrespect of the texts by individuals without the requisite preparation necessary to wield them with humility and accuracy can cause harm not only to those exposed, but also to the very fabric of the cultural institutions that grant them meaning. The Cherokee are not alone in asserting the potential damage that can result from unfettered access to culturally restricted material. Recent decades have seen extensive discussion and prolific literature about respectful treatment of documentation of Native culture, and I do not attempt to summarize the scholarship here.

The designation of the medical formulae as culturally sensitive is also not without disagreement. Jack and Anna Kilpatrick state in the introduction to their *Notebook of a Cherokee Shaman* that "the texts under consideration here are, from the Cherokee viewpoint, 'dead'; of no effect. Their power passed with their owner. The restoration of the powers of medicomagical writings whose original owner has died is accomplished by a previously unreported ritual whereby the materials, polluted by the death of the one who possessed them, are taken to running water and ceremonially cleansed."[12] The Kilpatricks, then, including Anna Gritts, who was related to the shaman in question, considered it uncontroversial to publish these "dead" texts. Their son Alan would reiterate this assertion twenty-seven years later in his monograph on Cherokee witchcraft and sorcery, stating that the texts therein are ritually "dead" and can only be revived by purification rites that he was sworn not to disclose.

Beinecke staff could have taken these statements as license to consider the entire corpus of medical formulae in their possession to be effectively inert and therefore safe to expose through digital presentation. Ongoing dialogue with Cherokee people, however, indicates that there is a diversity of beliefs on the best way to respect and protect these texts, and that at the very least the topic deserves our careful consideration before we digitize the medical texts and make them widely available. The librarian's dual obligations are to preservation and access, and in this case preservation includes the protection of the texts as culturally mediated content, not only as physical documents. In consultation with members of the Cherokee Nation, the United Keetoowah Band, and the Eastern Band of Cherokee Indians, Beinecke staff did not publicize the medical texts and focused instead on the remainder of the collection.

Beinecke does not restrict the use of medical texts in their reading room, nor does it restrict researchers from requesting copies of the material. A good-faith effort has been made, however, to assure that medical texts do not appear in any of the online tools that present digital collections to the public. Texts may have been misidentified, and readers who discover a medical text in the digital collections may contact the curator of Western Americana to request a takedown of the image(s). While the medical texts had previously received the majority of popular and scholarly attention, the remainder of the texts offer the best prospects for use in a wide range of contemporary contexts.

Beinecke staff seek to balance respect for the sensitive nature of the medical formulae with a desire to provide open access to a rich source of Cherokee cultural documentation. While the Kilpatricks were particularly interested in medical texts, they also collected historical and cultural documentation of a less sensitive nature, such as public obituary notices, church committee minutes, Christian hymns, shopping lists, and personal letters. This astonishingly varied trove of primary material will support current and future research endeavors without widely publicizing the medical texts. Lacking the subject knowledge to distinguish medical formulae from other content, however, Beinecke could not proceed with a plan to provide online access without first gaining basic intellectual control over the collection.

This intellectual control was achieved in three steps over two years. First, Beinecke invited two experts in Cherokee language to visit and begin to identify the material. The initial visit lasted one week and included Durbin Feeling, the world's foremost Cherokee linguist and author of the most comprehensive Cherokee dictionary, and Hartwell Francis, a linguist and educator who oversaw the Cherokee language program at Western Carolina University. Over the course of a week the two experts were able to identify about 5 percent of the collection, indicating a greater investment would be necessary in order to gain control over the material. Francis returned as a consultant and over the course of a month took meticulous notes to identify each of the over 1,800 manuscripts in the collection. He identified dates and authors, where present, and briefly summarized the content or genre of each text. During a third phase one year later, a graduate student who was learning Cherokee transformed Francis's notes into a finding aid. After two years of identifying the material, the library was ready in January 2015 to make the nonmedical texts accessible online and begin to gather information from Cherokee community members in order to build a community-based environment for interpreting the texts.

Use of the Texts in a Community-Based Context

The medical texts may be the most well-known and most requested aspects of the Kilpatrick collection, but they are not necessarily the most widely useful. The vernacular documentation of notes, lists, obituaries, and hymns could be applied in a variety of contexts, including classroom language learning, master-apprentice relationships, publicity and outreach, and historical, literary and linguistic inquiry. While the medical texts are written for a private audience, containing circumlocutions, abstract language, and obscure vocabulary, many of the others are written to be read. Shopping lists, public notices, committee meeting minutes, and letters containing news of family and friends were intended to be read and used and have emerged as vital, living documents. The diversity of the corpus lends itself to flexible adoption by audiences responding to the linguistic attributes of particular genres. Shopping lists, consisting of uninflected nouns identifying common everyday products, are appropriate for a beginning student; letters, with their conversational language and complete sentences, provide models for conversational construction to more advanced students. In addition to models for language learning, these seemingly mundane documents contain clues to family and community history. Personal names are identified throughout the corpus, including references that allow readers to identify dual names (English and Cherokee) for individuals. Obituary notices aid genealogists by identifying the parents of a deceased child, and the dates and addresses on letters and envelopes document where an individual was located at the time of the letter writing. Each of these areas provide hooks for Cherokee teachers to encourage interest among their students, as they uncover parallels to personal and family history. Because of Cherokee's unique literary history, literacy plays an important role in revitalization and language teaching.[13]

In addition to these pedagogical functions, the robust literature and commentary on the Kilpatrick texts in transliteration provides an opportunity to revisit these publications with a facsimile of the original manuscript at hand. Comparing the manuscripts to published translations or transliterations of the texts will result in valuable observations about vocabulary, linguistic features, and the editorial process and analysis of the Kilpatricks.[14] While digitization increases accessibility in a digital context, it also increases demand for the original paper documents. Digital access and engagement are appropriate outreach for today's younger students, but many of the people who can interact with the texts most meaningfully are Elders who express a preference for paper documents. Digitization also enables proliferation, and future prospects include the use of facsimiles in local exhibits that will provide better exposure outside of a digitally mediated space, promoting community engagement with the collection and dialogue about community-based archiving.

Community-Based Transcription

Given the distance of Beinecke from Cherokee speakers, Beinecke hoped to engage readers by enabling community-based transcription of the corpus. The open community approach allows for ease of entry into engagement with the manuscripts and the possibility for participants to build on one another's work. When examining the documentary editing and metadata practices of a variety of crowdsourcing sites in use, project stakeholders opted to encourage transcription in syllabary rather than a Latin script. Retaining the syllabary produces text that more closely replicates the original manuscript, since transliteration into a Latin script poses a series of potential pitfalls. There is a wide variety of Latin transliteration systems in use, and, since the syllabary ambiguously represents some features of the Cherokee sound system, a Latin transliteration would force the user to make analytical choices about the language being represented in syllabary. Transcribing in syllabary obviates this layer of analysis, thereby simplifying the process and encouraging consistency. The resulting digital corpus of syllabary text serves as a bridge and an aid to reading the manuscripts, and also as a data set that can be manipulated, searched, and reformatted. The choice of syllabary also makes an oppositional statement to previous presentations of Cherokee in scholarly contexts, asserting and respecting the primacy of the syllabary as the preferred medium for these Cherokee-language texts.

Some transcription sites are able to enforce rigorous documentary editing practices, using the Text Encoding Initiative to represent document structure and in-line semantic information. Instead of aiming to capture these categories of information, Transcribe@Yale simplifies the user experience and refrains from providing any instructions on how to structure or format the transcribed text. Since the knowledge barrier is already high in order to participate in this project (one must be interested in learning or already know Cherokee language), Beinecke did not want to add additional barriers to entry. The initial goals of the transcription site are modest: to produce unstructured machine-readable text and identify basic descriptive metadata. This initial corpus, though, will be a foundation for a progressive, multistep development of increasingly articulated documentation of the manuscripts, including identification of authors' identities and a better understanding of document genres. This iterative process will require input from diverse users over time. One user may be able to initiate a rough transcription of a text; a second may be able to provide confirmation of an unusual or uncertain word; and a third may be able to positively identify the author.

The initial test audience for Transcribe@Yale was a spring 2015 seminar class of undergraduate and graduate Yale students learning linguistic field methods, taught by Claire Bowern. Field methods is a topic that is typically taught by working with a speaker of an unfamiliar language in the classroom: students learn the skills of eliciting information about the sounds and structure of the language by engaging directly with a fluent speaker. Bowern, however, embraced an innovative approach to field methods by placing the archive at the center of the learning experience. The course met with a native speaker (Tom Belt of the Eastern Band of Cherokee Indians) and with Hartwell Francis (director of the Western Carolina University Cherokee Language Program) weekly via video call and used the Kilpatrick Collection to guide their learning sessions. The availability of the digitized manuscripts in an open transcription platform was part of this curricular innovation in academic programming.

In the spring of 2016 Transcribe@Yale was launched by expanding the base to known individuals who teach or study Cherokee language, publicizing the site through the language programs at the Cherokee Nation and Western Carolina University, and the John Hair Cultural Center of the United Keetoowah Band. After receiving user feedback and making slight modifications, the site was ready for wider publicity and adoption in the summer of 2016.

Engaging this user group to transcribe Cherokee manuscripts has resulted in a range of useful statements that scholars in the "crowd" make about collection, such as "The handwriting in document X is the same as that in document Y," or "Document X, which is undated, looks like it's from the same notebook as document Y, which has a date of 1923." The information allows Beinecke to better describe and provide access to these manuscripts. The raw text is keyword searchable on the site, and students and scholars can use the transcriptions to aid their language learning or philological analysis of the texts.

Mi'kmaw Hieroglyphic Texts

The second collection of texts featured in Transcribe@Yale is Mi'kmaw hieroglyphic manuscripts from various sources. Like Cherokee, the Mi'kmaw language thrives within proscribed contexts in Mi'kmaw communities and is being actively preserved, taught, and revived, but is ultimately endangered. Virtually all written sources in the Mi'kmaw language use some version of a Latin orthography, from the nineteenth-century writing system developed by the Baptist missionary Silas Rand, to a contemporary practical orthography that is easily typed using ASCII characters.[15]

There is, however, a hieroglyphic writing system documented in a small corpus of nineteenth- and early twentieth-century manuscripts and contemporary printed representations. These hieroglyphs (logographic by nature) display visual similarities to codified ideographs used in petroglyphs—that is, figures carved into stone that represent concepts and ideas. Mi'kmaw iconography also includes symbols found on birchbark manuscripts and maps, practices that informed the development of the codified hieroglyphic writing system. The surviving hieroglyphic texts of Catholic prayers are later copies of texts that can be traced to seventeenth-century encounters with French missionaries, most notably Chrestien Le Clercq (ca. 1630–ca. 1695), a Recollect, and Pierre Maillard (1710–1762), a Spiritan. There are no known surviving manuscripts from the French missionary period, though contemporary publications describe the hieroglyphs, most prominently Le Clercq.[16] There are very few surviving nineteenth-century manuscripts, and confirmed references to twentieth-century manuscripts number not more than a dozen.[17] The Beinecke Library acquired a nineteenth-century manuscript from a Philadelphia book dealer in 2015 (see fig. 2). The book dealer had acquired the manuscript at auction and was not able to confirm provenance of the manuscript from the auction house, but its authenticity is evident from its physical form and from comparison of the manuscript to contemporary specimens.[18] Almost all extant nineteenth-century manuscripts date between 1825 and 1850 and appear to contain selections of Catholic prayers, with the exception of the holdings of the APS, which include a map and an unanalyzed text, both possibly earlier than 1825.

The hieroglyphic writing system was in common use to record Catholic prayers in the nineteenth century, and in 1866 the German reverend Christian Kauder published what has become the most cited reference for the catechism in Mi'kmaw hieroglyphs; later sources are often copied from the printed work.[19] Manuscripts written after this source was published (such as that at the University of Massachusetts Amherst) may have used the print forms of the hieroglyphs as models, or may be simply fair copies of the book. Most scholarly analysis or reprints of the hieroglyphs are based on Kauder as well. Exemplars before this time are therefore key to understanding the origins and unique features of this writing system. The Transcribe@Yale site allows researchers to compare digital images of manuscripts from two institutions in a public forum for the first time. The tool is therefore being used to support a philological community devoted to the study of this unique and scantily documented manuscript tradition.

The activities of seventeenth- and eighteenth-century French missionaries are well recorded in their publications and in contemporary

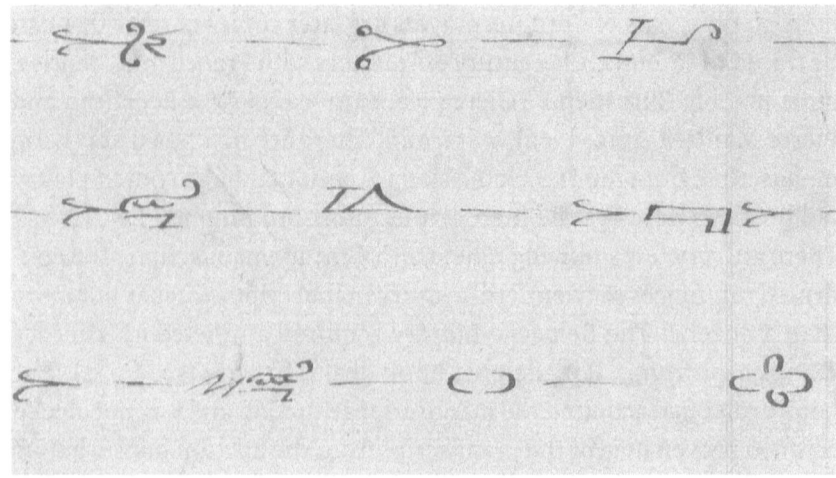

Fig. 2. Micmac Catholic Prayers (detail), undated (ca. 1825). General Collection, Beinecke Rare Book and Manuscript Library, Yale University.

analysis of their relationships with the Mi'kmaq people. The linguistic content of hieroglyphic texts, and a description of the nature of the system as an orthography, however, is virtually unexplored. In the absence of a strong continuing tradition of using the hieroglyphic writing system, digital access does not necessarily support pedagogy and revitalization, but instead the development of a nascent community of philologists exploring the nature of this tiny and unique corpus. This provides a sharp contrast to Cherokee, where the writing system continues to be in use today, playing a prominent role in revitalization programs.

Clearly the purpose and methods of publicizing the Mi'kmaw manuscripts are different than for the Cherokee. Because the Mi'kmaw corpus is so small, it is less compelling to create a machine-searchable textual corpus, and, because the writing system is not actively applied in a language learning environment, it is less relevant in a classroom outside of very specialized contexts. But, by pioneering open access to this genre of manuscript, Beinecke is stimulating research interest like never before. I expect that the platform will enable community discussion of the manuscripts that will contribute to a fuller understanding of their nature and use.

Conclusion

Cherokee and Mi'kmaw offer two case studies that share common elements: an Indigenous writing system with a purpose distinct from that of Latin-based orthographies in its documentation of Native culture. In the case of Cherokee, the texts document a wide range of personal and public history topics, whereas the Mi'kmaw texts reflect a specific manifestation of Native Catholicism. Both corpora, however, benefit from the openness and public collaboration offered by the Transcribe@Yale site.

NOTES

1. The author was affiliated with the Beinecke Library from 2007 to 2016.
2. See Brannon, "Metal Type," for an account of early printing of Cherokee language.
3. Kilpatrick and Kilpatrick, "Fountain of Life."
4. Kilpatrick and Kilpatrick, *Shadow of Sequoyah*, viii.
5. Mooney, "Sacred Formulas,"
6. For a detailed account of the textual editing process, see Olbrechts and Mooney, *Swimmer Manuscript*, 1–9.
7. Kilpatrick and Kilpatrick, *Shadow of Sequoyah*.
8. Kilpatrick and Kilpatrick, *Walk in Your Soul*.
9. Wahrhaftig, Albert, Review of *Walk in Your Soul*, 563.
10. For an investigation of differences between print and manuscript forms of Cherokee syllabary graphemes, see Anderson, "Cherokee and Dakota Language Letters"; and, for more on Cherokee handwriting, see Bender, *Signs of Cherokee Culture*.
11. Kilpatrick, "On Translating," 25.
12. Kilpatrick and Kilpatrick, *Notebook*, 85.
13. For an account of the role of literacy in Cherokee language revitalization, see Peter and Hirata-Edds, "Learning to Read."
14. For a case study on the value of revisiting published sources with contemporary speakers of endangered languages, see Feeling et al., "Why Revisit Published Data?"
15. Rand, *New Testament in the Micmac Language*.
16. LeClercq, *Nouvelle Relation*.
17. See Greenfield, "Mi'kmaq Prayer Book," for an account of nineteenth-century manuscripts. In addition to holdings at the APS and Yale, the Nova Scotia Museum has a collection, and the University of Massachusetts Amherst, the Newberry Library, Princeton University, and Cornell University each have a single manuscript. Others undoubtedly exist as well.
18. "Micmac Catholic Prayers."

19. See, for example, reference to the work of Silas Rand in Pilling, *Bibliography of the Algonquian Languages*, 426.

BIBLIOGRAPHY

Anderson, Laura. "Cherokee and Dakota Language Letters: Illustrations of Nineteenth-Century Discourse." PhD diss., University of Oklahoma, 1999.

Bender, Margaret. *Signs of Cherokee Culture*. Chapel Hill NC: University of North Carolina Press, 2001.

Brannon, Frank. 2009. "Metal Type from the Print Shop of the Historical Cherokee Phoenix Newspaper." *Papers of the Bibliographical Society of America* 123 (2009): 319–36.

Feeling, Durbin, Christine Armer, Charles Foster, Marcellino Berardo, and Sean O'Neill. "Why Revisit Published Data of an Endangered Language with Native Speakers? An Illustration from Cherokee." *Language Documentation & Conservation* 4 (2010): 1–21.

Greenfield, Bruce. "Mi'kmaq Prayer Book." In *The Language Encounter in the Americas, 1492–1800*, edited by Edward G. Gray and Norman Fiering, 189–211. New York: Berghahn, 2000.

Kauder, Christian. *Buch das gut: enthaltend den Katechismus, Betrachtung*. Vienna: Royal Printing House, 1866.

Kilpatrick, Alan. "On Translating Magical Texts." *Wicazo Sa Review* 14, no. 2 (1999): 25–31.

Kilpatrick, Jack, and Anna Gritts Kilpatrick. "'The Fountain of Life': The Cherokee National Ritual." *American Anthropologist* 66, no. 6 (1964): 1386–91.

——. *Notebook of a Cherokee Shaman*. Washington DC: Smithsonian Institution, 1970.

——. *Run toward the Nightland: Magic of the Oklahoma Cherokees*. Dallas: Southern Methodist University Press, 1967.

——. *Shadow of Sequoyah: Social Documents of the Cherokees, 1862–1964*. Norman: University of Oklahoma Press, 1965.

——. *Walk in Your Soul: Love Incantations of the Oklahoma Cherokees*. Dallas: Southern Methodist University Press, 1965.

Le Clercq, Chrestien. *Nouvelle Relation de la Gaspesie*. Paris: Amabele Auroy, 1691.

"Micmac Catholic Prayers." ca. 1825. General Collection, Beinecke Rare Book and Manuscript Library, Yale University, New Haven CT.

Mooney, James. "The Sacred Formulas of the Cherokees." *Seventh Annual Report of the Bureau of Ethnology* (1891): 301–97.

Olbrechts, Frans M., and James Mooney, ed. *The Swimmer Manuscript: Cherokee Sacred Formulas and Medicinal Prescriptions*. Bureau of American Ethnology Bulletin 99. Washington DC: Government Printing Office, 1932.

Peter, Lizette, and Tracy Hirata-Edds. "Learning to Read and Write Cherokee: Toward a Theory of Literacy Revitalization." *Bilingual Research Journal* 32 no. 2 (2009): 207–27.

Pilling, James Constantine. *Bibliography of the Algonquian Languages*. Washington DC: Government Printing Office, 1891.

Rand, Silas Tertius. *The New Testament in the Micmac Language*. Halifax NS: Nova Scotia Printing, 1874.

Schmidt, David L., and Murdena Marshall, ed. and trans. *Mi'kmaq Hieroglyphic Prayers: Readings in North America's First Indigenous Script*. Halifax NS: Nimbus, 1995.

Teuton, Christopher. *Deep Waters: The Textual Continuum in American Indian Literature*. Lincoln: University of Nebraska Press, 2010.

Wahrhaftig, Albert. Review of *Walk in Your Soul*. *American Anthropologist* 68, no. 2 (1966): 563–64.

PART 2

Revitalization Tools

Commentary by Bethany Wiggin

> Words were terribly important because they were formed with breath, with Sila, which was not specifically one's own, but was part of an amorphous whole, a great life force that a body sort of "borrowed" when animate.
> —Rachel Qitsualik

Scholars and students of translation rightly love the Italian phrase *traddutore-traditore*.[1] So close in sound, the pair of words reminds us that just a slip of the tongue turns a translator (*traddutore*) into a traitor (*traditore*). The homophones make plain the high stakes of translation. We are perhaps more accustomed to considering what we lose in translation. But, like slips of the tongue and other uncanny instances, translation can provide flashes of insight—of wit, in its many meanings. Its losses are more akin to the work of mourning than melancholia.[2] As philosopher Paul Ricoeur notes, "In translation too, work is advanced with some salvaging and some acceptance of loss."[3] The work of translation in other words can also *re-pair*, decoupling it from betrayal and linking it to reparation.

Translation offers, as the following chapters elaborate, the means for "mobilization." It literally requires movement, proceeding from a relationship to things past. It carries them over into the present, aiming at posterity. Futurity, we could say, is the "win" of translation, its other pair, providing with this re-pair the possibility of repair.

If translation is to be reparative, it needs an ethics. As Jennifer Carpenter and her coauthors foreground in chapter 4, "The answers to the questions raised in this chapter are not primarily technological, but rather social, cultural, political and economic." For translation cannot be a neutral, or invisible, tool: "In thinking about the translatability between historical languages, one cannot but consider the actual power relations that dictate the degree and magnitude of sacrifice that one language must make in order to achieve some level of commensurability with the other."[4] Reparative translations thus refuse to presume equivalence between languages and cultures. They recognize that "equivalence is not exactly something ready-made, like a preexisting or already-present condition, but rather something to be created."[5]

A reparative translation is akin to the everyday tools described by Michel de Certeau as tactics. Tactics are modest and purposefully nonheroic; they are situational and so need reinventing and constant repairing. They inscribe themselves in existing architecture and reconfigure the built environment for their own purposes. Tactics include poaching, and they are the tools of the historically disenfranchised. They can—as Jeffrey Davis's work in the archives of Plains Indian Sign Language shows in this volume—animate historical languages and archives, making them speak anew. "We are concerned with battles or games between the strong and the weak," De Certeau reminds us, "and with the 'actions' which remain possible for the latter."[6] It is the weak, as Rosi Braidotti suggests, who are "better placed to take the lead in the process of ethical transformation."[7] And, as Cathryn Stimpson continues, "the traumatized, as the pioneers of endurance, are the avant-garde of change. The safe and secure are too cocooned to bother."[8]

Today, in an era of human-made global climate change, climate migration, and climate refugees, we urgently need reparative tools. Such tools would build more cocoons (and for monarchs, too). "We *are* in a sense," Keith Basso writes, "the place-worlds we imagine."[9] Translating *sila*, the Inuit word in my epigraph, offers one tool to imagine other futures into being, breathing life. At their best, reparative translations animate other futures, repairing for a future that not only portends loss but one that suggests salvageable possibilities too.

NOTES

Epigraph: Qitsualik, "Word and Will—Part Two." My use of the critical concept of *sila* is indebted to Todd, "Indigenous Feminist's Take," 5–6.

1. See, for example, Chow, "Translator, Traitor."
2. Freud, "Mourning and Melancholia."
3. Ricoeur, *On Translation*, 3.
4. Lydia Liu, quoted in Chow, "Translator, Traitor," 9. See also Venuti, *Translator's Invisiblity*.
5. Chow, "Translator, Traitor," 74.
6. De Certeau, "Making Do," 34.
7. Rosi Braidotti quoted in Stimpson, "Nomadic Humanities."
8. Stimpson, "Nomadic Humanities."
9. Basso, *Wisdom Sits in Places*, 7.

BIBLIOGRAPHY

Basso, Keith. *Wisdom Sits in Places: Landscape and Language among the Western Apache*. Albuquerque: University of New Mexico Press, 1996.

Chow, Rey. "Translator, Traitor; Translator, Mourner (Or, Dreaming of Intercultural Equivalence)." *Not Like a Native Speaker: On Languaging as a Postcolonial Experience*. New York: Columbia University Press, 2014.

de Certeau, Michel. "'Making Do': Uses and Tactics." In *The Practice of Everyday Life*, translated by Steven Rendall, 29–42. Berkeley: University of California Press, 1984.

Freud, Sigmund. "Mourning and Melancholia." In *The Standard Edition of the Complete Psychological Works*, translated by James Strachey, 243–58. London: Hogarth, 1948.

Qitsualik, Rachel Attituk. "Word and Will—Part Two: Words and the Substance of Life." *Nunatsiaq News*, Nunavut Edition, November 12, 1998. http://www.nunatsiaqonline.ca/archives/nunavut981130/nvt81113_09.html.

Ricoeur, Paul. *On Translation*. Translated by Eileen Brennan. New York: Routledge, 2006.

Stimpson, Cathryn. "The Nomadic Humanities." *Los Angeles Review of Books*, July 12, 2016. https://lareviewofbooks.org/article/the-nomadic-humanities/#.

Todd, Zoe. "An Indigenous Feminist's Take on the Ontological Turn: 'Ontology' Is Just Another Word for Colonialism." *Journal of Historical Sociology*, 29, no. 1 (March 2016): 4–22.

Venuti, Lawrence. *The Translator's Invisibility*. 2nd ed. New York: Routledge, 2008.

CHAPTER 4

Locally Contingent and Community-Dependent

Tools and Technologies for Indigenous Language Mobilization

Jennifer Carpenter, Annie Guerin, Michelle Kaczmarek, Gerry Lawson, Kim Lawson, Lisa P. Nathan, Mark Turin

The Context

The vitality and expression of language within communities is a key aspect of the technoscape. Within Canada the concept of Indigenous communities is complex and dynamic, reflecting intricate relationships between familial, geographical, and political groups.[1] The legacy of suppression of Indigenous languages and knowledge is embedded within policy and legislation intended to break family and community cohesion. Technology has had a role in work undertaken by individuals and communities to maintain and restore these relationships.

In ways that challenge conventional representations of the "digital divide" as a split between the "technology haves and have-nots," Elders and youth in Indigenous communities are actively using and appropriating emerging technologies to strengthen their traditions and languages.[2] While technological efforts in the 1970s included specially modified typewriters and custom-made fonts to represent Indigenous writing systems, communities are now making use of online digital tools, internet radio, and mobile devices to nurture the continued development of Indigenous languages and cultures. Significantly undermined by colonial institutions and processes, Indigenous cultures have suffered systemic harm and marginalization. In Canada the documentation and revitalization of Indigenous languages and cultural knowledge are increasingly cited as priorities in support of well-being in Indigenous communities.[3]

Yet such interventions are not without risks and consequences for individuals, community organizations, and the Indigenous knowledge systems that are being mobilized. There is little agreement about what form an ideal presentation and dissemination platform for Indigenous cultural heritage organizations should take, and how it might work and be maintained and migrated over time. At the same time, Indigenous experiences with—and expectations of—technology can productively challenge normative Western understandings. While many research councils and libraries view the move toward open-access publishing to be of scientific and public benefit, Indigenous cultural and linguistic knowledge is often location-specific and community-internal, and not to be shared through an open portal.[4] Indigenous understandings of the responsibilities that accompany traditional knowledge offer rich insights into the different ways that intellectual property and ownership can function.[5]

Addressing the needs of policy makers within (and beyond) government for reliable data, this chapter aims to deepen the institutional understanding of the history of Canadian-Indigenous relations and expand the possibilities for new conversations that prioritize voices of Indigenous community members as creators, synthesizers, and mobilizers of emerging technologies. The experience of Indigenous and community-based scholars is not well reflected in the existing academic literature. Our environmental scan and knowledge synthesis establish that Indigenous cultural heritage organizations have sophisticated, complex, and multimodal technical needs that no single out-of-the-box solution has yet been able to address. Overall, Indigenous scholars and organizations are creators and innovators (and not just recipients or clients) of new technologies, particularly in the domain of cultural and linguistic heritage.

Heiltsuk First Nation Language and Culture Initiatives

The Heiltsuk Nation in Bella Bella, British Columbia, offers a compelling example of how Indigenous communities have long made use of emergent technologies to support language mobilization. Heiltsuk use of technology builds upon all of the front-line work Heiltsuk have done to document and reinvigorate their language in the face of oppressive forces, including refusing to be silent and speaking Heiltsuk to grandchildren;

taking advantage of (analog) recording devices to preserve these voices; bringing a linguist into the community and supporting him to stay for over a decade; collaboratively participating in creating dictionaries and grammatical instructions; recording autobiographies in Heiltsuk as a special project initiated by the Band Council; creating bilingual texts of transcripts and translations of audio recordings; modifying first typewriters and then computer fonts; and creating digital dictionaries with accompanying sound files. This is the story of all that Heiltsuk have initiated themselves—the wealth of voices and documents that they wish to make available to, first of all, the Heiltsuk Nation, to foster language learning, pride, and Heiltsuk worldviews.

The Heiltsuk Nation initiated extensive language research and documentation starting in 1973. Through its Heiltsuk Language Studies program, the Heiltsuk Cultural Education Centre has a mandate to continue the documentation and revitalization of the Heiltsuk language and has created and compiled extensive resources in the following focus areas:

> *Developing* a practical orthography (alphabet) for writing down the Heiltsuk language; recording and analyzing words in order to produce comprehensive word lists, bilingual dictionaries, and taxonomies; analyzing and identifying the basic structure of the Heiltsuk language; recording an extensive body of oral traditions, narratives, and discourses, as well as transcribing and translating these into English;
> *Assisting* and promoting the understanding and interpretation of Heiltsuk culture through linguistic analysis of information recorded or transmitted in Heiltsuk;
> *Promoting* and assisting in the development of Heiltsuk language instruction programs;
> *Maximizing* use of available and emerging technologies to promote the preservation of and access to Heiltsuk language materials.

In 1978 the Bella Bella Community School instituted Heiltsuk Language Instruction as a formal part of school curriculum and, since then, has focused its attention on curriculum development, Heiltsuk-language teacher certification, and the pursuit of effective language teaching strategies.

Through a memorandum of understanding signed in 2016, the Heiltsuk Cultural Education Centre, Bella Bella Community School, and the First Nations and Endangered Languages Program at the University of British Columbia (UBC) are partnering in an effort to collaboratively create new opportunities for speaking, writing, and reading Híłzaqvḷa (the Heiltsuk language) by expanding existing community language revitalization and cultural documentation in a digital environment.[6] This collaborative mobilization of existing language recordings and archival and cultural resources has resulted in the release of a cross-platform Híłzaqvḷa unicode keyboard and a beta version of a fully searchable online Híłzaqvḷa digital dictionary. Next steps include releasing the dictionary through Mother Tongues Dictionaries, a free, open-source language revitalization tool that visualizes lexical terms for community revitalization goals.[7]

The Digital Divide (Again)

Some of the earliest research in the emerging space around Indigenous uses of technologies explored how the internet could bring economic development to remote and rural areas. This early literature is often hopeful and speculative around the potential benefits and implications of internet access in Indigenous spaces.[8] Similarly, conversations from the late 1990s and early 2000s presupposed that universal internet connectivity was both imminent and inevitable, and that the rollout of all future technology would be predicated on stable, high-speed broadband across the global North.

Almost two decades later, many communities in Canada, the United States, and beyond are still waiting for the promised infrastructure backbone that will make affordable, stable high-speed broadband connectivity possible. While a presumed lack of proficiency in English was previously stated as a barrier to internet use for Indigenous people in Canada, in the interim (rather paradoxically) the conversation has shifted to explore how a more multivocal and multilingual internet can be tasked to support the revitalization of endangered and Indigenous languages that relies less on English.[9]

Indigenizing Colonial Thinking

This contribution demonstrates that Indigenous communities have always engaged with and made use of appropriate technologies to further community aims. Twenty years since the birth of the term "digital divide," an emphasis on simply providing and ensuring "access" has drawn criticism for the emptiness of its rhetoric and its enduringly paternalistic tone.[10] The underlying assumption that it is in the hands (and at the grace) of richer societies to initiate technological development on the other side of the divide fails to address the deeper, systemic social injustices that are embedded in technological developments. Moreover, the trickle-down model (from top to bottom, rather than anything more horizontal, let alone bottom to top) remains an inappropriate and unfortunate metaphor to describe how community development actually works.

Embedded at the core of such technologized ideologies lies an entrenched belief that Indigenous people always have been and always will be late to catch on to technological developments. For the greater part, "government agencies have taken on the servicing of Indigenous needs rather than encouraging communities to participate themselves," write Katina Michael and Leone Dunn, with remarkable restraint.[11]

Indigenous communities have long been engaged in the process of ensuring that technology platforms reflect and respond to their traditional ways, cultures, and languages. This fact is not well known by the wider public or government agencies. In large part this ignorance is the legacy of legislation that made Indigenous language and cultural practices illegal. However, some recent examples are better known, such as the work of language revitalization proponents in Hawaii that were quick to recognize the potential of ICTs to support, develop, and further strengthen the Hawaiian language. The 1993 deployment of Leokī is widely cited as the first electronic bulletin board system that was delivered entirely in an Indigenous language.[12] Since early advancements and uses of ICTs, Hawaiian has moved rapidly into cyberspace through negotiations and partnerships with Microsoft and Apple. The language is now offered as an option on most major operating systems, helping to normalize and in some ways equalize the language and increase its uptake, usability, and functionality in everyday life.[13]

Heartening examples aside, such work is almost by definition neverending and requires constant resourcing and vigilance to ensure that hard-won gains are not quickly lost. The path is long and the journey inevitably uphill, rooted in historical and institutional efforts to permanently eradicate Indigenous languages from everyday use. The irony of the new funding landscape has not escaped Indigenous scholars and activists who have spent years resisting punitive and racist government legislation designed to extinguish their languages and cultures, but who are now being courted by those very same agencies who — in the spirit of reconciliation — have pivoted to fund and support that which they earlier set out to destroy.

To that end, when the Social Sciences and Humanities Research Council of Canada (SSHRC) poses the question "How are First Nations, Inuit and Métis cultural heritage organizations responding to the opportunities and challenges of emerging technologies?," our response may be to invert and rather ask, "How are emerging technologies responding to the opportunities and needs of First Nations, Inuit and Métis cultural heritage organizations?"

Methodology

Technology-assisted language mobilization is a rapidly evolving field moving faster than most peer-reviewed journals can keep up with. Through collating knowledge and experiences over the last decade, including some very recent developments, we have looked beyond academic publications to more instant and sometimes ephemeral forms of information, as well as case studies and findings from community-based projects. To that end, we drew upon:

> Published research findings in the somewhat limited scholarly literature;
> "Grey literature": information produced and circulating outside of conventional academic distribution channels, such as projects within Indigenous communities;[14]
> Critical assessments and evaluations of a range of recent technical interventions.

In our search, we have considered the emerging technoscape both within and beyond Canada and have reflected on specific community-level tools as well as larger organizations that host, support, or promote multiple platforms and initiatives. By reviewing examples of relevant and recent technologically oriented projects in the area of language mobilization, we hope to have identified trends and successes alongside gaps in knowledge and attention.

Our methodology was necessarily flexible. We located published literature through database searches, reviewing recent publications and searching through promising citations. Grey literature and examples of technological interventions were more difficult to locate systematically, to which end we cast our net wider, using online resources, personal networks, and email fora—such as the excellent and active Indigenous Languages and Technology (ILAT) discussion list—to learn of projects that have so far escaped the attention of academic journals and scholarly publications.

Our approach was by no means comprehensive. We have not attempted to document every project, technology, or initiative. Instead, we have aimed for this chapter to be illustrative, representative, and generative. We document promising processes and approaches, successes and challenges, that may have traction beyond a special location, community, or time.

The emergent nature of the field entails that an inherent paradox is built into this document. As soon as this chapter is published it will cease to be current. It offers a glimpse into the technoscape of language revitalization in 2016, and all that we can hope—just like many of the publications that we have benefited from reading—is that this document will serve as a historical snapshot of the lay of the land at this time.

How can such diverse information best be organized, collated, and shared? We first thought to structure our findings according to the specific technology or platform being used, whether that was a mobile app, an interactive website, or an audio feed. Yet we quickly revised our thinking as it became apparent that such an approach embodied the very technological determinism that we reject.

It is not a particular technology that determines the outcome or success of an initiative, but a broader web of social, cultural, and often political factors that help to create (or constrain) a supportive environment for language revitalization. To that end, we organize our findings thematically, rather than by specific technologies, cutting across regions, applications, and communities. We believe that this better represents the flexibility and innovation of technology appropriation for culture and language mobilization in communities.

Findings

The Pace of Change: Speed and Obsolescence

Emerging technologies provide new opportunities and offer great possibilities. However, the pace of development also poses a challenge for communities, such as the Heiltsuk, who continue to be early adopters of emerging tools for language and culture work. A survey of literature over the last fifteen years demonstrates a series of rapidly changing uses, perceptions, and expectations of the internet.

In 1965 Intel co-founder Gordon Moore observed that the number of transistors per square inch on integrated circuits had doubled every year since the integrated circuit was invented. Now commonly referred to as "Moore's Law," it has become a truism to state that overall processing power for computers doubles every two years.

At the turn of the millennium, as availability and capability increased, the internet was largely discussed as a tool for delivering information and economic opportunity.[15] Rural and remote communities in Canada expressed frustration at the comparatively sluggish pace of infrastructure development, which failed to keep up with technological change. Yet, to this day, communities struggle with connectivity problems, and impatience with centrally organized infrastructure projects has fueled community-driven efforts to establish broadband and mobile networks. K-Net, for example, is a First Nations–owned ICT service provider that has established a cellular service, broadband connectivity, and online applications envisioned by and for rural and remote First Nations communities in Ontario.[16]

Since 2001 the internet has been increasingly conceptualized as a medium through which different and diverse tools function. The recent explosion of digital applications, prompted by the growing pervasiveness of mobile devices, is now shaping the future of the Web. This "appification" has fragmented digital functionality, assigning specific tasks to specific software, and it is not clear what the long-term consequences of this splintering will be.

Media technology is fast becoming asynchronous and individualized. In-flight entertainment systems on long-haul aircraft offer a lens through which we may observe this development. Films and television shows were first shown on one fixed screen, requiring that all passengers watch together. In the 1990s advances in technology, coupled with the demand for more personalized in-flight entertainment systems, prompted airlines to install individual screens, through which a sequence of films could be broadcast synchronously. In the early 2000s airline entertainment systems were upgraded to allow passengers to choose content from a wide selection, consume it when they liked, and pause programming as needed. The most recent trend in in-flight entertainment has individualized the experience even further, allowing (in some cases even forcing) passengers to access the system through their own digital devices, removing the costly requirement for screens in the back of each seat and pushing the service to passengers who use their computers, tablets and phones.

Such shifts offer an insight into the direction of individualized, customized digital experiences. We can now say with confidence that no two users of the internet use its services and consume content in the same way.

Free, Accessible, and Omnipresent Mobile Technologies

The availability of free, sometimes open-source, versatile, and mobile technologies has created high expectations, particularly among young people, in terms of what digital tools can do, how they function, and what they should look like. Many mobile (in all senses) users now rely exclusively on devices, such as smartphones and tablets, with operating systems that are app-driven. Users expect to realize all of their work through off-the-shelf systems, yet assumptions baked into many of these tools limit their functionality for different languages and across various operating systems. Basic research is critical to identify opportunities to increase the flexibility of such systems as they cross epistemological and ontological boundaries.

The development of cloud computing, which provides shared, internet-based processing and storage power on demand, presents a major reconceptualization of how hardware, firmware, and software technologies should be considered. Instead of relying on and committing to one expensive software tool locally housed within their device, users can now access, utilize, and save their licensed software in "the cloud," sometimes for free, other times for a fee. With this shift to multiple digital tools stored externally in third-party data centers, the issue of ownership and compatibility—already complex for Indigenous users—becomes even more intricate. Once located in the cloud, it is difficult to exercise control over a software platform, opening users up to unexpected vulnerabilities, changes, and updates, as well as new challenges in terms of backup and offline access.

Younger digital users have increasingly high expectations of what technology can do for them and how adaptive it is. Over the last decade we have witnessed a growth of immersive and interactive technologies that support such expectations. Yet, with the technological landscape moving so quickly, there is very little incentive to commit to tools that do not serve a user group's immediate needs. At the same time, although expectations for new technologies remain high, very few have the capacity to deliver everything that a user wants. An understanding of the range of available technologies and the ways they can be effectively combined to realize specific tasks is increasingly necessary to keep up with the needs of users. This process needs to be carefully explored to understand how choices are being made and what compromises, if any, are made along the way.

Harnessed through the use of free software, emerging technology is being used to support access to learning of Indigenous languages, such as UBC faculty member Candace K. Galla's project to teach Hawaiian hula lessons[17] over Skype.[18] Here follow a series of rich examples and illustrations of projects, programs, tools, and technologies that are being leveraged to assist communities reach their goals of language revitalization.

Waldayu (and its mobile counterpart, Waldayu Mobile) was the first dictionary app suite for endangered languages to combine a language agnostic design, customizable approximate search, cross-platform deployability (Web, Android, iOS), and open-source code.[19] Waldayu, meaning "word tool" in Kwak'wala, allows language communities with preexisting lexical data and materials to quickly create web and mobile apps that display their data in an engaging way. Additionally, Waldayu can be used on- or offline, making it especially useful for remote communities. Waldayu has been implemented and at the time of writing was in beta testing for over six languages from five different language families, including Tsimshianic, Wakashan, Salishan, Sino-Tibetan, and Iroquoian.[20]

FirstVoices is a suite of online and mobile app-based language archiving and learning tools developed for and available to Indigenous communities in Canada and administered by the First Peoples' Cultural Council.[21] Tools include a chat app with an orthography keyboard input system and language learning games. Language communities receive training and technical support to develop and manage their own language and culture archives and resources. The FirstVoices Keyboards app gives its users access to more than a hundred Indigenous languages—spoken in Canada, New Zealand, Australia, and the United States—through specialized keyboards that can be used within email, social media, word processing, and other apps on mobile phones. FirstVoices Chat was developed in response to Indigenous youth who want to communicate via social media in their own languages. This mobile app supports people who wish to compose and send text messages in the unique characters of their own Indigenous languages.[22]

The Resource Network for Linguistic Diversity is an international nonprofit organization founded in 2004 to advance the sustainability of the world's Indigenous endangered languages, and to support Indigenous people's participation in all aspects of language documentation and revitalization through training, resource sharing, networking, and advocacy.[23] The network hosts interactive online lists of Indigenous language projects, blogs, relevant links, and teaching resources to support language documentation and revitalization projects.[24] Haida-speaking Alaskan communities are engaging with multiple digital platforms,[25] including creating language-based YouTube videos to support Indigenous language learning.[26]

The multimodal ACORNS project supports the language revitalization efforts of the tribes of northern California and southern Oregon.[27] The ACORNS project provides free software to support teachers and learners of any language in building digital classes for language practice outside of the classroom.[28]

The Mi'gmaq language group developed an interactive language learning website, blog, talking dictionary, interactive Mi'gmaq wiki, Facebook, Instagram, Tumblr, and Twitter accounts to help language learners understand and speak the Mi'gmaq language on whichever platform or combination of platforms they feel best serves them.[29] The talking dictionary project, for example, has over 3,900 entries recorded by three different Migmaq-Mi'kmaq speakers, to assist with variations of pronunciation. These are then used in accompanying phrases to give learners the opportunity to distinguish individual words when they are spoken in a phrase.[30]

The Evaluation Gap

Despite the sharp uptake of digital tools to support endangered-language learning, there is little in the way of systematic and rigorous evaluation on the results of their use. In order for such technologies to have lasting and positive impacts on language revitalization, all stakeholders—communities, policy makers, and academics—need to know which tools are proving to be most effective, where, why, and how. For that, community-grounded, longitudinal case studies need to be commissioned that assess the success and review the impact of emerging technologies using criteria that are community-developed and locally appropriate.

In researching and preparing this chapter, examples of technological interventions for language mobilization were easy to find. Gauging their success and influence in supporting language preservation and use, however, has proved to be much more difficult. Few initiatives explicitly document and evaluate their effect on language use, and there is very little published research in this area. We therefore highlight the assessment and impact of revitalization technologies as a key knowledge gap to be addressed in future work.

We are not the first to highlight the lack of reporting on the evaluation, impact, and success of revitalization initiatives. While we found a general lack of evaluation programs in global as well as local contexts, previous research has highlighted that Canada in particular could do more to develop appropriate criteria to understand the impact of revitalization programs. Christopher Wetzel has observed that most research studies focus on the status of Indigenous languages, with little attention paid to revitalization efforts and their impact.[31] Little progress has been made in the intervening decade; Siomonn Pulla's Social Sciences and Humanities Research Council (SSHRC) knowledge synthesis report on mobile learning technologies found almost no research to report on.[32] Calling for more research in order to understand the impact of newer projects across the country, Pulla concluded that "Canada lags behind other countries in innovating, implementing and reporting on mobile learning for Indigenous people."[33]

More recently, Noelani Iokepa-Guerrero has noted that despite a range of programs designed to support Indigenous language learning, most programs do not document language use outcomes: "There is a wide variety of programs to teach traditional Indigenous languages. . . . However, most such programs have not explicitly documented language use impacts."[34] Greater knowledge in this area would help to identify successful strategies that could translate to other locations, with Onowa McIvor concluding that a great deal more could be learned about the "efficacy of Indigenous language revitalization strategies" from existing projects and programs.[35] Comparative evaluations based on locally relevant criteria to assess the functionality, technical architecture, and deployment of different software platforms and products have proven beneficial to communities when considering which resource management package to select and would likely also be of use in reviewing and selecting technologies that support language and culture.

The emergent nature of much of the technology is certainly one reason behind the apparent lack of evaluation. Since many language revitalization strategies are still relatively new, "few longitudinal studies are available to assess the impact on language vitality."[36] The press and public media also has a role to play. Articles and reports usually focus on technology rather than on the use, community, or relationships that underwrite a language context and thus perpetuate a form of technological determinism that is unnuanced and unhelpful. While we welcome the pivot away from sensationalist reports along the lines of "last speaker dies, language now extinct" to stories that are more positive and focus on Indigenous resurgence and vitality, mobile-phone apps and online dictionaries do not save languages any more than linguists do. Long-form investigative journalism has an important role to play, but even science reporters have an appetite for catchy headlines. The new online platform for increasing public engagement with anthropology, SAPIENS, recently published an article entitled "Can an iPhone App Help Save an Endangered Language?"[37] while the independent news and views web platform the Conversation led with an editorial entitled "Taking Indigenous Languages Online: Can They Be Seen, Heard, and Saved?" as we were finalizing this chapter.[38]

Understanding which stakeholders are actively involved in a specific project and making sense of how a collaboration progresses is not always easy. Relationships and dynamics within and between communities and outside partners are complex; technology projects often have an impact on these relationships and establish new power dynamics. Projects operating within a community informatics framework are more likely to be driven by community needs and agency. Projects that involve corporate bodies are frequently influenced by market forces. We would be well advised to be skeptical of headlines such as "Community Teams Up with Tech Company to Save Language," as there is often a backstory. Any account of a specific project, whether by academics, the media, or the community themselves, will be written from a certain subject position and agenda. The subjectivity of such representations is unavoidable and needs to be acknowledged and addressed.

Resisting Technological Determinism and Selective Use

Digital technologies do not, cannot, and will not save languages. Speakers keep languages alive. A digital dictionary on its own won't revitalize an endangered language, but speakers might use it to do work that will. At the same time, technology can be as symbolically powerful, as it is practically useful and often carries considerable political weight. In the English-dominant world of cyberspace, Indigenous communities are engaging with and disrupting technologies to create their own online presences. By generating their own digital visibility and legibility, Indigenous communities become present online and thereby exert increasing control over the terms of their own representation rather than be continually misrepresented by others.[39]

Some communities have chosen to resist engaging with certain technologies in order to retain control of their cultural knowledge and adhere to specific cultural sensitivities and protocols. What may therefore appear to outsiders as the nonpresence of an Indigenous community online is very often deliberate and thought out, a product of mindful resistance to a hegemonic representation rather than any kind of technological inexperience.

An example can be seen in how different communities have responded to British Columbia–based FirstVoices. Initiated by the First Peoples' Cultural Council, FirstVoices is a suite of web-based tools designed to support Indigenous people in language documentation, archivization, education, and revitalization. FirstVoices supports individual language communities to manage a space on their site to share language phrases, recordings, and teaching tools. The FirstVoices team have also developed and released an app for language learning and a keyboard and messaging app for texting and communicating in Indigenous languages.[40]

While many Indigenous communities in British Columbia have a presence on the FirstVoices website, others have chosen that their language not be included at this time. To note that even a system built with the needs of Canadian Indigenous people in mind may not meet the requirements of all communities is not intended as a criticism of the work undertaken by FirstVoices. Reasons are varied, but they may include policies around access to and ownership of information, specific structural design features that are not appropriate to certain languages and communities, or because communities are developing their own culture-specific digital tools. In addition, not all technologies allow for selectivity or value-driven adaptation by those trying to use them in different or unanticipated ways.[41]

Indigenizing Cyberspace

Historically, media technologies in English (or other colonial languages) informed the way settler cultures imagined Indigenous people, whether in print, photography, or film. The internet, initially envisioned to serve military functions, unexpectedly developed into a free and relatively open space, available to anyone with access to a computer and a level of comfort in one of its principal languages. Yet, just as Indigenous writers, photographers, and filmmakers have always carved out powerful Indigenous spaces in earlier media, so, too, Indigenous communities around the world are working to develop unique tools to reclaim cyberspace.

Within many English-dominated new media technologies, much free and open software actually asserts ownership and requires full access to all materials created by users or hosted through its architecture. Since the early 1960s Indigenous new media artists and programmers have been working to reclaim or "indigenize" technological spaces by generating their own sovereign spaces, on their own terms—what Mohawk artist Skawennati Tricia Fragnito and Swampy Cree artist Jason Lewis refer to as "Aboriginal Territories in Cyberspace."[42]

In isi-pîkiskwêwin-ayapihkêsîsak (Speaking the Language of Spiders),[43] Cree/Métis artist Ahasiw Maskegon-Iskwewhe created an interactive, interconnected web portal showcasing various Indigenous artists, with a focus on Indigenous culture and worldview as expressed by Indigenous languages.[44] In his artist statement on the website, Maskegon-Iswew outlines how "the underlying thematic context of the screenplay is based on an examination of the differences in worldview and the construction of reality that occur between cultures structured by First Nations languages and those constructed by English language."[45] The site was designed in 1996, the same year that the last Indian residential school in Canada closed.

Mohawk artist, writer, and independent curator Skawennati Tricia Fragnito's Cyber PowWow is a powerful and popular project that created an "Aboriginally-determined corner of cyberspace."[46] Part virtual gallery and part virtual chat room, Cyber PowWow was designed by emerging and established Indigenous writers and artists. Also launched in 1996, Skewennati's goal was to "overcome stereotypes about Aboriginal people;

to help shape the World Wide Web; and to generate critical discourse—both in person and online—about First Nations art, technology, and community."[47]

Never Alone, also known as Kisima Inŋitchuŋa (I am not alone), is a puzzle-platformer video game and a landmark in game development. Built in collaboration with the Iñupiat Nation in Alaska and made with contributions from around forty Alaska Elders, storytellers, and community members, Never Alone was produced by Upper One Games, the first Indigenous-owned commercial game company in the United States. Following an Iñupiaq girl named Nuna and her companion, an Arctic fox, the player completes puzzles in a story based on an Iñupiaq story told across eight chapters.[48] By developing a contemporary digital tool to present, represent, and engage people with Indigenous knowledge and culture, the designers made clear that "we are not a museum piece, the Iñupiat people are a living people and living culture."[49]

As unicode standards have extended and become more inclusive, and greater localization has enabled people around the world to use computers in any language, mainstream platforms such as Twitter have witnessed increased Indigenous presence in Indigenous languages. An example is the Twitter feed of Rory Housty, Heiltsuk community member from Bella Bella and staff member at the Heiltsuk College. Housty regularly tweets in Heiltsuk, often (but not always) with an English translation or an audio or a video file attached.[50] In a digital space so dominated by colonial languages, Housty's creation of an online presence for the language of his community serves both a pedagogical and political function. His Twitter feed is followed by many Heiltsuk community members, whose employment has taken them away from traditional territories, and provides them with a freely accessible and searchable archive of useful phrases. At the same time, by not translating all of his tweets into English, Housty is helping to create a distinct Indigenous online presence in Heiltsuk.

Technology Didn't Start with the Digital

We now live and work in such digitized spaces, with portable devices, databases, and materials present in all aspects of our lives, that the very word "digital" is becoming less relevant. While the term "digital humanities" still has traction in universities, we foresee a time in the not-so-distant future when the digital aspect of humanities scholarship will be implicit, and students will instead refer to an era of "analog humanities" before access to computing power was so widespread.

Our contemporary digital lives are the cumulative sum of the technologies of the past, and this layering shows no signs of slowing down. In language description, conservation, and revitalization, our current reliance on screen and keyboard derives from our earlier use of pen and paper, wax cylinders, reel-to-reel and other audio recording technologies, early videotape, and even specially modified typewriters with customized keys that could accurately represent Indigenous orthographies. In the 1960s and 1970s, for example, the Bell & Howell Language Master, used by communities in British Columbia, including Bella Bella, recorded on cards holding a magnetic tape with two three-second audio tracks—one for the language student and one for the teacher—allowing a comparison between student and teacher pronunciation.[51]

In the North American context in particular, with such a rich and deep history of language documentation and recording, we must be mindful to represent digital technologies for what they are: simply the most recent tools being harnessed to represent Indigenous languages, cultures, and worldviews. It is perhaps paradoxical to note that the depth and richness of cultural and linguistic documentation in North America makes the deployment of emerging digital technologies more complex, even if the promise of what can be achieved is all the more exciting. Any new technology, in the context of such a rich history of documentation, has to address the legacy of colonial collections and engage with a complex and problematic archival record.

The Dogma of Best Practice

Unworkable standards and a dogmatic insistence on "best practices" in digital technologies and language documentation set by scholars and funding agencies can have a disempowering effect on individuals and communities. Even well-funded academic research programs, archives, and library systems are not always able to adhere to the standards that they themselves promote and advocate. No surprise, then, that community-based language mobilization projects that utilize emerging technologies — often without sustainable funding and outside of academic research standards — risk being silenced in a culture that promotes unrealistic technical ideals. The First Nations in BC Knowledge Network, a hub for First Nations in the province to share ideas and tools on many aspects of governance and community development, encourages the creative term "inspired practices." Terms such as "evolving practice" and "inspired practice" in language mobilization move the conversation beyond the best practice of implementing a specific technological tool or platform to include a consideration of the complex social, cultural and historical contexts in which the work is being conducted.

Although rarely addressed in the scholarly literature, there are significant trauma-based barriers to language mobilization within Indigenous communities. As a result of the legacy of the system of Indian residential schools, many Indigenous language learners and teachers still carry feelings of distress and shame in relation to their language and can have a deeply emotional response to learning, hearing, and sharing their language. Intergenerational trauma and distress can lead to tensions and conflict over how or what to teach, particularly around the utility of writing systems versus the importance of oral transmission.

Such conversations are rooted in understandings that go far beyond simply building and implementing a curriculum, let alone an emerging digital tool or technical platform. These complicated and interconnected factors need to be better recognized by technologists, educators, and academics involved in language revitalization, and the power of language to work as a force for healing and well-being needs greater acknowledgement.

Implications

Our considered position is that Indigenous cultural insights can help to inform national policies around access to, and engagement with, emerging digital technologies. This section outlines some of the implications emerging from our environmental scan and some productive directions moving forward. Implications from this chapter can be organized around *community*, *funding*, and *technology*, with obvious intersections. In many of the most successful technology-based language initiatives, funding, technology, and community concerns are well aligned, working in common cause, with information and resources flowing freely. These implications speak to many diverse audiences, including, but not limited to:

Community organizations (e.g., cultural, political and educational);
Community groups (e.g., families, teachers, cultural practitioners);
Government (e.g., federal, provincial, funding bodies);
Academics (e.g., universities, faculty, staff, research NGOs).

These distinct groups are implicated by the outcomes of this chapter in the following ways:

> *Community-based language work needs significantly more resourcing.* Previous funding, largely focused on novelty, has resourced a series of pilot language projects in communities without the means for continuity, even when proven to be very effective. Sustained, multiyear funded support is required for community-based language revitalization, reclamation, and planning that is not necessarily tied to research or academic partnerships.
>
> *Sustainable funding models for continued technical infrastructure, development, and support at the community level are essential.* Most funding bodies reward novelty and innovation over preexisting projects that have a proven track record and community involvement. Communities cannot plan without secure funding for existing platforms and digital commitments. Short-term funding breeds self-contained, disconnected, poorly articulated, and often rushed time-bound projects that are hard to maintain and migrate forward. It is imperative that future funding models address this gap and target support for successful, ongoing community-led projects.
>
> *Connected initiatives that ground work within a community's specific revitalization environment are needed.* Technologies do not save languages; speakers do. Rather than discrete, independent technology installations, communities need integrated tools that engage with, reflect, and nurture the lived experience of language learners and teachers.
>
> *Not all work is research.* An overemphasis on academic funding mechanisms can divert energy and resources from community needs in order to

fulfill research requirements and strategic objectives within universities and colleges. While academic-driven projects can generate data sets that are useful to communities, they do not always do so and often prioritize research over applied, practical work and advocacy. In order to truly serve community needs through research, university-based academics and bodies that fund it must address the interests and needs of communities and be open to engaging in community-directed research agendas that offer tangible benefits to the communities themselves.

Platforms that better support Indigenous content must be explored and resourced. The last decade has seen an increase in language mobilizing technologies that are either very cheap or entirely free, considerably reducing the bar to entry. Users are multimodal, utilizing a wide array of technologies, which they combine to achieve broader tasks. Communities may no longer need to spend a great deal of money on specific customized software and the capital costs of hardware continue to decrease (but remain nontrivial). One consequence of the plurality of platforms is that little structured and experience-based guidance exists to support community members in choosing from a growing buffet of technologies that do not always interact or communicate well with one another. Herein lies an opportunity to develop platforms that better support Indigenous content. Further research that addresses knowledge security concerns to inform supportive policy and the development of appropriate applications is needed.

Unicode is central in achieving a core baseline agreement about digital language encoding. Customized and proprietary character sets and unique encodings pose barriers to digital language use and wider mobilization. Mobilization and rollout can only begin once unicode standardized encoding has been agreed on. It is likely that governing bodies such as the Unicode Consortium will need to continue to engage with localization requests and that community organizations will have to agree to adopt certain character sets and representations.

Support networks should be fostered to share expertise and experience within, across, and between communities. Inspiring and creative work is being undertaken in individual communities across Canada, but there are

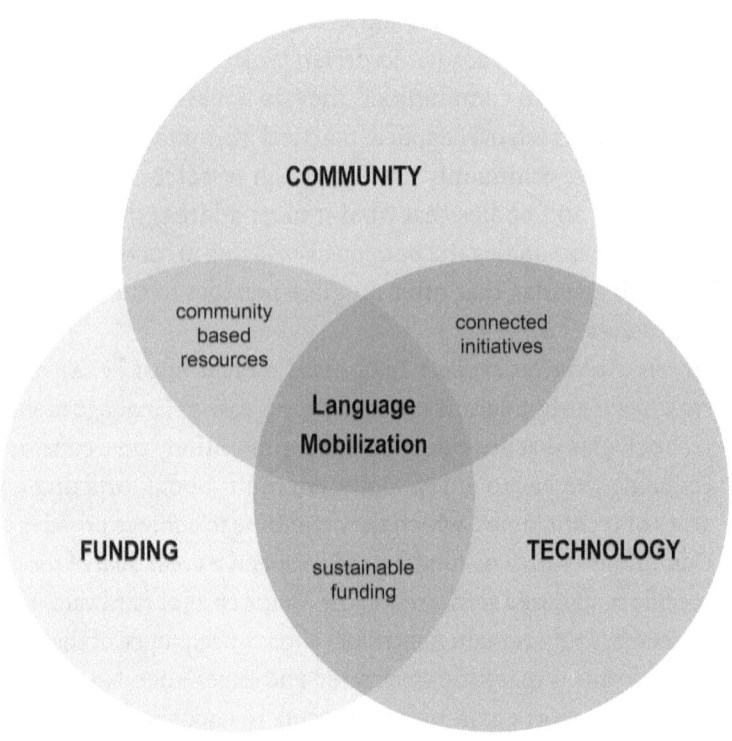

Fig. 3. Language mobilization nexus. Concept: Mark Turin 2016; implementation: Julia Schillo, 2019.

few structured spaces for sharing what people are learning or for seeking guidance. Technology platforms can build in channels of communication to support sustainability and community knowledge-sharing. In addition, structured knowledge-sharing provides an effective way to develop tools and criteria for evaluation that strengthen the support for effective language learning and mobilization at the community level. Support networks can be developed through existing networks, such as the Confederacy of Cultural Education Centers, the First Nations Schools Association, and the informal network of communities that have participated in Indigitization projects.

Community-grounded evaluation and impact assessments are needed. Despite the great variety of ways in which emerging technologies are being used by Indigenous communities and the fast rate of technological change and innovation, there is a surprising scarcity of published material reporting on the impact of such technologies. At this point it would be valuable to explore what has worked in the past. It should be noted that "inactivity" does not necessarily imply ineffectiveness; some good methods and technologies are defunct simply through lack of financial support or human resources. Independent studies are needed to review and evaluate the success of strategies such as dictionary apps and online learning modules, to offer just two examples. Researchers and communities conducting such evaluative work should be mindful to consider a number of criteria for how impact might be measured, including speaker proficiency, political impact, and symbolic value. At present, publications on Indigenous uses of technology for language mobilization are mostly sensational press reports that speak either of languages being "saved" by technology or, rather, predict doom, gloom, and extinction. More nuance and community-grounded, systematic review is needed.

Further Research

Computation, crowdsourcing, and crowdfunding offer promising emerging directions for future research. Unicode standards are now in place for many Indigenous languages, and some analysts see the next step to effective language mobilization being computational tools such as automated translation, optical character recognition, semantic interpretation, and speech recognition. Yet these developments are still very much in their infancy. Even in well-established Indigenous languages such as Hawaiian ('Ōlelo Hawai'i), most translation software can still only effectively manage individual words or short phrases.[52]

Collaborative technologies provide a means and a space for collecting and synthesizing knowledge. Ryan Henke, a doctoral candidate at the University of Hawaii, used Google Sheets to solicit input on and then compile a list of master-apprentice programs. The list is "intended to help serve as a first stop for linguists or language community members looking for answers to questions such as: Has the Master-Apprentice program been used for my language? For languages related to my language? For languages near my community?"⁵³ By sharing the document on LIST-SERVS, Henke has helped to crowdsource and synthesize information that would otherwise be difficult to locate.

Emerging technologies are also being leveraged to fund language revitalization initiatives. Crowdfunding websites such as Kickstarter provide a digital platform for people to campaign and raise resources for language programs, with filmmakers, artists, poets, and language teachers launching effective online campaigns to realize specific projects around language revitalization.⁵⁴

The answers to the questions raised in this chapter are not primarily technological, but rather social, cultural, political, and economic. Specifically, future research will need to address the following issues:

> *Sensitive, user-based, community-grounded evaluation and impact studies* must be commissioned to evaluate the effect of emerging technologies on projects that seek to revitalize Indigenous and endangered languages. These studies must be designed collaboratively with communities so that their methodologies and criteria are rooted in a recognition of cultural norms and community goals.
>
> *Further research is urgently needed on the state of digital media asset management in Indigenous communities* in order to better understand the barriers to effective mobilization and deployment of digital media for language revitalization and cultural work. Once again, this process should be comparative and community-driven, encouraging knowledge-sharing across and between Indigenous communities.
>
> Since evaluation and assessment have a bitter colonial legacy for many Indigenous communities, it is essential to *codesign methods and assessment tools that strengthen the work being undertaken in community rather than compromise it.* It is easy to forget that learning to read and write activates a different set of neural pathways than learning to hear, understand, and speak a language. Multiple longitudinal studies can help to identify areas where the development and deployment of digital platforms has brought or is bringing tangible benefit to community-based language revitalization programs. Specific areas to explore include applied language learning programs as well as language use in

natural cultural contexts, initiatives that have been designed to increase literacy and confidence, and programs that increase incentives through engaging technologies that help to generate prestige through digital access and ease of use in digital environments. Such impact studies should be publicly available in a central repository for easy access.

Conclusion

The Heiltsuk language, as with other Indigenous languages, is an integral component in Heiltsuk traditional and contemporary knowledge systems. Heiltsuk knowledge creation, development, dissemination, and intergenerational sharing is developed in—and carried through—varied modes of documentation and expression. These include spoken language, song, oral performance, ceremony, visual arts, architecture, fishing, and wood-working technologies. Heiltsuk knowledge exists in an intercultural and international context, and Heiltsuk people have a long, uninterrupted history of artistic innovation and cultural creation, sharing with and learning from other nations across the central coast. Similarly, Heiltsuk people and organizations have always adopted and adapted writing and media recording technologies.

Better resourcing language instructors in Indigenous communities and schools will promote stronger learning outcomes, language retention, and trust. Learning goals set by the community are more attainable, more credible, and have a higher chance of fulfillment.

The intellectual property and ownership implications of cloud-based storage and mobile language-learning apps are underexplored and central to ensuring that our shared digital future is a space of respectful coexistence.

Community-based language mobilization needs significantly more long-term, stable, and sustained funding. Simply put, Indigenous communities need more funding, dispersed in a better way, in order to plan strategically over the long term. Communities must not be positioned as competitors with universities for funding resources and visibility, but rather receive dedicated funding streams that will enable more equitable partnership.

Research agendas, funding needs, and success criteria must be designed, determined, and implemented by Indigenous communities themselves. Indigenous communities have long identified the language-related questions that they want research to answer and should be directly resourced to further develop and investigate these.

For Indigenous communities to continue to participate and cocreate our shared digital future, ongoing investment in the common digital backbone is essential. Infrastructure and capital costs are rarely one-off, and technology investments must be long-term and equitable — not only for communities themselves, but also for the organizations that support them.

The story of the resilience of Indigenous languages and cultural health in Indigenous communities is a story of local endurance and perseverance against enormous opposition. Indigenous scholars and organizations are creators and innovators (and not just recipients or clients) of new technologies, particularly in the domain of cultural and linguistic heritage. Direct provincial and federal investment in the research infrastructure and human capacity in Indigenous communities is therefore imperative and urgent.

ACKNOWLEDGMENTS

This research was supported by the Social Sciences and Humanities Research Council of Canada, through the Knowledge Synthesis program, Grant No. #421-2015-2076. We are grateful to members of the Heiltsuk Nation, in Bella Bella and beyond, for their gracious welcome and invitation to work in respectful partnership in their traditional territories. In Bella Bella we in particular wish to thank Janice Gladish, Rory Housty, Rex Slett and the staff of the Heiltsuk Cultural Education Centre, and the Bella Bella Community School for their contributions and support of this work. In addition, we are grateful to Heiltsuk Hereditary Chief and lifelong educator Chester Lawson for his insights and wisdom as this project took shape. At UBC, we are very grateful first and foremost to Pamela Brown at UBC's Museum of Anthropology for her generous guidance and profound counsel, as well as to Anne Kruijt and Aidan Pine for their careful reading and valuable editorial input, and to Emma Novotny, senior graphic designer in the Faculty of Arts, for kindly developing the layout for the original report on which this contribution is based and for assisting with its digital preparation.

NOTES

1. Of the many terms that are currently in use, we chose the term "Indigenous" for this article, with the exceptions of names of specific nations, communities, and organizations, such as the First Nations Technology Summit, First Nations Confederacy of Cultural Education Centre, and the Union of BC Indian Chiefs, or specific titles such as the Indian Act. Name changes from "Aboriginal" to "Indigenous" at Canadian postsecondary institutions (including at UBC) and in other Canadian contexts, such as at CBC News, reflect this wider discussion. For an exploration of these terms and their historical origins, see UBC Indigenous Foundations.
2. Howland, *Digital Divide*, 287–89.
3. Hallett, Chandler, and Lalonde, *Aboriginal Language Knowledge*, 392–99.
4. Nathan, *Access and Accessibility at ELAR*, 21–40.
5. Anderson, *Making of Indigenous Knowledge*, 347–73.
6. *Híłzaqv* means "native (of any place or country), aboriginal; (written with a capital letter:) Heiltsuk" while *híłzaqvḷa* means "one's native language, to speak one's native language; (written with a capital letter:) Heiltsuk language, to speak Heiltsuk."
7. Pine, "Waldayu."
8. Belanger, *Northern Disconnect*, 43–69.
9. Belanger, *Northern Disconnect*, 43–69.
10. Gurstein, *Effective Use*.
11. Michael and Dunn, *Information and Communication Technology*, 170–74.
12. Warschauer, *Technology and Indigenous Language Revitalization*, 139.
13. Galla, *Digital Futures*.
14. Banks, *Towards a Continuum of Scholarship*, 4–11.
15. Belanger, *Northern Disconnect*.
16. K-Net, "About K-Net."
17. University of British Columbia, "Hula Power."
18. University of British Columbia, "Hula Power."
19. Pine, "Mother Tongues."
20. Pine, "Waldayu."
21. First Peoples' Cultural Council, "FirstVoices."
22. First Peoples' Cultural Council, "FirstVoices."
23. Resource Network for Linguistic Diversity, "Sustainability of Indigenous Languages."
24. Resource Network for Linguistic Diversity, "Sustainability of Indigenous Languages."

25. Jenkins, "Reviving an Endangered Language."
26. Jenkins, "Reviving an Endangered Language."
27. Harvey, "ACORNS Overview," ACORNS Language Restoration Project.
28. Harvey, ACORNS Language Restoration Project.
29. Listuguj Education Directorate, "Introduction to Mi'gmaq."
30. Migmaq, "Migmaq Language Resources."
31. Wetzel, *Neshnabemwen Renaissance*, 61–86.
32. Pulla, *Mobile Learning and Indigenous Education*.
33. Pulla, *Mobile Learning and Indigenous Education*, iv.
34. Iokepa-Guerrero, *Revitalization Programs and Impacts*, 227.
35. McIvor, *Indigenous Language Revitalization and Maintenance*.
36. Whaley, *Future of Native Languages*, 967.
37. Arnold, *Can an iPhone App Help?*
38. Dickson, *Taking Indigenous Languages Online*.
39. Hennessy and Moore, *Language, Identity, and Community Control*, 189–91.
40. First Peoples' Cultural Council, "FirstVoices."
41. Nathan, *Sustainable Information Practice*, 2254–68.
42. Lewis and Fragnito, *Aboriginal Territories in Cyberspace*.
43. Maskegon-Iskwew, "Speaking the Language of Spiders."
44. Maskegon-Iskwew, "Speaking the Language of Spiders."
45. Maskegon-Iskwew, "Speaking the Language of Spiders."
46. CyberPowWow.
47. CyberPowWow.
48. Never Alone, "Cultural Insights."
49. Never Alone, "Cultural Insights."
50. @rhousty.
51. Waldbillig, "Bell & Howell Language Master."
52. Galla, *Digital Futures*.
53. Henke, "List of Master-Apprentice Approach Programs."
54. Brookes, "Right To Read."

BIBLIOGRAPHY

Anderson, Jane. "The Making of Indigenous Knowledge in Intellectual Property Law in Australia." *International Journal of Cultural Property* 12, no. 3 (August 2005): 347–73.

Arnold, Carrie. "Can an iPhone App Help Save the Chickasaw Language?" SAPIENS, September 7, 2016. http://www.sapiens.org/language/chickasaw-language-app/.

Banks, Marcus A. "Towards a Continuum of Scholarship: The Eventual Collapse of the Distinction between Grey and Non-Grey Literature." *Publishing Research Quarterly* 22, no. 1 (2006): 4–11.

Belanger, Yale D. "Northern Disconnect: Information Communications Technology Needs Assessment for Aboriginal Communities in Manitoba." *Native Studies Review* 14, no. 2 (2001): 43–69.

Brown, Pam, Jennifer Carpenter, Gerry Lawson, Kim Lawson, Lisa Nathan, and Mark Turin. "Uplifting Voices." In *Reflections of Canada: Illuminating Our Opportunities and Challenges at 150+ Years*, edited by Philippe Tortell, Peter Nemetz, and Margot Young, 264–69. Vancouver: Peter Wall Institute for Advanced Studies, 2007.

CyberPowWow. Accessed September 20, 2016. http://cyberpowwow.net/.

Dickson, Greg. "Taking Indigenous Languages Online: Can They Be Seen, Heard and Saved?" The Conversation, October 5, 2016. http://theconversation.com/taking-indigenous-languages-online-can-they-be-seen-heard-and-saved-64735.

First Peoples' Cultural Council. "FirstVoices." Accessed May 9, 2017. http://www.firstvoices.com/.

Galla, Candace. "'Digital Futures: Indigenous Language Revitalization in the 21st Century.'" Indigitization Futures Forum, June 11, 2017, University of British Columbia.

Gurstein, Michael. "Effective Use: A Community Informatics Strategy beyond the Digital Divide." *First Monday* 8, no. 12 (December 1, 2003): http://firstmonday.org/ojs/index.php/fm/article/view/1107.

Hallett, Darcy, Michael J. Chandler, and Christopher E. Lalonde. "Aboriginal Language Knowledge and Youth Suicide." *Cognitive Development* 22, no. 3 (July 2007): 392–99.

Harvey, Dan. ACORNS Language Restoration Project. 2012. http://cs.sou.edu/~harveyd/acorns/ (accessed August 20, 2020).

Henke, Ryan. "List of Master-Apprentice Approach (MAA) Programs." Google Docs. 2016. https://docs.google.com/spreadsheets/d/1rLfTi3gLmrHflnrz8kmeLkdOrtesrh7q1oddlhg1f4c/edit?usp=drive_web&usp=embed_facebook (site deleted).

Hennessy, Kate, and Patrick J. Moore. "Language, Identity, and Community Control: The Tagish First Voices Project." In *Information Technology and Indigenous People*, edited by Laurel Evelyn Dyson, Max Hendriks, and Stephen Grant, 189–91. London: IGI Global, 2007.

Housty, Rory [@rhousty]. Twitter, 2017. https://twitter.com/rhousty (accessed August 20, 2020).

Howland, J. S. "The 'Digital Divide': Are We Becoming a World of Technological 'Haves' and 'Have-Nots?'" *Electronic Library* 16, no. 5 (1998): 287–89.

Iokepa-Guerrero, Noelani. "Revitalization Programs and Impacts in the USA and Canada." In *Indigenous Language Revitalization in the Americas*, edited by Serafín M. Coronel-Molina and Teresa L. McCarty, 227. New York: Routledge, 2016.

Jenkins, Elizabeth. "Reviving an Endangered Language in the Age of Social Media." Alaska Public Media, November 24, 2015. http://www.alaskapublic.org/2015/11/24/how-to-revive-an-endangered-language-in-the-age-of-social-media/.

K-Net. "About K-Net." Last modified February 7, 2014. http://knet.ca/about_us.

Lewis, Jason, and Skawennati Tricia Fragnito. "Aboriginal Territories in Cyberspace." Cultural Survival, May 7, 2010. https://www.culturalsurvival.org/publications/cultural-survival-quarterly/canada/aboriginal-territories-cyberspace.

Listuguj Education Directorate. "Introduction to Mi'gmaq," June 15, 2015, http://www.learn.migmaq.org/units/1.1.html.

Maskegon-Iskwew, Ahasiw. "Isi-Pîkiskwêwin-Ayapihkêsîsak (Speaking the Language of Spiders)." Spider Language, December 11, 1996. http://www.spiderlanguage.net/ahasiw-statement.html.

McIvor, Onowa. "Strategies for Indigenous Language Revitalization and Maintenance." *Encyclopedia of Language and Literacy Development*. London, ON: Canadian Language and Literary Research Network, 2009.

Michael, Katina, and Leone Dunn. "The Use of Information and Communication Technology for the Preservation of Aboriginal Culture: The Badimaya People of Western Australia." In *Information Technology and Indigenous People*, edited by Laurel Evelyn Dyson, Max Hendriks, and Stephen Grant, 170–74. London: IGI Global, 2007.

"Migmaq Language Resources." Migmaq. Accessed September 20, 2016. http://migmaq.org/.

Nathan, David. "Access and Accessibility at ELAR, a Social Networking Archive for Endangered Languages Documentation." In *Oral Literature in the Digital Age: Archiving Orality and Connecting with Communities*, edited by Mark Turin, Claire Wheeler, and Eleanor Wilkinson, 21–40. Cambridge: Open Book, 2013.

Nathan, Lisa P. "Sustainable Information Practice: An Ethnographic Investigation." *Journal of the American Society for Information Science and Technology* 63, no. 11 (November 1, 2012): 2254–68.

Never Alone. "Cultural Insights." 2014. https://www.youtube.com/watch?v=e4iqq4_hoxk (video removed).

——— . "Never Alone." Accessed September 20, 2016. http://neveralonegame.com/game/.

Pine, Aidan. "Waldayu." Waldayu. Accessed May 9, 2017. http://waldayu.org/.

Pine, Aidan, and Mark Turin. "Language Revitalization." In *Oxford Research Encyclopedia of Linguistics*, edited by Mark Aronoff, https://oxfordre.com/linguistics/view/10.1093/acrefore/9780199384655.001.0001/acrefore-9780199384655-e-8?rskey=6VAErZ&result=1 (accessed August 19, 2020). New York: Oxford University Press, 2017.

Pine, Aidan, and Mark Turin. "Seeing the Heiltsuk Orthography from Font Encoding through to Unicode: A Case Study Using Convertextract." In *Proceedings of the LREC 2018 Workshop: "CCURL 2018–Sustaining Knowledge Diversity in the Digital Age,"* edited by Claudia Soria, Laurent Besacier, and Laurette Pretorius, 27–30. Paris: European Language Resources Association, 2018.

Pulla, Siomonn. "Mobile Learning and Indigenous Education in Canada: A Synthesis of New Ways of Learning." SSHRC Knowledge Synthesis Grant Final Report, 2015, Royal Roads University, Victoria, Australia.

Resource Network for Linguistic Diversity. Accessed September 21, 2016. http://www.rnld.org/.

Spider Language. Accessed May 9, 2017. http://www.spiderlanguage.net/domains.html.

University of British Columbia. "Hula Power." July 6, 2012. https://www.youtube.com/watch?v=fEzKo71xBdo.

Waldbillig, Larry. "The Bell & Howell Language Master." History's Dumpster. January 12, 2015. http://historysdumpster.blogspot.com/2015/01/the-bell-howell-language-master.html.

Warschauer, Mark. "Technology and Indigenous Language Revitalization: Analyzing the Experience of Hawai'i[1]." *Canadian Modern Language Review* 55, no. 1 (October 1998): 139.

Wetzel, Christopher. "Neshnabemwen Renaissance: Local and National Potawatomi Language Revitalization Efforts." *American Indian Quarterly* 30, no. 1/2 (2006): 61–86.

Whaley, L. "The Future of Native Languages." *Futures, Futures of Indigenous Cultures* 35, no. 9 (November 2003): 967.

CHAPTER 5

Translating American Indian Sign Language from the 1800s to the Present Day

Jeffrey Davis

This chapter features historical and contemporary documentation of American Indian signed-language varieties, which are broadly referred to as American Indian Sign Language (AISL).[1] It highlights the first fieldwork carried out in over fifty years to focus on the linguistic properties and current status of AISL — sometimes called "hand talk" or "sign talk" in Native American communities where it is used. Historically, signed language served various social and discursive functions among the highly nomadic American Indian communities of the Great Plains historical area and cultural groups bordering this geographic expanse. Currently, it is classified in the sign language family by *Ethnologue: Languages of the World* and considered to be a highly endangered language variety. Distinct from the American Sign Language (ASL) varieties used in deaf communities of the United States and Canada, AISL has undergone a dramatic decline since the nineteenth century, due in large part to its replacement by English, and, in some cases, ASL.[2] Today AISL is considered to be a highly endangered language variety, though mutually intelligible dialects and distinct varieties are still being used and learned by both deaf and hearing members of some Indian nations from Canada and the United States — namely, the Northern Cheyenne, Blackfeet-Blackfoot, Crow, Assiniboine, Nakoda-Lakȟóta, Madan-Hidatsa, Chippewa, Kutenai, Kalispel-Coeur d'Alene, Oneida-Haudenosaunee Shawnee, and others (see tables 1 and 2).

Although AISL is classified as a highly endangered language variety, the author's documentary linguistic fieldwork (2009–15) has identified twenty-five proficient native signers, and reportedly hundreds of tribal members are still learning and using the traditional ways of signing at varying degrees of proficiency.[3] Based on recent and ongoing AISL revitalization efforts among several Indian Nations in the United States (e.g., Northern Cheyenne, Blackfeet, Crow, Madan-Hidatsa) and First Nations in Canada (e.g., Blackfoot, Assiniboine, Oneida-Haudenosaunee Shawnee) shows that AISL has not vanished, but remains resilient, and members of several native communities and tribal nations are still keenly interested in learning and maintaining the traditional ways of signing. The documentary linguistics materials described in this chapter are of great relevance to members of communities where AISL varieties once thrived and contribute to the revitalization of indigenous signed language as well as several of the ambient indigenous spoken languages in communities with a tradition of sign language use. In some instances, depending on participants (deaf or hearing) and settings (in-group, between-group, or out-group), AISL may be signed in the accompaniment of a spoken indigenous language, or used to support the learning of one of the ambient spoken languages in pedagogical contexts. In such instances sign language plays an auxiliary or secondary role. However, AISL can also serve as a primary language and function independent of spoken language. Most often this is what happens with deaf Native Americans, who may have learned one or more of the AISL varieties, but not the ambient spoken language.

Globally, in the fields of anthropology, linguistics, and sign-language studies, there is a growing interest in areas of endangered language documentation, revitalization, applied linguistics, and second-language pedagogies. In brief, many individuals (deaf and hearing alike) from different backgrounds, especially in communities where indigenous sign language once flourished, are keenly interested in teaching, learning, or studying an indigenous language, whether it be one that is signed or spoken. With this in mind, in writing this chapter the author aspires to raise awareness about the historical and current linguistic status of AISL, and to show the significant connections between the disciplines of archival research, documentary linguistics fieldwork, and endangered-language revitalization. In this pursuit the author also traces the two-hundred-year history of indigenous signed and spoken language documentation and description, which typically go hand in hand. Notably, the archival collections of the American Philosophical Society (APS) contain some of the earliest known descriptions of indigenous signed and spoken languages in North America—for example, Stephen H. Long's papers and *Account of an Expedition from Pittsburgh to the Rocky Mountains* (1819–23), as well as earlier descriptions in diaries and journal entries from the Meriwether Lewis and William Clark expedition (1804–6). In fact, some of the Society's founding members were keenly interested in the subject and engaged in documenting and describing the Indian Language of Signs in the late 1700s and early 1800s (e.g., Thomas Jefferson and William Dunbar) as well as some of the first ethnologists, anthropologists, and linguists employed at the Smithsonian Institution's Bureau of Ethnology. These early scholars actively documented Indian Sign Language in the late 1800s and early 1900s, including the main progenitors of the fields of modern linguistics and anthropology, when the disciplines split from philology (e.g., Franz Boas, Albert Kroeber, Garrick Mallery, Hugh Scott, Carl Voeglin, and LaMont West). Thus one finds a long history of AISL documentation and research, spanning the eighteenth to the twenty-first centuries and continuing up to the present day.

AISL Documentary Linguistics and Archival Research

The corpus of AISL documentary linguistic materials central to the author's thirty-year research quest and findings reported here encompasses both legacy and contemporary historical documentary linguistic materials researched and collected from two main sources: first, extensive film footage of AISL native signers spanning more than eighty-five years (1930–2015), collected from anthropological, linguistic, and ethnographic fieldwork; and, second, AISL documentary materials from the late 1700s through the mid-1900s at the National Anthropological Archives, Smithsonian Institution.[4] Hence the AISL corpus central to this chapter spans the eighteenth to twenty-first centuries, represents many generations of signers, includes more than one endangered language, features a variety of dialects and discourse genres, and encompasses multiple linguistic modalities: written, spoken, and signed. Today many individuals are keenly interested in acquiring a first or second sign language and learning more about AISL and other indigenous languages, and it is anticipated that the indigenous sign language digital corpus and research findings reported here will promote the development of teaching curricula for younger generations while engaging key stakeholders from Native signing communities in documentary linguistic research.[5]

The Language Landscape

Linguistic and ethnographic documentation from historical accounts and contemporary fieldwork support that a highly conventionalized and linguistically enriched indigenous sign language once flourished and served a variety of discourse purposes across the vast North American landscape. Since the 1800s indigenous sign language has been well documented across the major American Indian geographic and cultural areas (e.g., the Great Plains, Great Basin, Southwest, Southeast, Northeast, Subarctic, and Mesoamerican). In previous times indigenous sign language was so prevalent and widespread that it was once used among many Indian nations as an international lingua franca. The historical and contemporary linguistic evidence suggest that indigenous sign language had already emerged prior to European contact and developed through pidginization and creolization processes—in other words, acquired natively and expanded lexically and grammatically.[6]

Historic and contemporary uses of signed language have been documented in at least one dozen distinct North American language families (phyla). Certainly, signing may have been used by more groups than these, but at least this many cases were documented in historical linguistic accounts. The archived data reveal that, regardless of hearing status, signing was used by members from approximately forty distinct American Indian spoken-language groups (see table 1).[7]

The Plains Indian Sign Language Variety

Historically and contemporarily, the best-documented cases of AISL have involved Indian tribes and nations of the Great Plains cultural area, centrally located on the North American continent, encompassing over 1.5 million square miles (4.3 million square kilometers), an area comparable to the size of Europe. This enormous geographic expanse spanned more than 2000 miles from the North Saskatchewan River in Canada to the Rio Grande in Mexico, and its east-west boundaries ranged from the Mississippi-Missouri valleys to the foothills of the Rocky Mountains. Over the years it has been well documented that a highly conventionalized and linguistically enriched sign language emerged as a common way of communicating among American Indian communities speaking so many different languages. Indigenous sign language was once so prevalent and widespread that it served as a lingua franca among many of the Indian nations of Native North America.[8]

Thus, speakers of mutually unintelligible American Indian languages to mediate contact often either adopted or developed a third language, which linguists called a "lingua franca." In addition to the three major North American Indian lingua francas—Mobilian, Chinook, and Plains Sign Language[9]—several European and Indian spoken languages may have historically served as lingua francas to varying degrees.[10] The "Plains sign lingua franca" was a variety of standard PISL commonly used among allies and trading partners to bridge linguistic barriers among individuals and groups. In previous times the lack of a single dominant language group in the Great Plains cultural area may have contributed to the emergence and widespread use of a sign-language lingua franca. In addition to its role as an intertribal and international lingua franca, sign language was also used intratribally and in-group to fulfill a variety of discourse purposes, such as storytelling, age or gender-specific activities, and at times when speech was difficult or taboo (e.g., during ritual practices, meetings of secret societies, or hunting expeditions). In this way signed language could be used when spoken language was possible but silence was preferred, as well as during international exchanges in ceremonial settings (i.e., in conjunction with formal oratory and during other forms of discourse). For many generations indigenous signed language has been acquired as a first, second, and third language and used both as an accompaniment or alternative to spoken language and as a separate language autonomous from speech. In other words, for hundreds of years and possibly longer, sign language has been used among individuals speaking different languages, as well as the same language, or different language dialects.

Although indigenous sign language is classified as an endangered language and the extant number of native signers is unknown, hundreds of North American Indians may still know and use it in some form and to varying degrees of proficiency. For example, the author has conducted fieldwork (2009–15) that documented the use of the PISL variety among both deaf and hearing Indians from several Indian nations of the United States and Canada First Nations, including different PISL dialects used among signers from four tribal nations representing the Blackfoot Confederacy (Niitsítapi) — namely, the Blood (Káínaa); Northern Piegan or Peigan (Aapátohsipikáni); Southern Piegan or Montana Blackfeet (Aamsskáápipikani); and Alberta, Canada, Blackfoot (Siksiká), as well as distinct PISL dialects used among Siouan groups: Crow (Apsaalooke), Mandan-Hidasta (Moennitarri), Assiniboine (A'aniinen), and Nakoda and Lakȟóta (Tetonwan; see table 2).[11]

While the largest number of signers have been identified from Indian nations of the Great Plains and surrounding cultural areas, not all Plains Indians or members of these tribes may have used or maintained the sign language. Still, it has been well documented that the PISL variety emerged as one of the historical lingua francas of the Great Plains and spread to cultural areas bordering this geographic region, and there are different PISL dialects (e.g., Blackfeet-Blackfoot, Crow, and Northern Cheyenne) used in Canada and the United States.

Indigenous sign language has also been documented in several native communities beyond the Plains cultural area. In recent times sign-language researchers have conducted fieldwork among signing communities such as the Inuit-Nunavut (Arctic, Canada); Navajo (Arizona); Keresan Pueblo (New Mexico); Maya of western Guatemala and the Yucatán, Chiapas, and Oaxaca states or regions of Mexico (Meso-America); and other American indigenous communities. Several other Indian nations or First Nations are revitalizing the traditional ways of signing, such as the Oneida (Onyota'a:ka) Nation of the Great Lakes region, southwestern Ontario, Canada, one of the five founding nations of the Iroquois (Haudenosaunee). Strikingly, in all of the cases reported here, deaf community members have played a significant role in the transmission and expansion of indigenous sign language.[12]

While the question of linguistic origins remains uncertain, several prominent anthropological and historical linguistic scholars have endorsed the hypothesis that sign language was already used among indigenous people across the North American continent prior to European contact. Its development into a lingua franca was likely enhanced by the postcolonization rise of horse nomadism and intensive language contact that ensued.[13] According to this hypothesis, sign language originated and spread from the Gulf Coast, becoming the intertribal lingua franca of the Great Plains and spreading throughout North America.[14] Conceivably, the use of sign language among indigenous groups could have been influenced by the need to communicate with the explorers and colonizers from diverse language backgrounds; individuals universally use gesture or pantomime in foreign language contexts. However, prominent anthropological linguist and scholar of Native American language Allan Taylor maintains that "the Spaniards did not invent the sign language—a hypothesis that is scarcely credible in any event—since the earliest Spanish penetration of the Plains area, that of Coronado in 1541–1542, encountered Indians who were using signs."[15] Taylor was responding to the assumption that European contact was necessary in order for sign language to have emerged.

Subsequently, Samarin challenged Taylor's hypothesis for the existence of a "pre-European contact sign language."[16] Samarin, however, offers no alternative interpretation, and merely alludes to the notion that Indian Sign Language somehow developed following the arrival of Europeans. On the other hand, several notable scholars have reexamined the historical documentation and, like Taylor, have presented evidence from additional historical sources that strongly favor the hypothesis for the existence of indigenous sign language prior to European contact.[17] Susan Wurtzburg and Lyle Campbell make a compelling case for there having been a preexistent, well-developed indigenous signed language across the Gulf Coast–Texas–northern Mexico area before European contact. In their historical study "North American Indian Sign Language," Wurtzburg and Campbell define "sign language" as "a conventionalized gesture language of the sort later attested among the Plains and neighboring areas."[18] Based on numerous early historical accounts, they report that the earliest and most substantive accounts come from the 1527 expedition for the conquest of Florida, led by the Spanish conquistador Álvar Núñez Cabeza de Vaca, who reported numerous occasions wherein native groups communicated with signs; according to the historical record, Cabeza de Vaca "also clearly distinguished which groups spoke the same language, which spoke different languages but understood others, and which groups did not understand others at all, except through the use of sign language."[19] Similar accounts were made by Coronado in 1541,[20] and subsequent reports were made in the eighteenth century (e.g., Santa Ana in 1740).[21] Ives Goddard and Wurtzburg and Campbell have published papers about the role served by indigenous signed language and some spoken native languages as lingua francas and have discussed the pidgins and trade languages used among Native American groups.[22] Again, the generally accepted hypothesis among scholars is that indigenous sign language originated and spread north from the Gulf Coast, becoming the intertribal lingua franca of the Great Plains and other cultural areas of Native North America.[23]

Hence, sign language was observed by many European explorers upon initial contact with native groups of North America and was well documented by early scholars.[24] These historical accounts remain open to different interpretations, such as on the spot use of gesture to enhance communication with foreigners, the ad hoc use of gestures in accompaniment with speech, or a gestural code shared among the native groups of these areas. However, based on numerous historical accounts, Wurzburg and Campbell conclude that "even if the Europeans started with ad hoc gestures, they soon learned the native system and used it for communication."[25] After all, there were already many separate languages spoken by numerous native groups, and sign language could just as easily have originally emerged in these North American multilingual communities without the influence of foreigners, explorers, or colonizers.

The question of origins and need to distinguish sign language and gesture continually arise, and the author has written extensively about this subject.[26] Whatever the origins, a signed lingua franca emerged and was used for many generations across a wide geographic expanse—a major outcome of intensive language contact following the postcolonization rise of horse nomadism and formation of military and trade alliances.

Historical Linguistic Accounts

Throughout the 1800s explorers, naturalists, ethnologists, and even U.S. military personnel, documented the use of Indian Sign Language for a variety of purposes. Documentation of Indian Sign Language continued through the 1900s, and the earliest anthropologists, linguists, and semioticians studied and described its linguistic structures.[27] Notably, many of these scholars served terms as presidents of learned societies like the American Anthropological Association, the American Philosophical Society, and the Linguistic Society of America. These pioneering scholars laid the groundwork for Indian Sign Language to be considered a preexistent, full-fledged language. As a result of their early research and fieldwork, there remains a rich linguistic and ethnographic legacy in the form of diaries, books, articles, illustrations, photographs, dictionaries, and motion pictures that document the varieties of indigenous sign language historically used among native populations. For the past three decades the author has been examining the veracity of these earlier claims, and at the same time working with members of Indian nations eager to reclaim this important part of their heritage, and exploring how these materials contribute to revitalization and multidisciplinary studies.

Earliest AISL Descriptions

The earliest known written descriptions of signs used by American Indians were made in the early 1800s and formed the basis of a paper titled "Sign Language of the Indian Nations to the West of the Mississippi River," which was presented by the president of the APS, Thomas Jefferson in January 1801, one month prior to his inauguration as the third president of the United States.[28] It contained copious descriptions of more than fifty signs used by members of the Indian nations, and its title, content, and timing reflect the fact that Jefferson was keenly interested in the subject and recognized the relevance of the sign language used by members of the "Indian Nations to the West of the Mississippi

River." Two years later, in 1803, the same year as the Louisiana Purchase, President Jefferson ordered an expedition from St. Louis, Missouri, to the Pacific Ocean led by Captains Meriwether Lewis and William Clark. Based on historical accounts, members of the expedition encountered sign language being used among members of the Indian nations. Furthermore, it has been well documented that Sacagawea, the sole Native American member of the expedition, played a pivotal role and served as an interpreter.[29] Sacagawea, a Shoshone, was about twelve years old when she was kidnapped by a war party of Hidatsa Indians and taken from her Rocky Mountain homeland to the Hidatsa-Mandan villages in what is today North Dakota. She was sold to a French-Canadian fur trader, Toussaint Charbonneau, who eventually claimed her as his wife. With the invaluable assistance of Sacagawea, Charbonneau served as an interpreter and guide for the expedition. The couple used Hidatsa (a Siouan language) to communicate with each other, and neither of them spoke English. Through Sacagawea's role as interpreter, the expedition was able to obtain horses from the Shoshones, her native people, in order to cross the vast western mountains. Without Sacagawea's contributions as an interpreter and her feats of bravery in moments of peril, many historians believe the expedition could have failed.

Reportedly the interpreting relay went this way: Sacagawea would translate Shoshone (a Uto-Aztecan language) into Hidatsa for her husband, who would then translate the message into French. Another member of the expedition would translate from French into English for Lewis and Clark.[30] The historical evidence indicates that Sacagawea used sign language on several occasions: she was raised Shoshone and later lived with the Hidatsa-Mandan, two nations in which sign language was widely used (see table 1). Members of these and other Indian nations, known to have used sign language, were frequently encountered during the expedition, and the use of Indian Sign Language was recorded in the original accounts on more than one occasion.[31] Moreover, the descriptions of how Sacagawea "gestured" when finally reunited with her Shoshone family offer additional support that she too used sign language.[32]

Due to the extreme hardships encountered by Lewis and Clark, there was a dearth of written documentation, especially in terms of indigenous languages. Another decade would pass before the next official expedition, in 1819, which originated in Pittsburgh, Pennsylvania, led by Major Stephen H. Long and continued well into western and northern regions of the Rocky Mountains. In striking contrast to the Lewis and Clark expedition, during the Long expedition extensive written documentation was made about the languages and ways of life of the Indians. The essential role that sign language served was described in the published accounts of the expedition, including more than one hundred descriptions of Indian signs.[33]

The Natural Language of Signs

It is also historically significant that Thomas H. Gallaudet, co-founder of the first school for deaf students in the United States in 1817, used the early descriptive accounts of Indian signs to make a case for "The Natural Language of Signs" for teaching and communicating with people who are deaf. Gallaudet's first published papers (1847–52) advocated the use of the natural language of signs to teach children who were deaf. His essays on this subject featured detailed descriptions of some of the signs used by the "aboriginal Indians" based largely on Long's account.[34] It is clear from his writings that Gallaudet considered Indian Sign Language, like the sign language of deaf people, to be a natural language. The historical evidence suggests that frequent contact occurred between signing Native American and deaf groups, and that American Indian signs were introduced to people who were deaf. Most notably, Gallaudet's attention to Indian Sign Language in early publications and dissemination of descriptions of Indian signs to educators of deaf people through one of the nation's earliest scholarly and this subject was often discussed in articles published during the nineteenth century,[35] as well as in published accounts of contact between deaf people and American Indians who signed AISL during this historical period.[36] This reflects the importance of archival materials in carrying out historical linguistics research.

To address the question of historical relatedness, the author conducted preliminary lexical similarity studies of PISL (the most widely used variety) and ASL from comparable historical periods.[37] The author's studies identified 50-percent lexical similarity between historical varieties of ASL and PISL, which suggests these are separate languages—that is, unlikely to be genetically related or to have a common language ancestor. Still, 50 percent is a high degree of lexical similarity, which suggests that lexical borrowing likely occurred as a result of signed language contact between members of Native American and deaf communities. However, it should be noted that historical connections between signed languages are not that easily traced. This is due to the greater potential for shared visual symbolism between genetically unrelated signed languages (i.e. the iconicity factor) and also because signed languages have not been written down like many spoken languages have been historically. Nevertheless, 50 percent is a relatively high degree of lexical similarity and suggests possible lexical borrowing that could be attributed to language contact between American Indians and individuals who were deaf.

The author also conducted preliminary lexical similarity studies to determine if PISL constitutes one language with many dialects, or a variety of distinct signed languages.[38] This has involved linguistic assessments of more than one thousand lexical signs extracted from written, illustrated, and filmed sources documenting PISL from five historical periods (1800s, 1820s, 1920s, 1930s, and 2000s). The author's comparisons have found an 80- to 92-percent range of lexical similarity (cognates) between historical and contemporary PISL varieties (see tables 1 and 2). The high percentage of lexical similarity suggests that the PISL varieties compared are dialects of the same language from similar origins—that is, genetically related members of the same language family. Thus, one finds different PISL dialects among signers from four tribal nations representing the Blackfoot Confederacy (Niitsítapi)—namely, the Blood (Káínaa), Northern Piegan or Peigan (Aapátohsipikáni), Southern Piegan or Montana Blackfeet (Aamsskáápipikani), and Alberta, Canada Blackfoot (Siksiká); as well as different PISL dialects being used among Siouan groups: Crow (Apsaalooke), Mandan-Hidasta (Moennitarri), Assiniboine (A'aniinen), and Nakoda and Lakȟóta (Tetonwan; see table 1).

The author's preliminary lexical similarity studies are among the largest of this kind, although further research is needed before more definitive conclusions can be reached about the number of distinct American Indian signed languages and number of dialects. Still, given the pattern of language replacement and endangerment due to pressures to use English (or, in some instances, ASL), it is striking that the core lexicon of PISL appears to have remained relatively stable for at least the past two hundred years. The high percentage of lexical similarity between the sign lexicons from signers of different spoken-language families (e.g., Algonquian and Siouan) illuminates the question of mutual intelligibility and number of different sign language dialects that are evident. Specifically, the large number of cognates suggests that these shared lexical signs could have been commonplace during the historical period when the use of Plains sign language lingua franca was widespread. Remarkably, today it continues to serve a role in international arenas shared among members of multiple language groups between Canada and the United States. For example, among Algonquian and Siouan language families, which include dozens of distinct spoken languages and numerous dialects (see tables 1 and 2). The Blackfoot language (Siksiká) has four major dialects used by the four tribal nations comprising the Blackfoot Confederacy (Niitsítapi): the Blackfeet Nation of northern Montana, and Kainai, Piikani, Siksiká Nations from different regions of the Canadian Province Alberta. Today we find great interest among the Indian nations of Canada and the United States to maintain both spoken and signed indigenous languages. In fact, signed language is often used to buoy the learning of the ambient spoken language, thus contributing much to language revitalization.[39]

National Treasure

The documentary and historical linguistics research findings reported in this chapter are grounded in the AISL documentary linguistics corpus described here. From 1990 to the present the author has been conducting research in the National Archives and Smithsonian Archives, especially the National Anthropological Archives, Human Studies Film Archives (originally the Bureau of American Ethnology). The Smithsonian archives are recognized as one of the world's greatest resources for the study of American Indian languages and cultures. Many of the languages that the first ethnologists (now recognized as anthropologists) documented and described have long since vanished, and most of the remaining

American Indian languages are currently endangered. Although much of this research was carried out during the late nineteenth and early twentieth centuries, these legacy materials remain a national treasure—an irreplaceable source for further studies and means to study and revitalize American Indian cultural traditions and languages. Even though the author has been conducting research in these archives for thirty years, only the tip of the iceberg has been touched. The most rewarding part of this research has been to share these findings with native community members and with those most interested in studying and revitalizing these endangered languages.

Garrick Mallery (1831–94) was one of the greatest early contributors to the Smithsonian's collection of American Indian spoken- and signed-language documentary materials, including a wealth of legacy material about pictographs and other semiotic representational systems (e.g., codes, signals, signs, gestures).[40] Recognized today as the largest collection of its kind, Mallery's body of work remains of great interest to contemporary scholars.[41] As one of the first ethnologists employed at the Bureau of Ethnology, established by an act of the U.S. Congress in 1879, Mallery served a major role. During this period he had a great deal of political clout in Washington, DC, and throughout his time at the Smithsonian (1879–94) Mallery carried out an enormous amount of research, published many important works, mentored many other ethnologists, and helped promote legislation that led to the passage of several acts of Congress.[42]

To summarize, Mallery's research concentrated on the study of Indian Sign Language, pictographs, and other semiotic forms relevant to language and culture. He made substantive contributions as author and editor to dozens of research publications. For example, the Bureau of Ethnology's first major publication devoted 280 pages (two-thirds of the volume) to the subject of sign language that Mallery authored. He and his fellow ethnographers as well as numerous collaborators in the field collected vast amounts of data on Indian signs, pictographs, and other forms of early writing that otherwise would have been lost. His work encompassed both the signed and spoken languages of North American Indians (see table 1).[43]

Mallery's research on sign language and pictographs was rigorously executed and grounded in empiricism. He aimed to dispel numerous common myths about American Indians, sign language, and pictographs, avoiding "mystic symbolism as a canon of interpretation; he presented the facts simply as facts."[44] Mallery chaired the anthropological section of the American Association for the Advancement of Science (AAAS) in 1881, and the following year the AAAS formally recognized the field of anthropology. Mallery was elected president of the Philosophical Society of Washington in 1888, and his presidential address was titled "Philosophy and Specialties" and published in 1889. Hence, he was a principal founder, officer, and author of the constitutions and histories for several scientific, philosophical, and literary societies of the late nineteenth century. His work preceded, and contributed to, the establishment of American Anthropology, Archeology, and Linguistics Societies.[45]

In many ways, Mallery was one hundred years ahead of his time, particularly in his views about signed language, pictographs, and the subject of semiotics. He appears to be one of the first American scholars to approach the study of language, and its representational systems, from the perspective of semiotics, which is a recurrent theme in his writings. Thomas A. Sebeok wrote a substantive essay on Mallery's theoretical contributions in his book *Semiotics in the United States*, in which he calls Mallery "the first American grand master of the realm."[46] Jean Umiker-Sebeok and Thomas Sebeok state that "Mallery's comparison of aboriginal sign languages . . . with other auditory and visual systems in terms of a broad semiotic typology has in many respects yet to be surpassed."[47] Although generally considered to be in the philosophic realm, semiotics is highly multidisciplinary and has informed the fields of linguistics, pragmatics, translation and interpretation, communication, and mass media.

In brief, research of AISL would only be resumed for a short period by John Harrington (1938), one of the Smithsonian's first academically trained anthropological linguists. However, the level of scholarship produced by Mallery on the subject of sign language remained unparalleled until the work of Albert Kroeber, Carl Voegelin, and LaMont West in the late 1950s, seventy-five years following Mallery's death, and the extinction of numerous American Indian languages later.[48]

Film Dictionary of Indian Sign Language

Following the extensive linguistic corpus of lexical descriptions, texts, illustrations, and photographs documenting the sign language varieties used among American Indians produced by Mallery during his years at the Smithsonian, several researchers supported by the Smithsonian Institution's Bureau of American Ethnology continued to document cases of sign language use among American Indians—for example, Franz Boas, Esther Goldfrank, John Harrington, and Hugh Scott (great-grandson of Benjamin Franklin). Additionally, one of the richest sources of historical sign language documentation comes from the motion pictures produced by an act of Congress, passed in 1930 to support the production of a *Film Dictionary of Indian Sign Language*—the first such dictionary of its kind.[49]

Indian Sign Language Council of 1930

Unfortunately, by the 1900s the use of Indian Sign Language was greatly diminished and endangered. Recognizing the endangered status of Indian Sign Language, in 1930 General Hugh L. Scott proposed a motion picture preservation project that was funded and completed by an act of Congress.[50] This effort resulted in the Indian Sign Language Conference that was filmed on September 4–6, 1930, in Browning, Montana—the largest intertribal meeting of Indian chiefs, Elders, medicine men, and other representatives ever filmed. There were eighteen official participants, including chiefs and leaders from a dozen different tribes and language groups from the Plains, Plateau, and Basin cultural areas. A permanent monument to the Indian Sign Language Council signifying the importance of this gathering was established at the conference site, and each of the council members had their footprints placed in bronze as a part of the monument. Subsequently, the Museum of the Plains Indian was constructed on this site. The purpose of the 1930 conference was to document and preserve the traditional ways of signing that had been a vital part of North American Indian cultural and linguistic heritage. The films show the Native American participants engaged in lively, natural, and unrehearsed signed language discourse covering a wide range of topics, including anecdotes, jokes, metaphors, and stories.[51]

The spontaneity and variety of discourse types shown in these films offer abundant evidence of a full-fledged natural sign language.[52] The oldest participants appeared to be the most proficient in sign language. For example, Mountain Chief (Nena-es-toko) from the Kaini or Blood tribe and leader of the Blackfoot nation was eighty-two years old at the time. The ages of the other participants were not reported, but the youngest participants appeared to be in their forties, with several of the others approaching their sixties and seventies. Age is significant because the older participants probably learned to sign in the mid-1800s, before the decline of many Indian languages and traditions that occurred in the late 1800s, brought on by the construction of the first cross-continental railroad and the rapid Western expansion by Anglo-Americans. This decline is reflected in one of the statements signed by General Hugh Scott during the opening remarks: "The young men are not learning your sign language and soon it will disappear from this country. It is for us to make a record of it for those who come after us before it becomes lost forever." Indian Schools were established during the post–Civil War reconstruction era, and it became commonplace for Indian children to be taken from their families and placed in these residential schools. Native languages and cultural customs were forbidden in these schools, and the only language allowed was English. Consequently, such pressures inhibited the acquisition of indigenous sign language among subsequent generations In brief, the Indian Sign Language films and *Dictionary of Indian Sign Language* was a highly experimental "cinematic dictionary" project launched at the Smithsonian Institution's Bureau of American Ethnology. This project represents one of the earliest known attempts to use motion picture film for the purpose of documentary linguistics fieldwork and PISL revitalization. Although long overlooked by historians of ethnographic cinema, Scott and Sanderville's (1930–34) collaborative work to document the PISL variety represents an enduring legacy and major contribution to the modern enterprise of language preservation.[53]

Hugh Lennox Scott (1853–1934) was seventy-eight years old at the time of the conference and had been signing for more than fifty years. Scott's contribution to the Indian Sign Language film dictionary included several short signed narratives and 358 proper noun signs for tribes and geographic location. As testimony to his sign language skills, Scott provided voice-over translations for the films made during the 1930 conference, which were professionally dubbed during subsequent production stages in 1934. Richard Sanderville, Scott's chief collaborator and interpreter from the Blackfoot nation, returned to the Smithsonian Institution following Scott's death in 1934 and was filmed producing 790 signs and several signed narratives. The scope and discourse coherence of the signed narratives in the 1930 and 1934 films provides evidence of the use of a language, not just a collection of gestures.

While doing research in the National Archives in 2002, I identified Sanderville's contributions that were filmed at the Smithsonian in the early 1930s. Unfortunately, the only preservation copies available were either poorly processed or produced in an outmoded format. Following two years of painstaking analysis to decipher what remains of Sanderville's contribution to the film dictionary, more than two hundred PISL signs and idioms signifying a variety of lexical categories have been identified, including abstract nouns, classifier predicates, and noun and verb modifiers. Elsewhere, the author reports that Sanderville's contributions constitute a type of "Rosetta Stone"—that is, the lexical inventories documented in these films, combined with the original translations provided by Scott and Sanderville, offer keys to translating what the original participants at the council were signing.[54] Additional translations of the narratives filmed during the 1930 gathering and those of Richard Sanderville produced at the Smithsonian Institution in 1934 are underway. Further restoration of the historical films in digitized formats with open captions is needed to provide greater access to the content being conveyed.

In short, the variety of sociolinguistic contexts, participants, and discourse types that are captured in the corpus of documentary materials described here supports that PISL was (and still remains) a full-fledged language. Elsewhere, I have described how PISL demonstrates phonological, morphological, and syntactic patterns that are consistent with those evident for full-fledged signed languages.[55] PISL involves the same lexical categories (e.g., nouns, verbs, adjectives, adverbs) and basic grammatical features as any human language (e.g., tense, questions, topics, negation, pronouns, as well as singular, plural, possessive forms). There are also many examples of rich use of metaphor in the PISL corpus, including metonyms, hyponyms, and hypernyms, as well as compounds, polysemous forms, and a variety of linguistic features that are common among sign languages of the world (e.g., predicates composed of indicating and depicting signs, and rich use of visual, gestural, and spatial properties). Analysis of these linguistic properties and other grammatical features are ongoing.[56] The documentary linguistic fieldwork and research findings reported in this chapter have aimed to advance the understanding of the linguistic underpinnings of indigenous signed languages like PISL, as well as to draw attention to other dialects or varieties that could still be learned and used today.

After three decades of archival research and fieldwork, the author has collected and maintained a substantial amount of culturally and linguistically relevant data documenting both historic and current use of AISL varieties (see tables 1 and 2). The sheer magnitude of these historical and contemporary data point to the need for other scholars and stakeholders to be involved and to establish an open-source database to provide access for others to study, teach, and research both Native American signed and spoken language varieties. Hence, the documentary linguistic materials described in this chapter could contribute much to language revitalization efforts. While efforts are ongoing to develop an open-source database, illustrations, photographs, sample video clips of historical sign language use can be viewed online at the author's research website.[57]

Summary and Conclusions

The corpus of AISL documentary materials described in this chapter encompasses both historical and contemporary uses of American indigenous signed and spoken languages. It embodies extensive archival research of legacy materials spanning three centuries (1800s to present), encompassing over ten-thousand lexical descriptions and including material from more than twenty-five years of ethnographic fieldwork involving Native American collaborators. Since the early 1990s the author has been collaborating with members of Native sign language communities and conducting research in major archival collections like the

National Archives, Smithsonian Archives, and the National Museum of Natural History's National Anthropological Archives and Human Studies Film Archives. Over the years, while researching rare and fragile legacy materials documenting indigenous signed language, the author has also conducted ethnographic fieldwork documenting contemporary cases of American indigenous signed language. The chief aim has been to help preserve these rare and precious documentary materials, to raise awareness about endangered languages, and to create greater academic and community access to the corpus of AISL documentary materials. This has involved extensive collaboration with scholars from around the world and members of Native American communities with a tradition of sign language use for the purpose of language documentation, description, and revitalization, and to draw attention to this important, yet sometimes overlooked, part of Native American cultural and linguistic heritage.

In conclusion, the study of indigenous signed languages is illuminating historical linguistic and sociolinguistic questions about language origins, spread, contact, and change. Although certain challenges arise when documenting an endangered language and we encounter misconceptions about sign language, there is an ever-growing interest in sign language studies and indigenous language revitalization. Generally, Native American leaders and members of communities with sign language traditions have recognized and embraced the need to record and preserve their languages and cultural practices for this and future generations, as long as the documentary materials are studied and treated with respect when made available outside of Native communities. The corpus of indigenous sign language documentary materials and research findings reported here advances scholarship and contributes to the development of teaching materials to support language revitalization efforts. Among the First Nations of Native North America are descendants and stakeholders keenly interested in in teaching and learning the traditional ways of signing. Moreover, both deaf and hearing tribal members are continuing to play a vital role in the transmission of sign language. Hopefully, the international and intertribal connections and continuation of historical traditions into modern times will enable indigenous signed and spoken languages to be learned, used, studied, and maintained for future generations.

Appendix

Table 1. Historical and contemporary documentation of American Indian Sign Language

Language Phyla and Group	Published Sources
1. ALGIC = ALGONQUIAN	Campbell (2000), Mithun (2001)
1. Arapaho	Clark (1885), Mallery (1881), Scott and Sanderville (1934)
2. Blackfeet = Piegan Blackfoot = Blood	**Davis (2011, 2014, 2015)**, Mallery (1881), Scott and Sanderville (1934), **Weatherwax (2002)**
3. Northern Cheyenne	**Davis (2011, 2014, 2015), Davis and McKay-Cody (2010)**, Burton (1862), Mallery (1881), Scott and Sanderville (1934), Seton (1918)
4. Cree (media reports, 2019)*	Long (1823), Mallery (1881), Scott and Sanderville (1934)
5. Fox = Sauk-Kickapoo	Long (1823), Mallery (1881)
6. Ojibwa = Chippeway*	Hofsinde (1956), Long (1823), Mallery (1881)
7. Shawnee	Burton (1862), Harrington (1938), Davis (2017)
2. ATHABASKAN-TLINGIT	Campbell (2000), Mithun (2001)
8. Navajo = Diné	**Davis and Supalla (1995)**
9. Plains Apache = Kiowa	Hadley (1891), Harrington (1938),
10. Apachean	Mallery (1881),
11. Chiricahua-Mescalero	Scott and Sanderville (1934)
12. Sarcee = Sarsi	Scott and Sanderville (1934)
3. SIOUAN-CATAWBAN	Campbell (2000), Mithun (2001)
13. Crow	Burton (1862), **Davis (2014, 2015)**, Mallery (1881), **Real Bird (2012)**, Scott and Sanderville (1934)
14. Hidatsa = Gros Venture	Scott and Sanderville (1934), **Real Bird (2012)**

15. **Mandan**	Scott and Sanderville (1934), **Real Bird (2012)**
16. **Dakotan = Sioux = Lak(h)ota**	Burton (1862), **Farnell (1995)**, Long (1823), **Real Bird (2012)**, Seton (1918), Tompkins (1926)
17. **Assiniboine, Alberta**	**Farnell (1995)**, Scott and Sanderville (1934)
18. Omaha-Ponca	Long (1823), Mallery (1881)
19. Osage = Kansa	Harrington (1938), Long (1823)
20. Oto = Missouri = Iowa	Long (1823), Mallery (1881)
4. CADDOAN FAMILY	Campbell (2000), Mithun (2001)
21. Caddo	Harrington (1938)
22. Wichita	Harrington (1938), Mallery (1881)
23. Pawnee	Burton (1862), Mallery (1881)
24. Arikara	Mallery (1881), Scott and Sanderville (1934)
5. KIOWAN-TONOAN	Campbell (2000), Mithun (2001)
25. Kiowa	Hadley(1891), Mallery (1881)
26. Tonoan = Hopi-Tewa	Goddard (1979), Mallery (1881)
6. UTO-AZTECAN	Campbell (2000), Mithun (2001)
27. Shoshone = Shoshoni	Burton (1862), Mallery (1881), Scott (1934)
28. Comanche	Harrington (1938), Mallery (1881)
29. Ute = Southern Paiute	Burton (1862), Mallery (1881)
30. Northern Paiute, Bannock	Mallery (1881)
7. SHAHAPTIAN	Campbell (2000), Mithun (2001)
31. Nez Perce	Scott and Sanderville (1934)
32. Sahaptin	Mallery (1881)
8. SALISHAN	Campbell (2000), Mithun (2001)
33. **Coeur d'Alene**	Teit (1930), Thompson (2007)
34. **Flathead, Spokane, Kalispell**	Scott and Sanderville (1934), Thompson (2007)

35. Shuswap, Columbia	Boas (1890)
9. ESKIMO-ALEUT	Campbell (2000), Mithun (2001)
36. Inuit, Inupiaq-Inuktitut	Hoffman (1895); **Schuit (2012)**
10. IROQUOIAN FAMILY	Campbell (2000), Mithun (2001)
37. Huron-Wyandot	Mallery (1881)
38. Iroquois	Mallery (1881)
11. ZUNI	Campbell (2000)
39. Zuni	Mallery (1881)
12. KERESAN = KERES	**Campbell (2000)**
40. Laguna Pueblo	Goldfrank (1923)
41. **Keresan Pueblo**	**Kelly and McGregor (2003)**

Note: Table features Indian nations, language families, and tribal communities in which indigenous sign language has been documented historically. North American Indian communities where sign language is known to be used, learned, or revitalized in recent times are indicated in **bold**. Language phyla and group names follow conventions for the classification of North American language families based on Campbell (2000) and Mithun (2001).

* 2019–20 public and social media outlets have reported sign language revitalization efforts underway among Cree and Ojibwa-Chippeway First Nations of Canada: reportedly, the Plains Indian Sign Language (PISL) variety.

Table 2. Documentary linguistic fieldwork of the PISL variety (Davis, 2009–15)

Language Family	Cultural and Geographic Area
Algonquian	**Northern Great Plains**
Blackfeet [Aamsskáápipikani = Amskapi Piikani]	Blackfeet Nation, northern Montana
Blackfoot [Aapátohsipikáni = Piikáni = Pekuni]	Piikani Nation of Alberta, Canada
Bloods [Káínaa = Kainai = Kainah]	Kainai Nation of Alberta, Canada
Siksiká [Tsuu T'ina]	Blackfoot Nation of Alberta, Canada*
Northern Cheyenne [Tse'tsehestahese]	N. Cheyenne reservation, southeastern Montana

Siouan	Great Plains
Crow [Apsaalooke]	Crow Reservation, Montana
Mandan-Hidasta [Moennitarri]	Ft. Berthold Reservation, North Dakota
Assiniboine [A'aniinen]	Ft. Belknap Reservation, Montana, and Indian Reserves in Saskatchewan and Alberta
Nakoda and Lakȟóta [Tetonwan]	Ft. Belknap and Ft. Peck Reservations in Montana and Indian Reserves in Saskatchewan and Alberta

* Four tribal nations compose the Blackfoot Confederacy (Niitsítapi) — namely, the Blood (Káínaa), Northern Piegan or Peigan (Aapátohsipikáni), Southern Piegan or Montana Blackfeet (Aamsskáápipikani), and Alberta, Canada, Blackfoot (Siksiká).

NOTES

1. The author of this chapter follows wording and naming conventions established in contemporary sign language linguistics and indigenous language research literature. Generally, "signed" is used in parallel constructions with "spoken": for instance, "both *signed and spoken* languages are being documented and revitalized." Also, when used as a common noun or adjective without reference to a cultural group or specific language — the terms "indigenous," "nation," "native," and "sign language" are not capitalized. However, uppercase "Native" or "Indian" are sometimes used as the shorter form of "Native American Indian" and refer to genetic heritage and indigenous cultural background of a person or people. In contrast, the lowercase form "native" refers to acculturation or language acquisition from birth through early childhood. While "Native American" and "American Indian" are used interchangeably, ideally it is best to ask individual members of the language community their naming preferences. In this chapter, tribal affiliation and cultural-linguistic group designations are acknowledged to the extent possible.

2. In recent times an increasing number of anthropologists, linguists, and other scholars have been studying indigenous and "village" types of sign languages worldwide (Davis, "North American Indian Sign Languages"; Davis, *Hand Talk*; Davis, "Discourse Features"; Pfau, Steinbach, and Woll, *Sign Language*; Zeshan and de Vos, *Sign Languages in Village Communities*). Paradoxically, the endangerment of indigenous and village-based signed languages is most likely due to the success and spread of urban sign languages such as ASL, as well as intense social and educational pressures (lack of dual-language and multilingual teaching approaches in place) leading deaf indigenous community members to abandon

their native indigenous signed languages in favor of the more predominately used signed languages of urban Deaf communities (Davis, "American Indian Sign Language").

3. Davis, "American Indian Sign Language." The linguistic term "variety" refers to "varieties" of a historically and genetically related language. Thus, British and American English are varieties of the same language, but British Sign Language (BSL) and American Sign Language (ASL) are distinct languages, including different dialects or varieties (sometimes called vernaculars). For example, Australian (Auslan) and New Zealand Sign Language (NZSL) are varieties of BSL (i.e., historically and genetically related), and there are several varieties of ASL, including Caribbean and African American varieties. See Davis, *Hand Talk*; Davis, "American Indian Sign Languages"; and Davis, "Native American Signed Languages," for further distinctions and descriptions along these lines.

4. Garrick Mallery Collection on Sign Language and Pictography, Numbered Manuscripts 1850s–1980s, MS 2372, National Anthropological Archives and Human Studies Film, Smithsonian Institution, Washington DC.

5. The author acknowledges grant and fellowship support from the Office of Research and Engagement at the University of Tennessee, National Endowment for the Humanities, and National Science Foundation's Documenting Endangered Languages Program, Division of Behavioral and Cognitive Sciences (BCS-0853665, BCS-1027735, BCS-1110211, BCS-1160604, and FN-50127–14), awarded to him as principal investigator between 2009 and 2015 to carry out the archival research, documentary linguistics fieldwork, AISL corpus linguistics development, and sign-language linguistics research work reported here. This has involved intensive collaboration with numerous scholars, students, and Native American leaders and members of communities where AISL continues to be used and learned today. Although the funding was not specifically for the purpose of language revitalization, the research outcomes have contributed much to these efforts. I am most grateful to the Native signers, collaborators, archivists, and participants who have shared their expertise and knowledge of indigenous signed language and for participating in the documentation of the AISL variety. I take responsibility for the descriptions and interpretations presented in this chapter.

6. Campbell, *American Indian Languages*; Davis, *Hand Talk*; Davis, "Discourse Features"; Davis, "Plains Indian Sign Language"; Mithun, *Languages of Native North America*; Taylor, "Indian Lingua Francas;" and Taylor, "Nonspeech Communication Systems."

7. Although language documentation and description for the purpose of revitalizing an endangered language represent enormous undertakings, there continues to be an urgency to do so (Crystal, *Language Death*). The fact that indigenous languages have survived and continue to be learned and used is remarkable,

considering the pressures for linguistic and cultural assimilation historically imposed on Native American groups to acquire and use the dominant languages of the larger society or community. Strikingly, the Native American communities and nations with a long history of sign language use have remained among the most linguistically resilient.

8. Campbell, *American Indian Languages*; Davis, "Historical Signed Lingua Franca"; Davis, *Hand Talk*; Davis, "American Indian Sign Language"; Mithun, *Languages of Native North America*; Taylor, "Indian Lingua Francas"; Taylor, "Nonspeech Communication Systems"; Umiker-Sebeok and Sebeok, *Aboriginal Sign Languages*.
9. Taylor, "Indian Lingua Francas."
10. See Mithun, *Languages of Native North America*.
11. See Davis, "American Indian Sign Language."
12. Davis, *Hand Talk*; Davis, "Discourse Features"; Davis, "American Indian Sign Language"; Davis and Supalla, "Sociolinguistic Description"; Fox Tree, "Meemul Tziij"; Kelly and McGregor, "Keresan Pueblo Indian Sign Language"; Le Guen, "In the Domain of Time"; and Schuit, "Signing in the Arctic."
13. Davis, *Hand Talk*.
14. Campbell, *American Indian Languages*; Mithun, *Languages of Native North America*; Goddard, "Languages of South Texas"; Taylor, "Nonverbal Communication"; Taylor, "Nonspeech Communication Systems"; Wurtzburg and Campbell, "North American Indian Sign Language."
15. Taylor, "Nonverbal Communication," 224.
16. Samarin, "Demythologizing."
17. Bonvillian et al., "Observations"; Goddard, "Languages of South Texas"; Mithun, *Languages of Native North America*; Wurtzburg and Campbell, "North American Indian Sign Language."
18. Wurtzburg and Campbell, "North American Indian Sign Language," 160.
19. Wurtzburg and Campbell, "North American Indian Sign Language," 154–55.
20. Taylor, "Nonverbal Communication."
21. Mithun, *Languages of Native North America*.
22. Goddard, "Languages of South Texas"; Wurtzburg and Campbell, "North American Indian Sign Language."
23. See Campbell, *American Indian Languages*; and Mithun, *Languages of Native North America*.
24. Boas, "Sign Language"; Clark, *Indian Sign Language*; Dunbar, "On the Language of Signs"; Gallaudet, "Natural Language of Signs"; Long, *Account of an Expedition*; Mallery, "Of the North American Indians."
25. Wurtzburg and Campbell, "North American Indian Sign Language," 164.
26. Davis, *Hand Talk*; Davis, "Discourse Features"; Davis, "American Indian Sign Language"; Davis, "Linguistic Vitality."

27. Boas, "Sign Language"; Dunbar, "On the Language of Signs"; Kroeber, "Sign Language Inquiry"; Mallery, "Among North American Indians"; Umiker-Sebeok and Sebeok, *Aboriginal Sign Languages*; Voegelin, "Sign Language Analysis."
28. Dunbar, "On the Language of Signs."
29. Goff-Paris and Wood, *Step into a Circle*; Karttunen, *Between Worlds*.
30. Karttunen, *Between Worlds*.
31. Karttunen, *Between Worlds*, 30, 44.
32. Davis, *Hand Talk*, 21–22.
33. Long, *Account of an Expedition*, 378–94.
34. Long, *Account of an Expedition*.
35. *American Annals for the Deaf and Dumb*, vols. 1–35, 1847–90.
36. Mallery, "Of the North American Indians."
37. Davis, "Signed Language Varieties"; Davis, *Hand Talk*; Davis, "Discourse Features."
38. Davis, "Signed Language Varieties"; Davis, *Hand Talk*; Davis, "Discourse Features."
39. Real Bird, *Crow and Hidasta-Mandan Sign Language*; Weatherwax, *Indian Sign Language*.
40. Garrick Mallery was from Philadelphia, the son of Judge Garrick Mallery Sr., a state legislator, Supreme Court justice, and chief justice for several years prior to his death in 1866. At that time Judge Mallery was the oldest active member of the bar in Philadelphia. Following in his father's footsteps, the young Mallery entered Yale College at the age of fifteen and graduated in 1850; he was recognized as being gifted in languages and mathematics. After graduating from Yale, he returned to Philadelphia to study law at the University of Pennsylvania and interned with his father. Three years later, at the age of twenty-two, he was admitted to the bar and established a legal career in Philadelphia. Mallery's background in law served him well and was evident in his work at the Bureau of Ethnology and his career in anthropology. For example, he was a principal founder and author of the constitutions and histories for several scientific, philosophical, and learned societies of the late nineteenth century, and he was actively involved in the passage of several acts of the U.S. Congress (Davis, *Hand Talk*).
41. Carayon, "Gesture Speech of Mankind"; Davis *Hand Talk*; Hochman, *Savage Preservation*; Kolodny, "Fictions of American Prehistory."
42. See Davis, *Hand Talk*. The acts of Congress with which Mallery was involved included federal legislation during Civil War Reconstruction that led to the establishment of the U.S. Signal Corps, Bureau of Freedmen and Refugees, Bureau of Ethnology at the Smithsonian, as well as Howard College and Columbia College (for the Deaf, now Gallaudet University), and work that eventually led to the passage of the American Antiquities Act.
43. Mallery, Boas, and their fellow ethnographers were members of the APS and actively involved in the establishment of several learned societies. Mallery's

long list of scholarly contributions, besides many publications, include being a founding member and serving as an officer for learned societies like the American Philosophical Society and Anthropological Society of Washington, DC—the first anthropology association in the United States. Mallery authored the constitution for the society, which served as a model for other newly formed scholarly societies nationwide, preceding the establishment of the American Anthropological Association by more than two decades (see Boas, "Foundation").

44. Hinsley, *Savages and Scientists*, 168.
45. Mallery's life was cut short at the age of sixty-three, due to chronic illnesses and injuries he had sustained as a union officer and prisoner of war during the American Civil War. Even though he produced an enormous amount of work, Mallery might have produced more, had he lived longer and not had chronic health issues in the years following the Civil War. During this historical period few American universities offered the PhD degree, and most of those academic programs were suspended during the Civil War (see Davis, *Hand Talk*). Hence, Mallery never held a university academic position, the modern fields of anthropology and linguistics had not yet emerged, and such degrees were not offered at American universities until the early twentieth century. I believe this could be why it has taken longer for Mallery's body of work and significance of his contributions to be recognized. On the other hand, his younger protégé Franz Boas enjoyed a long academic career and continued to work into his eighties, and Boas's students did much to help carry forward and maintain his enormous body of work and further develop his theories (most notably, A. L. Kroeber, Ruth Benedict, Edward Sapir, Margaret Mead, Zora Neale Hurston, Esther Goldfrank, among many others), and he is recognized as having a tremendous impact on subsequent generations of anthropologists and linguists. In brief, Franz Boas (German-born and educated) came to be recognized as the "Father of American Anthropology" and as the progenitor of cultural relativism, which maintains that cultures cannot be objectively ranked as higher or lower, or better or more correct, but that all humans see the world through the lens of their own culture, and judge it according to their own culturally acquired norms.
46. Sebeok, *Semiotics in the United States*, 16.
47. Umiker-Sebeok and Sebeok, *Aboriginal Sign Languages*, xx.
48. Elsewhere, the author has written extensively about Mallery's contributions and how his research of sign language remained unparalleled for the next one hundred years (Davis, *Hand Talk*). In the 1970s a major resurgence of sign language linguistic research commenced, focusing on the sign language of deaf communities. That is when the preeminent neurobiologist Ursula Bellugi established the Laboratory for Cognitive Sciences at the Salk Institute in La Jolla, California. Around the same time, William Stokoe (then a professor of English

and linguistics), established the Sign Language Research Laboratory at Gallaudet College in the 1970s. In Stokoe's case, as it had been in the past and even the present, sign language was often viewed as a speech surrogate, not a "real" language and an interference with (or competitor of) speech acquisition—fallacies that have been dispelled in the discipline of modern linguistics. These scholars have been forerunners in the field of linguistics, making enormous scholarly contributions, advancing research, and promoting the academic acceptance of signed languages.

49. Scott and Sanderville, *Film Dictionary*.
50. General Hugh L. Scott had considerable political clout and diligently led the Indian Sign Language preservation effort until his death in 1934. He attended Princeton University, graduated from West Point in 1876, and began his military career as a lieutenant in the U.S. Calvary. He was promoted to major general in 1915, then served as secretary of war in Woodrow Wilson's cabinet. He was responsible for the passage of the Selective Service Act and the appointment of General Pershing as commander in chief. After he had officially retired from military and civil service, Scott remained extremely active as a member of the Board of Indian Commissioners and as chairman of the New Jersey Highway Commission, and he spent the remainder of his life studying, lecturing, and writing about Indian Sign Language. He also received honorary doctorate degrees from both Princeton and Columbia Universities. In testimony to the respect held for him by tribal leaders, he was made an honorary member of various Indian tribes. Scott worked with the Indians for more than fifty years and was known as "Mole-I-Gu-Op," signifying "one who talks with his hands." See Meadows, *Through Indian Sign Language*; Hochman, *Savage Preservation*; and Davis, *Hand Talk*, for more information about Scott's Indian Sign Language film dictionary and extensive ethnographic documentation of Plains Indian Sign Language.
51. Davis, "Evidence"; Davis, "Historical Linguistic Account"; Davis, *Hand Talk*; Davis, "Discourse Features"; Davis, "American Indian Sign Language"; Davis, "Native American Signed Languages."
52. Davis, "Evidence"; Davis, "Historical Linguistic Account"; Davis, *Hand Talk*; Davis, "Discourse Features."
53. Davis *Hand Talk*; Hochman, *Savage Preservation*.
54. Davis, *Hand Talk*.
55. Davis, *Hand Talk*.
56. Davis, *Hand Talk*; Davis, "Discourse Features"; 2014; Davis, "American Indian Sign Language"; Davis, "Linguistic Vitality."
57. http://pislresearch.com/.

BIBLIOGRAPHY

Boas, Franz. "The Foundation of a National Anthropological Society." *Science* 15 (1902): 804–9.

——— . "Sign Language." In *Aboriginal Sign Language of the Americas and Australia, Vol. 2*, edited by Jean Umiker-Sebeok and Thomas A. Sebeok, 19–20. New York: Plenum, 1978. Reprinted from the *Report of the Sixtieth Meeting of the British Association for the Advancement of Science* (1890), 638–641. London: John Murray.

Bonvillian, John D., Vicky L. Ingram, and Brendan M. McCleary. "Observations on the Use of Manual Signs and Gestures in the Communicative Interactions between Native Americans and Spanish Explorers of North America: The Accounts of Bernal Díaz del Castillo and Álvar Núñez Cabeza de Vaca." *Sign Language Studies* 9, no. 2 (2009):132–65.

Burton, R. F. *The City of the Saints and Across the Rocky Mountains to California*. New York: Harper, 1862.

Campbell, Lyle. *American Indian Languages*. New York: Oxford University Press, 2000.

Carayon, Celine. "The Gesture Speech of Mankind: Old and New Entanglements in the Histories of American Indian and European Sign Languages." *American Historical Review* 121 (2016): 461–91.

Clark, William P. *The Indian Sign Language*. Philadelphia: Hamersly, 1885.

Crystal, David. *Language Death*. New York: Cambridge University Press, 2000.

Davis, Jeffrey E. "American Indian Sign Language: Documentary Linguistic Methodologies and Technologies." In *Endangered Languages and New Technologies*, edited by Mari C. Jones, 161–78. Cambridge: Cambridge University Press, 2015.

——— . "Discourse Features of American Indian Sign Language." In *Discourse in Signed Languages; Sociolinguistics in Deaf Communities, Vol. 17*, edited by Cynthia B. Roy, 179–217. Washington DC: Gallaudet University Press, 2011.

——— . "Evidence of a Historical Signed Lingua Franca among North American Indians." *International Journal of Deaf Studies* 21, no. 3 (2005): 47–72.

——— . *Hand Talk: Sign Language among American Indian Nations*. Cambridge: Cambridge University Press, 2010.

——— . "A Historical Linguistic Account of Sign Language among North American Indians." In *Multilingualism and Sign Languages: From the Great Plains to Australia*, edited by Ceil Lucas, 3–35. Washington DC: Gallaudet University Press, 2006.

——— . "The Linguistic Vitality of American Indian Sign Language: Endangered, Yet Not Vanished." *Sign Language Studies* 16, no. 4 (2016): 535–562.

——— . "Native American Signed Languages." Oxford Handbooks Online. Oxford University Press, 2017, https://www.oxfordhandbooks.com/view/10.1093/oxfordhb/9780199935345.001.0001/oxfordhb-9780199935345-e-42 (accessed August 19, 2020).

———. "North American Indian Signed Language Varieties: A Comparative Linguistic Assessment." In *Sign Languages in Contact: Sociolinguistics in Deaf Communities*, edited by David Quinto-Pozos, 85–122. Washington DC: Gallaudet University Press, 2007.

———. "Plains Indian Sign Language: The Legacy of Documentary Linguistics." In *Keeping Languages Alive: Documentation, Pedagogy, and Revitalization*, edited by Mari C. Jones and Sarah Ogilvie, 69–82. Cambridge: Cambridge University Press, 2014.

Davis, Jeffrey E., and Melanie McKay-Cody. "Signed Languages and American Indian Communities: Considerations for Interpreting Work and Research." In *Sign Language Interpreting in Multilingual, Multicultural Contexts; Studies in Interpretation, Vol. 7*, edited by Rachel Locker McKee and Jeffrey Davis, 119–57. Washington DC: Gallaudet University Press, 2010.

Davis, Jeffrey E., and Samuel Supalla. "A Sociolinguistic Description of Sign Language Use in a Navajo Family." In *Sociolinguistics of the Deaf Community*, vol. 1, edited by Ceil Lucas, 77–106. Washington DC: Gallaudet University Press, 1995.

Dunbar, William. "On the Language of Signs among Certain North American Indians." *Transactions of the American Philosophical Society* 6, no. 1 (1801): 1–8.

Farnell, Brenda. *Do You See What I Mean? Plains Indian Sign Talk and the Embodiment of Action*. Austin: University of Texas Press, 1995.

Fox Tree, Eric. "Meemul Tziij: An Indigenous Sign Language Complex of Mesoamerica." *Sign Language Studies* 9 (2009): 324–366.

Gallaudet, Thomas H. "Indian Language of Signs." *American Annals of the Deaf and Dumb* 4 (1852): 157–171.

———. "On the Natural Language of Signs; and Its Value and Uses in the Instruction of the Deaf and Dumb. Part I." *American Annals of the Deaf and Dumb* 1 (1847): 55–60.

———. "On the Natural Language of Signs; and Its Value and Uses in the Instruction of the Deaf and Dumb. Part II." *American Annals of the Deaf and Dumb* 2 (1848): 79–93.

Goddard, Ives. "The Languages of South Texas and the Lower Rio Grande." In *The Languages of Native America: Historical and Comparative Assessment*, edited by Lyle Campbell and Marianne Mithun, 70–132. Austin: University of Texas Press, 1979.

Goddard, Ives, ed. *Handbook of North American Indians, 17: Languages*. Washington DC: Smithsonian Institution Scholarly Press, 1996.

Goff-Paris, Damara, and Sharon Wood. *Step Into the Circle: The Heartbeat of American Indian, Alaska Native and First Nations Deaf Communities*. Monmouth OR: AGO, 2002.

Goldfrank, Ellen. "Notes on the Two Pueblo Feasts." *American Antiquity* 25 (1923): 193–95.

Hadley, Lewis F. *Indian Sign Talk*. Chicago: Baker, 1891.

Harrington, James P. "The American Indian Sign Language." In *Aboriginal Sign Language of the Americas and Australia, Vol. 2*, edited by D. Jean Umiker-Sebeok and Thomas A. Sebeok, 109–56. New York: Plenum, [1938] 1978.

Hinsley, C. *Savages and Scientists: The Smithsonian Institution and the Development of American Anthropology, 1846-1910*. Washington DC: Smithsonian Institution, 1981.

Hochman, Brian. *Savage Preservation: The Ethnographic Origins of Modern Media Technology*. Minneapolis: University of Minnesota Press, 2014.

Hofsinde, R. *Indian Sign Language*. New York: William Morrow, 1956.

Karttunen, Frances. *Between Worlds: Interpreters, Guides, and Survivors*. New Brunswick, NJ: Rutgers University Press, 1994.

Kelly, Walter P., and Tony L. McGregor. "Keresan Pueblo Indian Sign Language." In *Nurturing Native Languages*, edited by J. Reyhner, O. Trujillo, R. L. Carrasco, and L. Lockard, 141-48. Flagstaff: Northern Arizona University Press, 2003.

Kolodny, Annette. "Fictions of American Prehistory: Indians, Archeology, and National Origin Myths," *American Literature* 75, no. 4 (2003): 693-772.

Kroeber, Albert L. "Sign Language Inquiry." *International Journal of American Linguistics* 24 (1958): 1-19.

Le Guen, Olivier. "An Exploration in the Domain of Time: From Yucatec Maya Time Gestures to Yucatec Maya Sign Language Time Signs." In *Endangered Sign Languages in Village Communities: Anthropological and Linguistic Insights*, edited by Ulrike Zeshan and Connie de Vos, 209-50. Berlin: Mouton de Gruyter/Ishara, 2012.

Long, Stephen H. *Account of an Expedition from Pittsburgh to the Rocky Mountains*. Philadelphia: Edwin James, 1823.

Mallery, Garrick. "Sign Language among North American Indians." In *First Annual Report of the Bureau of Ethnology of the Smithsonian Institution for 1879-1880*, edited by John W. Powell, 263-552. New York: Dover, [1881] 2001.

———. "The Sign Language of the North American Indians." *American Annals of the Deaf and Dumb* 25 (1880): 1-20.

Meadows, William C., ed. *Through Indian Sign Language: The Fort Sill Ledgers of Hugh Lenox Scott and Iseeo, 1889-1897*. Norman: University of Oklahoma Press, 2015.

Mithun, Marianne. *The Languages of Native North America*. Cambridge: Cambridge University Press, 2001.

Pfau, Roland, M. Steinbach, and Bencie Woll, eds. *Sign Language: An International Handbook*. Berlin: Mouton de Gruyter, 2012.

Real Bird, Lanny. *Crow and Hidasta-Mandan Sign Language Teaching Materials*. Crow Agency MT: Little Big Horn College, 2012.

Samarin, William J. "Demythologizing Plains Indian Sign Language History." *International Journal of American Linguistics* 53, no. 1 (1987): 65-73.

Scott, Hugh L., and Richard Sanderville. *Film Dictionary of the North American Indian Sign Language*. Washington DC: Smithsonian Institution, 1931-34.

Sebeok, Thomas A. *Semiotics in the United States*. Bloomington: Indiana University Press, 1991.

Seton, E. T. *Sign Talk: A Universal Signal Code, Without Apparatus, for Use in the Army, Navy, Camping, Hunting, and Daily Life. The Gesture Language of the Cheyenne Indians.* New York: Doubleday, Page, 1918.
Schuit, Joke M. "Signing in the Arctic: External Influences on Inuit Sign Language." In *Sign Languages in Village Communities*, edited by Ulrike Zeshan and Connie de Vos, 181–208. Berlin: Mouton de Gruyter, 2012.
Taylor, Allan R. "Indian Lingua Francas." In *Languages in the USA*, edited by Charles Ferguson and Shirley B. Heath, 79–95. Cambridge: Cambridge University Press, 1981.
———. "Nonspeech Communication Systems." In *Handbook of the North American Indian: Vol. 17. Languages*, edited by Ives Goddard, 275–89. Washington DC: Smithsonian Institution, 1996.
———. "Nonverbal Communication in Aboriginal North America: The Plains Sign Language." In *Aboriginal Sign Languages of the Americas and Australia: Vol. 2*, edited by D. Jean Umiker-Sebeok and Thomas A. Sebeok, 223–44. New York: Plenum, 1978.
Teit, James A. *The Salishan Tribes of the Western Plateau: 45th Annual Report of the Bureau of American Ethnology.* Washington DC: U.S. Government Printing Office, 1930.
Thompson, Sally. *Tribes of Montana* [film series]. Helena: Montana Office of Public Instruction, Indian Education for All Program, 2007.
Tomkins, William. *Universal Indian Sign Language of the Plains Indians of North America.* New York: Dover, [1926] 1969.
Umiker-Sebeok, Jean, and Thomas Sebeok, eds. *Aboriginal Sign Languages of the Americas and Australia.* Vols. 1 and 2. New York: Plenum, 1978.
Voegelin, Carl. "Sign Language Analysis: On One Level or Two?" *International Journal of American Linguistics* 24 (1958): 71–77.
Weatherwax, Marvin. *Indian Sign Language.* Videotape. Department of Blackfeet Studies, Blackfeet Community College, Browning MT, 2002.
West, LaMont. "The Sign Language: An Analysis." PhD diss., Indiana University, Bloomington, 1960.
Wurtzburg, Susan, and Lyle Campbell. "North American Indian Sign Language: Evidence of Its Existence before European Contact." *International Journal of American Linguistics* 61 (1995): 153–67.
Zeshan, Ulrike, and Connie de Vos, eds. *Sign Languages in Village Communities.* Berlin: Mouton de Gruyter, 2012.

PART 3

Power and Language

Commentary by Diana E. Marsh

Perhaps more than any other set of chapters in this volume, the three on power and language make direct connections with the exhibition that inspired the symposium of the American Philosophical Society (APS). The exhibition, *Gathering Voices: Thomas Jefferson and Native America* (April–December 2016), explored Jefferson's early effort to collect Native American and Indigenous languages and its legacy at the Society.[1] One of the most important goals of the exhibition was to showcase the ways in which Native American and Indigenous people maintained or asserted agency in the process of language collecting and during American assimilation efforts. Likewise, each of these chapters eschews reductionist readings of colonial narratives in favor of more nuanced interpretations of transcultural encounter.[2]

Sean P. Harvey's chapter illustrates the central role of the APS, under the leadership of Peter S. Du Ponceau and in the spirit of Jefferson's initial program, in building a network of scholars and informants in pursuit of language collecting. As president of the APS, Jefferson had encouraged the collecting of Native American vocabularies and artifacts. To this end Du Ponceau aided him in forming the Historical and Literary Committee, devoted to collecting "American Antiquities"—that is, the languages, histories, and cultures of Native America. Later, Du Ponceau expanded Jefferson's project by collecting samples of languages from across the globe. Du Ponceau utilized a network of correspondents to

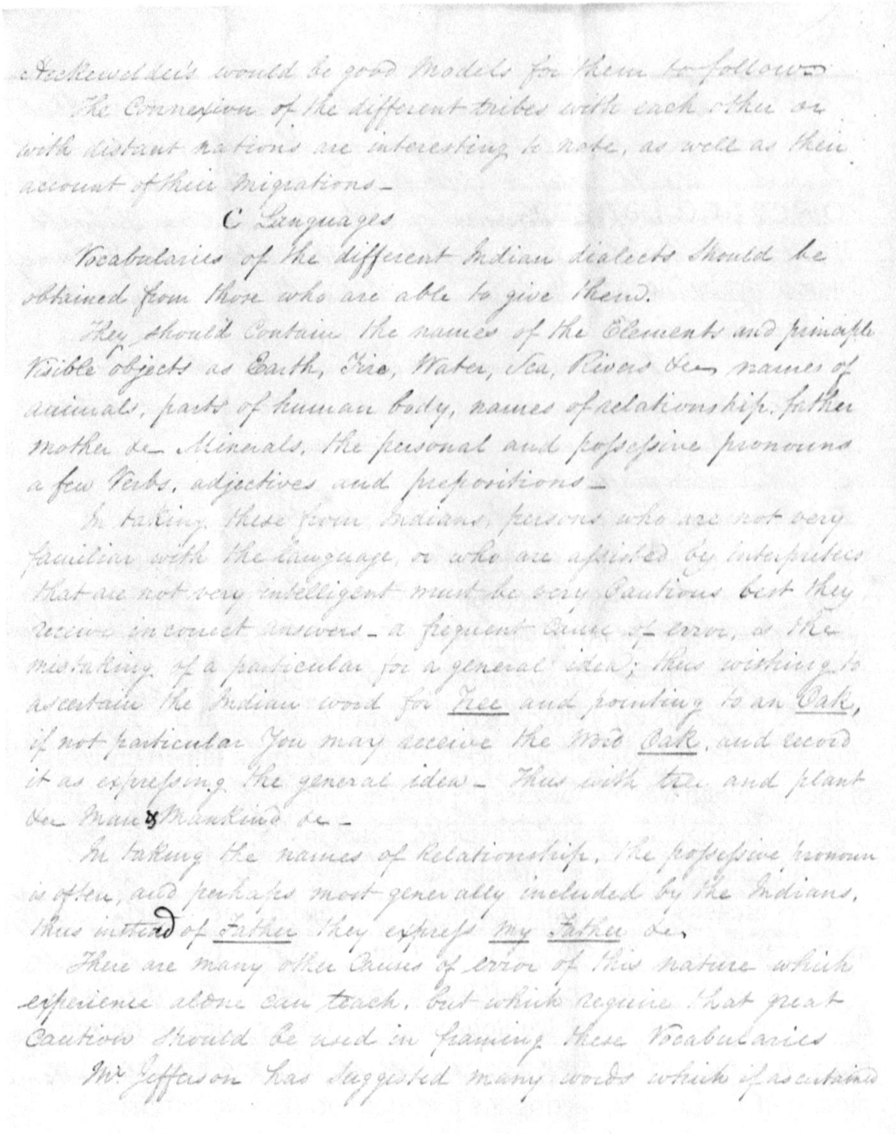

Heckewelder's would be good models for them to follow—

The Connexion of the different tribes with each other or with distant nations are interesting to note, as well as their account of their Migrations—

C Languages

Vocabularies of the different Indian dialects should be obtained from those who are able to give them.

They should contain the names of the Elements and principle visible objects as Earth, Fire, Water, Sea, Rivers &c— names of animals, parts of human body, names of relationship, father, mother &c— Minerals, the personal and possessive pronouns, a few Verbs, adjectives and prepositions—

In taking these from Indians, persons who are not very familiar with the language, or who are assisted by interpreters that are not very intelligent must be very cautious lest they receive incorrect answers— a frequent cause of error, is the mistaking of a particular for a general idea; thus wishing to ascertain the Indian word for _tree_ and pointing to an _Oak_, if not particular you may receive the word _Oak_, and record it as expressing the general idea— Thus with tree and plant &c— Man & Mankind &c—

In taking the names of relationship, the possessive pronoun is often, and perhaps most generally included by the Indians, thus instead of _father_ they express _my father_ &c.

There are many other causes of error of this nature which experience alone can teach, but which require that great caution should be used in framing these Vocabularies

Mr Jefferson has suggested many words which if ascertained

Fig. 4. (APS) Historical and Literary Committee to George Izard, May 6, 1825. No. 29, 30, Mss.497.V85, American Philosophical Society Historical and Literary Committee, American Indian Vocabulary Collection, APS.

collect information, including APS members such as J. G. E. Heckewelder. The committee also offered advice to correspondents on how to collect languages in the field.

Harvey argues that the idea that Native people and languages were dying out in favor of English language and culture was pervasive; at the same time, Du Ponceau, like others of his time, in fact "misunderstood the evidence before him." In this context Harvey takes a closer look at the power dynamics of Du Ponceau's project. Power was distributed among a "strikingly inclusive" range of participants involved in this complex knowledge exchange, including "missionaries, Indian agents, military officers, territorial governors, and others near Native communities." Close attention to that network helps account for Native resistance and agency in such linguistic projects, even though it was Du Ponceau who "gained scholarly prestige." Harvey's chapter thus illuminates the agency of the full range of actors engaged in language collecting projects—a concept that is very difficult to convey in an exhibition.[3] Harvey's close analysis of correspondence shows the capacity of archival collection to reveal quieter actors, even in the named archival collections of those otherwise assumed to wield the most power.

The next two chapters, by Anne Keary and by Gwen N. Westerman and Glenn M. Wasicuna, explore the legacy of such early eighteenth-century projects. As the nineteenth century progressed, more missionaries, linguists, and Native communities worked to develop writing systems to record and translate Indigenous languages. A close look at many of these projects likewise complicates the notion of a unilinear, top-down, colonial imposition of power. Rather, as Keary observes, deeper exploration reveals the "complicated dynamics of the interplay between colonial and Indigenous engagements with the written word."

Keary shows how *Numipuain Shapahitamanash Timash*, a primer designed to teach Nimiipuu people to read and write their language, was at the same time part of a systematic missionary-led Indigenous literacy campaign and an example of Indigenous agency and collaboration. Looking closely at this primer—its content and its collaborative production—reveals a complex cross-cultural settler-Native encounter. While, for instance, many animal stories included in the primer attempt

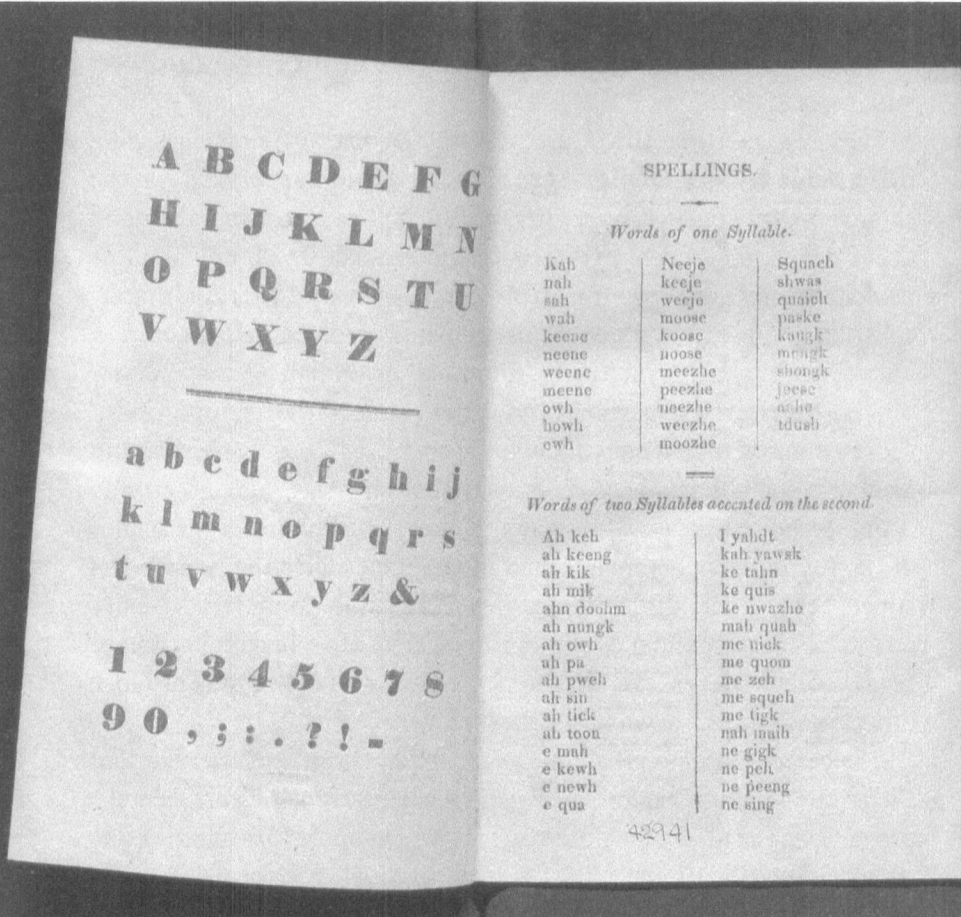

Fig. 5. *Spellings for the Schools in the Chipeway (Chippewa) Language*, Canada Conference Missionary Society, 1828, APS.

to correct and "improve" Indigenous worldviews, a few stories adopt Nimiipuu modes of oral storytelling. The collection also features a hymn that, rather than being a simple translation of Protestant beliefs, is in fact a transcultural composition, melding Nimiipuu and Christian conceptions of divine power.

According to Westerman and Wasicuna's chapter, the scholarly edition of Dakota letters from 1838 to 1878 will explore this period of drastic

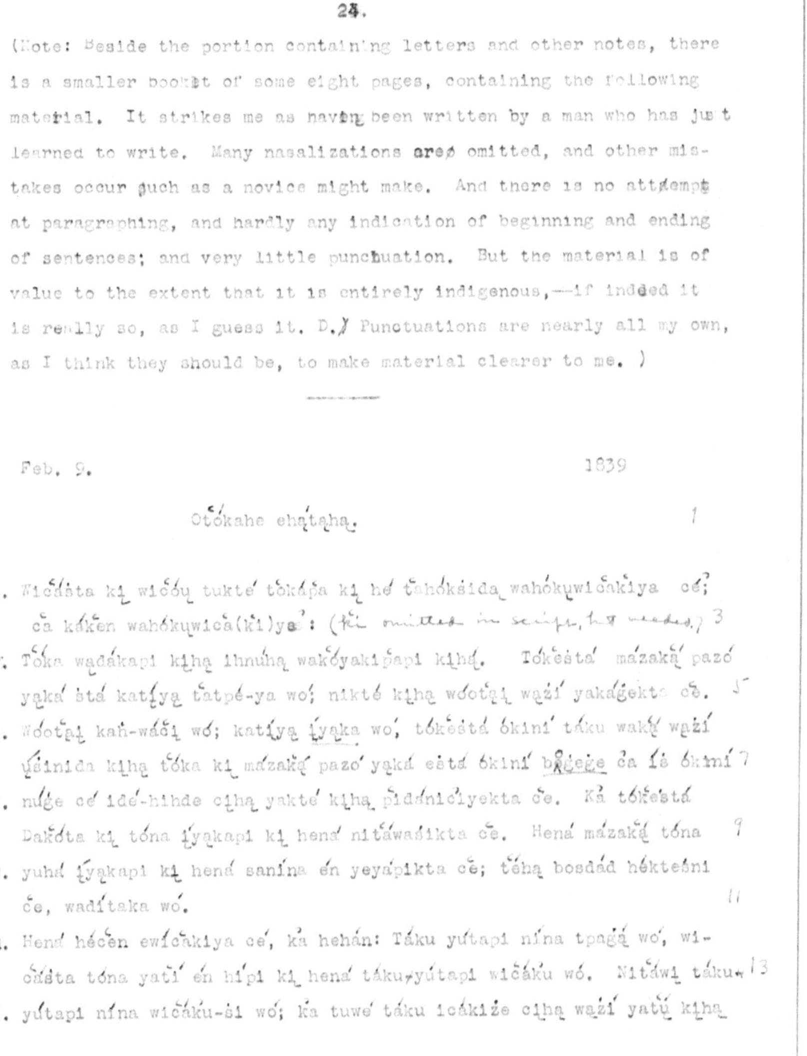

24.

(Note: Beside the portion containing letters and other notes, there is a smaller booklet of some eight pages, containing the following material. It strikes me as having been written by a man who has just learned to write. Many nasalizations are omitted, and other mistakes occur such as a novice might make. And there is no attempt at paragraphing, and hardly any indication of beginning and ending of sentences; and very little punchuation. But the material is of value to the extent that it is entirely indigenous,—if indeed it is really so, as I guess it. D.) Punctuations are nearly all my own, as I think they should be, to make material clearer to me.)

Feb. 9.   1839

Otókahe ehą́tąhą.   1

1. Wičášta ki wičóų tukté tókápa ki hé tųhókšida wahókųwičakiya ce;
   ča káken wahókųwiča(ki)yą²: (ki omitted in script, he needed.) 3

3. Tóka wadákapi kįhą ihnuhą wakóyakipapi kįhą. Tókéstá mázaką́ pazó
   yąká štá katíya tatpé-ya wo; nikté kįhą wóotą́i wąží yakágekta ce. 5

5. Wóotą́i kah-wáči wó; katíya iyąka wo, tókéšta ókiní táku waką́ wąží
   ysinida kįhą tóka ki mázaką́ pazó yąká eštá ókiní bšdęgę ča iš ókiní 7

7. nuǧe ce idé-hihde ciha yakté kįhą pidániciyekta ce. Ká tókéšta
   Dakóta ki tóna íyąkapi ki hená nitáwašikta ce. Hená mázaką́ tóna 9

9. yuhá íyąkapi ki hená sanína én yeyápikta ce; téhą bosdád héktešni
   ce, wadítaka wó.   11

10. Hená héčen ewíčakiya ce, ka hehán: Táku yútapi nína tpąǧá wo, wi-
    čášta tóna yatí én hípi ki hená táku yútapi wičáku wó. Nitáwį táku 13

13. yútapi nína wičáku-ši wó; ká tuwe táku ičákiže ciha wąží yatų́ kįhą

Fig. 6. Letters in Dakota from various Indians educated at the mission school, translated by Ella C. Deloria. x8a.20: Letters and miscellaneous materials in Dakota from the Minnesota, Mss.497.3.B63c, American Council of Learned Societies Committee on Native American Languages (ACLS Collection), APS.

change and epistemicide from the Dakota point of view.[4] Just as Keary showed in the Nimiipuu context, writing was not an unfamiliar technology to the Dakota when settlers arrived. In both cases Native communities were exposed to writing through colonial trade networks. Whereas Keary focuses on one example of a missionary-driven movement and text, Westerman and Wasicuna show how the language assimilation process impacted power relations in the drafting of treaties and escalation of the U.S.-Dakota War of 1862. While much of the published and archival record has privileged the settlers' Anglophone interpretation of these events, the scholarly translation project, "This is Who We Are," is beginning to reveal the first-person perspectives and everyday lives of Dakota people during this period.

Together, the chapters also show how colonial archives can be reinterpreted. Like the encounters that produced them, archival collections embody complex networks of people and things that accrued over time. As Jane Anderson and James E. Francis Sr. note in their chapter, many archival systems, categories, and legal frameworks prioritize colonial collectors and provenance, and many Native and Indigenous speakers are left out of the archival record. Closer analysis of these records, and projects such as those described here, can expose and give voice to such silences. With an institutional commitment to inviting and incorporating community voices—through new subject guides and metadata based on Indigenous knowledge, CNAIR's collaborative projects, and exhibitions like *Gathering Voices*—the American Philosophical Society can build on Du Ponceau's project to facilitate new networks and relationships for the twenty-first century.

NOTES

1. For a summary of the exhibition, see Regouby and Marsh, "Curating Gathering Voices."
2. On "transculturation" in various "contact zones" as a dual movement, and how "metropolitan modes of representation" were not only disseminated to, but also received and reappropriated by, peripheral people, see Pratt, *Imperial Eyes*. On "in-between" spaces as "innovative sites of collaboration and contestation," see Bhabha, *Location of Culture*, 1–2. On earlier anthropological approaches to cultural change as "externally induced yet indigenously orchestrated," see Sahlins, *Islands of History*, vii.

3. Bruchac, "Ephemeral Encounters and Material Evidence." On other failings of the exhibition to communicate these narratives, see Fowler Williams, "Review of Gathering Voices."
4. On "epistemicide" as the "murder of knowledge," see de Sousa Santos, "Fall of the Angelus Novus," 103.

BIBLIOGRAPHY

Bhabha, Homi K. *The Location of Culture*. New York: Routledge, 1994.
Bruchac, Margaret. "Ephemeral Encounters and Material Evidence." *Anthropology News* 57 (2016): 218–22.
de Sousa Santos, Boaventura. "The Fall of the Angelus Novus: Beyond the Modern Game of Roots and Options." *Current Sociology* 46, no. 2 (1998): 81–118.
Fowler Williams, Lucy. "Review of Gathering Voices: Thomas Jefferson and Native America." Exhibit at the American Philosophical Society Museum. Philadelphia PA: April 10–December 30, 2016." *Museum Anthropology* 40 (2017): 185–86.
Pratt, Mary Louise. *Imperial Eyes: Travel Writing and Transculturation*. New York: Routledge, 1992.
Regouby, Lynette, and Diana E. Marsh. "Curating Gathering Voices." *Anthropology News* 57 (2016): 59–60.
Sahlins, Marshall. *Islands of History*. Chicago: University of Chicago Press, 1985.

CHAPTER 6

"The Indian Republic of Letters"

Scholarly Networks and Indigenous Knowledge in Philology

Sean P. Harvey

On consecutive days in mid-December 1817, on behalf of the Historical and Literary Committee (HLC) of the American Philosophical Society (APS), Peter S. Du Ponceau wrote two letters that indicate the circuits through which linguistic information about Natives traveled in the early nineteenth century and the ways in which the exchange of ideas entailed the exchange of physical objects. The first letter was to Frederick Adelung, a German philologist in St. Petersburg, Russia. His father had been the author of the most important polyglot compilation of the early nineteenth century, *Mithridates* (4 vols., 1806–17), and the son was "one of the men who give the lead to public opinion in matters of science."[1] Adelung had presented the APS with two works of philology, and other "magnificent present[s] of precious and rare books in diverse languages" followed. Expressing gratitude for the gifts and for the post-Napoleonic peace that had allowed philosophical exchanges to flourish, Du Ponceau ventured to recommend an "interchange of ideas" that could "unite the two hemispheres in joint efforts to promote a Science, the utility of which is equally felt by the learned of your country and the students of our own." To reciprocate the gift, he sent Adelung his own recent essay of sounds in English. The subsequent correspondence allowed Du Ponceau entrance to the circle of Continental philologists, elevating his prestige and fueling further publication. When he reviewed one of Adelung's gifts, a book on Russian and Sanskrit, in the pages of the Philadelphia *Port-Folio*, he proudly declared the United States a "tribunal ... the self-created judge" of European scholarship.²

The day after he wrote to Adelung, Du Ponceau penned a letter to the missionary Eleazer Williams, a Mohawk ministering to Oneidas in central New York. He sought materials respecting the languages of the Haudenosaunee, since, as he had complained to a collaborator, for all that was known of Algonquian languages, "there was hardly any thing to be found of the Iroquois." He told Williams, who had authored a Mohawk spelling book and translated several religious texts, the "languages of the American Indians will probably be lost in process of time" and urged a cooperative "endeavor to preserve some memorials of them." The notion that Native languages were dying, verbal manifestations of a physically doomed people or of a savagery destined to vanish before civilization, to be replaced by English as a necessary part of assimilation, was pervasive among scholars and within the broader public.³ Du Ponceau misunderstood the evidence before him. Williams produced varied Mohawk texts precisely because his native tongue still thrived. Yet one wonders if Du Ponceau's elegiac tone was persuasive. Williams, for a time, did contribute to the philological studies of Du Ponceau as well as to other scholars, sending books and clarifying questions related to Mohawk sounds and grammar. Philologists cited Williams as an authority on Mohawk.⁴

These letters and the subsequent exchanges between their author and recipients are emblematic of the study of Native languages in the early nineteenth century. Scholars sought to forge connections to Continental philologists on the one hand, and on the other to those who lived near or among Indigenous people. Despite their divergent paths, toward Europe and toward "Indian Country," these variegated letters were part of a mutually supportive enterprise. As Du Ponceau told Adelung in 1821, revealing both the stereotypes and the sources of scientific authority that underlay philology, he would send "notices on the languages of our savages, which I believe can be useful to you, and that one can obtain only on the spot."⁵

Knowledge of languages was closely linked to power. Yet the dynamics were complex, since power was diffused among the many participants who played some role in the creation of linguistic knowledge and throughout the relationships that bound together what Du Ponceau dubbed "the Indian Republic of Letters."[6] Scholarship on philology has stressed its diverse functions as a culturally nationalist pursuit for U.S. scholars, a description of "savage" tongues to justify dispossession, and a growing field of knowledge with ramifications for European understanding of languages, minds, and bodies. Indigenous speakers also resisted such linguistic projects. While it is crucial to understand the role of linguistic information and language ideologies in the imposition and experience of colonialism, a topic I have treated elsewhere, there were limits to colonial knowledge and power.[7] Some of those limits are especially legible through an examination of the networks that scholars constructed as they pursued and disseminated what they learned.

Scholars who were professionally and socially prominent, and situated in port cities, went to great lengths to construct extensive networks that stretched to Russia, Iroquoia, and beyond. As work on learned societies and intellectual practices has shown, these circuits extended to individuals whose labor, vocation, appointment, or personal situation placed them in or near Indigenous communities, who could provide scholars with desired information and who willingly leveraged collection into cultural prestige and social connections. Collectors transmitted information that allowed scholars, often affiliated with local learned societies, to establish a reputation through publication.[8] Taking part in a global philosophical, literary, or scientific project, in turn, provided a basis for enhancing their own national and international networks of statesmen and savants.[9] Careful cultivation of epistolary relationships bound this far-flung philological community together, but assiduous letter writing, within and far beyond national boundaries, existed in a complex relationship with local institutions and an expanding and increasingly variegated print culture. Neither scholarship on eighteenth-century Atlantic epistolary networks nor on the nineteenth-century U.S. postal system has examined the proliferation of transatlantic ties among the learned in the nineteenth century or how they were maintained.[10] A closer look at scholarly practices—not simply a close reading of a dense learned essay or an especially revealing line in a private letter, but rather the more mundane work of maintaining correspondence—provides a rich sense of who was participating in the creation of linguistic knowledge and on what terms.

Focusing on the work of Du Ponceau, especially, to build a scholarly network, this essay will examine the work of synopsis, clarification, criticism, debate, encouragement, and gossip that fill the manuscripts of philologists. The networks that resulted were inclusive—linking North America and Europe, east and west, male and female, white and Native—but decidedly unequal. Even as they offered avenues for well-situated individuals to contribute to prestigious, cosmopolitan projects, white and Indigenous participants often chafed at the terms of that incorporation. Focusing on the deep correspondence that Du Ponceau maintained with a small number of scholars provides a clear view of the varied dynamics of scholarly relationships and, in turn, the diffuse power that shaped knowledge of Native languages.

Mindful of the efforts of the learned in Massachusetts and New York to preserve historical materials and pursue their study, members of the APS determined to create a committee for "history, moral science, and general literature" in August 1815. The committee's corresponding secretary was Peter S. Du Ponceau, an established lawyer who had been corresponding secretary for other Philadelphia associations, such as the Democratic Society of Pennsylvania and the French Benevolent Society.[11] The Historical and Literary Committee's several letter books reveal the efforts he made to establish himself and the new group in the world of learned exchange. In the first year or so Du Ponceau wrote to Thomas Jefferson, a former APS president and collector himself; Elias Boudinot, a proponent of the Lost Tribes theory who was among the founders of the American Bible Society; and other locally prominent men identified with philosophical and philanthropic pursuits. These letters announced the committee's existence, explained its purpose, and solicited communications on subjects "worthy of the attention of every Citizen who unites leisure to talents & patriotism."[12]

At its conception the committee pursued a nationalistic salvage project, but it became increasingly focused on Natives once Du Ponceau opened a correspondence with John Heckewelder, a retired Moravian missionary to Delawares (Lenni Lenapes). By early 1817 the committee "particularly turned their attention to the languages of our Indian nations," Du Ponceau informed Jefferson, who had recommended linguistic collection four decades earlier.[13] Diplomatically, Du Ponceau asked Jefferson for "hints ... upon the subject," though he knew that Jefferson's actual knowledge of Native languages was negligible. Delicate negotiation of the competing imperatives of respect due to age and status and the need for scholarly rigor suffused the committee's correspondence.[14] As Du Ponceau turned his attention to acquiring Native linguistic materials, the individuals that he wrote to on behalf of the HLC became more geographically distant and socially varied. Looking past local elites, Du Ponceau posted letters to missionaries, U.S. Indian agents, military officers, territorial governors, and others near Native communities. Though he usually wrote to men as members of his scholarly network, he occasionally reached out to women, as when he assured Eliza C. Tunstall, "Madam, no one is better able than you to supply the deficiency" with respect to southeastern Indigenous languages.[15] Revealing the scope of his ambition, he sent requests to government officials in Quebec and Mexico as well.[16]

Some of these correspondents became essential to Du Ponceau's researches, and to the committee's profile among the literati. John Heckewelder provided the foundation for Du Ponceau's philology. The retired missionary offered skill in spoken Delaware and access to the Brethren's deep archive of linguistic materials, and he described what they had collected. Finally, he connected Du Ponceau to other Moravians in North America and the Caribbean and guided him in utilizing those connections, alerting his new friend of the unreliability of certain contacts (one missionary, for instance, possessed a drinking problem, "Vanity—& a share of Avarice"). The exchange and resulting publications, beginning with the inaugural *Transactions of the Historical and Literary Committee of the American Philosophical Society* (1819), had tremendous consequences for Euro-American understanding of Native languages, and for missionary-led projects to use them for evangelizing. Heckewelder offered these sundry scholarly services because he saw philology as an opportunity to cultivate better opinions about Natives among whites, though, like Du Ponceau, he also anticipated setting "Linguists in Philada.—Boston—Germany, Russia &c. a going." Du Ponceau did not trust all that Heckewelder said, and, though he tried to filter out what seemed to an armchair scholar like bias or conjecture, the new philology's missionary foundations remained a source of criticism for those who sought to debunk it.[17] Nevertheless, Du Ponceau's close relationship with Heckewelder convinced others of philology's philanthropic worth, and many of its supporters valued that feature more highly than its technical rigor or transatlantic prestige.

Du Ponceau's other most important correspondent was a fellow philologist, John Pickering. It is striking that the secretary of the Democratic Society of Pennsylvania and the son of the High Federalist Timothy Pickering should have formed so close a bond, but they were congenial spirits who shared literary and professional interests.[18] References to Homer, Augustine, Dante, Montaigne, and Rousseau are sprinkled throughout a warm and wide-ranging correspondence that also divulges their hopes, personal tribulations, roles in local civic associations, and political and legal opinions. From the outset their relationship was one of exchange and collaboration. Initiating the correspondence in 1818, Du Ponceau sent his essay on English sounds, and Pickering reciprocated with works of his own on Americanisms in English and on pronunciation in Greek.[19] Receiving the HLC *Transactions* sparked Pickering's interest in Native languages, and he reviewed the volume glowingly in the *North American Review*. In 1820 he sent Du Ponceau an essay published in the *Memoirs of the American Academy of Arts and Sciences* on a uniform orthography for recording unwritten Native languages, which U.S. missionaries came to use widely. Du Ponceau heaped praise on Pickering's system and forwarded it to European philologists.[20] Du Ponceau and Pickering extracted material from books and manuscripts for one another, or at least directed someone else to do it for them. (In one letter Du Ponceau revealed the usually silent work of a clerk, Jacques Julien Robert Malenfant, who performed the actual manual labor.)[21] They also collaborated on a new edition of John Eliot's mid-seventeenth century Massachusett grammar, published in the *Collections of the Massachusetts Historical Society*, with an introductory essay and copious explanatory notes that incorporated new information and cited the authority of Indigenous consultants such as David Brown, a Cherokee. Publications, in turn, circulated among savants at home and abroad, connecting disparate learned societies and prompting reviews and other publications.[22] The close friendship and collaboration with Pickering propelled the rapid dissemination of the new philology.

The two men also aided one another as each negotiated cosmopolitan exchanges among philologists. Du Ponceau sought out foreign journals that he could not obtain in Philadelphia and informed his friend when he received a "large packet of German books." At least once Pickering explicitly requested "the favor to introduce me" to a European correspondent.[23] Each shared the news when they had been elected to foreign learned societies. Pickering expressed particular pride when he learned that the renowned philologist Franz Bopp had proposed Pickering's membership in the Berlin Academy after Therese Robinson, the daughter of a German professor and wife of an American biblical scholar, translated one of Pickering's essays—which incorporated, without citation, substantial Cherokee grammatical information obtained from David Brown—into German.[24] They also shared candid impressions of European philology, including a French prize question that Du Ponceau dismissed as "silly" and a review that Pickering wrote "to 'show up'" English scholars.[25] Their relationship brought ostensibly disinterested scholarship and philanthropy as well as nationalist literary ambition to bear on a broader project among moderate Republicans and Federalists to transcend sectional divisions and old partisan animosities just a few years removed from the War of 1812.[26]

Such exchanges were limited by the political and economic obstacles that scholars faced. In 1818 Du Ponceau informed John Quincy Adams, secretary of state and APS member, that his committee found it "sometimes difficult to transmit their communications to the different parts of Europe, particularly Germany and Russia," so he requested that they be sent through State Department officials. Oddly, given the War Department's authority in Indian affairs, Du Ponceau also hoped that State might help the HLC reach "Indian Country" too.[27] Customs duties set by Congress on imported books presented another obstacle and scholars lobbied, unsuccessfully, for the free importation of books in foreign languages since, as Pickering complained, "our booksellers ... reprint none of the ones we want."[28] In addition the U.S. post office charged much higher rates for sending personal correspondence than for newspapers and other printed matter, and postmasters had the "vile practice" of charging letter postage on "loose printed sheets."[29] Finally, with no aristocratic patrons in the republic and government patronage politically divisive and liable to stoke individual and institutional jealousy, there were few opportunities to secure financial support for research. Lacking the means to make a living as scholars, philology and legal practice detracted from one another. Pickering worried that he had "suffered much in my professional business, from having . . . acquired something of the character of a litterateur." Similarly, Du Ponceau lamented to the German philologist Johann S. Vater that, "whenever I have devoted much of my time to any literary pursuit, I have always found my book of receipts diminished by at least one half."[30]

Du Ponceau's efforts to cultivate correspondences with Continental philologists such as Vater is especially revealing of less material factors that produced inequalities in the philological republic of letters. As coauthor of *Mithridates* and a professor at the esteemed Prussian university of Konigsberg, and as the European scholar who had undertaken the deepest comparative study to date of the Indigenous languages of the Americas (aided by the materials given him by his countryman, the explorer Alexander von Humboldt), Vater was a valuable correspondent. Between October 1819 and October 1821, Du Ponceau deluged Vater with several shipments of materials that included at least eight U.S. books on philology, language philosophy, and archaeology, including the HLC's *Transactions* and the initial volume of the American Antiquarian Society's *Archaeologia Americana*; Moravian materials, including a printed spelling book and book of sermons as well as manuscript dictionaries and grammars; and no fewer than two dozen manuscript vocabularies, including ten "before unknown" that had been collected, at Du Ponceau's urging, on the Long Expedition, a federal exploration of the Missouri Valley as far as the Rocky Mountains.[31]

Exchange between Philadelphia and Konigsberg shows clearly how Euro-American language learning and linguistic collection depended upon Native participation. While figures like the missionary John Heckewelder, the Indian agent Benjamin Hawkins, or naturalists on federal exploring expeditions such as Thomas Say sent those vocabularies to scholars, Du Ponceau's records contain numerous details on the Native figures who were the ultimate source of linguistic knowledge. A Creek vocabulary came from "one of their greatest Orators. Aided by other Chiefs selected for the purpose." A Choctaw vocabulary came from a "lad of that nation, who spoke English." One Chickasaw vocabulary came from "a native Chickasaw," and another was provided by "a Chickasaw family who passed an evening" with a white Tennessean. A "Nanticoke Chief who spoke both languages," perhaps Samuel White, provided a comparative vocabulary of Nanticoke and Ojibwe. A vocabulary of Mohegan came from "the mouth of one of that nation, who had been in Connecticut." The renowned chief Little Turtle contributed to a Miami vocabulary. A Yankton Sioux vocabulary, one of the fruits of the Long Expedition, came from J. B. Dorion, a Métis man.[32] White collectors named few of these consultants, but the degree to which philologists depended upon Native people not only for their own studies but also for the ability to establish and maintain scholarly connections an ocean away is clear.

For all his efforts to correspond with the Konigsberg philologist, Du Ponceau was disappointed by Vater's infrequent responses, likely illustrating their unequal statuses in the republic of letters. Du Ponceau was sometimes self-deprecating and occasionally chided his counterpart for his neglect, but he continued to send staggering quantities of script and print and flattered the professor by translating Vater's essay on Natives' origins. When they finally arrived, Vater's letters were frequently accompanied by gifts, such as a philological bibliography (an "Index linguarum") or Vater's translation of an important comparative work by the Danish scholar Rasmus Rask.[33] Grateful for the token of recognition and eager to reaffirm his own and his country's standing, Du Ponceau redoubled his efforts. To elevate his value as a correspondent in Vater's eyes, he demonstrated the reach of his own network. Describing how Don Pedro Perez, a Peruvian mestizo learned in Quechua and Latin, had corrected one of Du Ponceau's published assertions gave Du Ponceau the opportunity both to display his character as a scholar more eager to find the truth than to defend a theory, and to reflect that the "independence of the Spanish Continental Colonies, will open here a fruitful source of information." To indicate his broad interests and philological virtuosity, Du Ponceau disclosed that he had begun studying Basque, and he casually indicated his knowledge of languages spoken in southern Africa and Oceania. Besides illustrating his industriousness in pursuing philology in rare moments of leisure, Du Ponceau even presented his professional business as revealing of his character and cosmopolitanism. The particular legal questions that occupied his time — stemming from of the country's tumultuous commercial relations amid European war in the 1790s–1810s — concerned what Du Ponceau called a civil, rather than political, law of nations, which "treats the rights of individuals out of their own country." He also sent still more materials, including several books and fourteen manuscript vocabularies.[34]

With other foreign correspondents, relations were more equal. Such was the case with a man whom Du Ponceau considered "the most learned orientalist in Europe," Joseph Von Hammer. Du Ponceau informed the Austrian of his election to the APS, and Von Hammer offered a token of thanks by presenting a copy of a cuneiform inscription. Over many years they wrote and exchanged books frequently, and over time it may have been Von Hammer who was the more eager correspondent. He wrote to Du Ponceau in English; he expressed the opinion that philology in Berlin dwarfed his own Vienna as much as it did Philadelphia; and he shared gossip involving animosites and accusations among European philologists. In 1840 Von Hammer complained that a "whole year passed since I have received any token of your remembrance." By then Du Ponceau had established himself in the eyes of Von Hammer and other European philologists "amongst the first philologists not only of the new but also of the antient world."[35]

Communications with these German-speaking philologists represented one facet of a broader effort to cultivate new intellectual ties. The old mother country, in the estimation of Du Ponceau and others, was "queer" in its philological backwardness, and, as Du Ponceau told Pickering, "we can only get a national spirit of character in literature, by looking beyond England, and Germany is the nearest to us in language & current of thought."[36] German states also lacked a history of American colonization, though large numbers of German speakers had colonized Pennsylvania and other parts of North America. The centrality of Moravian materials to Du Ponceau's philology and to the gifts he sent to Europe underscored the point. It was an especially opportune moment to connect the United States to central Europe, since increasing numbers of American students were traveling to Berlin and other German cities, where they found an audience interested in U.S. scholarship. Through the aegis of the future historian George Bancroft, for instance, Wilhelm von Humboldt—an established philologist and brother to the explorer—learned of American philology by reading one of Pickering's reviews and subsequently opened a correspondence. Amid their exchange Humboldt expressed the hope that Pickering could track down a few American books—inadvertently answering the sneering question an English reviewer had asked in 1820, "In the four quarters of the globe, who reads an American book?" Pickering passed Humboldt's request to Du Ponceau, who seized the opportunity by sending the HLC and AAS volumes as well as several other philological and antiquarian titles.[37] While Du Ponceau valued the sophistication, and the reputation, of German philologists, he used his correspondence to demonstrate his own and his countrymen's attainments and liberality.[38]

Once Du Ponceau established himself among European philologists, and after he ascended to the presidency of the APS in 1827, his less well-placed countrymen in the United States sought to establish themselves in his eyes. Although Du Ponceau may have occasionally felt distant from the centers of European philology, from elsewhere in the United States Philadelphia looked like a privileged place in the republic of letters. In early 1827 Edwin James, a U.S. army surgeon in northern Michigan, submitted a manuscript on Menominee. The APS declined to publish the essay, but James eagerly corresponded with Du Ponceau anyway. Due to his "remoteness and . . . almost inaccessible position," James's scholarly opportunities were "necessarily limited," though it would be a "pleasure" to send what he could.[39] A fellow man of letters, the Prussian immigrant Francis Lieber, expressed similar views from Columbia, South Carolina. He felt "the most chilling want of interest" in philology there and lamented, "You have at least an easy communication with Europe, you read what the European scholars are doing, you have materials around you, you see at least some people. I am an exile. Believe me, that in the same degree as you may feel lonely in Philadelphia, if you direct your look eastward, so do I feel lonely if I think of Philadelphia." The pang of isolation was especially keen because he recalled that the APS had never invited him to become a member.[40] The reputations that philologists acquired, which stemmed not only from their authorship in the United States but also from their illustrious epistolary connections across the sea, allured and frustrated those who were excluded.

A European philological contest, the Prix Volney, provides a remarkable glimpse into the unequal statuses of individuals and learned societies in the philological republic of letters and the tangled weave of handwritten and printed texts that connected them to one another. Despite writing "French like an *Iroquois*" after a half-century in the United States, Du Ponceau had tried for the prize a decade earlier, without success. With the 1835 prize calling for an essay on the grammatical structure and relations of North American Indian languages, Du Ponceau was better positioned than most, but he was ambivalent. Unable to "bear that any but an American should get that prize," he also worried that "no man should seek fame out of *his own country*."[41] As it turned out, Du Ponceau faced limited competition for the prize. Edwin James had considered trying for it, but his "slovenly" effort could not meet the contest's rules (which required submissions to be written in French or Latin).[42] The only other entrant was Constantine S. Rafinesque, a Philadelphian excluded from APS membership—and even from public acknowledgment despite his repeated efforts to secure Du Ponceau's recognition and patronage. Rafinesque's submission for the prize included a fraudulent Delaware pictographic text, cobbled together from the work of Du Ponceau, Heckewelder, James, and others. The *Walum Olam*, as he called it, was a brazen ethnological hoax premised on the illusion of access to Native historical and linguistic knowledge.[43]

Du Ponceau's winning essay was built on Native knowledge, but only Du Ponceau gained scholarly prestige and 1200 francs. The Moravian materials that Heckewelder had provided, themselves rooted in what Native Brethren had shared with missionaries, were a crucial resource. Du Ponceau, however, needed more on the languages spoken around the Great Lakes. If not for Augustin Hamelin Jr. (Kanapima), an Odawa who had studied in Rome and provided him a vocabulary, Du Ponceau admitted, "we should yet know nothing of the Outawa."[44] Edwin James sent information on Menominee, Ojibwe, and the Athapaskan language Chipewyan that he had acquired from John Tanner, a former captive whom Anishinaabeg had taught their language; from at least one Menominee consultant; and from a Hudson's Bay Company trader married to a Chipewyan woman.[45] Du Ponceau also solicited material from the Indian agent at Sault Ste. Marie. Although Henry R. Schoolcraft had not yet established a wide reputation as an ethnologist, Du Ponceau trusted his philology because he knew Schoolcraft had a *"Chippeway wife."*[46] As in other aspects of his philology, Du Ponceau's *Memoire sur le système grammatical des langues de quelques nations indiennes de l'Amérique du Nord* (1838) relied on the network that he had stitched together letter by letter, built on the deeper foundation of Indigenous knowledge and the decisions of Native consultants to share what they knew with white collectors and scholars.

In some scholarly relationships, lines of reciprocity and authority were especially complex, and these provide an important window into the exchanges that disseminated linguistic knowledge and motivations of those who participated in them. An exchange of more than thirty letters, and accompanying manuscripts and books, between Du Ponceau and Albert Gallatin in spring 1826 provides an important example. They had known each other for decades by that point. In 1786 Gallatin had used Du Ponceau's legal services in a matter related to an inheritance, and the lawyer was among those who could publicly affirm, contrary to a story printed in a Virginia newspaper, that Gallatin had not been killed by Natives while surveying and speculating in western lands. With Gallatin's appointment as secretary of the treasury in 1801, Du Ponceau wrote to him on behalf of Federalist officeholders and foreign friends, again provided legal services, and requested of a copy of one of his reports that Congress had published in 1808.[47] The correspondence became more scholarly once Gallatin returned from a seven-year stint as U.S. minister to France. While in Paris, Gallatin had become close friends with Alexander von Humboldt, with whom he shared ethnographic and antiquarian interests.[48] Gallatin penned a "sketch of a synopsis of our

Indian tribes arranged as far as practicable, according to languages" in 1823, which Humboldt passed along to Adrien Balbi, an Italian geographer who included its information in his *L'Atlas ethnographique* (1826). Gallatin told Du Ponceau of his interests when he presented the APS (of which he was a member) with an annotated copy of a 1632 edition of Champlain's *Les Voyages de la Nouvelle France*, though Gallatin declined Du Ponceau's invitation to write something for the HLC's *Transactions*.[49] Instead, in spring 1826 Gallatin solicited information from Du Ponceau that would allow him to classify Native languages and understand social development—the interests that would guide Gallatin's philology and ethnology for the next two decades—to send to Humboldt for inclusion in a new edition of the explorer's *Political Essay on New Spain*.[50]

The three months of correspondence was remarkably deep. Gallatin initially wrote to Du Ponceau to communicate taxonomic findings, particularly related to the people of the Southeast and the Great Plains. In early writings Du Ponceau and Heckewelder had speculated that there was a single "Floridian" group of languages in the Southeast and that the languages spoken among the Sioux were related to those spoken among the Iroquois. By the time Gallatin wrote, Du Ponceau had already published a correction of the latter view on the basis of materials that he had urged the War Department to collect on the Long Expedition.[51] In opening his correspondence with Du Ponceau, Gallatin affirmed Du Ponceau's revised opinion and shared his own taxonomic views, particularly related to the Creeks, a polity in which several Muskogean languages were spoken as well as Yuchi and Natchez, two tongues unrelated to one another or to any other known languages. Gallatin also notified Du Ponceau that he had embarked upon a project to push the War Department to extend its efforts at linguistic collection and publication. He sought Du Ponceau's aid in finishing what he intended to send to Humboldt and in guiding the new federal project.[52]

That missive led to dozens more. "Secluded on the Monongahela," Gallatin was especially grateful for Du Ponceau's willingness to send his own and the HLC's materials, sometimes after having had extracts made, and to inform him of publications that he had missed.[53] They discussed philological problems, shared scholarly judgments, and rehearsed views that they would later publish.⁵⁴ Conflict also emerged in their intense exchange. Each expressed frustration with what the other did not know. Du Ponceau, for instance, found Gallatin's knowledge of American philology since 1819 to be disturbingly incomplete, while Gallatin thought that Du Ponceau should have paid closer attention to colonial-era Jesuit writings. Occasionally tempers flared, usually politely, though once Du Ponceau felt the need to apologize for an indecorous letter after the death of his only daughter and the grave illness of her son had "shattered my nerves and fevered my temper."⁵⁵ They also butted heads on what constituted useful publications, on the proper relationship between learned societies and the federal government, on the best means to obtain the desired information, and on the haste with which Du Ponceau thought Gallatin wanted to finish his work.⁵⁶ Their exchange deepened nonetheless. Their efforts produced few immediate results, but the collaboration was significant. By sharing their knowledge, materials, and criticisms while working together to produce the vocabulary and sample sentences that the War Department distributed to its Indian agents and missionaries receiving federal money, the two philologists established their scholarly authority in one another's eyes, expanded the range of linguistic knowledge that would allow them to further pursue their studies and enhance their reputations at home and abroad, and augmented the linguistic knowledge available to scholars and the administrators of colonialism.⁵⁷

Just as it was for Du Ponceau, Indigenous knowledge proved important for Gallatin. After he found a "copious" vocabulary of Cree (then commonly called "Knistenaux") in Daniel Williams Harmon's *Journal of Voyages and Travels into the Interior Part of North America* (1820), Gallatin contacted the U.S. senators from Vermont to open a direct correspondence with the author, a former clerk with the North West Company who now lived in that state. As he told Du Ponceau, "His wife is an Indian of that tribe, said to be a sensible woman," and both were "respectable."⁵⁸ More directly, Gallatin capitalized on a Creek delegation then in Washington City protesting the Treaty of Indian Springs (1825), an illegitimate removal treaty. The "Chiefs," Gallatin related, "assured" him that Hitchiti, Alabama, and Koasati were each "a dialect, though remote" of Muskogee, the multiethnic nation's dominant language.⁵⁹ Gallatin and

Du Ponceau were each especially interested in Yuchi and Natchez. Du Ponceau had only a "meagre" vocabulary of the former, and there were no known vocabularies of the latter. Through the offices of John Ridge, a missionary-educated Cherokee who acted as secretary for the Creek delegation, Gallatin received a Yuchi vocabulary, but he wanted to augment it. Articulating his sense of authority over his consultant, Gallatin told Du Ponceau, "I will make the Uchee chief repeat the sounds in my hearing."[60] Gallatin was also able to obtain a Natchez vocabulary directly "from the lips" of Is-ah-laktih, an "intelligent & good humoured" Natchez chief.[61] Du Ponceau was surprised. As he told Gallatin, "I thought that nation entirely lost—It does you great honor to have resuscitated it."[62] Given the prevalence of the notion that Native languages were dying tongues, the metaphor is striking, but inaccurate. Gallatin did not revive Natchez; he merely wrote down the words of a man whose people had successfully maintained their tongue against pressure from both English speakers and the Muskogee majority among the Creeks.[63] Gallatin could do so only because Is-ah-laktih was willing to share his time and knowledge.

Countless other Native consultants made similar decisions. Each had reasons of their own, undoubtedly, and the limits of the sources can make those intentions difficult to trace. A tremendous amount of linguistic knowledge emerged from Christian missions, and, in those instances, Native participation in the creation and dissemination of linguistic knowledge was most often a decision, primarily, to aid missionaries, and subject to the host of spiritual and temporal considerations that guided such decisions.[64] At other times, from the Ohio River to the Gila River, Miamis, Maricopas, and others chose to exchange linguistic information for money or food.[65] Other Indigenous consultants, such as Eleazer Williams and David Brown, sought scholarly reputations, aiding white collectors and philologists, and authoring their own philology as well.[66]

An exchange that Gallatin had with another Native consultant suggests an additional reason, linked to struggles over Native autonomy amid colonialism even more explicitly than what is extant in Du Ponceau's papers.[67] In addition to vocabularies of languages spoken among Creeks and Cherokees, Gallatin wanted John Ridge to provide him with a description of Cherokee society. Ridge ignored Gallatin's request for a year. At the limits of his patience, apparently, Gallatin contacted the director of the Indian office, hoping that he would intercede on Gallatin's behalf. To the director, Thomas L. McKenney, Gallatin framed what he hoped would be a persuasive case. It was in Ridge's interest to comply, Gallatin explained, because of "the favourable effect which, if published by Humboldt, this essay written by a native Indian may have on public opinion both here and abroad... and I may add that it gives an opportunity to Mr Ridge to obtain a general reputation which he may not again meet with." Although we should be wary of ascribing Gallatin's view to Ridge himself, it is striking that, after that note, Ridge provided the essay and another vocabulary within days.[68] Although many of his philological contemporaries mentioned their reliance on Native participation, and some expressed misgivings about the conduct of Indian affairs, Gallatin here expressed a rare understanding that power shaped what philologists could study. The opportunity to influence "public opinion"—in the United States and in Europe—just as Congress was considering a removal bill in 1826 was not lost on Ridge, and he took it, just as he and other Cherokee activists sought to publicize Cherokee "civilization" to combat removal for the next decade.[69] At the same time, without Native participation, U.S. philologists would not have been able to produce the scholarship they produced and they would not have been able to establish themselves as securely in Atlantic scholarly networks.

Metaphors of dying languages and a resuscitated language bookend this essay. They speak to prevailing, power-laden prejudices, but also to the unexpected results that philology could produce. Euro-American knowledge of Native languages was always embedded in power. The sources of information that scholars relied upon—missionaries, traders, Indian agents, military officers, and, most important, Native people themselves—illustrate the braided strands of philology and colonialism. While the power directly exercised by those figures was most significant to the colonized, other power relations pervaded philology as well. Those power relations, this essay has argued, can be best understood by examining the networks that scholars such as Peter S. Du Ponceau constructed as they pursued research and disseminated what they learned.

Philologists of unequal standing and from distant places wrote letters to one another to share information about their own or others' researches, and to engage in the scholarly work of synopsis, clarification, criticism, and debate. They also exchanged daunting masses of manuscripts and books. Even as colonizers pursuing varied schemes used philology as an instrument of power against Native communities, U.S. philologists wielded it to establish themselves as equal scholars in a European-led linguistic project. Close examination of the scholarly correspondence and related papers clearly reveal the degree to which Indigenous participation was central not only to linguistic description and theorization but also to relations among Euro-American scholars pursuing a global project that was cosmopolitan in aspiration and, in North America, colonialist in practice. The motives, and even identities, of many of the Native consultants can be difficult to recover—though each of the innumerable instances that can be found in diverse archives presents a potential avenue of further research.

NOTES

1. Peter S. Du Ponceau to Thomas Jefferson, December 11, 1817, Letter Books of the Historical and Literary Committee (HLC Letter Books), American Philosophical Society (APS), 1:61–63. On *Mithridates*, see Robins, *Short History of Linguistics*, 59–60, 194.
2. Du Ponceau to Frederick Adelung, December 16, 1817, March 17, 1821, HLC Letter Books, 2:1–2, 39. The relevant portion of 1821 letter, originally in French, reads: "Magnifique présent de livres précieux et rares en diverses langues." For the review, see [Peter S. Du Ponceau], "For the Port Folio," *Port-Folio* (April 1818), 276–77. On Du Ponceau's authorship of the review, see Levette Harris to Du Ponceau, April 23, 1818, Peter S. Du Ponceau Collection, APS. Du Ponceau sent "English Phonology; Or an Essay towards an Analysis and Description of the Component Sounds of the English Language," *Transactions of the American Philosophical Society* 1 (1818).
3. Du Ponceau to John Heckewelder, August 3, 1816, HLC Letter Books, 1:42–43; Du Ponceau to Eleazer Williams, December 17, 1817, HLC Letter Books, 2:3. See also Jason Chamberlain to Du Ponceau, August 28, 1817, in Du Ponceau Collection, APS. On linguistic collection as a "science of the vanished," see Gray, *New World Babel*, 112–38. For a critique of the way linguists' metaphors obscure colonialism, see Perley, "Zombie Linguistics," 133–149, especially 137–41.

4. For Williams's philological contributions, see Samuel F. Jarvis to Du Ponceau, January 11, 1820, Peter S. Du Ponceau Papers, Historical Society of Pennsylvania (HSP), Box 1, Folder 3; Jarvis, "Indian Tribes of North America," 234, 246–248; Lewis Cass to Eleazer Williams, July 13, 1825, Lewis Cass Papers, Clements Library, vol. 3; [Peter S. Du Ponceau], "Philology," vol. 10 (1832), 86. See also Harvey, *Native Tongues*, 102, 111, 133–34, 160. On Williams's life, see Oberg, *Professional Indian*.
5. Du Ponceau to Adelung, March 17, 1821, in HLC Letter Books, 2:39. The original reads: "Vous fournir les notices sur les langues de nos sauvages, que je croirai pouvoir vous etres utiles, et qu'on ne peut obtenir que sur les lieux."
6. Du Ponceau to Albert Gallatin, March 12, 1835, Du Ponceau Papers, HSP.
7. Gray, *New World Babel*, 85–158, has cataloged ideas of "savage" tongues, stressed scholars' preoccupation with preserving specimens of dying languages, and Du Ponceau's romantic-nationalist poetics. On cultural nationalism, see also Greene, *American Science*, 376–408; and Andresen, *Linguistics in America*, 22–135. On the epistemological consequences of such projects, see Rivett, *Unscripted America*. Harvey, *Native Tongues*, stresses the framework of colonialism in terms of ongoing missionary projects, justifications for dispossession, administratively useful classifications, and the significance of linguistic ideas for ideas about race. For comparative purposes, see Errington, *Linguistics in a Colonial World*; and Turner, *Philology*.
8. For studies of early U.S. science that stress cultural nationalism, see Hindle, *Pursuit of Science*; and Greene, *American Science*. On professionalization, see Daniels, *American Science in the Age of Jackson*. For case studies of particular institutions, see Oleson and Brown, *Pursuit of Knowledge*. On conflict over institutions and authority, see Baatz, "Philadelphia Patronage," 111–38; and Lewis, *Democracy of Facts*. For a recent historiographic review, see Valencius et al., "Science in Early America," 73–123.
9. On extending the concept of a republic of letters to the mid-nineteenth century, see Burke, "Republic of Letters," 397–99. On transatlantic power imbalances, see Dierks, "Letter Writing," 167–98; and Yokota, *Unbecoming British*, 153–225. See also Winterer, "Where Is America," 597–623. For work that has stressed the significance of Indigenous knowledge, see Parrish, *American Curiosities*; and Safier, "Global Knowledge," 133–45.
10. On eighteenth- and early nineteenth-century epistolary culture, see Bannet, *Empire of Letters*; Dierks, *In My Power*; and Pearsall, *Atlantic Families*. On the shifting purpose of the postal system toward linking a nation of letter readers and writers, as opposed to the earlier focus on linking representatives and constituents and newspaper readers across the country, see Henkin, *Postal Age*.
11. The Massachusetts Historical Society was established in 1791, the New York Historical Society was established in 1804, and the American Antiquarian Society

was established in 1812. On Du Ponceau's place in Philadelphia's broader associational life, see Koschnik, *Let a Common Interest*, 23–26, 186, 195, 220–22; and Furstenberg, *When the United States Spoke French*, 106–7, 242–43.

12. Du Ponceau to Thomas Jefferson, November 14, 1815, in HLC Letter Books, 1:1–2; Du Ponceau to Elias Boudinot, November 17, 1815, HLC Letter Books, 1:2–3. See also Du Ponceau to Benjamin R. Morgan, December 2, 1815, in HLC Letter Books, 1:7–8.
13. Du Ponceau to Jefferson, February 17, 1817, in HLC Letter Books, 1:57–59.
14. Jefferson to Du Ponceau, November 7, 1817, in Jackson, ed., *Letters of the Lewis and Clark Expedition*, 631–33; Du Ponceau to Jefferson, January 22, 1818, HLC Letter Books, 2:6–7. Jefferson had asserted that a recently acquired Nottoway vocabulary was spoken by a "component" of the "Powhatan confederacy," but Du Ponceau assured him of its "decided Iroquois physiognomy." See Jefferson to Du Ponceau, July 7, 1820, in Thomas Jefferson Papers, APS; and Du Ponceau to Jefferson, July 12, 1820, HLC Letter Books, 2:32–33.
15. Du Ponceau to Eliza C. Tunstall, January 11, 1819, in HLC Letter Books, 2:23. See also 2:12–14, 16–21, and 3:3–5.
16. Du Ponceau to Monsieur le Vicar General du Diocese du Quebec, March 30, 1818, in HLC Letter Books, 2:10–11; Du Ponceau to Poinsett, August 15, 1827, in Joel Roberts Poinsett Papers, HSP, 4:125–126.
17. Heckewelder to Du Ponceau, November 8, 1818, March 21, July 18, 1819, in John Gottlieb Ernestus Heckewelder Letters to Peter Stephen Du Ponceau, 1816–22, APS. The missionary in question was Frederick Christian Dencke. For other original correspondence, see HLC Letter Books, 1:11–12, 39–52; John Gottlieb Ernestus Heckewelder, "Communications to the Historical and Literary Committee of the American Philosophical Society," APS; Peter S. Du Ponceau Letters, Wisconsin State Historical Society. The highly edited published version can be found in Du Ponceau, "Correspondence," 358–59. For the significance of this project in light of missionary efforts, see Harvey, *Native Tongues*, 80–181.
18. Du Ponceau to John Pickering, March 3, 1820, in Du Ponceau Papers, HSP, Box 3.
19. Du Ponceau to Timothy Pickering, October 28, 1817, Timothy Pickering Papers, 16:229, Massachusetts Historical Society; Du Ponceau to Pickering, June 6, 1818, February 13, 1819, Du Ponceau Papers, HSP, Box 3; Pickering, *Life of John Pickering*, 266–80.
20. Pickering, *Life*, 281–90.
21. Du Ponceau to Pickering, June 3, 1822, in Du Ponceau Papers, HSP Box 3. Malenfant was also mentioned in Du Ponceau to Gallatin, May 2, 1826, Peter Stephen Du Ponceau Letters, 1801–43, to Albert Gallatin (Mss.Film.541), APS . One can find Malenfant's full name as a witness in a nonphilological matter in Du Ponceau to Albert Gallatin, July 10, 1797, Papers of Albert Gallatin (PAG), New York University and National Historical Publications Commission Microfilm Set, Reel 3.

22. For the dynamics of philology and print culture, see Harvey, *Native Tongues*, 102, 110–14, 120–23, and 153.
23. Du Ponceau to Pickering, November 20, December 29, 1825, June 23, 1828, Pickering to Du Ponceau, September 22, 1840, Du Ponceau Papers, HSP, Box 3. Pickering sought to correspond with the biblical scholar and philologist Freidrich Schleiermacher.
24. Du Ponceau to Pickering, August 22, 1839, Pickering to Du Ponceau, April 17, 1840, Du Ponceau Papers, HSP, Box 3. See also Pickering, *Life*, 409; Voigt, "Life and Works of Mrs. Therese Robinson," 59–63.
25. Du Ponceau to Pickering, July 15, 1826; Pickering to Du Ponceau, January 1, 1839, Du Ponceau Papers, HSP, Box 3.
26. See Foletta, *Coming to Terms with Democracy*; and Koschnik, *Let a Common Interest*, 184–227. More broadly, on party amalgamation in this era, see Livermore Jr., *Twilight of Federalism*; and Hofstadter, *Idea of a Party System*, 170–211.
27. Du Ponceau to John Quincy Adams, February 16, 1818, in HLC Letter Books, 2:9.
28. Pickering to Du Ponceau, December 12, 1820, in Pickering, *Life of John Pickering*, 290.
29. Du Poneau to Pickering, January 14, 1823, Du Ponceau Papers, HSP, Box 3. See also John, *Spreading the News*, 25–63.
30. Pickering to Du Ponceau, October 5, 1835, Du Ponceau Papers, HSP, Box 3; Du Ponceau to Vater, March 13, 1822, HLC Letter Books, 3:6–7. For fears of rivalries over federal patronage, see Gallatin to Du Ponceau, April 17, 1826, Du Ponceau Papers, HSP, Box 1, Folder 8. On American complaints about professional obligations interfering with research, see Dierks, "Letter Writing," 173–74. Although it inexplicably neglects philology, see also Ferguson, "Emulation of Sir William Jones," 2–26. On the problem of patronage in the arts and sciences in the early republic, see Ellis, *After the Revolution*, 23–39.
31. Du Ponceau to J. S. Vater, October 6, 1819; February 2, 1820; February 16, March 29 ("before unknown"), September 9, September 13, and October 5, 1821, in HLC Letter Books, 2:25, 27–28, 38, 41–42, 54–55, 57–58, 59. On the university at Konigsberg, see Lifschitz, *Language and Enlightenment*, 65. On the APS and the Long Expedition, see "Concerning Inquiries"; and U. S. War Department to Robert Walsh, April 7, 1819, in APS Archives, Record Group 3.
32. The sources for these vocabularies can be found in Du Ponceau, "Indian Vocabularies," 19, 26–27, 53, 57, 61, 86, and 114.
33. Du Ponceau to Vater, March 13, October 20, 1822, in HLC Letter Books, 3:6–7, 15–17. On the "Index linguarum," see Du Ponceau to Vater, February 2, 1820, in HLC Letter Books, 2: 27–28. On equal correspondence as the expectation among equals, see Dierks, "Letter Writing," 173–74. On Vater, see Robins, *Short History of Linguistics*, 59–60, 194; and Turner, *Philology*, 125–26.

34. Du Ponceau to Vater, October 20, 1822, in HLC Letter Books, 3:15–17. On this project, see also Du Ponceau to Gallatin, May 13, 1826, Du Ponceau Letters to Gallatin, APS.
35. [Peter S. Du Ponceau], "Babylonian Bricks," 49 ("most learned orientialist"); Du Ponceau to Joseph von Hammer, April 25, December 22, 1822; January 5, 1823, in HLC Letter Books, 3:10–12, 20–21, 32; von Hammer to Du Ponceau, February 1819, in Du Ponceau Papers, HSP, Box 1, Folder 2; von Hammer to Du Ponceau, September 30, 1821, in Du Ponceau Papers, HSP, Box 1, Folder 5; von Hammer to Du Ponceau, March 21, 1824; April 25, 1825, in Box 1, Folder 7; von Hammer to Du Ponceau, November 30, 1828 ("amongst the first philologists"), in box 1, Folder 10; von Hammer to Du Ponceau, February 1840, in box 2, Folder 10. See also F. C. Schaffer to Du Ponceau, April 7, 1820, in box 1, Folder 3. On Von Hammer-Purgstall, see Marchand, *German Orientalism*, 70–73, 87, 98–104.
36. Du Ponceau to Gallatin, April 2, 1835, Du Ponceau Letters to Gallatin, APS; Du Ponceau to Pickering, September 4, 1828, Du Ponceau Papers, HSP, Box 3. Du Ponceau shared such views with Frederick Christian Schaffer, the editor of the *German Correspondent*, who had initiated an exchange with him. See, for instance, Schaffer to Du Ponceau, February 16, Aug. 6, 1820, in Du Ponceau Papers, HSP, Box 1, Folder 3. See also Du Ponceau, *Discourse on the Necessity*, 24.
37. Du Ponceau to Wilhelm von Humboldt, July 28, 1821, HLC Letter Books, 48–49. On a report that the Prussian king's council sought to acquire U.S. books, see Du Ponceau to Alexander von Humboldt, July 27, 1821, in HLC Letter Books, 2:43–44. On the beginning of the Pickering-Humboldt correspondence, see George Bancroft to John Pickering, April 12, 1821, in Pickering, *Life of John Pickering*, 299–301; Wilhem von Humboldt to Pickering, February 24, 1821, in Müller-Vollmer, ed., "Wilhelm von Humboldt." See also Sweet, *Wilhelm von Humboldt*, vol. 2, 398–406. The English reviewer's question is quoted in Green, "Rise of Book Publishing," vol. 2, 106.
38. Du Ponceau to John Vaughan, April 9, 1838, Du Ponceau Collection, APS. On the complex dynamics of American participation in transatlantic natural history networks, see Parrish, *American Curiosities*; and Yokota, *Unbecoming British*, 153–225.
39. "A.P.S. Report of Committee on Dr. Edwin James's Communication of the Menomonie Indians, c. February 1827," APS Archives; James to Du Ponceau, June 16, 1827, Gratz Collection, HSP, Case 7, Box 23; James to Du Ponceau, January 19, 1828, Michigan Papers, William L. Clements Library, Ann Arbor. See also Edwin James, "Some Account of the Menomonies with a Specimen of an Attempt to form a Dictionary of their Language, by Edwin James, an Assistant Surgeon of the U. S. Army" (1827), APS; James to Du Ponceau, May 10, 1828, Du Ponceau Papers, HSP. Although the focus is on archaeology, Lewis, *Democracy of Facts*, 72–106,

explores the relationship between western collectors and eastern scholars and institutions.

40. Francis Lieber to Du Ponceau, May 9, June 3, 1837, Gratz Collection, Case 6, Box 32.
41. Du Ponceau to Pickering, September 27, July 23, 1835; August 28, 1834, Du Ponceau Papers, HSP, Box 3. For both of Du Ponceau's Prix Volney treatises as well as essays on their place in the history of linguistics, see Leopold, ed., *Early Nineteenth-Century Contributions to Amerindian and General Linguistics*.
42. Edwin James to Du Ponceau, December 12, 1835, Du Ponceau Papers, HSP. See also Du Ponceau to Pickering, August 28, 1834.
43. A "translation" of the Walum Olam can be found in Rafinesque, *American Nations*. See also Rafinesque, "Important Historical and Philological Discovery," 2. For records of Du Ponceau keeping what Rafinesque sent, see Historical and Literary Committee Vocabularies and Miscellaneous Papers Pertaining to Indian Languages, nos. 25–26, APS; Peter S. Du Ponceau, Notebooks on Philology, 6:29–38, APS. On the hoax, see Oestreicher, "Roots of the Walam Olum."
44. Du Ponceau to Gallatin, April 22, 1835, PAG, supplement reel. See also Peter S. Du Ponceau, "Indian Vocabularies Collected September 1820," no. 74, APS. On Hamelin, see McKenney, *History of the Indian Tribes*, 3 vols., 1:263–65.
45. James sent at least eleven letters in the latter half of the year, including a comparative vocabulary of those tongues and, in a letter on especially large and thick pages, a table containing the various conjugations of an Ojibwe verb. See James to Du Ponceau, June 27, July 24, September 22, October 2, November 11, November 19, November 22, November 28, December 1, December 2, December 29, in Du Ponceau Papers, HSP, Box 2, Folder 5. The detail of the HBC factor and his Chipewyan wife is in James to Du Ponceau, November 8, 1828, Gratz Collection, HSP, Case 7, Box 23.
46. Du Ponceau to Gallatin, April 22, 1835, PAG, supplement reel; Henry R. Schoolcraft to R. Wilmot Griswold, October 28, 1841, in Gratz Collection, HSP, Case 7, Box 9. See also James to Du Ponceau, January 19, 1828, Michigan Papers, Clements Library.
47. Peter S. Du Ponceau to John Jay, May 14, 1786, in PAG, Reel 1; Du Ponceau to Gallatin, February 1, December 13, 1801; July 28, August 11, 1804; May 28, 1808, Du Ponceau Letters to Gallatin, APS.
48. Alexander von Humboldt to Albert Gallatin, [1822?], in Schwarz, ed., *Alexander von Humboldt und die Vereinigten Staaten von Amerika Briefwechsel*, 160 ("très mal rédigée"). For Du Ponceau's shipment of that volume, see Du Ponceau to Humboldt, July 27, 1821, in HLC Letter Books, 2:43–44.
49. Gallatin to Du Ponceau, March 20, 1826, Du Ponceau Papers, HSP, Box 1, Folder 8; Du Ponceau to John Vaughan, July 17, 1823, APS Archives, Record Group 3. See also Gallatin, "Synopsis of the Indian Tribes," 1.

50. Humboldt to Gallatin, February 22, 1825; Gallatin to Humboldt, February 23, March 24, 1826, in Schwarz, ed., *Alexander von Humboldt*, 169, 173, 175–79.

51. Du Ponceau rejected his previous belief in a "chain of connection" that linked Iroquoian and Siouan languages, and he asserted that Sioux and Pawnee were "the two great *Ultra-Mississippian* Languages." See Ponceau, quoted in [Pickering], "Explanatory Remarks," 149. For their earlier speculations, see Du Ponceau, "Report of the Corresponding Secretary," xxxiii–xxxv; and Heckewelder, "Account of the History," 105, 112–14.

52. Gallatin to Du Ponceau, March 20, 1826, Du Ponceau Papers, HSP, Box 1, Folder 8. Gallatin had only recently become aware of Du Ponceau's correction. See Gallatin to Humboldt, February 23, 1826, in Schwarz, ed., *Alexander von Humboldt*, 173. For differing interpretations of this War Department project, see Harvey, *Native Tongues*, 77–78, 154–55; and Strang, "Scientific Instructions and Native American Linguistics in the Imperial United States," 399–427.

53. Du Ponceau to Gallatin, March 22, 1826, Du Ponceau Letters to Gallatin, APS; Gallatin to Du Ponceau, April 3, 1826 (quote), Du Ponceau Papers, HSP, Box 1, Folder 8. On extracts, see Du Ponceau to Gallatin, May 2, 16, 1826, Du Ponceau Letters to Gallatin, APS.

54. On reading, see Gallatin to Du Ponceau, March 29, April 4, 1826, Du Ponceau Papers, HSP, Box 1, Folder 8. On judgments, see Du Ponceau to Gallatin, March 22, April 2, April 18, 1826, Du Ponceau Letters to Gallatin, APS; Gallatin to Du Ponceau, April 24, May 17, 1826, Du Ponceau Papers, HSP, Box 1, Folder 8. On rehearsals for later publication, see Gallatin to Du Ponceau, March 20, 29, May 9, 17, 1826, Du Ponceau Papers, HSP, Box 1, Folder 8; and Du Ponceau to Gallatin, April 6, April 18, 1826, Du Ponceau Letters to Gallatin, APS.

55. Du Ponceau to Gallatin, April 17, 1826, Du Ponceau Letters to Gallatin, APS. On each other's ignorance, see Du Ponceau to Gallatin, April 6, 1826, Du Ponceau Letters to Gallatin, APS; Gallatin to Du Ponceau, May 5, 1826, Du Ponceau Papers, HSP, Box 1, Folder 8.

56. On useful publications, see Du Ponceau to Gallatin, March 22, 1826, Du Ponceau Letters to Gallatin, APS; Gallatin to Du Ponceau, March 29, 1826, Du Ponceau Papers, HSP, Box 1, Folder 8. On federal roles, see Gallatin to Du Ponceau, March 20, 1826, Du Ponceau Papers, HSP, Box 1, Folder 8; Du Ponceau to Gallatin, April 15,1826, Du Ponceau Letters to Gallatin, APS. On the particulars of collecting, see Du Ponceau to Gallatin, April 2, 1826, Du Ponceau Letters to Gallatin, APS; Gallatin to Du Ponceau, April 17, 1826, Du Ponceau Papers, HSP, Box 1, Folder 8. On Gallatin's haste, see Du Ponceau to Gallatin, April 2, 15, 1826, Du Ponceau Letters to Gallatin, APS.

57. Du Ponceau to Gallatin, May 13, 1826, Du Ponceau Letters to Gallatin, APS.

58. Gallatin to Du Ponceau, May 2, 1826, Du Ponceau Papers, HSP, Box 1, Folder 8.

59. Gallatin to Du Ponceau, March 20, 1826, Du Ponceau Papers, HSP, Box 1, Folder 8.
60. Du Ponceau to Gallatin, May 13, March 22, 1826, Du Ponceau Letters to Gallatin, APS; Gallatin to Du Ponceau, March 29, 1826, Du Ponceau Papers, HSP, Box 1, Folder 8.
61. Gallatin to Du Ponceau, March 29, April 12, 1826, in Du Ponceau Papers, HSP, Box 1, Folder 8; Gallatin, "Synopsis of the Indian Tribes," 97.
62. Du Ponceau to Gallatin, April 26, 1826, Du Ponceau Letters to Gallatin, APS.
63. For a Natchez view of Creek diversity, see Stiggins, "Historical Narration," 1–47, at 19–31. For a consideration of this account's significance, see Harvey, "Native Views of Native Languages," 651–84, especially 670–73.
64. For an examination of decisions regarding "affiliation" with Christian missions, see Fisher, *Indian Great Awakening*, 7–8. The literature on missionary linguistics is large and growing. To start, see Harvey and Rivett, "Colonial-Indigenous Language Encounters," 442–73, especially 454–59.
65. On paying Native consultants, see, for example, Charles C. Trowbridge to Lewis Cass, March 6, 1826, in Trowbridge, *Meearmeear Traditions*, ed. Vernon Kinietz, *Occasional Contributions from the Museum of Anthropology of the University of Michigan*, no. 7 (Ann Arbor: University of Michigan Press, 1938), 1; and Bartlett, *Personal Narrative*, 452–53.
66. D. S. Butrick and D. Brown, *Tsvlvki Sqclvclv. A Cherokee Spelling Book, for the Mission Establishment at Brainerd* (Knoxville, 1819); Eleazer Williams, "Grammar of the Mohawk Dialect of the Iroquois Language," Mss. Film 578, APS. For Brown's unattributed work on a Cherokee grammar, see Pickering, *Life of John Pickering*, 332–33. On Williams's unsuccessful effort to get the APS to publish it, see Eleazer Williams to Du Ponceau, June 24, 1838, in Gratz Collection, HSP, Case 8, Box 20; Meeting, July 10, 1840, in Minutes of the Historical and Literary Committee, July 10, 1840–November 8, 1843, 2; Williams to secretary of the APS, April 18, 1854, in APS Archives, Record Group 2E. For a consideration of Native struggles for "proprietary authorship," see Round, *Removable Type*, 150–72.
67. Precisely because of the way Gallatin's scholarship benefited from colonialist pressures and aided facets of colonialism as diverse as evangelization and administrative taxonomy, I do not go as far as Strang, "Scientific Instructions," in interpreting Gallatin as "anti-imperial."
68. Gallatin to Thomas L. McKenney, March 4, 1826, PAG, Reel 36. See also McKenney to Gallatin, April 1825, PAG, Reel 36; Gallatin to Du Ponceau, March 29, April 12, 1826, in Du Ponceau Papers, HSP, Box 1, Folder 8. Ridge's essay can be found in Sturtevant, ed., "John Ridge on Cherokee Civilization," 79–91.
69. On such efforts, see Konkle, *Writing Indian Nations*, 78–96; Wyss, *English Letters and Indian Literacies*, 150–210; and Harvey, *Native Tongues*, 124–32.

BIBLIOGRAPHY

Andresen, Julie Tetel. *Linguistics in America, 1769-1924.* London: Routledge, 1990.

American Philosophical Society, Philadelphia (APS).
- APS Archives, Record Group 2E
- APS Archives, Record Group 3
- Communications to the Historical and Literary Committee of the American Philosophical Society
- Eleazer Williams, "Grammar of the Mohawk Dialect of the Iroquois Language," Mss. Film 578
- Historical and Literary Committee Letter Books
- Historical and Literary Committee Vocabularies and Miscellaneous Papers Pertaining to Indian Languages
- Indian Vocabularies, 1820-1844
- John Gottlieb Ernestus Heckewelder Letters to Peter Stephen Du Ponceau
- Peter Stephen Du Ponceau Collection
- Peter Stephen Du Ponceau Letters, 1801-43, to Albert Gallatin (Mss.Film.541)
- Peter Stephen Du Ponceau Notebooks on Philology
- Some Account of the Menomonies with a Specimen of an Attempt to form a Dictionary of their Language, by Edwin James, an Assistant Surgeon of the U. S. Army
- Thomas Jefferson Papers

Baatz, Simon. "Philadelphia Patronage: The Institutional Structure of Natural History in the New Republic, 1800-1833." *Journal of the Early Republic* 8 (1988): 111-38.

Bannet, Eve Tavor. *Empire of Letters: Letter Manuals and Transatlantic Correspondence, 1680-1820.* New York: Cambridge University Press, 2005.

Bartlett, John Russell. *Personal Narrative of Explorations and Incidents in Texas, New Mexico, California, Sonora, and Chihuahua, connected with the United States and Mexican Boundary Commission, during the years 1851, '51, '52, and '53.* New York: Appleton, 1854.

Burke, Peter. "The Republic of Letters as a Communication System: An Essay in Periodization." *Media History* 18, nos. 3-4 (2012): 397-99.

Butrick, D. S., and D. Brown. *Tsvlvki Sqclvclv. A Cherokee Spelling Book, for the Mission Establishment at Brainerd.* Knoxville TN: F. S. Heiskell & H. Brown, 1819.

Daniels, George. *American Science in the Age of Jackson.* New York: Columbia University Press, 1968.

Dierks, Konstantin. *In My Power: Letter Writing and Communications in Early America.* Philadelphia: University of Pennsylvania Press, 2009.

———. "Letter Writing, Masculinity, and American Men of Science, 1750-1800." *Pennsylvania History* 65 (1998): 167-98.

[Du Ponceau, Peter S.] "Babylonian Bricks." *German Correspondent,* May 23, 1820, n.p.

———. "A Correspondence between the Rev. John Heckewelder, of Bethlehem, and Peter S. Du Ponceau, Esq., . . . Respecting the Languages of the American Indians." *Transactions of the Historical and Literary Committee of the American Philosophical Society*, 1 (1819): 351–448.

———. *A Discourse on the Necessity and Means of Making Our National Literature Independent of That of Great Britain, Delivered Before the Members of the Pennsylvania Library of Foreign Literature and Science, on Saturday, February 15, 1834*. Philadelphia: E. G. Dorsey, 1834.

———. "English Phonology; or An Essay towards an Analysis and Description of the Component Sounds of the English Language." *Transactions of the American Philosophical Society* 1: (1818): 228–64.

———. "For the Port Folio." *Port-Folio*, April 1818, 276–77.

———. "Philology." In *Encyclopedia Americana: A Popular Dictionary of Arts, Sciences, Literature, History, Politics and Biography, Brought Down to the Present Time; Including a Copious Collection of Original Articles in American Biography; On the Basis of the Basis of the Seventh Edition of the German Conversations-Lexicon*. Vol. 10. Edited by Francis Lieber, 81–93. N.p., 1832.

———. "Report of the Corresponding Secretary." In *Transactions of the Historical and Literary Committee of the American Philosophical Society* 1 (1819): xvii–lvi.

Ellis, Joseph J. *After the Revolution: Profiles in Early American Culture*. New York: Norton, [1979] 2002.

Errington, Joseph. *Linguistics in a Colonial World: A Story of Language, Meaning, and Power*. Malden MA: Blackwell, 2008.

Ferguson, Robert A. "The Emulation of Sir William Jones in the Early Republic." *New England Quarterly* 52 (1979): 2–26.

Fisher, Linford D. *The Indian Great Awakening: Religion and the Shaping of Native Cultures in Early America*. New York: Oxford University Press, 2012.

Foletta, Marshall. *Coming to Terms with Democracy: Federalist Intellectuals and the Shaping of American Culture*. Charlottesville: University of Virginia Press, 2001.

Furstenberg, François. *When the United States Spoke French: Five Refugees Who Shaped a Nation*. New York: Penguin, 2014.

Gallatin, Albert. "A Synopsis of the Indian Tribes within the United States East of the Rocky Mountains, and in the British and Russian Possessions in North America." *Archaeologia Americana: Transactions of the American Antiquarian Society* 2 (1836): 1–422.

Gray, Edward G. *New World Babel: Languages and Nations in Early America*. Princeton NJ: Princeton University Press, 1999.

Green, James N. "The Rise of Book Publishing." In *An Extensive Republic: Print, Culture, and Society in the New Nation, 1790–1840*, edited by Robert A. Gross and Mary Kelley, 75–126. A History of the Book in America, vol. 2. Chapel Hill: University of North Carolina Press, 2010.

Greene, John C. *American Science in the Age of Jefferson*. Ames: Iowa State University Press, 1984.

Harvey, Sean P. *Native Tongues: Colonialism and Race from Encounter to the Reservation*. Cambridge MA: Harvard University Press, 2015.

——— . "Native Views of Native Languages: Communication and Kinship in Eastern North America, ca. 1800–1830." *William and Mary Quarterly* 75, no. 4 (October 2018): 651–84.

Harvey, Sean P., and Sarah Rivett. "Colonial-Indigenous Language Encounters in North America and the Intellectual History of the Atlantic World." *Early American Studies* 15, no. 3 (Summer 2017): 442–73.

Heckewelder, John. "An Account of the History, Manners, and Customs, of the Indian Nations, Who Once Inhabited Pennsylvania and the Neighbouring States." *Transactions of the Historical and Literary Committee of the American Philosophical Society* 1 (1819): 1–347.

Henkin, David M. *The Postal Age: The Emergence of Modern Communications in Nineteenth-Century America*. Chicago: University of Chicago Press, 2006.

Hindle, Brooke. *The Pursuit of Science in Revolutionary America, 1735–1789*. New York: Norton, 1974.

Historical Society of Pennsylvania, Philadelphia (HSP).
    Gratz Collection
    Joel Roberts Poinsett Papers
    Peter S. Du Ponceau Papers

Hofstadter, Richard. *The Idea of a Party System*. Berkeley: University of California Press, 1969.

Jackson, Donald, ed., *Letters of the Lewis and Clark Expedition with Related Documents, 1783–1854*. Urbana: University of Illinois Press, 1962.

Jarvis, Samuel F. "A Discourse on the Religion of the Indian Tribes of North America." *Collections of the New York Historical Society* 3 (1821): 183–268.

John, Richard R. *Spreading the News: The American Postal System from Franklin to Morse*. Cambridge MA: Harvard University Press, 1995.

Kinietz, Vernon. *Meearmeear Traditions*. Occasional Contributions from the Museum of Anthropology of the University of Michigan, no. 7. Ann Arbor: University of Michigan Press, 1938.

Konkle, Maureen. *Writing Indian Nations: Native Intellectuals and the Politics of Historiography*. Chapel Hill: University of North Carolina Press, 2004.

Koschnik, Albrecht. *Let a Common Interest Bind Us Together: Associations, Partisanship, and Culture in Philadelphia, 1775–1840*. Charlottesville: University of Virginia Press, 2007.

Leopold, Joan, ed. *Early Nineteenth-Century Contributions to General and Amerindian Linguistics: Du Ponceau and Rafinesque*. The Prix Volney, vol. 2. Dordrecht: Kluwer, 1999.

Lewis, Andrew J. *Democracy of Facts: Natural History in the Early Republic.* Philadelphia: University of Pennsylvania Press, 2011.
Lifschitz, Avi. *Language and Enlightenment: The Berlin Debates of the Eighteenth Century.* New York: Oxford University Press, 2012.
Livermore, Shaw, Jr. *The Twilight of Federalism: The Disintegration of the Federalist Party.* Princeton NJ: Princeton University Press, 1962.
Marchand, Suzanne L. *German Orientalism in the Age of Empire: Religion, Race, and Scholarship.* New York: Cambridge University Press, 2010.
Massachusetts Historical Society.
    Timothy Pickering Papers.
McKenney, Thomas L. *History of the Indian Tribes of North America, with Biographical Sketches and Anecdotes of the Principal Chiefs.* 3 vols. Philadelphia: Rice, Rutter, 1870.
Müller-Vollmer, Kurt, ed. "Wilhelm von Humboldt und der Anfang der amerikanischen Sprachwissenschaft: Die briefe an John Pickering." In *Universalismus und Wissenschaft im Werk und Wirken der Brüder Humboldt*, 259–316. Frankfurt am Main: Vittorio Klostermann, 1974.
New York Historical Society.
    Papers of Albert Gallatin (New York University and National Historical Publications Commission Microfilm Set)
Oberg, Michael Leroy. *Professional Indian: The American Odyssey of Eleazer Williams.* Philadelphia: University of Pennsylvania Press, 2015.
Oestreicher, David M. "Roots of the Walam Olum: Constantine Samuel Rafinesque and the Intellectual Heritage of the Early Nineteenth Century." In *New Perspectives on the Origins of Americanist Archaeology*, edited by David L. Browman and Stephen Williams, 60–86. Tuscaloosa: University of Alabama Press, 2002.
Oleson, Alexandra, and Sanborn C. Brown. *The Pursuit of Knowledge in the Early American Republic: American Scientific and Learned Societies from Colonial Times to the Civil War.* Baltimore: Johns Hopkins University Press, 1976.
Parrish, Susan Scott. *American Curiosities: Culture of Natural History in the Colonial British Atlantic World.* Chapel Hill: University of North Carolina Press, 2006.
Pearsall, Sarah M. S. *Atlantic Families: Lives and Letters in the Latter Eighteenth Century.* New York: Oxford University Press, 2010.
Perley, Bernard. "Zombie Linguistics: Experts, Endangered Languages and the Curse of Undead Voices." *Anthropological Forum* 22, no. 2 (2012): 133–49.
[Pickering, John.] "Explanatory Remarks on the Preceding Comparative Vocabulary." *Collections of the Massachusetts Historical Society*, 2nd ser., vol. 10 (1823): 146–57.
Pickering, Mary Orne. *The Life of John Pickering.* Boston: John Wilson & Son, 1887.
Rafinesque, C. S. *The American Nations; or, Outlines of a National History; of the Ancient and Modern Nations of North and South America.* 2 vols. Philadelphia: C. S. Rafinesque, 1836.

———. "Important Historical and Philological Discovery. To Peter Duponceau." *Saturday Evening Post*, January 13, 1827, n.p.

Rivett, Sarah. *Unscripted America: Indigenous Languages and the Origin of an American Literary Nation*. New York: Oxford University Press, 2017.

Robins, R. H. *A Short History of Linguistics*. 4th ed. London: Longman, 1997.

Round, Phillip H. *Removable Type: Histories of the Book in Indian Country, 1663–1880*. Chapel Hill: University of North Carolina Press, 2010.

Safier, Neil. "Global Knowledge on the Move: Itineraries, Amerindian Narratives, and Deep Histories of Science." *Isis* 101, no. 4 (December 2010): 133–45.

Schwarz, Ingo, ed. *Alexander von Humboldt und die Vereinigten Staaten von Amerika Briefwechsel*. Berlin: Akademie Verlag, 2004.

Stiggins, George. "A Historical Narration of the Genealogy Traditions and Downfall of the Ispocaga or Creek Tribe of Indians, Written by One of the Tribe." In Theron A. Nunez Jr., "Creek Nativism and the Creek War of 1813–1814." *Ethnohistory* 5, no. 1 (Winter 1958): 1–47.

Strang, Cameron. "Scientific Instructions and Native American Linguistics in the Imperial United States: The Department of War's 1826 Vocabulary." *Journal of the Early Republic* 37, no. 3 (Fall 2017): 399–427.

Sturtevant, William C., ed. "John Ridge on Cherokee Civilization." *Journal of Cherokee Studies* 6 (Fall 1981): 79–91.

Sweet, Paul R. *Wilhelm von Humboldt: A Biography*. Columbus: Ohio State University Press, 1980.

Turner, James. *Philology: The Forgotten Origins of the Modern Humanities*. Princeton NJ: Princeton University Press, 2014.

Valencius, Conevery Bolton, et al. "Science in Early America: Print Culture and the Sciences of Territoriality." *Journal of the Early Republic* 36, no. 1 (Spring 2016): 73–123.

Voigt, Irma Elizabeth. "The Life and Works of Mrs. Therese Robinson (Talvj)." PhD diss., University of Illinois, 1913.

William L. Clements Library, Ann Arbor, Michigan.
    Lewis Cass Papers
    Michigan Papers

Winterer, Caroline. "Where Is America in the Republic of Letters." *Modern Intellectual History* 9, no. 3 (2012): 597–623.

Wisconsin State Historical Society, Madison.
    Peter S. Du Ponceau Letters

Wyss, Hillary. *English Letters and Indian Literacies: Reading, Writing, and New England Missionary Schools, 1750–1830*. Philadelphia: University of Pennsylvania Press, 2012.

Yokota, Kariann. *Unbecoming British: How Revolutionary America became a Postcolonial Nation*. New York: Oxford University Press, 2011.

CHAPTER 7

Literacy, Cross-Cultural Interaction, and Colonialism

The Making of a Nineteenth-Century Nez Perce Mission Primer

Anne Keary

In February 1840, in the Nez Perce village of Lapwai, a lay mission assistant with the American Board of Commissioners for Foreign Missions (ABCFM) printed off eight hundred copies of a small book entitled *Numipuain Shapahitamanash Timash* (A Book to Teach Reading for the Nez Perce).[1] The book, a literacy primer, was intended for instructing the Nez Perce or Niimíipuu people to read in their own language. As such it was both one of the earliest books printed in the Pacific Northwest and one of a large number of Indigenous-language reading books printed at Protestant mission stations across North America in the first half of the nineteenth century.[2] Of these mission books, *Numipuain Shapahitamanash Timash* is one of the first to have been translated into English and, in this case, also contemporary Nimipuutímt. This work was undertaken by the Niimíipuu Elders Florene Davis and Vera Sonneck, as well as the late Bessie Scott, Cecil Carter, and Horace Axtell, working together with linguist Harold Crook. Now, over one hundred and seventy years after its first printing, the text and its translation provide a new resource for the future and the ongoing work of revitalizing Nimipuutímt, and a new window onto the past and the history of the Niimíipuu encounter with alphabetic literacy and Euro-American book culture.

This chapter sets out to explore that past. The story to be told here is specific to the Niimíipuu, but it has implications for understanding the history of Euro-American attempts to introduce books and literacy to Indigenous people across North America. Generally speaking, scholars of Indigenous encounters with alphabetic literacy have focused either on mission literacy instruction in the colonial period or on the boarding school experiences of Indigenous children in the later nineteenth and twentieth centuries. The former have tended to focus on missionary attempts to translate and transcribe Native languages and Native efforts to adopt and adapt writing to suit their own needs as they navigated their way in a newly colonized world;[3] the latter have more often focused on the colonial and anticolonial uses of English-language literacy in the boarding school environment and beyond.[4]

The Indigenous-language literacy campaign of antebellum missionaries has, however, been largely ignored, even though it was through this campaign that many Indigenous people, particularly in the prereservation West, first encountered and contended with the written word in a sustained way.[5] The translation of *Numipuain Shapahitamanash Timash* thus presents a unique opportunity to look at how this campaign was enacted on the ground—in this case, Niimíipuu ground. In what follows I situate the making of *Numipuain Shapahitamanash Timash* in the context of the colonial and cross-cultural histories that were brought together on its printed pages: the history of the antebellum missionary literacy campaign; the emergence of a Niimíipuu interest in acquiring a knowledge of books and literacy for their own purposes; and the evolution of Niimíipuu-missionary relations. I then present a reading of the primer itself that aims to elucidate the ways in which the text worked both as an instrument of colonial mission instruction and as a product of dynamic cross-cultural exchange.

The ABCFM Literacy Campaign

The literacy campaign of the ABCFM had deep roots in the long history of Euro-American missionizing to Indigenous people, but it was also significantly shaped by shifts in early nineteenth-century American literate culture. Established in 1810 as an interdenominational Protestant organization, the ABCFM looked back to the literacy work of the Puritan missionaries, and to John Eliot in particular. Eliot, with the assistance of Native-language teachers, had produced the first Massachusett translation of the Bible in 1663 and, in 1669, the very first *Indian Primer*.[6] Nineteenth-century evangelical writers praised Eliot for his work in "propagat[ing] the gospel among the heathen" and upheld his efforts to get the written word into Indigenous hands as a model to be continued.[7] Like their seventeenth-century forebear, they believed that literacy instruction was a necessity if Native people were to have access to the Bible and, through the Bible, God's saving grace.

But while there were certain similarities between the work of Eliot and the plans of the ABCFM missionaries, there were also important differences. Between the seventeenth century when Eliot was active and the early nineteenth century when the ABCFM was founded, the meanings and practice of Euro-American literacy changed. The first significant shift occurred in the period following the American Revolution when campaigns led by patriot leaders to create a unified and educated citizenry endowed literacy with a new ideological significance as necessary not only to the practice of religion but to the health of republican civic life.[8] With the establishment of common schools, the promotion of national literature, and efforts to institute uniform language use led by educational reformers like Noah Webster, literacy also became increasingly tied to a new and more secular nationalism. Then, during the 1820s and 1830s, the very decades in which the ABCFM was establishing its "Indian missions," the massive expansion of the print marketplace led to further changes in American literate culture. The diversification of print materials in this period brought new sources of literary entertainment to a growing number of readers. It also gave them access to information on an increasingly broad array of topics, a development widely hailed in the popular press as bringing about a "general diffusion of knowledge" that would inform and elevate the population at large.[9]

Given the multilayered ideological significance of literacy for American evangelicals, it is not surprising, then, that the ABCFM devoted considerable attention to the question of literacy instruction at its mission stations, and that they did so with the view that literacy was necessary not only so that Indigenous people could access the Scriptures but so that they could increase their "sources of knowledge and means of improvement."[10] At first the board directed its missionaries to undertake literacy instruction in English in order that Native people might access English print materials, but by the late 1820s a growing emphasis on the primacy of evangelization, combined with the successful translation of the Bible into Cherokee (1825) and then Hawaiian (1829) led the board to change course and direct its missionaries to teach literacy in Native languages instead.[11] This shift in policy required resources. To advance the work of transcribing Indigenous languages, the board recommended that its missionaries use the Roman-letter based "Uniform Orthography for the Indian Languages of North America" that the American philologist John Pickering had devised at the board's request.[12] And, to get print materials more speedily into the hands of Native people, the board began providing its mission stations with printing presses. The secretary for Indian missions on the board, David Greene, made a point of emphasizing, however, that missionaries should use these presses to print reading books before attempting translations of the Bible.[13] As he put it in a letter to the missionaries to the Niimíipuu: "Print only small elementary books at first."[14] And, notably, the model for these elementary books was not Eliot's *Indian Primer* (with its catechism, Apostles' Creed, and Lord's Prayer), but the more eclectic and secular reading books produced for early nineteenth-century common schools, books that included lessons on history, geography, and natural history, as well as stories and moral lessons for the edification of young readers.[15] The mission primers produced for Indigenous people in the antebellum period were, in short, books produced with the goal of introducing not just alphabetic literacy, but modern Euro-American book culture as well.

Niimíipuu Encounters with Alphabetic Literacy

Books were not, however, entirely new to the Niimíipuu. In fact, when the ABCFM missionaries arrived, they encountered a people who were already somewhat familiar with the written word and who had their own reasons for being interested in books and alphabetic literacy. The Niimíipuu had first encountered Euro-American writing on the trade objects they acquired in the eighteenth century, and they had first witnessed Euro-Americans engaged in the practices of reading and writing when the explorers Lewis and Clark stayed with them in 1805.[16] Then, when the Hudson's Bay Company established its network of trade posts through the Columbia Plateau region, including Fort Nez Perces in 1818, their encounters with the written word increased. Some Niimíipuu began serving, on occasion, as couriers for the traders' handwritten messages.[17] And, in the 1820s, when the traders began inviting the Niimíipuu and other Plateau peoples to attend Sunday gatherings at which Euro-Americans read from the Bible and the Book of Common Prayer with the aid of interpreters, the people were introduced to printed books as well.[18]

It was during this period that one trader, Samuel Black, recorded what he believed were Nez Perce words for "to write," and "paper": "timet" and "timash," respectively. (He recorded similar words for the Walla Walla and Cayuse languages too.)[19] The "timet" Black recorded may have been the Sahaptin *tímat*, which is perhaps what he heard, but it is also related to the Nimipuutímt *tíim'e* ('to write, make a mark, stamp, brand') and to *tíim'enin'*, a word the Niimíipuu used to refer to "war paint," "petroglyphs," and "pictographs."[20] The extension of these words to refer to alphabetic writing suggests, at the very least, that the Niimíipuu and other Plateau people had come to view Euro-American forms of graphic communication as comparable to their own. Black's noting of "timash" or *tíim'es* to refer to "paper" is even more notable, as this word was also used by the Niimíipuu to refer to "book." The Niimíipuu-Cayuse scholar Phillip Cash Cash argues that this particular word, which had no other referent in the culture, had made its appearance earlier in the context of a prophetic movement that began in the late eighteenth century, a period marked by smallpox epidemics and significant social and cultural change.[21] The movement involved the performance of dances and songs about upheaval, renewal, and the acquisition of new spiritual powers, and one of these songs, later recorded by the anthropologist Deward Walker, included the refrain "Hiya Hiya. Now in the heavens coming towards us, That's what the [book] *ti-mes* tells us."[22] In 1831 interest in this prophetic movement, combined with interest in the preaching of a Salish man, Spokan Garry, who had received instruction at the Hudson Bay Company's Red River School, prompted a Niimíipuu council to send a delegation to St. Louis to specifically request teachers with knowledge of a special *tíim'es*, a request understood by the Americans as a request for the Bible.[23]

It was, at least in part, in response to the news of this delegation that the ABCFM sent missionaries to the Niimíipuu and other Plateau peoples in 1836, and the missionaries' early accounts indicate that the Niimíipuu were indeed interested in their *tíim'es*.[24] One of these missionaries, Henry Harmon Spalding, claimed that "as soon as one gets hold of a book who is able to spell out a few words, he immediately searches for the name of God, Jesus Christ, and the Holy Spirit."[25] He also reported that, when he drew up pictures of biblical stories on paper, Niimíipuu headmen took his pictures (which they also called *tíim'es*) back to their camps in order to retell the stories in their own way.[26] Spalding's missionary colleague Asa Bowen Smith, who was roundly critical of this practice, asserted that the headmen manifested "a great fondness for hearing something new and telling of it," and that they did so in order to "increase their influence ... among the people."[27] From a Niimíipuu perspective, however, the headmen were likely simply incorporating a novel element, the pictures on paper or *tíim'es*, into an established Indigenous practice: that of sharing and telling stories as a means of creating relationships and making sense of the new.[28] A similar process of appropriation occurred when the missionaries began teaching literacy at the mission's school. According to Spalding, whenever the Niimíipuu were left on their own in the schoolroom they "assembled in clusters, with one teaching a number of others.... To-day a stranger will enter the room, not knowing a letter, tomorrow he will be teaching the others."[29] Spalding was probably exaggerating, but his reports indicate that from the outset the Niimíipuu were interested in adopting and adapting Euro-American ways of communicating on paper for their own purposes.

The Making of *Numipuain Shapahitamanash Timash*

It was in this context that *Numipuain Shapahitamanash Timash* was composed. The book's principal author was Spalding's critic, Asa Bowen Smith, but Smith was not the sole author. He was aided by a lay missionary assistant, Cornelius Rogers, and Hallalhotsoot, a Niimíipuu-Salish man also known as "Lawyer," who was the missionaries' principal language teacher. Each brought different interests and perspectives to the task. Smith was an erudite man who had moved from Lapwai to the village of Kamiah in 1839 in order to better learn the language. As the literate grammarian that he was, he did so by assiduously transcribing Nimipuutímt and analyzing its grammatical structures.[30] Alarmed by the Niimíipuu response to Spalding's use of pictures and the autonomy the headmen exercised in running the school, it seems likely that Smith hoped that by "mastering" the language and composing the primer, he could reassert control over the meaning and purpose of the written word among the Niimíipuu. Rogers, on the other hand, acquired his knowledge of Nimipuutímt not through analytical study but through conversation with the Niimíipuu during his travels with a summer buffalo-hunting party.[31] As a result, as Smith himself acknowledged, the parts of the primer that Rogers "prepared" were "in a more easy style & more according to the idiom of the language."[32] In other words, it appears that Rogers brought to the making of the primer the skills he had acquired not only as a translator between English and Nimipuutímt, but also as a mediator between Euro-American and Indigenous modes of communicating.

Meanwhile, although Hallalhotsoot was not explicitly acknowledged by either Smith or Rogers as a contributor—a common practice among colonial Euro-Americans who tended to privilege their own translation work over that of Indigenous people—it can nevertheless be assumed that as the missionaries' language teacher he, too, assisted. By all accounts, Hallalhotsoot was an able and ambitious man and a skilled linguist who spoke Nimipuutímt, Salish, and some English. According to Smith, he had been given the name "Lawyer" by the fur traders on account "of his knowledge of different languages & his talent in public speaking." Smith also described him as "the best teacher that could be obtained in the country."[33] With his language skills, his evident curiosity about the Euro-Americans, and his connections to Indigenous Plateau peoples, Hallalhotsoot would have been a particularly useful instructor and interpreter for the missionaries as they worked together on composing a primer for a Niimíipuu audience.

At first glance the book these men produced appears to be similar to Euro-American English-language primers of the period. It consists of a pronunciation guide, lists of numerals and letters, a syllabarium, and thirty lessons on such topics as the value and purpose of books and reading, various Euro-American material objects, Western ways of measuring time and space, the uses and characteristics of different animals, and moral values. References to the Christian god and Protestant principles are scattered throughout the text, but they are few. Evidently, Smith and (to some extent) Rogers were primarily interested in instructing the Niimíipuu in the secular knowledges and ways of knowing associated with early nineteenth-century Euro-American book culture.

But if the text was informed by the missionaries' colonial interest in remaking Niimíipuu lives and ways of thinking, it was also shaped by the processes of cross-cultural translation and interaction. At Kamiah the ABCFM missionaries were not in a position of colonial dominance, and, as much as they sought to instill Euro-American modes of knowing, they had to compose their book in Nimipuutímt, work with Hallalhotsoot, and appeal to potential Niimíipuu readers who had their own reasons for being interested in the written word. A close reading of *Numipuain Shapahitamanash Timash* reveals it to be very much a hybrid text, inevitably informed by the missionaries' evangelical and colonial project of instructing the Niimíipuu in alphabetic literacy, but not reducible to the terms of that project. In the discussion that follows, I attempt to illuminate the complicated colonial and cross-cultural dynamics of the primer's composition. Focusing on selections from the text while also outlining broader themes and patterns, my reading aims to show how the primer's lessons worked as confrontations with—or, in some cases, adaptations to—different ways of knowing, relating, and communicating.

Literacy and Book Culture

The first lesson in the primer dedicated to explaining the purpose of books and literacy to Niimíipuu readers is *Himte'ke's* (Lesson) V. Entitled "Timash"—that is, "*Tíim'es*" or "Book"—the lesson is revealing of the ways in which the missionary authors sought both to appeal to and assert their authority over the meanings of books and literacy in Niimíipuu life. In free translation, this lesson reads:

Now this has become my new book. One is writing many different things in it.

Who gave it to you?

My older brother gave it to me. It was just recently made. It was made for me. This is the way he does it, the way that he writes various things.

Whatever will you do with that book then?

I am just pondering it. Just now I have only a little knowledge, but maybe soon I will know much.

Always take care of it. Read it with clean hands lest you smudge it.

Books are precious. They are for learning everything. One very good book is Jehovah's. For that knowledge, you will continue reading this book.[34]

This lesson opens with the narrator inviting the reader to consider a new book that has been given to him or her, not—notably—by a missionary, but by an older brother who made the book "for me." These first lines, then, appear to reference a Niimíipuu interest in appropriating books and passing them on through their own channels of communication and kinship networks. But the voice of the missionary teacher intervenes, first cautioning, "Always take care of it. Read it with clean hands lest you smudge it"; then informing the reader that books "are for learning everything," for "knowledge"; and, lastly, urging the reader to continue learning to read so that he or she will be able to read the most important *tíim'es*: "Jehovah's." With this transition, the context of familial gift-giving falls away, and the Niimíipuu reader is repositioned as a pupil subordinate to a missionary teacher and redirected toward a particularly Euro-American complex of ideas about books and alphabetic literacy: that books should be kept clean and treated with care; that reading books is *the* way to acquire knowledge; and, ultimately, that learning to read was the way to a knowledge of Jehovah.

In the other lessons on literacy—Himte'ke's XV, XVI, XVII—this set of ideas is repeated and reinforced, and, as the lessons proceed, they become more disciplinary in tone and more explicitly colonial in their message. The acquisition of literacy, Niimíipuu readers were informed, required obedience to missionary authority; adoption of a Euro-American code of conduct in which the care and keeping of books functioned as a sign of personal virtue; and acceptance of the Euro-American contention that the possession of print-based knowledge was the cause of their self-proclaimed superiority.[35] "In the Americans' land," readers were told, "they are learning at the same age as you boys are and the same age as you girls are. Because of that they are becoming smart from a young age."[36] In a sense this was, of course, the central message of the primer and certainly central to its purpose of directing the Niimíipuu toward Euro-American literate ways of knowing. But even as the missionary authors pressed this message, their felt need to appeal to the Niimíipuu by referencing aspects of their social world—as shown in their first of their lessons on the book—also persisted.

History, Geography, and Material Culture

In the set of lessons on material culture, the transition from an engagement with Niimíipuu life to an insistence on the adoption of Euro-Americans ways is repeated, but in these lessons the missionary authors make use of the transition itself by historicizing it. This tactic is evident, to varying degrees, in the lessons on writing surfaces, houses, and paper-making. In each the missionaries refer to Niimíipuu objects, thereby grounding the lessons in Niimíipuu life, but then proceed to present these objects as precursors to Euro-American objects in an ongoing history of material progress. For instance, in Himte'ke's VI, on writing implements and surfaces, they inform readers that "that is not the only way people used to write long ago; they wrote in other ways. One way was they used to write on stone. Then they used to write on wood and on tree bark and on thin softened hide. A book on hide can last a long time."[37] And, in Himte'ke's XIII, entitled 'iníit (House), they write: "Some people make houses of cattail, tules, and rye grass. Then some have houses of uncured hide.... Americans' and French Canadians' houses are of stone, wood, and burned mud bricks." They then suggest, "Perhaps you will come to have some kind of house, you who are reading this."[38] In this way the missionary authors repositioned the Niimíipuu within a unilinear and universalizing Western historical narrative and, in the same move, introduced a distinctly Western mode of historical thinking. Indeed, in this regard, it is possible that the missionaries sought to present petroglyph-making as the precursor to writing on paper in the knowledge, perhaps acquired from Hallalhotsoot, that the people had extended the word they used to refer to the making of rock art to refer to alphabetic writing. The implication of charting this shift as an historical trajectory was that to write on paper was itself an act of participating in historical progress.

In other lessons the missionaries' attempt to introduce Western historical thinking is complemented by an attempt to impress the Niimíipuu with Euro-American geographical knowledge. While there are a few references to Niimíipuu places, these are outnumbered by references to "the lands of the Americans and the French," to Spain, to Africa, and, significantly, to the "many lands that you do not yet know the names of."[39] While the missionaries' historicized transitions from Niimíipuu to Euro-American ways positioned the Niimíipuu in a Western narrative of historical progress, their references to other lands "you do not yet know the names of" positioned the people within Euro-American geographical space. Heedless of their own ignorance of Niimíipuu country, the missionary authors' references to Western geography were no doubt intended to convey a sense of Euro-American spatial mastery, a mastery predicated on a print-based knowledge of the globe that the Niimíipuu, the missionaries remind them, did not possess.

'Iceyéeye (Coyote)

Given the missionaries' interest in promoting Euro-American print knowledge and Western conceptions of history and geography, it is especially interesting to turn to Himte'ke's X, their lesson on 'Iceyéeye (Coyote). In Niimíipuu life *Iceyéeye* is the creator trickster figure whose activities, along with those of other Animal People, shaped the Plateau world and gave its creatures their form and character. The *titwatináawit*, or Coyote stories, are therefore integral to Niimíipuu conceptions of history and geography, to their understanding of the spiritual dimensions of life, and to their ways of knowing and relating to their world in all its particularity and diversity. Passed on as oral traditions the *titwatináawit* also provide important moral teachings about how to live properly in relation to the land and to all living beings.[40] From the perspective of the missionaries, therefore, *titwatináawit* were a major obstacle to their efforts to instruct the Niimíipuu in

Christianity and literate Euro-American ways of knowing. Their lesson on *Iceyéeye* is thus particularly significant. It reads, in part, in free translation:

> They used to say, they used to tell stories, the coyote long ago was a person. That one was crafty. That's how the forefathers used to tell stories. However, they were foolish. That same one he just stayed a coyote and animals and all the others which are here on the land.
>
> Moreover they used to say, The coyote, the grizzly, the hoofed animals, the crow, the bald-eagle, they speak to a person, yet all of these just make non-human sounds.
>
> Maybe we have believed that they are intelligent, the grizzly and other things, but all over the earth they are just completely uncomprehending.[41]

Here are highlighted those aspects of the *titwatináawit* that so troubled the missionaries: first, the authority of these oral traditions and the Elders who told them, for this was an authority that challenged the missionaries' own and countermanded their assertions about the superiority of book knowledge; and, second, the understanding, central to all *titwatináawit*, that animals as the original Animal People possessed the ability to communicate in language. For the missionaries this went to the heart of the matter, as such a notion challenged everything they understood about the nature of knowledge, the workings of language, and what it meant to be human. Marcus Whitman, Smith and Rogers's colleague, also reported being deeply troubled by the peoples' beliefs, writing that their "legend is that the present race of beasts birds reptiles & fish were once a race of men who inhabited the globe before the present race.... they were doomed to their present state... but... still their language is retained & these beasts birds reptiles & fish have the power to convey this language to the people into whom they transfix themselves."[42] This last was a reference to the vision quests in which young Niimíipuu individuals would be endowed with special powers or gifts by a *weeyekin* (guardian spirit), who often appeared in an animal form.[43] For the missionaries, however, the very notion that humans could enter into relations with animal spirits, or that humans and animal spirits might share, or once have shared, the status of persons possessed of language, was an affront to their deepest beliefs about the sacred order of the world. According to their own origins story, God had brought the animals to Adam for him to name. Human language thereby established knowledge of, and authority over, nonhumans; it did not enable communication with them. For the missionaries, therefore, their assertion that "coyote, grizzly bear, hooved animals, crow, bald eagle" had only ever made animal sounds—*hiinmiya'íiktan'ix*—and were completely uncomprehending of human language, was a necessary and forceful condemnation of what they took to be the fallacies of Niimíipuu ways of knowing and relating to the world. Such ways should be considered, as they presented it, as the ways of the past, what the "forefathers" used to do. Implied here is a trajectory from a past in which Elders told Coyote stories to an enlightened future in which the people will receive instruction from the missionaries and their books.

Animals and Animal Stories

It is not surprising that the majority of lessons on animals that follow—and indeed almost a third of the primer is comprised of lessons on animals—are aimed at "correcting" Niimíipuu ideas about human-animal relations and introducing Euro-American ways of knowing them. In lessons on the cow, the horse, the ass, the sheep, the cat, and the bee, the missionaries press Nimipuutímt into the plain language of factual statements to render these animals into objects: sets of facts made knowable through books, rather than active, knowing subjects. And, against the notion that humans and animals might share any attributes, the missionary authors repeatedly present them solely as resources for human use, valuable only insofar as they served human purposes: "Sheep's wool is good for shirts, for pants, for coverings, and for making many things."[44] The cow is "good for milk. Always at dawn and at evening a person extracts the milk. The milk is valuable to a person for butter and for food."[45]

However, and significantly, there are three lessons—on the lion, the elephant, and the whale—where the relationship between Euro-American literate culture and Niimíipuu orality is turned about. In these lessons the missionaries' concern to establish the superiority of a literate knowledge of animals gives way to an interest in engaging the Niimíipuu with stories about animals. The fact that these animals were all undomesticated and therefore, from the Euro-American perspective, not creatures whose human uses needed describing but rather animals whose more exotic status made them suitable subject material for stories was no doubt an important factor. Here the Nimipuutímt written word is put to new purposes. The composition of Himte'ke's XXI on the lion is a good example. Although the lesson includes conventional instruction on the physical appearance and geographic location of the lion, most of it is taken up with stories, including a story that had previously appeared in Euro-American books under the title "The Hottentot and the Lion," which must have been either known to the missionaries or in their possession. A colonial tale, this story concerns an African man who realizes he is being tracked by a lion and decides to trick the animal by putting his shirt on a stick near the edge of a cliff. When the lion rushes in to attack the stick figure, he tumbles over the cliff to his death. A comparison of the original with the version in the primer is revealing. Of the man's thoughts upon realizing he was being tracked, for instance, the original reads: "But as he was well acquainted with the nature of the lion, and the manner of its seizing upon its prey; and at the same time had leisure to ruminate on the ways and means in which it was most likely that his existence would be terminated, he at length hit on a method of saving his life."[46] In *Numipuain Shapahitamanash Timash*, however, the story reads very differently, as is evident even in free translation:

> One time a man was traveling where there were no houses. There he saw a lion on the road; but it was already evening. Then he thought, "Now then it is about to get dark and it is about to track me down to kill me." At twilight he arrived at a bluff, and then he thought, "Now what am I going to do? It is surely tracking me." Then he thought, "Surely now, it has tracked me." Then he removed his shirt and then he stuck a piece of wood in the ground on the bluff top and then he put his shirt on it and put his hat on it.[47]

Here, rather than being described in literary language for the reader's consideration, events are presented with an immediacy that commands the reader's attention. Indeed, the narrator invites the reader to enter into the drama of the story much in the way a storyteller might invite listeners to participate in an oral narration, even of a Coyote story. The man's thoughts are represented as reported speech, a narrative mode commonly used in Niimíipuu oral stories in order, as Phillip Cash Cash has put it, "to impart volition and animacy in the immediate reality of the perceiving agent."[48] And the reader also follows as the man considers the thoughts and actions of the lion as well. Indeed, toward the end of the story, the reader is momentarily invited to adopt the lion's viewpoint as he "tracked [the man] by his tracks," and then to sense his surprise when discovers the stick "was only the shirt." Further, the original is characterized by the repeated use of "*kawá*," or "then," a linguistic marker frequently employed in Sahaptin oral narratives, as the linguist Dell Hymes has noted, to mark "sequences of action" and shape the text "to expressive purpose, as it proceeds, arousing and fulfilling expectations, as is the case with all traditional literary forms."[49] In this story it is used in a pattern typical of Niimíipuu narratives in particular—that is, to mark "a sequence of three steps with a sense of outcome in the third."[50] All of these elements suggest that the printed story may, in fact, have been transcribed from an actual oral retelling, possibly by Rogers, or possibly by Hallalhotsoot, after first having heard it from the missionaries.

Morality Tales

Significantly, this use of the performative and interactive devices of Niimíipuu storytelling is also evident in two of the lessons that convey moral instruction: Himte'ke's XXX, entitled *Miséemt* (Lying), and Himte'ke's XXIX, entitled *Toq'óoxnin* (Blind-in-one-eye). In Lesson XXIX the links between the written composition and oral narration are particularly striking. The lesson, which presents a story about a boy who defies his parents and secretly acquires a gun only to lose his eye when he fires it, opens with the line "A person blind in one eye *said*."[51] The lesson then proceeds as a story "told" by an older man about his younger self: "Then I brought the gun from the house, and then I loaded it almost completely full. Then I fired it. Boom!"[52] The language is immediate and expressive. The "Boom," or, in Nimipuutímt, *t'óox!*, evokes the sound a storyteller would make to mimic the sound of gunfire.

Additionally, both morality tales display elements of an Indigenous moral sensibility. In "Lying," which was, like the story about the man and the lion, based on a previously published tale,[53] the reader is invited not to simply condemn the boy who lies to his mother (as in the original), but rather to sympathize with or at least understand him when he thinks, "Let me pretend to be sick and then she will give me good medicine, that very good one she medicated me with only yesterday."[54] And in the story of "Blind-in-one-eye" the reader is similarly asked to understand the boy's desire for the gun, as he was "exceedingly fond of playing with gunpowder."[55] In this respect the stories more closely resemble the stories of Niimíipuu culture, which tended to encourage sympathetic amusement at the failings of others and to acknowledge the difficulty of living a moral life, rather than the more didactic tales common to Euro-American primers of the period.[56] It is also notable that the elderly narrator of "Blind-in-one-eye" concludes his story with the lines "Now, when I see children when they disobey I think, then I think in this way I made myself blind in one eye, and perhaps they will similarly make themselves miserable by being disobedient."[57] With this the moral "lesson" of the story is grounded in relationships between the narrator, the reader or listener, and the children. Although the more abstract principle—("Don't disobey your father and mother. No one ever became good through disobedience")—concludes the lesson, as it would in a typical Protestant morality tale, the preceding statements are those of an older man who would like to convey his learned wisdom to a younger audience.[58] The story as a whole also affirms the significance of a moral value—respect for one's elders—that was important to the Niimíipuu. In all of these ways, the composition of this story suggests some attunement, on the part of the authors, to an Indigenous moral order.

Taken together these morality tales and animal stories reveal a different dynamic at work in the making of the primer, a dynamic shaped neither by the missionaries' interest in asserting colonial forms of authority nor by their insistence on the superiority of literacy and Western knowledge, but rather by a shared interest in stories and storytelling, even if this interest was not shared for the same reasons. The missionaries no doubt viewed the stories primarily as a means of engaging the Niimíipuu and thereby drawing them into the realm of written communication and book culture. As they had learned, stories for the Niimíipuu were a means of forging relations with others and heightening one's status. As Smith himself had noted, the "principal men manifest a great fondness for hearing something new & telling of it & by so doing they ... increase their influence ... among the people."[59] Quite possibly the missionary authors, perhaps Rogers in particular, were looking to adapt Niimíipuu ways of exercising authority by using stories that would increase their own "influence among the people." Through the work of relating, translating, and transcribing these stories with Hallalhotsoot and for a Niimíipuu readership, they were evidently moved to adapt to and adopt elements of the Niimíipuu storytelling culture of which they were otherwise critical. In the stories literacy is not opposed to Niimíipuu orality but partakes of it. The written word is not aimed at suppressing the voices, modes of expression, and sensibility of Niimíipuu oral life, but is put into play with them. And here the relationship between Niimíipuu orality and alphabetic literacy is not configured as a trajectory in which readers must reject the oral ways of the past and adopt the literate ways of the future; rather, the relationship is adaptive and interactive, open to other possibilities.

The Final Hymn: A Song of Creation

The primer's final lesson includes a hymn that also bears traces of Indigenous influence and the effects of cross-cultural engagement. Entitled *Yehóova 'óykalanm hanyaw'aat*—in English, "Jehovah Is Everything's Creator"—the hymn reads, in free translation:

> We are Jehovah's making,
> the same all over;
> This land and animals,
> he made all by himself.
>
> Likewise for us he made,
> the trees in the same way:
> the garden grows
> by his law

He alone has the authority
over us, over everything:
It is for life he speaks to us
Let us listen to him.⁶⁰

The overall message of the hymn would appear to be undeniably colonial. To claim that Jehovah was the sole creator of the land and animals was, of course, to supplant the creative activities of Coyote, who shaped the world first brought into being by the Creator. And to insist that the world was made by Jehovah "for us" was to assert a distinctly instrumental Euro-American view of the natural world and its creatures.⁶¹ But if these were the claims that the missionaries made, they were also the grounds on which they made their final appeal, and in making this appeal there are indications that Smith and Rogers understood, perhaps through their interactions with Hallalhotsoot, that elements of their hymn made sense in Niimíipuu terms. It is notable, for instance, that in the only lesson in the primer dedicated to teaching the people about the Christian god, the missionaries chose to present their god not as the judge of souls—a conception of the deity that Smith otherwise favored—but as a creator who brought the land and the animals into being according to his law, *tamáalwit*.⁶² Although it is impossible to know the missionaries' intentions here, this representation of Jehovah as a creator whose law was made manifest in his creation would almost certainly have resonated with Niimíipuu understandings of *tamáalwit* as the law "thrown down" at creation, the law that established the purpose and "rules to live by" for all beings.⁶³ Further, it is surely significant that the missionaries chose to end their literacy primer, with all of its lessons on the importance of the written word, with a song to be sung. Song was, and is, a spiritually powerful form of communication among the Niimíipuu: vision seekers revealed the identity of their *wéyekin* through song, and songs, such as songs for the arrival of first foods, were a means of expressing and sustaining relations to the created world.⁶⁴ Possibly the missionaries, who had long been aware of Indigenous interest in song, hoped that the addition of the hymn would heighten the significance and appeal of the book for the

Niimíipuu. Interestingly, the missionaries concluded the song itself with a statement about the value and power of oral communication with Jehovah: "for life he speaks to us, let us listen to him." The message here is that a knowledge of Jehovah is to be obtained, in the end, not from the Book but by actively singing and listening to him. This was, to be sure, in keeping with a Protestant understanding of the need for believers to have a personal and intimate relationship with their god, but it is also suggestive of Indigenous understandings of connections between speech, active listening, and the reception of spiritual power. In composing this final hymn, then, it appears that Smith and Rogers, working with Hallalhotsoot, were drawn into creating a cross-cultural composition, a composition in which Protestant and Niimíipuu conceptions of creation were linked, albeit partially, and in which the written word was used to convey the living power of oral communication.

Aftermath: The Meanings of Nimipuutímt Literacy

As an artifact of the evangelical campaign to bring alphabetic literacy and literate culture to Indian country, *Numipuain Shapahitamanash Timash* cannot, in the end, be understood in the terms the missionaries themselves had outlined. Far from being an instrument in any unilinear history of "progress," or "improvement" for the Niimíipuu, the primer was a product of, and integral to, a complicated history of colonial and cross-cultural interaction. For all Smith and Rogers's evangelical interest in transforming Niimíipuu ways of thinking and knowing, they had to work with Hallalhotsoot, compose their lessons in Nimipuutímt, and seek to engage a Niimíipuu audience. In the process they were moved, on occasion, to reference an Indigenous social world, acknowledge elements of Indigenous life, and even adapt to Indigenous modes of narration. Stories and song, in particular, promised a means of appealing to potential Niimíipuu readers, but in composing them the missionaries were drawn into creating texts that challenged the hierarchies they otherwise sought to institute. On the printed pages of the primer, the missionaries pressed transcribed Nimipuutímt words to the purpose of condemning and "correcting" Niimíipuu ways and asserting the superiority of Euro-American book knowledge, but in writing in Nimipuutímt for Niimíipuu people they also found themselves inscribing Indigenous modes of knowing and relating and, to some extent, accommodating Indigenous values.

In the years after the printing of *Numipuain Shapahitamanash Timash*, Nimipuutímt literacy continued to be shaped by the complicated colonial and cross-cultural dynamics of Niimíipuu-missionary relations. Unfortunately, there are no direct reports of how the Niimíipuu received the primer itself. In 1841 Asa Bowen Smith left the mission, and two years later Cornelius Rogers drowned in a canoeing accident.[65] However, the records of the other ABCFM missionaries, principally the Spaldings, reveal that there was an increased interest in receiving literacy instruction among the Niimíipuu in the early 1840s, particularly at the Spaldings' school at Lapwai. Notably, Hallalhotsoot himself began attending, and, according to Eliza Spalding, he became "deeply interested in learning to read."[66] When a class in writing was established, Henry Spalding further reported that Hallalhotsoot and other leading men made "it their business to learn & seem all absorbed in the undertaking."[67] Just as before, it appears that these Niimíipuu headmen were interested in making literacy their own. In 1842 Henry Spalding reported that "the chiefs govern the school," and the following year he observed that "the people evidently think more of the books they print themselves than of those from the press."[68] He went on to claim that "about 100 are printing their own books with a pen," and many were taking these books "home at nights," so that "every lodge becomes a school room."[69] In many respects these developments would seem to be a continuation of the headmen's earlier practice of retelling the missionaries' biblical stories in their villages with pictures on paper in hand, only now they were reading and teaching, using their own methods from books they had handwritten themselves. Clearly, then, for all the missionaries' interest in using *Numipuain Shapahitamanash Timash*, the Niimíipuu remained intent on taking alphabetic literacy into their own hands.

Fortunately, two of these handwritten books, or *tíim'es*, survive, and the composition of one is particularly suggestive. Both consist mostly of handwritten copies of translated passages from Scripture, but in one of them the writer has also drawn a series of designs of various kinds alongside and between the Christian texts. These designs take a variety of forms — some are very simple curvy or dashed lines, others are more elaborate—and, while their precise meaning cannot be determined, it seems clear that they were created with intent, and that they likely possessed symbolic meaning for their Niimíipuu maker. In figure 6, for instance, the writer has drawn a striking geometric design of lined shapes connected to a rayed circle, a symbol found in Plateau rock art that is understood to "symbolically represent the concept of supernatural power."[70] It is one of two rayed circles in the book. The composition as a whole, however, is different from most Plateau rock art forms, indicating, perhaps, that the writer innovated in creating these designs for a *tíim'es*. His placement of the design is also strongly suggestive of meaningful purpose. The graphic forms are situated between translations of the Ten Commandments and the Lord's Prayer, each of which is, in turn, separated from other texts by patterned lines. Such a placement suggests that the writer wished to highlight the significance of these particular texts and, at the same time, literally reframe them and thereby resituate them within an Indigenous interpretative space. Certainly, it seems likely that he wanted them to be seen by other Niimíipuu readers, possibly by those whom the writer taught when he took his books "home at nights." One might speculate here that to the extent that any of the designs reference Indigenous rock art, the writer was relating, in some way, the Euro-American practice of reading Scripture to the Niimíipuu practice of reading the *tíim'enin'* that connected the people to the stories and spiritual beings active in their landscape, and thereby to other sources of spiritual power, but this is by no means clear. More certainly, and at the very least, it can be said that the designs link Indigenous and Euro-American forms of graphic communication, not as a historical progression, as the missionaries might have hoped, but as forms that might coexist or "speak" to each other on the page.[71]

Over the following years, the meanings of Nimipuutímt literacy continued to change, and increasingly they were shaped both by shifts in relations between the Niimíipuu and incoming Euro-American settler colonists, and by divisions among the Niimíipuu themselves. After the institution of a set of written laws by a U.S. Indian subagent in 1842 and the appointment of Ellis, a literate Niimíipuu man, as head chief, writing became ever more linked to the imposition of colonial power. At the same time, many among

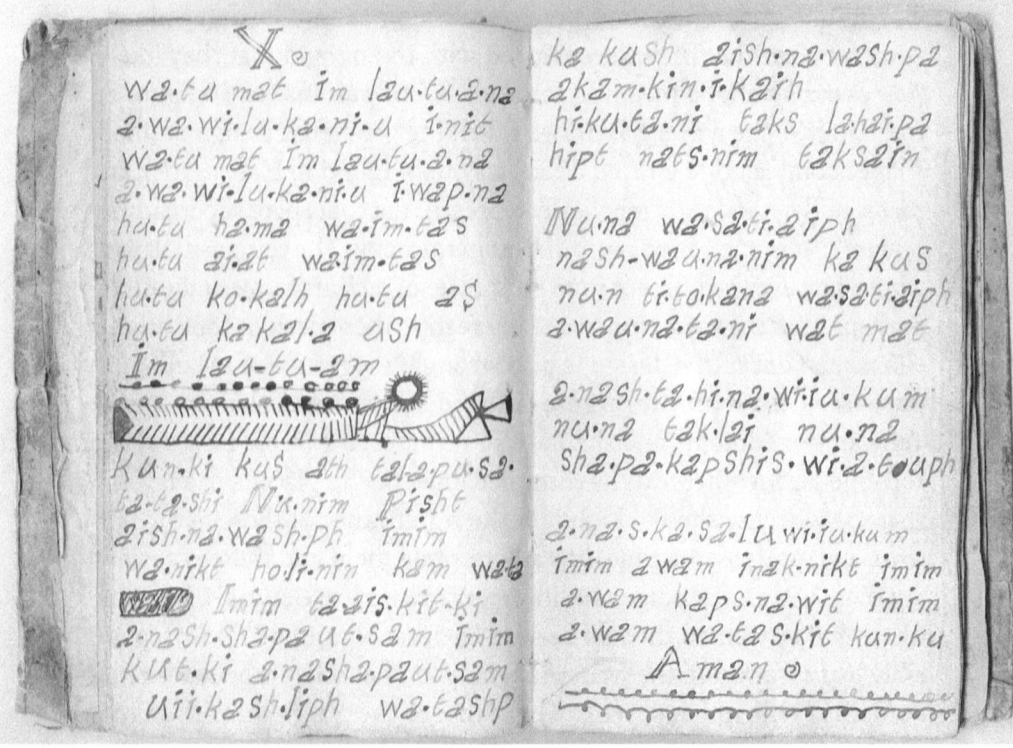

Fig. 7. This Lapwai mission school notebook ca. 1842 is characterized by the inclusion of some distinctive graphic designs. On these pages the Niimíipuu writer has inserted the designs between translations of the Lord's Prayer and the Ten Commandments. University of Idaho, Special Collections and Archives, MG 5144.

the Niimíipuu, particularly those interested in Christianity, looked to use the written word in developing new forms of political authority for themselves. These two developments were related but not seamlessly aligned. They were also the source of growing divisions among the Niimíipuu. At the Treaty Council of 1855, Hallalhotsoot, who had risen to prominence in large part through his skills as an intermediary with the Euro-Americans and his knowledge of literacy, was recognized as head chief by American officials. In accepting this title he made a show, according to the records, of reading to the Niimíipuu from "a book containing in their own language the advice left to them by their Great Chief Ellis."[72] With this act Hallalhotsoot accepted a position created by the colonial powers, but he was also asserting a new kind of Niimíipuu authority predicated on the use of written Nimipuutímt for a Niimíipuu audience. Hallalhotsoot's assertion was not, however, accepted by those who supported the established Niimíipuu leaders chosen by the Elders and the people, and his subsequent actions were the cause of much loss and conflict. In arguing for acceptance of this and later treaties, the former language teacher would go on to play a significant role in the cession of Niimíipuu lands to the colonizers and the imposition of colonial written rule over Niimíipuu lives.

The full history of the Niimíipuu encounter with books and alphabetic literacy in this period remains to be explored. What is clear is that it is a history of many dimensions, and that understanding this history—and others like it—will require attention to both the colonial and cross-cultural dynamics at work. Certainly it will entail examining the ways in which the introduction of books and alphabetic literacy was linked to colonial missionary efforts to negate Indigenous knowledges and orient Niimíipuu people toward, and position them within, literate Euro-American knowledge systems, particularly Euro-American history, geography, and Christianity. It will also entail exploring how these efforts were related to subsequent Euro-American campaigns to institute the rule of colonial written law in Niimíipuu life. But, in addition, it will require an ethnographic attention to the particulars of Niimíipuu cultural and communicative practices and to the ways in which Niimíipuu people both influenced missionary uses of literacy and sought to acquire and use the written word for their own purposes. The relationship between colonial and Indigenous engagements with the written word was complicated. As I hope this study of *Numipuain Shapahitamanash Timash* has shown, close attention to Indigenous language sources can offer new insights into the dynamics of the interplay between them.

ACKNOWLEDGMENTS

I would like to thank Harold Crook and the Niimíipuu Elders Florene Davis, Vera Sonneck, and the late Bessie Scott, Horace Axtell, and Cecil Carter for their translation of *Numipuain Shapahitamanash Timash* and their dedication to this project. I would also like to express my gratitude for their generosity and hospitality during my visits to Lapwai. In addition, I would like to thank the organizers and participants of the American Philosophical Society Conference Translating across Time and Space: Endangered Languages, Cultural Revitalization, and the Work of History, where I first had the opportunity to present this essay.

APPENDIX

The free translations presented in the body of the essay are the work of Harold Crook and Anne Keary in consultation with Florene Davis and the late Bessie Scott. This appendix presents the translations completed by Harold Crook and the Niimíipuu Elders Florene Davis, Vera Sonneck, and the late Bessie Scott, Cecil Carter, and Horace Axtell. The first line is the original as it appeared in *Numipuain Shapahitamanash Timash*; the second line of bold text provides the contemporary Nimipuutímt translation; and the third line of italic text provides the English translation.

Himte'ke's V [from note 34]

Wako   kiak   inim   kimtih   timash   witsash   Ilahni
   pamanama   hiwitimasa
Wáaqo' kíyex   'íinim   kímti   tíim'es   wíc'es   'iléx̣ni
   pamnáma   hiwíitim'ece
now   me   my   new   book   mine is become   many
   different things   one is writing

Ishinm   atka   hinia   timash   ioh?   Naiasam   hinia
   Atsispama   hanit   hiwash   Hahnan-im
'isíinm   'étke   hi'níiye   tíim'es   yox̣?   Na'yáacam   hi'níiye
   'ec'íicpeme   háanit   híiwes   Haanyáanim
who   because gave   book   that   my older brother   he gave
   from recently   made   it is   he made for me

Ki   kush   hiwiusha   hiwitimasa   Kaua   manama
   kutatasha   kunki   timash-ki?
Kii   ku'ús   hiwíiwse   hiwíitim'ece   Kawá   manáma
   kutet'éese   konkí   tíim'eski?
this   thus   he does variously   he writes variously   then   whatever
   you will do   by that   by book

Kala   asilausukuatatasha   Kos   kala   milas   sukua   matu
   paish   ilahni   sukuata-tasha   miwaspa
Kalá   'ecilewcukwetet'éese   Qo'c   kaľa   míiľac   cúukwe   mét'u
   pay's   'iléx̣ni   cukwetet'éese   míiw'acpa
just   I am just pondering it   still   just   little   knowledge   but
   maybe   much   I am about to know   in short time

Aiiianu   a   kunku   Wapaikishki   a   hita-manu
   kainam   tukapsimuku
'a'íiyano'   'ee   kúnk'u   Wapa'áyqi'ski   'ee   hitéemenu'
   kéenem   tukéepcimuku'
you care for it   you   always   with clean hands   you   you will read
   as you   you will smudge

Hatau   hiwash   timash   Uiikalaain   su-kuanash   hiwash
     timash   Naks   tahsnih
**Heté'ew   híiwes   tíim'es   'óykala'ayn   cúukwen'es   híiwes
     tíim'es   Naaqc   ta'sníx**
precious   it is   book   for everything   knowledge   it is
     book   one   very good

hiwash   timash   Iehovanm   Kuniain   su-kuanash   a   kinia
     wiahitamasa
**híiwes   tíim'es   Yehovanm   Ko'ny'áyn   cúukwen'es   'ee   kínye
     wiyehitéemece**
it is   book   Jehovah's   for that   knowledge   you   this
     you continue reading

Himte'ke's VI [from note 37]

Watu	mish	kushpaisim	hitimananihna	titokan	wakepa
ki	ka	kushpa	hitimasa		
Wéet'u	**mi's**	**ku'speycíim**	**hitíim'ene'nixne**	**titóoqan**	**waqíipa**
kii	**ke**	**ku'spé**	**hitíim'ece**		
not	at all	same way only	they used to write	people	long ago
this	which	thus	it writes		

Naks	pishwapa	hitimananihna	kaua	naks	hatsupa
wah	taulikinm	pakatpa	wah	tualpishpa	
Naaqc	**piswéepe**	**hitíim'ene'nixne**	**kawá**	**naaqc**	**hecúupe**
wax̣	**tewlikínm**	**peqétpe**	**wax̣**	**tiw'alpíispa**	
one	on stone	they used to write	then	one	on wood
and	tree's	on bark	and	on softened hide	

hawakespa	Lahai	hiutsah	timash	tualpishpa
hawaq'íispa	**Leehéy**	**hiwc'áax̣**	**tíim'es**	**tiw'alpíispa**
on thin	long time	it can stay	book	on softened hide

Himte'ke's X [from note 41]

Hinanihna   hittiwatianihna   titokan   hi-waka wakepa   isaiaia
Hi'ne'níixne   hittiwatiyáan'ixne   titóoqan   hiwéeke waqíipa   'iceyéeye
They used to say   they used to tell stories   person   he was long ago   coyote

Naks   sikauish   hiutsakana   Kush   hittiwatianihna nokunmam
Naacqc   cikáaw'is   hiwc'áaqana   Ku'ús   hittiwatiyáan'ixne nokóonmam
one   crafty   he used to be   thus   they used to tell stories forefathers

Met ata   palaipalai   hiushina   Kushanih   ata   hiutsaia isaisaia   wak   imash   uiikala   ka   kala
Met'éete   peléypeley   hiwsíine   Ko'saníx   'éete   hiwc'eeye 'iceyéeye   waẋ   'ímes*   'oykala   ke   kál'a
however   foolish   they were   that same   surely   he became coyote   and   deer/animals   all   which   just

hiwash   kina   watashpa
híiwes   kíne   wéetespe
It is   here   in land

Inaki   hinanih   titokana   pataniuatatu patunm   isaiaianm   hahasnim   patunm
'inekíix   hii'neníix   titóoqana   petenw'yúutetu pet'úunm   'iceyéeyenm   ẋáẋaasnim   pe'túunm
moreover   they used to say   person   it talks to him something   coyote   grizzly   something

waiu-talikinm   kokohnim   shakantaihnim   sauin   kala
naksnih   hinimiaiiktanih   kima   uiikala
weyúutelikinm   qoqóoxnim   saq'ant'áayx̱nim   c'awíin kal'a
naqsníix   hiinmiya'íiktan'ix   kíime   'óykala
hooved animals   crow   bald-eagle   yet   just
each one   they make animal cries   these   all

Ku wat   kinaisim   panaks   wapsuh   hiutsah   hahas
  patu   metu   kala   mashtapsh   tamau-nin
Kú'weet   kínaycim   péeneks   wepcúux   hiwc'áax̱ x̱áx̱aac
  pe'túu   mét'u   kál'a   mástaps   tamáwnin'
maybe   this only   we have believed   smart   it may be grizzly
  things   but   just   unhearing   exceedingly

kaua   uiikashlih   watash
kawá   'óykaslix   wéetesx
then   all over   earth to

*Harold Crook points out that Nimipuutímt does not have a general word for "animal," so the missionaries used the word *ímes* or "deer" as a term to refer to all animals, following the older English usage of "deer" to designate any animal.

Himte'ke's XXI [from note 47]

Kuna naks hama hikiaiikshana ka kuna saiau init aushina
Koná náaqc háama hikiyéeyiksene ke koná cá'yaw 'iníit 'ewsíine
there one man he was traveling where no house his was

Kuna pahnakauna laiana iskitpa metu wako kulawit hiwaka
Koná páaxnaqawna láyana 'iskítpe mét'u wáaqo' kuléewit hiwéeke
there he really saw it lion in road but already evening it was

Kaua kuna hinaka "kakaua taks hisahamtatasha
Kawá koná hinéeke "ka kawá taqc hicehemtet'éese
then there he thought when surely it is about to get dark

kaua kiah hikpikaiktatasham wapsiaunash" Sahaham tilelpa hipaina
kawá kíyex hikpike'yktet'éesem wáapciy'awn'as" Cehehém tiléelpe hipáayna
then me it is about to track me to kill twilight at bluff he arrived

kaua kuna hinaka nasmanama in kutatasha
kawá koná hinéeke nacmanáma 'iin kutet'éese
then there he thought now how I am going to do

256 KEARY

kah   hikpikaikluaktam"   Kaua   hinaka   "Kah wakat
kex   hikpike'yklúu'ktem"   Kawá   hinéeke   "Kex wáaqit
surely me it shall track me   then   he thought   surely me I live

kush   kush   kah   hikpikaikluaktam"   Kaua   shamh hinkakawalka
ku'us   ku'us   kex   hikpike'yklúu'ktem"   Kawá   sam'x̱ hinkáaq'ołka
thus   thus   surely me   it shall track me   Then   shirt he removed

kaua   hatsuna   papalikasia   tilautoiam   kaua   pashamkia   kaua   pashapatakmahlhia
kawá   hecúune   pe'pelíikseye   tilátoyam   kawá   páasam'qiya   kawá   páasapataqmałiya
then   wood   he it put in ground bluff top   then he dressed it   then he hatted it

LITERACY, INTERACTION, COLONIALISM   257

Himte'ke's XIII [from note 38]

Tatoshm titokan muhshnim init hanianih wah tukunm wah shushainim Kaua
Tato'ósm a titóoqan múuxsnim 'iníit haanyan'íix wax tok'óonm wax suse'éynim Kawá
some people cattail house they make and tule and rye-grass then

tatoshmam piahs-init autsanih
tató'smam piyéxs'iniit 'ewc'en'íix
some rawhide-house theirs is

Suiapum wak Alaimam autsanih hatsunm init kaua pishwanm kaua hanaka
Sooyáapoom wax 'aláaymam 'ewc'en'íix hecúunm 'iníit kawá piswéenm kawá héenek'e
Americans' and French Canadians' theirs is wood house then stone then also

shitahnim apanm lunishnim
sitéxnim 'apáanm líwni'snim
mud bricks burned

Kupam wak itunm init witstatashih imam kapam kinia ahitamasih
Kú'pem wax 'itúunm 'iníit wic'etet'esíix 'iméem kepém kínye 'ehitéemecix
maybe-you and some kind house yours it is about to be yours which this you read it

Himte'ke's XI [from note 39]

Kala	ilahnipa	wataspa	kapam	kunia	watu	kos	wanikt
awisukuanaishih							
Kaľa	**'ilex̣níipe**	**wéetespe**	**kepém**	**konyá**	**wéet'u**	**qo'c**	**we'níikt**
'ewíicukweney'six							
just	in many	in lands	that you	that	not	yet	name
you know theirs							

Himte'ke's XIV [note 36]

Ki   kapam   kikashl   washih hahaswal   kaua
Kii   kepém   kikásł   wasíix hahácwal   kawa
Now which you this size you are boys   then

ki   kapam   kikashl   imanku   pipitin   washih kuna
   Suiapum   watashpa   timashna
kii   kepém   kikásł   'iméenk'u' pipít'in'   wasíix* koná
   Sooyáapoom wéetespe tíim'esne
this which you   this size you also   girls   you are there
   Americans'   in land   book

pasukuatanih   Kunki   wapsuh   hiutsatanih   hahaswal
   wah   pipitin   kikuskusap   kinih
péecukweten'ix   Konki   wepcúux   hiwc'éeten'ix   hahácwal
   waẋ   pipít'in'   kikuckucéep   kin'ix
they are learning it by that smart   they are becoming boys
   and   girls   small age   from

Himte'ke's XX [from note 44]

Tahs   autsatatu   shipnim   tahai   shamkain   tohonain
    takaiain   wah   patuain   hanitash
**Ta'c   'ewc'éetetu   síipnim   téhey   sam'q'áyn   tohón'ayn
    téekey'ayn   waẋ   pe'túu'ayn   haníit'as**
Good   it is   sheep's   wool   for shirts   for pants
    for covering   and   for things   making

Himte'ke's XXII [from note 45]

Tahs	hiwash	kokalh	kahasain	Kunku	wiakaaupa	wah
Ta'c	**híiwes**	**qoq'áalx̱**	**qahás'ayn**	**Kúnk'u**	**wiyáakaa'awpa**	**wax̱**
good	it is	ox	for milk	always	every dawn	and

Wiakulawitpa	titokanm	pashapattatatu	kahas	Titokanm
wiyéekulewitpe	**titóoqanm**	**paasapa'tato**	**qáhas**	**Titóoqanm**
every evening	person	she extracts it	milk	person

hatau	autsatatu	kahas	waiiktain	wah	hiptain
heté'ew	**'ewc'éetetu**	**qáhas**	**we'ikt'áyn**	**wax̱**	**hipt'áyn**
valuable	its is	milk	for butter	and	for food

Himte'ke's XXX [from note 54]

kaua hinaka iokopi haswal "kah wakat inokomaiksh
kawá hinéeke yoq'opí háacwal "kex wáaqit 'inóok'omayks
then he thought that very boy "let me well then make myself sick

kaua taks saikiptatash hiniu iokopi tahs kah
kawá ta'c sáykiptat'as hi'niyú' yoq'opí ta'c kex
then good medicine she-will-give that very good which I

kunki watish maua hisaikiptashaka"
konkí watíisx máwa hisáykiptasaqa"
by that yesterday when she medicated recently

Himte'ke's XXIX [from note 51]

Hihina	naks	tokohnin
Hihíne	**náaqc**	**toq'óoxnin**
He said	one	blind in one eye

Himte'ke's XXIX [from note 52]

init	kinik	inahnana	timuni	kaua	itia	kakamamu itia
'iníit	**kin'ix**	**'inéhnene**	**tim'úuni**	**kawá**	**'íteye**	**kakamámo' 'íteye**
house	from	I brought	gun	then	I loaded	full completely I loaded

witas	Kaua	alaki	atsuptaia	tuh!
wíit'ec	**Kawá**	**'aláaki**	**'ecú'pt'eye**	**t'óox̣!**
almost	then	by fire	I struck it	boom!

Himte'ke's XXIX [from note 55]

Kah kaua   kuskus   haswal   waka   hatau   tamaunin
waka   pohpokashki   hailawit
Kax kawá   kúckuc   háacwal   wéeke   heté'ew   tamáwnin'
wéeke   poxpok'láaski   x̣eeléewit
when I   small   boy   was   precious   exceedingly
was   by gunpowder   playing

Himte'ke's XXIX [from note 57]

Ki   kahkaua   anashaktatu   mamaiasna   kakaua himtsitpashwitanih
Kii   kexkawá   'enéeshektetu   mamáy'asna ka kawá himc'itpáaswitan'ix
this(-time) when I   I see them   children   when they disobey

kaua   kunai   in   naktatu   kushki tokohnin   inashapautsaia
kawá   koná   'iin   nektéetu   ku'ski toq'óoxnin'   'inéesepewc'eye
then   there   I   think   by thus blind in one eye I made myself

wah   paish   kushtita   iiawis   imamashapautsashih   kinki mitsitpashwitki
wax̣   páy's   ku'stíite   yiyéew'ic 'imeméesepewc'esix   kínki mic'itpáaswitki
and   perhaps   same way   pitiful   themselves are making   by this by disobedience

Himte'ke's XXIX [from note 58]

Watmet pisht wah pika pamtsitpashwianih Watu maua naks tahs hiutsaia
Wéetmet pist waẋ píke pamc'itpáaswiyan'ix Wéet'u máwa naaqc ta'c hiwc'éeye
not ever father and mother you disobey not ever one good one-became

mitsitpashwitki
mic'itpáaswitki
by disobedience

Yehóova 'óykalanm   hanyaw'aat [from note 60]

Iehovanm   hanit   nun   washih kushtit   uiikashlih
Yehóovanm   háanit   nuun   wisíix   ku'stíit   'óykaslix
Jehova's   making we   we are same   all over

Kinia   watashna   wak imashna   Ips'   watnim   panima
kínye   wéetesne   waẋ 'iméesne   'ipci   wáatẋnim   páanima
this   land   and   animals   by himself   he   made it

Nunimain kushna panima   kushtit   taulikina   tamanikt
     hipiimtatu   ipnim   tamalwitki
Non'máyn ku'sné   páanima   ku'stíit   tewlikíne   temeníikt
hipʔyímtetu 'ipním   tamáalwitki
For us   thus it   he made it same   trees   garden
     it grows   his   by law

Ipnimsim   ush tamalwitash nunimph   uiikalaph
'ipnimcíim   'uus tamáalwit'as núunimpx   'óykalapx
Only his   his is authority   to ours   to all over

Wakeshain   kia   hitanuasham   kanm   amtsitatashih
waq'íis'ayn   kíye   hiten'weséem   kéenm   'amc'itat'asíix
for life   we all   he tells us   let us   we listen to him

NOTES

1. Marcus Whitman to David Greene, March 1840, quoted in Schoenberg, *Lapwai Mission Press*, 27.
2. For listings of the primers and elementary readers produced by missionaries in Indigenous languages in this period see Schoolcraft, *Bibliographic Catalogue of Books*, and the many bibliographic works of James Pilling. Schoolcraft's by no means exhaustive bibliography lists fifty-two elementary reading books in Indigenous languages that were printed by missionaries in the first half of the nineteenth century. Pilling lists twenty-one such books in his *Bibliography of Iroqouian languages* alone. Other Pilling bibliographies indicate that the numbers of these books were similar for other language groups. Indeed, there were probably more: Pilling only lists two of the four primers produced on the Lapwai mission press.
3. For studies that examine both missionary efforts to introduce alphabetic literacy and the Indigenous adoption and use of alphabetic texts in the colonial period, see Bragdon and Goddard, *Native Writings in Massachusett*; Bragdon, "Native Languages as Spoken and Written"; Brooks, *Common Pot*; Brown, *Pilgrim and the Bee*, 179–207; Cogley, *John Eliot's Mission*, 117–26; Greenfield, "Mi'kmaq Hieroglyphic Prayer Book"; Jaskoski, *Early Native American Writing*; Monaghan, "She Loved to Read"; Peyer, *Tutor'd Mind*; Round, "From Performance to Print"; Rice, "To Save Their Substance"; Rivett, *Unscripted America*; Round, *Removable Type*; Silverman, "Indians, Missionaries, and Religious Translation"; Valentine, *Making It Their Own*; Warkentin, "In Search of 'The Word of the Other'"; Wogan, "Perceptions of European Literacy"; Wyss, *Writing Indians*; Wyss, *English Letters*; and Wyss and Bross, *Early Native Literacies*.
4. For studies of the colonial and anticolonial uses of alphabetic literacy in boarding schools and beyond, see Donaldson, "Writing the Talking Stick"; Emery, *Recovering Native American Writings*; Goodburn, "Literacy Practices"; Klotz, "Impossible Rhetorics"; Lyons, "Rhetorical Sovereignty"; Morgan, *Bearer of This Letter*; and Warrior, *People and the Word*.
5. There are some exceptions to this relative lack of interest in Indigenous-language literacy in the antebellum period. First, there are some important studies of the creation and use of the Cherokee syllabary—see, in particular, Bender, *Signs of Cherokee Culture*; and Cushman, *Cherokee Syllabary*. There are also a small number of studies of Indigenous-language book production in this period, but, for the most part, these studies focus on the interests and ideologies of the Euro-Americans involved rather than the processes of cross-cultural interaction and translation entailed in the making of these texts. Sean P. Harvey discusses missionary language ideologies and their efforts to produce orthographies in *Native Tongues*, 115–24; and in Phillip H. Round provides an account of the printing

and circulation of Indigenous-language books in this period with some analysis of Indigenous attitudes toward these texts (*Removable Type*, 73–96). However, he only briefly discusses their content and his section on the books produced by the ABCFM missionaries among the Plateau tribes is unfortunately marred by errors regarding their language and authorship. Separately and more specifically, Albert Furtwangler writes about the ABCFM missionaries' interest in instructing the Niimíipuu and other Plateau tribes in literacy, but he has little to say about Indigenous involvement in, or response to, the creation of the books they printed. See Furtwangler, *Bringing the Indians*, 115–57. On the other hand, Phillip Cash Cash, a Niimíipuu-Cayuse scholar and linguist, has presented an important interpretation of the Niimíipuu encounter with — and conceptualization of — literacy in the context of early prophetic movements; however, his section on Niimíipuu relations with the missionaries focuses only on their efforts to introduce religious texts and the 1842 laws, rather than their creation of literacy primers. See Cash Cash, *Timnakni Timat*, 28–48.

6. For a list of Eliot's translations and an account of this work, see Swiggers, "Bones and Ribs."
7. Moore, *Memoirs of the Life*, 163. For an example of the ways in which nineteenth-century evangelicals claimed Eliot as a foundational figure, see Tracy, *History of the American Board*, 3–7. On the ideological uses of John Eliot in the nineteenth century more generally, see Bellin, "Apostle of Removal."
8. On the literacy campaigns of the early republican period, see Warner, *Letters of the Republic*; Kramer, *Imagining Language in America*; and Kaestle, *Pillars of the Republic*.
9. On the specialization and circulation of print knowledge in this period, see Brown, *Knowledge Is Power*; and Burke, *Social History of Knowledge*, 160–83. On the expansion of the print marketplace in early nineteenth-century America more generally, see Loughran, *Republic in Print*. On the extensive involvement of evangelical organizations in American print capitalism, see Brown, *Word in the World*; Nord, *Faith in Reading*; Moore, *Selling God*; and Wosh, *Spreading the Word*.
10. "Report of the American Board for 1816," quoted in Anderson, *Foreign Missions*, 98.
11. On this shift in policy, see Hutchison, *Errand to the World*, 65–69; and Round, *Removable Type*, 81–82.
12. The orthography was first used by the ABCFM missionary Hiram Bingham, who took a copy of Pickering's orthography with him to Hawaii in 1820. Pickering had been a correspondent with Bingham and with the ABCFM missionaries among the Cherokee. See Stevens, "John Pickering's Uniform Orthography." On the relationship between Pickering and the ABCFM, see Harvey, *Native Tongues*, 120–24.

13. As corresponding secretary of the board for Indians missions from 1832 to 1848, David Greene was an active proponent of Indigenous-language literacy instruction for Indigenous people. In 1834, in a letter to the secretary of war, Lewis Cass, Greene explained that "while the primary object of the Board, is the introduction among heathen & other unevangelized tribes Christian knowledge with all the blessing which flow from it to individuals & communities, the Board also aims to promote intellectual & social improvement generally; being fully persuaded that an intelligent Christianity can never prevail in a community or exert a controlling permanent influence over it, without the establishment of schools, the reading of the Scriptures, and the diffusion of general knowledge and of the arts of civilized life" (Greene to Cass, January 2, 1834, quoted in Jensen, *Pawnee Mission Letters*, xvi). For his views on the uses of printing presses at mission stations, see Greene, "Employment of the Press."
14. David Greene to Spalding and Whitman, January 7, 1837, in Hulbert and Hulbert, *Marcus Whitman Crusader*, 263. To aid them, Greene sent them some mission primers printed in the Ojibwe, Sioux, and Seneca languages.
15. On the production and composition of children's readings books in the late eighteenth and early nineteenth centuries, see Crain, *Story of A*, 55–101; Venezky, "History of the American Reading Textbook"; Hall, "Uses of Literacy in New England"; and Davidson, *Revolution and the Word*, 66–68. On the increased emphasis on secular knowledge in elementary school books in this period, see Bruckner, *Geographic Revolution in Early America*, 99–171; and Gilmore, *Reading Becomes a Necessity of Life*, 310–11.
16. It is also possible that they heard about the practice of this particular form of graphic communication well before they first observed people actually engaged in it when they met with Lewis and Clark in 1805. It is very likely that Watkuweis, a Niimíipuu woman who had been captured and taken to Canada, had witnessed Euro-Americans reading and writing. Watkuweis was instrumental in securing a friendly reception for the explorers. See Ronda, *Lewis and Clark among the Indians*, 159–60; and Pinkham and Evans, *Lewis and Clark among the Nez Perce*, 37–38.
17. Fur traders' dependence on Indigenous messengers to carry their letters is abundantly clear from their journals. Alexander Ross, for instance, Hudson's Bay Company (HBC) trader at Fort Nez Perces, claimed that "a Columbia Indian was always ready to start in the capacity of courier" (*Fur Hunters of the Far West*, 108). It is important to note that the traders' use of Indigenous couriers was developed on the back of on established Indigenous system for transmitting news and information.

18. On the initiation of Sunday gatherings at the trade posts and the Hudson Bay Company's policy of Christianization, see Oliphant, "George Simpson and Oregon Missions"; Stern, *Chiefs and Change*, 2–8; Chance, *Influences of the Hudson's Bay Company*, 75; and Cebula, *Plateau Indians*, 76–78.
19. Samuel Black, "Report," Hudson's Bay Company Archives (HBCA).
20. Aoki, *Nez Perce Dictionary*, 746. On the relationships between Sahaptin and Nimipuutímt and on the Sahaptin word timat in particular, see Cash Cash, *Timnakni Timat*, 7–11, 25.
21. Cash Cash, *Timnakni Timat*, 28–48.
22. Quoted in Walker, *Conflict and Schism*, 35. The origins of the prophetic movement and its relationship to direct and indirect contact with Euro-American culture has been much debated. It was clearly deeply rooted in Indigenous culture and experience, but the movement also changed over time and in response to contact. Deward Walker has argued that it became increasingly concerned with an interest in acquiring the spiritual powers of the wealthy and disease-free traders ("New Light"). Other scholars have argued for its precontact origins, linking it to hopes for renewal following a major volcanic eruption in 1800 or the devastation of smallpox epidemics in the late eighteenth and early nineteenth centuries. See Cebula, *Plateau Indians*, 45–51; and Vibert, *Traders' Tales*, 50–83.
23. On the St Louis delegation, see Josephy, *Nez Perce Indians*, 97–102. It should be noted that some Niimíipuu today believe that the delegation went east not to obtain a copy of the Christian book but to obtain an instruction in literacy itself. According to Allen Pinkham, a former tribal chairman, "They didn't go there for the Bible. . . . They went to learn how to communicate with written words. They wanted the technology of writing that they'd first seen with Lewis and Clark, not the Christian faith." Quoted in "Niimipuu: A Way of Life Unravels," in the *Idaho Statesman*, September, 2005, 11.
24. For accounts of the establishment of the ABCFM missions in Niimíipuu territory, see Josephy, *Nez Perce Indians*, 120–252; and Stern, *Chiefs and Change*, 42–78. See also the many works of Clifford Drury, but especially *Diaries and Letters*.
25. Spalding, "Indians West of the Rocky Mountains," 499–500.
26. In that same February 1837 letter to Greene, Spalding explained his method of preaching with the drawings: "We have represented in paintings, several events recorded in the Scriptures, such as the passage through the Red Sea, the crucifixion of Christ, etc. These I explain first to my crier. I then go over the subject to the people the crier correcting my language and carrying out my history." After he finished preaching, he reported that the people then returned "to their tents, and sometimes spend the whole night in perfecting

what they but partly understood on the Sabbath." Further, he wrote, "if one is to leave camp for some distant part of the country, my crier and the paintings are sent forth and the whole night spent in going over with the subjects, to prepare himself to instruct others" ("Indians West of the Rocky Mountains," 499). In 1838 Spalding, probably with assistance from Hallalhotsoot, translated a speech given by a Spokane headman about Spalding's own preaching activities. Published in an essay in the *Hawaiian Spectator* by Hiram Bingham, the speech included the lines: "I see you give books to your children. I hear them read with you. I see these good books (the paintings)." This suggests that Plateau people may well have used the same term for pictures on paper and books. Hiram Bingham, "Introduction of the Gospel to North America," *Hawaiian Spectator* 1, no. 4 (October 1838): 382.

27. Smith to Greene, August 27, 1839 in Drury, *Diaries and Letters*, 107. These paintings, it should be noted, were not the same as the "Protestant Ladder" that Spalding and his wife Eliza made in 1845.

28. On the ways in which Plateau people shared stories and songs at trade and fishing gatherings, see Turner and Loewen, "Original 'Free Trade,'" 53. The importance of story persists. As a contemporary Plateau storyteller has put it: "The stories are what we have to explore with." Quoted in Frey, *Stories that Make the World*, 172.

29. Spalding, "Indians West of the Rocky Mountains," 499.

30. For a biography of Smith, see Drury, *Diaries and Letters*, 31–36. Working with Hallalhotsoot, Smith produced a grammatical "sketch" of the language in 1840. See Asa Bowen Smith, "Peculiarities of the Nez Perce Language," in Papers of the American Board of Commissioners for Foreign Missions. For a discussion of Smith's linguistic work, see Mackert, "First Grammatical Sketch."

31. Smith reported that in 1839 Rogers went "with the Indians to buffalo . . . & has made great proficiency in the language. He has a natural talent for acquiring language & it is probably that he has surpassed all other white men in the acquisition of the Nez Perce language." Smith to Greene, August 27, 1839, in Drury, *Diaries and Letters*, 110. On Rogers's early life, see Drury, *Mountains*, 269–71.

32. Smith to Greene, February 6, 1840, in Drury, *Diaries and Letters*, 133.

33. Smith to Greene, August 27, 1839, in Drury, *Diaries and Letters*, 103–4. For an account of Hallalhotsoot's life, see Drury, *Chief Lawyer*.

34. Smith and Rogers, *Numipuain Shapahitamanash Timash*, 8. See appendix, Himte'ke's V.

35. As Karen Sánchez-Eppler notes, in the nineteenth century a child's relation to books was often taken "as the surest sign of personal virtue." See Sánchez-Eppler, *Dependent States*, 8.

36. Free translation of an excerpt from Himte'ke's XIV, in Smith and Rogers, *Numipuain Shapahitamanah Timash*, 20. For the original and the interlinear translation, see Himte'ke's XIV in the appendix.
37. Free translation of an excerpt from Himte'ke's VI, in Smith and Rogers, *Numipuain Shapahitamanah Timash*, 9. For the original and the interlinear translation, see Himte'ke's VI in the appendix.
38. Free translation of an excerpt from Himte'ke's XIII, in Smith and Rogers, *Numipuain Shapahitamanah Timash*, 18. For the original and the interlinear translation, see Himte'ke's XIV in the appendix.
39. Free translation of an excerpt from Himte'ke's XI, in Smith and Rogers, *Numipuain Shapahitamanah Timash*, 9. For the original and the interlinear translation, see Himte'ke's XI in the appendix. For references to other Euro-American nations, see *Numipuain Shapahitamanah Timash*: 11, 29, 34.
40. On the significance of Coyote stories for the Niimíipuu and other Plateau peoples, see Frey, *Stories that Make the World*; Ramsey, *Reading the Fire*; and Walker and Matthews, *Nez Perce Coyote Tales*.
41. Free translation of an excerpt from Himte'ke's X, in Smith and Rogers, *Numipuain Shapahitamanah Timash*, 14. For the original and the interlinear translation, see Himte'ke's X in the appendix.
42. Marcus Whitman to David Greene, 7 April 1843, in Hulbert and Hulbert, *Marcus Whitman Crusader*, 298–99.
43. On the central role of *wéyekin* in Plateau cultures, see Walker, *Conflict and Schism*, 18–24; Josephy, *Nez Perce Country*, 18–19; and Nabokov, *Where the Lightning Strikes*, 150–55. Youths would only reveal the identity of their *wéeyekin* when they sang their spirit songs at winter spirit dances.
44. Free translation of an excerpt from Himte'ke's XX, in Smith and Rogers, *Numipuain Shapahitamanah Timash*, 27. For the original and the interlinear translation, see Himte'ke's XX in the appendix.
45. Free translation of an excerpt from Himte'ke's XXII, in Smith and Rogers, *Numipuain Shapahitamanah Timash*, 31–32. For the original and the interlinear translation, see Himte'ke's XXII in the appendix.
46. Bingham, *American Preceptor*, 159. This story was much reprinted but seems to have first appeared in Georg Forster, *Voyage to the Cape of Good Hope*, 47.
47. Free translation of an excerpt from Himte'ke's XXI, in Smith and Rogers, *Numipuain Shapahitamanah Timash*, 29. For the original and the interlinear translation, see Himte'ke's XXI in the appendix.
48. Cash Cash, "*Ke yox hitamtaaycaqa ciiqinpa*," 79.
49. Hymes, "Particle, Pause, and Pattern," 24. With thanks to Michael Silverstein for this reference and to Elizabeth Ellis for pushing me to further analyse the use of *kawá* in this text.

50. Hymes, *Now I Know Only So Far*, 235–36.
51. Free translation of an excerpt from Himte'ke's XXIX, in Smith and Rogers, *Numipuain Shapahitamanah Timash*, 45 (emphasis added). For the original and the interlinear translation, see Himte'ke's XXIX in the appendix.
52. Free translation of an excerpt from Himte'ke's XXIX, in Smith and Rogers, *Numipuain Shapahitamanah Timash*, 46. For the original and the interlinear translation, see Himte'ke's XXIX in the appendix.
53. The story appeared in 1812 under the title "The Lie" in Crabb, *Tales for Children*, 88–95. It was widely reprinted.
54. Free translation of an excerpt from Himte'ke's XXX, in Smith and Rogers, *Numipuain Shapahitamanah Timash*, 48. For the original and the interlinear translation, see Himte'ke's XXX in the appendix.
55. Free translation of an excerpt from Himte'ke's XXIX, in Smith and Rogers, *Numipuain Shapahitamanah Timash*, 45. For the original and the interlinear translation, see Himte'ke's XXIX in the appendix.
56. As a number have scholars have noted, rather than spelling out a moral code, as nineteenth-century American writers were wont to do, Coyote stories showed people, with humor, how difficult it could be to live up to that code. As Jarold Ramsey has argued, "Through the mediation of the Trickster, the people could in effect have their traditional morality both ways, at least in the imagination—familiar with [Coyote's] stories, they knew that his reckless hedonistic conduct would come to no good end, according to tribal values—but before these ends arrived, episodically, they could richly enjoy themselves, as if on holiday!" (*Reading the Fire*, 32). See also Kroeber, *Artistry in Native American Myths*, 224–251.
57. Free translation of an excerpt from Himte'ke's XXIX, in Smith and Rogers, *Numipuain Shapahitamanah Timash*, 46. For the original and the interlinear translation, see Himte'ke's XXIX in the appendix.
58. Free translation of an excerpt from Himte'ke's XXX, in Smith and Rogers, *Numipuain Shapahitamanah Timash*, 47. For the original and the interlinear translation, see Himte'ke's XXX in the appendix.
59. Smith to Greene, August 27, 1839, in Drury, *Diaries and Letters*, 107.
60. Free translation of *Yehóova 'óykalanm hanyaw'aat*, in Smith and Rogers, *Numipuain Shapahitamanah Timash*, 52. For the original and the interlinear translation see the final hymn in the appendix.
61. On Plateau conceptions of an original creator, see Cash Cash, *Núunim Titwatíitin? Wéetes*, 21.
62. After the printing of the primer, Smith, still frustrated by the people's persistent interest in stories, decided to focus his preaching on the principles of Christianity as he saw them. In a letter to Greene he outlined the topics of his sermons: "The

topics on which I have dwelt have been the law of God, the transgression of the law & the consequent condemnation, ruin & guilt of mankind, the provision of salvation through Christ & the conditions on which sinners may become partakers of this great salvation." Smith to Greene, September 28, 1840, in Drury, *Diaries and Letters*, 183.

63. On this point, see Trafzer, "Presence of *Tamanwít*," 77.
64. On the importance of song in Plateau cultures, see Hammill, *Songs of Power*, 63–84. Phillip Cash Cash has also made the point that song, like story, was a form of communication that could be employed to record and make sense of the new. See Cash Cash, "Oral Traditions of the Natíyatma," 15.
65. The reasons for Smith's departure were numerous. They included his wife's poor health, conflicts with some of the headmen at Kamiah and, perhaps above all, his despondency about the possibility of finding words in Nimipuutímt to translate the fundamental principles of Christianity. See Drury, *Letters and Diaries*, 209–12. Spalding reported on Smith's concerns about the language in a letter to Greene; see Spalding to Greene, July 12, 1841, in "Oregon Indians 1838 to 1844," Papers of the American Board of Commissioners for Foreign Missions.
66. Eliza Spalding to Mrs Sara Smith, February 14, 1842, Spalding Papers, Washington State University Archives, Cage 143, Box 2, Folder 26.
67. Spalding to D. Allen, February 18, 1842, Spalding Papers, Washington State University Archives, Cage 143, Box 2, Folder 26.
68. Spalding to D. Allen, February 18, 1842, Spalding Papers; Spalding to Greene, February 26, 1843, American Board of Commissioners for Foreign Missions Records, Oregon Historical Society, Mss 1200 (typescript), Box 9.
69. Spalding to Elijah White, n.d., in White, *Concise View of Oregon Territory*, 21.
70. Keyser, *Indian Rock Art*, 71. In this particular case, James Keyser observed that the composition as a whole was atypical of Plateau rock art designs. Keyser, personal communication, April 21, 2017.
71. It should be noted, nevertheless, that the practice of transferring rock art motifs to paper was not unknown. Phillip Cash Cash has pointed to a more recent example of a Niimíipuu writer using rock art markings in the margins of a letter alongside a Nimipuutímt text. See Cash Cash, "Tíim'enin,'" 147.
72. U.S. Department of the Interior, *Certified Copy of the Original Minutes of the Official Proceedings at the Council in Walla Walla Valley*.

BIBLIOGRAPHY

Anderson, Rufus. *Foreign Missions: Their Relations and Claims*. New York: Charles Scribner, 1869.

Aoki, Haruo. *Nez Perce Dictionary*. Berkeley: University of California Press, 1994.

Bender, Margaret Clelland. *Signs of Cherokee Culture: Sequoyah's Syllabary in Eastern Cherokee Life.* Chapel Hill: University of North Carolina Press, 2002.

Bellin, Joshua. "Apostle of Removal: John Eliot in the Nineteenth Century." *New England Quarterly* 69, no. 1 (March, 1996): 3–32.

Bingham, Caleb. *The American Preceptor.* Cincinnati OH: Oliver Farnsworth, 1825.

Bingham, Hiram. "Introduction of the Gospel to North America." *Hawaiian Spectator* 1, no. 4 (October 1838): 382.

Black, Samuel. "Report by Chief Trader Samuel Black to the Governor and Committee of the Hudson's Bay Company, 1829." Hudson's Bay Company Archives, B146/e/2. Microfilm IM101, Manitoba, Winnipeg.

Bragdon, Kathleen. "Native Languages as Spoken and Written: Views from Southern New England." In *The Language Encounter in the Americas: 1492–1800: A Collection of Essays*, edited by Edward G. Gray and Norman Fiering, 173–88. New York: Berghahn, 2000.

Bragdon, Kathleen, and Ives Goddard. *Native Writings in Massachuset:* Parts 1 and 2. Memoirs of the American Philosophical Society, vol. 185. Philadelphia: American Philosophical Society, 1988.

Brooks, Lisa Tanya. *The Common Pot: The Recovery of Native Space in the Northeast.* Minneapolis: University of Minnesota Press, 2008.

Brown, Candy Gunther. *Word in the World: Evangelical Writing, Publishing, and Reading in America, 1789–1880.* Chapel Hill: University of North Carolina Press, 2004.

Brown, Matthew P. *The Pilgrim and the Bee: Reading Rituals and Book Culture in Early New England.* Philadelphia: University of Pennsylvania Press, 2007.

Brown, Richard D. *Knowledge Is Power: The Diffusion of Information in Early America, 1700–1865.* Oxford: Oxford University Press, 1991.

Bruckner, Martin. *The Geographic Revolution in Early America: Maps, Literacy, and National Identity.* Chapel Hill: University of North Carolina Press, 2006.

Burke, Peter. *The Social History of Knowledge II: From the Encyclopedia to Wikipedia.* Cambridge: Polity, 2012.

Cash Cash, Phillip E. "*Ke yox hitamtaaycaqa ciiqinpa* (that which is reported in talk): Reported Speech in Nez Perce." *Coyote Papers: Working Papers in Linguistics, Special Volume Dedicated to the Indigenous Languages of the Americas* 13 (2004): 75–85.

―――. "Núunim Titwatíitin? Wéetes 'Our Storied Earth.'" In *Cáw Pawá Láakni / They Are Not Forgotten: Sahaptian Place Names Atlas of the Cayuse, Umatilla, and Walla Walla*, edited by Eugene S. Hunn, E. Thomas Morning Owl, Phillip E. Cash Cash, and Jennifer Karson Engum, 21–24. Pendleton OR: Tamástslikt Cultural Institute, 2015.

―――. "Oral Traditions of the Natiyatma." In *Wiyaxayxt / Wiyaakaa'awn / As Days Go By: Our History, Our Land, Our People—the Cayuse, Umatilla and Walla Walla*, edited by Jennifer Karson, 5–19. Seattle: University of Washington Press, 2006.

———. "Timnakni Timat (Writing from the Heart): Sahaptin Discourse and Text in the Speaker Writing of Xiluxin." MA thesis, University of Arizona, 2000.

———. "Tíim'enin': Indigenous Conceptions of Columbia Plateau Rock Art." In *Talking with the Past: The Ethnography of Rock Art*, edited by George R. Poetschat, Michael W. Taylor, and James D. Keyser, 143–57. Portland: Oregon Archaeological Society, 2006.

Cebula, Larry. *Plateau Indians and the Quest for Spiritual Power, 1700–1850*. Lincoln: University of Nebraska Press, 2003.

Chance, David H. *Influences of the Hudson's Bay Company on the Native Cultures of the Colville District*. Northwest Anthropological Research Notes, Memoir 2, Vol. 7, no. 1, part 2. Moscow: University of Idaho Press, 1973.

Cogley, Richard W., *John Eliot's Mission to the Indians before King Phillip's War*. Cambridge MA: Harvard University Press, 2009.

Crabb, Maria. *Tales for Children in a Familiar Style*. London: Darton, Havery & Darton, 1812.

Crain, Patricia. *The Story of A: The Alphabetization of America from the New England Primer to the Scarlet Letter*. Stanford CA: Stanford University Press, 2000.

Cushman, Ellen. *The Cherokee Syllabary: Writing the People's Perseverance*. Norman: University of Oklahoma Press, 2011.

Donaldson, Laura E., "Writing the Talking Stick: Alphabetic Literacy as Colonial Technology and Postcolonial Appropriation." *American Indian Quarterly* 22, nos. 1–2 (Winter–Spring 1998): 46–62.

Davidson, Cathy N. *Revolution and the Word: The Rise of the Novel in America*. Oxford: Oxford University Press, 2004.

Drury, Clifford M. *Chief Lawyer of the Nez Perce Indians, 1796–1876*. Glendale CA: Arthur H. Clark, 1979.

Drury, Clifford M., ed. *The Diaries and Letters of Henry H. Spalding and Asa Bowen Smith relating to the Nez Perce Mission 1838–1842*. Glendale CA: Arthur H. Clark, 1958.

———. *The Mountains We Have Crossed: Diaries and Letters of the Oregon Mission, 1838*. Lincoln: University of Nebraska Press, 1966.

Emery, Jacqueline, ed. *Recovering Native American Writings in the Boarding School Press*. Lincoln: University of Nebraska Press, 2017.

Forster, Georg. *A Voyage to the Cape of Good Hope: Towards the Antarctic Polar Circle, and Round the World: But Chiefly into the Country of the Hottentots and Caffres from the Year 1772 to 1776*. Vol. 2. London: G. G. J. & J. Robinson, 1785.

Frey, Rodney. *Stories That Make the World: Oral Literature of the Inland Peoples of the Northwest*. Norman: University of Oklahoma Press, 1999.

Furtwangler, Albert. *Bringing the Indians to the Book*. Seattle: University of Washington Press, 2005.

Gilmore, William J. *Reading Becomes a Necessity of Life: Material and Cultural Life in Rural New England, 1780–1835*. Knoxville: University of Tennessee Press, 1992.

Goodburn, Amy. "Literacy Practices at the Genoa Industrial Indian School." *Great Plains Quarterly* 19 (Winter 1999): 35–52.

Greene, David. "The Employment of the Press in Promoting Missionary Work." *Report of the American Board of Commissioners for Foreign Missions* 31 (1840): 48–50.

Greenfield, Bruce. "The Mi'kmaq Hieroglyphic Prayer Book: Writing and Christianity in Maritime Canada, 1675–1921." In *Language Encounter in the Americas, 1492–1800: A Collection of Essays*, edited by Edward G. Gray and Norman Fiering, 189–211. New York: Berghahn, 2000.

Hall, David D. "The Uses of Literacy in New England, 1600–1850." In *Cultures of Print: Essays in the History of the Book*, edited by David D. Hall, 36–78. Amherst: University of Massachusetts Press, 1996.

Hammill, Chad S. *Songs of Power and Prayer in the Columbia Plateau: The Jesuit, the Medicine Man, and the Indian Hymn Singer*. Corvallis: Oregon State University Press, 2012.

Harvey, Sean P. *Native Tongues: Colonialism and Race from Encounter to the Reservation*. Cambridge, MA: Harvard University Press, 2015.

Hulbert, Archer, and Dorothy Printup Hulbert, eds. *Marcus Whitman Crusader: Part One, 1802–1839*. Overland to the Pacific, Vol. 6. Denver: Stewart Commission of Colorado College, Denver Public Library, 1936.

Hutchison, William. *Errand to the World: American Protestant Thought and Foreign Missions*. Chicago: University of Chicago Press, 1993.

Hymes, Dell. *Now I Know Only So Far: Essays in Ethnopoetics*. Lincoln: University of Nebraska Press, 2003.

——— . "Particle, Pause, and Pattern in American Indian Narrative Verse." *American Indian Culture and Research Journal* 4, no. 4 (1980): 7–51.

Jaskoski, Helen ed. *Early Native American Writing: New Critical Essays*. Cambridge: Cambridge University Press, 1996.

Jensen, Richard E., ed. *The Pawnee Mission Letters, 1834–1851*. Lincoln: University of Nebraska Press, 2010.

Josephy, Alvin. *Nez Perce Country*. Lincoln: University of Nebraska Press, 2007.

——— . *The Nez Perce Indians and the Opening of the Northwest*. Boston: Houghton Mifflin Harcourt, 1997.

Kaestle, Carl. *Pillars of the Republic: Common Schools and American Society, 1780–1860*. New York: Hill & Wang, 1983.

Keyser, James D. *Indian Rock Art of the Columbia Plateau*. Seattle: University of Washington Press, 1992.

Keyser, James D., and David S. Whitley. "Sympathetic Magic in Western North American Rock Art." *American Antiquity* 71, no. 1 (Jan. 2006): 3–26.

Keyser, James D., Michael W. Taylor, and George Poetschat. *Echoes of the Ancients: The Dalles-Deschutes Region*. Portland: Oregon Archaeological Society, 2004.

Klotz, Sarah. "Impossible Rhetorics of Survivance at the Carlisle School, 1879–1883." *College Composition and Communication* 69, no. 2 (2017): 208–29.

Kramer, Michael P. *Imagining Language in America: From the Revolution to the Civil War.* Princeton NJ: Princeton University Press, 1992.

Kroeber, Karl. *Artistry in Native American Myths.* Lincoln: University of Nebraska Press, 1998.

Loughran, Trish. *The Republic in Print: Print Culture in the Age of U.S. Nation Building, 1770–1870.* New York: Columbia University Press, 2013.

Lyons, Scott Richard. "Rhetorical Sovereignty: What Do American Indians Want from Writing?" *College Composition and Communication* 51, no. 3 (2000): 447–68.

Mackert, Michael. "The First Grammatical Sketch of Nimipuutímt (Nez Perce)." In *... and the Word Was God: Missionary Linguistics and Missionary Grammar*, edited by Even Hovdhaugen, 45–76. Munster: Nodus Publikationen, 1996.

Monaghan, E. Jennifer. "'She Loved to Read in Good Books': Literacy and the Indians of Martha's Vineyard, 1643–1725." *History of Education Quarterly* 30, no. 4 (Winter 1990): 493–521.

Moore, Martin. *Memoirs of the Life and Character of Rev. John Eliot, Apostle of the N. A. Indians.* Boston: T. Bedlington, 1822.

Moore, R. Laurence. *Selling God: American Religion in the Marketplace of Culture.* Oxford: Oxford University Press, 1994.

Morgan, Mindy J. *The Bearer of this Letter: Language Ideologies, Literacy Practices, and the Fort Belknap Indian Community.* Lincoln: University of Nebraska Press, 2009.

Nabokov, Peter. *Where the Lightning Strikes: The Lives of American Indian Sacred Places.* New York: Viking, 2006.

Nord, David Paul. *Faith in Reading: Religious Publishing and the Birth of Mass Media in America.* Oxford: Oxford University Press, 2004.

Oliphant, J. Orin. "George Simpson and Oregon Missions." *Pacific Historical Review* 6, no. 3 (1937): 215–19.

Papers of the American Board of Commissioners for Foreign Missions, Mission to the Oregon Indians. ABC 18.5.3, Vol. 1, Microfilm Reel 783.

Peyer, Bernd. *The Tutor'd Mind: Indian Missionary Writings in Antebellum America.* Amherst: University of Massachusetts, 1997.

Pilling, James. *Bibliography of the Algonquian Languages.* Washington DC: Government Printing Office, 1891.

——— . *Bibliography of the Athapascan Languages.* Washington DC: Government Printing Office, 1892.

——— . *Bibliography of the Chinookan Languages.* Washington DC: Smithsonian Institution, 1893.

——— . *Bibliography of the Eskimo Languages.* Washington DC: Smithsonian Institution, 1887.

———. *Bibliography of the Iroquian Languages*. Washington DC: Smithsonian Institution, 1888.

———. *Bibliography of the Muskoghean Languages*. Washington DC: Smithsonian Institution, 1887.

———. *Bibliography of the Salishan Languages*. Washington DC: Smithsonian Institution, 1893.

———. *Bibliography of the Siouan Languages*. Washington DC: Smithsonian Institution, 1887.

———. *Bibliography of the Wakashan Languages*. Washington DC: Government Printing Office, 1892.

Pinkham, Allen V., and Steven R. Evans. *Lewis and Clark among the Nez Perce: Strangers in the Land of the Nimiipuu*. Washburn ND: Dakota Institute, 2013.

Ramsey, Jarold ed. *Reading the Fire: The Traditional Indian Literatures of America*. Seattle: University of Washington Press, 1999.

Rice, Alanna. "'To Save Their Substance That They May Live Together': Rethinking Schooling and Literacy in Eighteenth-century Algonquian Communities in Southern New England." *American Indian Culture and Research Journal* 34, no. 3 (2010): 47–70.

Rivett, Sarah. *Unscripted America: Indigenous Languages and the Origins of a Literary Nation*. Oxford: Oxford University Press, 2017.

Ronda, James P. *Lewis and Clark among the Indians*. Lincoln: University of Nebraska Press, 2002.

Ross, Alexander. *Fur Hunters of the Far West: A Narrative of Adventures in the Oregon and Rocky Mountains*. Vol. 1. London: Smith, Elder, 1855.

Round, Phillip H. "From Performance to Print in the Native Northeast." In *Cultural Narratives: Textuality and Performance in American Culture before 1900*, edited by Sandra M. Gustafson and Caroline F. Sloat, 97–117. Notre Dame IN: University of Notre Dame Press, 2010.

———. *Removable Type: Histories of the Book in Indian Country, 1663–1880*. Chapel Hill: University of North Carolina Press, 2010.

Sánchez-Eppler, Karen. *Dependent States: The Child's Part in Nineteenth-Century American Culture*. Chicago: University of Chicago Press, 2005.

Schoenberg, Wilfrid P. *The Lapwai Mission Press*. Boise: Idaho Center for the Book, 1994.

Schoolcraft, Henry. *A Bibliographic Catalogue of Books, Translations of the Scriptures, and Other Publications in the Indian Tongues of the United States with Brief Critical Notices*. Washington DC: Alexander, 1849.

Silverman, David J. "Indians, Missionaries, and Religious Translation: Creating Wampanoag Christianity in Seventeenth-Century Martha's Vineyard." *William and Mary Quarterly* 62 (April 2005): 141–74.

Smith, Asa Bowen, and Cornelius Rogers. *Numipuain Shapahitamanash Timash*. Lapwai ID: n.p., 1840.
Spalding, Henry Harmon. "Indians West of the Rocky Mountains" (reprint of a letter from Henry Harmon Spalding to David Greene, February 16, 1837). *Missionary Herald* 33, no.12 (December 1837): 497–501.
Spalding Papers. Manuscripts, Archives, and Special Collections, Terrell Library. Washington State University, Cage 143, Box 2, Folder 26.
Stern, Theodore. *Chiefs and Change in the Oregon Country: Indian Relations at Fort Nez Percés*. Vol. 2. Corvallis: Oregon State University Press, 1996.
Stevens, C. J. "John Pickering's Uniform Orthography." *Quarterly Journal of Speech* 42, no. 2 (1956): 139–43.
Swiggers, Pierre. "'Bones and Ribs': Morphosyntax in John Eliot's Grammar of Massachusett." In *Missionary Linguistics/Lingüística Misionera: Morphology and Syntax: Selected Papers from the Third and Fourth International Conferences on Missionary Linguistics, Hong Kong/Macau, 12–15 March 2003*, edited by Otto Zwarties, Gregory James, and Emilio Ridruejo, 41–58. Philadelphia: John Benjamins, 2007.
Tracy, Joseph. *History of the American Board of Commissioners for Foreign Missions*. New York: M. W. Dodd, 1842.
Trafzer, Clifford. "The Presence of *Tamanwit* at the Treaty Council." In *Wiyaxayxt / Wiyaakaa'awn / As Days Go By: Our History, Our Land, Our People—the Cayuse, Umatilla and Walla Walla*, edited by Jennifer Karson, 77–81. Seattle: University of Washington Press, 2006.
Turner, Nancy J., and Dawn C. Loewen. "The Original 'Free Trade': Exchange of Botanical Products and Associated Plant Knowledge in Northwestern North America." *Anthopologica* 40, no. 1 (1998): 49–70.
U.S. Department of the Interior. Bureau of Indian Affairs. *Certified Copy of the Original Minutes of the Official Proceedings at the Council in Walla Walla Valley, Which Culminated in the Stevens Treaty of 1855*. Portland OR: Bureau of Indian Affairs, 1953.
Valentine, Lisa. *Making It Their Own: Severn Ojibwe Communicative Practices*. Toronto: University of Toronto Press, 1995.
Venezky, Richard L. "A History of the American Reading Textbook." *Elementary School Journal* 87, no. 3 (1987): 246–65.
Vibert, Elizabeth. *Traders' Tales: Narratives of Cultural Encounters in the Columbia Plateau, 1807–1846*. Norman: University of Oklahoma Press, 1997.
Walker, Deward E. *Conflict and Schism in Nez Perce Acculturation: A Study of Religion and Politics*. Moscow: University of Idaho Press, 1985.
———. "New Light on the Prophet Dance Controversy." *Ethnohistory* 16, no.3 (1969): 245–55.

Walker, Deward E., and Daniel N. Matthews. *Nez Perce Coyote Tales: The Myth Cycle.* Norman: University of Oklahoma Press, 1998.

Warkentin, Germaine, "In Search of 'The Word of the Other': Aboriginal Sign Systems and the History of the Book in Canada." *Book History* 2, no. 1 (1999):1–27.

Warner, Michael. *The Letters of the Republic: Publication and the Public Sphere in Eighteenth-Century America.* Cambridge MA: Harvard University Press, 1990.

Warrior, Robert. *The People and the Word: Reading Native Nonfiction.* Minneapolis: University of Minnesota Press, 2005.

White, Elijah. *A Concise View of Oregon Territory: Its Colonial and Indian Relations: Compiled from Official Letters and Reports, Together with the Organic Laws of the Colony.* Washington DC: T. Barnard, 1846.

Whitley, David S. "Rock Art and Rites of Passage in Far Western North America." In *Talking with the Past: The Ethnography of Rock Art,* edited by George R. Poetschat, Michael W. Taylor, and James D. Keyser, 295–326. Portland: Oregon Archaeological Society, 2006.

——— . "Sympathetic Magic in Western North American Rock Art." *American Antiquity* 71, no. 1 (January 2006): 3–26.

Wogan, Peter. "Perceptions of European Literacy in Early Contact Situations." *Ethnohistory* 41, no. 3 (Summer 1994): 407–29.

Wosh, Peter J. *Spreading the Word: The Bible Business in Nineteenth-Century America.* Ithaca NY: Cornell University Press, 1994.

Wyss, Hilary E. *English Letters and Indian Literacies: Reading, Writing, and New England Missionary Schools, 1750–1830.* Philadelphia: University of Pennsylvania, 2012.

——— . *Writing Indians: Literacy, Christianity, and Native Community in Early America.* Amherst: University of Massachusetts Press, 1998

Wyss, Hilary E., and Kristina Bross. *Early Native Literacies in New England: A Documentary and Critical Anthology.* Amherst: University of Massachusetts Press, 2008.

CHAPTER 8

Across Space and Time

Letters from the Dakota People, 1838–1878

Gwen N. Westerman and Glenn M. Wasicuna

> All language is a longing for home.
> —Jalaluddin Rumi

Our project "This Is Who We Are: Letters from the Dakota People, 1838–1878" will result in a critical edition of English translations of first-person narratives of those Dakota men and women writing in their own language during the mid-nineteenth century. The translation from Dakota to English, along with historical and biographical context, will provide access to a body of work previously unavailable to students and scholars of Dakota history and culture, of Minnesota history, and of American Indian policies during the Civil War. Beyond local and regional interest, these translated letters may also have significance for scholars of internment camp studies, truth commissions, and reconciliation, as well as broader histories of the military, the United States, and colonization. Additional contributions may be made in other fields where theories of borderlands, resistance, subaltern states, and center and periphery come into play.

The resulting scholarly edition will also provide evidence of the eloquence of the language and the diversity of perspectives of Dakota people regarding the events happening around them, including the U.S.-Dakota War of 1862, often referred to as the "Sioux Uprising" or the "Dakota Conflict."[1] The letters have not been translated in a critical mass that would provide access to interested researchers and general audiences who do not speak or read the Dakota language. The period selected for this project encompasses the years of most drastic change for Dakota people: of treaty negotiations, land loss, war, imprisonment, exile, and the beginnings of recovery. As such, many of the voices represented in these letters have been silent for more than 140 years.

As interpretations of causes of cultural clash and change have undergone several shifts, the prevalent narrative of the Dakota people, and especially of the U.S.-Dakota War, has been more closely examined. In the late nineteenth century, historians, ethnographers, and anthropologists viewed Indigenous people as wild savages, defeated in "battles" by the U.S. Army: illiterate, ignorant, and unable to be civilized. Some of those attitudes receded when children's stories and memoirs, such as those written by Charles Eastman, great-grandson of Dakota chief Maḣpiya Wicaṡta (Cloud Man), began to appear in the early twentieth century and romanticized the vanishing lifestyles of the "red man."[2] In 1956, when William Folwell published the revised first volume of *A History of Minnesota*, Dakota people were cast in an insignificant role in the state's development and their oral histories and traditions relegated to folktales and fanciful myths.[3]

Numerous books about Dakota history and culture have been published in the past fifty years, including Roy Meyer's *History of the Santee Sioux* ([1968], 1993), and Gary Clayton Anderson's *Kinsmen of Another Kind: Dakota White Relations in the Upper Mississippi Valley, 1650–1862* (1984). A new state history, *North Country: The Making of Minnesota*, written in 2010 by Mary Wingerd, covers the events that shaped the region from 1650 to the onset of the U.S.-Dakota War. The process of Minnesota statehood, begun in 1848, was devastating for Dakota people and others, as Wingerd explains: "In just twelve short years, the onslaught of settlers and speculators had transformed the region: the rich multicultural world of the borderland was eradicated; and history, as written by the winners, began."[4] The commemoration of the sesquicentennial of the U.S.-Dakota War prompted more publications. Despite the renewed interest in Dakota and Minnesota history in 2012, few of those books and articles used primary Dakota sources, and even fewer had access to translations of the letters written in Dakota language between 1862 and 1865.

The Minnesota History Center holds in its collections more than three hundred untranslated letters written in the Dakota language between 1838 and 1878. Most of these letters were written to missionaries and government agents during imprisonment and removal, which is reflected in the letters' content and tone. They provide insights into the daily lives of prominent and ordinary Dakota people, their opinions about their relationships with the federal government, and their attempts to negotiate the rapid changes brought on by farming, Christianity, settlers, and removal in 1863. A Dakota perspective—via observations of the world written in their own words in their own language—will challenge accepted representations of Dakota issues and concerns and may influence the way scholars and students understand how their Dakota history has been written for them predominantly by others.

These Dakota men and women write about their families and relatives, their living conditions, their desire to be good people, and their concerns about their future in their homeland after their removal. While we had a preliminary idea of the content of the letters going into the first phase of this project, we were amazed at the depth and breadth of historical and cultural information revealed as we began the translation process. We realized within the first six months that the original goal of publishing only seventy-five letters with one historical chapter was far too limited in scope. The project was then organized into three periods, to adequately address the substantial amount of material involved: 1838–51, 1852–62, and 1863–78.

1838–51: The Development of Dakota Writing

Writing was not a new concept to Dakota people when the Protestant missionaries arrived in Mni Sota Makoce in the early nineteenth century. Before explorers and missionaries came to this region, Dakota people were recording information on "bark, skin, tabular pieces of wood, or smooth faces of standing rock," and other materials with pictographs and additional symbols.[5]

They were familiar not only with their own forms of writing, but also with documents in French and English from their encounters with the French and the British in Canada. Missionary Samuel Pond reported that

Fig. 8. Detail of a Dakota song stick. National Museum of the American Indian (NMNH) Collections. Photo courtesy of Gwen Westerman.

when he and his brother Gideon arrived in 1834 the Dakota communities "occasionally made use of picture-writing, drawing figures on bark or on a tree that had been peeled, and could in this way convey to others considerable information."[6] The Ponds were eager to learn the Dakota language and adapted the English alphabet for recording it during the summer of 1834, with the goal of being able to preach to and convert Dakota people to Christianity using their own language.

By 1836 the missionaries had developed a spelling book, followed by "Bible passages," a catechism, a reader, and a hymnal. One key to their success was Joseph Renville Sr., a Dakota-French trader who lived near Lac qui Parle. Educated in Canada, Renville spoke Dakota, French, and English. Missionary Thomas Williamson read aloud passages from a French Catholic bible, and, after some negotiation of French dialects, Renville dictated the Dakota translation, with missionary Stephen Return Riggs and the others attempting to write it down (a full translation of the Bible took the missionaries forty years to complete). Once they had books and materials in the Dakota language, the missionaries set about teaching the people in Maḣpiya Wicasta's village to read and write.

From the outset the missionaries saw the use of Dakota language as a temporary means to an end. Sixteen years after the mission started, the men had completed a grammar and a dictionary containing fifteen thousand words. However, in a letter to his brother in 1851, Samuel Pond remarked on what he considered the inferiority of Indian languages: "All

SOUNDS OF THE POND ALPHABET.

A	sounds as *a* in far.	O	sounds as *o* in go.
B	" *b* in but.	P	" *p* in pea.
C	" *ch* in cheat.	Q	indescribable.
D	" *d* in deed.	R	high guttural.
E	" *a* in say.	S	sounds as *s* in sea,
G	low guttural.	T	" *t* in tea.
H	" *h* in he.	U	" *oo* in noon.
M	" *m* in me.	Z	" *z* in zeta.
N	" *n* in neat.		

Fig. 9. Pond alphabet. Pond, *Two Volunteer Missionaries among the Dakotas*, 52.

missionaries who have acquired sufficient knowledge of an Indian language to know what it is and is not fit for, are convinced that the Indians can never have either science or literature in their own language, and can never be a civilized and enlightened people until they adopt the English language."[7] Riggs particularly thought that its days as a living language were numbered. In the introduction to *Dakota Grammar with Texts and Ethnography*, he defended the publication because "the work might prove useful to future philologists after the language itself died out."[8]

Regardless of the conversion plans, Dakota individuals gave the missionaries names in their language, as was their custom in developing kinship ties. Samuel Pond was Wambdi Duta, or "Red Eagle," and Gideon Pond was Mato Ḣota, or "Grey Bear." Thomas Williamson was known as Pejihuta Wicasta, or "Medicine Man," because he was a physician, and Riggs was given the name Tamakoce, "His Country." One of the earliest Dakota writers and a cousin of Joseph Renville was Wanmdi Okiya. In August 1837 he wrote a letter to Mato Ḣota, *Mita koda* ('my friend'), and explained Dakota traditions: "This is what we believe as Dakotas: be

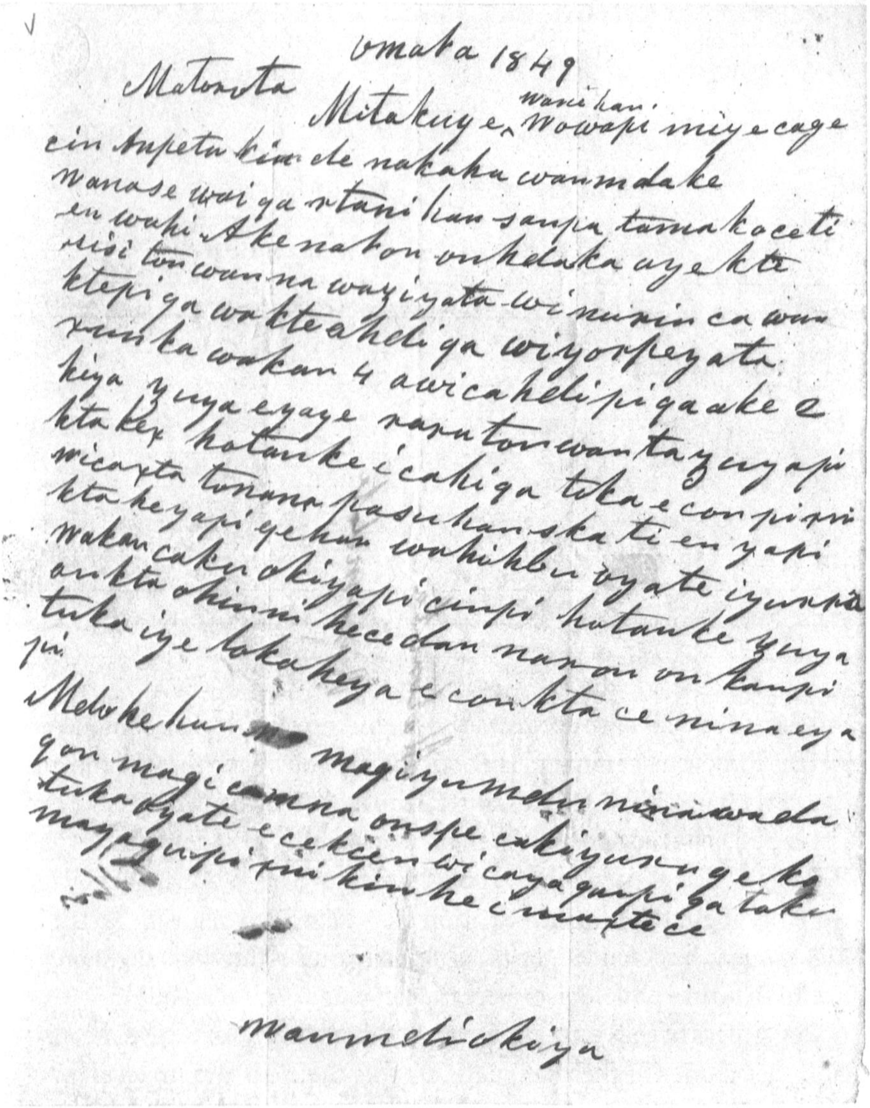

Fig. 10. Wanmdi Okiya's letter to Mato Ḣota, ca. 1849. Pond Family Papers (P437 box 3), Minnesota Historical Society.

generous; and think not on evil; give feasts for others; scout actively during a war and be diligent about carrying away whoever is wounded in battle; do not hurt the feelings of anyone; feed whoever comes to your home; and be kindly disposed toward all your relatives."[9] Wanmdi Okiya's letter provides a description of Dakota life and expresses the importance of reciprocal kinship, as well as the changes occurring around him, including the effects of trader debt upon Dakota society.

Wanmdi Okiya was also wary of the missionaries and their motivations in coming to Mni Sota Makoce. He was not hesitant to confront them when necessary:

> When you first settled here and taught us writing, and you said you were going to teach us everything, at that time, I alone listened to all you said, and you in no way help those who listened to what you had to say. . . . I suppose that because you taught me writing I am even worse off. As for me, I know why you are living here but you keep it hidden. When we sell this land, then money will be given to you. That is why you came. That is how it is, but you say you pity us, therein you are false.[10]

Because he was among the best students learning to read and write, and despite his direct challenge to the missionaries' motives, by 1839 Williamson encouraged him to work as a traveling teacher among the Sisseton and Wahpeton bands at Lake Traverse.

Those same missionaries and translators were essential to treaties between the Dakota bands and the United States as they were negotiated and written in the nineteenth century. Riggs, along with the trader Alexander Faribault, served as an interpreter during the negotiations of the 1851 Treaty of Traverse des Sioux. Even though he had been summoned to be a translator, his only mention of the process in his memoir is that "it gave me an opportunity of seeing the inside of Indian treaties."[11] According to the 1851 treaty journal, during the negotiations commissioner Luke Lea ordered that the treaty be read aloud in Dakota language. As a result a written record of the Dakota language version was preserved, in Riggs's handwriting. This was the version translated back into English for the first

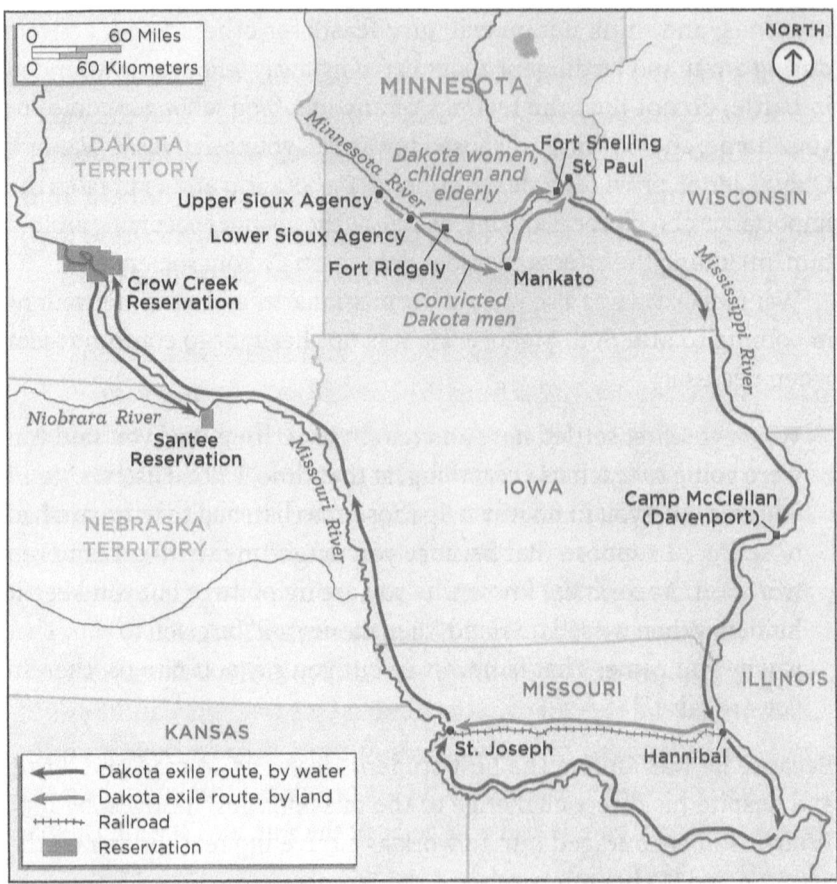

Fig. 11. Map of 1863 Dakota removal from Minnesota. Dakota Exile Route, *Northern Lights: The Stories of Minnesota's Past*, 186.

time in *Mni Sota Makoce: The Land of the Dakota* by project collaborator and fluent first-language speaker Glenn Wasicuna.

Obligations of reciprocal kinship were added to the treaty language that do not exist in the legal English-language version. Article 1 of the 1851 Treaty begins with "It is stipulated and solemnly agreed that the peace and friendship now so happily existing between the United States and the aforesaid band of Indians, shall be perpetual." Riggs translated this passage as "The people of the US and the Wahpeton and Sisseton

Dakota people, those named, help each other and are allied with each other; earlier this day they purposefully resolved and concluded forever from this time to hold each other's hearts."[12] Riggs had lived among his Dakota relatives long enough to know the significant reciprocal kinship obligations implicit in "holding each other's hearts."

The task of writing down the Dakota language transformed it. The people who translated it did not fully understand the deep cultural meanings within Dakota as it was meant to be spoken. A standard treaty term word like "article" posed difficulty. The word Riggs chose, *oehde*, means the physical action of "setting down" something, from the verb *ehde*. In the *Dakota-English Dictionary*, Riggs translated the noun as "a setting down; a saying, a verse, a sentence."[13] However, as with other translations, he seems to have added meaning to a Dakota word that did not convey the same sense as the English word he wanted to bring to it. In some cases he overcame these challenges by simply omitting passages. The language in Article 4 states that $1,360,000 would "remain in trust with the United States, and five percent interest thereon to be paid, annually, to said Indians for the period of fifty years, . . . which shall be in full payment of said balance." That annual distribution was to pay for, among other services, a "civilization fund" and meant in effect that the principal would never be paid directly to them. Riggs simply dropped this detail from the Dakota-language version.[14]

Therefore, translation of the letters written during this formative period is an important part of the story of the transformation of the Dakota people between 1838 and 1851. Translations and representations made by the missionaries and others need to be compared with original Dakota accounts. The critical edition that results from this project will help tell more of these stories.

1852–62: The Reservation Period and the War

The 1851 Treaty resulted in a series of land cessions that relegated the Dakota bands to a 10-mile-wide by 150-mile long strip of land on both sides of the Minnesota River. After the treaty was ratified by Congress in 1858, the lands reserved for the Dakota communities were reduced to those on the south side of the river. As a result of successive droughts, settler encroachment on their lands, overhunting of natural resources, and undelivered government annuities and rations, by 1862 they were starving. The strained relationship between the Dakota people and the United States was compounded by the government's attentions to the Civil War. Rations for the Dakota families were in storehouses at the Lower Sioux and Upper Sioux agencies, but the Indian agents refused to distribute them until the annuity payments arrived, and Congress held up the payments because of ongoing arguments over sending the Indians paper money or gold. When they finally settled on a gold payment in early August 1862, it was too late. Many of the Dakota bands—traditional, farmer, Christian—responded by fighting for what was rightfully theirs.

The war lasted six weeks. At the height of the conflict and spurred on by outraged Minnesotans, governor Alexander Ramsey declared on September 9 that "the Sioux Indians of Minnesota must be exterminated or driven forever beyond the borders of the state."[15] Though they sustained an embarrassing defeat at the Battle of Birch Coulee, the U.S. Army overpowered the Dakota soldiers on September 23. Nearly 2,000 Dakota people surrendered, expecting to be treated humanely as prisoners of war and as noncombatant "loyalists," based on Colonel Henry Sibley's promise that he would protect them. Almost 400 Dakota men were put on trial over six weeks, and as many as 42 were tried in a single day, with Riggs serving once again as interpreter for the government. According to Riggs, the greater part of them "were condemned on general principles, without any specific charges proved," a comment for which he was severely condemned.[16] Of those arrested, only 8 were released, 69 were acquitted, 20 sentenced to unspecified prison terms, and 303 condemned to die.[17]

The women and children were separated from the men at Camp Release. When the trials were over in November, 1,700 Dakota people—mostly women, children, and old people, along with about 250 guiltless men— were force-marched to a prison camp at Fort Snelling. The 4-mile-long train of people and wagons was attacked by mobs along the journey 150 miles downriver, which took seven days.[18] The 303 condemned men, along with 15 to 20 of their wives, were held in a prison at Mankato. Wakiyehdi, who had been among the Dakota leaders who had petitioned the American Board of Foreign Missions in 1854 for a missionary to come

Omaka 1849	Year 1849
Mato hota	Grey Bear
Mitakuye wanihan wowapi miye cage cin anpetu kin de nakaha wanmdaka. wanase wai qa htanni han sampa tamakoce ti en waki. Ake nakon unhdaka aye kte sisitonwanna waziyata winuhinca wa ktepi qa wakte ahdi qa wiyohpeyata sunkawakan 4 awicahdipi qa ake 2 kiya zuya eyaye "hahuton" wanta zuyapi kta kes hotanke icahi qa tuka econpi sni. Wicasta tonana pasu hanska ti en yapi kta keyapi kehun wahibdu. Oyate iyunhpa wakan canku okiyapi cinpi. Hotanke zuya au kta ohinni heceda nahon unkanpi. Tka iye tokaheya econ kta ce nina eyapi. mdokehanna magi yumbdu nina wada. Quon magicamna onspe caki yuhungeka tuka oyate ecekcen wicayakupi qa taku mayakupi sni kin he imaste ce.	My relative, last winter you wrote to me I just saw it today. I went on a buffalo hunt and two days ago I got to Tamakoce's place. Again they will be moving. A Sisseton woman was killed up north they brought her home. they brought back four horses from the west and two groups went to war they want to fight the Ojibwe but they are mixed in with Ho Chunk and they did not. Some men said they were going to Pasu Hanske place and Wahihbu Oyate, all of them, want to help Wakan Canku. We always hear the Ho Chunk are going to make war on us. They have to make the first move we said. Last summer I kept asking for a plow and also hoe, fish hook, but you gave them out to certain people and gave me nothing. I am embarassed and shamed by that.
Wanmdi okiya	Wanmdi Okiya

Fig. 12. Transcribed and translated letter of Wanmdi Okiya, 1849. Courtesy of Gwen Westerman.

to their village, expressed his concern in a letter to Riggs: "My relative, Tamakoce, I do not know why I was jailed but it has happened and I am suffering. But I heard they want to keep me here a long time. I want you to find out why. I am not strong anymore. I do not want to get in the way. My children, my wife, what are they going to live on, and who is going to care for them? I am thinking about this and it is hard to bear."[19] The men, including those who had "actively assisted endangered whites and protected captives from harm," were held for weeks without knowing what would happen to them, until the list came from president Abraham Lincoln with the names of those who were to be hanged.[20]

The end of this war culminated in the hanging of thirty-eight Dakota men on December 26, 1862, in Mankato, Minnesota, which remains the largest mass execution in the history of the United States. In the spring of 1863, the remaining men were sent to a military prison in Davenport, Iowa, and the noncombatants—women, children, and old people—were transported by steamboat and train from Minnesota to Crow Creek, Dakota Territory. Three years later survivors were relocated to the Santee reservation near Niobrara, Nebraska. A 2012 episode of *This American Life* recounts this history, of which many people in Minnesota and the rest of the country are still not aware today.[21]

1863–78: Exile, Imprisonment, Recovery

During this turmoil Icarapi and Tatepiyawin were separated in the spring of 1863, when the men were sent to Davenport and their families to Crow Creek. They wrote letters promising to see each another again soon that were carried by missionary John Williamson between the prison and the settlement on a weekly basis. However, Williamson appears to have been reading what was being sent. He wrote to his father that "there was a letter came here from Icarapi for his wife by the last mail but none from you. Icarapi says to his wife that he will see her either in the harvest or in the fall. I couldn't make anything else out of it but that he intended to run off. So I wish you would see to this matter. I scratched it off as I thought it would create talk among the Indians."[22] It is impossible to know what other redactions were made in the personal correspondence between family and friends during this time, and it was not the first or the last time the missionaries and translators controlled critical information.

Even in the desperate conditions of the Iowa prison, the Dakota men and women continued to write to each other and to the missionaries about rumors they heard and news they received. On April 17, 1865, Moses Ite Wakan Hdi Ota wrote to Riggs about the assassination of President Lincoln. Moses was among the condemned Dakota men sent there, many with their families, after the U.S.-Dakota War:

> My relative, we heard the news that they killed the President. But it seems anyone can tell us anything, and I want to hear from you. The

President treated us with compassion and that is why we are still alive. But now it seems they have killed him and we are heartbroken. Tell me, how will the Americans view us now? I want to hear exactly how they killed the President, that is why I am writing this letter. Every Sunday, I do my best to preach to the people. That is all I will say. I hold everyone's hands. I am Moses Ite Wakan Hdi Ota.[23]

Regardless of how they had been treated, Moses and other Dakota men in prison at Davenport recognized that they had been spared by the president's actions, and that their future was even more uncertain; as Moses asks, "How will the Americans view us now?" The missionaries were the intermediaries in language, in treaty negotiations, in trial testimonies, and in prison—how often were they acting on behalf of the Dakota people, and how often in their own best interests? The letters written during this time period are especially revealing when compared to the reports, memoirs, and books written by the missionaries and others.

The Translation Project

The scholarly edition we are developing will have a general introduction that provides historical and interpretive information, including explanations of events and historical figures relevant to an understanding of the importance of the letters and how they came to be written. Currently, only two published works include firsthand Dakota narratives of this time period. *The Dakota Prisoner of War Letters* contains fifty letters written between 1863 and 1866 by Dakota men imprisoned in Davenport, Iowa, after the 1862 war. The translators converted the original Dakota text into what they call Dakota English, "known colloquially as 'Rez English.'"[24] The other text, *Through Dakota Eyes: Narrative Accounts of the Minnesota Indian War of 1862*, presents thirty-six transcribed testimonies—given in English—taken in 1901 at hearings in the U.S. Court of Claims. The Sisseton and Wahpeton Dakota bands were asking for restoration of their annuities provided by the 1851 Treaty, which was abrogated after the war in 1862. However, almost fifty years after the war, anti-Indian sentiment was still so intense in Minnesota and racism so pervasive in

American society that the Dakota men testifying there knew there was little, if any, sympathy for their claims.[25]

In addition to the general introduction, the edition will also contain a statement on the history of the letters, their physical form, and the construction of the volume of collected letters. This statement will explain annotations to various words and passages, as well as discuss the composition of the letters, including variants in spelling, methods of formal address, and possible readings. Many of the letters in the Minnesota History Center and other collections are fading and almost unreadable without the aid of high-resolution scanning. One goal of this project is to publish digital reproductions of selected letters and make digital reproductions of as many as possible available online through digital archives and the holding repositories where appropriate.

Previously completed research on this project created an inventory of the existing manuscripts of letters of Dakota people currently in the archives of the Minnesota Historical Society (MNHS). The inventory is organized by sender's name, recipient's name, date, and location within the MNHS collections. The letters are held in various manuscript collections and family papers throughout the archives and had not been inventoried within the collections or through a comprehensive catalog or finding aid until this project began.

Our project has been organized in three stages: first, compilation of letters and identification of their authors; second, translation from Dakota to English; and, third, research and writing of cultural and historical context for the collection. Between April 2011 and April 2012, the selected letters in manuscript collections of the MNHS were copied and scanned; biographical research was conducted; and photographs or images of the authors located. Eight letters were transcribed using the standard orthography and a font currently used for Dakota language. Then a literal translation was produced, with the final product being a translation in conventional English; Glenn Wasicuna was the lead translator for this process. The result was a small set of transcribed, translated, contextualized letters ready for further research and publication, which led to the award of a two-year grant from the Scholarly Editions and Translations Program of the National Endowment for the Humanities.

To maximize results for the two years of the 2016–17 grant period, the scope of the search for additional letters in Dakota language from 1838–78 was limited to the following locations: the National Archives, the Center for Western Studies at Augustana College, the Franz Boas Papers at the American Philosophical Society, and the Abraham Lincoln Papers at the Library of Congress. Due to the lack of familiarity with Dakota language or recognition of their historical importance, collections staff at repositories seldom catalog these letters with any level of detail. Many have been found in general correspondence files or labeled as miscellaneous documents or misfiled, which is why it is important that the collections be physically inspected whenever possible.

By the start of the grant period in January 2016, most of the existing letters at the Minnesota Historical Society were identified, and 122 were collected. Transcription was more labor-intensive than we had anticipated for the project team as it was originally developed; consequently, we hired a graduate student for that task, which significantly boosted project productivity. Rachel Schienke transcribed the original letters, then worked with lead translator Glenn Wasicuna to correct the letter transcriptions, transcribed the translations, and created an abstract and an index for each letter. In this case unfamiliarity with Dakota language was an asset, as she transcribed what she saw without the distraction of trying to understand the content of the letters. Variation in handwriting of the originals is still a challenge at times for the entire project team.

To produce an accurate text for the collection and to provide consistency in translations, the project team also has the support of a formal advisory board. Members of the board were selected for their combined qualifications of editorial and translation experience, and backgrounds in the language, history, culture, and literature of Native Americans, especially of the Dakota people. The board includes fluent Dakota speakers, Dakota-language teachers, a digital archivist, and editors knowledgeable in preserving and publishing Native-language materials. The Dakota speakers will also serve as reviewers of the translations.

The significance of the letters for this scholarly edition is that they will complement, challenge, and expand relevant studies in the humanities by providing the first-person narratives of Dakota people in the mid-nineteenth century who were directly involved in historical events. These letters have yet to be translated in a critical mass to provide access to interested researchers who do not speak or read the Dakota language, and it is anticipated that this will be a major contribution to the body of translated Dakota narratives published in English.

> Wanmdiokiya just received Grey Bear's letter. W says he was at Tamakoce's place and heard everyone will be moving again. A Sisseton woman has been killed up north, so T's group brought four horses and two groups went to war. The group wanted to fight the Ojibwe but couldn't because they are mixed with the Ho Chunk. Some are headed to Wahihbu Oyate to help Wakan Canku. There are rumors that the Ho Chunk want war, but the Dakota are waiting for their first move. W asked for a plow, hoe, and fish hook, but didn't get them and is embarrassed and shamed because he has been left out.
> —Transcribed and translated letter of Wanmdi Okiya, 1849, MNHS Collections

As we worked through the first phase of this project, we adapted our methods as we became more familiar with the process of translation. The need for an abstract for each letter was almost immediately evident, as was the indexing of each letter. These steps are completed as each letter is translated rather than waiting until later phases of the manuscript process. As of December 2019, we have completed translation of 348 letters. Additional letters will be selected based upon availability of biographical information and identifiable photographic images collected from tribal and state archives. It is our intent that images of the letter writers be included to ensure that the writers are seen as real people. The print edition of this project will be organized to reveal an expanded narrative from multiple perspectives that documents the lives of Dakota people in the period before and after land loss, war, and exile. Additionally, the edition will be extensively indexed by writer, topic, and date so that multiple writers addressing the same situation or event can be read together. The criteria for selecting those documents to be edited and published will include legibility of the original document, identification of the author and availability of biographical information, the author's role in critical historical events, and representation of cultural aspects of Dakota life at that time.[26]

The methods for this project follow the guidelines set by the Modern Language Association Committee on Scholarly Editions and strive for consistency and explicitness. Each letter selected for translation is digitally photographed or scanned and then transcribed from the digital copy. During the transcription process, the project team determines the letter's content and records additional information about the topic and author. The transcription is checked against the original, and potentially significant texts are collated. Literal translations were not generated because of the limited time frame, so we began with transliterations, followed by a final version in conventional English that achieves an equivalent level of eloquence with the original. The letter is then indexed, and an abstract is created.

A general critical introduction to the edition will provide historical and interpretive information about the letters and their authors, including annotations of various words, as well as variant spellings of names, events, and historical figures about which the intended audience may need more background information. These annotations may include informative notes and descriptions providing more detail, with references to outside sources on Dakota language or history. This introduction will be complemented by a textual essay that describes how the edition was constructed, provides a clear statement of the editorial principles and methods, and gives a physical description of the manuscript letters. An index will be developed with sufficient detail and appropriate terminology for the subject and intended readers, as well as entries reflecting variant spelling of names and places. We have made the deliberate decision not to translate personal Dakota names into English because we do not have—in most cases—the context of the original meanings. It is our position that literal translations do a disservice to the significance of naming in our Dakota culture and traditions.

Particular problems posed by the translation of these letters include a range of nineteenth-century penmanship styles, unrecognizable words in the manuscripts, references to unidentifiable persons or places, inconsistent spellings and word breaks, as well as use of words that are archaic to contemporary Dakota speakers. For example, earlier writers from 1835 to about 1851 use variant spellings for the same sounds. These kinds of issues were resolved by referring back to the initial alphabet and dictionary developed by the missionaries and logging the spelling variations. In some cases annotations will have to be added to explain possible variant readings or the inability to provide a definitive translation for a word or term. Providing annotated transcriptions will give readers useful information within the well-researched and balanced context that is necessary to understand the complexities of the historical record. Thus, the project will offer students, educators, researchers, Dakota descendants, and the general public visual and intellectual access to significant historical knowledge for the purposes of learning, teaching, scholarly analysis, and research.

Despite the historical and linguistic significance of this collection of letters, it will be extremely important to provide a critical introduction to establish the historical and intellectual contexts as well. Knowing the extreme conditions under which many of the letters were written and the ultimate removal of the Dakota people from their homeland will contribute to a better understanding of the texts. Digital reproductions of the original letters will support the literacy and eloquence of Dakota men and women, and American Indians as a group, during a period in history when they were thought to be illiterate. Perhaps even more significant is the representation of distinct and diverse perspectives among this group of Dakota people that demonstrates their understanding of the events affecting them, as well as their agency in expressing their concerns in their own words. It is time for their voices to be heard.

NOTES

1. Numerous books have been written about the "Dakota Conflict" or "Sioux Uprising." For more information about Dakota history and events leading up to the U.S.-Dakota War of 1862, see Meyer, *History of the Santee Sioux*; Wingerd, *North Country*; and Westerman and White, *Mni Sota Makoce*.
2. Among Charles Eastman's many works are *Indian Boyhood* (1902), *Wigwam Evenings* (1909), and *From the Deep Woods to Civilization* (1916).
3. Folwell, *History of Minnesota*.
4. Wingerd, *North Country*, xvi–xvii.
5. Schoolcraft, *Information*, 277.
6. Pond, *Dakota Life in the Upper Midwest*, 78.

7. Samuel Pond to Gideon Pond, January 5, 1851, MHSP.
8. Meyer, 53–54.
9. Wanmbdi Okiya to Mato Ḣota, August 1837, EDP.
10. Wanmbdi Okiya to Mato Ḣota and Amos Huggins, May 1838, EDP.
11. Riggs, *Mary and I*, 116.
12. Westerman and White, *Mni Sota Makoce*, 176.
13. Riggs, *Dakota-English Dictionary*, 348.
14. Westerman and White, *Mni Sota Makoce*, 178.
15. Ramsey, "To a Special Session," 64–66.
16. Riggs, *Mary and I*, 208.
17. Wingerd, *North Country*, 314.
18. Wingerd, *North Country*, 319.
19. Wakiyehdi to Tamakoce, undated 1862, MHSR. Wasicuna-Westerman translation.
20. Wingerd, *North Country*, 324. Lincoln's original list was forty, including Joseph Godfrey, a former enslaved African married to a Dakota woman, who provided testimony against many Dakota men during the trials. His sentence was commuted by the military commission, and he served three years in prison with the Dakota people. Another Dakota man Tatemina (Round Wind) was granted a reprieve based on the pleas of Thomas Williamson and his wife (Meyer, *History of the Santee Sioux*, 127–28).
21. "Little War on the Prairie."
22. John Williamson to Thomas Williamson, undated, from Sioux Agency, MHSW.
23. Ite Wakan Hdi Ota to Tamakoce, April 7, 1865, MHSR. Wasicuna-Westerman translation.
24. Canku and Simon, *Dakota Prisoner of War Letters*, xxii.
25. Anderson and Woolworth, *Through Dakota Eyes*, 2–3.
26. Any information in these letters identified as culturally sensitive by the cultural advisors, reviewers, or preservation officers will not be published in print or online.

BIBLIOGRAPHY

Anderson, Gary Clayton, and Alan R. Woolworth, eds. *Through Dakota Eyes: Narrative Accounts of the Minnesota Indian War of 1862*. St. Paul: Minnesota Historical Society, 1988.

Canku, Clifford, and Mike Simon. *The Dakota Prisoner of War Letters*. St. Paul: Minnesota Historical Society, 2013.

Ella Cara Deloria Papers (EDP). Letters & Misc. Materials from the Minnesota Mss. American Philosophical Society Library, American Philosophical Society, Philadelphia.

Folwell, William. *A History of Minnesota*. Vol. 1. Rev. ed. St. Paul: Minnesota Historical Society, 1956.

"Little War on the Prairie." *This American Life*, Episode 479, November 23, 2012. https://www.thisamericanlife.org/479/little-war-on-the-prairie.

Meyer, Roy W. *History of the Santee Sioux: United States Indian Policy on Trial, Revised Edition*. Lincoln: University of Nebraska Press, 1993.

Minnesota Historical Society (MHSP).
Gale Family Library
    Pond Family Papers (P437)
    Stephen R. Riggs and Family Papers (144.G.7.1B)
    Thomas H. Williamson Papers (P726)

Pond, Gideon W. *Dakota Life in the Upper Midwest*. St. Paul: Minnesota Historical Society, 1986.

Ramsey, Alexander. "To a Special Session of the Minnesota Legislature, September 9, 1862." Minnesota Executive Documents, 1862, 64–66.

Riggs, Stephen R. *A Dakota-English Dictionary*. St. Paul: Minnesota Historical Society, 1992.

——— . *Mary and I: Forty Years with the Sioux*. Boston: Congregational Sunday School & Publishing Society, 1887.

Schoolcraft, Henry Rowe. *Information Respecting the History, Condition and Prospects of the Indian Tribes of the United States*. Vol. 2. Philadelphia: Lippincott, Grambo, 1853.

Westerman, Gwen, and Bruce M. White, *Mni Sota Makoce: The Land of the Dakota*. St. Paul: Minnesota Historical Society, 2012.

Wingerd, Mary Lethert. *North Country: The Making of Minnesota*. Minneapolis: University of Minnesota Press, 2010.

PART 4

Landscape and Language

Commentary by Michael Silverstein

One of the critical issues for academic scholars working to "revitalize" American Native languages and sociocultural traditions is how to avoid metaphorically compounding the various colonizing and subordinating projects of the settler state in efforts to support and assist Indigenous groups. In matters of language, the Euro-American and Canadian scholarly tradition has worked in terms of documentation of grammatical structure and dictionary. And, until very recently, partly as a function of technical infrastructures, actual discourse—language in use—could be rendered only from narrative monologue transcribed live or from audio recordings. These have been published in print editions of "texts" or exist as collections in field archives awaiting such treatment. To be sure, great figures such as Franz Boas drew Native American people into this documentary work (the Fox scholar William Jones and the Nez Perce scholar Archie Finney did anthropology PhDs under Boas at Columbia; the Yankton Dakota woman of letters Ella Deloria worked with him for her EdD at Teachers College, Columbia), but their work was in the main shaped by academic disciplinary professional consciousness.

In relation to projects of Native American and First Nation communities, these collections of material have themselves become useful in new ways: as resources not merely for various scholarly and scientific projects but also for the people whose linguistic and cultural heritage they instantiate and exemplify. Communities have in various ways been able to draw on both published and unpublished resources as they develop their local practical consciousness of heritage and ways of keeping it vital or returning it to vitality for present and future generations. What "language" means for the work of the anthropological linguist and what "culture" means for that of the sociocultural anthropologist do not necessarily approximate the reflexive understandings by which Indigenous people value these materials and their possible reimmersive uses in creative projects focused on heritage that both of the following contributions exemplify. Both emphasize language as living discourse within the social space-time of a morally and ethically suffused cosmos.

Tsal'áł, the territory of the present-day Upper St'át'imc (Lillooet) people is, like that of many people, a living landscape, a manifest endpoint of a local sweep of creation and transformation in which biota, including people, have come to interact according to their several ways of being, their intersecting cycles of life, sustenance, reproduction, and death. Much of the textual material documented by James A. Teit and others concerns the prehistory and rationale of such relationships among people and other species, especially the "landlocked kokanee salmon" — *Gwenis* in the local language — so that such material exemplifies a set of propositions descriptively true to those who know the conceptual vocabulary and narrative coherence that amounts to a social ecology focused on salmon harvesting by humans, blue herons, and other wildlife in increasingly threatened lake waters of present-day British Columbia.

Into this threatened — indeed, disintegrating — ecology, as Sarah Carmen Moritz reports, a sense of urgency among the St'át'imc leaders has resulted in the *Papt ku Gwenis* (Gwenis Forever) initiative that is revitalizing the social ecology by raising consciousness of its locally understood narrative form: the stories or tales are understood to be prescriptions for a sustainable way of life as the culmination of a long, still ongoing cosmogonic process, one that must be documented and discussed, ritually propitiated, and, especially, emphasized for young people in such projects as "culture camp" organized on the land. Here, seeing the interrelationships of humans and others in the overall way of life specific to the lacustrine environment informs the way young people are invited into activities and St'át'imcets vocabulary and expressions, as well as to explanations of the importance of keeping their way of life, of understanding that they are centrally involved in keeping Gwenis "forever." The wisdom of putting the language back into the cultural environment, the "place" it both makes and describes, couldn't be clearer.

A very different accommodation of discourse and text, to making place is the focus of Bernard C. Perley, Margaret Ann Noodin, and Cary Miller's account of creating an exhibit space in Milwaukee, Wisconsin, designed to affirm and raise consciousness of what we might consider an outside and an inside space-time. The space is the North American continent; the time is—at least at first—the history of settler-state colonization and appropriation thereof (which, as we saw in respect to the Dakota Access Pipeline, continues apace). The exhibit was constructed as an enclosure composed of four walls of verbal and pictorial material on both faces of each wall, oriented by the four cardinal directions. As one approaches the enclosure from outside, one is informed of the political and ideological forces of settler perspectives on the history of transcontinental expansion at the expense of Indigenous people. Represented in the central immersive epistemic space, by contrast, are enduring value systems of a number of people now associated with territory in the State of Wisconsin, Oneidas, long ago resettled there from current New York State, as well as Menominees and Anishinaabemowin (Ojibwas); Perley's Maliseet people from Maine and New Brunswick (he is a faculty member at University of Wisconsin–Milwaukee) are represented also.

This space, too, is rendered as a "place," an organized locus of sociocultural practice, by emphasizing a shared text, one that bespeaks an outlook on and sense of the world. It is taken from the Mohawk Prayer of Thanks that Perley had translated into Maliseet, and here, for this space, fashioned to stimulate and celebrate epistemic empathy for (and from) an Indigenous point of view, stanzas of the prayer are translated into the three other languages and mounted, one on each of the interior walls. The prayer descriptively creates a self-standing cosmos, starting (in Menominee) with stars, sun, and moon; continuing (in Oneida) with flora giving life and well-being, and (in Anishinaabemowin) with fauna such as forest animals, fish, and birds; and concluding (in Maliseet) with wind, earth, and water. A visitor paying attention to the text—really, an intertext comprising a newfound unity in diversity—is indeed transported to this inner place that revitalizes a sense that what has come from the outside, figured on the exterior of this sanctum, cannot penetrate this cosmos.

CHAPTER 9

Cúzlhkan Sqwéqwel ('I Am Going to Tell a Story')

Revitalizing Stories to Strengthen Fish, Water, and the Upper St'át'imc Salish Language

Sarah Carmen Moritz

Papt ku Gwenis as Revitalization and Decolonization

"This is the land of the Tsalálhmec, the 'blue heron' or 'crane people,' the 'people of the lake,' as James Teit chalked it up," Elder and Grand Chief Desmond Peters Sr. of Tsalálh (Shalalth) and Tskwáylacw (Pavilion) explained while pointing toward Seton and Anderson Lake in the Interior of British Columbia (BC), which means home to five hundred St'át'imc Interior Salish families at present.[1] The heron Desmond mentions relies on the water, fish, air, forest, and practical stewardship and knowledge of the land to live well, nest, and survive as a species. Reciprocally, the blue heron people share the same reliance on other beings that allows them to maintain *t'aks ta amha swa7*, or a good-quality way of life in St'át'imcets. This chapter illustrates the socially entangled needs, visions, actions, and laws that derive from this interwoven heritage. It will outline the ways we, as a community-academic alliance, seek to bolster these entanglements through respectful reliance on local knowledge, St'át'imcets (a.k.a Lillooet) language, and governance processes. Specifically, this chapter highlights some of the promising decolonial practices for revitalizing language, lakes, and livelihoods that may inspire future initiatives and generations. These practices are now emerging from an innovative multigenerational community project entitled *Papt ku Gwenis* (Gwenis Forever), and related seasonal land-based camp activities for intergenerational teaching.[2]

In keeping with the teachings shared by Lekwungen (Esquimalt and Songhees) community organizer Cheryl Bryce and Cherokee Indigenous governance professor Jeff Corntassel, this type of revitalization starts with "protecting the land, reinstating traditional roles, and practicing everyday acts of resurgence."[3] Importantly, we engage these discourses without mobilizing antithetical assimilative salvage notions and prophecies of extinction, loss, or irreversible endangerment of language, land, people, community, or culture.[4] Drawing on local St'át'imc research methodologies and storytelling practice, this chapter is written in a style that highlights a variety of voices of those who participate in *Papt ku Gwenis* and culture camp activities. As some Indigenous scholars have suggested, it is vital that we open academic spaces up to include forms of knowledge exchange such as storytelling that matter in Indigenous communities.[5]

Tsal̓álh families have thrived in governing their traditional fisheries, lands, waters, and intertribal relationships for centuries.[6] It is understood that this is not just because there were certain St'át'imc laws and social institutions in place, but because these laws and institutions are grounded in a particular way of thinking about, communicating with, and honoring the water and fish. A rich social metaphorical and metonymic lore exists in regard to fish, lakes, and rivers in and around Tsal̓álh's home.[7] These are vivid tropes to "live by" that order one's relationships to land, other beings, the past, and the future.[8] For example, one may frequently hear statements in both English and St'át'imcets such as "Fish is there for our descendants!"[9]; "Fishing is life";[10] "Fishing is our life's blood";[11] or "We are the salmon people."[12] We, the *Papt ku Gwenis* co-organizers, take these tropes and their narrators seriously, embracing metaphorical, symbolic, and literal understandings in the same multifaceted way St'át'imc narrators listen and speak to one another, both within the human and nonhuman worlds.[13] We pay particular attention to what we can learn about the instructive social concepts of "respect," "reciprocity," "kindness," and "sharing" in strengthening land, language, and community well-being. Thus, this work explores the quality of this relational ontology via such social metaphors while examining their application as communicative frameworks for ecological knowledge, stewardship, resurgence, and governance practices.[14]

The St'át'imc way of life was and continues to be cultivated through a complex knowledge and governance system by maintaining land-based stories, laws, ceremonies, foods, and territorial visions of autonomy and posterity.[15] In the face of colonial, neoliberal, and large-scale industrial (especially hydroelectric) mining and logging impacts, St'át'imc families are consistently challenged to creatively envision, protect, restore, and maintain *t'aks ta amha swa7*—a "good quality of life"—in their traditional territory.[16] This chapter provides a salient snapshot of these practices.

This chapter shows, through cogent examples, that the current collaborative reassessment and recontextualization of previously inaccessible archival materials related to Franz Boas and James Teit such as unpublished field notes, manuscripts, and correspondence—particularly regarding language, transformer, animal, and origin stories—can constructively fuel complex revitalization processes. Sacred and culturally sensitive knowledge is frequently archived in institutions without consent and removed from its origins. By and large both Boas and his Indigenous partners considered Indian-language materials to reveal Indigenous perspectives and philosophies with accuracy. These texts, embodying the thought and experience of their producers, may now be employed for ongoing social, political, and ceremonial agendas. Despite utilizing research methods endorsed in their days but considered largely unethical today (e.g., handling of human remains or ceremonial objects), Boas and Teit spearheaded respectful collaborations and a requisite and dialogic focus on both Indigenous and non-Indigenous perspectives.[17]

This chapter will reflect on some of the specific benefits and challenges of working with materials from the American Philosophical Society (APS), among other archives, and the virtual and practical implications of retelling, remapping, and reinscribing of evocative place names, as well as mythological and transformer stories, onto the landscape and back into people's minds and the current vernacular. We further consider the possible pedagogical, grassroots, and political uses of this work in translating, renaming, and reclaiming on the ground.

Spreading Our Wings: Methodologies for Change

The method underlying *Papt ku Gwenis* is defined by an intercultural, interdisciplinary collaboration that brings together community members, community institutions, and academic institutions. This relationship is rooted in St'át'imc Tsal̓álhmec protocol, the "laws of the land," that encompass practical knowledge and the social ethics of long-term enduring and reciprocal relationships.[18]

I, Sarah Moritz, position myself relationally, as my research accentuates forms of knowledge coproduction that promote relational and social justice while respecting long-standing and current St'át'imc perceptions of their lives, rights, social and environmental responsibilities.[19] My research follows in the tradition of a reflexive, relational, and decolonial action anthropology method for conducting fieldwork, in following the work of anthropologist Sol Tax.[20] This methodology protects the interests of community research partners, follows a community-defined research agenda, and focuses on the results of the research being directly beneficial to the communities and their chronicled self-determination efforts.[21]

As such, this work is deeply grounded in Indigenous resurgence,[22] decolonization, and current truth and reconciliation guiding principles,[23] as ways that communities can assert their own sustainable futures and "life projects" while realizing alternative, intrinsic models of development and growth, based on complex notions of "living well" and a "good life."[24] It also positions myself, the researcher, in a facilitating but not hierarchical leadership or expert role through techniques like open-ended, narrative-style interviewing and colearning rather than formal time-constrained consultations, allowing for less mediated responses and dialogues to emerge.[25] To ensure genuinely engaged and collaborative research partnerships, I conducted extensive preliminary research and consulted with many St'át'imc individuals across various communities on what comprises meaningful and adequate research following local protocols and priorities.[26]

In the Land of the Blue Heron People (Tsal'álh)

The Seton and Anderson Lakes deep-spawning Gwenis, also known as "landlocked kokanee salmon" (*Oncorhynchus nerka*), and the local lakes

Fig. 13. Gwenis washed ashore at Anderson Lake, Seton Portage, Tsal̓álh. Photo: Willie Terry Sr.

environment sustain(ed) the people of the lake or the blue heron people (*Tsalálhmec*), providing staple food during harsh, long, and lean winters.[27] During the postspawning season, in late fall and early winter, Gwenis ascend to the surface with an inflating air sac, float ashore animated by warm, dry Chinook wind gusts. They are then picked up by harvesters or predators such as bald eagles, wolves, herons, cougars, seagulls, or even bears that would specifically interrupt hibernation to feast on the fish.[28] Generally, the arrival of *neqw ta qaptsák7a* ('the warm south and north winds') are known to announce the Gwenis season and are traditionally a sign that the *tmicw* ('the land') and *kukwpi7* ('the creator') looks after its people.[29]

Currently, Anderson and Seton lake are thought to have severely depressed populations compared to historical records with fewer predators and a frequent absence of the formerly more predictable wind. This, following St'át'imc Eco Resources (SER) officer Rod Louie, is certainly a sign that the climate is changing too fast, and we need to address this plight collectively on all levels of governance and direct action.[30]

The Gwenis population and particularly Seton Lake are thought to be severely impacted by BC Hydro's operations, mining activities, forestry, municipal and Canadian National Railway (CN Rail) activities with a loss of land and shore access to key fishing sites, decreased water quality, and overall little or no compensation or mitigation activities to address these detrimental cumulative impacts.[31] Gwenis are granted no special attention in the water-use planning processes, which are supposed to be conducted collaboratively and sustainably with BC Hydro.[32] Industrial and other impacts on fish and water include, for example, mining effluent and train car derailments with effluent; herbicide and pesticide use along transmission lines; historical impacts through hatcheries and aquaculture experiments on the lakes by fisheries officers such as John P. Babcock;[33] changing water temperatures; quality and availability of food such as zooplankton or bullhead fish; sturgeon feeding on the Gwenis; and side casting from railway activities disturbing critical spawning habitat and times.[34]

Both 2014 and 2015, which were early years of *Papt ku Gwenis*, have been particularly poor years with hardly any or no Gwenis observed or harvested. Only one child was served Gwenis for supper.[35] Over the last years, only a few children could learn about, harvest, and taste Gwenis and participate in harvesting them. This is particularly detrimental, as Gwenis are an "acquired taste"—a way of life that must be taught from early on. Without this experience you will not make connections and tastes committed to memory, which implies that one day "it is just one of those things you remember," to quote Elder Desmond Peters Sr.[36] "Elders love the Gwenis but for them it is often an issue of access and getting them. All generations must work together," Desmond's daughter thoughtfully remarked.[37]

Some local families and leaders emphasize that Gwenis can teach us about reciprocity, respect, sharing, generation, traditional fishing laws, human-fish social relationships, continuities in a fishing way of life, and stewardship principles.[38] Knowledge and history regarding Gwenis and the lakes may be key to environmental conservation and rejuvenation of traditional knowledge, fisheries, and language in and for all of the territory.[39] This may be especially true in the face of large-scale industrial and resource-extractive impacts and an overall decline of fisheries. The Fraser River sockeye salmon fishery has been increasingly dismal, with the worst return on record in 2016, which left many St'át'imc hungry for fish and camp life.

Practicing Reciprocity, Sharing, and Posterity

To address this plight, together with a diverse and multigenerational group of Tsal'álh community organizers including an Elder, a hereditary chief, a leader and St'át'imc title and rights activist, a comprehensive community planner seeking to resuscitate a hereditary governance structure, and Tsal'álh Chief and Council support, we have set up the *Papt ku Gwenis* (Gwenis Forever) project, which began in the winter of 2014–15. The project is planned to run for several years and will ideally yield sustainable change as we document and present the social, ecological, economic, and spiritual significance and status of Gwenis and their lake environments. Building on these insights, a next step is the devising of strategies and actions for Gwenis and lake environment protection and enhancement. Overall, we seek to bolster local language, knowledge, laws, and governance practices regarding water, fish, stories, and land use. As one Tsal'álh Elder remarked, "All our stories are supposed to teach us things," and we base our attention on this methodological and ethical insight.[40]

For the project, we have collectively drafted a vision statement as follows:

> Papt ku Gwenis is a local research project that documents the past and future of the Gwenis in Tsal'álh's watersheds to increase knowledge and stewardship strategies to ensure their existence as food source and a way of life for future generations. Recent years have seen a steady decline of the Gwenis, predators such as bald eagles, herons, bears and the warm south wind that allows them to float ashore in the winter months. Gwenis used to be a very important winter staple food for Tsal'álhmec, for many animals such as eagles and herons and an integral part to a healthy ecosystem. We base this project on our Elders' call: "If we stop fishing, the fish will stop coming!"

Fig. 14. Watching for Gwenis at shore of Anderson Lake. Photo: Willie Terry Sr.

To ensure that our research is informed by local grassroots processes and the deepening of community-based capacity, we have created integrated research roles and training components for the documentation and promotion of St'át'imc knowledge through written, cartographic, video, and audio accounts.[41] Generally, we are relying on qualitative and ethnographic methods compatible with "local ways of knowing" and metacommunication that allows for accurate, dialogical, and diverse documentation sensitive toward the complexity that represents "community."[42]

Elder Willie Terry Sr., a passionate Tsaĺálhmec Gwenis harvester who ventures out almost every day during the winter to observe and to access the lake by boat and canoe and prepares winter fires at the beach to cook Gwenis, is mandated during spawning and harvesting season to concentrate his observations on Gwenis and the lakes. This includes a focus on Gwenis and their predator numbers, their health and behavior not only during the season but also year-round. It also includes a long-term assessment of the wind and water quality and their interaction. Willie captures his observations through a waterproof camera that functions both on land as well as underwater, and in a Gwenis diary that he carries with him on trips to the lake. In addition, a reporting sheet to assess various water, fish, predator, and wind qualities was designed through *Papt ku Gwenis* to be completed by volunteers who also go out regularly during Gwenis season.

The Tsalálhmec Gwenis and Lakes community call for submissions, which was sent out to all households, was designed to encourage community members to contribute their respective knowledge, stories, videos, audio files, pictures, drawings, and poetry regarding Gwenis' and the lakes' significance and health, locations of spawning grounds, harvesting practices, and visions for stewardship and protection. As part of this, we are also collecting spatial data points using the Global Positioning System (GPS) and maps on land use and places of significance, now a key method for community-based data collection in Indigenous contexts.[43]

Currently we are in the process of compiling, transcribing, translating, mapping, and visualizing people's contributions on what the land used to be like, what it is like now, and what it should be like in both languages to devise protection strategies. So far we have identified the need for more people to fish more often and the need to reclaim the sacred by conducting a sacred first fish ceremony, specifically focusing on the human-fish-water-health correlation and the need to physically reclaim land from CN Rail, BC Hydro, mining, forestry, and the government of BC territorially and through specific sites. We are asking about continuities and changes in this relationship, and we are reenergizing the transformative elements in this relationality by employing digital technologies in a way that enables an integrative living process and dialogue. We hope to achieve such a living discourse through digitally linking, mapping, and juxtaposing a unique plethora of stories and story versions across time and space. For this purpose we are in the process of putting together a *Tsalálhmec Úxwal* ('home of the Tsalálh') digital heritage repository that seeks to connect materials on a given topic, place, or story and make them searchable through multilingual meta tags and cross-links. This could either function as stand-alone or become part of a Tsalálh heritage centre or museum that is currently envisioned as community-driven decolonial architecture and designed as repurposed healing space, housed in an old abandoned Indian Day School.

On various occasions I have provided ethnographic, anthropological, and ethnohistorical research training to my *Papt ku Gwenis* community research associates, especially for Morris Prosser, a young local leader of Tsal̓álh who assisted in planning, designing, interviewing, fundraising, and evaluating material. Collaborating this way on the research design enabled insightful dialogues and storytelling adequately attuned to the specific event, place, or person to be engaged. Having a young Tsal̓álhmec seek mentorship this way honored Elders as, to quote Morris Prosser's eloquent reflection, "coming to seek knowledge from them is a gift for them, learning is one for me."[44]

Elders' Stories vis-à-vis Franz Boas and James Teit

As an editorial member of the Franz Boas Papers: Documentary Edition Project (FBP) led by Regna Darnell at the University of Western Ontario (UWO) and as a consulting scholar for the Center for Native American and Indigenous Research (CNAIR) at the American Philosophical Society (APS), I have been afforded comprehensive access to various archives in the United States, Canada, Great Britain, and Germany of the writing and work of Franz Boas and his associates, particularly that of James Teit, who have conducted extensive ethnographic, ethnobotanical, political-activist, and linguistic work in the area, commonly referred to as the "Interior Plateau" (ethnographic) region. A majority of this material, especially unpublished material, has not been reviewed or integrated into St'át'imc community or nation efforts. *Papt ku Gwenis*, we realized, is uniquely positioned to bridge this gap.

With the support of a number of Elders, fluent and active language speakers, we first conduct an open-ended life history, mapping biography interviews and storytelling sessions to document passed-down stories and knowledge both in St'át'imcets and English. These include stories Elders deem relevant to be remembered and used to inform community action and strategy for and beyond this project. Stories shared so far have included, for instance, Tsal̓álhmec retellings and new versions of *sptákwalh* (oral traditions or 'ancient stories forever') and *skwékwel* (true stories after mythological time), origin and creation stories ("The Flood," "Creation of the Lakes"; "Distribution of the People of the Land"), transformer stories ("Coyote, Bear, and Driftwood Salmon"; "Coyote, Mink, and Black Bear"; "Old Man Comes to Earth"; "The Salmon Men"), personal and family stories ("Fishing with My Brother"), stories about outsiders and newcomers ("Simon Fraser Traveling Through"; "Indian Agents Stopping Fishing"), as well as stories about colonial and residential school impacts ("Unlearning Love"; "Leaving Home").[45]

For *Papt Ku Gwenis*, for example, we also started working with correspondence, unpublished manuscripts, ethnographic and language materials such as the "Salish Notes" and Salish (Lillooet) vocabulary lists from the American Council of Learned Societies (ACLS) collection at the APS and the BC archives.[46] Working with these materials typically involved my reading words, stories, or story parts and then receiving Elders' and other people's commentary, ranging from approval and correction to confusion or disbelief. It allowed for an in-depth resuscitation, assessment, and recontextualization of content, as well as its accuracy and importance in past, present, and future settings. This allowed for vivid dialogues and elicited many insightful memories, stories, and anecdotes, which we preserved for future generations.

In small focus groups or individual interview settings with Elders and other community members, we specifically set out to retell and review versions of transformer stories—for example, of how salmon became people and how the origin of humans and salmon are entangled in space and time.[47] In the St'át'imc relational world, plants, animals, rocks, and significant places were and are included in St'át'imc reckoning of kin.[48] In this regard St'át'imc scholar and writer Joanne Drake-Terry notes that the Lillooet tribal territory sustained generations of people with lakes, rivers, creeks, rocks, and mountains named as defining social features or "places" of the territory.[49]

Such local "traditional" stories, folklore, and oral history accounts tell of a time in history when powerful transformers and tricksters traveled the earth, most commonly Nk̓yap (Coyote).[50] According to one of many stories, transformers were sent to Earth by Old Man to prepare it and make it habitable. James Teit writes:[51]

Coyote, Mink and Black Bears travel from Lower (Southern) St'át'imc territory on Lillooet lake into Upper St'át'imc. Along the way they instructed people how to engage essential activities such as catching and processing fish. They created beneficial and peaceful relations between the Lower and Upper families. In another story, Old Man visits the Earth to complete the work of the transformers by turning bad people into birds, rocks and animals and providing others with places to dwell.[52]

Xaxlíp (Fountain) former chief and council member Art Adolph explains the importance of St'át'imc principles derived from such stories:[53]

> Our values: We are St'át'imc. In regards to our land—we don't take more than we need. Our principles: Managing lands and resources so that they are still there for future generations. We really need to take a look at our sptákwalh our oral traditions—and how to incorporate them. A lot of them are about Nk̓yap, Coyote. In many, Coyote dies because he's done something wrong and it takes another Coyote to make right . . . if we really read into the sptákwalh we learn. He's done something wrong. You need to understand that if you're doing this, there are consequences.

Frequently, discussing such *sptákwalh* as part of our research has turned into Boas material reading sessions and spoken word performances that involved one person or a whole family translating individual words and landmarks and discussing the accuracy of what was recorded, which practices are still present and where, and which ones should be returned to and how.

During one such storytelling afternoon, Tsal̓álh Elder Pete Alexander was inspired to share with us a story that was particularly impelling and poignant regarding our *Papt ku Gwenis* objectives.[54] A *sptákwalh* transformer story on "The Gwenis Lady That Turned into a Rock" was shared with us as follows:

> This story involves a group of three powerful á7xa7s [Indian doctors with great supernatural talent and transformative spiritual powers], two male and one female, who travelled up the valley on one of the lakes,

Anderson Lake, in a dugout canoe [lifts arm, points at lake behind his house]. They came from Pemberton or Indian Meadows down south. As they were travelling across, the two male á7xa7s transformed the female into a rock when reaching the shore because she was making disrespectful demands and would not attend to their need for silence. She had asked for a drink of water as she was very thirsty. The á7xa7s had the powers to do so as it was their will. She stood as a large rock by the cottonwood trees, her forehead, her eyebrows, her nose and mouth clearly distinguishable [points at features on his face]. She would still talk and lament her unresolved situation, she was still thirsty. Some people from Tsal̓álh who unsuccessfully tried to find food and fish by the lake during one harsh winter encountered the rock lady, noticed her face and heard her talking. She still had certain powers and could rouse the wind by whistling. She asked for water because she was thirsty. She promised the men to teach them successful fishing in return. The men went to the lake, collected some water and brought it to her to drink. They brought it to her lips. In return, she called the wind to bring ashore the floaters, the Gwenis for the men to harvest. From then onwards, every winter, to honour and open Gwenis season, the people would have to splash the lady with water to feed her and fulfil her needs so the Gwenis would come for those who fish. Henceforth, she was known as the Gwenis Lady who turned into a rock. This ritual taught subsequent generations to ensure the abundant return and harvest of the Gwenis in the lakes.

"If the rock was still there now, we'd splash the Gwenis Lady and wind and Gwenis would appear to us," Pete concluded with a kind, reticent smile on his lips. Much of the rock, however, was blasted and submerged a few years ago by CN Rail's construction for both freight and rail-tour development such as the Rocky Mountaineer. This story, we realized, is not well known, and very few contemporary people could relate to it once we shared it in the community. People who could remember the story well were around Pete's age and were taught about the rock, Gwenis, and the Gwenis Lady at a young age to learn how to honor it at the beginning of each Gwenis season.[55] Generally, listeners were mesmerized and enchanted, and they wished for the story to be shared and remembered more widely.

Elder Pete, just like his younger brother Qwa7yán'ak (Elder Carl Alexander), added pensively that Teit and Boas seemed to make a reasonable effort at capturing some of the transformer stories and stories of the Animal People, but they should have pointed out that these powers are ongoing, not a bygone, obscured thing of the past.[56] They could have done so, for example, by illustrating in depth more of the context and the ways contemporary storytellers engage the stories. How are these stories kept alive and what visions exist(ed) for their future use to deal with colonial impacts? Even now there are people, places, rocks and, beings that exhibit powerful transformer qualities that are individual and complex.[57]

Furthermore, Pete noted that "this story is uniquely about our people, from our people for our people, it has nothing to do with any neighbors, the coast or exchanging of stories. The Gwenis, the lakes are unique in all of this country." He added: "When the Sama7 [white man] came, they didn't know what to call the ones who transformed peoples into a rock, they didn't know or use our languages properly, so they simplified them into 'transformers' or those who transform. Teit and Boas tried it seems, a reasonable effort. Transformer is an action word, it doesn't work as a name. We'd like to call them á7xa7, people with great spiritual powers, a named people, a people with a name." Through these conversations we grasped that Teit and Boas approached this story through profiling the blue heron people and the way they used the lakes and lakeshores, but it was not fleshed out as much as it could have been.[58] What made them miss or neglect this story?

As a general comment, Qwa7yán'ak noted that James Teit did very well with his people: he spoke the language, he lived there, worked the land, and showed good will.[59] This is exemplified by Teit's political-activist support of the charter *Declaration of the Lillooet Tribe* in 1911, a formal collective St'át'imc assertion of sovereignty over territorial lands and strong opposition to the confiscation of land by non-St'át'imc settlers and governments around the early twentieth century. Engaging ethnographer James Teit as secretary-treasurer and special agent in 1909, the Interior

Tribes of BC made a number of appeals to the Honour of the Crown.[60] These appeals were based in the ideals of truth, justice, and reciprocity and called for their land, title, and rights to be ensured.[61] Xwísten (Bridge River) author Joanne Drake-Terry highlights the fact that James Teit's engagement as secretary and interpreter for many Interior tribal chiefs established him as key witness in the political arena.[62]

For Boas and Teit,[63] also concerned with historical and German diffusionism against hierarchical racist social evolutionist principles, this story would have likely been slightly at odds with their generalizing argument that "the Lillooet tales show a strong infusion of coast elements."[64] The Elder left us with the general instruction that the story's complexity and its nuances have to be fleshed out more in the *Papt Ku Gwenis* work to affect change in people's minds and for relationships to be charted on a map.[65]

When discussing Teit and Boas materials pertaining to St'át'imc and the Lillooet Tribe, another Elder remarked critically, "Well, there is so much information out there on us. Take Teit's stories on us. Where did all this information come from? From whom specifically? It is not clear to me. Where is this information? He had good mentors. Let's show the sources, honour it. We can show different views. Let's do that now in our times."[66] Thus, it became crucial for us to contemplate the specific benefits and challenges of working with archival documents from relevant institutions such as the APS and to think carefully about the virtual and practical implications of the remapping or reinscribing of certain mythological transformer stories onto the landscape and back into people's daily lives and to do so while honoring all its various contexts from its origins to its (re)tellings.

Participating in regular lands and resources as well as culture and heritage (LRCH) meetings in Tsal'álh, we had a chance to involve many chief and council and LRCH members and to present and discuss ideas, findings, and visions for the project. One of the challenges that emerged from these meetings was the importance of shaping the project to include insights on water use and fisheries from the perspective of other nonhuman beings—the land, eagles, fish, bears, deer, herons, wolves, coyotes, cougars, ravens, the wind, and so on. This was considered paramount, to ensure that we do not create hierarchies and biases that center and augment humans. I also used these occasions to discuss specific archival material and older research of interest on the Tsal̓álh traditional area, especially Boas and Teit's focus on the fish, water, and lakes through, for instance, the "Origin of the Skimqai'n People."[67] Skimqai'n is now a contested area, historically a key fishing location for Tsal̓álhmec along the lakes, which has been appropriated, conceptually removed from its original owners, and never adequately returned or reclaimed.[68] Revisiting Teit and Boas in this regard, with the vision for reclaiming the land and setting the record straight, has been "most eye-opening and helpful," to quote Tsal̓álh former chief and council member Qwalqwalten Garry John as he reflected on one of my presentations.[69]

During such a meeting, given the transformative power of "The Gwenis Lady That Turned into a Rock" and the fact that CN Rail blasted most of the Gwenis Lady rock, we were considering the application of this knowledge beyond community and educational use to prevent CN Rail and a recent application for Tsal̓álh's permission to further side cast, upgrade, and develop in the area. "The rock is still there, even if partially destroyed, it maybe still has powers and if they do not listen to land, beings, spirits, and don't get the spiritual dimension, they may listen to us, humans, I wonder?" asked Morris Prosser.[70] In this regard Elder Pete also envisions a commemorative plaque, a UNESCO or local heritage designation, and regular gatherings at the site to remind people of the story and powers of the Gwenis Lady to bolster the relationship between á7xa7s-people-fish-water.[71] This would educate all local and incoming people on its importance and maybe instill some respect for the protection of land, water, people, and fish.

As Pete's younger brother Qwa7yán'ak reflected, transformer stories should ideally be told one to one, around a fire, between a mentor and an apprentice.[72] This is where they transfuse true meanings. If the story is mobilized to protect the water, the fish, and the people, it should be put forth on a heritage, health, and overall ownership basis. Youth and Elders agree that to "own the land" one needs to get back to using it regularly, to belong to it.[73] The revitalization of the charter 1911 Declaration of the Lillooet Tribe and Teit's exemplary activist support thereof

Fig. 15. Sacred winter fire for the Gwenis season. Photo: Willie Terry Sr.

is an important element of this effort to remember, reclaim, reengage, and reown. Accordingly, another related work-in-progress became the evaluation of measures such as seeking Species at Risk Act (SARA) designation for Gwenis, providing legal means to protection and challenging of infringements thereof.[74]

In addition to summary reports, another objective became independent toxicology reports of fish and water quality to assess human and environmental health impacts and bolster other documentation. We are also composing an interactive map of the lakes with key sites, place names, and storied descriptions taken from interviews, Gwenis diaries, and both archival and reporting material. All of these collated elements allow us to achieve a spatial and temporal synergy. A workshop is planned for the next years to teach traditional willow shoots traps to catch prespawner Gwenis and strengthen community relationships with both fish and fishing.

In line with this suggestion, *Papt ku Gwenis* continues to take place around an ongoing sacred winter fire (see fig. 15) during harvesting season with an annual Papt ku Gwenis Day and festival to gather; to share knowledge, stories, and food; and to honor fish and waters.

The Láwa Gwenis Ceremony (First Salmon Ceremony)

As already indicated above, a practice that should be participated in more frequently is the formal first Láwa Gwenis Ceremony, a first fish ceremony that seeks to connect fishing people to the master spirit of the fish, to offer respect and proper treatment, and to ensure regular and abundant returns.[75]

For a typical first fish ceremony, humans are required to *think* themselves into the ancestors, the fish, the water, the wind, and to *conceive of* life in the water, to see, smell, and feel its movement and temperature.[76] This way one may be encouraged to understand what adversity fish face to be or return "home." Such a ceremony offers the place and time to be of *pala kalha muta7 sptínusem ama*—one, good, and acceptable mind, body, breath, and thought, to connect to the spirit of the king salmon, the creator, and to respect the way of the land.[77] The primacy of the fish in this positive reciprocal relationship sustains the livelihood and well-being of the Tsal'álh community, which is highly endangered in times of fluctuation in fish populations, in destruction of habitat and in the absence of mitigation activities offered or supported by the government, industry, or scientific agents thought to be largely responsible for this predicament. Through mutual engagement in these dialogues, the Tsal'álh collectively become able to understand, share, and act upon all the different meanings of their home and futures.

For St'át'imc, Boas and Teit summarized human-salmon entanglements and a formal first fish (salmon) ceremony in their "Salish Notes" as follows:

> Salmon which have been caught in the rivers become men. They return to the sockeye country. If they should throw them away, they become angry and take revenge. If they look after them carefully, they will have good luck. When the first salmon is caught, the fisherman takes it to the house and gives it to the chief. He is put on a new mat or a good board. Then the chief's wife cuts and washes it. She holds it with her

foot and sayu. Who sent you here to make us happy. Which chief sent you. Then she cuts it. She holds taul [sic] with foot. She must not turn it but rinse and then sit down at the head and end hold its head with her foot. They are put over fire. When one side is done it is turned over and skin and bone are left on it. Then all the people are invited and the chief says: take medicine and they take pepekoi and equisetum. They rub it in the basket and drink. Then everybody eats part of the salmon.[78]

In a concerted effort to think about the revitalization of such material, we have revisited and discussed elements from the Boasian record, compared it directly to past and current community practice to assess which elements have remained the same, changed, or need to be further bolstered. For example, Qwa7yán'ak appreciates Teit and Boas's notes of the first salmon ceremony and the instructions on how to communicate with the fish and wonders how we can be empowered through memory and praxis to educate people on the importance of this ceremony, to encourage participation without putting out calls out with the character of a McDonald's advertisement.[79] As I will explain in more detail below, this is mainly because, in his mind, people should know in quietness that this ceremony is necessary, and is happening, and has been happening for a long time, as the written and oral record clearly illustrates.

The impacts of processes of colonization, residential schooling, and attempted assimilation on language and oral accounts have been immense and violent.[80] Thus, as part of *Papt ku Gwenis*, we want to think carefully about how to respect sensitive elements of the ceremony and devise strategies for regulating access to the knowledge we generate. The following section illustrates creative knowledge generation as an effort to counter these forces in a particular pedagogical context.

Language Revitalization through a Tsal'álhmec Children's Story

Revitalizing language, contriving stories, and learning the *Nt'átkmens* (the 'good ways') and *Nxékmens* (the 'laws of the people') with the children we seek to reconnect with Gwenis entail a plethora of didactic opportunities and challenges.[81] The good things include hereditary and traditional forms of governance, reciprocity, language, positive family relations, name giving, spiritual and cultural training for different roles, or inherent gifts that include dreaming, sensing, knowing, and feeling—the ability to do things in a good way.[82]

A common way to define a "good way of life" for St'át'imc is as follows:

Palla7míntwal' lhkalh tmícwa we snímulh cw7aoz kwelhkálh ka kelhaw'silca lhélta tmícwkalha.

Tákem i stám'a lta tmícwkálha wa qwéznem. Wa7lhkalh tsunam'entwal' ts7a ama nt'ákmen.

(We the St'át'imc are one with the land and we cannot be separated from the land. We make use of everything on our land. We teach each other this good way of life.)

A practical example of efforts to ensure a maintenance of the good way of life involves teaching children and youth in specific ways. Tsal'álh community organizers hold the annual Sqay't (Mountain Top) Summer Culture Camp, intended to bring young people "into balance with St'át'imc values, nature and promote health" within the traditional hunting, fishing, and food gathering areas. Camp activities include talking circles, storytelling, hiking, trail building, flint knapping, fishing, hand drumming, hunting, bathing for spirit cleansing, basketry, drying meat, traditional games and skinning, gutting and cutting of game, and identifying animal tracks. Other pursuits include the gathering of traditional medicines and food plants; drying and preparing plants for teas or ointments; learning to identify culturally modified trees (CMTs); promoting and encouraging St'át'imc ecology, land use, and wildlife practices; storytelling; and practicing St'át'imcets with fluent speakers.

At a recent annual camp, Elders, adults, and myself, as cosupervisors, practiced St'át'imcets with children aged seven to sixteen during hikes while gathering medicine, identifying animal tracks, fishing, and hunting, as well as sitting around the fire before meals to share prayers. Only two fluent speakers attended, alongside a few adult learners. Childrens' experience with St'át'imcets was almost exclusively based on limited curriculum lessons and time with Elders and fluent speakers, so camp provided unique opportunities for embodied and communal learning.

In regards to teaching and practicing St'át'imcets, a few of the camp days were particularly telling. One particular day, returning from fishing and hunting, we gathered around the fire and started reflecting on our day. Memories were vivid, fresh, and true. We also occupied ourselves picking up a variety of rocks, which we found around the fire pit and began seeing faces, animals, scenes, land features, and curious symbols. Someone ran to the main cabin and brought back permanent markers while others used charcoal from the fire's ashes as pencils.

We began drawing on the rocks while talking about our individual designs. Elder and language teacher Aggie Patrick and I translated single words and sentences from English to St'át'imcets, which the children repeated, accepted, or amended and wrote on the rocks. This developed into a dynamic dialogue about design choices and how some words translate well and some do not, gaining or losing certain meanings. Rock designs ranged from scenes of where the blue heron people originate ("there were the sun and the moon people, the people of the land"), to seasonal events ("chickadee was calling the summer") to activities we had just engaged in during camp ("Rain is busy fishing") taking us through space and time. Our mouths were filled with laughter.

We also discussed why we seem to remember some words more than others—for instance, why do we only seem to know the term St'át'imc *súxwem̓* ('balsamroot', *Balsamorhiza sagittate*) for a native flower but not the English word? Why is it difficult to remember the St'át'imcets word for "sockeye salmon"? We agreed that it has to do with how often we hear a word, how and when we use it, how easy it is to pronounce, and who teaches us. For the entire process we all became designers, teachers, learners, storytellers, translators, and artists. After a long joy-filled artistic activity around the fire and inside the main cabin during a torrential downpour, we then aligned and numbered the rocks chronologically into a story (see fig. 16).

The idea that you see the ghost or spirit in the exact the moment you shoot the deer and it dies came from the youngest child and storyteller (see fig. 17). Teit's traditions of the Lillooet Indians of the *Jesup*

Pixem muta7 I7was

A story about fishing and hunting

Fig. 16. *Pixem muta7 i7was* title page. Courtesy Willie Terry Sr.

North Pacific Expedition AMNH *Memoir Volume* IX, plate 9 and pictograph drawings were on hand and served as accessible and visual inspiration for children learning about animal tracks and rock paintings and pondering their rock story designs.[83] The children were particularly fond of the animal tracks and human and animal symbols (see figs. 18 and 19). Children also assessed the accuracy and ongoing importance of these representations for today's usage and emulated or amended their own designs accordingly. Rocks, we established, are as telling and sacred as ever; they help us connect and communicate with ancestors, land, and animals through time and space. They inspire.

This way, we employed traditional ideas and our own lived experience during camp days to cocreate and perform storied elements. We

Ni muta7 spaqw sas ta cwel'alpa
———
He is also looking at the ghost in this moment

Fig. 17. *Pixem muta7 i7was* example page. Courtesy Willie Terry Sr.

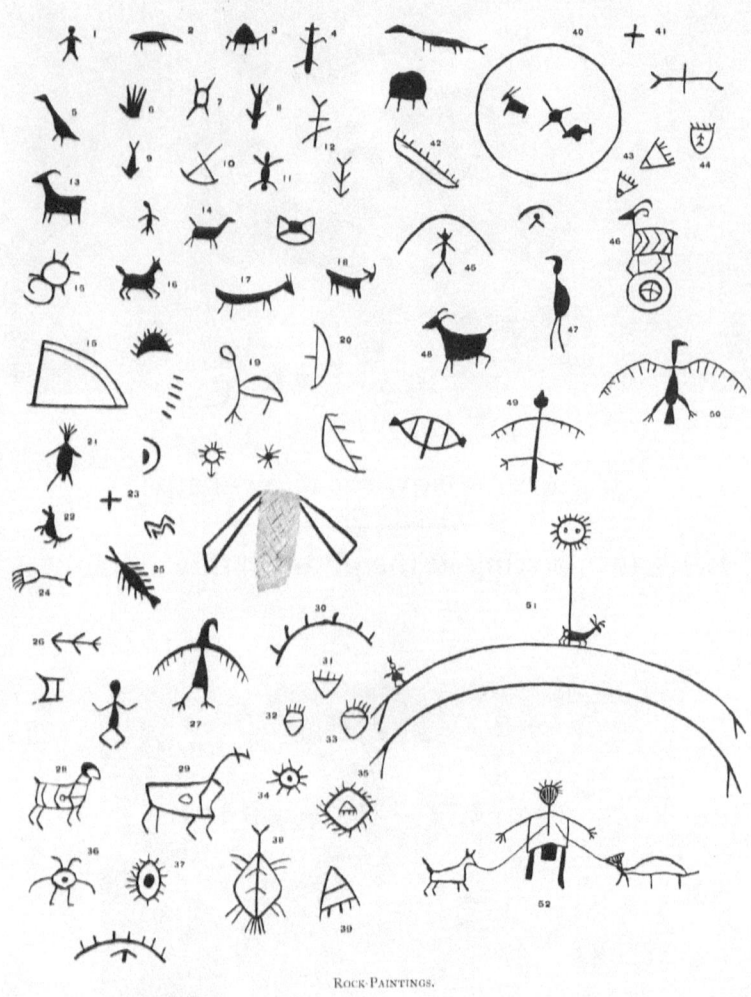

Fig. 18. *Lillooet Pictographs* by James Teit, Jesup North Pacific Expedition, vol. 2, plate 9, of *Two Volunteer Missionaries among the Dakota The Lillooet Indians: Memoirs of the AMNH*, James Teit, vol. 4, plate 5, American Museum of Natural History (AMNH). Used with permission.

Ats'xnas I mixalhena

He saw bear tracks

Fig. 19. *Lilloeet Pictographs* by James Teit, bear paws inspiration, vol. 2, plate 9, AMNH. Used with permission.

subsequently captured the rock story in a coedited booklet titled *Pixem muta7 17was* (A story about fishing and hunting) and began envisioning storied performances and reinterpretations at future communal events. Together we also contemplated the future life and spirit of this particular story. What will happen if we transplant it to other contexts, situations, minds and hearts? Will we uproot it? Will it be instructive and help people—especially youth—appreciate the content and feel encouraged to walk the land and fish and hunt, following the good ways and laws of the land? Will people be encouraged to speak, read, perform, and share this story onward? We imagined its application in community classrooms, at meetings and birthday parties, or during bedtime rituals or everyday family activity. The overall creation process and design steps could serve as innovative instruction kit for teachers, parents, and educators to replicate.[84]

On the last day of camp, the youngest fellow camp participant left us with an important vision: "I wish culture camp was every day!" With this wish in mind, we returned to the valley and our *Papt ku Gwenis* project wondering how we may salvage this spirit and ensure Packhorse Mountain camp life within the home valley. Generally, we are hopeful that the good ways—speaking the language, owning and using the land, surviving on foods from the land, knowing how to move around the land, and passing on this knowledge—are skills and gifts that could be included more in everyday activities by way of our project and the legacy it aspires to inscribe into land, lakes, and livelihoods in Tsal'álh.

Conclusions: Rebuilding the Nest and Fishing Again

Exploring the design, spirit, and implementation of *Papt ku Gwenis* and seasonal camp activities with youth, this chapter has illustrated a variety of methods for meaningful, culturally appropriate, and community-engaged health, language, and cultural revitalization advocacy.

Papt ku Gwenis exemplifies how Indigenous groups can play a significant steering role within a diverse working group. This work directly contributes to the existing literatures that explore the importance of solidaristic relationship building, the revitalization of Indigenous knowledge, and the modern historiographic, historicist, and revisionist uses of the Boasian record and archival institutions that ideally help set the table for the wider goal of reconciliation, heritage preservation, and peaceful coexistence.[85]

Papt ku Gwenis is one of the few collaborative projects that foregrounds St'át'imc knowledge, protocol, and method in design, implementation, and purpose and does not privilege Western science as authoritative, cardinal, and (a more) valid method. Neither need to validate the other, but they should coexist.[86]

With the rapid and devastating decline of the Fraser River sockeye salmon, which most St'át'imc families rely on as a main source of protein, alternatives are being sought to try and protect the remaining fisheries and ensure that all families may continue this way of life. Maybe *Papt ku Gwenis* can help St'át'imc communities refocus their fishing on the Gwenis and Tsal'álh or as a strategy and blueprint on how to deal with loss, decline, scarcity, and uncertainty, as Xwísten lands and resources coordinator Gerald Michel has suggested.[87] These are ongoing conversations that may benefit from *Papt ku Gwenis*, and its facilitative goals and visions.

Challenges we could identify overall when working with archival records include the fact that we often have a static written version of a normally performed or performative story, and we frequently lack enough context, detail, and the spirit of a person, thing, or animal whose ancestor's knowledge is captured on paper and thereby quarantined from lived contexts. Therefore, we are not always able to trace back sufficiently enough to determine when, who, or where something was shared and how to map it (back) onto the land, animal, or family histories accurately and respectfully. We are further encountering difficulties trying to disentangle generalized terms and groupings such as "Lillooet People" and are left pondering in regards to what they include and exclude. Elders are noting difficulties with translated versions of a story that in the process of retranslating may lose or change meaning and that in itself will need support and endorsement from more than one person. Qwa7yán'ak, among others, has observed that it is crucial to have written versions of transformer and other long-standing stories, as they help to preserve, cultivate, and refresh the memories of those who went to residential school and were forced to forget.[88] Frequently, however, the written record as colonial tool retraumatizes some people, and, he argued, stories should really be told from me to you around a fire, should be read by you and practiced in dialogue with all witnesses—human and otherwise—where they are written on the land. With kindness in his voice, he added that, for pragmatic purposes of revitalization and healing, exceptions must be made.

Thus, within *Papt ku Gwenis* we are always pondering how to use video and audio recordings, texts, and interactive storied maps in dialogue that teach us stories in adequate complexity, help us re-create its context, practice the language, and encourage others to participate and join forces. Throughout the project and beyond we are encouraged to pay particular attention to the way in which we document and promote descriptions, place names, and storied practice as this awareness also modifies how we relate and act upon these elements on the ground, while fishing, teaching children about Gwenis or reclaiming places and sites.

In anything you do, given these concerns, Qwa7yán'ak alerted us, remember to respect and honour the seven sacred St'át'imc laws of the land.[89] They include: *gelp* ('health'), *tśíl* ('happiness'), *nmuzmitáṅ* ('generosity'), *i ts7ása úcwalmicw* ('generation'), *múzmit.s* ('pity'), *nsná7em* ('power'), and *těktkem* ('quietness'). For example, "We had *múzmit.s* ('pity') on the starving fur traders that came to us, we were *nmuzmitáṅ* ('generous') and shared our fish with them at Fort Kamloops so they could survive," he remarked during the annual first fish ceremony. I was considerably puzzled by the last law—*těktkem* ('quietness'). How can you have a relationship, a dialogue with someone without speaking? Qwa7yán'ak explained, "I don't need to go around telling people that a first salmon ceremony is needed to honor and appease the master spirit of the salmon so many would return and feed us. That the people should not be greedy and just fish for themselves without respect. That they should join me in ceremony and that this is necessary to ensure our collective health." That must be, ideally, an implicit, intrinsic, latent, and deep-rooted understanding of the knowledge, behavior, and relationality required to live well as people of the land was the key message to take away from this decree of quietness.

Silence or quietness is manifest in other contexts, also. For example, human thoughts and language at the lakes and rivers and on the land, must be reticent and cognizant. Fish, the water, the land, the ancestors might listen and understand their quiet inward and visceral language and thoughts.[90] St'át'imcets utterances, deductions, and prayers are all understood by them as the diversiform language of *Úcwalmicw* ('the people of the land'). Therefore, one shall be reticent when discussing, thinking of, and addressing them in any context.[91] Both may embody life, death, or (master) spirits holding or taking knowledge through space and time. Therefore, encounters between them and people occur within a generalized conversable scheme governed by principles of aloofness, closeness, care, respect, and precision.

In speaking with young leader Morris Prosser about this law of quietness and the ritualistic first fish ceremony, he replied that he was not aware of this taking place, and that it is important to be educated about it, which is probably true for many other younger people. But there is a need and a willingness to learn if stories are shared again and life breathed into them.[92] Morris's statement summarizes our *Papt ku Gwenis* project's inclusive resolve and broadly, cultural, socioecological, and language revitalization work in St'át'imc territory. We are hopeful that we are contributing earnestly to the rebuilding of the nest of the blue heron people and the fish and waters on which they used to thrive.

With the encouragement and support of organizations like the APS — important archival repositories that house many of the unpublished documents that will aid in bringing back St'át'imc versions of the material such as the Coyote and Salmon People stories and language — we are confident that we will realize our goal in protecting the land and its past, as well as its contemporary and future inhabitants. Spreading our wings to embrace and bring about change so far has been rewarding and challenging in unforeseen ways.

ACKNOWLEDGMENTS

The author is profoundly grateful to the following individuals and organizations, without whom this work would have been impossible to complete: Elders Qwa7yán'ak (Carl Alexander) of Xwísten (Bridge River); Desmond Peters Sr. of Tsal'álh (Seton Lake-Shalalth) and Ts'k'wáylacw (Pavilion);

Aggie Patrick and Pete Alexander of Tsal̓álh (Seton Lake-Shalalth); Art Adolph of Xaxlíp (Fountain); Gerald Michel of Xwísten; the *Papt ku Gwenis* coorganizers and supporters, including Tiiya7 (William Alexander of Tsal̓álh), Morris Prosser (Tsal̓álh), Qwalqwalten (Garry John of Tsal̓álh), Willie Terry Sr. (Tsal̓álh), hereditary and elected kukwpi7 Randy James, former chief and councillor Ida Mary Peter, former chief and councillor Larry Casper, Rodney Louie, and many more Tsal̓álhmec individuals, who have provided invaluable storytelling, research design, protocol awareness, and translation assistance in the preparation of research and this chapter: *Kukwstum'úlhkal'ap!*

This work was generously funded and supported by the SSHRC Partnership Grant (895-2012-1001) funded Franz Boas Papers: Documentary Edition; the European Research Council advanced grant Arctic Domus; the Centre for Indigenous Conservation and Alternative Development (CICADA); the Indigenous Stewardship of the Environment and Alternative Development (INSTEAD) project; the Vanier Canada Graduate Scholarship (CGS); the Tomlinson Doctoral Fellowship; and the Firebird Foundation for Anthropological Research. The author acknowledges the profound gifts that Elders and youth continue to share with Indigenous and settler communities — my guiding inspiration.

NOTES

1. Personal communication, Elder Desmond Peters Sr., August 2014; see also Davis and Van Eijk, "Lillooet Bird Terminology."
2. There are approximately only fifty fluent St'át'imcets speakers, and most of them are older than sixty years of age. This makes language revitalization and education an urgent key priority for all St'át'imc communities. However, there are comparatively few children and youths that are learning and using the language on a regular basis. Some preschools and community schools have specific courses to learn and conduct annual education camps, such as the Sqayt Culture Camp described here. The Upper St'át'imc Language Culture and Education Society (USLCES), a local language authority founded in 1991, supports and urges learning and passing on of St'át'imcets, in both classroom and land-based settings. Therefore, the author will consistently employ "we" as the personal plural pronoun in cases of *Papt ku Gwenis* co-organizers' shared a perspective.

3. Corntassel and Bryce, "Practicing Sustainable Self-Determination," 158; Archibald, *Indigenous Storywork*; Battiste, *Indigenous Knowledge and Pedagogy*; Deloria, *Custer Died for Your Sins*; Simpson, "Anticolonial Strategies."
4. Perley, *Zombie Linguistics*.
5. Kovach, *Indigenous Methodologies*; Kulnieks et al., *Re-indigenizing Curriculum*; Smith, *Decolonizing Knowledge*.
6. Drake-Terry, *The Same as Yesterday*; Prentiss and Kujit, *People of the Middle Fraser Canyon*; SLRA, "St'át'imc Preliminary Draft Land Use Plan."
7. See Scott, "Ontology and Ethics in Cree Hunting," for a telling (James Bay) Cree example. Crucially, in arguing presence, temporal priority, belonging, and proprietary relationships for homelands that are not perceived or perceivable through (Western) ontological divisions that have the potential to (permanently) separate people from fish, lands, and so on, many Indigenous people resort to strategically deploying social metaphors that illustrate valid ways of conceptualizing and using their lands, and some of these are metaphors to live by (Lakoff and Johnson, *Metaphors We Live By*; Scott, "Ontology and Ethics in Cree Hunting").
8. Lakoff and Johnson, *Metaphors We Live By*.
9. Personal communication, Elder Desmond Peters Sr., June 2012.
10. Personal communication, Xaxlíp Chief Art Adolph, June 2013.
11. SGS (St'át'imc Government Services), "St'át'imc."
12. Teit, *Lillooet Indians*; Teit, *Traditions of the Lillooet Indians*; SGS, *St'át'imc*.
13. Cruikshank, *Life Lived Like a Story*.
14. Johnsen, "Salmon, Science, and Reciprocity"; Lévi-Strauss, "Principle of Reciprocity"; Mauss, *Gift*; Nadasdy, "Gift in the Animal"; Scott, "Science for the West, Myth for the Rest?" This relationality emerges as a fundamental critique of the Cartesian and Kantian nature and culture dichotomy that sustains the Western constitution of modernity and thought since the European Enlightenment (Horkheimer et al., *Dialectic of Enlightenment*; Latour, *We Have Never Been Modern*; Latour, *Agency at the Time of the Anthropocene*).
15. SLRA, "St'át'imc Preliminary Draft Land Use Plan."
16. Moritz, *St'át'imc Self-Determination*.
17. Smith et al., *Franz Boas Papers, Vol. 1*. The author is affiliated with the Franz Boas Papers: Documentary Edition project at the University of Western Ontario and the Center for Native American and Indigenous Research (CNAIR) at the APS that seek to connect a variety of audiences, especially Indigenous descendant communities of those under scrutiny by Franz Boas and his associates, creating resources for the extensive unpublished materials to make them relevant and useful for contemporary audiences.

18. Smith, "Our Stories Are Written on the Land"; SLRA, "St'át'imc Preliminary Draft Land Use Plan"; SCC, "St'át'imc Code Nxékmens I St'át'imca."
19. Lassiter et al., "Collaborative Ethnography and Public Anthropology."
20. Tax, *Action Anthropology*; Lurie, *Action Anthropology and the American Indian*; Smith, *Political Thought of Sol Tax*.
21. Asch, "Anthropology, Colonialism, and the Reflexive Turn"; Asch, *On Being Here to Stay*; Corntassel, "Re-envisioning Resurgence"; Lurie, *Action Anthropology and the American Indian*; Mulrennan et al., "Revamping Community-based Conservation"; Noble, "Consent, Collaboration, Treaty"; Tax, *Action Anthropology*.
22. Borrows, *Recovering Canada*; Borrows, "Earth-Bound"; Simpson, *Lighting the Eighth Fire*.
23. TRC, *Honouring the Truth*.
24. Blaser, "Life Projects"; Feit, "James Bay Crees' Life Projects." Analytical and grassroots conceptualizations of the term "life projects" are increasingly employed persuasively in comparative work on Indigenous self-determined responses to expansive neoliberal and industrial development, pertinent economic growth models, and adversarial colonial(ist) governments in both Canada and Latin America (Escobar, "Reflections on 'Development'"; Borrows, *Recovering Canada*; Blaser, "Life Projects"; Feit, "James Bay Crees' Life Projects"). The notion draws attention to various directions of life that emerge from Indigenous histories that are not isolated from outside influences and universalist agendas but are unique and sovereign in their configuration. Suggestive notions of "living well" or of the "good life" have been employed analogously.
25. Davies, *Reflexive Ethnography*; Cruikshank, *Life Lived Like a Story*.
26. Lassiter et al., "Collaborative Ethnography and Public Anthropology"; Sillitoe, *Indigenous Studies and Engaged Anthropology*; Wilson, *Research Is Ceremony*.
27. Personal communication, Tiiya7 William "BJ" Alexander (Tsal'álh), August 2014.
28. Personal communication, Xwísten Elder Albert Joseph, July 2016.
29. Personal communication, Xaxlíp former chief and councillor Art Adolph, June 2013.
30. Personal communication, Rod Louie (Tsal'álh), July 2016.
31. Canadian National Railway Company (CN Rail).
32. Moritz, *St'át'imc Self-Determination*; personal communication, Tsal'álh leader Ida M. Peter, June 2016.
33. Babcock Papers, University of Washington Archives, 0860-001, Box #1, Folder: 1, 13-15C.
34. Personal communication, Tiiya7, July 2016; personal communication, Xwísten (Bridge River) Lands and Resources councillor Gerald Michell, June 2016.
35. Personal communication, Willie Terry Sr., August 2016.
36. Personal communication, Desmond Peters Sr., July 2016.

37. Personal communication, Tsk̓wáylacw S. Peters, July 2014.
38. Personal communication, Art Adolph (Xaxli'p), June 2013.
39. Personal communication, Gerald Michell (Xwisten), August 2016; personal communication, Art Adolph, June 2013.
40. Personal communication, July 2016.
41. Deloria, *Custer Died for Your Sins*; Escobar, "Reflections on 'Development'"; LaDuke, *Recovering the Sacred*; Simpson, *Anticolonial Strategies for the Recovery*.
42. Cruikshank, *Life Lived Like a Story*; Lassiter et al., "Collaborative Ethnography and Public Anthropology"; Turner et al., "Traditional Ecological Knowledge and Wisdom."
43. Caquard and Cartwright, "Narrative Cartography"; Tucker and Rose-Redwood, "Decolonizing the Map?"
44. Personal communication, Morris Posser, July 2016.
45. Huijsmans et al., "Papers for the International Conference," 211–12. Boas posits that, from a cognitive stance, Lillooet folklore, while belonging to the Interior Salish, shows a strong infusion of coastal elements. Therefore, Boas considered it important to follow the lineages of transformer myths that have become significant in the interior but may originate in coastal areas. Such local "traditional" stories, folklore, and oral history accounts tell of a time in history when powerful transformers and tricksters traveled the earth (Boas, *Transformer Myths*; Teit, *Traditions of the Lillooet Indians*; Bouchard and Kennedy, *Lillooet Stories*; Prentiss and Kuijt, *People of the Middle Fraser Canyon*).
46. Boas, "Salish Notes," Boas, Lillooet vocabulary; Teit, Lillooet vocabulary, APS.
47. Teit, *Thompson Indians of British Columbia*. In the words of amateur anthropologist Charles Hill-Tout (Maud, *Salish People*) on the Lillooet Indians and their relationship to fish and other resources guided by an ethic of respect and sharing: "Nothing that the Indian of this region eats is regarded by him as mere food and nothing more. Not a single plant, animal or fish, or other object upon which he feeds, is looked upon in this light, or as something he has secured for himself by his own wit or skill. He regards it as something which has been voluntarily and compassionately place in his hands by the good will and consent of the 'spirit' of the object itself, or by the intercession and magic of his culture heroes, to be retained and used by him only upon the fulfilment of certain conditions. These conditions include respect and reverent care in the killing or plucking of the animal or plant and proper treatment of the parts he has no use for, such as the bones, blood and offal; and the depositing of the same in some stream or lake, so that the object may by that means renew its life and physical form."
48. Hallowell, "Ojibwa Ontology, Behavior, and Worldview."
49. Drake-Terry, *Same as Yesterday*.

50. Boas, "Salish Notes," APS; Teit, *Traditions of the Lillooet Indians*; Adolph, "Anthropology of Space and Place"; Bouchard and Kennedy, *Lillooet Stories*; Prentiss and Kuijt, *People of the Middle Fraser Canyon*; Van Eijk, *These Are Our Legends*; Van Eijk and Williams, *Lillooet Legends and Stories*. An influential collection of *Lillooet Stories*—by Elders Charlie Mack, Baptiste Richie, Sam Mitchell, Slim Jackson, and Francis Edwards, collected and edited by Dorothy Kennedy and Randy Bouchard (1972) as part of the *Indian Language Project*—emphasizes that Lillooet people are part of creation, which encompasses the Great Spirit, other spirits, fish, animals, plants, air, sun, stars, moon, water, mountains, land, and all other forms of existence.
51. James Teit, *Traditions of the Lillooet Indians*, 292.
52. According to St'át'imc *sptákwalh* "knowledge rooted in ancestral mythological accounts," Nk̓yap (Coyote) along with other transformers created the land and river formations in St'át'imc territory. Specifically, Xaxlíp (Fountain) former chief and councilor Art Adolph ("Anthropology of Space and Place," 2) notes a place of significance in Upper St'át'imc Territory called Sxetl' ('drop-off'), which tells of a generational recital of how Nk̓yap (Coyote) brought the salmon from the ocean into St'át'imc territory, created the land formations at the Six Mile Rapids, and left his footprints and seat mark embedded in the nearby rocks that now illustrates a landscape culturally produced by mythical forces.
53. Personal communication, Art Adolph, June 2011.
54. Personal communication, Pete Alexander, July 2016.
55. Personal communication, Pete Alexander, July 2016.
56. Personal communication, Qwa7yán'ak Elder Carl, August 2016.
57. Hallowell, "Ojibwa Ontology, Behavior, and Worldview."
58. Teit, "Lillooet Indians."
59. Personal communication, Qwa7yán'ak, July 2016.
60. Galois, "Indian Rights Association."
61. Ware, *Five Issues, Five Battlegrounds*.
62. Drake-Terry, *Same as Yesterday*, 246.
63. Boas and Teit, *Traditions of the Lillooet Indians*, 288.
64. For Boas, as for his students, (German) diffusion as a key mechanism of history provided a methodological framework to attack the premises of the evolutionary method that claims superiority for certain species or humans along a ladder of progressive developmental civilization and assimilation processes. This is true especially for the idea of independent inventions on the basis of an *Elementargedanken* (psychic unity of mankind), the idea that all individuals share a set of innate elementary ideas, as postulated most famously by German ethnologist Adolf Bastian (Darnell, *Invisible Genealogies*, 48; Koepping, *Adolf Bastian and the Psychic Unity of Mankind*).

65. Personal communication,, July 2016.
66. Personal communication, August 2016.
67. Teit, "Traditions of the Lillooet Indians," 364–68.
68. Personal communication, Desmond Peters Sr., June 2014.
69. Personal communication, Qwalqwalten Garry John, August 2016.
70. Personal communication, Morris Posser, August 2016.
71. Personal communication, Pete Alexander, August 2016.
72. Personal communication, Qwa7yán'ak, July 2016.
73. Personal communication, Morris Prosser, August 2016; Elder Dez Peters Sr., July 2016.
74. Formally, Canada's Species at Risk Act (SARA) [S.C. 2002, c. 29] represents "an Act respecting the protection of wildlife species at risk in Canada," further noting that "the roles of the aboriginal peoples of Canada and of wildlife management boards established under land claims agreements in the conservation of wildlife in this country are essential."
75. Boas, "Salish Notes," APS; Amoss, *Fish God Gave Us*; Boas, *Indian Tribes of the Lower Fraser River*; Boas, "Ethnology of the Kwakiutl"; Gunther, "Analysis of the First Salmon Ceremony"; Gunther, "Further Analysis"; Hill-Tout, "Report on the Ethnology of the Stlatlumh"; Hill-Tout, *Salish People*; Teit, "Lillooet Indians"; Teit, "Traditions of the Lillooet Indians"; Teit, "Notes on Songs of the Indians of British Columbia."
76. Personal communication, Qwa7yán'ak, July 2016.
77. Personal communication, Qwa7yán'ak, July 2016; Siragusa, Westman, and Moritz, "Shared Breath."
78. Boas, "Salish Notes," APS.
79. Personal communication, Qwa7yán'ak, July 2016.
80. TRC, "Honouring the Truth."
81. SCC, "St'át'imc Code Nxékmens I St'át'imca."
82. SCC, "St'át'imc Code Nxékmens I St'át'imca."
83. Teit, "Lillooet Indians," 285.
84. Personal communication, Elder and language teacher, July 2016; personal communication, Morris Prosser, August 2016.
85. Corntassel and Bryce, "Practicing Sustainable Self-determination."
86. Personal communication, Tiiya7, June 2016.
87. Personal communication, Gerald Michel, August 2016.
88. Personal communication, Qwa7yán'ak, July 2016.
89. Personal communication, Qwa7yán'ak, July 2016.
90. Personal communication, St'át'imc Elder, July 2014.
91. For a Cree example, see Darnell, "Thirty-nine Postulates."
92. Personal communication, Morris Posser, August 2016.

BIBLIOGRAPHY

Adolph, Arthur. "The Anthropology of Space and Place: Sxetl'." Unpublished paper, Anthropology Department, Thompson Rivers University, 2009.

American Museum of Natural History. Jessup North Pacific Expedition Archive (1897–1902). Vol. 9. New York.

American Philosophical Society (APS). Boas, Franz. "Salish Notes." S. 19. Franz Boas Professional Papers. Roll 372–15. BC Archives MS-1425, Reel A236, 1910a. American Philosophical Society, Philadelphia.

——— . Boas, Franz. Lillooet vocabulary. S1A.2. American Council of Learned Societies (ACLS) Committee on Native American Languages, MS-372, Reel 17, 1910B. American Philosophical Society, Philadelphia.

——— . Teit, James A. Lillooet vocabulary. S1A.1. American Council of Learned Societies (G) Committee on Native American Languages, MS-372, Reel 17, 1910. American Philosophical Society, Philadelphia.

Amoss, Pamela T. "The Fish God Gave Us: The First Salmon Ceremony Revived." *Arctic Anthropology* (1987): 56–66.

Archibald, Jo-Ann. *Indigenous Storywork: Educating the Heart, Mind, Body, and Spirit*. Vancouver: University of British Columbia Press, 2008.

Asch, Michael. "Anthropology, Colonialism, and the Reflexive Turn: Finding a Place to Stand." *Anthropologica* 57, no. 2 (2001): 481–89.

——— . *On Being Here to Stay: Treaties and Aboriginal Rights in Canada*. Toronto: University of Toronto Press, 2014.

Battiste, Marie. *Indigenous Knowledge and Pedagogy in First Nations Education: A Literature Review with Recommendations*. Ottawa: Apamuwek Institute, 2002.

Blaser, Mario. "Life Projects: Indigenous Peoples' Agency and Development." In *In the Way of Development: Indigenous Peoples, Life Projects, and Globalisation*, 26–47. New York: Zed, 2004.

Boas, Franz. *Ethnology of the Kwakiutl: Bureau of American Ethnology 35th Annual Report, Parts 1 and 2*. Washington DC: Smithsonian Institution, 1921.

——— . "The Indian Tribes of the Lower Fraser River." *Report of the 64th Meeting of the British Association for the Advancement of Science* (1884): 454–63.

——— . "Transformer Myths." In *Tsimshian Mythology (in) Thirty-First Annual Report of the Bureau of American Ethnology to the Secretary of the Smithsonian Institution 1909–1010*, edited by Franz Boas, 586–610. Washington DC: Government Printing Office, 1916.

Borrows, John. "Earth-Bound: Indigenous Resurgence and Environmental Reconciliation." In *Resurgence and Reconciliation: Indigenous-Settler Relations and Earth Teachings*, edited by Michael Asch, John Borrows, and James Tully, 49–81. Toronto: University of Toronto Press, 2018.

―――. *Recovering Canada: The Resurgence of Indigenous Law*. Toronto: University of Toronto Press, 2002.

Bouchard, Randy, and Dorothy Kennedy, eds. *Lillooet Stories*. Victoria BC: Aural History, Provincial Archives of British Columbia, 1977.

Caquard, Sébastien, and William Cartwright. "Narrative Cartography: From Mapping Stories to the Narrative of Maps and Mapping." *Cartographic Journal* 51, no. 2 (2014): 101–6.

Corntassel, Jeff. "Re-envisioning Resurgence: Indigenous Pathways to Decolonization and Sustainable Self-determination." *Decolonization: Indigeneity, Education & Society* 1, no. 1 (2012): 86–101.

Corntassel, Jeff, and Cheryl Bryce. "Practicing Sustainable Self-Determination: Indigenous Approaches to Cultural Restoration and Revitalization." *Brown Journal of International Affairs* 18 (2011): 151–62.

Cruikshank, Julie. *Life Lived Like a Story: Life Stories of Three Yukon Native Elders*. Lincoln: University of Nebraska Press, 1990.

Darnell, Regna. *Invisible Genealogies: A History of Americanist Anthropology*. Vol. 1. Lincoln: University of Nebraska Press, 2001.

―――. "Thirty-nine Postulates of Plains Cree Conversation, 'Power,' and Interaction: A Culture-specific Model." In *Papers of the Twenty-second Algonquian Conference*, edited by William Cowan, 89–102. Ottawa ON: Carleton University Press, 1991.

Davies, Charlotte Aull. *Reflexive Ethnography: A Guide to Researching Selves and Others*. Abingdon: Routledge, 2008.

Davis, Henry, and Jan P. Van Eijk. "Lillooet Bird Terminology." In "Papers for the 47th International Conference on Salish and Neighbouring Languages," *Vancouver: University of British Columbia Working Papers in Linguistics* 32 (2012): 13–33.

Deloria, Vine Jr. *Custer Died for Your Sins: An Indian Manifesto*. Norman: University of Oklahoma Press, 1969.

Drake-Terry, Joanne. *The Same as Yesterday: The Lillooet Chronicle-The Theft of Their Lands and Resources*. Lillooet BC: Lillooet Tribal Council, 1989.

Escobar, Arturo. "Reflections on 'Development': Grassroots Approaches and Alternative Politics in the Third World." *Futures* 24, no. 5 (1992): 411–36.

Feit, Harvey A. "James Bay Crees' Life Projects and Politics: Histories of Place, Animal Partners, and Enduring Relationships." In *In the Way of Development: Indigenous Peoples, Life Projects, and Globalisation*, 92–110. New York: Zed, 2004.

Galois, Robert M. "The Indian Rights Association, Native Protest Activity, and the 'Land Question' in British Columbia, 1903–1916." *Native Studies Review* 8, no. 2 (1992): 1–34.

Gunther, Erna. "An Analysis of the First Salmon Ceremony." *American Anthropologist* 28, no. 4 (1926): 605–17.

———. "A Further Analysis of the First Salmon Ceremony." *Washington Historical Quarterly* 19, no. 4 (1928): 306.
Hallowell, A. Irving. "Ojibwa Ontology, Behavior, and Worldview." In *Contributions to Anthropology: Selected Papers of A. Irving Hallowell*, 357–90. Chicago: University of Chicago Press, 1976.
Hill-Tout, Charles. "Report on the Ethnology of the Stlatlumh of British Columbia." *Journal of the Anthropological Institute of Great Britain and Ireland* 35 (1905): 126–218.
———. *The Salish People: The Local Contribution of Charles Hill-Tout, Vol. II: The Squamish and Lillooet*. Edited by Ralph Maud. Vancouver: Talonbooks, 1978.
Huijsmans, Marianne, et al. *Papers for the International Conference on Salish and Neighbouring Languages 51, University of British Columbia Working Papers in Linguistics*. Vol. 42. Edited by Marianne Huijsmans, Thomas J. Heins, Oksana Tkachman, and Natalie Weber, 2016.
Horkheimer, Max, Theodor W. Adorno, and Gunzelin Noeri. *Dialectic of Enlightenment*. Stanford CA: Stanford University Press, 2002.
Johnsen, D. Bruce. "Salmon, Science, and Reciprocity on the Northwest Coast." *Ecology and Society* 14, no. 2 (2009): http://www.ecologyandsociety.org/vol14/iss2/art43/ (accessed August, 27, 2020).
Koepping, Klaus-Peter. *Adolf Bastian and the Psychic Unity of Mankind: The Foundations of Anthropology in Nineteenth Century Germany*. Berlin: LIT Verlag, 2005.
Kovach, Margaret Elizabeth. *Indigenous Methodologies: Characteristics, Conversations, and Contexts*. Toronto: University of Toronto Press, 2010.
Kulnieks, Andrejs, Dan R. Longboat, and Kelly Young. "Re-indigenizing Curriculum: An Eco-hermeneutic Approach to Learning." *AlterNative: An International Journal of Indigenous Peoples* 6, no. 1 (2010): 15–24.
LaDuke, Winona. *Recovering the Sacred: The Power of Naming and Claiming*. New York: South End, 2005.
Lakoff, George, and Mark Johnson. *Metaphors We Live By*. Chicago: University of Chicago Press, 1980.
Lassiter, Luke Eric, Samuel R. Cook, Les Field, Sjoerd R. Jaarsma, James L. Peacock, Deborah Rose and Brian Street. "Collaborative Ethnography and Public Anthropology." *Current Anthropology* 46, no. 1 (2005): 83–106.
Latour, Bruno. "Agency at the Time of the Anthropocene." *New Literary History* 45, no. 1 (2014): 1–18.
———. *We Have Never Been Modern*. Cambridge MA: Harvard University Press, 1993.
Lévi-Strauss, Claude. "The Principle of Reciprocity." In *The Gift: An Interdisciplinary Perspective*, edited by A. Komter, 18–26. Amsterdam: Amsterdam University Press, 1996.
Lurie, Nancy O. "Action Anthropology and the American Indian." In *Anthropology and the American Indian*, 5–15. San Francisco: Indian Historian, 1973.

Maud, Ralph. *The Salish People: The Local Contribution of Charles Hill-Tout, Vol. II: The Squamish and Lillooet*. Vancouver: Talonbooks, 1978.

Mauss, Marcel. *The Gift: Forms and Functions of Exchange in Archaic Societies*. New York: W. W. Norton, [1925] 1967.

Mulrennan, Monica E., Rodney Mark, and Colin H. Scott. "Revamping Community-based Conservation through Participatory Research." *Canadian Geographer/Le Géographe canadien* 56, no. 2 (2012): 243–59.

Moritz, Sarah C. "Tsuwalhkálh Ti Tmícwa (The Land Is Ours): St'át'imc Self-Determination in the Face of Large-Scale Hydro-electric Development." MA thesis, University of Victoria, 2012. https://dspace.library.uvic.ca/bitstream/handle/1828/4215/Moritz_Sarah_ma_2012.pdf?sequence=3&isAllowed=y (accessed August 27, 2020).

Nadasdy, Paul. "The Gift in the Animal: The Ontology of Hunting and Human-Animal Sociality." *American Ethnologist* 34, no. 1 (2007): 25–43.

Noble, Brian. "Consent, Collaboration, Treaty: Toward Anti-Colonial Praxis in Indigenous-Settler Research Relations." *Anthropologica* 57, no. 2 (2015): 411–17.

Perley, Bernard C. "Zombie Linguistics: Experts, Endangered Languages, and the Curse of Undead Voices." *Anthropological Forum* 22, no. 2 (2012): 133–49.

Prentiss, Anna Marie, and Ian Kuijt. *People of the Middle Fraser Canyon: An Archaeological History*. Vancouver: University of British Columbia Press, 2012.

Scott Colin. "Ontology and Ethics in Cree Hunting: Animism, Totemism, and Practical Knowledge." In *The Handbook of Contemporary Animism*, edited by Graham Harvey, 159–66. Durham NC: Acumen, 2013.

———. "Science for the West, Myth for the Rest? The Case of James Bay Cree Knowledge Construction." In *Naked Science: Anthropological Inquiry into Boundaries, Power, and Knowledge*, edited by Laura Nader, 69–86. Abingdon: Routledge, 1996.

Sillitoe, Paul. *Indigenous Studies and Engaged Anthropology: The Collaborative Moment*. Abingdon: Routledge, 2016.

Simpson, Leanne. "Anticolonial Strategies for the Recovery and Maintenance of Indigenous Knowledge." *American Indian Quarterly* 28, no. 3 (2004): 373–84.

Simpson, Leanne, ed. *Lighting the Eighth Fire: The Liberation, Resurgence, and Protection of Indigenous Nations*. Winnipeg: Arbeiter Ring, 2008.

Siragusa, Laura, Clint Westman N., and Sarah C. Moritz. "Shared Breath: Human and Non-Human Co-presence through Ritualized Words and Beyond." *Current Anthropology* 61, no. 4 (forthcoming).

Smith, Joshua. "The Political Thought of Sol Tax: The Principles of Non-Assimilation and Self-Government in Action Anthropology." *Histories of Anthropology Annual* 6, no. 1 (2010): 129–70.

Smith, Joshua, Regna Darnell, Robert LA Hancock, and Sarah Moritz. "The Franz Boas Papers: Documentary Edition." *Journal of Northwest Anthropology* 48, no. 1 (2014): 93–106.

Smith, Linda Tuhiwai. "Decolonizing Knowledge: Toward a Critical Indigenous Research Justice Praxis." *Research Justice: Methodologies for Social Change* (2012): 205–10.

Smith, Trefor. *Our Stories Are Written on the Land: A Brief History of the Upper St'át'imc 1800-1940*. Lillooet BC: Upper St'át'imc Language, Culture, and Education Society (USLCES), 1998.

St'át'imc Chiefs Council (SCC). *Nxékmens I St'át'imca* (Draft: St'át'imc Code). Lillooet BC: SCC, 2006.

St'át'imc Land and Resource Authority (SLRA). *Nxekmenlhkala lti tmicwa: St'át'imc Preliminary Draft Land Use Plan, Part 1*. Lillooet BC: Lillooet Tribal Council, 2004.

St'át'imc Government Services (SGS). *St'át'imc: The Salmon People*. Film. Lillooet, 2016. https://www.youtube.com/watch?v=kmtdVqhdrwc (accessed August 27, 2020).

Tax, Sol. "Action Anthropology." *Current Anthropology* 16, no. 4 (1975): 514–17.

Teit, James A. "The Lillooet Indians." *Memoirs of the American Museum of Natural History* 4, no. 4 (1906): 193–300.

——— . "Notes on Songs of the Indians of British Columbia." Canadian Ethnology Service, Canadian Museum of Civilization, Gatineau ON, n.d..

——— . "The Thompson Indians of British Columbia." In *The Jesup North Pacific Expedition*, edited by Franz Boas, 167–392. New York: AMS, 1900.

"Traditions of the Lillooet Indians of British Columbia." *Journal of American Folklore* 25, no. 98 (1912): 287–371.

Truth and Reconciliation Commission (TRC) of Canada. *Honouring the Truth, Reconciling for the Future: Summary of the Final Report of the Truth and Reconciliation Commission of Canada*. Ottawa: Truth and Reconciliation Commission of Canada, 2015.

Tucker, Brian, and Reuben Rose-Redwood. "Decolonizing the Map? Toponymic Politics and the Rescaling of the Salish Sea." *Canadian Geographer/Le Géographe canadien* 59, no. 2 (2015): 194–206.

Turner, Nancy J., Marianne Boelscher Ignace, and Ronald Ignace. "Traditional Ecological Knowledge and Wisdom of Aboriginal Peoples in British Columbia." *Ecological Applications* 10, no. 5 (2000): 1275–87.

Van Eijk, Jan P. *Nilh Izá Sptákwlhkalh/These Are Our Legends*. Regina SK: University of Regina Press, 2015.

Van Eijk, Jan, and Lorna Williams. *Cuystwí Malh Ucwalmícwts: Lillooet Legends and Stories*. Mount Currie BC: Ts'zil, 1981.

Ware, Reuben. *Five Issues, Five Battlegrounds: An Introduction to the History of Indian Fishing in British Columbia 1850-1930*. Chilliwack BC: Coqualeetza Education Training Centre for the Stó:lō Nation, 1983.

Wilson, Shawn. *Research Is Ceremony: Indigenous Research Methods*. Halifax NS: Fernwood, 2008.

CHAPTER 10

No Time Like the Present

Living American Indian Languages, Landscapes, and Histories

Bernard C. Perley, Margaret Ann Noodin, and Cary Miller

On Temporality

The proverb "There is no time like the present" is ostensibly a recommendation for taking immediate action. Regarding the immediate global language extinction crisis, the proverb's sentiment is not only apropos, but serves as a call to arms for language scholars, advocates, and activists. The authors of this chapter recognize the import of the proverb and the potentially efficacious actions that may be taken to revitalize endangered languages. We approach the proverb with critical appraisal because we understand it to be embedded in a cultural context that coalesces particular ideologies and actions based on particular linguistic and cultural precepts. The authors share their approach to actualizing the agentive potential of the proverb for creative interpretations that complicate expected understandings and actions; doing so makes room for Indigenous interventions that play on the polysemic potential of the proverb while allowing alternative practices for rethinking prevailing discourses on language revitalization, endangerment, and extinction. The authors argue that the phrase "There is no time like the present" can, on the one hand, be taken literally, such that the separation of the past, the present, and the future relegates these temporalities as distinct and ideologically incommensurable. On the other hand, the authors suggest that the phrase can also be interpreted to position the present as the condition through which all temporalities are coexistent and codependent as a complex relationship of emergent vitalities. The complexities of these relations are compounded by the strategies and stances between colonial and Indigenous worlds.

In his 1991 foreword to Peter Nabokov's *Native American Testimony*, Vine Deloria Jr. observes, "Standard textbooks and histories concern themselves with the arrangements of historical artifacts-the dates, policies, movements, and institutions which mark the progress of the human transformation of the North American continent. Anthologies, for the most part, attempt to illustrate a general theme of the conflicting values that characterize the settlement of America. The missing dimension in our knowledge is the informality of human experience, which colors all our decisions and plays an intimate and influential role in the historical experiences of our species."[1] The authors have taken Deloria Jr.'s critical stance and collaborated on presenting the textbook histories and anthologies into an experiential space where all observers can experience the juxtaposition of histories and representations together with personal experience. The goal of the resultant installation piece, titled *Experiencing Native North America*, was to bring diverse audiences into the coordinated histories to promote mutual understanding from common experience. This is crucial in enabling us, as Deloria Jr. states, "to transcend the limitations of time and space and participate in the meaning of life as others who have come before us have known it. Thus the joy and tragedy of the past enable us to renew the clouded but intense vision of our own lives; as we walk with our ancestors through incidents of the past, we come to a realization of the underlying meaning of human activities."[2] The installation is intended to evoke an encounter that embodies the meaning of Deloria Jr.'s words—to cause the viewer to experience the joy and tragedy of life through an Indigenous temporal lens in which the individual present and the past of our ancestors are concurrent and equally meaningful. Living *minobimaadiziwin* ('a good life'), as embodied by the interior of the installation cannot be undertaken without concurrent awareness of the pressures, successes, and losses of Indigenous history impinging on our experience from without.

Fig. 20. Collaborative installation *Experiencing Native North America*. Photo by author.

The authors take up Deloria Jr.'s vision of experiential history by emphasizing the entangled legacies of colonialism and Native American survivance in the installation piece so that the experiential superimposition of temporalities marked by joy as well as tragedy transcend the limitations of our simultaneous but separate epistemic perspectives. As Deloria Jr. notes, "Provocations of emotion are much superior to provocations of the mind alone, and these selections are designed to burst sterile barriers of communication and lead the reader through the twists and turns of human life. The assumptions that one party or the other was fated to arrive at its present condition eliminates any possibility of understanding how events occurred and what people felt in the immediate situation and upon later reflection."[3] *Experiencing Native North American* is a physical construction of experiential historical space where "the twist and turns of human life" invite all readers and participants to transcend communicative barriers in search of mutual understanding and respect.

NO TIME LIKE THE PRESENT 351

On Translation

When the proverb "There is no time like the present" is translated into Anishinaabemowin and Maliseet, we find that translation must work across temporalities, cultural precepts, languages, and histories. Although our sample is only two languages, we find that the work of translation from English into Anishinaabemowin and Maliseet requires thoughtful conceptual gymnastics. For example, when Bernard Perley asked Margaret Noodin to provide a translation of the English proverb, she commented, "I could just disagree because we know there are other worlds and facets of reality that might allow us to see other times parallel to, or opposite from, or pulling on and influencing this moment we are acting in right now. So, my first sense is to say, 'I would never say that'; 'privilege English and be as literal as possible'; and 'I could privilege the Anishinaabemowin.'"[4] Similarly, when Perley asked a Maliseet Elder how she would translate the proverb, she had to think for a moment. Initially she responded, "There a number of ways you can approach that." Then she offered a few phrases that translate as "It will happen right now"; "We can proceed right now" (followed by a comment about the phrase requiring the proper context); and "The two (or more) of us will work on it." After considering the English idiomatic usage, the Elder offered the following English glosses: "Might as well work on it now," and "Let's work on it right now."[5] In both cases the Anishinaabemowin and Maliseet speakers attempt to transcend the limitations of both linguistic—better yet, experiential—worlds to arrive at some approximation of common experience that can translate into understanding. The processes of translation were less about a linguistic word-for-word translation and more about thinking in terms of trans-relations and common ground for understanding. The tension between the kinds of relationships that settler-colonial society has with language, time, and action as characterized by the proverb create challenges for American Indians in approximating similar experiences. The significance of these trans-relations offers insights into the authors' argument that all translations are trans-relations that emphasize living languages, landscapes, and histories.

Experiencing Native North America

The challenge the authors tackled was imagining, constructing, and sharing a provocative experience for educators teaching about Wisconsin's American Indian history, culture, and vitality in K–12 schools in Wisconsin. The effort required each author to transcend academic boundaries by organizing the "knowledge" about American Indians in their respective fields into an Indigenous practice of knowledge sharing. The result of their efforts is an immersive epistemic space that may seem "interdisciplinary" from the Western academic perspective but were intended to bridge experiential worlds. Rather than focus on distinct programs of knowledge, the authors emphasize that all forms of knowledge are integrated into our daily lives as living languages, landscapes, and histories. Not only are the epistemic systems living and robust fields of knowledge, but they are emergent embodiments of shared knowledge that superimpose temporal, physical, and ideational relationships. The authors share their perspectives of how the installation addresses the translations of language, landscape, and history as a provocation toward mutual respect and understanding.

Living Language

The interior of the installation synchronizes multiple forms of balance and offers a counterpoint to the overall impact of cultural collision, colonization, settlement, and capital gains. More than just a soothing glimpse of nature, the words and images offer an antidote to violence and trauma. What began as an exercise in translation quickly evolved into a reflection of cosmic equations. What follows is the story of how words given to a group can help viewers glimpse patterns of language, landscape, and the balance of life.

At the core of the installation is an idea represented in English by the word "thank." Because English, for reasons explained by history, is the shared lingua franca of the contemporary creators and audience, it is worth pausing to note the origins of the term, which ripples through the centuries as *poncian* in Old English, *thancon* in Old Saxon, *þakka* in Old Norse, *danchon* in Old High German and several other languages, back to the Proto Indo European root *tong*, which means "to think." This morpheme, depending on which archeologists and linguists one follows, was first used somewhere in the Eurasian steppes, possibly five thousand years ago, where a need arose to combine the notion of "thought" and "thanks." In our story here, it becomes the charged particle at the center of our constructive collaboration.

One of the project's primary objectives is to recognize the indigenous voice of a place—in this case, the land and waterways between the Atlantic Ocean and the Great Lakes. We want the idea of "thanks" to take shape in a woodland space on a continent with its own ancient human history and networks of being. Even more than that, the intent was to reinforce a network of people and place that is drawn between the Milwaukee Indian Community School and several sovereign nations. The Milwaukee Indian Community School is an urban private school run by an American Indian board of directors who annually steward roughly two hundred acres of land and three hundred students, who come from many nations and are mostly multiethnic. The school makes a continual effort to provide instruction in local Indigenous languages, in part to maintain the connection to similar revitalization efforts on contemporary nearby nations, but also to retain an ancestral connection to the knowledge that sits in the space now occupied by the modern school.

Bernard Perley began by giving three other teachers a bilingual version of the Maliseet Prayer, which was an act of collective defiance and incredible hope. His community had taken the Mohawk Prayer of Thanks and, with the help of Henrietta Black, created a Maliseet version to give children a way to express thanks for the world around them in the language of their ancestors. As he states in his book *Defying Maliseet Language Death*, "The odds seem to be overwhelmingly against revitalizing the Maliseet language. But that is no reason to give up"; he reports that "there are a number of community members who are defying the odds and have initiated creative Maliseet language, culture, and identity projects that could collectively reverse language shift from endangerment to revitalization."[6] The core of the installation is the echo of that first project in thanks and translation.

The Maliseet are, in their own language, the Wolastoqiyik, which is their name for the river that they live with, between the lakes in what is now Maine, New Brunswick, Quebec, and the Atlantic coast. Relevant to the conversation of balance and perpetual motion, the discharge point of the Wolastoqiyik River (also known as the St. John's River) is one of the places on earth where the variation between high tide and low tide is greater than almost anywhere else. Here in the northern heart of the Wabanaki Confederacy, where the tides shift the location and perception of shore, is where the translation of "thanks" begins.

It might be logical to mention next the other languages in the same family as Maliseet, but, in this story, the counterbalance to the Maliseet, which sits in the north, is Oneida. Viewers who enter the space and read the Maliseet will have the Oneida translation directly behind them. Some stories say the Abenaki Confederacy was created to answer the strength of the Iroquois Confederacy, also called the Haudenosaunee: seven groups who share the traditions of the longhouse. They most certainly have existed for many centuries as neighbors and their languages, cultures, and social systems are fascinatingly different. What they have in common is an understanding of the same surface of the globe. Therefore, when Renee Pfaller translates a part of the prayer into Oneida, she is moving words across old enemy lines, finding alliance in a universal perspective. The Oneida, known as the people of the Standing Stone, or Ukwehùwé, speak a language in the Iroquoian family while all the other languages in the project are in the Algonquian family. Oneida is now spoken in three primary locations that have been fractured by colonization and relocation. Most speakers and teachers are still in the east, but the group that was moved to Wisconsin has worked hard to ensure that the language is spoken on the reservation and in the city of Milwaukee, where Wisconsin Oneida leaders built a network of economic influence in the middle of the twentieth century. The interjection of this diversity is important and signals the complexity of many patterns in nature and human social systems.

The eastern and western sections of the installation are translations of Maliseet into Anishinaabemowin and Mamaceqtaw. In some ways they are close cousins; in other ways they offer another stark contrast. Menominee holds the eastern position as viewers interact with the images, which is poignant, because the installation was created in what is now Wisconsin, home to the only Menominee Nation on earth and among the first Native nations in the United States to be terminated by the U.S. government in 1961. In spite of great odds, the people have never left their home at the mouth of the Fox River, which is the source of their creation story and home to gardens blooming from the descendants of thousand-year-old seeds. Today Mary Warrington is the only fluent teacher who learned the language as a child, and a small group of dedicated second-language learners are now working with her to create a bilingual environment with as many immersion spaces as possible for nurturing the language. Readers who examine the Menominee and Anishinaabemowin translations closely will see that the words echo one another with many cognates and a similar structure. The languages are so close that students of Menominee and Anishinaabemowin would often pause to sound out one another's language and were often sure they could recognize parts of words, but never fully understand each other without help.

The prayer offers thanks for days, nights, the land, the sea, and everything that rotates together through these motions. As the stanzas rotate, so does a viewer's understanding of space. The Menominee stanza invokes the dawn of our galaxy and the way night continues to turn into day:

Thank you for the stars, for their twinkling.

Waewaenen anāhkok wāqsapāehkasowak.

Thank you for the sun, it gives us light and keeps us warm.

Waewaenen kēsoq mēnāew wāqsahkonāenekāew mesek mēnāew apāqnahsōw.

Thank you for the moon, it gives us light at night.

Waēwāenen kēsoq, wāqsekōhtaew nīpātepaeh.

The Oneida recognizes the literal power of the earth by speaking for the medicines harvested in the region:

We greet and thank the grass, especially sweetgrass.

Waʔtkwanuhwela·tú tsiʔ oneklʔshúha otokʌ́·u waneklasláthehteʔ

We greet and thank the plants that give us medicine and food.

Waʔtkwanuhwela·tú tsiʔ yaʔtekayʌthóhslake yukhiya·wíheʔ yukwanúhkwaʔt ókhaleʔ yukwá<u>khwa</u>ʔ

We greet and thank the trees, especially the fir and the ash.

Waʔtkwanuhwela·tú tsiʔ kaluteshúha otokʌ́·u kahuwe·yá·ókhaleʔ ohnéhtaʔ nikalutó·tʌhseʔ

The Anishinaabemowin reminds viewers of animacy and agency beyond humanity, thanking all of the manidoog, or spirits, surrounding the entire ecosystem:

We thank the animals, they keep the forests clean.

Gimiigwechiwiaanaanig aweiinyensag, mitigwakiwan biinitoowaad.

We thank the fish, they keep the waters clean.

Gimiigwechiwiaanaanig giigoonyag, nibiin biinitoowaad.

We thank the birds and their beautiful songs.

Gimiigwechiwiaanaanig bineshiiyag nitaanagamowaad.

The Maliseet brings the circle to a pause in the north that many of these nations view as home and the source of winter, which is viewed by each of these cultures as a time for reflection and storytelling:

Thank you for the wind, it makes us breathe clean air.

Wəliwən ciw wocawsən, wellam kisi wəlatəmohtipən.

Thank you earth for all the good things you have given and done for us.

Wəliwən skitkamikw, ciw psiwte kekw eli wəleyowinekw.

Thank you for the water so that no one will be thirsty.

Wəliwən ciw samakwan matehc wən kətəwehsmiw.

As viewers interact with the words and images there is a sense of sustainable exploration and restoration, of stretching the limits and sources of information beyond what is immediate and can be touched, what can be observed and what can be heard, into the spaces of collective memory, emotion, and interpretation, where space is translated into culture.

In that space between language, landscape, and culture are lessons about the world that extend beyond words to illustrate what is beautiful or functional and what is broken or out of balance. This particular project centers on an interactive translation of "thanks." When mathematicians speak of iterative functions, they represent the world around us in equations that summarize and help explain or predict past and future patterns. These iterative functions are part of dynamic systems, and at the core of each one is a periodic point: a point the system returns to after a certain number of function iterations or a certain amount of time. Periodic points play a role in the theories of fractals, which are unfolding fiddleheads of cause and effect. In the many ways we can look at the patterns of nature, we are able to recognize order and come to appreciate the necessity of chaos.

Whether viewers find solace in the visible passing of time, or are inspired to see "there is no time like the present," depends on many variables of each personal equation. Some may have the ability to speak one of the languages represented; others may have heard stories of the burning stars, pine relations, animal voices, or climate elements. An intersection of both groups will show that all are now impacted by the imbalance of capitalism and its emphasis on possession and capital gains. The installation shows how indigenous relationships between culture and landscape can address the issues of our time from immunity to sustainable use of resources.

Living Landscape

Bernard Perley is Maliseet and a guest in the Anishinaabe homeland. Perley's first act of respect as a guest was to visit Lizard Mound State Park in Washington County, north of Milwaukee, Wisconsin. His visit served as an acknowledgement of the Indigenous ancestors who inscribed their presence in their sacred landscape, and Perley honored them by creating a painting that hangs in his office at the University of Wisconsin-Milwaukee. The painting is a prayer of thanksgiving to the ancestors and commitment to respecting their sacred landscape. An important aspect of the prayer is Perley's ongoing public presentation of the importance of the effigy mound sites as evidence of the deep history of Indigenous habitation in the Wisconsin area. That commitment led to the coordinated participation of his coauthors as well as the teachers at the Milwaukee Indian Community School, along with the principal and her staff. The efforts of all participants resulted in an installation of forty-eight canvases, mounted to create an epistemic space of living translations of experience.

The installation features an interior space and an exterior space arranged in a large twenty-foot square. The sides of the square are aligned to the cardinal directions. The exterior eastward arrangement depicts "Empire" and reflects the European invasion from the east. The central interior panel reflects the first line of the prayer giving thanks to the sun and is flanked by panels, one on the right and one on the left, reflecting the lines of the prayer giving thanks to the stars and the moon. These are presented in Menominee, our hosts in this sacred landscape. The exterior south-facing arrangement is representation of manifest destiny as a genocidal project. The interior panels present the importance of plants to the Native people as sustenance and medicine. Those stanzas of the prayer are presented in Oneida. The west-facing exterior panels present the unconscionable government attempts to terminate the Menominee and other tribes. The interior panels provide Anishinaabemowin prayer stanzas that acknowledge our living relatives, the fish, the animals, and the birds. Finally, the north-facing panels represent the ongoing trauma of neocolonialism that continues to undermine the health and well-being of America's Native people. The interior panels provide Maliseet translation of the key elements for sustaining life-water, earth, and air. Together, the arrangement creates a sacred space that brings parallel places and temporalities together into a common experience.

Deloria Jr.'s provocation of emotion to elicit everyday experience from historical artifacts is his attempt to draw empathy from readers. The installation is a similar provocation, inviting participants to share their experience with one another. The organization of the installation is designed as permeable histories, landscapes, and experiences. The exterior are four walls of colonial pressures bearing inward against American Indian worlds; the interior is a celebration of the interconnectedness of American Indian languages, landscapes, and deep history. The bifurcation of interior and exterior is less about the incommensurability of settler-colonial and American Indian worlds. Rather, the design presents gaps between the cardinal directions to structurally represent the permeability of supposed separate histories and experiences. Despite Deloria Jr.'s claim that "provocations of emotion are superior to provocations of the mind," the installation demands that the participant think about the differences of representation and feel the emotive power of the tensions between tragedy and joy, the contemporaneity of past and present, and the emergent condition of translating experience. Experiencing the entire installation requires weaving in and out while reading and interpreting all texts, signs, and symbols until the participant has completed their engagement with the installation. The provocations of emotion and mind are brought together as the embodied practice of understanding the trans-relations between inside and outside, English and American Indian languages, and historical space and sacred space. In short, the physical arrangement of the installation is translation as experience.

The authors' assertion of the interior space as sacred space is crucial to promoting the emotive provocation of Deloria Jr. to "burst sterile barriers of communication." When standing in the center and surveying the panels from east to south to west to north and back to east, the participant views a map of the effigy mounds from Lizard Mound State Park. The interior space honors the ancestral sacred lands by superimposing the four American Indian languages onto the local landscape. The mounds map is painted over raised delineations of chevrons that represent the upper world and horizontal lines that represent the lower world in the pottery of ancestral people. A third element, double-curve motifs, represents the confluence of the Wolastuk (St. John) and Tobique rivers that define the point of Tobique First Nation. This superimposition of traditional landscapes integrates American Indian landscapes together as sacred landscapes. The prayer translated into four American Indian languages asserts the sacredness of Indigenous landscapes that transcend the temporal barriers of past, present, and future. The top-most panels reflect the dawn, midday, dusk, and night to create another temporal reminder of the daily renewal of our relationship to our languages, landscapes, and histories. The experiential theme of the interior is the integration of temporalities, religious and spiritual practices, linguistic vitalities, and histories in an immersive space that reinforces the coexistence of parallel experiences that can be shared by everyone.

The exterior panels invite participants to share a different experience, one marked by colonial history and the tragedy and trauma that history continues to impose on American Indians. Four themes depict four traumatic episodes of history that are ostensibly separated by dates and events, relegating those traumas and tragedies to the past—a convenient distancing. The final episode is the crucial link that refuses to treat the earlier episodes as distant and distinct. The title "neocolonialism" asserts the authors' position that those tragedies and traumas of the past are still with us today. The external forces of colonialism continue to exert pervasive and insidious pressures that undermine American Indian language, landscape, and historical vitality.

The installation is provocation by emotion and by mind: an invitation to bring the experiences of both settler-colonial societies and American Indian societies together in the same epistemic and experiential space so that our common experience can promote conversations that work toward mutual respect and understanding. The provocation the installation is designed to promote is to make "the twists and turns of human life" the common ground from which we draw understanding from common experience.[7]

Living History

For Indigenous people, the experience of history is a living, breathing thing steeped in the landscape that surrounds us, inscribed and reinscribed by our oral traditions. While Wisconsin retains many of its Indigenous place names, for most these words now inscribed on maps and road signs have become disembodied from the land losing their connection to Indigenous stories, setting them adrift from their original identities. As new cultures settled here with a different understanding of history, they brought their own stories of place and location, celebrating pioneer narratives that often ignored and displaced Indigenous knowledge of place in the public sphere as they plowed the mounds of our ancestors and brought with them invasive species that have challenged our Indigenous foods and medicines as the settlers themselves challenged our sovereignty.

Native communities remember the stories that connect them to place and their responsibilities to all the beings that live there: an animate world of plant, animal, stone, and water relations, described in an animate language of interconnected being. These relationships are binding and continue to inform the choices Native communities make to protect places from external encroachment and development. This is at once a different experience of history and a different ascription of historical meaning and importance to place than that recognized by those who have settled amongst us.

Senator Ron Johnson of Wisconsin while running for reelection in 2016 suggested that colleges and universities do not need history teachers, as everything we need to know is found in documentaries.[8] This public perception that there is only one experience of history—a perception that the full-year omnibus-textbook full of facts and dates approach to K-12 historical instruction contributes to—ignores concurrent historical narratives, whose suppression results in cognitive dissonance between individual experience of historical narrative and the public historical discourse. Individual and community identity is embedded in history; these are the origin stories that we define as true, as opposed to those that are considered part of a mythic past or religious theology. For dominant cultures whose identity is further reinforced by these narratives, embedded not only in textbooks and documentaries but in the architecture and public statues of our cities, and even referenced in popular culture through TV shows, commercials, Broadway musicals, and sports mascots, these narratives are part of the comforting background noise of lived experience—rarely considered but constantly reassuring. Individuals and communities whose personal, family, or community experience deviates significantly from this public historical narrative are daily assaulted by attempts to redefine or discredit their identities, giving rise to an anxiety and alienation we have come to call "historical trauma." This trauma is ever present, not only due to our awareness of it when exposed to ubiquitous and often misrepresented historical references, but also because we are constantly called upon to interpret and explain our alternative narrative experience. As not only a historian of American Indian history but also an individual of Anishinaabeg descent, I constantly find myself instructing others on historical misrepresentation and omission, not only in the classroom, but in casual conversation at a grocery store, the DMV, or with a contractor fixing my house. But the ultimate societal implications of this are more severe than these everyday encounters; for populations whose experience of history deviate from the dominant narrative, the historical misperceptions represented lead to societal ignorance undermining the ability of health professionals to treat illnesses, politicians to develop responsible laws, and police to conduct traffic stops without violence.

The quotes and images on the exterior of the installation are intended, as Deloria Jr. recommends, to provoke not only the mind but also the emotions of the viewer in an effort to visually translate experience. As such the installation depicts historical trauma on two different levels. On one level it critiques some of the most prevalent historical myths in our society—that a benign age of colonial empire was launched when Columbus discovered an Edenic America whose empty lands cried out for civilized use and occupation; that "manifest destiny" was not only an opportunity but an obligation to settle an empty landscape with little consequence; that any Indians left in America can and should have their ethnic and political identity terminated while their cultural and historical images are appropriated and distorted in a modern neocolonial experience, all of which, as Deloria Jr. suggests, are assumed to be fated, preordained, inescapable. On another level the installation depicts the way that these narratives are all around us, imposing a daily burden of historical experience, making the interior space of cultural identity all the more important. Likewise, language loss, destruction of sacred spaces like the effigy mounds, and continued cultural attack circumscribe the availability of this space, this haven, as historical trauma pushes in from without.

As a specific example of this experiential contrast—between the historical experience of Native people and the public historical narrative that is a catalyst for historical trauma—let us briefly examine one of the most iconic historical identity narratives of the United States: the American Revolution. It is a historic moment, celebrated and commemorated as a great victory in the public sphere, defined as a moment when a ragtag group of underdogs disgruntled over unfair taxation and limited representation determined to set off on a course toward liberty, sovereignty, and self-determination, which was achieved after passing through a crucible of war. So iconic is this interpretation that in 2009 the Tea Party movement within the Republican Party, whose goals are small government and elimination of taxes, arose and consciously wrapped themselves in the imagery and terminology of this history, including resistance to the "tyranny" of America's first Black president, Barack Obama, which was often expressed in racialized as well as political terms. Yet this narrative of America's birth as a rejection of tyranny, taxation, and lack of representation is incomplete; it obscures as much if not more than it tells. The American Revolution was not an isolated incident but, rather, part of a series of imperial conflicts involving England, France, Spain, American Indian tribes, and colonial settlers for more than a century. American Indians participated in these conflicts not as dependent imperial subjects, but as independent sovereign nations making choices based on their own needs and strategic position.[9] For Native people choice of ally generally rested with the power most supportive of Indigenous sovereignty and land rights. They would have drawn very different maps than the ones appearing in many textbooks that suggest European fantasy and political rhetoric rather than the reality of Indigenous sovereignty and power. Leaving aside discussions of how agreements were perceived, overlooked, or abused in Europe, the key issues for Native people at the time of the American Revolution were preventing further European expansion while maintaining tribal sovereignty.

While Native people fought on both sides of the Seven Years' War, a larger number of tribes chose to ally with the French rather than the English. As much as the American colonies sparked the imperial war by overreaching with their territorial claims, Native people also perceived the war as a vital contest over land and resource rights, and, in some regions, like Pennsylvania, the local conflicts between tribes and settlers dominated the territory and regional negotiations.[10] England ultimately won the Seven Years' War by diplomatically convincing tribes to abandon the French, who could no longer maintain gifting relationships due to English naval blockades, but not before emptying treasuries in both France and England in the process. While this would set the stage in France for their own revolution as they increased taxation on their immediate subjects, England determined to pay debts from the war by taxing the colonists who had gotten them into the conflict in the first place.

Following the war, the English began to implement a frontier policy intended to minimize disagreements with Indian tribes that could again erupt into costly warfare. The tribes themselves underlined the need for these provisions when they engaged in Pontiac's Revolt in 1763, seizing all but three of the English forts in the Great Lakes region, when British officials began to renege on trade and land agreements made during the conflict. While the split between the interests of the American colonies and England had begun to appear prior to the Seven Years' War, these interests were brought into sharp relief thereafter. The colonists, long perceiving the presence of the French as the chief barrier to expansion, now expected no barriers to westward settlement. Poor, landless colonists expected a quick road to financial improvement while the wealthy speculated in western land futures. However, the crown imposed the Line of Proclamation in 1763, returning to its promise to tribes to restrict European settlement to the eastern side of the Appalachian Mountains and agreeing that tribes had the right to deport any illegal immigrants who settled west of the line.[11] This did not discourage the settlers, resulting in smoldering conflicts along the line for the next decade, along with colonial resentment at the crown's lack of military aid in these skirmishes.

The proclamation had also created a temporary government for the newly acquired French territories, which the crown determined to formally establish in the 1774 Quebec Act, restoring the French form of civil law for residents and providing religious freedom, at least for adherents of Catholicism, in the new colony of Quebec, defined as eastern Canada south to the lands between the Mississippi River and the Ohio River (today's states of Ohio, Indiana, Illinois, Michigan, Wisconsin, and part of Minnesota). It was the land provisions of this act that angered colonists the most; many colonial charters used the Mississippi River as a western boundary, with the result that the Quebec Act was viewed as violating these agreements. Further, wealthy men who had invested in land futures in the Ohio River Valley such as the Washington family, the Jefferson family, the Lee family, the Paine family, and Benjamin Franklin, whose investments in the Ohio Company, the Loyal Company of Virginia, and the Grand Ohio Company now faced considerable jeopardy. In the Declaration of Independence a number of complaints that relate to these issues of the crown's attempt to control settler expansion are enumerated:

> He [the king] has endeavoured to prevent the population of these States; for that purpose obstructing the Laws for Naturalization of Foreigners; refusing to pass others to encourage their migrations hither, and raising the conditions of new Appropriations of Lands.
>
> For abolishing the free System of English Laws in a neighbouring Province, establishing therein an Arbitrary government, and enlarging its Boundaries so as to render it at once an example and fit instrument for introducing the same absolute rule into these Colonies:
>
> For taking away our Charters, abolishing our most valuable Laws, and altering fundamentally the Forms of our Governments:[12]
>
> He has abdicated Government here, by declaring us out of his Protection and waging War against us.
>
> He has excited domestic insurrections amongst us, and has endeavoured to bring on the inhabitants of our frontiers, the merciless Indian Savages, whose known rule of warfare, is an undistinguished destruction of all ages, sexes and conditions.[13]

While only the final complaint explicitly mentions Native people, all of these complaints relate to issues of expansion, particularly concerns resulting from the Line of Proclamation and the Quebec Act, while at the same time covering other unrelated issues. Still, this means that the public discourse of the American Revolution as a war against taxation without representation skews the historical narrative, obscuring less savory motivations that sought to gain liberty for one people at the expense of another. Only one complaint in the declaration concerns taxation while at least four concern expansion.

As revealed in the Declaration of Independence, the American Revolution itself was at once both a war for independence from Britain and a war of settler expansion against Indigenous populations. Very few tribes supported the American cause, and those who did largely chose to do so due to proximity to the colonies, in hopes that siding with their American neighbors would keep conflict out of their communities. Nonetheless, the war brought brutal campaigns against Indigenous populations seldom discussed in textbooks or public discourse. When the dominant narrative moves from the military successes in the north to the final victories in South Carolina, discussion of the 1779 Sullivan-Clinton campaign, which destroyed nearly sixty Iroquoian towns with thousands of acres of supporting crops and orchards, are usually omitted. Washington and his advisors committed 6,200 men—nearly a quarter of the Continental Army—to this action, with the following orders:

> The immediate objects are the total destruction and devastation of their settlements, and the capture of as many prisoners of every age and sex as possible. It will be essential to ruin their crops now in the ground and prevent their planting more. I would recommend that.... parties should be detached to lay waste all the settlements around, with instructions to do it in the most effectual manner, that the country may not be merely overrun, but destroyed. But you will not by any means listen to any overture of peace before the total ruinment of their settlements is effected.[14]

These actions earned Washington the Iroquoian name "Town Destroyer." The Iroquois not only suffered the economic loss of their settlements and crops, but when over 5,000 men, women, children, and Elders arrived at British Fort Niagara as refugees, many died from starvation and disease during an exceptionally severe winter, which saw five feet of snowfall in the region. While most of the villages were abandoned before the soldiers reached them, Washington's directive to capture as many prisoners of every age and sex as possible reflects another general feature of colonial warfare: that thousands of Native Americans were captured and sold into slavery following military conflicts. While Washington's directive here could be seen as due to his identity as a plantation owner, the reality is that the capture and sale of Native American prisoners had been a feature of English warfare and colonial economics for more than a century. And England was not alone in this regard. Indeed, Columbus's first observations of Hispaniola express his opinion that the people he encountered there "ought to make good slaves." Most students I encounter are shocked to hear of this practice; Indigenous people who know their history are not.

When the American Revolution between the colonies and England concluded, it continued in Indian country. The new nation determined to fund itself largely through land sales, with the first debt owed to soldiers promised land for service. Washington intended to settle these men on his Ohio claims and pursued three conflicts with allied Great Lakes tribes in the 1790s to achieve this goal, before finally negotiating a land cession treaty in 1795. As a result Native people view the American Revolution and its legacy through a very different lens. For tribes in New York and Ohio, this was not a war for independence but a war of disenfranchisement, impoverishment, and land loss following which even Indigenous place names for towns, rivers, and lakes were erased. Even tribes that supported the United States in the revolution as soldiers and scouts, like the Oneida, Stockbridge, and Brotherton communities, lost some or all of their land during or after the war. The U.S. Constitution went on to define Native people as noncitizens, placing our communities beyond the protections of the bill of rights until 1924.[15]

Teaching about this moment in history without discussing its impact on Native nations distorts the truth not only for American Indians, but for all Americans. What does it mean for a nation's identity when its origin narrative has been purged of unflattering elements? Does this contribute to a national sense of exceptionalism and superiority at odds with historical and current reality? Does this blind modern Americans to the consequences of global economic and political expansion? These questions suggest that ignorance of history will impact current actions. One of the most important components of a functioning democracy is an informed electorate. By misinforming generations of Americans about the experience of American Indians in U.S. history, we not only amplify historical trauma for Indigenous persons, but we also hamstring our collective decision-making at today's voting booth. There is absolutely no time like the present to correct these narratives, precisely because misperceptions of this history inform our nation's actions today.

Native people continue to live and breathe their history in landscapes defined by reciprocal relationships. These relationships include ways to use and harvest from the land sustainably and inform tribal decisions to fight to maintain treaty rights to hunt, fish, and gather; and to block drilling, mining, hydroelectric, and pipeline projects that threaten to destroy sacred places inscribed with story and ancestral burial grounds imbued with history, as well as poison waters that have nourished and protected their communities. The historical knowledge of how easily rights and homelands can be lost, and the weight and gaze of ancestors who lost their lives in the past to protect what remains to us, drives current generations to social and political activism. In 2016/17 in North Dakota, families from tribes across the country gathered to support the Standing Rock community in their protests against the Dakota Pipeline currently under construction. There they prayed in many Indigenous languages, saying thanks for our water, thanks for our land, and thanks for our people. In 2019 in Canada, as the Wet'suwet'en protested lack of consultation for the expansion of a different pipeline, First Nations across Canada blocked railroads crippling the country's commerce and supply chains. In both countries media and everyday people reacted in surprise—a surprise only possible because the collective histories that give rise to these conflicts have been misrepresented or forgotten.

Conclusion

The authors realize that essays, chapters, and papers are expected to come to a conclusion. This chapter, too, will end with a period. But the work of provocation will continue. The coordinated efforts to enhance the vitality of American Indian languages, landscapes, and histories as living and embodied experiences will continue to resist the ongoing periodization of settler-colonial history and its propensity to relegate American Indian worlds as a thing of the past. The authors celebrate their American Indian ancestral languages, landscapes, heritage, and histories as integral aspects of present and contemporaneous embodiments of American Indian life. The translations across disciplines and settler-colonial and American Indian worlds is less about idiomatic comprehensibility and more about the building of trans-relationships of respect and understanding. That requires a commitment to *remembering Indigenous worlds* and *living as we act*.

Remembering Indigenous Worlds

Deloria Jr. may characterize this essay as another academic example of "provocations of the mind." The authors understand that limitation of text, but they recognize the importance of provocations of the mind to serve as a catalyst for provocations of emotion. The authors wanted to address not isolated readers but community members such as Wisconsin schoolteachers, their students, and American Indian community leaders. The installation has been shared with attendees of the conferences of the Wisconsin Indian Educators of Wisconsin and the Educators for Social Justice Network, as well as with University of Wisconsin-Milwaukee faculty, staff, and students. Among the results of sharing the installation with these diverse audiences are the collaborations that arise from the conversations that were generated from the common experience. The coordination of knowledge systems and experiences across disciplines, experiences, and communities are the respectful but necessary translations that must take place so that not only do we share common experiences, but we come to mutual understanding.

Living as We Act

When Bernard Perley asked Margaret Noodin to translate "There is no time like the present" Margaret Noodin provided two options. Option one she explained as:

> If I take it as the "carpe diem" "now or never" dare I say it "good day to die" proverb of inspiration I could privilege English and be as literal as possible—
> Noongom gaawiin wiikaa waa ezhiwebsinoon.
> Today will never happen again.[16]

Margaret Noodin was uncomfortable with the "English privilege version" and she offered a second translation:

> Or I could privilege the Anishinaabemowin and say
> Nimaadizimin ezhi-ezhichigeyaang.
> We live as we act.
> I think the second one sounds better in Anishinaabemowin and is made of verbs and would make clear the present is singularly defined by what we do in it.

The authors' insistence on focusing on the present is to argue that the discourses of language endangerment and of historical trauma are couched in ideologies of linear temporalities that distance settler-colonial societies from the horrors of the past while casting American Indian experiences of those horrors and traumas as distinct and distant periods of history. The discursive strategies used by language experts as they exhort language advocates to preserve—or save—endangered languages imply the same linearity of past, present, and future. Unfortunately, the trajectory they emphasize is one that leads to language death and extinction; the temporal framing has all but relegated those languages to silence. As Noodin states, "The present is singularly defined by what we do in it." The authors recognize the pressures colonial histories have brought to bear on American Indian lives, but they also assert that those pressures have inflicted tragedy and trauma on contemporary American Indian experience. One-sided histories and loss of heritage languages and traditional lands inscribe colonial pasts onto the American Indian present. Despite colonial privilege, American Indian communities celebrate the joys and the solace of integrated knowledge systems that do not isolate language, landscape, and history. The daily activity of experiencing American Indian knowledge systems is a celebration of life. The authors coordinated their knowledge and experience to create the installation to invite all participants to share a common experience of Native North America. The installation, as an immersive experiential space of knowledge sharing, is the authors' admonition to "live as we act." In doing so our acts of sharing and understanding will not only define the present, but also shift our translation practices toward establishing trans-relationships.

ACKNOWLEDGMENTS

The authors want to acknowledge the contributions of the Menominee and Oneida language teachers at the Milwaukee Indian Community School. We also want to thank Michael Zimmerman for his contributions to Anishinaabemowin translations and Henrietta Black for her contributions to Maliseet translations. We also express our sincere thanks to the teachers, administration, and staff at the Indian Community School for their generous time and assistance. The authors acknowledge the profound gifts that our Elders have and continue to share with our communities. Miigwech. Woliwon.

NOTES

Epigraph: Deloria, "Foreword," xviii. Italics in the original.
1. Deloria, "Foreword," xvii.
2. Deloria, "Foreword," xvii.
3. Deloria, "Foreword," xix.
4. Personal communication, August 14, 2016.
5. Personal communication with Henrietta Black of Tobique First Nation on August 14, 2016. Note also that Henrietta Black is Bernard Perley's mother.
6. Perley, *Defying Maliseet Language Death*, 186.
7. Deloria, "Foreword," xix.
8. "GOP Senator Suggests Swapping College Instructors for Videos," Associated Press, August 22, 2016, https://apnews.com/b3d9a41e764b433b9fd251a52cda4c7d/gop-senator-suggests-swapping-college-instructors-videos.
9. See White, *Middle Ground*; and McDonnell, *Masters of Empire*.
10. In the same month of 1754 that Benjamin Franklin drafted the Albany Plan for Unity—an early recommendation for colonial confederacy to defend against Indigenous attacks on illegal settlements—twenty-two-year-old Lieutenant George Washington of the Virginia militia led an exploratory party into what is today southwestern Pennsylvania to establish claims based on a very questionable treaty between Virginia and the Iroquois confederacy ceding land actually occupied and used by the Shawnee and Delaware, who were French allies. The Iroquois claimed the land based on their seventeenth-century expansion, which these other tribes with French support had curbed and turned back, resulting in the 1701 Peace of Montreal. Washington ran afoul of a French foraging party, and shots were fired that drew England and France into war. This is the first of the seventeenth-century wars fought in North America to originate on this continent rather than spilling over to North America from contests for various crowns in Europe.

11. "And. We do further strictly enjoin and require all Persons whatever who have either wilfully or inadvertently seated themselves upon any Lands within the Countries above described. or upon any other Lands which, not having been ceded to or purchased by Us, are still reserved to the said Indians as aforesaid, forthwith to remove themselves from such Settlements.... And whereas great Frauds and Abuses have been committed in purchasing Lands of the Indians, to the great Prejudice of our Interests. and to the great Dissatisfaction of the said Indians: In order, therefore, to prevent such Irregularities for the future, and to the end that the Indians may be convinced of our Justice and determined Resolution to remove all reasonable Cause of Discontent, We do. with the Advice of our Privy Council strictly enjoin and require. that no private Person do presume to make any purchase from the said Indians of any Lands reserved to the said Indians, within those parts of our Colonies where, We have thought proper to allow Settlement: but that. if at any Time any of the Said Indians should be inclined to dispose of the said Lands, the same shall be Purchased only for Us, in our Name, at some public Meeting or Assembly of the said Indians, to be held for that Purpose by the Governor or Commander in Chief of our Colony respectively within which they shall lie." Royal Proclamation, October 1, 1763.
12. Both the Massachusetts Bay Company Charter and the Virginia Company Charter had been revoked roughly a century before for inciting significant and expensive warfare with neighboring tribes over expansion.
13. This is a mischaracterization of Indian warfare; women and children were generally abducted, not killed. Declaration of Independence, Philadelphia, 1776.
14. George Washington to Major General John Sullivan, May 31, 1779.
15. Article 1 section 2, of the U.S. Constitution excludes Native people from counting toward the apportionment of representatives. This is the same clause that defines African Americans as counting as three-fifths of a person. Article 8 states that the federal government shall have the right to regulate commerce "with foreign Nations, and among the several States, and with the Indian Tribes," which courts interpreted in the 1830s to mean that tribes are noncitizen "domestic dependent nations."
16. Personal communication, August 14, 2016.

BIBLIOGRAPHY

Deloria Jr., Vine. "Foreword." In *Native American Testimony*, rev. ed., edited by Peter Nabokov, xvii–xix. New York: Penguin, 1991.

McDonnell, Michael. *Masters of Empire: Great Lakes Indians and the Making of America*. New York: Hill & Wang, 2015.

Perley, Bernard C. *Defying Maliseet Language Death: Emergent Vitalities of Language, Culture, and Identity in Eastern Canada*. Lincoln: University of Nebraska Press, 2011.

White, Richard. *The Middle Ground*. Cambridge: Cambridge University Press, 1991.

PART 5

Creative Collaborations

Commentary by Regna Darnell

Although both chapters in this section describe collaborative projects in language revitalization, there are considerable differences between the two contexts. Sara Snyder Hopkins relies on the linguistic, cultural, and musical intuitions of contemporary Elders at Western Carolina University in a relatively homogeneous Cherokee home territory (despite forced relocation of Cherokees to Oklahoma in Indian removal policies of the 1830s) to interpret song texts recorded in 1846 by missionary Samuel Worchester. Justin Spence and his coauthors, linguistics graduate student Kayla Begay and high school teacher Cheryl Tuttle, employ archival texts from Wailaki encounters with outsiders to reawaken a language that has no known living speakers but whose recovery is of critical importance to descendants of the traditional community. The Wailaki, one of many such small tribes within the cultural and linguistic diversity of Indigenous California, spoke a Dene (Athabascan) language and were seminomadic hunters and gatherers intermarrying extensively with closely related groups. The Cherokee were settled horticulturalists speaking an Iroquoian language.

How, then, do we situate the Wailaki experience alongside that of the Cherokee, when their surface features are so different? How can we extend the commonalities of language revitalization across these two groups to gain insight into language revitalization in general? That language revitalization movements are now widespread across the Americas demonstrates that Indigenous communities themselves are searching for ways to reclaim aspects of traditional identity that have been lost or permanently changed as a result of colonization and its assimilation policies, which were designed to separate them from these traditions. Details differ across the continent, but all tribes have suffered the degradations of cultural loss, poverty, and marginalization. Decolonization is a goal with diverse details and challenges in different places, but clear parallel intentions. These Indigenous communities share the empowering belief that heritage languages are integral to contemporary identity; the languages are merely "sleeping" and can be reclaimed with sufficient determination. The exercise of local agency through language revitalization cannot erase the ongoing effects of colonialism, but it can restore pride and agency and provide resources for resisting and subverting its legacy.

Ethnographic research and community collaboration are qualitative methods whose insights are transportable or generalizable to other situations and contexts. The more we know about the variables that coalesce in a particular case or cases, the more precise the questions we can ask to further our understanding of other cases where similar variables intersect in different ways. Surface examination of diversity or quantitative comparison alone will not produce such an explanatory analytic.

Criticism of non-Indigenous scholars is rife, and much of it is well deserved. Both of the projects described in this section, however, productively engage the skills and resources of outsiders alongside knowledge from within the contemporary community. Capacity building in communities (e.g., training in linguistic and archival skills) is integral to most successful revitalization projects. Linguists can be of considerable assistance to community agendas in contexts including language description, inference from limited data, and culturally appropriate teaching materials and pedagogical methods—as long as they work within the frameworks set out by the community and its goals. Some results are unlikely to come from within the communities. Historical linguistic reconstructions, for example, reveal migration patterns, tribal relationships, and epistemological underpinnings of attested speech that prove useful for such issues as land claims, ecological stewardship, land use patterns, and self-government, in addition to language revitalization in the narrow sense.

Language is the mode through which all else is done, most important, perhaps, in expressing the relationship of human persons to land, animals, and plants. For some Cherokee who learn to listen, the knowledge encoded in the language and its metaphors remains available to contemporary speakers. Cherokee knowledge-keeper, fluent speaker, and language teacher Tom Belt emphasizes the inherent violence embedded in the hierarchical power relations of missionary translations designed to restructure the metaphorical and epistemological resources of Cherokee converts; comparable violence is entailed by the contemporary imposition of external forms of curriculum and pedagogy. Belt's "acoustic epistemology" of Cherokee terms and their metaphorical resonance counters with a systematic culturally appropriate alternative—that is, a Cherokee theory of sound. The investigation of musical terminology and its underlying assumptions is coterminous with the overarching values of Cherokee culture: for example, balance, recognition of plurality facilitating accommodation of diversity, and polyvalence of linguistic and cultural forms. The revitalization of language and culture is inextricable from the process of decolonization.

Methods of revitalization depend on local circumstances. Ideally, however, community-based collaborative projects draw on all available sources. Not every community has fluent speakers, but contemporary Elders and knowledge-keepers everywhere can examine archival sources and fill in their gaps by bringing back to memory what they were taught by the Elders in their own childhoods. Archival texts record much that has been lost, but they also misinterpret much of the cultural and linguistic meaning traditionally coded in the concepts, stories, narratives, and histories from oral tradition; therefore, they cannot be taken at face value. This is where the Elders (and the linguists) come in. Many of the texts created in the so-called salvage era of Americanist anthropology and linguistics are being revitalized by awakening their proper meanings, which are still understood within present-day communities, even though the product will not precisely replicate the linguistic and cultural forms of prior generations.

There has been much criticism of salvage research for its now patently false assumptions about the "disappearing savage." Linguists operating under this outdated paradigm aspired to reconstruct a pure language as it might have been spoken prior to contact, as though languages have not always changed along with their speakers and contemporary speech were somehow inauthentic. Along with the search for purity, linguists have hoped to find single representations of "the language" extrapolated from diverse sources of varying quality. When the Wailaki project was confronted by different orthographic transcriptions, translations, and interpretations, the authors emphasized the linguistic quality of Li Fang-Kuei's texts over those of C. Hart Merriam, Pliny E. Goddard, and other early recorders, but the earlier documents, despite their inadequacies of both transcription and interpretation, include information that has been lost over time and that document the time and place of their recording. It is crucial to use all that is available and seek a pragmatic convergent coherence epitomizing the American Philosophical Society's mandate to seek "useful knowledge." Contemporary Americans do not speak the English of their ancestors in 1492, so why should we expect Indigenous languages to remain static? Collaborative projects in language revitalization counter all narratives of deficit by insisting on the legitimacy of their knowledge and enact its utility to the present and future aspirations of their communities.

CHAPTER 11

"Going Over" and Coming Back

Reclaiming the *Cherokee Singing Book* for Contemporary Language Revitalization

Sara Snyder Hopkins

In a letter to the American Board of Commissioners for Foreign Missions in the 1820s, missionary to the Cherokee Nation Samuel Worcester writes the following about translating the concept of "baptism" into the Cherokee language:

> We could adopt a *noun* from another language as in some instance we have done; but to introduce a verb, and Cherokeeize it, is an impossibility. Where a new idea is introduced, which the language has not hitherto expressed, and which is to be expressed by a verb the only possible course is to use an old verb with a new shade of signification, and let that signification be learned by use and explanation. This has been done in a multitude of cases, as civilization and religion have introduced new ideas... Your inquiry has led me to ask Cherokees to whom I have access respecting the meaning of the word [for Baptism], and in doing so I have learned, that the Cherokee conjurers, as they are called, have a ceremony of washing persons, in which the person *usually* goes into the water, but sometimes is only washed in some part, e.g., the hands or face; and the ceremony, however performed, is designated by the same word by which we translated baptize.[1]

In this excerpt Worcester, who worked closely with native Cherokee speaker Elias Boudinot,[2] makes explicit the ideological and linguistic processes by which missionaries and Indigenous Christians purposely modified semantic and pragmatic elements of an Indigenous language in situations of language contact and colonization.[3] The word "baptize"[4] is itself metaphorical of the conversion of a target language term to form a new equivalence to a meaning in the source language.[5] Through such commensuration, or "linguistic conversion," the translators attempted to detach Cherokee words from their connections to non-Christian religious practices and reorient them to Christian theological concepts.[6]

Evangelical Christian missionaries such as Worcester have prioritized the development of literacy and Bible translation into Indigenous languages based on the belief that Christian beliefs can be expressed and practiced in any language.[7] However, Indigenous languages must be brought into alignment with the dominant contact language of the missionaries such that meaning can transfer from source language to the target language. This process of commensuration often creates a "translanguage," or a specialized set of terms lifted from the target language and imbued with new, Christian meanings.[8] In theory true commensuration is equally bidirectional: Language 1 = Language 2 and Language 2 = Language 1. In practice social conditions and language ideologies (re)produce translational asymmetries, where the resulting translation can omit and silence that which is incommensurate to the source meaning; the perspectives most often rendered invisible or irrelevant belong to those with the least social power.[9]

Indigenous languages suffer semantic and epistemic violence in situations of language contact and colonization, often becoming extinct or endangered as communities shift to the dominant colonial language. Language revitalization initiatives undertaken in Indigenous communities seek to reclaim not only the grammatical systems of endangered languages, but also the knowledge, epistemologies, and ontologies they convey. In an ironic twist, archival documents and translations created by missionaries (both settlers and Indigenous converts) are now being circulated anew as valuable resources for linguistic and cultural revitalization. In this chapter I argue that revisiting Native language documents from archives and retooling them for contemporary use requires looking beyond the equivalencies of translation to the incommensurate knowledges that persist between the lines of translation. We can rekindle some of the epistemologies and ontological orientations that were stifled by processes of commensuration. To illustrate I will explore Cherokee Indigenous conceptualizations of space and sound through a close analysis of the Cherokee language of the *Cherokee Singing Book*, a translation project undertaken by Samuel Worcestor for teaching music in Cherokee churches, with less than a thousand copies produced in a single printing in 1846; existing original printings of the text are contained in a handful of archives across the United States.[10] The terms used to describe music and sound in the *Singing Book* retain semantic connections to pre-Christian Cherokee epistemologies despite the text being a product of broader social processes that attempt to semantically separate the Cherokee language from traditional modes of knowledge. I pair linguistic analysis of concepts from the *Singing Book* with historical and contemporary ethnographic data to gain insight into how some Cherokee-language speakers conceptualize and experience the world through music and sound. This process demonstrates a way that scholars and community language activists can work with remaining fluent speakers to reclaim Indigenous modes of thought *through* the language "preserved" within archival texts.

Cherokee Translation and Commensuration

Scholars of Christianization and translation often privilege missionaries' ideologies and perspectives of translation over Native theories of translation. This is in part because, in situations of colonialization, written records were kept by literate settlers; therefore, their perspectives remain in archival record. However, in the 1820s the Cherokees adopted a written syllabary for their language that was completed by Sequoyah (George Guess) in 1821. In the decades that followed, the Cherokee Nation published numerous texts in the syllabary, including a bilingual Cherokee-English newspaper (the *Cherokee Phoenix*) and the Christian New Testament. Thus Cherokee language records exist from the period of increased colonization and contact with European settlers. Moreover, because they had their own institutionalized writing system during the period of highest colonization, Cherokee translators had the "final authority" over biblical translations and other texts, and Christianity therefore "came to the Cherokee on their own terms, not those of the missionaries."[11] Alan Kilpatrick (Cherokee Nation) states that, in order to become "theologically" literate, Cherokee translators had to undergo a "complex psycholinguistic process" to create equivalencies between English and Cherokee religious terms.[12] Cherokee Christian translators, in collaboration with missionaries, were often the ones driving semantic changes and were also largely responsible for the syllabary's adoption as a national writing system for the tribe. This literary history means that Cherokees themselves have long-standing theories of translation that must be accounted for when examining archival documents in their language.

Tom Belt (Cherokee Nation), Cherokee-language program coordinator at Western Carolina University and fluent Cherokee speaker, describes two kinds of translation from a Cherokee perspective. The first is *ahnetlatanv'i*, which roughly glosses as "to say it in the way the person speaking (the translator) would say it."[13] This type of translation could be thought of as interpretation or paraphrase and privileges the translator's perspective on the information being conveyed.

ahnetlatanv'i interpretation
SOURCE TRANSLATOR LISTENER (target audience)
What the translator thinks the information conveyed means

Ahnetlatanv'i contrasts with *gawohiltanv'I*, or "going over" (to how the source would say it). *Gawohiltanv'i* is related to *gawohilosga* ('he is going over') and represents a translator's attempt to remain as true as possible to what the source expressed and how it was expressed. The same verb is used to describe the 1838 Cherokee Removal (the Trail of Tears), *tsiduniwohiltanv'i* ('when they went over'), and for the Cherokee name of Reverend Evan Jones, *gawohilosgi*, meaning "he who goes overhill." Jones was a prolific Welsh American preacher who became fluent in Cherokee, translated the Bible into the Cherokee language, and led a group of Cherokees from North Carolina to Indian Territory in what is present-day Oklahoma during Removal in 1838.

gowohiltanv'i going over
SOURCE TRANSLATOR LISTENER (target audience)
Translator adheres as closely as possible to content and style of source

In this second kind of translation, the translator is charged with remaining as close to the original source material as possible. A translator must "go over" to the perspective and language of the source.

"Going over" resonates with the concept of commensuration (and I acknowledge that this comparison is itself commensuration). Yet, even in the most exacting translations, words and phrases from the source language fail to form perfect equivalences to words in the target language. There are always remainders, or incommensurable elements. Incommensurability refers to "a state in which an undistorted translation cannot be produced between two or more denotational texts."[14] Where it is impossible to translate between two languages without extreme slippages of meaning, then metalanguage, language about language, enters in the form of inter- and intralingual glosses to establish mutual intelligibility.[15] This produces neologisms that themselves can become a new register in the target language. Moreover, this process can involve semantic extensions of existing words to new concepts.

To illustrate the latter, Tom Belt has discussed how the word "covenant" in the Bible was translated to *kanohedv datlohisdv'i* in Cherokee. This Cherokee phrase roughly means "the story of when they crossed" (or 'met'). This echoes the Latin *convenire* root of "covenant," meaning "come together," also found in the word "convene." However, the Cherokee word has the sense of two parts being tied or bound together as a belt is tied together. Indeed, the word for "belt," *adadlohisdi*, is from the same word root and glosses as "to cross itself," as a belt wrapped around a body and tied to itself does. Furthermore, traditional (precontact) Cherokee laws were inscribed in wampum belts in a time when religion, law, and medicine were not conceptually separate for Cherokees. The word *datlohisdv'i* was an obvious choice for "covenant," which indicates the Christian god's agreement with and laws for his people. However, this new meaning for *datlohisdv'i* is not identical to the previous one for Cherokees, and, as evangelicals pushed Cherokees to abandon their old ways, the previous meanings of the word were likely supplanted by Christian ones for Cherokee speakers who did not follow traditional customs. This example and the opening example of Samuel Worcester's translation for "baptism" illustrate how Cherokee words were reshaped and reoriented to English-language concepts.

Christian missionary approaches to converting Cherokees to Christianity varied across denominations and pastors, but were almost always aligned with federal policies for "civilizing" Native Americans, which entailed wide-scale social reorganization; the path to salvation entailed dressing, acting, living, speaking, and singing as the colonizers. The *Cherokee Singing Book* was created by Protestant missionaries and thinkers whose theological orientation called for supplanting Cherokee traditional ways of life and belief systems with rigidly defined Christian practices. Therefore, it is not surprising that the *Singing Book* is devoid of any overt reference to traditional music that would have been associated with pre-contact religious practices. Nonetheless, the *Singing Book* hints toward Cherokee Indigenous ways of knowing and provides some insight into the multilayered experiences of Cherokee people in the mid-nineteenth century.

Cherokees were generally far more accommodating of diversity of religion and thought than their neighboring Christian settlers and missionaries. Despite efforts to reorder Cherokee society around Christian practices through the surveillance of religious and cultural practices, many Cherokees continued in their traditional beliefs and practices alongside Christian ones.[16] Ethnologist James Mooney noted that many medicine men of the Eastern Band of Cherokee Indians (the community of Cherokees who remained in North Carolina after Removal in 1838) were also respected Methodist ministers. Mooney described Christianity as a "thin veneer" over traditional practices.[17] Mooney understood religion through the Christian concept of conversion: you were either one thing or another. This contrasted at the time with many Cherokee spiritual leaders, who adopted Christianity as another tool in a spiritual arsenal. Cherokee medicine men frequently used terms associated with Christian practices in their traditional practices and vice versa; thus Cherokees consistently resisted the wholesale semantic reorientation of their language for Christian practices and concepts. This resonates with the plurality expressed in Cherokee concepts of translation described earlier and indicates that Cherokees recognized multiple perspectives and approaches in many domains of life. Cherokees' privileging of diverse perspectives rested upon the polyvalence of linguistic signs, which allow for and invite pragmatic slippages of meaning or the incomplete commensuration of terms. Also, the fact that most Cherokee nouns are derived from verbs preserves meaning in instances where the same translation processes may have eradicated original meanings in other languages.

As an example, the Cherokee word used in the *Singing Book* to translate a note in musical notation is *ganoyvlisdodi*, which glosses as "it is used (by him or her) to make a sound." This noun is derived from the verb *ganoyvlisdiha* ('he is making it make a sound'). The derived noun encodes the action of the verb in the noun by retaining the same verb base. Explicating these kinds of connections between verbs and nouns provides more information about Cherokee conceptualizations of music notation than simply glossing *ganoyvlisdodi* as "note" would. In revisiting Cherokee texts, these imperfect equivalencies of translation open up ambiguous spaces where the remainders of Indigenous modes of thought persist, allowing us to decolonize such texts and reclaim Indigenous epistemologies. I now turn to some of those jagged edges of meaning by explicating the musical terminology in the *Cherokee Singing Book*.

The *Cherokee Singing Book*

The *Cherokee Singing Book*, published in 1846, is a collection of hymns with Cherokee texts, as well as an introduction to the elements of written music. The book was assembled and partially authored by longtime missionary Samuel Worcester, in consultation with prominent nineteenth-century music educator Lowell Mason, whose hymns and pedagogical approach were foundational to the work. Princeton-educated Cherokee Stephan Foreman translated the elements of the musical rudiments from portions of Lowell Mason's *Choir* and the *Manual of the Boston Academy*, which was itself translated from a German text by G. F. Kübler.[18]

Unsurprisingly, given the content, concepts of space and time are prevalent throughout the text. In some instances Cherokee and English concepts align seamlessly; pitch moves up (*galvladi*) and down (*eladi*) in space (as notes on a staff). However, where English talks about low and high voices (as in "bass" and "soprano"), the Cherokee text describes "large" (*udvna*) and "small" (*usdi*) men's or women's voices. Both English and Cherokee describe musical time as moving laterally in space (as in reading music across a page). The term for "measure" is *atlitlosv'i*, which likewise means "that which is measured," and *digalvsdodi* is used for barline, but glosses literally as "the thing which you use to climb laterally." A "step" (the distance from one adjacent note to the next on the staff) is *alasinvhi*, which glosses as "stepped" and comes from the same word as *alasiti* ('one step' or a 'measured foot'). The term used for "interval" is *nidudatlv*, which can be described as "next to each other but with equal space in between" or "intermittent"; this is nearly perfectly aligned with the English "interval," which comes from the Latin *intervallum*, meaning "spaces between the ramparts" (the spaced openings in a castle wall).

As in English, time can be visualized as divided across space—as one might think of a calendar. For instance, a person can ask "*tsadlanvd-vde'itsu?*" which would mean "Do you have space for it?" (as opposed to the more frequent question in English: "Do you have time for it?") Space and time can be metaphorically synonymous in Cherokee as well. This verb appears in the *Cherokee Singing Book* as *udlanvdv* and means "it is devoid of anything," and is the word used for a space on the music staff. In the *Singing Book* the process of commensuration brings Cherokee terms to bear on Euro-American musical concepts. And while it assures that musical concepts are interpreted through a Cherokee lens, it also alters the Cherokee language by providing new references for Cherokee words. The Cherokee terms discussed thus far appear to commensurate without significant distortion with the English source-language terms. However, some Cherokee words used to discuss sound carry additional meanings in Cherokee and hint at a broader conceptualization of sound and Cherokee ontologies.

Many languages incorporate the metaphor of sound as water or liquid. In English, for instance, sound "flows" and travels in "waves." Cherokee classifies things in the world according to five categories: solid, long and rigid, animate, flexible, and liquid.[19] These five categories are reflected by certain verbs that have different bases for different kinds of objects in each category. For instance, when pouring or spilling water, a person would use a term for a liquid: *atsv'vsga* ('he's pouring it'). However, to describe a waterfall, one would say *gado'osga*, meaning "it (flexible) is falling off." Water can be a liquid or a flexible object, depending on its physical presentation and how it is manipulated.

According to fluent Cherokee speakers Tom Belt (Cherokee Nation) and Myrtle Driver (Eastern Band of Cherokee Indians [EBCI]), Cherokees consider sound a flexible object like a waterfall. This is revealed in the *Singing Book* text by the term *unosdv ganoyvlisdodi* ('whole note'). *Unosdv* means a "whole, flexible object." The term is used by Cherokees living in Oklahoma to mean a dollar bill: *sogwu unosdv* ('one dollar'). The word can also refer to a hide or animal pelt, which would be flexible. The image of sound as a flexible object like flowing water is further strengthened by the translation of "staff" as *gagusdvdi*, which can be translated as "foundation," but is akin to the term used for a kitchen strainer or a filter, *gvgusdadi*. This evokes an image of sound as a flexible thing flowing vertically down the *agilawisdiyi* ('scale' or, literally, the 'thing that you climb on vertically') while the staff catches some notes from this flow.

The syllable *-no-* found in *unosdv* ('whole flexible object') may connect the flexible class of objects to verbs having to do with sound:

*u**no**hyvga*   it is making a sound
*deka**no**gi'a*   he is singing
*ka**no**heda*   news (it is said)

Many verbs in the Cherokee language have *-no-* somewhere in the verb stem; therefore, it is impossible to determine a definitive connection. However, given the established fact that Cherokees speak of sound as a flexible object, it bears speculation.

Cultural Metaphors of Sound

Language about music describes sound phenomena in metaphorical terms; in fact, it would be impossible to talk about music without using metaphors. Metaphors reflect theoretical conceptualizations of the world and how things work within it. Shared cultural metaphors systematize and structure experiences of music and sound; they are the foundation of "cultural understandings" of music-sound systems. Language about music and sound, therefore, allow speakers of a language to communicate with each other about sound phenomena and musical practices in ways that are unique to members of that language who have a shared history of cultural practices. Semantic categories used to describe music and sound "are embodiments of cognitive arrangements now made available at the surface level."[20] The words used to discuss music, then, can be understood not as a "list" for things in the world, but as representing "a set of metaphors interlocking the terms with principles of systematic thought."[21] A system of thought around a practice or phenomenon is a "theory"; therefore, Cherokee conceptualizations of music and sound in the words discussed in this article hint toward an Indigenous theory of sound and music as culturally organized sounding practices. But, more broadly, these kinds of connections between the natural world, sound, and sociality coalesce into an "acoustemology," or acoustic epistemology.[22] Acoustemology is knowing through sound, where "local acoustic ecology can thus be considered a kind of aesthetic adaptation" or "ecological and aesthetic co-evolution."[23]

Some terms from the *Singing Book* point toward a Cherokee acoustemology that demands the ontological and linguistic knowledge of a fluent speaker to decode. For example, to discuss consonant and dissonant intervals, the Cherokee text uses *dinadoligi* ('they recognize each other') and *nidanadoligvna* ('they don't recognize each other'). According to Tom Belt, "If they don't recognize each other, they don't balance," and things out of balance create conflict. A consonant "sounding together" ratio would constitute a "balance of sound." Consonant and dissonant intervals can be mathematically depicted as more or less well-balanced fractions, or as anthropomorphized entities who may or may not know each other.

Belt likens the idea of sounds "recognizing" each other to Amazonian shamans who find plants to treat sicknesses by recognizing that the plants were "singing" a song that matched the "song" of a particular sickness.[24] As with many other Indigenous groups, Cherokees have understood the voices of human beings to be only one small part of the larger ecological soundscape of speech and song. Trees, plants, rivers, animals, and rocks could also speak or sing. Belt related the following story about a Cherokee-speaking friend who was visiting North Carolina from Oklahomas:

We went down to Kituwah the last time they were here, and we got out.²⁵ I noticed he was looking around. He was looking over in the bushes and stuff like that. He never said anything. Then later on that night he said, "when we got there, we stepped out, and I could hear people singing Stomp Dance songs."²⁶ He said, "I could hear water running. I thought it was somebody on down the other side of the field maybe practicing... but I figured you'd tell us if it was somebody down there practicing. But since you didn't, it could have been not really there." You know, *something else*. He can hear stuff like that. I don't think that it's paranormal, ghost stuff. I don't think it is. I think that sound is inherently there. Those kinds of sounds are inherently there. I think that's where we learned them maybe, from the world itself, from the very ground itself. Maybe from the plants. We always said plants could talk to us if they wanted.

This story reflects a Cherokee worldview about sound and music, where humans learned their songs from the natural world. James Mooney relates the story of how Cherokees received disease from the animals then medicine from the sympathetic plants:

When the Plants, who were friendly to Man, heard what had been done by the animals, they determined to defeat the latter's evil designs. Each Tree, Shrub, and Herb, down even to the Grasses and Mosses, agreed to furnish a cure for some one of the diseases named, and each said: "I shall appear to help Man when he calls upon me in his need." Thus came medicine; and the plants, every one of which has its use if we only knew it, furnish the remedy to counteract the evil wrought by the revengeful animals. Even weeds were made for some good purpose, which we must find out for ourselves. *When the doctor does not know what medicine to use for a sick man the spirit of the plant tells him* (emphasis added).²⁷

For some Cherokees, human beings are not the only beings who speak and sing in the world. The plants and animals and the immortal *nvnehi* can be heard singing, for they are the ancestors who are always here. There are the *yvwi tsunsdi*, the little people who dwell in caves but sometimes come to help or play tricks on us humans. There is Long Person, *yvwi gvnahida*, spirit of the sacred rivers. In one sacred formula, "the song would appear to partake somewhat of the nature of an invocation to the spirit of running water, a circumstance which strongly suggests that after each recitation of the conjuration and delivery of the song, the patient is blown with 'live water.'"[28] The world is alive and speaking and singing if one knows how to listen.

Translation and Culturally Based Education

Thus far I have explored a "decolonizing" approach to archival texts: connecting Cherokee words for Euro-American concepts to broader Cherokee epistemologies and ontologies as a means for understanding how Cherokees experienced the world. The goal of this kind of work is not to produce a finite product, but rather to explicate a process for reclaiming cultural knowledge from archival texts for contemporary use in linguistic and cultural revitalization efforts. Now the question stands: How can knowledge gleaned from archival documents be applied to teaching the Cherokee language and producing Cherokee language materials for language revitalization? I will conclude by making some suggestions based on my own ethnographic observations and teaching experiences.

From 2011 through 2016 I conducted ethnographic fieldwork at New Kituwah Academy, the Eastern Band of Cherokee Indians' language immersion school located in Cherokee North Carolina. The program serves children from preschool through sixth grade. During my years as ethnographic observer and participant, I worked for the program as the elementary and middle school music and arts teacher. In my current position as director of the Cherokee Language Program at Western Carolina, I continue to work with language revitalization efforts in the region. The goal for second-language teachers such as myself at New Kituwah was to present as much material as possible in Cherokee. Generally, curriculum materials were expected to adhere to federal education standards per requirements for North Carolina charter schools, and the program administers standardized tests based on this content. As in other tribally operated charter schools, New Kituwah staff and parents negotiate a balance between the goals of their community and the federal and state requirements.[29]

As the previous discussion of translation practices demonstrates, not all translations are created equally. Taking terms from an Indigenous language and applying them to non-Indigenous knowledge frameworks can sever knowledge of the Indigenous worldview originally associated with those concepts. In situations of language revitalization and immersion, if students learn Cherokee words for non-Indigenous concepts without retaining knowledge of their Indigenous meanings, then language immersion programs are inadvertently participating in their own cultural erasure. In many ways state and federal education standards covertly demand the kind of forced assimilation instituted by the federal boarding schools of preceding generations, which were often operated by missionary organizations. Such imposed standards, even when curriculum materials are translated into the Cherokee language, often displace Indigenous knowledge, ways of understanding, and educational strategies, and therefore perpetuate "civilizing" and assimilationist processes that have contributed to the imminent complete language shift to English for most Cherokee people. There are currently fewer than two hundred fluent first-language speakers of Eastern Cherokee remaining, and nearly all of them are older than sixty.

The manner in which scholars and community language activists use archival materials for language revitalization has direct implications for the education of Indigenous children. The central goal of many Indigenous communities operating their own schools is to exercise educational sovereignty over the educational goals, strategies, curricula, and operations of their own institutions.[30] Indigenous schools often seek to create and implement holistic and culturally based curricula based on Indigenous ways of knowing and learning. Many Native American communities, including the Cherokee, have traditionally viewed human beings as part of a larger world of sound and life; humans are connected to and part of the whole ecology, not its apex.

Human-centric perspectives of biology are socially constructed and learned. Such conceptualizations are underscored by the prevalence of anthropocentric media (e.g., television shows, movies, and books) such as animals wearing clothes and speaking English in children's stories. Seldom do dominant, mainstream media depict people *with* animals, sharing habitats with animals in realistic ways. Euro-American orientations toward the world often portray humans as separate from nature, as existing outside of it and having dominion over it, whereas Native American people often position human beings as part of a natural ecosystem.[31]

The Western concept of "science" places some epistemologies above others in their contributions to human knowledge. Native ways of knowing should not be valued as merely folk wisdom that is validated or invalidated by "real science." They are not simply conglomerations of facts, either. Rather, Native epistemologies are entire systems of thought that shape a person's experience of the world. Science is not divorced from other domains of knowing; for example, when a person understands plants to be relatives, their relationship to the natural environment changes. In one study Menominee students interacted with a garden that included medicinal and ceremonial plants. Students "visited" with their "relative" plant each day and learned about it. They made observations of their plant through various senses and also gathered "scientific" data such as soil pH and and rate of growth. Students were never asked to collect specimens from their plants.[32] In pluralistic approaches to education, culturally based activities can be integrated with standard science and art curricula. Such activities can revitalize traditional perspectives as living tools for understanding the contemporary world through Native eyes.

The *Cherokee Singing Book* is useful for teaching the elements of (Western) music at New Kituwah Academy and other Cherokee-language programs in North Carolina and Oklahoma. During my tenure there as researcher and music educator, I used terms from the *Singing Book* to teach students about music notation. In the tradition of Cherokee pluralism, students also learned traditional songs and dances from Cherokee men who worked for the program (as a non-Cherokee person, I did not teach traditional music). The question, of course, is how we can teach the music terms from the *Singing Book* while also connecting them to other domains of Cherokee knowledge and thought they imply. I would suggest two approaches.

First, making time for stories and narratives in Indigenous schooling is paramount. Stories are powerful epistemological tools, and "Cherokee songs and stories model the valuable experience of passing from ignorance to wisdom. They offer accounts of the resources and strategies of Cherokee lifeways and world view."[33] Thus it is important for immersion students to hear traditional and contemporary stories from fluent speakers. When students learn stories such as the one cited above, about the plants giving medicine to cure the diseases caused by the animals, they begin to develop a conceptual framework for considering musical consonance as recognition and balance; students without a concept of humans as embedded within a broader ecology may not conceive of musical sound originating from nonhuman actors. Second, students must develop the linguistic resources to differentiate certain categories of thought. Being able to conceptualize of sound and water as flexible within a broader sound ecology requires students to have ecological awareness as well as the knowledge of classificatory verbs in order to be able to make those connections. Such a depth of knowledge and worldview cannot be taught in a single classroom but demands a truly holistic Indigenous education based on fluency in the Indigenous language specific to Indigenous domains of knowledge. Where Euro-American education segments knowledge areas—science, medicine, religion, and music—a culturally based Indigenous education may connect these under a single domain of practice, making ecological connections that may otherwise have been invisible.

Imposed educational standards are systematized orders of thought that can supplant Indigenous ways of knowing unless care is taken to balance perspectives in educational practice. Translation practices of the past and present are partially responsible for the silencing of Indigenous epistemologies and ontologies. In order to reclaim Indigenous modes of knowledge from the gaps of translation, those working with and learning Indigenous languages must develop a sense of how Indigenous communities have been and continue to be intimately connected with their sounding ecological environments. We must "go over" and come back again.

Table 3. Selected terms from the *Cherokee Singing Book*

Cherokee	English	Gloss
diganoyvlisdod	notes	'it is used (by him or her) to make a sound'
gagusdvdi	staff	'foundation' or 'strainer' or 'filter'
atlilo'v'sv'i	measure	'that which is measured'
atsawesolvsdodiyi	rest	'the thing used to indicate a resting place'
asdayidisdi	time signature	'that which is tightened'
oweyeni vtelvhvsga	conduct	'one shakes [moves] one's hand'
agilawisdiyi	scale	'stairs' or 'the thing that you climb on'
alasinvhi	step	'stepped', related to body part *alasideni* (foot), *alasiti* (one measured step)
unosdv alasinvhi	whole step	'complete [step]'; *unosdv* used in Oklahoma to mean "complete flexible form," as in a hide, pelt, or dollar bill
ayeli iyalasinvhi	half step	'half [amount] step'
dasdanvnv	lines (bar)	'lines'
dudlanvdv	spaces	'area void of anything'
tsusquala dasdanvnv	ledger lines	'short [horizontal] lines'

nidudatlv	intervals	'next to each other, but space in between', 'intermittent', 'measured space'
dinadoligi	consonant	'they who recognize each other'
nidanadoligvna	dissonant	'they don't recognize each other'
hilvsgi nanadadisgv dininogisgi	vocal parts (i.e., SATB)	'several singers in equal parts that do not separate themselves [from the rest]'
digudadvsgi	grand staff	'it is connected', 'it bonds with something'
anigeyv tsuninogisdi	treble clef (soprano and alto)	'that which women sing'; *anitsutsano* ('and boys')
anisgaya usdi dininogisgi tsuninogisdi	treble clef (tenor)	"for small (voice) men singers sing"
anisgaya udvna dininogisgi tsuninogisdi	bass clef	'for large (voice) men singers to sing'
taline iya:sti atlilosdiyi	interval (second)	'second like-as-in-time measurement'; use ordinal numbers for other intervals
digalvsdodi	barline	'that which climbs [laterally]'
gvgutilosgi	repeat sign	'looper', *gvgotiloda* ('he loops it')
alewisdodi	fermata	'the thing used to stop'

alasadisgv	sharp	'it raises it'
eladi igvnehi	flat	'it makes it low'
nigada diganoyvlisdodi agilawisdiyi	chromatic scale	'all notes stairs'
agilawisdiyi adanetliyvsgv'i	key signature	'changing stairs'

Note: All words were transliterated from the syllabary to simple phonetics.

NOTES

1. Bass, *Cherokee Messenger*, 240.
2. Cherokee Elias Boudinot (1802–39) was raised as a Christian and was the the founding editor of the *Cherokee Phoenix* newspaper in 1828.
3. See Samuels, "Bible Translation and Medicine Man Talk"; and Hanks, "The Space of Translation," for discussion of similar processes.
4. The Cherokee word Worcester coopted for the Christian concept of baptism is *gawo'a*, which now carries the dual meanings "he is bathing him" and "he is baptizing him."
5. Gal, "Politics of Translation."
6. Hanks, *Converting Words*.
7. Schram, "Tapwaroro Is True."
8. Schram, "Tapwaroro Is True."
9. Espeland, "Commensuration as a Social Process."
10. Lee, "Lowell Mason, the Cherokee Singing Book."
11. Owens, "Bible Translation and Language Preservation."
12. Kilpatrick, *Night Has a Naked Soul*, 390.
13. *ahnetsatanv'i* in the Eastern dialect. I have chosen to represent the Cherokee language in this document using "simple phonetics" in order to make the Cherokee terms in the text more accessible to general readers.
14. Povinelli, "Radical Worlds," 320.
15. Hanks, "Space of Translation."
16. Perdue, *"Mixed Blood" Indians*.
17. Mooney, *Cherokee History, Myths, and Sacred Formulas*, 312.
18. Lee, "Lowell Mason, the Cherokee Singing Book."
19. For further discussion of Cherokee classificatory verbs, see Kilarski, "Cherokee Classificatory Verbs"; Blankenship, "Classificatory Verbs in Cherokee"; Scancarelli, "Another Look at a 'Primitive Language,'"; and Uchihara, "Cherokee Noun Incorporation Revisited."
20. Feld, "Flow Like a Waterfall," 23.

21. Feld, "Flow Like a Waterfall," 23.
22. Feld, "A Poetics of Place"; and "Acoustemology."
23. Feld, "From Ethnomusicology to Echo-muse-ecology."
24. Jauregui et al., "Plantas con madre"; and Callicott, "Interspecies Communication in the Western Amazon."
25. A Cherokee sacred mound site in Swain County, North Carolina, considered the Cherokee mother town.
26. Cherokee Stomp Dances are considered a traditional religious practice.
27. Mooney, *Cherokee Myths*.
28. Kilpatrick and Kilpatrick, *Notebook*, 110.
29. McCarty and Lee, "Critical Culturally Sustaining/Revitalizing Pedagogy."
30. Lomawaima and McCarty, "When Tribal Sovereignty Challenges Democracy."
31. Medin and Bang, *Who's Asking?*
32. Bang and Medin, "Cultural Processes in Science Education."
33. Meredith and Meredith, *Reflections on Cherokee Literary Expression*, 97.

BIBLIOGRAPHY

Bang, Megan, and Douglas Medin. "Cultural Processes in Science Education: Supporting the Navigation of Multiple Epistemologies." *Science Education* 94, no. 6 (2010): 1008–26.

Bass, Althea. *Cherokee Messenger*. Norman: University of Oklahoma Press, [1936] 1996.

Blankenship, Barbara. "Classificatory Verbs in Cherokee." *Anthropological Linguistics* 29, no. 1 (Spring 1997): 92–110.

Callicott, Christina Maria. "Interspecies Communication in the Western Amazon: Music as a Form of Conversation Between Plants and People." *European Journal of Ecopsychology* 4, no. 1 (2013): 32–43.

Espeland, Wendy Nelson, and Mitchell L. Stevens. "Commensuration as a Social Process." *Annual Review of Sociology* 24, no. 1 (1998): 313–43.

Feld, Steven. "Acoustemology." In *Keywords in Sound*, edited by David Novak and Matt Sakakeeny, 12–21. Durham NC: Duke University Press, 2015.

——— . "'Flow Like a Waterfall': The Metaphors of Kaluli Musical Theory." *Yearbook for Traditional Music* 13 (1981): 22–47.

——— . "From Ethnomusicology to Echo-muse-ecology: Reading R. Murray Schafer in the Papua New Guinea Rainforest." *Soundscape Newsletter* 8 (1994): 4–6.

——— . "A Poetics of Place: Ecological and Aesthetic Co-evolution in a Papua New Guinea Rainforest Xommunity." In *Redefining Nature: Ecology, Culture, and Domestication*, edited by R. F. Ellen and Katsuyoshi Fukui, 61–87. Oxford: Oxford International, 1996.

Hanks, William F. *Converting Words: Maya in the Age of the Cross*. Berkeley: University of California Press, 2010.

———. "The Space of Translation." *Hau: Journal of Ethnographic Theory* 4, no. 2 (2014): 17–39.

Jauregui, X., Z. M. Clavo, E. M. Jovel, and M. Pardo-de-Santayana. "'Plantas con madre': Plants that Teach and Guide in the Shamanic Initiation Process in the East-Central Peruvian Amazon." *Journal of Ethnopharmacology* 134, no. 3 (2011): 739–52.

Kilarski, Marcin. "Cherokee Classificatory Verbs: Their Place in the Study of American Indian Languages." *Historiographia Linguistica* 36, no. 1 (2009): 39–73.

Kilpatrick, Alan. *The Night has a Naked Soul: Witchcraft and Sorcery Among the Western Cherokee*. Syracuse NY: Syracuse University Press, 1997.

Kilpatrick, Anna Gritts, and Jack Frederick Kilpatrick. *Notebook of a Cherokee Shaman*. Smithsonian Contributions to Anthropology 2, no. 6 (1970).

Lee, William R. "Lowell Mason, the Cherokee Singing Book, and the Missionary Ethic." *Quarterly* 3, no. 3 (1992): 14–23.

Lomawaima, K. Tsianina, and Teresa L. McCarty. "When Tribal Sovereignty Challenges Democracy: American Indian Education and the Democratic Ideal." *American Educational Research Journal* 39, no. 2 (2002): 279–305.

McCarty, Teresa, and Tiffany Lee. "Critical Culturally Sustaining/Revitalizing Pedagogy and Indigenous Education Sovereignty." *Harvard Educational Review* 84, no. 1 (2014): 101–24.

Medin, Douglas L., and Megan Bang. *Who's Asking?: Native Science, Western Science, and Science Education*. Cambridge MA: MIT Press, 2014.

Meredith, Mary Ellen, and Howard L. Meredith. *Reflections on Cherokee Literary Expression*. New York: Edwin Mellen, 2003.

Mooney, James. *Cherokee History, Myths, and Sacred Formulas*. Clyde NC: Cherokee, 2006.

Owens, Pamela Jean. "Bible Translation and Language Preservation: The Politics of the Nineteenth Century Cherokee Bible Translation Projects." *Bible Translator* 57, no. 1 (2006): 1–10.

Perdue, Theda. *"Mixed Blood" Indians: Racial Construction in the Early South*. Athens GA: University of Georgia Press, 2003.

Povinelli, Elizabeth A. "Radical Worlds: The Anthropology of Incommensurability and Inconceivability." *Annual Review of Anthropology* 30, no. 1 (2001): 319–34.

Samuels, David W. "Bible Translation and Medicine Man Talk: Missionaries, Indexicality, and the 'Language Expert' on the San Carlos Apache Reservation." *Language in Society* 35, no. 04 (2006): 529–57.

Scancarelli, Janine. "Another Look at a 'Primitive Language.'" *International Journal of American Linguistics* 60, no. 2 (1994): 149–60.

Schram, Ryan. "'Tapwaroro Is True': Indigenous Voice and the Heteroglossia of Methodist Missionary Translation in British New Guinea." *Journal of Linguistic Anthropology* 26, no. 3 (2016): 259–77.

Uchihara, Hiroto. "Cherokee Noun Incorporation Revisited." *International Journal of American Linguistics* 80, no. 1 (2014): 5–38.

CHAPTER 12

Teaching Wailaki

Archives, Interpretation, and Collaboration

Kayla Begay, Justin Spence, and Cheryl Tuttle

In precontact times California was one of the most linguistically diverse places in the world, with at least eighty distinct languages belonging to approximately twenty language families.[1] California remains incredibly linguistically diverse to this day, but radically reconfigured as successive waves of settlers speaking a variety of exogenous languages—beginning with Spanish in the late eighteenth century, eventually English, and dozens of others—have displaced Indigenous people and their languages. As colonizing powers established control of the region, policies explicitly designed to eradicate Indigenous autonomy and cultural distinctiveness included prohibitions on using languages other than English in the boarding school system established and operated by the U.S. federal government.[2] Over time the Indigenous languages of California were relegated to the margins of particular communities, known primarily by a small number of elderly people, or restricted to highly specialized contexts of use such as ceremonies.[3]

Today many Native communities in California are actively resisting wholesale loss of their languages through a variety of revitalization efforts designed to develop new generations of fluent speakers. Hopeful signs can be found throughout the state that Native American languages are again becoming an important part of people's lives and beginning to be spoken in the home once more.[4] The challenges facing such efforts are daunting, especially in communities where ancestral languages ceased to be spoken some decades ago. This is the situation for Wailaki, a Dene (Athabaskan) language of northwestern California. As far as is known, there are no people alive today who grew up speaking this language.[5] Wailaki therefore qualifies as what was traditionally known in the academic literature as an "extinct" language, although we here adopt the preferred term "sleeping" to refer to a language like Wailaki with substantial documentation and contemporary communities that consider it their ancestral language—that is, one that is a potential target for language reclamation.[6] Many people with Wailaki heritage have become interested in reconnecting with their history and culture by means of the language, as evidenced by their enthusiastic participation in the biennial Breath of Life language workshops held at the University of California, Berkeley.[7] The immediate issue that learners face, however, is that they do not have any contemporary speakers to learn from. Instead, language revitalization must proceed entirely based on a finite corpus of documentation collected in the past.

This chapter outlines the authors' recent collaborative effort to work with the existing documentation of Wailaki as one of us (Tuttle) implements a new classroom-based revitalization program at Round Valley High School (RVHS) in Covelo, California. Our aim is not to evaluate the program itself or to document student learning outcomes, except in a general sort of way. Instead, we highlight how we have approached various problems related to interpreting written documents as the primary source of information about the language, focusing especially on aspects of the work that may be applicable in other contexts. The discussion is structured as follows. First, the chapter provides an overview of the Wailaki language, the Round Valley community, and the project to date; next, it considers how the project is using philological methods to address the main problems encountered with the available materials. The chapter goes on to highlight some aspects of our approach to collaboration, and it concludes by addressing how our project relates to two general issues commonly found in language revitalization efforts: how to approach language pedagogy when the descriptive understanding of the language is still being developed, and how problematic notions of "authenticity" come into play.

Background

Language

Wailaki is a Dene (Athabaskan) language of northwestern California whose closest linguistic relatives are three other adjoining languages: Hupa-Chilula to the north, Mattole-Bear River to the west, and Kato to the south. Estimates of the precontact population of Wailaki-speaking communities range from three thousand to over ten thousand.[8] According to census data, by 1910 only approximately three hundred Wailaki individuals still remained, two hundred of whom resided on the Round Valley Indian Reservation.[9] These figures, as well as personal accounts by remaining speakers, underscore the violence experienced by Wailaki people during and after the California Gold Rush.[10] As a result of the extreme hardships endured in this period, today the language for all practical purposes can be classified as "sleeping" in the sense defined above.

The documentation of Wailaki is substantial, but far from ideal. The only existing audio recordings of Wailaki are of songs instead of spoken language, so written materials, mostly collected prior to the 1930, serve as the basis for all revitalization efforts. The majority of this documentation is unpublished, the main exception being thirty-six texts narrated by Captain Jim and transcribed by P. E. Goddard, published in 1923.[11] There is little additional published Wailaki material available, other than vocabulary lists and two short texts originally transcribed by Li (discussed below).[12] In addition to these published resources, there is extensive unpublished Wailaki material held by archives and individual scholars, exhaustively described by Golla.[13] The two main archival sources that we have relied on for this project were collected by C. Hart Merriam and Li Fang-Kuei. Merriam, a renowned naturalist, collected vocabulary lists from Wailaki speakers in the years 1920–24.[14] Although his transcriptions are unreliable, they are important for understanding dialect differences among Wailaki groups in the 1920s because Merriam worked with speakers from several communities. Li's unpublished work with Wailaki speaker John Tip in 1927 is the most extensive and careful documentation of the language. Li produced a total of 431 notecards, many of which are full of targeted elicitations of verb paradigms. In addition, there are twenty-four texts and an extensive analyzed list of noun and verb stems. Li's transcriptions are highly accurate and often include prosodic patterns within words (probably stress) that are not represented by other researchers. For many years Li's material was in the personal collection of William Seaburg, who published annotated editions of two of the texts.[15] The Cultural Resources Center at Humboldt State University has recently produced digital copies of some of Li's materials, which became available to us late in 2014, a few months after our project got underway.

Community

Wailaki is one of the heritage languages of the present-day Round Valley Indian Tribes (RVIT) in Covelo, California. RVIT tribal members are descended from a number of distinct language groups: Yuki-speaking people indigenous to the Covelo region, as well as speakers of Wailaki, Northern Pomo, Achumawi (Pit River), Nomlaki, and Konkow who were forcibly resettled to Round Valley in the mid-nineteenth century.[16] Over the years the community has shifted from their ancestral languages to English as the primary language of everyday communication. In the contemporary "unified community" that has emerged since the establishment of the reservation, Wailaki is just one of several ancestral languages that are potential loci for revitalization.[17] The Wailaki classes discussed in this chapter are very much a test case for a more expansive set of programs involving additional languages that may be developed in the future.

The program we describe here is based at Round Valley High School (RVHS), part of the publicly funded Round Valley Unified School District. The fact that RVHS is a public school is important, since Native American–language programs must adhere to curricular and certification requirements that meet local and state standards, issues that might not apply to programs established in tribally run schools or outside of classroom settings altogether. According to data provided by the school district, in 2013–14 there were ninety-nine students enrolled at RVHS, 64 percent of whom identified as American Indian or Alaska Native.[18] The same report indicates that students at RVHS perform below statewide averages on standardized tests in English, mathematics, and science, and that the school's graduation rates are much lower than are found elsewhere in California. These data can be interpreted in many ways, but they suggest that students at RVHS face significant challenges that affect academic performance. Language revitalization efforts in the school thus need to be responsive to the fact that a relatively high proportion of students struggle academically. At the same time, one of the motivations for teaching Wailaki in this setting is to develop a more culturally relevant curriculum that might appeal to students who feel alienated from mainstream subjects offered at the school, likely due in part to the academic setting itself being tainted by a legacy of institutional engagement with Native American communities that has historically been destructive to culture, community, and identity.

This new program should not, however, be understood as a radical shift in thinking about the importance of ancestral languages. Rather, it can be seen as a contemporary manifestation of long-standing interest in preserving Wailaki and other ancestral languages of RVIT. A curriculum for Yuki, the language of Round Valley's inhabitants in precontact times, was developed in the 1970s.[19] For the past several years, a number of Wailaki descendants have participated in events such as the Breath of Life workshops (described below). Even from the earliest days, individuals like Captain Jim, John Tip, and Lucy Young devoted considerable amounts of time and energy to working with the anthropologists and linguists who transcribed and translated—however imperfectly—their knowledge of Wailaki language, culture, and history. These individuals, having survived the most violent period in their people's history, no doubt recognized that the old language was slipping away in their communities, and they took full advantage of one of the few avenues available to them to ensure that their knowledge would survive into the future. Without this incredible foresight, their lived experiences, often as the sole family survivors of violent ethnic cleansing, might go unrecognized.[20] Certainly today's language revitalization efforts would not be possible, and Wailaki would indeed be an extinct language.

Project

Like many language revitalization projects involving professional linguists and California's Native communities, our collaboration started at the Breath of Life Language Restoration Workshop, which supports people who are working to revitalize their ancestral languages using archival documentation.[21] Organized by the nonprofit Advocates for Indigenous California Language Survival (AICLS) and hosted at the University of California, Berkeley, Breath of Life has been held every two years since the early 1990s. With support from the Round Valley community and administrators in the Round Valley Unified School District, Tuttle and teaching assistant Rolinda Want attended the 2014 iteration of Breath of Life. Tuttle, a member of northern California's Native American community, has spent her career working for social justice in the region; although not from Round Valley, she has worked there as a teacher for fourteen years. She had not previously studied Wailaki, but she had experience as a learner of Tolowa, another Dene language of California. Tuttle and Want were partnered with Spence, a former UC Berkeley graduate student who had recently joined the Native American studies faculty at UC Davis, and Lorenzo Tlacaelel Lambertino, a graduate student in linguistics at San Jose State University. Spence's PhD dissertation had focused on historical linguistic topics in the Dene languages of California and Oregon, and he was already familiar with the Wailaki documentation and some of the idiosyncrasies of early transcribers.[22]

Tuttle and Want made clear from the outset of the workshop that their ambitious goal was to have an introductory-level Wailaki language program in place in the upcoming academic year. Although recognizing that it would be better to have more time to plan and prepare the curriculum, they indicated that the alignment of community and administrative support for starting the program demanded an accelerated schedule for implementation. As discussed later in the chapter, this required rethinking several key assumptions that typically guide curriculum planning, a situation that is not atypical in revitalization situations, where there are few, if any, preexisting pedagogical resources or fluent speakers of a language who are qualified to teach it.[23] After a productive week at Breath of Life, Tuttle and Spence agreed to stay in regular communication. An introductory Wailaki 1 class was offered as an elective at RVHS in the fall of 2014, with an initial enrollment of twelve students. In these first several months, Tuttle and Spence would meet online for approximately two hours each week to work through materials and develop a basic curriculum. The Wailaki I course was again offered in the 2015–16 academic year, with an enrollment of nine students, and Wailaki 2 was offered with an enrollment of six students.

Also in 2014, Begay, a graduate student in the Department of Linguistics at UC Berkeley, was actively exploring potential dissertation topics related to Dene languages of California. Begay is from Hoopa Valley in Humboldt County, north of Round Valley. Her family has been active in language revitalization activities for more than two decades, and she grew up with extensive exposure to Hupa, a Dene language closely related to Wailaki. In pursuing tertiary degrees in linguistics, Begay focused explicitly on developing expertise that can be brought to bear in support of language revitalization efforts for Hupa and other languages of California. In recent years she has taken on leadership roles in organizations such as AICLS. In 2012 Begay mentored a woman who was learning Wailaki at that year's Breath of Life workshop. From that experience she gained an appreciation of the dearth of materials available to learners of the language and the difficulties associated with accessing and interpreting the documentation that does exist. Begay decided to pursue a grammar of Wailaki as her dissertation topic (with Spence as one of her committee members), the goal being to fill in a gap in the academic literature that would have applied value as well. It was a happy coincidence that Begay chose this topic at approximately the same time that Tuttle and Want were getting the Wailaki language revitalization program started in Round Valley, as it was a priority for all of them to assemble the disparate strands of Wailaki documentation and put them in a format that would make them available for analysis. Begay and Tuttle have also stayed in regular communication, sharing resources and insights about the language.

Revitalization from a Finite Corpus

Like many other revitalization programs we are familiar with, the Wailaki language classes have had to address a number of challenges. Some of them are social and political in nature and fall beyond the scope of this chapter, where we consider more strictly linguistic issues that arise from the available documentation of the language.

Applied Amerindian Philology

Contemporary methods in linguistics assume the reliability of written representations of language that are the basis of analysis; training in descriptive linguistics seeks to assure that this accuracy is achieved when transcriptions are created. When working with older documentation of Native American languages, one enters the realm not of linguistics per se, but rather what Krauss called "Amerindian philology."[24] Krauss considered the development of this science (as he called it) essential for making better use of older materials, with all of their attendant uncertainties, than would otherwise be possible. Ives Goddard defines philology as "that part of the discipline of linguistics that is concerned with getting from texts and other recorded attestations of languages systematic information that is not directly conveyed by such records as they stand."[25] When the accuracy of transcriptions is in doubt, philology becomes a means to determine "just what the facts of the primary record are, . . . the degree to which the record is dependable, and . . . exactly what can or cannot be concluded from it."[26]

Goddard rightly laments the lack of attention paid to philological concerns in academically oriented Americanist linguistic research. We echo this sentiment from the more applied perspective of language revitalization work. As more Native American communities turn to early documentation as sources of information about their languages, establishing a systematic statement of what works and what doesn't—and why—when interpreting such materials becomes an increasingly pressing need. We adopt Krauss's "Amerindian philology" as a label for the research methods we have employed, but, given our focus on developing resources that are intended primarily for pedagogical purposes, we augment it with the term "applied." While philological methods in service of academically oriented research versus the needs of language revitalization are broadly similar, differences in their respective goals might lead to corresponding differences of application. This is especially true with regard to the degree of residual uncertainty that can be tolerated: whereas philological interpretation informing other modes of linguistic research might set a very high threshold of evidence for accepting the validity of interpreted forms, language revitalization is driven by the need to have the full expressive potential of human language available for learners. Even where a high degree of certainty is elusive, for revitalization purposes it is sometimes necessary to fall back on educated guesses in order to provide learners with the means to say what they want to say.

Morphological Complexity

A typical Dene language, Wailaki is characterized by a much higher degree of morphological complexity than is encountered in English and other Indo-European languages.[27] This is especially the case for verbs, which are composed of a root and a number of prefixes encoding information such as voice and valence, aspect and mode, the path or goal of motion, and agreement with subject, object, and oblique arguments. Idiosyncratic "thematic" prefixes combine with roots to create complex and often discontinuous lexical units known as themes in the Athabaskanist literature. There are also a number of suffixes and enclitics encoding tense, aspect, and evidentiality. A polymorphemic verb such as (1) is not atypical; words with a larger number of morphemes are common as well:[28]

(1) nɑɫ nın ya tɛl tɛñ
'it will follow you'[29]

This example can be analyzed as <nɑ> '2sg', <ɫ> 'with' (likely a proclitic), <nın> 'perfective', <ya> 'go (sg.)', and <tɛl tɛñ> 'future'—a more literal translation is "it will go with you."

As we have worked through the Wailaki materials, we have adopted the principle that each word in the corpus must be carefully scrutinized and exhaustively parsed morphologically in order to ensure that all transcribed elements have an explanation given the gloss and context of use. In example (1), many of the letter combinations happen to be identical with other morphemes transcribed elsewhere by Goddard. The verb root <ya> resembles a plural agreement prefix <ya>; in the future tense suffix <tɛl tɛñ>, <l> could be mistaken for a detransitivizing voice/valence prefix <l> preceding a classificatory verb root <tɛñ> 'handle a living being'. This analysis of (1) is incorrect, but illustrates how each word has many possible "garden path" alternative analyses, sometimes quite plausible and tantalizing, that must be eliminated in order to arrive at the correct one. The morphological complexity of Wailaki makes polymorphemic words common, thus ensuring that there will often be a large number of alternatives that must be adjudicated, greatly slowing the pace of analysis.

Interpreting Attested Forms

As alluded to above, one of the most obvious ways that the documentation of Wailaki is difficult to use is the variety of transcription conventions employed by different researchers. Goddard uses a variant of the Boasian system developed by Alfred Kroeber and his associates and found in much of the early research on languages of California.[30] Li's transcriptions reflect some of these same conventions, but they also have features that are transitional to the Americanist system used in contemporary sources. Merriam's transcriptions are famously idiosyncratic: his insistence on using only English-based transcription symbols means that his system was incapable in principle of adequately representing all of the contrastive sounds of Wailaki.[31] Table 1 illustrates some of the differences between the systems as well as how we decided to represent them in the practical orthography developed for the RVHS classes (based on similar ones used for Hupa and Tolowa).

Table 4. Transcriptional correspondences in Wailaki documentation

IPA	Merriam	Goddard	Li	Practical
ŋ	ng	ñ	ŋ	ng
tʃ	ch, tch	tc	tc	ch
ɬ	hl, sl	ł	ł	lh
iː	ē	i	i·	ii

Such differences in transcription practices are par for the course in any linguistic research that considers data from different decades. Goddard considers this to be one of the main problems for philological interpretation: setting aside questions of particular researchers' accuracy, the fact that one encounters so many "idiosyncratic modifications" even to putatively standardized conventions, and that the conventions themselves have been subject to "the shifting caprice of fashion" over time, can create considerable confusion.³² These problems loom especially large in language revitalization efforts based on archival materials, since researchers often use nonstandard symbols that they do not define in their field notes (which were not intended to be accessed by others), but might have had they published their material.

Quite apart from the differences between transcription conventions is the highly variable quality of the transcriptions themselves. Of the researchers who transcribed any significant quantity of Wailaki material, only Li can be said to be adequate in this regard. By his own admission, Goddard did not transcribe glottalized consonants consistently, and he typically omits [ʔ] and [h] in syllable codas.³³ Thus, for example, if Goddard transcribes a syllable <to>, in principle this could represent [tʰo], [tʰoʔ], [tʰoh], [t'o], [t'oʔ], or [t'oh]. Such ambiguities multiply in longer words, making the interpretation of any given word fraught with numerous alternative analyses, as noted above.

Another kind of interpretive difficulty involves the sparseness of translations, which often fail to capture what one can reasonably suspect are important nuances of meaning. This is found in Goddard's texts especially, where the same interlinear English gloss is often used to render distinct Wailaki words, and different tokens of the same Wailaki word are often given different English interlinear glosses. For example, Goddard provides the gloss "I eat" for several distinct words: <kɛł tsɛ>, <tcɑg gai yañ>, <tcɑt tañ dɛ> and <a cɑn nɑñ>. Whatever the differences between these words, they are not reflected directly in the interlinear glosses and must be inferred from context or by other means.

Our overall approach to resolving issues of interpretation has been twofold. First, we have come to rely on Li's material as much as possible, simply because it is so much more accurate than other sources. When we find words or phrases in other sources that we want to use, we immediately attempt to analyze them in relation to Li's material. We are not always successful in this, but it does offer a starting point for removing some of the many uncertainties encountered in materials transcribed by Goddard and Merriam. Lurking in the background here is the nontrivial assumption that at least some differences between Li and other transcribers are likely due to transcription errors rather than to genuine variation in the language. It is possible, for example, that Captain Jim, who worked with Goddard, might actually have omitted coda [ʔ] and [h] in some contexts where John Tip, who worked with Li, produced them. However, the assumption of uniformity seems preferable to a dubious alternative assumption that transcriptions from Goddard and Merriam are entirely faithful representations of the sounds produced by speakers they worked with.

It was only several months into the classes at RVHS that Li's material became available to us; up to that point, we had relied mainly on Goddard, and on Merriam for topics covered extensively in his vocabularies (e.g., plants and animals). Faced with the same transcriptional ambiguities that we later would view through the lens of Li's more accurate documentation, we adopted several heuristics for dealing with them. Primary among these was a comparative approach where we relied on our understanding of other Dene languages (Tolowa and Hupa). This helped in a general sort of way, insofar as we expected to find certain linguistic features in Wailaki, such as templatic morphology, a set of classificatory verbs found throughout the family, inflectional and derivational morphology realized with cognate morphemes (e.g., 2SG subject *n*-), and so on. It was also a way to disambiguate transcriptions. For any given word transcribed by Goddard or Merriam, we attempted to locate a cognate word in Hupa and Tolowa, or cognate component morphemes when we were exploring the plausibility of a given morphological analysis. If Goddard transcribed a syllable <to> glossed "water," we can identify the <t> as aspirated [tʰ] and eliminate glottalized [t'] based on the cognate word *to* "water" in Hupa; likewise, we can eliminate interpretations ending in [ʔ] or [h].

The second strategy that we used to deal with potentially inaccurate transcriptions was by reconstitution, collating examples of the same or similar words within a single source.[34] By this method it has sometimes been possible to infer features that tend not to be transcribed by Goddard and Merriam. To take a relatively straightforward example, there is an element at the end of verbs that Goddard often transcribes as <tsɛ> or <sɛ>, with "I hear..." or "I feel..." typically included in the interlinear English gloss:

(2) a din tsɛ
'I heard you say'³⁵

This is clearly cognate with the nonvisual evidential enclitic-*ts'eh* in Hupa. Identifying this cognate establishes that the same element in Wailaki is also likely to have been glottalized [ts'] rather than aspirated [tsʰ], but there still may be doubt about whether or not the final [h] present in Hupa is also found in Wailaki. Examination of multiple tokens of the enclitic reveals that it frequently occurs before another enclitic element most commonly transcribed by Goddard as <αñ> (approximately [əŋ]), with the consonant of a preceding stem syllabifying with it. This same enclitic is transcribed <hαñ> following <tsɛ>, as in (3):

(3) tcαk ɢa lɛ tsɛ hαñ
'I hear him walking'³⁶

This shows that <tsɛ> does indeed have a final [h], transcribed accurately by Goddard when the addition of a vowel-initial enclitic makes it a syllable onset. This is a relatively straightforward case because the element is common and glossed consistently enough that multiple tokens can be easily located, and there is a clear cognate in the closely related language Hupa. Many cases do not have as much supporting evidence, but this example illustrates the general principles involved in arriving at an accurate reconstituted interpretation of relatively impoverished transcriptions.

Filling in Gaps

Just as pressing as interpreting words attested in the Wailaki corpus is the problem of filling in gaps in the documentation: clearly it is not sufficient for most purposes to be limited to saying only exactly what was said in the past in precisely the same way. This topic has been much discussed with respect to vocabulary in the language revitalization literature.³⁷ Learners working toward "situational fluency" in historically repressed Indigenous languages often find that formerly everyday activities easily described in the language (e.g., acorn processing, plant gathering) are no longer done regularly and perhaps are even reserved for special occasions. Furthermore, contemporary everyday activities, like using a computer or sending a text message, lack ready-made vocabulary to promote language use rooted in daily situations. Words designating new items or describing new daily situations must be created, or existing words must be adapted accordingly, and this is one of the biggest initial barriers for people who want to reintroduce an ancestral language into everyday life in the contemporary world.

Following lexicalization strategies that can be found in many Dene languages, we have tended to avoid borrowing English words to fill lexical gaps, preferring instead to use Wailaki's own lexical and morphological resources—coining new words, or adapting the meanings of existing ones.[38] In some cases we have explicitly done this on the model of words that have been created in Hupa or Tolowa. For example, Tuttle has created Wailaki versions of familiar card games. The four playing card suits, rendered in the practical orthography, are *bu-jii'* 'hearts' (lit., 'its heart'), *see lhchiit* 'diamonds' (lit., 'red stones'), *dai'-ki-ling* 'spades' (lit., 'arrowheads'), and *bin-da-che bu-ke'* 'clubs' (lit., 'bobcat's foot'). The word for "clubs" was adapted from a Hupa word, *bo:se mixe'* (lit., 'cat's paw'), substituting the Indigenous-sourced word meaning "bobcat" for the English-sourced loanword *bo:se* (< pussy) found in Hupa, and applying the regular sound correspondence Hupa [x] ~ Wailaki [kʰ] to *-ke'* 'foot'. Similarly, in creating language to be used when reclaiming cooking and mealtimes as a domain for revitalization, Tuttle has devised locative and instrumental nominalizations such as *bulh yaang* 'silverware' (lit., 'with it-one eats') and *bu-k'ut yaang* 'table' (lit., 'on it-one eats'), again modeled on similar words found in Tolowa and Hupa, respectively.[39]

Another important aspect of filling gaps in the documentation is having the ability to generate new inflected forms of words, whether they are attested in the existing corpus or new ones created as outlined above. Begay's dissertation project seeks to infer enough details of Wailaki grammar implicit in the documentation, especially the complex verb morphology, to be able to generate new forms.[40] Analysis of attested forms in paradigms, whether explicitly elicited as such in sources like Li or assembled on an ad hoc basis from texts, can lead to educated guesses about what unattested inflected forms of Wailaki words most likely were.[41]

These guesses may, of course, be incorrect in some cases—perhaps a given verb in Wailaki was irregular in some way that is not reflected in the documentation—but they at least ensure that something approximating a viable Wailaki inflected word will be generated more often than not. Here again a comparative perspective is helpful. For example, formation of the progressive aspect in Hupa involves the addition of a prefix *wi-* together with a suffix *-il/-ił*. Knowing this not only helps interpret a verb transcribed by Li as <naɪ'ɪɣʷo't'oł> 'you (pl.) set a snare right along', with Wailaki ɣʷo- cognate with the progressive prefix *wi-* in Hupa, and *-ł* cognate with the Hupa progressive suffix *-il/-ił*, but it also indicates how progressive aspect could be applied in other verb paradigms.

While it is possible to fill in some kinds of gaps in the documentation, it is important to note that there are areas where the documentation of Wailaki is not sufficient to do this in highly principled ways. With regard to linguistic form, even Li's very best segmental transcriptions are merely written representations of sounds with all of their attendant deficiencies. This issue is nicely summarized in the Yuki pedagogical materials produced in Round Valley in the 1970s: "The written form of a language is like a picture of the language. The picture is not as complete as the real thing. It is flat while the real thing is three-dimensional, and it is black-and-white while the real thing is colored."[42] Prosody offers a prime example. Li and Merriam use accent marks to indicate prosody, presumably stress, but inconsistently. While the broad outlines of Wailaki stress patterns are discernable, it remains unclear which phonetic correlates of stress (whether pitch, duration, or intensity) might be involved, and to what degree.[43] In none of the available transcriptions are intonation or other aspects of phrasal prosody represented.

Similar considerations apply for the kinds of subphonemic phonetic features that are known to be subject to variation in the Dene language family. For example, McDonough and Wood show that there are significant differences in average voice onset time (VOT) durations for stop consonants in different Dene languages.[44] When Li transcribes aspirated <t'> in a given Wailaki word, there is no way to know whether the VOT in that token was 50ms, 80ms, or some other value. Because there are no viable audio recordings of Wailaki, this information cannot in principle be recovered from the existing documentary record. For both prosody and subphonemic phonetic tendencies a comparative approach can again be adopted, with reference to published studies of other Dene languages from the region—in effect encouraging new learners of Wailaki to speak the language with an accent strongly colored by languages like Tolowa and Hupa.[45] This approach may be preferable to being satisfied to have learners transfer their English speech patterns into Wailaki. Even so, Wailaki as spoken in the revitalization context is almost certain to sound different from how it might have sounded when spoken a century ago.

The problem of gaps is pervasive in other, perhaps less obvious ways as well, notably in the domain of word sense and usage, due primarily to the small size of the Wailaki corpus. Consider the case of the verbs glossed "I eat" given above. It would be surprising indeed if there were no differences in meaning or usage between them, but what basis will there be for deciding which word with this gloss new learners of the language should use? Would their choice be the same as one made by fluent speakers who lived a century ago? Ideally one would address these questions by gathering numerous tokens of each word, examining the contexts in which they are typically used, and from that inferring general properties that distinguish them—the principles of phonetic reconstitution outlined above applied to lexical semantics. The problem with this approach is a general one encountered in any corpus-based linguistic research: even if a corpus happens to contain an example of every possible word in a given language, the frequency of all but the most common words will be so low that there will not be sufficient information to draw general conclusions about them.[46] Comparative data from Hupa or other Dene languages might shed light on some particular cases, but analyses of those languages will similarly be limited by the small size of the corpora from which inferences about meaning and usage are being made.

The upshot is that revitalizing a language like Wailaki entirely from a finite corpus of written documentation means that there will *necessarily* be gaps that cannot be filled in a straightforward manner. If this sounds pessimistic, this is not our intent, since our experience with Wailaki has been that there is a great deal that can be learned from such materials with a reasonably high degree of certainty. This issue does, however, raise questions about the "authenticity" of languages revitalized from documentary sources that cannot be avoided.[47] We return to this issue later in the chapter.

Collaboration

Ever since this project first got underway in 2014, many aspects of the resulting collaboration have been productive and rewarding for all of us. An important part of this is the background and the skill sets that each of us brings to the project. Two of us (Tuttle and Begay) are members of northwestern California's Native American community. Although neither is from Round Valley, both have spent much of their lives working towards social justice on behalf of Native people in the region. Tuttle is a veteran teacher who has worked in Round Valley for over a decade, and her experience there—knowing her students, their families, and their motivations for participating in language classes—has made it possible for her to sustain students' interest in the Wailaki revitalization efforts. Two of us (Begay and Spence) are also members of the university academic community, both having completed PhDs in linguistics. All three of us in various ways came to the Wailaki project with significant experience with other Dene languages from the region and had previously participated in language revitalization programs, whether as learners (Tuttle, Begay), as researchers (Begay, Spence), or as organizers (Begay is a board member of AICLS). This convergence of interests and expertise may not be exactly reproducible in all cases, but it serves as an example of the kinds of complementary professional experience that can help make such collaborations fruitful.

Another key aspect of our collaboration is the use of digital resources in ways that would have been inconceivable as recently as ten years ago. Our regular meetings have been conducted almost exclusively online, using videoconferencing software such as Skype; Tuttle and Begay frequently communicate with one another using social media platforms such as Facebook; we use cloud-based file storage to share digital images of archival resources as we obtain them. Begay invested many hours in assembling the disparate strands of Wailaki documentation and creating machine-readable transcriptions of materials, which greatly speeds up the process of locating information in the source documents. These digital representations of the main Wailaki data are stored in the shared online Google Sheets environment, which has made them instantly accessible to Tuttle, even while still in progress. We are able to search, edit, and annotate these resources collaboratively during online meetings, and they have formed the basis for the beginnings of an online dictionary and text concordance that we continue to develop. The use of digital resources such as this will continue to play a large role in our own efforts for Wailaki, as they surely will in other revitalization efforts as well.

Conclusions

At the time of writing, the Wailaki language classes at RVHS are approaching the end of their fourth year of existence. What long-term effect they will have on bringing the language back into everyday use remains to be seen, but certainly they are an important starting point for developing a more broad-based language revitalization effort that permeates beyond the walls of the school. To conclude we highlight two points that emerge from our experience with the Wailaki revitalization effort thus far: how the development of the Wailaki language curriculum and our understanding of the language have proceeded apace, and our views on concerns that are sometimes raised about the legitimacy of the revitalized form of a language.

Teaching While Learning

Perhaps the biggest ongoing challenge for this project has been the disconnect between what we understand well about the language versus the needs on the ground for implementing a curriculum on a day-to-day basis—a common issue in language revitalization.[48] As discussed earlier, the alignment of community and administrative support for the program favored moving forward on an accelerated schedule, seizing the opportunity when it presented itself. Certainly this approach had its drawbacks: especially in the first few months after the Breath of Life workshop, it was an ongoing challenge to prepare enough material with enough certainty to have new things to present in class each day. Moreover, as our understanding of the language evolved, it was sometimes necessary to revise and reteach material based on better information. Ideally, of course, we would have waited until we had a better understanding of the language before proceeding. However, we did not want to fall into the trap of placing too much emphasis on developing a perfect analysis of every aspect of the language before anything could be taught. Indeed, such an understanding is certainly many years away, and, as noted earlier in the chapter, there are aspects of the language where that understanding may never be possible given the limitations of working with a small, finite corpus.

Despite the drawbacks of moving forward with the program while the linguistic analysis was not yet complete, we discovered certain unintended benefits to our approach. Since Tuttle and teaching assistant Rolinda Want were effectively learning Wailaki at the same time as their students, it put them in the role of colearners and facilitators, which created a productive classroom dynamic that students responded to well. It required the curriculum to be flexible enough to focus initially on areas that could be learned easily through existing documentation, deferring topics that required more detailed analysis; both the students and the teachers had to be willing to accept revisions to the pedagogical targets as ongoing analysis of materials led to a more refined understanding of the language. This rendered transparent to students how the content they were encountering in class was subject to revision as the result of inquiry and research. This supported broader pedagogical goals of developing active, engaged learners who think critically about information presented to them and who recognize the iterative process involved in research. The cloud of uncertainty associated with the documentation of Wailaki, in other words, did have something of a silver lining.

Authenticity

We argued above that language revitalization proceeding from a small, finite corpus will necessarily have gaps that cannot be filled in a principled way, and the revitalized language is thus virtually guaranteed to be different in certain respects from the way it was spoken in the past. The obvious question this raises is the following: Does it matter? The short answer that we give here is that it does, but not as much or for the same reasons that skeptics of language revitalization sometimes offer.[49] We take as a starting point the assumption that the primary aim of language revitalization is not merely to develop fluency or communicative competence in the target language. This is especially the case for languages like Wailaki, where there currently isn't a population of living speakers to connect and communicate with (though becoming that resource to new generations of speakers is a goal among learners using all available means). Rather, language revitalization efforts like the ones undertaken in Round Valley offer students the chance to connect on a personal and emotional level with aspects of their family's cultural legacy, to reclaim and assert a presence for Indigenous knowledge systems in the contemporary world, especially in institutions that played a key role in creating their current precarious status, and to reflect critically on the legacy of colonization that has ensured that Wailaki rather than English satisfies a foreign-language requirement in their school.[50] These aims can be achieved even if students impose English-based prosodic interference on their Wailaki utterances, undershoot average VOT targets for aspirated stops, or never develop a nuanced understanding of different ways of saying "I eat" and instead use whichever word happens to be easiest to remember, inflect, spell, or pronounce.

It is true that some of these broader goals could be addressed in the absence of any particular linguistic content, but activities promoting fluency and communication play an important role in bringing the issues into sharp focus. The RVHS Wailaki curriculum does emphasize practical language that can be deployed in everyday situations outside the classroom, so developing communicative competence and approximating the language as spoken in generations past are certainly important considerations. Thus, we are not suggesting that Native American languages being revitalized, whether from written documentation or otherwise, cannot have relevance for everyday communication, or that in the long run the bar for endangered language pedagogy should be lower than the standards set for other languages that are taught in classroom settings. Rather, we simply maintain that even if those particular communicative goals cannot be achieved neatly within a couple of short years, getting students as close to them as possible is time well spent.

ACKNOWLEDGMENTS

We wish to thank people whose enthusiasm for Wailaki language, culture, and history have inspired us: Perry Lincoln, Mike Lincoln, Ron Lincoln Sr., Ron Lincoln Jr., Rolinda Want, Lorenzo Tlacaelel Lambertino, Tichetsa Thelili, Lewis Lawyer, and Julie Ngo. Thanks are also due to audiences at the 2015 Language Is Life conference in Wonder Valley, California, and the Translating Across Time and Space symposium at the American Philosophical Society in 2016, who provided helpful feedback on earlier versions of this chapter.

NOTES

1. Golla, *California Indian Languages*, 1–2.
2. Crawford, "Endangered Native American Languages," 10–12.
3. Hinton, *Flutes of Fire*, 14, 247.
4. See Hinton, *Bringing Our Languages Home*.
5. Golla, *California Indian Languages*, 81.
6. Hinton, "Sleeping Languages"; Leonard, "Challenging 'Extinction.'"
7. Hinton, "Use of Linguistic Archives."
8. Kroeber, *Handbook of the Indians of California*, 883; Baumhoff, "California Athabaskan Groups," 216.
9. Kroeber, *Handbook of the Indians of California*, 154, 883.
10. Young and Murphey, "Out of the Past"; Bauer, *California through Native Eyes*.
11. Goddard's field notebooks containing the original transcriptions of these texts are archived with the American Philosophical Society (Na20c.1).
12. Curtis, "Wailaki," 201–7; Essene, "Culture Element Distributions"; Kroeber, "Goddard's California Athabascan Texts."
13. Golla, *California Indian Languages*, 79–81.
14. Merriam's notes are archived with the Bancroft Library (BANC FILM 1022), and copies with substantially similar content are also at the Library of Congress (MSS32698). Digital images of the Bancroft copies are easily accessed through the Internet Archive website, https://archive.org/ (accessed August 21, 2020).
15. Seaburg, "Man Who Married a Grizzly Girl"; Seaburg, "Wailaki (Athabaskan) Text with Comparative Notes."
16. Round Valley Indian Tribes, "About Us."
17. Round Valley Indian Tribes, "About Us."
18. Round Valley High School, Student Accountability Report Card.
19. Britton, McLane, and Wenger, *Learning to Speak Yuki*.
20. Miranda, *Bad Indians*; Bauer, *California through Native Eyes*.
21. Hinton, "Use of Linguistic Archives."

22. Spence, "Language Change, Contact."
23. Hinton, "How to Teach When the Teacher Isn't Fluent."
24. Krauss, "Na-Dene," 293.
25. Goddard, "Philological Approaches," 73.
26. Goddard, "Philological Approaches," 74.
27. Begay, "Wailaki Grammar," provides a detailed description of Wailaki morphology.
28. Examples are rendered according to the source transcription. When presented inline in the text, such forms are enclosed in angle brackets <>. Forms intended to be phonetic representations are enclosed in square brackets [], and forms in Wailaki and Hupa practical orthographies are italicized.
29. Goddard, "Wailaki Texts," 106.
30. Golla, *California Indian Languages*, 283–286.
31. Golla, *California Indian Languages*, 43.
32. Goddard, "Wailaki Texts."
33. Goddard, "Wailaki Texts."
34. Broadbent, "Rumsen I"; Goddard, "Philological Approaches."
35. Goddard, "Wailaki Texts," 108.
36. Goddard, "Wailaki Texts," 90; Compare Hupa *ch'iqa:l* 'someone walks along', *-e:* 'there'.
37. See, for example, Hinton and Ahlers, "Issue of 'Authenticity'"; and Warner, Luna, and Butler, "Ethics and Revitalization."
38. Ahlers, "Metonymy and the Creation"; Rice, "Our Language is Very Literal"; Peterson and Webster, "Speech Play and Language Ideologies"; Spence, "Lexical Innovation and Variation in Hupa (Athabaskan)."
39. Ahlers, "Metonymy and the Creation."
40. Begay, "Wailaki Grammar."
41. Li, Wailaki noun and verb stem list.
42. Britton, McLane, and Wenger, *Learning to Speak Yuki*.
43. Begay, "Wailaki Grammar."
44. McDonough and Wood, "Stop Contrasts of Athabaskan Languages."
45. Bright, "Phonology of Smith River Athapaskan"; Gordon, "Phonetic Structures of Hupa"; and Gordon and Luna, "Intergenerational Investigation of Hupa Stress."
46. For discussion, see Sinclair, "Corpus and Text."
47. Warner, Luna, and Butler, "Ethics and Revitalization."
48. Hinton, "How to Teach When the Teacher Isn't Fluent"; Szoboszlai, *Mutsun Reclamation Continued*.
49. See Edwards, "Language Revitalization and Its Discontents."
50. See Hinton and Ahlers, "Issue of 'Authenticity'"; Warner, Luna, and Butler, "Ethics and Revitalization"; Szaoboszlai, *Mutsun Reclamation Continued*; and, especially, Leonard, "Challenging 'Extinction.'"

BIBLIOGRAPHY

Ahlers, Jocelyn C. "Metonymy and the Creation of New Words in Hupa." In *Proceedings of the Twenty-Second Annual Meeting of the Berkeley Linguistics Society: Special Session on Historical Issues in Native American Languages*, edited by David Librik and Roxane Beeler, 2–10. Berkeley CA: Berkeley Linguistics Society, 1996.

Bauer, William Jr. *California through Native Eyes*. Seattle: University of Washington Press, 2016.

Baumhoff, Martin A. "California Athabaskan Groups." *University of California Anthropological Records* 16, no. 5 (1958): 157–237.

Begay, Kayla. "Wailaki Grammar." PhD diss., University of California, Berkeley, 2017.

Bright, Jane O. "The Phonology of Smith River Athapaskan (Tolowa)." *International Journal of American Linguistics* 30, no. 2 (1964): 101–7.

Britton, Donna, Linda McClane, and Pat Wenger. *Learning to Speak Yuki*. Covelo CA: Covelo Indian Community Council, 1978.

Broadbent, Sylvia M. "Rumsen I: Methods of Reconstitution." *International Journal of American Linguistics* 23, no. 4 (1957): 275–80.

Crawford, James. "Endangered Native American Languages: What Is to Be Done, and Why?" *Bilingual Research Journal*. 19, no. 1 (1995): 17–38.

Curtis, Edward. "The Wailaki." *The North American Indian: Being a Series of Volumes Picturing and Describing the Indians of the United States, the Dominion of Canada, and Alaska*, vol. 14, edited by Frederick Webb Hodge, 21–38. Norwood MA: Plimpton, 1924.

Edwards, John. "Language Revitalization and Its Discontents: An Essay and Review of *Saving Languages: An Introduction to Language Revitalization*." *Canadian Journal of Applied Linguistics* 10, no. 1 (2007): 101–20.

Essene, Frank. "Culture Element Distributions: XXI. Round Valley." *University of California Archaeological Records* 8, no.1 (1942): 85–89.

Goddard, Ives. "Philological Approaches to the Study of North American Languages: Documents and Documentation." In *Native Languages of the Americas*, edited by Thomas A. Sebeok, 73–91. New York: Plenum, 1976.

Goddard, Pliny Earle. "Wailaki Texts." *International Journal of American Linguistics* 2, nos. 3–4 (1923): 77–134.

Golla, Victor. *California Indian Languages*. Berkeley: University of California Press, 2011.

Gordon, Matthew. "The Phonetic Structures of Hupa." *UCLA Working Papers in Phonetics* 93 (1996): 164–87.

Gordon, Matthew, and Edmundo Luna. "An Intergenerational Investigation of Hupa Stress." In *Proceedings of the 30th Annual Meeting of the Berkeley Linguistics Society*, edited by M. Ettlinger, N. Fleischer, and M. Park-Doob, 105–17. Berkeley CA: Berkeley Linguistics Society, 2005.

Hinton, Leanne. *Flutes of Fire: Essays on California Indian Languages*. Berkeley CA: Heyday, 1993.

———. "How to Teach When the Teacher Isn't Fluent." In *Nurturing Native Languages*, edited by Jon Reyhner, Octaviana V. Trujillo, Roberto Luis Carrasco, and Louise Lockard, 79-92. Flagstaff: Northern Arizona University, 2003.

———. "Sleeping Languages: Can They Be Awakened?" In *The Green Book of Language Revitalization in Practice*, edited by Leanne Hinton and Kenneth Hale, 413-17. Boston: Brill, 2001.

———. "The Use of Linguistic Archives in Language Revitalization: The Native California Language Restoration Workshop." In *The Green Book of Language Revitalization in Practice*, edited by Leanne Hinton and Kenneth Hale, 419-23. Boston: Brill, 2001.

Hinton, Leanne, ed. *Bringing Our Languages Home: Language Revitalization for Families*. Berkeley CA: Heyday, 2013.

Hinton, Leanne, and Jocelyn Ahlers. "The Issue of 'Authenticity' in California Language Restoration." *Anthropology & Education Quarterly* 30, no. 1 (1999): 56-67.

Hinton, Leanne, and Kenneth Hale, eds. *The Green Book of Language Revitalization in Practice*. Boston: Brill, 2001.

Krauss, Michael. "Na-Dene." In *Linguistics in North America*, edited by Thomas A. Sebeok, 903-78. Current Trends in Linguistics 10. The Hague: Mouton, 1973.

Kroeber, Alfred L. "Goddard's California Athabascan Texts." *International Journal of American Linguistics* 33, no. 4 (1967): 269-75.

———. *Handbook of the Indians of California*. Bureau of American Ethnology Bulletin 78. Washington DC: Government Printing Office, 1925.

Leonard, Wesley. "Challenging 'Extinction' through Modern Miami Language Practices." *American Indian Culture and Research Journal* 35, no. 2 (2011): 135-60.

Li, Fang-Kuei. Wailaki notecards, 1927. Digital access copy available from the Cultural Resources Center, Humboldt State University. Unpublished.

———. Wailaki noun and verb stem list, n.d. Photocopy of original manuscript in the possession of Victor Golla, Humboldt State University. Unpublished.

McDonough, Joyce, and Valerie Wood. "The Stop Contrasts of Athabaskan Languages." *Journal of Phonetics* 36 (2008): 427-49.

Miranda, Deborah A. *Bad Indians: A Tribal Memoir*. Berkeley CA: Heyday, 2013.

Peterson, Leighton C., and Anthony K. Webster. 2. "Speech Play and Language Ideologies in Navajo Terminology Development." *Pragmatics* 23, no. 1 (2013): 93-116.

Rice, Sally. "'Our Language is Very Literal': Figurative Language in Dene Sųłiné [Athapaskan]." In *Endangered Metaphors*, edited by Anna Idström and Elisabeth Piirainen, 21-76. Philadelphia: John Benjamins, 2012.

Round Valley High School. Student Accountability Report Card. 2013-14; 2014-15. http://www.roundvalleyschools.org/pages/uploaded_files/14%20sarc_rvusd _Round%20valley%20hs(1).pdf (link deleted).

Round Valley Indian Tribes. "About Us." 2016. http://www.rvit.org/about.php (accessed August, 21, 2020).

Sapir, Edward, and Victor Golla. "Hupa Texts, with Notes and Lexicon." In *Collected Works of Edward Sapir, Vol. 14: Northwest California Linguistics*, edited by Victor Golla and Sean O'Neill, 19–101. New York: Mouton de Gruyter, 2001.

Seaburg, William R. "The Man Who Married a Grizzly Girl." In *Northern California Texts*, edited by Victor Golla and Shirley Silver. *International Journal of American Linguistics Native American Texts Series* 2, no. 2 (1977): 114–120.

———. "A Wailaki (Athabaskan) Text with Comparative Notes." *International Journal of American Linguistics* 43, no. 4 (1977): 327–32.

Sinclair, John. "Corpus and Text: Basic Principles." In *Developing Linguistic Corpora: A Guide to Good Practice*. 2004. https://ota.ox.ac.uk/documents/creating/dlc/chapter1.htm (accessed August 21, 2020).

Spence, Justin. "Language Change, Contact, and Koineization in Pacific Coast Athabaskan." PhD diss., University of California Berkeley, 2013.

———. "Lexical Innovation and Variation in Hupa (Athabaskan)." *International Journal of American Linguistics* 82, no. 1 (2016): 72–93.

Szoboszlai, Lajos. "Mutsun Reclamation Continued: Four Years in a Learner's Effort to Acquire Language." PhD diss., University of California, Davis, 2017.

Warner, Natasha, Quirina Luna, and Lynnika Butler. "Ethics and Revitalization of Dormant Languages: The Mutsun Language." *Language Documentation and Conservation* 1, no. 1 (2007): 58–76.

Young, Lucy (T'tcetsa), and Edith V. A. Murphey. "Out of the Past: A True Indian Story Told by Lucy Young, of Round Valley Indian Reservation." *California Historical Society Quarterly* 20, no. 4 (1941): 349–64.

PART 6

Transforming Collecting

Commentary by Jennifer R. O'Neal

I imagine a world in the not-so-distant future, where Indigenous history and ways of knowing are at the center of all humanity's existence. Where Native people do not have to constantly struggle to explain our beautiful and complex history of being here since time immemorial. Where, rather than having our cultures and peoples studied because others find us so fascinating and do not quite understand our world, we are respected and given our space to freely practice our cultures, tell our stories the way we want them told, and determine how we want our history and culture preserved for future generations. Moreover, I hope for a world where humanity is brought into the professions that research and work with our tribal communities. We are a people who once lived peacefully and accordingly to our own laws but, since the arrival of outsiders, have struggled for hundreds of years due to forced colonization, removal from our traditional homelands, cultural and physical genocide, assimilation, and loss of identity. Due to the U.S. federal government's lack of a formal reconciliation policy for the atrocities done to Native American people, it then rests with communities, professions, and individuals to make a difference in ensuring that there is some restitution, in bringing some justice to this very unfortunate and complex colonial history.

Thus, it is heartening to see the amazing work being done by historians, anthropologists, curators, and archivists. It gives me hope to see that such important and meaningful work is being accomplished by these individuals and groups who have shared their personal stories about their projects in this section, especially as many of them work for larger national and federal repositories or museums, where it can often be challenging to move forward with projects that often push the boundaries of organizations still tied to a colonial history. As seen in these chapters, it takes a concerted effort on the part of an individual, groups, researchers, or a community of curators to put forward major change in these large repositories and institutions, by implementing shared stewardship and curation through building strong, respectful, and reciprocal relationships with Indigenous communities and centering Indigenous ways of knowing through decolonization frameworks.

At the core of each of these chapters is the importance of centering traditional Indigenous knowledge in collections and research. It is imperative, as one embarks on any project involving Indigenous collections and histories, to remember the very complex and settler-colonial ways that collectors and repositories acquired Indigenous cultural heritage, often taking items far from their traditional homelands, out of the control of Indigenous communities, and then centering them into Western ways of managing collections, directly decentering Indigenous ways of knowing. As noted in Gwyneira Isaac's chapter, a major factor affecting the management of Indigenous collections and information relates directly to the way the intersectionality of power and knowledge dynamics has influenced this work. Isaac's argument for a multisited, comprehensive, and pluralistic approach to the anthropology of knowledge systems is much needed and long overdue for institutions working in preexisting salvage paradigms. Isaac's work with Gabriela Perez-Baez on the Recovering Voices program within the National Museum of Natural History provides a tangible example of how even a program at a very large complex federal repository with historic colonial collecting has begun to make substantial changes to their collaborative stewardship and relationship-building policies. It shows, further, that it is only through building these very important and meaningful relationships that curators and museums will come to understand and receive the true Indigenous history and knowledge of objects from the experts themselves: the tribal community members. This is shown, for example, with the Hopi Pottery Oral History Project, through the reciprocity that is essential in Hopi cultural protocol. These projects exemplify that, when working with Indigenous communities, curators and researchers must recognize, center, and respect Indigenous ontologies and knowledge systems.

The key practice of relationship building is exemplified by the work of Craig Mishler and Kenneth Frank, as they share their stories of collaborating on the Gwich'in language documentation. Their innovative approach to language documentation that centers the tribal Elders and language speakers reflects the respect and shared understanding for the Indigenous history, culture, and people who are the knowledge-bearers for this language. Mishler and Frank keenly reflect that, although there would always be some degree of tension, they tried to set aside their differences and place their friendship and Frank's Indigenous perspective and knowledge at the core of the project. It is this humanistic approach that made the project so successful. Although this approach and these types of projects can be challenging, it is imperative to center the Indigenous perspective to build strong relationships for a respectful and reciprocal project.

It is heartening to see such meaningful work occurring between large repositories and tribal communities regarding language, culture, and history preservation to ensure that Indigenous perspectives and knowledges are respected and recentered. These chapters reflect what is possible when we are brave and move this work forward. If you are wondering or considering whether or not to begin a similar project, I encourage you not to wait for someone else to implement changes or for someone to come to do this work. If you have the desire or see changes that should be implemented in the management of collections, say and do something about it. To make a significant change in collecting, we must bring humanity into this work. We have hundreds of years of colonization to undo, and it is time to place Indigenous knowledge systems where they have been since time immemorial—at the center of our universe.

CHAPTER 13

Museums and the Revitalization of Endangered Languages and Knowledge

Gwyneira Isaac

Our home among the dinosaurs poses challenges. The iconic stars of natural history museums, dinosaurs are the main draw for the majority of the public, and, as a result, they are the top predators eating up huge amounts of funding, space, staff attention, and airtime. I experience this firsthand—recently, during a public program we were hosting on cultural revitalization partnerships with Native American communities. Rather than engage with the selection of Hopi pottery we had on display, a visitor stops to ask me, "Can you tell me where the dinosaurs are?" I would like to answer, "They are extinct, madam. They have been for some sixty-five million years—but join us, instead, in a workshop to celebrate cultural diversity." Nonetheless I don't. I see that she has a small child tugging at her sleeve who is eager to see these ancient creatures, and I sense instinctively that I cannot compete with dinosaurs—at least, not in this particular time and space. I am, however, left feeling even more determined to find appropriate methods and arenas in which to address the needs of Indigenous communities in their cultural revitalization efforts. I must also ask—as many still house large collections related to the Indigenous people of the world—what role can natural history museums play in this endeavor?

It is this complex territory that we, Recovering Voices—a cultural and language revitalization program in the National Museum of Natural

History (NMNH) at the Smithsonian Institution—occupy. It is a terrain with a particular history, one in which Native American communities have been the subjects of colonial regimes, cultural assimilation policies, and nineteenth- and twentieth-century concepts of and interests in science. This territory is now actively being questioned and reshaped by Indigenous communities for the purposes of cultural revitalization. Revisiting the history of the NMNH and the problematic power inequities of the past and present, as well as the current and future role of an anthropology department in a natural history museum, is at the heart of Recovering Voices' endeavors. More important, this effort is understood to be a joint project with Indigenous communities to reimagine the future of this institution, and to change the role museums in general play in supporting the work of Indigenous people in sustaining their cultural traditions and languages.

As language retains and shapes all of our worldviews and transmits this knowledge down through the generations, it is the adhesive that links all elements—human philosophies, living beings, and our understanding of natural forces and our histories over time.[1] For many of the communities with whom Recovering Voices works, language is also seen as the breath of life that brings the world into being. While the study and documentation of language should not be limited to textual methods, often for the sake of analysis it is distilled to and materialized as written vocabularies and dictionaries. Certainly these research objects are central to archives housed in libraries, universities and museums. Yet, because the National Anthropological Archives (NAA) and Recovering Voices are nested within a natural history museum, their location has expanded our responsibilities, which now cover a vast nexus of diverse knowledges, both disciplinary and cultural. This environment has demanded that we forge collaborative, interdisciplinary, multimodal research with diverse communities, partnering with Indigenous scholars and working across a vast array of natural history and archival and ethnographic collections that include plants, animals, minerals, arts, games, music, dance, technology (including the knowledge and raw materials used to make pottery), baskets, clothing, and the specialized expertise needed to farm or hunt. This world includes linguistic manuscripts, film and sound archives, photographic collections, and public outreach efforts through education centers, such as Q?rius at the NMNH, and the Mother Tongue Film Festival (MTFF), which links diverse units across the Smithsonian.

Our position in the museum world also requires reconciling our problematic past—with its violent cultural subjugation and forced assimilation of Native Americans—and the present, in which these collections provide a lens on cultural and environmental changes over time and, therefore, reflective resources for revitalization efforts. At the same time, this effort faces countless contemporary issues that contribute to language endangerment, including economic pressures on communities, the politics of language, and a lack of funding to build more adaptive infrastructures for the sustaining of traditional knowledges in institutions such as schools and museums.[2] As argued by one of our Recovering Voices team members, Tim McCoy, a member of the Miami Tribe of Oklahoma and a curator in mineral sciences at NMNH, "Putting a rover on Mars was one of the hardest and most intellectually challenging things I have been involved in—but revitalizing a dormant language is proving to be a thousand times harder."

Although the situation of Recovering Voices in a natural history museum has introduced particular challenges, it has also resulted in the program gaining invaluable lessons. These are explored here as a means to ask: What role can museums play in language and cultural revitalization efforts? What kinds of traits do these institutions bring to this endeavor and what do they gain in return? What particular features do natural history museums bring to these efforts? Moreover, how is their role in cultural revitalization shaped by Indigenous communities, and what does this mean for the future of this endeavor?

The Origins of Recovering Voices

In 2008 the then-director of the NMNH, Cristian Samper, solicited proposals that envisioned ways of building projects that would transcend different divisions at the museum and advance its interdisciplinarity. A group of anthropology, botany, and mineral science curators joined with colleagues from the National Anthropological Archives (NAA) and the National Museum of the American Indian (NMAI) to submit a proposal to highlight Smithsonian collections as a means of advancing collaborative research and revitalization work on endangered languages and Indigenous knowledges.[3] This materialized as the Recovering Voices initiative, and in 2009 the group hosted a three-day symposium to which linguists, community experts, and researchers from a wide range of fields were invited to share their work on endangered languages, as well to envision what a program might look like that would continue this effort at the Smithsonian. The initiative was supported by the NMNH's executive team, and in 2010 a curator of linguistics and a curator for North American ethnology were hired to join Recovering Voices. This collaborative group then worked with Samper and development officers to raise an endowment that could support this vision. An endowment was established in 2012 through the WEM foundation that enabled the hire of a coordinator for community-based research projects on collections and a program manager, as well as funds to support community visits to the Smithsonian to work on collections.

There have been rising concerns that, although languages have historically changed over time, the decline in the vitality of the languages of the world in the last five hundred years has occurred at an unprecedented rate. It is estimated that one-third of the world's languages are in some state of language shift,[4] and forecasts indicate that within this century as many as 90 percent of the world's languages could go silent.[5] Exactly how we conceive of this loss of the world's diversity in languages is evaluated differently and according to the various ways it is seen to affect the wellbeing of communities around the world,[6] associated knowledge systems,[7] and science's ability to advance our understanding of what it means to be human.[8]

Ten years since its inception, Recovering Voices has established its mission as one of using collections to foster innovative collaborative research with Indigenous communities to revitalize endangered languages and traditional knowledge. This work is being done through three programmatic branches: the Community Research Program (CRP), which includes an annual competitive funding program that enables Indigenous communities to visit Smithsonian collections; the Mother Tongue Film Festival (MTFF), which bridges units across the Smithsonian to showcase films and communicate to the wider public the problems of language endangerment and the importance of cultural diversity and sustainability; and the National Breath of Life Archival Institute for Indigenous Languages (BOL), which is the biennial mentoring workshop funded through the NSF, bringing Native American community members and linguists together to work on archives.

As far as we understand, the CRP is currently one of the only language and cultural revitalization programs situated within a natural history museum, and therefore it has expanded the types of collections that are used as revitalization resources. The CRP encourages proposals from communities working on revitalizing language and traditional knowledge, such that projects on canoe building, fishing technology, clothing construction, quillwork, beading, weaving, basketmaking, pottery techniques, and traditional games have been part of the program. In addition it facilitates work with natural history collections, such as birds, mammals, and plants, and this approach has proved invaluable for communities such as the Wauja from Brazil, who have suffered the effects of deforestation and climate change and therefore chose during their research visit to include the natural world as part of their documentation of knowledge and language for future generations of Wauja.

Recovering Voices must also be understood according to its context within the longer history of language research at the Smithsonian Institution. The Smithsonian itself exemplifies a particular relationship that emerged between the philosophies of the Enlightenment and explorations of the New World. During this time attention was given not only to the study of natural history, but also to the history of the original people of the Americas. From the start this included linguistic surveys of North American tribes pursued by Henry Rowe Schoolcraft (1793–1864) and then–secretary of state Thomas Jefferson (1743–1826). During the first meeting of the Board of Regents of the Smithsonian Institution, Schoolcraft advocated for the establishment of a library of philology, arguing that language was a critical means to comprehending Native American societies. As a result the study and collection of materials relating to Native American languages in the New World became a foundational cornerstone in the development of the Smithsonian Institution.

The present-day collections of the NMNH reflect these multiple past avenues of collecting during the eighteenth, nineteenth, and twentieth centuries, from the original philological library collections—which include some of the earliest bibles and publications printed in Native American languages—to seeds, raw materials, and natural history specimens collected by naturalists, who, at times, included their cultural uses and nomenclature. Under John Wesley Powell's leadership, in 1879 the newly established Bureau of American Ethnology (BAE) acquired the corpus of anthropological research conducted by federal geological surveys and expanded to encompass vast collections of ethnographic materials from across the continent. This included increased documentation that focused on North American languages and cultures through BAE fieldwork and researchers external to the Smithsonian, By 1965 the BAE had been integrated into the United States National Museum (USNM)— now the NMNH—and joined the Department of Anthropology, with the BAE records becoming part of the NAA. The NAA holdings now include 1 million photographs (among them, early images of Indigenous people worldwide); 20,000 works of Native art; 11,400 sound recordings; and more than 8 million feet of original film and video materials.

The NMNH collections must also be understood as products of their time—a period of immense social change in which Native Americans had to face the traumas of western expansion in the United States. By the 1880s ethnologists and museums argued for more resources for intensive collecting methods, as they believed they were racing against what they saw as the inevitable destruction of these cultures by colonial forces and rapidly expanding settler communities. This approach, now known as "salvage ethnology,"[9] included exhaustive collecting techniques that, in some contexts, resulted in the almost wholesale removal of cultural artifacts from Native American communities.[10] Under this school of thought, scholars advocating for the relocation of cultural objects to centralized institutions subscribed to the belief that the scientific methods of the day were the most suitable for the study and classification of both the natural and human world, as well as for the preservation of these specific aspects of Indigenous cultures.

As a result these collections largely represent that window of time between the 1870s and the 1930s. Museum collecting of ethnographic objects declined following World War II, owing to colonized countries gaining independence and increasing criticism by Indigenous scholars of scientific and anthropological methods. The postparadigm period that followed introduced postcolonialist and postmodernist schools of thought that contributed to pluralistic approaches to knowledge production.[11] Throughout the 1960s the objectivity of fieldwork methods was reexamined, with critics arguing that these held biases originated from the political and cultural positions of the ethnographer. Demands by Indigenous people to acknowledge their values and approaches to knowledge and cultural heritage has resulted in the growth of museums developed by communities for communities, as well as the emergence of frameworks and studies in decolonization, which advocate Indigenous ontologies as primary principles in the restructuring of museum practices.[12]

Since the 1960s tribally initiated self-determination and self-governance movements in the United States have been of critical importance to shaping heritage preservation efforts in Native American communities. Interests in reestablishing Indigenous values and knowledge as central to decision-making in tribal governments, education, and law has also been accompanied by a wide range of language programs, schools, and camps[13] and by the development of tribal museums and cultural centers, as well as tribal heritage and preservation offices (THPOs).[14] While it would be true to say that anthropology and museums have a long history of collaboration with Native American communities, with whom they now work together on cultural revitalization projects, it is key to recognize that the lion's share of the efforts behind revitalization have come from the communities themselves.[15] The role national museums and collections can play in this endeavor, however, may be meaningful not only in terms of providing further insight into the history of cultural and environmental change over time, but in helping to address the problems of the past by enabling community-led curatorial input and therefore continuity to the areas of cultural disruption in which museums played a part.

Museums as Nexus for Collaborative Revitalization

One of the first groups that Recovering Voices partnered with is a research collective known as the Great Lakes Research Alliance for the Study of

Aboriginal Art and Culture (GRASAC). GRASAC was established in 2005 as a program to help coordinate the research on and documentation of collections and archives relating to the Indigenous communities of the Great Lakes region that had been scattered among geographically disparate institutions around the world. The concept of the consortia revolves around group visits to museums and archives to review and input collections into the GRASAC knowledge-sharing database (GKS) and, through this process, reestablish and revitalize knowledge about Anishinaabeg history and culture.

In 2012 members of the GRASAC consortia from the Anishinaabeg community—Alan Ojiig Corbiere (Anishinaabemowin Revival Program, M'Chigeeng First Nation), Myna and Theodore Toulouse (M'Chigeeng First Nation), Crystal Migwan (Columbia University), and Mary Ann Naokwegijig-Corbiere (University of Sudbury)—joined with the linguist Rand Valentine (University of Wisconsin Madison), art historian Ruth Phillips (Carleton University), Gwyneira Isaac (NMNH), and Judith Andrews (NMNH)—to work on NMNH collections relating to Anishinaabeg history, language, and culture.

During this visit the group convened around objects, and the discussions about the materials, designs, and iconography, as well as the meanings and history behind the objects, were recorded on video. The majority of the discussions were in Anishinaabemowin, and the linguists, Corbiere and Valentine, annotated specific terminology for use in the database. The objects reviewed had been selected by the group beforehand and consisted of clothing, wampum, birchbark *biting art*, or *mazinibaganjiganan*, as well as quillwork baskets, of which Myna Toulouse is a distinguished expert.

While organizing the GRASAC visit, Myna requested that her husband, Ted, accompany her. As an Elder she did not want to undertake the long journey alone. While the majority of her visit centered around talking about quillwork, once Ted encountered a series of cabinets containing birchbark containers and historic equipment used to make maple syrup he and Alan Corbiere enthusiastically started recording his knowledge about the traditional process of syrup collecting. Ted excitedly shared with the group that he had not seen these things since he was a boy, and

Fig. 21. GRASAC visit, 2012. *Left to right*: Myna Toulouse, Mary Ann Corbiere, Ruth Phillips (*background*), Theodore Toulouse, and Alan Corbiere. Photo by Judith Andrews, Recovering Voices, NMNH.

that they brought back powerful memories and knowledge that he was now inspired to share with the youth of his community. He explained how birchbark was collected and re-collected from the same trees, and how you could tell if a birchbark container was a "first" or "second" sourcing of bark. In the case of the Toulouses, Ted is the person who sources the raw materials (e.g., quills, bark) for Myna's quillwork boxes. As a couple they represent an important union of artistic, cultural, and environmental knowledge. Myna, however, is often the individual who is brought to museum collections, because, as an artist, she is recognized by museum staff as having the required expertise to help them work with the objects.

Many of the objects GRASAC worked on at NMNH had been collected in the early 1900s by the ethnomusicologist Frances Densmore. Yet it took Ted opening and engaging with these long-overlooked cabinets of historic equipment to reveal to Recovering Voices the specific niche they potentially hold in cultural revitalization efforts. This is now understood to be the rejoining of elements from Indigenous worlds that have been divided up according to disciplines, scientific categories, knowledge systems, and institutional foci. Group discussions enacted through the Recovering Voices methodology of videotaping discussions, as well and the diverse and intergenerational expertise from an Indigenous community, has brought into relief the need to find mechanisms that encourage engagement across cultural, linguistic, and environmental worlds. The breadth of knowledge and language needed to understand the value of, for example, quillwork, as not only an art object, but a cultural practice situated in a specific cosmology and landscape, is an approach that museums will need to further explore as part of revitalization endeavors. While Native American communities *clearly* understand the interconnectedness of all things through their cosmologies and have repeatedly asked for this philosophy to be implemented in museums, the ways in which museums themselves divide up art, science, natural history, and culture has further impeded a holistic understanding of these Indigenous worlds. We also learned, following this visit, that Ted and Alan have been working together to record traditional knowledge in Anishinaabemowin about maple syrup collection alongside the stories that teach knowledge about the animal world. Their approach ties together environmental, behavioral, artistic, social, and spiritual values and philosophies, and these videos are being used as part of the Anishinaabemowin Revival Program.[16]

Environmental change and habitat destruction have also become central features of collaborative projects initiated through Recovering Voices. In 2016 we worked with three individuals, Atapucha, Kuratu, and Tukupe, from the Wauja community of the Upper Xingu area in the northern Mato Grosso region of Brazil. In partnership with the anthropologist Emmeline Ireland, who for the past forty years has been working closely with the Wauja, a project was devised to help the community record important cosmological knowledge for younger generations, as well as to explore how knowledge is embodied in material culture and the natural world. As the Wauja face tremendous challenges in coming to Washington, DC—such as obtaining passports and making an arduous journey from a remote region of Brazil with few roads and no public transport—their project spanned a longer period of two months at the NMNH. Ireland's collection of important Wauja material culture from the community in the 1980s became the foci of the project, with objects becoming mnemonics for stories and rituals they felt were at risk of being lost. These objects have also now been donated to the NMNH collection following the Wauja visit and recording of stories related to them.

During their visit the Wauja asked to view collections of birds, insects, and mammals from the Upper Xingu region. Ireland and the Recovering Voices team recorded these visits on video. Discussions around the animals were twofold: first the Wauja recorded their concerns about how these beings were now either gone or had migrated due to deforestation and habitat destruction, and, second, how the animals were not just representative of an ecosystem, but the teachers of morals and behavior for the Wauja. The pitfalls of jealousy, greed, and aggression, as well as the rewards of generosity, loyalty, and unity, are the lessons learned from these animals. This visit alerted the Recovering Voices research team to the endangerment issues beyond language loss that many Indigenous communities are facing. Ireland summarizes this value of belonging for the Wauja: "The Wauja's land provides far more than food, tools, and shelter. It is the dwelling place of the spirits who guide them, the birthplace of their children, and the resting place of their ancestors. It is the sacred landscape of all their poetry, stories, songs, and prayers; it is their one place upon the earth. Everything needed for human life, everything sacred and precious, flows from that land."[17]

During their visit the Wauja also made a plea to the Department of Anthropology to help them in their efforts to survive the current violent degradation of their world by deforestation and the encroachment of ranchers. This engaged and vested the NMNH in conversations beyond preservation of objects and language, and into the realm of survival. The Wauja also requested to meet with the delegation from the Pueblo of Zuni that was at NMNH at the same time as part of a Recovering Voices project. As the Zuni had experienced colonization under both the Spanish and the U.S. government, during this meeting the Wauja asked for help in setting up a community museum for their youth and for advice on how to deal with missionaries. Interestingly, this became a practical session between Indigenous communities about surviving colonization, a feat that the Wauja deemed the Zunis successful.

Fig. 22. Wauja visit, 2016. *Left to right*: Phil Tajitsu Nash, Emi Ireland, Atapucha (*holding bird*), Kuratu, and Tukupe. Photo by Judith Andrews, Recovering Voices, NMNH.

Another project that offers insight into a community's resilience to the challenges presented by environmental and cultural change comes from the Wanapum Tribe of Priest Rapids in Washington State. The Wanapum originally inhabited the Hanford region of the Columbia River, but were relocated in the 1940s when this area was allocated to the U.S. government to build a nuclear production complex for the Manhattan Project. Parts of this area are now opening up, and, in order to access this area and the river, the Wanapum have initiated a project to bring back the traditional fishing technology of this region. While Elders remember some of the fishing techniques, their specific technology had not been used for sixty years and required research and a system for transmitting it to younger generations.

Wanapum fishing technology includes ring net fish weights, of which only four are known to exist—all of them housed in museums—and two of which are at the Smithsonian. Recovering Voices worked with community experts to dissect and replicate these objects. This included figuring out the materials used, their preparation, and the knots used to fasten the various parts of the stone weight. The Wanapum are now in the process of making replicas based on this research that will enable them to fish in this region again using their traditional methods.

From this partnership Recovering Voices staff learned about the sophistication of the technology needed to fish in this particular area of the Columbia River. These ring weights are designed to bounce along the bottom of the riverbed so the nets do not get caught on the many boulders specific to this portion of the river. The rings are weighted in such a way that they can "swim" and stay parallel to the current, thereby enabling the net to glide slowly down river. They also have a spring mechanism so that they flex and do not break when they hit boulders in the riverbed. There are also distinct sizes of rings and weights used in different seasons, as the river varies according to snowmelt and rainfall. This project facilitated the sharing of multiple layers of knowledge and language to younger generations of Wanapum regarding their fishing technology, as well as asserting ideas of sovereignty that affirmed their intimate relationship to this particular section of the river and their understanding of its specific personality.

One of the longest-running interdisciplinary projects of Recovering Voices has been the Diidxaza dictionary that is being compiled by Gabriela Perez Baez. In 2013 Baez, the then-curator of linguistics for the Department of Anthropology, developed a project in collaboration with the La Ventosa Diidxaza community and the botany department of the NMNH to record traditional knowledge and terminology about the flora of the region. Diidxaza is the Zapotec language spoken in the Isthums of Tehuantepec region of the southern state of Oaxaca in Mexico. Documentation of the flora, the lexicon, and associated knowledge required an interdisciplinary team that included community knowledge bearers, linguists, botanists, and a photographer. Botanical documentation included the collection of fertile plant samples (with flower and fruit) to record the referents of the Diidxazá plant names. From 2013 to 2014 the team documented 284 plant names, 1,361 herbarium samples, and more than 5,000 high-resolution photographs and 200 audio files, with Diidxazá descriptions and their cultural relevance.[18] The botanical samples were then deposited in both U.S. and Mexican herbaria.[19]

Fig. 23. Wanapum visit, 2015. Patrick Wyena (*with magnifying glass*) and Clayton Buck. Photo by Gwyneira Isaac, Recovering Voices, NMNH.

A critical outcome of the project was a database that organized data in such a way as to satisfy the rigors of linguistic, botanical and cultural documentation, without obscuring the local taxonomic principles. The linguistic, audio, and photographic data were accessioned into NMNH's collection system (EMu), which required the bridging of distinct ontological systems and their management by experts, who at the start of the project were largely conversant in only one system. Lexical, phonological, and grammatical information for each Diidxazá plant name was systematically coded alongside the Linnean taxonomic categories of family, genus, and species, in addition to standard botanical descriptors.[20] The organization of any data output can now be produced from any one of these ontological schemas, while relating each of these different ontological units to the others. Using this data management tool, the team could consider different types of analytical outputs. For example, trees were given different uses in the system, including medicinal and practical. With the opportunity to view a wide a range of these, the team discovered a previously undocumented Diidxazá category, *yaga la guitu*, which is based on the *architecture* of the tree—that is, the thickness of the branches, the curved upward direction of the branches, and the average number of primary branches. This elucidated the importance of geometry as a classificatory principle for speakers of Diidxazá.

Following the documentation portion of this project, community collaborators explained that they wanted to prevent the loss of botanical knowledge and the silencing of the Diidxazá language. This led to the formulation of workshops for children to access linguistic and botanical knowledge from the project. These were so well attended they became a research priority, and subsequently two of the linguists with training in educational linguistics developed curricula for twelve monthly workshops that are currently going into their third year of operation. This is also combined with efforts to expand dedicated literacy classes in Diidxazá, language classes for adults, and the development of a Diidxazá library, as well as teaching and administrative positions. A set of fact cards were produced that focus attention on the local botanical classification system, but do not exclude the Linnean taxonomy. Consequently, these are suitable for use in science courses within the community and allow for the introduction of the local botanical knowledge and language into the classroom.[21] Throughout this project the interdisciplinarity and diversity of ontologies generated insights into human-environment interactions, which in turn were critical for the understanding of categorization principles.

Another long-term project that originated out of the CRP and is centered on outreach and mobilizing collections beyond the museum and within communities is the Hopi Pottery Oral History Project (HPOHP). The HPOHP was developed to address concerns within the Hopi community about access to heritage pottery collections and is led by Karen Charley and Valerie Kahe (Hopi potters from the First Mesa community of northeastern Arizona), Lea McChesney (curator of ethnology from the Maxwell Museum of Anthropology, University of New Mexico), Leigh Kuwanwisiwma (former director of the Hopi Cultural Preservation Office, HCPO), Stewart Koyiyumtewa (current director of the HCPO), and Gwyneira Isaac (this author, and curator of North American ethnology from the Smithsonian's NMNH). It has its origins in a Recovering Voices grant that allowed Charley, Kahe, and McChesney to visit the Smithsonian, after which Charely and Kahe articulated to the HCPO the necessity of hands-on community access to historic collections. The priorities then became the dissemination of traditional knowledge of pottery to younger generations of Hopis, with Charley and Kahe suggesting they could conduct interviews, each focusing on their respective peer groups—a research phase that is currently ongoing.

The principles underlying the HPOHP also grew out of Hopi cultural protocol emphasizing "paying back"—in other words, the giving-back process essential to relationships of reciprocity. Hopi ideals about exchange and reciprocity incorporate everyone with whom Hopi interact, including Hopis and non-Hopis. Paying back is viewed as a practice that establishes basic principles for the generation and regeneration of Hopi society.[22] Reciprocal obligations from gift exchanges can extend over generations, so that they develop enduring interactions between families and clan members. The HPOHP explores in particular how Hopi pottery plays a critical role in maintaining matrilineal relationships, as well as the idea of nurturing people and friendships. As Charley and McChesney explain, the "blush" acquired on Hopi pots is a chemical reaction that develops through the potter's relationship with the clay—her skill in shaping and firing the pot—and is likened by Hopi potters to the warmth felt during an emotionally meaningful interaction between people.[23] As such the pots "materialize and make accessible and durable an otherwise fleeting, highly valued human experience: the warm sensation of happiness in mutually satisfying intimate social relations."[24]

In reflecting on its partnership with the NMNH, the HPOHP reconsidered the nature of fieldwork practices that deposit research within the museum and therefore follow the salvage-ethnology paradigm. The group explored ways of addressing this and, consequently, focused attention on dynamics that enabled transmission between community members and between generations and according to Hopi values. With the salvage paradigm premised on "loss," the team chose to prioritize Hopi views on the cyclical nature of life, emphasizing the recirculation and mobility of the pottery and the regeneration of knowledge between generations.

To meet this goal in 2017 the HPOHP, the HCPO, Mesa Media (a not-for-profit Hopi organization providing Hopi language programming), and Recovering Voices organized the First Annual Intergenerational Hopi Pottery Festival at the Veteran's Wellness Center in Hopi. Preparation included the production and distribution of a Hopi Pottery workbook with a selection of the NMNH pottery collections. Two panels of experts gave presentations, with the first, "Tracing Hopi History Through Pottery," being led by the director of HCPO, Leigh Kuwinwiwsma, and the archaeologist Kelley Hays-Gilpin. The second panel, "The Social Value of Hopi Pottery," included twelve potters from First Mesa.[25] Each potter shared thoughts on their mentors and factors enabling them to learn how to make traditional Hopi pottery. For Hopis learning to make pottery is akin to shaping a Hopi citizen who can engage with and nurture others; each finished pot becomes a gift representing the warmth created through close relationships and exchange.[26] The need for intergenerational mentoring was discussed, with Darlene James pointing out, "I am a fifth-generation potter. I learned from my grandmother after school. She was my babysitter and she taught us.... When I was eleven, we had to go get clay and I was shocked that we were going to go collect it out on the mesa. I thought you just went to the store and bought it. We hiked out and my grandmother told us to remember our surroundings. She said: 'Just look at the landscape—everything you need for the pottery is out here.' She was very humble with us. Every summer I would go to her to learn to make pottery."[27] The festival was held again in 2018 and included discussions about apprenticeships that could create personalized and effective mentoring environments for elder potters and Hopi youth. As Hopi potter Larson Goldtooth pointed out, "We are warmed by the pottery and we want to sustain that gift and we want a younger generation to have this."[28] Although the HPOHP and its partnership with Recovering Voices is in its infancy, project leaders in Hopi have allied it to the development of a cultural center in Hopi and the chance to bring the pottery from the NMNH to the community for long-term programming and care according to Hopi protocol and values in order to teach younger generations about their heritage.

Mapping Museums within Revitalization Movements

The idea of using museums as part of cultural revitalization efforts is not a new one. Archaeological repositories established by Native American communities have acted as catalysts for the building of cultural centers, such as the Makah Cultural and Research Center in Neah Bay in Washington State, and the AkChin HimDak Ecomuseum in Maricopa in Arizona. In Canada the repatriation of potlatch items led to the foundation of the U'mista Cultural Center in Alert Bay in British Columbia, where the term *U'mista* aptly means "the return of something important." In terms of projects done in collaboration with national museums, in the 1980s a program was developed in the Pueblo of Zuni, through which Margaret Hardin and Zuni high school students worked with museum collections to revitalize Zuni pottery practices. Similarly, JoAllyn Archambault (NMNH) worked in the latter part of the 1980s and the early 1990s with Rose Wyaco, Joseph Dishta, and Otto Lucio, also from Zuni, to duplicate photographs from the NAA and send these to Zuni. This collection became the foundation of the A:shiwi A:wan Museum and Heritage Center.[29]

Cultural revitalization programs can be seen as the products of a long history of Native American self-determination movements in the United States. Seen through this lens, they should also be understood as emerging from the communities themselves, and not out of the disciplines of anthropology or museology, although there is overlap. As a result revitalization programming is changing these disciplines in terms of the kinds of collaborative work that is being done and the priorities of research.[30] Hence, changes to the museum concept are largely due to pressure from Native American communities to acknowledge their value systems, a process that has been facilitated from within by museum staff and researchers, although there are still areas of resistance. It is also worth noting that cultural revitalization movements have been viewed as an Indigenous critique of the past practices of anthropology and colonialism.[31] Similarly, cultural revitalization values are seen by anthropologists to "mesh well with anthropological ones," as "cultural revitalization is stimulated by cross-cultural exchange."[32] Consequently, there has been an increase in museums and Indigenous communities collaborating around revitalization efforts.

Over the past two decades, the ways in which historic collections are being used within museums has shifted toward an increased recognition and acknowledgment of Indigenous value systems.[33] Moira Simpson argues that "contemporary museology has undergone a significant shift, from practices and purposes based on ideas of heritage as evidence of the past—valued for its historical research potential and as the basis for a thriving heritage industry—to recognition of the contemporary value of heritage for living cultures."[34] Accordingly, repatriation is understood as a form of cultural renewal, such that objects once returned "assist indigenous peoples in continuing... practices essential to their cultural and ceremonial life and can contribute to community healing as part of contemporary life," and, as a result, repatriation becomes "the ultimate form of cultural preservation."[35]

The emergence of this kind of collaborative anthropology has been accompanied by debates about the extent to which this approach can in fact democratize anthropology, museums, and research more broadly, as well as improve relationships between communities and museums.[36] Accordingly, problems arise in collaborative projects due to the unequal management and distribution of funds,[37] differing concepts of reciprocity,[38] issues around sustainability and the maintaining of social capital, and, last but not least, contrasting agendas within anthropology and museums themselves.[39] Similar debates are also ongoing in linguistics,[40] with continued efforts to arrive at a standard of best practices that direct and accommodate a diversity of cultural ontologies and expectations.[41]

Comparable discussions have also shaped the discipline of linguistics, especially around the role and purpose of collecting linguistic knowledge from Indigenous communities. To address past inequities, contemporary ethics in linguistics' field research advocate against "extractive linguistics" that only benefit the researcher.[42] In response an ample and growing body of literature proposes models of research aimed at ensuring benefits to the language community.[43] Among practitioners in this field, there is increasing agreement that the interests of both language community members and community-external researchers can be satisfied through culturally appropriate, mutually agreed upon collaborative approaches.[44]

In making sense of the politics of revitalization programs within the museum context, insight comes from looking at parallel issues relating to language revitalization writ large. For instance, debates have fulminated over the extent to which language is correlated with culture,[45] or is a factor in authenticating indigeneity,[46] or part of proving rights to land,[47] or the extent to which research on language is affected by salvage and urgency metaphors.[48] Combine this volatile context of language politics with the equally problematic legacy of museums—institutions often labeled as the "handmaidens of colonialism"—and you encounter a provocative arena in which museum-based revitalization programs operate.

Yet the value of the reintegration of once-separated knowledge components into Indigenous worlds and cosmologies becomes apparent from these community research projects at NMNH. The Recovering Voices projects with communities through the CRP highlight the value of Indigenous people reclaiming their knowledge through the use of museum collections—a process that is understood to also be about affirming and asserting their identity and culture within a national museum space. While many of the tasks of revitalization have not yet been fully realized in terms of restructuring the museum to meet these new needs, projects like the Diidxazá ethnobotanical database also reveal the potential for reorganizing knowledge according to Indigenous ontologies and correlating or situating it alongside scientific knowledge.

Conclusions

Museums are valued in Anglo-European societies according to their ability to provide a designated space for the long-term retention of objects, manuscripts, and the like. The concept of a repository relies on ideals and practices that privilege the preservation and stability of objects, alongside ongoing maintenance of associated documentation. These ideals are usually achieved by limiting the use and movement of these objects. Revitalization efforts, in contrast, are designed to draw out dormant knowledge from an object or archive and mobilize it, striving to build connections and networks that will keep that knowledge in motion and in use. Revitalization efforts such as Recovering Voices foster a particular type of reintegration and reclaiming of knowledge according to the values of their community of origin. In practice, in the museum, this requires the mobility of knowledge across disciplinary, technological, and institutional boundaries, such as between botany and anthropology, as well as between museums and communities.

Without these revitalization programs, museums will not experience the same level of vitality in their collections and the reconvening of separately categorized collections according to Indigenous ontologies—an endeavor only achieved through partnership with Indigenous communities. Revitalization efforts are also predicated on the idea that the Indigenous ontologies are the primary frameworks for the maintenance of traditional knowledge, language, and well-being, especially if these are to be sustainable, living languages. Consequently, these efforts not only increase mobility of museum collections and related knowledge; they result in the productive cross-pollination of ideas and an awareness of unique knowledge ecosystems that are critical to understanding the distinctive worlds that coexist and that, as a whole, provide insight into our overall humanity and future on this planet *together*.

Language revitalization programs partnering with archives such as BOL have largely focused on historic manuscripts and records, including those needed for the grammatical reconstruction of dormant languages. In some cases these may be the *only* written records, and they can be critical in reconstructing and reclaiming languages: their words, grammars, and orthographies, as well as the specific historical contexts in which they had been documented and the individuals involved. The role archives play in this process is twofold. First, they are accountable to the extent to which records and materials are accessible to Indigenous communities and linguists; this includes the level of operability of online databases and search functions for different users, such as revitalization linguists, tribal linguists, and archivists. Second, their institutional efficacy depends on the level of support they provide for community visits and follow-up, including the digitization and duplication of archival documents for use in communities.

In recent years databases designed specifically for language reconstruction and revitalization based on archival records such as the Miami-Illinois Digital Archive (MIDA) have been developed to address the problems of managing large amounts of archival, digital, and linguistic data. In conjunction with Recovering Voices and with funding from the NEH, the MIDA database has been expanded to become the Indigenous Language Digital Archive (ILDA), making it available to other Indigenous communities working in language revitalization. As a specialized tool for use within the archival context, it helps to fill "the software tool gap between archives, linguists and revitalizationists,"[49] allowing for "the organization, storage and retrieval of digital copies of linguistic archival materials."[50] The partnership between the Miami-Illinois tribal linguists, Recovering Voices, and the NAA helped to realize the potential of archival records within the revitalization process.

The work of Recovering Voices within broadly defined revitalization efforts—language *and* culture, as well as how these are interrelated—inherently spans diverse collections, including film, ethnographic objects, zoological specimens, archives, and botanical specimens. This breadth is a result not only of the program's position within the NMNH, but also Indigenous communities' interests in exploring and communicating cultural and environmental relationships. The role of natural history museums in revitalization efforts potentially includes expanding into diverse types of materials and knowledges, as well as serving as a nexus for convening these according to Indigenous value systems—a process that is critical for Indigenous communities who are reclaiming their culture and language for their own uses. It is important to note that, from the start, Recovering Voices chose to define its parameters as including both language *and* knowledge revitalization, to highlight the importance of linking language with other cultural practices such as farming, art, and music, as well as support groups working in revitalization that was not focused solely on language. As a result this wider purview has revealed the potential of natural history museums in advancing collaborative, multimodal, and interdisciplinary research in revitalization efforts that are being expanded to meet the diverse needs of Indigenous communities.

Through the Recovering Voices program, we have observed the significance of using material culture alongside archives and natural history specimens, and to situate these objects as mnemonics that are critical in the production and reproduction of collective knowledge. The role of objects as mnemonics and catalysts for "collective memory" making has been well documented,[51] alongside the ability of objects to record and recall place names,[52] and their use in remapping and reconnecting memories of communities that have been relocated.[53] The use of objects as part of collaborative museum projects with Native American communities has been recognized as critical in building relationships,[54] and their use in cultural revitalization efforts has also been documented.[55] In a parallel study to the work being done in Recovering Voices, the examination of language revitalization using material culture and the building of "collective networks" has been undertaken in a case study of the Smithsonian Institution's Arctic Studies Center in Alaska.[56] This example highlights the importance of intangible cultural heritage (ICH), maintaining that museums need "to focus on the documentation and preservation of language as intangible cultural heritage (ICH) because of the vital connection between language and culture."[57]

The CRP division in particular builds on this area of research and engagement by fostering age diversity within the visiting community groups, in order to increase the likelihood of the intergenerational transmission of knowledge. Through these collaborative projects and visits, Recovering Voices has documented how engagement with historic objects has not only helped to reawaken dormant knowledge in individuals, whose memories may not have been recalled without access to and handling of these objects; as this knowledge is enacted and shared as a group, this engagement process becomes a crucial step in rebuilding collective memory and knowledge, often using the Indigenous language to describe cultural practices, context, and value systems. This type of knowledge rebuilding and revitalization should awaken museums as well as to their responsibilities in partnering with communities to ensure that these cultural heritage objects are not only accessible, but resocialized, both literally and figuratively, back into the Indigenous communities from which they originated. We also observed that these intergenerational and collective knowledge-building processes fostered respect for the older generations with the younger generations. For the younger generations, their inclusion in these encounters helped to provide them with mentors and ways of envisioning professional career paths in cultural revitalization within their schools, museums, and community-based programming. In honoring this collective knowledge and memory, these revitalization projects based around diverse collections are also about empowerment—defining how this knowledge is used and enacted, for what purposes, and by whom.

In practice, Recovering Voices has become an endeavor in collaborative, interdisciplinary, multimodal revitalization work. The reawakening and sharing of knowledge and narratives around diverse kinds of collections has involved orality, textual documentation, video, and material culture studies, as well as areas introduced through diverse disciplines such as anthropology, linguistics, environmental studies, mineral science, and zoology. This approach has also called upon a wide range of participants to think about how the various elements function together and, therefore, the philosophical links and adhesive that keeps an Indigenous cultural system of knowledge operational and in use. Thus, revitalization work in museums also encourages Indigenous values to be materialized, enacted, realized, and reclaimed. In short, this endeavor is about Indigenous worlds that are spoken into being again to ensure their use by future generations. What is more, these actions are in defiance of dinosaurs.

ACKNOWLEDGMENTS

Although revitalization efforts may be beset with challenges, the people invested in these endeavors continually amaze me with their tireless energy, generosity of mind, and vision for the future. This chapter is built on the insights of many people and represents only a small portion of their expertise, yet it would not have been possible without them. Gabriela Perez Baez, who coauthored the first version of this chapter for the APS panel, shared her in-depth knowledge of language revitalization in Mexico. The NMNH Recovering Voices staff—Judith Andrews, Joshua A. Bell, Laura Sharp, Tim McCoy, Igor Krupnik, and many invaluable staff members at NMNH—all helped to build the problem and keep it running. Contributing collaborative partners include Karen Charley, Valerie Kahe, Lea McChesney, Leigh Kuwanwisiwma, and Stewart Koyiyumtewa, all of whom continue to work with Recovering Voices on the Hopi Oral History Project. Alan Corbiere, Myna and Ted Toulouse, Mary Ann Corbiere, Rand Valentine, Crystal Migwams, Ruth Phillips, Crystal Migwam, Emmeline Ireland, Atapucha, Kuratu, Tukupe, Rex Buck Jr., Patrick Wyena, Clayton Buck—you and many other partners too long to list here have helped bring Recovering Voices to life. Thank you.

NOTES

1. Maffi, *On Biocultural Diversity*.
2. Simons and Lewis, "World's Languages in Crisis."
3. The first iteration of the RV team was led by the curators Ives Goddard, Igor Krupnik, William Merrill, and Joshua Bell (NMNH Anthropology), Tim McCoy (NMNH Mineral Sciences), Larry Dorr (NMNH Botany), Robert Leopold (NAA), Michael Mason (NMNH Exhibits), Doug Herman and Fred Nawooksie (NMAI), and Marjorie Hunt (Folklife). Gabriela Perez Baez (NMNH) and Gwyneira Isaac (NMNH) joined in 2010. Following the endowment of the initiative, Judith Andrews and Laura Sharp joined the team, and following Mason and Leopold's move to Folklife in 2014, they were later joined by the curators Mary Linn and Amalia Cordoba.
4. Simons and Lewis, "World's Languages in Crisis."
5. Hale et al., "Endangered Languages."
6. Whalen et al., "Healing Through Language."
7. Maffi, *On Biocultural Diversity*.
8. Hale et al., "Endangered Languages."
9. Gruber, "Ethnographic Salvage."
10. McChesney and Isaac, "Paying Back."
11. Marcus and Fischer, *Anthropology as Cultural Critique*.
12. Isaac, *Mediating Knowledges*; Lonetree, *Decolonizing Museums*; Silverman, *Museum as Process*.
13. Hinton, "Language Revitalization"; McCarty, *Language Planning and Policy*.
14. Fuller and Fabricius, "Native American Museums and Cultural Centers"; Archambault, "American Indians and American Museums."
15. Bruchac, *Savage Kin*.
16. Toulouse, Corbiere, and Owl, "Gete-Neamaakwaan."
17. Ireland, "Neither Warriors nor Victims."
18. Pérez Báez, "Interdisciplinary Documentation."
19. U.S. National Herbarium at the NMNH and other Mexican herbaria including Mexico's National Herbarium (MEXU), the Jardín Botánico de Oaxaca, and the Sociedad para el Estudio de los Recursos Bióticos de Oaxaca.
20. The plant determination is ongoing at the moment. 60 percent of the collection of collected samples has been identified to species. Current efforts are aimed at reaching 80 percent determination of the collection to species.
21. Two hundred and fifty sets of fact cards were produced in high quality, laminated, full color 8.5" x 14" format. These sets were costly, and, as such, their distribution is reserved primarily for schools and cultural and educational centers. A more affordable version was designed in the form of a bingo-style game, *chalupa*, that is very popular in the region. Five hundred copies of the full-color game set

were produced for more ample distribution to households. The set includes one photograph per plant and all the cultural and taxonomic information as the fact cards. Both sets point the users to a website where the entire set of documented plants can be consulted in Diidxazá in addition to Spanish and English. Included are high-resolution images of the digital surrogates of herbarium samples and the entire collection of photographs as well as audio files in Diidxazá. The site is at www.neho.si.edu (accessed August 21, 2020).

22. Whitely, "Ties That Bind."
23. Charley and McChesney, "Form and Meaning."
24. McChesney and Isaac, "Paying Back."
25. First Mesa potters that contributed to the Social Value of Hopi Pottery session at the festival included Karen Charley, Ramona Ami, Darlene James, Grace Tahbo, Fawn Navase, Emiline Nahe, Adele Lalo, Gloria Mahle, Gwen Stefala, Valerie Kahe, Alice Funk, and Larson Goldtooth.
26. Charley and McChesney, "Form and Meaning."
27. James, "Social Value of Hopi Pottery."
28. Goldtooth, "Social Value of Hopi Pottery."
29. Isaac, *Mediating Knowledges*.
30. In 2016 Isaac surveyed articles published in the journal *Museum Anthropology* from its inception in 1976 to 2016 to understand the evolution of concepts such as "repatriation" and "collaboration." It became clear in the context of this journal, with a few exceptions (Ames 1992), that the majority of museum anthropologists from 1976 to the late 1980s fought the idea of repatriation. Once it had been introduced in the 1990s, however, museum anthropologists began to see and write about the benefits, and how it introduced further collaboration models that helped to revitalize museums.
31. Willow, "Cultivating Common Ground."
32. Willow, "Cultivating Common Ground," 54.
33. Isaac, *Mediating Knowledges*; Lonetree, *Decolonizing Museums*.
34. Simpson, "Museums and Restorative Justice," 122.
35. Simpson, "Museums and Restorative Justice," 128.
36. Moreno-Black and Homchampa, "Collaboration, Cooperation, and Working Together"; Colwell-Chanthphonh, "Problems of Collaboration?"; Campbell and Lassiter, "From Collaborative Ethnography."
37. McMullen, "Currency of Consultation and Collaboration."
38. McChesney and Isaac, "Paying Back."
39. Contreras and Griffith, "Action-Research Collaborative"; Swan and Jordan, "Contingent Collaborations."
40. Benedicto and McLean, "Fieldwork"; Benedicto et al., "Model of Participatory Action Research."

41. Pérez Báez, "Addressing the Gap"; Bischoff and Jany, *Insights from Practices*.
42. Dwyer, "Ethics and Practicalities."
43. Cameron et al., *Researching Language*; Benedicto, Dolores, and McLean, "Fieldwork as a Participatory Research Activity"; Benedicto et al., "Model of Participatory Action Research"; Crippen and Robinson, "In Defense of the Lone Wolf"; Czaykowska-Higgins, "Research Models, Community Engagement"; Dobrin, "From Linguistic Elicitation"; Dwyer, "Ethics and Practicalities"; England, "Mayan Language Revival"; Gerdts, "Beyond Expertise"; Grenoble and Furbee, *Language Documentation*; Grinevald, "Language Endangerment in South America"; Hale, "Ulwa (Southern Sumu)"; Rice, "Ethical Issues in Linguistic Fieldwork"; Rice, "Documentary Linguistics and Community Relations"; Yamada, "Collaborative Linguistic Fieldwork."
44. Bischoff and Jany, *Insights from Practices*.
45. Muehlman, "Spread Your Ass Cheeks"; Perley, "Defying Maliseet Language Death."
46. Rogers, "Indigenous Authenticity."
47. Field, *Abalone Tales*.
48. Perley, "Zombie Linguistics"; Crippen and Robinson, "In Defense of the Lone Wolf"; Bowern and Warner, "'Lone Wolves' and Collaboration"; Robinson and Crippen, "Collaboration"; Newman, "Law of Unintended Consequences."
49. Baldwin, "Myaamiaataweenki eekincikoonihkiinki eeyoonki aapisaataweenki," 394.
50. See website for the National Breath of Life Archival Institute for Indigenous Languages, http://miamioh.edu/myaamia-center/breath-of-life/index.html. (accessed May 11, 2019).
51. Connerton, *How Societies Remember*; Hoskins, *Biographical Objects*.
52. Kerlogue, "Memory and the Material Culture."
53. Cassidy, "Recalling Community."
54. Brown, "Co-Authoring Relationships."
55. Brown and Peers, *Pictures Bring Us Messages*; Krmpotich and Peers, *This Is Our Life*.
56. McClain, "Language and Museums."
57. McClain, "Language and Museums," ii.

BIBLIOGRAPHY

Archambault, JoAllyn. "American Indians and American Museums." *Zeitschrift fur Ethnologie*, 118 (1994): 7–22.
Baldwin, Daryl, David J. Costa, and Douglas Troy. "Myaamiaataweenki eekincikoonihkiinki eeyoonki aapisaataweenki: A Miami Language Digital Tool for Language Reclamation." *Language Documentation & Conservation* 10 (2016): 394–410.

Benedicto, Elena, Demetrio Antolín, Modesta Dolores, M. Cristina Feliciano, Gloria Fendly, Tomasa Gómez, Baudillo Miguel, and Elizabeth Salomón. "A Model of Participatory Action Research: The Mayangna Linguists' Team of Nicaragua." In *Proceedings of the XI FEL Conference on "Working Together for Endangered Languages—Research Challenges and Social Impacts,"* edited by Maya Khemlani David, Nicholas Ostler, and Caesar Dealwis, 29–35. Kuala Lumpur: SKET, University of Malaya and Foundation for Endangered Languages, 2007.

Benedicto, Elena, Modesta Dolores, and Melba McLean. "Fieldwork as a Participatory Research Activity: The Mayangna Linguistic Teams." In *Proceedings of the Twenty-Eighth Annual Meeting of the Berkeley Linguistics Society: General Session and Parasession on Field Linguistics (2002),* edited by Julie Larson and Mary Paster, 375–86. Berkeley: University of California at Berkeley, 2002.

Bischoff, Shannon, and Carmen Jany, eds. *Insights from Practices in Community-Based Research: From Theory to Practice Around the Globe.* Boston: de Gruyter Mouton, 2018.

Bowern, Claire, and Natasha Warner. "'Lone Wolves' and Collaboration: A Reply to Crippen & Robinson (2013)." *Language Documentation & Conservation* 9 (2015): 59–85.

Brown, Alison K. "Co-Authoring Relationships: Blackfoot Collections, UK Museums, and Collaborative Practice." *Collaborative Anthropologies* 9, nos. 1–2 (2016): 117–47.

Brown, Alison K., and Laura Peers, with Members of the Kainai Nation. *Pictures Bring Us Messages: Photographs and Histories from the Kainai Nation.* Toronto: University of Toronto Press, 2006.

Bruchac, Margaret M. *Savage Kin: Indigenous Informants and American Anthropologists.* Tucson: University of Arizona Press, 2018.

Cameron, Deborah, Elizabeth Frazer, Penelope Harvey, M. B. H. Rampton, and Kay Richardson. *Researching Language: Issues of Power and Method.* London: Routledge, 1992.

Campbell, Elizabeth, and Luke Eric Lassiter. "From Collaborative Ethnography to Collaborative Pedagogy: Reflections on the Other Side of the Middletown Project and Community-University Research." *Anthropology and Education Quarterly* 41, no. 4 (2010): 370–85.

Cassidy, Lawrence. "Recalling Community: Using Material Culture and Digital Archives in Salford." *Gateways: International Journal of Community Research and Engagement* 5 (2012): 166–82.

Charley, Karen K., and Lea S. McChesney. "Form and Meaning Is Indigenous Aesthetics: A Hopi Perspective." *American Indian Art Magazine* 32, no. 4 (2007): 84–91.

Colwell-Chanthphonh, Chip. "The Problems of Collaboration? Reflections in Engagements of Inclusivity, Reciprocity, and Democracy in Museum Anthropology." *Western Humanities Review* 64, no. 3 (2010): 49–63.

Connerton, Paul. *How Societies Remember.* Cambridge: Cambridge University Press, 1989.

Contreras, Ricardo, and David Griffith. "Building a Latino-Engaged Action-Research Collaborative: A Challenging University-Community Encounter." *Annals of Anthropological Practice* 35, no. 2 (2011): 96-111.

Crippen, James A., and Laura C. Robinson. "In Defense of the Lone Wolf: Collaboration in Language Documentation." *Language Documentation & Conservation* 7 (2013): 123-35.

Czaykowska-Higgins, E. "Research Models, Community Engagement, and Linguistic Fieldwork: Reflections on Working within Canadian Indigenous Communities." *Language Documentation & Conservation* 3, no. 1 (2009): 15-50.

Dobrin, Lise. "From Linguistic Elicitation to Eliciting the Linguist: Lessons in Community Empowerment from Melanesia." *Language* 84, no. 2 (2008): 300-324.

Dwyer, Arienne M. "Ethics and Practicalities of Cooperative Fieldwork and Analysis." In *Essentials of Language Documentation*, edited by Jost Gippert, Nikolaus P. Himmelmann, and Ulrike Mosel, 31-66. New York: de Gruyter Mouton, 2006.

England, Nora C. "Mayan Language Revival and Revitalization Politics: Linguists and Linguistic Ideologies." *American Anthropologist* 105, no. 4 (2003): 733-43.

Field, Les. *Abalone Tales: Collaborative Explorations of Sovereignty and Identity in Native California*. Durham NC: Duke University Press, 2008.

Fuller, Nancy, and Susanne Fabricius. "Native American Museums and Cultural Centers: Historical Overview and Current Issues." *Zeitschrift fur Ethnologie* 117 (1992): 223-37.

Gerdts, Donna. "Beyond Expertise: The Role of the Linguist in Language Revitalization Programs." In *Endangered Languages: What Role for the Specialist? Proceedings of Second Foundation for Endangered Languages Conference*, edited by Nicholas Ostler, 13-22. Bath: Foundation for Endangered Languages, 1998.

Goldtooth, Larson. "The Social Value of Hopi Pottery." Panel discussion, First Annual Hopi Pottery Festival, Hopi Wellness Center, Third Mesa AZ, April 2017.

Grenoble, Leonore A., and N. Louanna Furbee, eds. *Language Documentation: Practice and Values*. Philadelphia: John Benjamins, 2010.

Grinevald, Colette. "Language Endangerment in South America: A Programmatic Approach." In *Endangered Languages: Current Issues and Future Prospects*, edited by Lenore A. Grenoble and Lindsay J. Whaley, 124-59. Cambridge: Cambridge University Press, 1998.

Gruber, Jacob W. "Ethnographic Salvage and the Shaping of American Anthropology." *American Anthropologist* 72, no. 6 (1970): 1289-99.

Hale, Ken. "Ulwa (Southern Sumu): The Beginnings of a Language Research Project." In *Linguistic Fieldwork*, edited by Paul Newman and Martha Ratliff, 71-101. Cambridge: Cambridge University Press, 2001.

Hale, Ken, Michael Krauss, Lucille J. Watahomigie, Akira Y. Yamamoto, Colette Craig, LaVerne Masayesva Jeanne, and Nora C. England. "Endangered Languages." *Language* 68, no.1 (1992): 1-42.

Hinton, Leanne. "Commentary: Internal and External Advocacy." *Journal of Linguistic Anthropology* 12, no. 2 (2002): 150–56.

———. "Language Revitalization: An Overview." In *The Green Book of Language Revitalization in Practice*, edited by L. Hinton and K. Hale, 3–18. San Diego: Academic Press, 2001.

Hoskins, Janet. *Biographical Objects: How Things Tell the Stories of People's Lives*. London: Routledge, 1998.

Instituto Nacional de Lenguas Indígenas (INALI). *Catálogo de las lenguas indígenas nacionales: variantes lingüísticas de México con sus autodenominaciones y referencias geoestadísticas*. Diario Oficial de la Federación, 14 de marzo de 2008 (Sección 1: 31–78, Sección 2: 1–96, Sección 3: 1–112), 2008. http://www.inali.gob.mx/pdf/clincompleto.pdf (accessed August 19, 2016).

———. Población de 5 años y más hablante de alguna lengua indígena por variante lingü.stica según bilingüismo lengua indígena-español. http://site.inali.gob.mx/pdf/estadistica/variante/variante_c3_monolinguismo.pdf (accessed August 19, 2016).

Isaac, Gwyneira. *Mediating Knowledges: Origins of A Zuni Tribal Museum*. Tucson: University of Arizona Press, 2007.

Ireland, E. "Neither Warriors nor Victims, the Wauja Peacefully Organize to Defend Their Land." *Cultural Survival Quarterly* 15, no. 1 (1991): https://www.culturalsurvival.org/publications/cultural-survival-quarterly/neither-warriors-nor-victims-wauja-peacefully-organize (accessed August 21, 2020).

James, Darlene. "The Social Value of Hopi Pottery." Panel discussion, First Annual Hopi Pottery Festival, Hopi Wellness Center, Third Mesa AZ, April 2017.

Kerlogue, Fiona. "Memory and the Material Culture." *Indonesia and the Malay World* 39, no. 113 (2011): 89–101.

Krmpotich, Cara, and Laura Peers. *This Is Our Life: Haida Material Heritage and Changing Museum Practice*. Vancouver: University of British Columbia Press, 2014.

Lonetree, Amy. *Decolonizing Museums: Representing Native America in National and Tribal Museums*. Chapel Hill: University of North Carolina Press, 2012.

Maffi, Luisa, ed. *On Biocultural Diversity: Linking Language, Knowledge, and the Environment*. Washington DC: Smithsonian Institution, 2001.

Marcus, George E., and Michael M. J. Fischer. *Anthropology as Cultural Critique: An Experimental Moment in the Human Sciences*. Chicago: University of Chicago Press, 1999.

McClain, Heather. "Language and Museums: Supporting Alaska Native Languages through Collaborative Networking." MA thesis, University of Denver, 2014.

McCarty, Teresa L. *Language Planning and Policy in Native America: History, Theory, Praxis*. Buffalo NY: Multilingual Matters, 2013.

McChesney, Lea, and Gwyneira Isaac. "'Paying Back': The Hopi Pottery Oral History Project." In *Giving Back: Research and Reciprocity in Indigenous Contexts*, edited by Doug Herman, 55–85. Corvallis: Oregon State University Press, 2019.

McMullen, Ann. "The Currency of Consultation and Collaboration." *Museum Anthropology Review* 2, no. 2 (2008): 54–87.

Moreno-Black, Geraldine, and Pissamai Homchampa. "Collaboration, Cooperation, and Working Together: Anthropologists Creating a Space for Research and Academic Partnerships." NAPA *Bulletin* 29, no. 1 (2008): 87–98.

Muehlman, Shaylih. "'Spread Your Ass Cheeks': And Other Things that Should Not Be Said in Indigenous Languages." *American Ethnologist* 35, no. 1 (2008): 34–48.

Newman, Paul. "The Law of Unintended Consequences: How the Endangered Languages Movement Undermines Field Linguistics as a Scientific Enterprise." Presentation at the Hans Rausing Endangered Languages Program, October 15, 2013. https://www.youtube.com/watch?v=xzieO8ozQok.

Pérez Báez, Gabriela. "Addressing the Gap between Community Beliefs and Priorities and Researchers' Language Maintenance Interests." In *Language Documentation and Revitalization in Latin American Contexts*, edited by Gabriela Pérez Báez, Chris Rogers, and Jorge Emilio Rosés Labrada, 165–94. Boston: de Gruyter Mouton, 2016a.

———. "The Interdisciplinary Documentation of the Flora of La Ventosa and Associated Lexicon and Knowledge: A Pilot for the National Ethnobotanical Herbarium Online." *Taxon* 65, no. 2 (May, 3 2016b): 425–26.

Perley, Bernard C. *Defying Maliseet Language Death: Emergent Vitalities of Language, Culture and Identity in Eastern Canada*. Lincoln: University of Nebraska Press, 2011.

———. "Zombie Linguistics: Experts, Endangered Languages, and the Curse of Undead Voices." *Anthropological Forum* 22, no. 2 (2012): 133–49.

Pretty, Jules, Bill Adams, Fikret Berkes, Simone Ferreira de Athayde, Nigel Dudley, Eugene Hunn, Luisa Maffi, Kay Milton, David Rapport, Paul Robbins, Eleanor Sterling, Sue Stolton, Anna Tsing, Erin Vintinner, and Sarah Pilgrim. "The Intersections of Biological Diversity and Cultural Diversity: Towards Integration." *Conservation and Society* 7, no. 2 (2009): 100–112.

Rice, Keren. "Documentary Linguistics and Community Relations." *Language Documentation & Conservation* 5 (2011): 187–207.

———. "Ethical Issues in Linguistic Fieldwork: An Overview." *Journal of Academic Ethics* 4, nos. 1–4 (2006): 123–55.

Robinson, Laura, and James Crippen. "Collaboration: A Reply to Bowern & Warner's Reply." *Language Documentation & Conservation* 9 (2015): 86–88.

Rogers, Chris. "Indigenous Authenticity as a Goal of Language Documentation and Revitalization: Addressing the Motivations in the Xinkan Community." In *Language Documentation and Revitalization in Latin American Contexts*, edited by Gabriela Pérez Báez, Chris Rogers, and Jorge Emilio Rosés Labrada, 247–72. Boston: de Gruyter Mouton, 2016.

Silverman, Raymond, ed. *Museum as Process: Translating Local and Global Knowledges*. London: Routledge, 2015.

Simons, Gary F., and M. Paul Lewis. "The World's Languages in Crisis: A 20-Year Update." In *Responses to Language Endangerment. In Honor of Mickey Noonan*, edited by Elena Mihas, Bernard Perley, Gabriel Rei-Doval, and Kathleen Wheatley, 3–19. Amsterdam: John Benjamins, 2013.

Simpson, Moira. "Museums and Restorative Justice: Heritage, Repatriation and Cultural Education." *Museum International* 61, nos. 1–2 (2009): 121–29.

Swan, Daniel, and Michael Paul Jordan. "Contingent Collaborations: Pattern of Reciprocity in Museum-Community Partnerships." *Journal of Folklore Research* 52, no. 1 (2015): 39–82.

Toulouse, Theodore, Alan Ojiig Corbiere, and Albert Owl. "Gete-Neamaakwaan: Traditional Spile." Anishinaabemowin Revival Program, July 25, 2019. https://www.mchigeeng.ca/negamakwaan.html.

Whalen, D. H., Margaret Moss, and Daryl Baldwin. "Healing through Language: Positive Physical Health Effects of Indigenous Language Use." *F1000Research* 5 (2016): 852.

Whiteley, Peter. "Ties That Bind: Hopi Gift Culture and Its First Encounter with the United States." *Natural History*, November 2004, 26–31.

Willow, Anna J. "Cultivating Common Ground: Cultural Revitalization in Anishinaabe and Anthropological Discourse." *American Indian Quarterly* 34, no. 1 (2010): 33–60.

Yamada, Racquel-Maria. "Collaborative Linguistic Fieldwork: Practical Application of the Empowerment Model." *Language Documentation and Conservation* 1 no. 2 (2007): 257–82.

CHAPTER 14

Shriniinlii ('Fix It')

The Grease Mechanics of Translating Gwich'in

Craig Mishler and Kenneth Frank

For the past seven years, we have been collaborating on a Gwich'in language documentation project funded by the National Science Foundation. The Gwich'in homeland stretches across a vast territory covering part of eastern Alaska, the northern Yukon, and the Northwest Territories. It is a severely endangered northern Dene language with fewer than four hundred fluent speakers, the youngest of whom are now in their mid-thirties.

Our project is called Linguistic Anthropology: Gwich'in Caribou Anatomy and Cultural Ecology (NFS Award No. ARC-1162600). In the course of our fieldwork, we made numerous audio and video field recordings of twelve Alaskan and Yukon Elders, living in four villages, on their knowledge of caribou. Vadzaih or caribou are a keystone species, ensuring human survival in the subarctic for millennia, so our goals in this project are to document Gwich'in traditional knowledge of these intelligent animals in the Gwich'in language for the benefit of Gwich'in speakers; help revitalize Gwich'in language and culture; and, finally, make that knowledge more accessible to the wider world of English-language speakers.

Over the millennia these Gwich'in have developed a detailed knowledge of caribou—not only sundry names and uses for caribou body parts, but a series of traditional stories, songs, tools, games, toys, family names, beliefs, and ceremonies associated with them. While moose and Dall sheep are also important large game animals, and some Gwich'in communities lie outside of the Porcupine caribou herd migration area, it is caribou that have gradually come to symbolize the Gwich'in way of life.

Our recordings have helped us produce a wide variety of mediated performance texts on hunting, butchering, and transporting and storing meat, as well as cooking and eating it. We have also managed to elicit a number of traditional Gwich'in folktales about caribou. With the assistance of two younger scholars on our team, Crystal Frank and Allan Hayton, who transcribed the recordings, we have invested hundreds of hours translating and editing transcripts online in real time to produce a corpus of bilingual texts in Gwich'in and English.

The theme of the American Philosophical Society conference Translating Across Time and Space describes exactly what we do: we upload our documents to Google Drive and translate them while talking on Skype. As the senior author, I (Craig Mishler) reside in Anchorage, Alaska, or Las Cruces, New Mexico, while Kenneth resides in Fairbanks or Arctic Village. Kenneth is an Elder and a fluent speaker of Gwich'in, while I am a longtime friend of the Gwich'in and a student of their language.

In an earlier paper we defined the larger methodological process of recording, transcribing, translating, and editing that we developed for our collaborative research on the web.[1] This entire process was illustrated with a step-by-step flow chart. The present chapter, by contrast, is reflexively focused on the detailed hands-on way we get from Gwich'in to English in a slow, mutually satisfying way, consciously teaching one another. A flow chart is relatively useless here, because we resort to a wide variety of techniques for representing Gwich'in thoughts in English, and any one or several of the techniques may be invoked in the moment. Improvisation and paradigmatic thinking govern.

Following Dell Hymes's way of measuring and recasting oral narratives as verbal art, we begin decoding Gwich'in texts with Kenneth's fairly literal interlinear translations, and then we transform these sentences into formal ethnopoetic lines based on grammatical clauses, punctuating as needed.[2] In essence we see the translator's work as similar to that of the poet—playing with words and rearranging them. Next and most important, as word mechanics we negotiate syntactic and lexical choices: What will work best here? Our online Google Drive manuscripts are interlinear, but for final presentation and publication we download and separate the two languages, numbering the lines so that the finished texts are parallel and evenly matched on facing pages.

We believe that in order for Gwich'in to maintain its aesthetic integrity, independence, and flow, it needs to stand by itself and be seamlessly connected to itself as a uniform code, so that readers are not constantly distracted and forced to switch back and forth between languages. This is a practice we began back in the 1990s with the book *Neerihiinjìk: We Traveled from Place to Place: The Gwich'in Stories of Johnny and Sarah Frank*.[3] Interlinear translations distract from this kind of flow, although they are still a popular format with some well-recognized scholars.[4]

In this chapter we focus on our efforts to translate several problematic passages: places where we got stuck, rather than where we translated cleanly and smoothly. There is actually very little to say about the great majority of lines, which unravel rather seamlessly; in them Gwich'in and English seem fairly congruent, and cross-culturally transparent. To entextualize the oral, many times all we have to do is generate a literal translation from the Gwich'in transcript and transpose a couple of words or a phrase, tinkering with a synonym or two, making sure the wrench is snug and tight before letting go.

But, by drawing on detailed examples from eight problematic passages—passages where we were at least temporarily stumped—we are able to discuss our praxis for collaborating. Our full box of tools ranges from proofreading, relistening, searching bilingual dictionaries and other publications, inverting syntaxes, locating idioms, and finding synonyms to consulting with additional Gwich'in and English speakers, surfing the Web to find scientific names for plant and animal species, recognizing the features of idiolects and dialects, and annotating with footnotes. Mainly, we want to talk about how we negotiate solutions in a tenacious, engaging, and diplomatic way.

A few words are in order about our base metaphor of tools and grease mechanics. This is a decidedly masculine way of conceptualizing what we do, and we defend that genderization because we are both men who were raised with hammers, saws, vises, screwdrivers, and wrenches. But, as

Katie Collins reminds us in a recent essay, women may well prefer to use a different kind of controlling metaphor, such as sewing and needlework, where piecing, creating seams, cutting fabric, and following threads of thought may be more suitable.[5] Whatever the case, it is vitally important to think about translation as hard work, because it is.

Text Samples

Some obstacles are fairly simple, such as finding the best gloss for a Gwich'in word that has no clear English counterpart. This usually requires going through a list of synonyms, but it can also extend beyond that. Other obstacles are more complex and dynamic, because they require restructuring a clause or a sentence, or inverting the syntax. They may also require tinkering with tense and aspect or modality in such a way that the Gwich'in utterance cannot be translated word for word. Although we prefer facing page translations, we have gone interlinear in this chapter to achieve an economy of pages.

Example 1: Unraveling a Mysterious Key Word

This first sample comes from Kenneth Frank's (KF47) personal experience story on how to cook caribou ribs when no firewood is available.[6]

> Geetak hee vadzaih tr'aahk'ee dai' traa chan kwaa zhyaa ddhah laii kak goo'aii ts'ą',

> Sometimes when we shoot caribou up on the mountain tops where there's no firewood,

> łuu'ah zhrih gwanlii, ddhah kak gwa'an *łuu'ah* tr'al.

> There's nothing around there but a lot of *łuu'ah* brush.

When we first encountered the word *łuu'ah*, we were unable to translate it because it was one of many species of brush found growing on the mountain tops in Gwich'in country, and the word was not contained in any of the three Gwich'in dictionaries available to us.[7] To find its English equivalent, we did an online Google search for photo images of "tundra plants." By sharing our computer screens in real time, we were able to scroll down and locate photos of plants known to Kenneth as *łuu'ah*. It turned out that in Latin and English these shrubs are called *betula nana* ('dwarf birch') or *betula glandulosa* ('American dwarf birch'). For the second line we eventually settled on "There's nothing around here but a lot of dwarf birch brush."

Another example of an unidentified species we encountered was the name of a tiny freshwater fish called *ch'ihtł'eevihtr'ii*, named in another one of Kenneth's caribou stories. We had to scour the Web once again by doing a Google search for images of "Arctic freshwater fish" to discover that this was indeed the tiny slimy sculpin, not identified in any of our dictionaries. The second part of the sculpin's name, *-vihtr'ii*, means "obsidian," perhaps because metaphorically it is the size and shape of a black volcanic rock arrowhead.

Example 2: Noting the Nuances of a Single Word or Phrase

Hunter, trapper, and fisherman, Robert Frank has served as Venetie village first chief numerous times and has also been elected to the Venetie IRA Council. As the older first cousin of Kenneth, Robert is a veteran of the Alaska National Guard, a respected storyteller, and a teacher of traditional ways, well known for his humor. Many times there are words that cannot be translated without the addition of crucial context. A good example of this comes from Robert's (2012A) discussion of aural camouflage while hunting caribou, where he says:

Geetee *dink'ee ki*[1] shriidaanch'yaa ts'ą',

And sometimes when they have rifle shells in their ammo pouch,

tł'yahthaa zhik gaa giiyaałąįį k'it[2], digiyahnyaa.

They say they make a noise pretending to be like caribou.

This passage is footnoted twice. *Dink'ee ki'* (lit. 'gun arrow') in the first line is the hunter's everyday metaphor for a rifle shell or bullet, presumably coined shortly after guns were introduced to the Gwich'in in the early nineteenth century. To say that *dink'ee ki'* glosses freely as "rifle shells" is accurate but misses a very important historical fact—namely, that the

Gwich'in extended the arrowhead of aboriginal times to name a radical new hunting tool. Even though they are made of brass, copper, steel, lead, or tungsten, rifle shells are still figuratively visualized as arrows. It's clear that, functionally, arrows and bullets are both projectiles and accomplish the same task of killing or wounding animals, so the first note here helps us understand how the Gwich'in language has adapted and evolved in response to technological change.

The second note, attached to most of the entire second line, explains more precisely what the sound of the rattling rifle shells recreates. The sound of the bullets bumping up against each other in an ammunition pouch or rolled together in a hunter's hand is mimetic, reproducing the natural sound made by caribou hooves clicking as they walk. To say "they make a noise pretending to be like caribou" is fully accurate but terribly understated. For Gwich'in hunters this comparison of the two sounds is all too obvious, but to most non-Natives it would be totally lost without an explanatory note.

Example 3: Inverting the Syntax

Elder Maggie Roberts (1935–2013) was born in Fort Yukon and raised at Gold Camp by her parents, Johnny and Sarah Frank. Gold Camp is a small home place on the banks of the K'aii'eechų'njik River about thirty miles north of the village of Venetie. As the mother of nine children, Maggie was famous for her warm hospitality and for tanning skins. She was Kenneth Frank's father's younger sister, and we recorded her at her home in Venetie over a three-day period. In English she is thought of as Kenneth's aunt, but in the Gwich'in way he always referred to her and addressed her as shitsuu ('my grandmother').

In translating the following statement by Maggie (13F), we started out by sticking to the original word order, allowing the phrasing of the English to be parallel to the Gwich'in. The resulting first draft translation, while easily understood, sounds stilted because the subject of the sentence gets repeated. At the same time, we lose something in the second draft translation by discarding the Gwich'in way of speaking, of organizing thought. For aesthetic reasons we finally recast the sentence and shortened it, but the first draft might actually do more to convey

Gwich'in grammatical structure and oral conversational style. There are good arguments to be made for both translations.

> Ch'itrih choh, aii giizhit ch'itrik tthak tr'ilii i'. [*Original Gwich'in*]
>
> The big rumen stomach, we take all the digesta out of it. [*1st draft translation*]
>
> We take all the digesta out of the big rumen stomach. [*2nd draft translation*]

Example 4: Deciphering Quoted Speech, Direct and Indirect

Here Maggie Roberts (1F) is telling the legendary story about the Brush Man who saved a band of people from starvation. The difficulty with translating this passage goes well beyond knowing the vocabulary. Ch'anzhaldǫǫ, the mysterious Brush Man, gave an old woman instructions to pass along to the rest of the travelers so that he would not be observed when he was sharing his food with them.

The main problem in this passage lies in deciphering the difference between direct or reported speech (where we hear someone's exact words) and reporting speech (where we find out who said it), which is complicated by the fact that the Brush Man is asking the old woman to relay his orders to the rest of the group. As one of us observed many years ago, verbs of saying are important rhythmic and poetic devices not only in Gwich'in but in many other Native American languages.[8] They are central to the discourse, but often get neglected or dropped altogether in translations.

For the sake of comparison, here are three drafts of the translation, which evolved over the course of four days.

TRANSLATION DRAFT 1, JULY 28, 2016

> "Dzaa gwee'an neegogǫǫya' shro'," yahnyaa łee.
>
> "Don't let them come around here," he told her. [*Direct*]
>
> "Jyaa govahąįįjyaa yuu, dzaa gwee'an neegogǫǫya' shro'."
>
> "Tell them not to come around here." [*Indirect*]

There is a mismatch here between the draft translation for the first line and the translation for the second line, even though the Gwich'in words are clearly identical. This issue had to be resolved.

TRANSLATION DRAFT 2, JULY 29, 2016

"Dzaa gwee'an neegogǫǫya' shro'," yahnyaa łee.

"Don't [let them] come around here," he told her,

Jyaa govahąįįjyaa yuu, "Dzaa gwee'an neegogǫǫya' shro'."

Tell them, "Don't come around here." [*Partly Direct*]

Kenneth resolved this by saying that although the highlighted Gwich'in clauses are identical, their intent was actually different, in that the old woman was expected to pass on what the Brush Man said to the whole band. Therefore we decided to put "let them" in brackets, to show that it was understood that the Brush Man's instructions "Don't come around here" were not intended solely for the old woman, but for her and the entire band she was traveling with. One puzzle we had with this passage was deciding where to put the quotes, especially in the second line of the Gwich'in.

TRANSLATION DRAFT 3, AUGUST 2, 2016

"Dzaa gwee'an neegogǫǫya' shro'," yahnyaa łee.

"Don't [let them] come around here," he told her,

Jyaa govahąįįjyaa yuu, "dzaa gwee'an neegogǫǫya' shro'."

"Tell them, 'Don't come around here.'" [*Direct and embedded*]

Here I realized that the Brush Man's words to the old woman were slightly different from his words to the rest of the band because he was instructing her to relay the warning. It becomes quite tricky, since he told her exactly what to tell them. The solution we found after about thirty minutes of deliberation was to add an interior single quote inside a double quote.

The punctuation acts as a lubricant to preserve the original dramatic structure of the dialogue.

Since we often go back and revisit trouble spots like this one, one benefit of our collaborative work on documents uploaded to Google Drive is that we can go back and see all of the revisions each of us has made chronologically day by day. The ability to revisit translated documents in the cloud and review all the previous edits has, moreover, both facilitated and informed the writing of this chapter.

Example 5: Pondering the Small Words

Here Maggie Roberts (13F) is talking about how she makes a meat soup. I noticed that some words were not included in Kenneth's initial translation, and I drew attention to the words *tsal* ('small' or 'little') and *chan* ('also') and asked, "Small pieces of fat or a small amount of fat?" Kenneth said, "Small pieces of fat." And then I asked, "Do you want to translate that final 'ts'ą' as 'so'?" In this case, Kenneth said, "Go ahead."

> Ch'ik'eh, ch'ik'eh dal *tsal chan* vitee t'ihłik *ts'ą'*. [*Gwich'in original*]

> I add pieces of diced fat into it. [*1st draft translation*]

> The fat, I add small pieces of diced fat into it. [*2nd draft translation*]

> *So* I *also* add *small* pieces of diced fat into it. [*3rd and final draft*]

The repetition of *ch'ik'eh* ('the fat') is fully acceptable in oral performance for Gwich'in, the source language, but it seems unnecessary and redundant in English.

This example highlights Maggie's rather unique way of speaking—her idiolect—by the way she often ends her sentences with *ts'ą'* ('and' or 'so'). Most other fluent speakers we know will begin rather than end their sentences with *ts'ą'*. But in English it's simply not acceptable to end a sentence with "and" or "so," and we were pretty much forced to move it to the beginning of the sentence. Other speakers we interviewed like to end their sentences with discourse particles such as *reh, roh, ni', no', i'*, or *o'*, which are not really translatable at all. They serve more as punctuation than as words, orally marking the ends of sentences.

Example 6: Embedding with -*nyaa* 'saying'

Here Kenneth Frank is talking again to Maggie Roberts (4F), about the disagreeable rutting taste of bull caribou meat in the fall. At first Maggie calls it "Ch'atsanh," but then she changes the word to "Datsanh." Kenneth points out this disparity to her and says:

> Diinyaa t'iinyaa noihnyaa geh'an t'ihnyaa.
>
> The reason I'm saying that is I'm not sure what you were saying.

This sentence is extremely difficult to translate because it's a Gwich'in tongue twister, and there are four forms of the verb -*nyaa* ('to say') within a single sentence. The artistry and playfulness of such a line is quite profound, but, when rendered literally, it comes out as "What you were saying I'm not sure the reason I'm saying," which in English just doesn't make any sense. With a little more tinkering we recast it more freely as "The reason I'm saying that is I'm not sure what you were saying."

In Gwich'in oral tradition, -*nyaa* is one of the most important verbs.[9] It is used to identify who said what, and we have documented close to eighty inflections within the paradigm. These verbs of saying are important and nuanced in that they allow us to distinguish what constitutes traditional knowledge from what comes directly from the personal experience of the speaker. When they are doubled up or compounded like this, they also have a rhythmic effect. The end result is rather comical and mind teasing, even in translation.

Example 7: Consulting a Fluent Speaker of the Language

In one of our recordings, Maggie Roberts relates a story of how a young boy, her older brother Dan Frank, once killed a caribou with just his pocketknife. Snaring caribou and moose is an ancient and vital form of subsistence for Gwich'in people, but it is not practiced in contemporary Anglo-American culture. As Maggie tells the story, Dan went out one morning to check the family snares and discovered that a caribou had been caught in one of them. Snares are big loops made out of rawhide that are attached to a tree as an anchor. The snares are set in an opening in the brush where there is a caribou trail, and when an animal walks through the opening, it sticks its neck into the loop, pulls against the loop, and the noose quickly tightens around its head or its antlers.

When Dan encountered the snared caribou, he realized that he couldn't approach the animal without being kicked or trampled, so he began to approach it slowly from behind. He noticed that as he approached the animal quickly retreated from him, and, as it did so, it began to wind the tether of the snare around the tree. So he kept this up until the caribou eventually shortened its tether so much that it couldn't move any further. At that point he walked right up to it and jabbed it under the foreleg with his pocketknife enough times that he eventually killed it.

The problem we faced here is translating the line "Ts'ą' t'ee khaihłak nilii o'." Kenneth's first suggestion was "So the caribou was stuck right next to the tree." However, "stuck" did not seem appropriate as a verb, because the caribou was not actually covered with pitch or another sticky substance, and it was not impossible for it to walk backwards and unwind its tether.

After two more days had passed, I finally asked my wife, Barbara, how she would describe the caribou's predicament. She quickly offered yet another take: "So the caribou was joined to the tree." Both Kenneth and I immediately felt that this new verb "joined" captured the essence of the situation and quickly agreed to adopt it, with one minor change. Because the sentence does not actually include *vadzaih*, the word for "caribou," even though it is understood, we needed to write it as "So it [the caribou] became joined to the tree." Here the value of an outside opinion proved to be extremely valuable in brokering the translation. In other cases Kenneth has often successfully consulted his wife, Caroline, for concrete suggestions on how to translate Gwich'in words and phrases.

Example 8: Backtranslating

As we were preparing the chapters of our forthcoming book on caribou, it occurred to me that in addition to the introduction, there was also a need to introduce and focus on the fundamental unifying story called "The Man Who Became a Caribou," which also serves as the title to the book.[10] Facing an organizational imperative, my first idea was to call this section the "prologue," but of course Kenneth had never heard of such a word, and it was very challenging for us to come up with a Gwich'in equivalent to it. I explained that a prologue is a section of a book that comes near the beginning, before all of the chapters of stories that we had collected from Elders on various topics such as hunting methods, butchering techniques, meat transportation, and food preparation and storage.

After a few minutes of discussion, Kenneth offered up the simple but remarkable Gwich'in phrase *Tr'ookit Gwandak Gwehkii* ('Before the first story'). At that moment I realized that the prologue was itself a story, so it couldn't come *before* the first story. It *was already* the first story. And the obvious solution was to call it that. We agreed to drop the "prologue" concept and simply call it "Tr'ookit Gwandak: The First Story." That in turn made it possible for us to use Kenneth's initial suggestion, "Tr'ookit Gwandak Gwehkii," as the title of the introduction, since the introduction logically comes *before* the first story. In this way we brainstormed to arrive at appropriate titles for both the introduction and the lead-off story.

Breakthrough

One of the first tasks we tackled in our project was compiling Gwich'in names for all the body parts of the caribou. All of these names, with the single exception of *ch'ikiidruu* ('the first rib'), also apply to the body parts of other large game animals such as moose and Dall sheep. In order to elicit the names of these animal body parts we looked for and found sketches of caribou skeletons. After trying out another sketch that was not adequately detailed, we commissioned one to be done by the osteologist and illustrator Lee Post of Homer, Alaska. Post's sketch (fig. 24) shows all of the caribou's bones in elegant detail and was excellent as an interview prompt. We then set forth to attach Gwich'in labels to each bone. For comparison we used a duplicate of the same basic sketch for the corresponding English and scientific names. The Gwich'in-labeled sketch is shown here. Of course, after labeling all of the bones, antlers, and hooves, we then proceeded to identify all of the muscles, internal organs, and other tissues.

To make a long story short, we used these anatomical sketches as primary models for Gwich'in caribou anatomy for the first three years of our project. Only when we began to compile a spreadsheet comparing

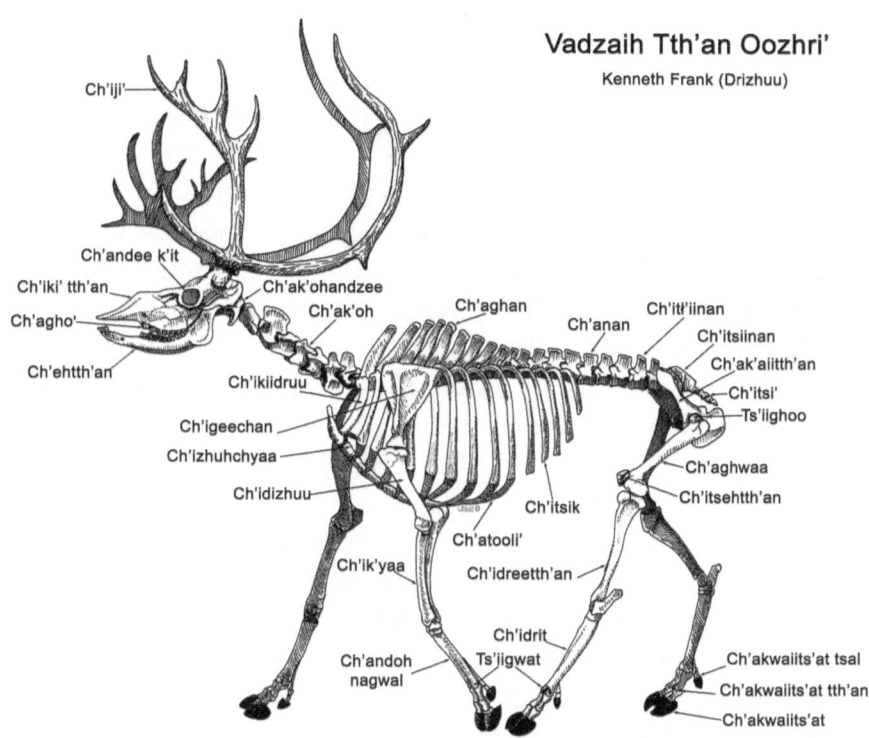

Fig. 24. Vadzaih Tth'an Oozhri': Caribou bone names. Illustration by Lee Post.

different Elders' names for these body parts did we make a key discovery. It was not a discovery for Kenneth, but it was for me. What suddenly dawned on me one day was that in Gwich'in the names of most of the bones of the caribou are actually the names for the bones and the meat together. The *ch'idrit*, for example, is not simply the metatarsal bone shown in the sketch but also the skin, meat, and tendons on that bone and the delicious marrow found inside it.

The reason my own understanding was held back for years is due to the visual influence of published anatomical sketches by Lee Post,[11] and by twentieth-century zooarchaeologists such as Lewis Binford and Arthur Spiess, two scientists who were interested in studying the faunal remains and butchering methods of caribou excavated in situ.[12] But Gwich'in hunters and processors seldom see animal bones as skeletons or fossils unless they have been bleaching and weathering for many years on the surface of the tundra. They see bones primarily as they are dissected from freshly killed animals, still encased in flesh and skin.

The Gwich'in also see game animals as cut up into sections as well as into single bone joints. My initial typology put the meat and bones into separate categories, separate word lists. This discovery meant that I had to reconceptualize all of the parts of the caribou, and subsequently it affected the way we translated and classified the Gwich'in names of the 150 or so body parts identified for us by the consulting Elders. This was, in no small way, quite a revelation.

Verbal Negotiations

We conclude this essay by discussing how we use the language of negotiation and diplomacy to improve our communication and reduce conflicts. Due to culture-specific discourse patterns, as Ron and Suzanne Scollon showed us so convincingly many years ago, Athabaskan-English interethnic communication, like many others, is fraught with pitfalls.[13] Gwich'in speakers think that English speakers talk too much, and English speakers think that Athabaskans have nothing to say—a tension created by differing discourse patterns and expectations. There is always some degree of it, but neither one of us wants to alienate the other, because our friendship is too important, and, since Gwich'in is Kenneth's first language, I often defer to him when we are unable to agree. Our egos cannot be completely discarded, but they can be minimized or set aside until things cool off. Who is right cannot be the central issue.

The negotiating process begins with both of us looking at the same document in Google Drive and both of us connected to live audio via Skype. Kenneth generally takes the initiative with a literal English translation of a Gwich'in sentence. I wait and give him time to revise the translation. Then I will respond with a suggested revision. After making a verbal suggestion or two and then typing it in to Google Drive, I often say, "Does that work for you?" or "Are you with me?" Or I may simply say, "You can't say it that way in standard English." Or, then again, I might say of a specific edit, "I can live with it like that if you can." And Kenneth might say something like "No, no. Take it out," or "Leave it alone." In these latter two cases, I recognize that there is no path to compromise. I take my suggestion off the table, and I wait for Kenneth to come up with a countersuggestion or just let the existing text stand as is. One of the keys is to be patient and give each other time to think, so there are often long pauses when neither of us says anything.

Nevertheless, there are many occasions when we have worked on a sentence for some time and have the general thought expressed in English, yet I will announce that "it's still pretty awkward like that." At this point Kenneth is likely to say "Fix it!" In Gwich'in the imperative verb for "fix it" is *shriniinlii*. This means he trusts me to recast the line or the sentence to make the English smoother and more intelligible.

To buy additional time to think something through, Kenneth may say, "Let me see. Hold on." This call for a time-out may last just a few minutes or may be extended to the next day or days, especially if he wants to consult with another fluent speaker for a better gloss or an alternative spelling. If we need to come back and revisit a word or a line, we highlight it in red. We realize that such time-outs are necessary to save us from getting mired down for so long that we get tired and frustrated. There are always bigger fish to fry.

Keeping in mind that we want to define lines of text by clauses that act as units of translation, we will often suggest breaking up an existing sentence. "Let's bring that part down," we'll say, meaning that we want to break up an existing line and begin a new line. This usually results in one of us inserting a period or a comma at the end of the first line. The visual pauses represented by these periods and commas supply the reader with balanced lines containing both a subject and a predicate.

In conclusion we find that, by collaborating orally on translations, we play to each other's strengths. For nuts-and-bolts word mechanics this may be the most important tool of all. Of course there are exceptional individuals who are fully fluent, fully literate, and well read in two languages and can easily move back and forth between them, but that's not us. So we think that the next best thing is to pair up a fluent literate speaker of the source language with one who is fully fluent in the target language and trained as an ethnographer. That has been our immense good fortune, bringing together the very best of both our worlds in an ongoing dialogue of mediation.

ACKNOWLEDGMENTS

We wish to thank fellow APS Symposium participant Anne Keary for reading an earlier draft of this chapter and making a wealth of constructive comments for its improvement.

NOTES

1. Mishler, Frank, and Hayton, "Collaborating in Gwich'in."
2. Hymes, *"In Vain I Tried to Tell You."* See also Hymes, *Now I Only Know So Far*.
3. Mishler, *Neerihiinjìk*. A new, 3rd edition is forthcoming.
4. See, for example, Kari, *Ahtna Travel Narratives*. Also Cowell, Moss Sr., and C'Hair, *Arapaho Stories, Songs, and Prayers*.
5. Collins, "Materiality of Research."
6. Throughout this manuscript we have added internal references to our field recordings in parentheses. (KF47), for example, is Kenneth Frank's own recording no. 47. We expect to donate all these recordings to the Alaska Native Language Archive at the University of Alaska Fairbanks in the near future.
7. The three Gwich'in dictionaries available to us are: 1) Alexander and Alexander, comps., *Gwich'in to English Dictionary*; 2) James and Mueller, *Western Gwich'in Topical Dictionary*; and 3) Katherine Peter, *Dinjii Zhuh Ginjik Nagwan Tr'iłtsaii*.
8. Mishler, "He Said, They Say," 239–49.
9. Mishler, "-Nyaa, Just Saying."
10. Mishler and Frank, *The Man Who Became a Caribou*.
11. Lee Post, *Moose Manual*. See also the Boneman [Lee Post], Bone Building Books, http://www.theboneman.com/ (accessed August 21, 2020).
12. See Binford, *Nunamiut Ethnoarchaeology*; and Spiess, *Reindeer and Caribou Hunters*.
13. Scollon and Wong-Scollon, "Athabaskan-English Interethnic Communication."

BIBLIOGRAPHY

Alexander, Virginia, and Clarence Alexander, comps. *Gwich'in to English Dictionary*. Fort Yukon AK: privately printed, 2005.
Binford, Lewis. *Nunamiut Ethnoarchaeology*. New York: Academic Press, 1978.
Collins, Katie. "The Materiality of Research: Woven into the Fabric of the Text: Subversive Material Metaphors in Academic Writing." London School of Economics and Political Science, May 27, 2016. https://blogs.lse.ac.uk/lsereviewofbooks/2016/05/27/the-materiality-of-research-woven-into-the-fabric-of-the-text-subversive-material-metaphors-in-academic-writing-by-katie-collins/.

Cowell, Andrew, Alonzo Moss Sr., and William J. C'Hair. *Arapaho Stories, Songs, and Prayers: A Bilingual Anthology*. Norman: University of Oklahoma Press, 2014.

Hymes, Dell. *"In Vain I Tried to Tell You": Essays in Native American Ethnopoetics*. Philadelphia: University of Pennsylvania Press, 1981.

———. *Now I Only Know So Far: Essays in Ethnopoetics*. Lincoln: University of Nebraska Press, 2003.

James, Lillian, and Richard Mueller, comps. *Western Gwich'in Topical Dictionary*. Fairbanks: Alaska Native Language Center and Summer Institute of Linguistics, 1994.

Kari, James, ed. *Ahtna Travel Narratives: A Demonstration of Shared Geographic Knowledge among Alaska Athabascans*. Fairbanks: Alaska Native Language Center, University of Alaska, 2010.

Mishler, Craig. "'He Said, They Say': The Uses of Reporting Speech in Native American Folk Narrative." *Fabula* 22, nos. 3–4 (1981): 239–49.

———. *Neerihiinjìk: We Traveled from Place to Place: The Gwich'in Stories of Johnny and Sarah Frank*. 2nd ed. Fairbanks: Alaska Native Language Center, 2001.

———. "-Nyaa, Just Saying: Functional and Artistic Uses of a Gwich'in Verb Stem." Paper presented at the Alaskan Anthropological Association Annual Meeting, Anchorage, March 22, 2018.

Mishler, Craig, and Kenneth Frank, eds. *The Man Who Became a Caribou: Gwich'in Stories and Conversations from Alaska and the Yukon*. 2nd ed. Hanover NH: International Polar Institute, 2020.

Mishler, Craig, Kenneth Frank, and Allan Hayton. "Collaborating in Gwich'in on the Web: Khahłok Gwitr'it'agwarah'in." In *Working Papers in Athabaskan (Dene) Languages, 2013*, vol. 12, 22–29. Fairbanks: Alaska Native Language Center, University of Alaska Fairbanks, 2014.

Peter, Katherine, comp. *Dinjii Zhuh Ginjik Nagwan Tr'iłtsaii: Gwich'in Junior Dictionary*. Anchorage AK: National Bilingual Materials Development Center, 1979.

Post, Lee. *The Moose Manual: How to Prepare and Articulate Large Hoofed Mammal Skeletons: Vol. 6*. Homer AK: Lee Post, 2004.

Scollon, Ronald, and Suzanne Wong-Scollon. "Athabaskan-English Interethnic Communication." In *Cultural Communication and Intercultural Contact*, edited by Donald Carbaugh, 259–86. New York: Psychology Press, [1981] 2009.

Spiess, Arthur E. *Reindeer and Caribou Hunters: An Archaeological Study*. New York: Academic Press, 1979.

Conclusion

The Power of Words, Relationships, and Archives

Mary S. Linn

It is difficult to have the last word in a volume that is so rich in content and so complete in commentary. This volume encompasses the main issues surrounding archival contributions to language reclamation and, more important, on language reclamation's impact on archives. I am using the term "reclamation" not in the sense of the renewal of sleeping languages with the help of archival language materials—although that is included—or as a synonym for revitalization, but as the empowerment of Indigenous and autochthonous communities in regaining rights over their language, land, and wellness and setting their own goals in these regards. Reclamation is representative of a change of perspective from colonialization to Indigenous.[1] The authors in this volume provide strong case studies and often personal arguments for why indigenizing language archives and methodologies in documentary linguistics is necessary and even natural. The outcomes constitute a transformative recentering around respect and reciprocity and in thinking about everything we do as recognizing, building, and sustaining relationships that benefit originating communities and archives alike.[2]

Indigenizing language archives and archival research has been taking place quietly (like everything in the archive world), yet also at an uncharacteristically fast pace. Archives are generally not seen as initiators of social change, but I believe that language archives have been at the forefront of change in linguistics: from demanding metadata that allows discoverability to embracing Indigenous methodologies as core. Ryan Henke and Andrea Berez-Kroeker provide an excellent historical overview of the growth of endangered- and minoritized-language archives.[3] They distinguish four periods, and I will use their framework for putting this volume into context while providing community responses to these changes, and—more crucial—influences on archives.

The first period is early analog. It lasted from the inception of repositories such as the American Philosophical Society Library (APS), through the massive collecting period of Franz Boas and Edward Sapir and their students, up to the early 1990s. The early period is characterized by physical archive collections and spaces in grand natural history museums and libraries. Mirroring language documentation methodology, the archival focus was on the collector, who was considered *the* expert on the language and provided all of the content metadata and context of the collection. Academics knew of these collections through word of mouth or from academic advisors, and one could access the collections only by visiting the archives themselves. Thus, archives were virtually closed off to originating communities, and indeed many young or underemployed academic researchers as well. This period, which continues to embody the popular image of archives to this day, built the legacy of exclusiveness and ownership as well as an imposing space that all memory institutions allied with or participating in reclamation must work against today.

A second period of dedicated language archives began in the 1990s, a decade that saw the rapidly increased awareness of language endangerment by both academics and communities. In academia this began a push to put language documentation and description back into consciousness and coursework.[4] With this came an increased focus on finding where existing collections were located and how to locate this information easily, otherwise known as "discoverability." There was also a push for preservation through improved digitization of language collections. Parallel to archives, at least in North America and Australia, documentary and descriptive linguists began moving toward more collaborative methodology and a focus on collecting natural language that is immediately usable for community revitalization efforts.[5]

The increased awareness of language endangerment also saw the rapid growth of community action. With roots in the cultural revolution of the late 1960s, isolated revitalization efforts began growing into a global language revitalization movement.[6] Communities started to make decisions about what would be documented based on what they wanted to be able to say or pass on to the next generations, as opposed to what was typologically unique or theoretically challenging. They also adhered to their internal restrictions of what should not be recorded or accessed by outsiders and began requiring the same respect from linguists, with several emerging language archives, such as the Survey of Californian and Other Languages (now the California Language Archive) at the University of California, Berkeley, and the Alaska Native Language Archive at the University of Alaska, Fairbanks, responding as well. Significantly, in 1995 the Advocates for Indigenous California Language Survival partnered with the University of California at Berkeley to hold the first Breath of Life Institute (BOL). Geared toward communities with few or no fluent first-language speakers, the goal of the institute was to "assist the participants in exploring and utilizing the vast archives of California Indian languages and materials for their own efforts in language reclamation."[7] This was a departure from most approaches, which were focused on developing immersion curriculum and teacher training and where most funding and media attention was located. It was, however, an honest appraisal of their resources and needs. So communities with sleeping languages consciously embarked on a multigenerational experiment in language renewal with archives. Collections became not just relevant, but necessary to communities.

Starting in the early twenty-first century, a third period focused on technological advancements, including digital archiving, organized development of standards of archival practice, and higher levels of discoverability. For the first time, there was worldwide financial support of language documentation and revitalization projects. Funders such as the U.S. National Science Foundation and National Endowment for the Humanities' Documenting Endangered Languages grants and the

Endangered Languages Documentation Programme (ELDP) grants at the School of Oriental and African Languages in London focused on documentation, but required grantees to include archival plans as part of their applications. To prepare linguists to be able to archive materials, ELDP holds archival training workshops for grantees, and, to make archiving part of the documentation process from the beginning stages, the Collaborative Language Research Institute (CoLang) teaches archival methods to students and active linguists, both community members (Indigenous, minoritized, autochthonous, or small-language community members) and noncommunity members, from around the world.[8]

This third period also saw exponential growth of Indigenous archives and archivist and archival organizations. As collaborative methodologies were influencing archives, so were Indigenous methodologies. An important contribution on Indigenous archival organizations, their inspirations, impact, and needs going forward can be found in Jennifer R. O'Neal's essay "'The Right to Know': Decolonizing Native American Archives."[9] In 2006 the Administration for Native Americans and the Smithsonian National Museum of the American Indian published a reference guide, *Native Language Preservation, Establishing Archives and Repositories*. Indigenous archival organizations, such as the Association for Tribal Archives, Libraries, and Museums (ATALM), fueled more impetus to have protocols for "culturally responsible care and use" of Indigenous materials.[10] Many non-Indigenous language archives responded. The Digital Endangered Languages and Musics Archives Network (DELAMAN), founded in 2003, has twelve full-member language archives and three associate-member archives, representing the largest holders of Indigenous language materials throughout the world. The DELAMAN constitution includes seven objectives, the first being the ethical care and preservation of digital materials, and the second objective "to promote access to archival material by originating communities."[11]

The contribution of the BOL workshops and institutes to indigenizing methodology is understated in most narratives. In the early 2000s BOL spread from California to institutes held in Washington State, Oklahoma, British Columbia, and the National Breath of Life in Washington, DC. In addition to impacting communities, Baldwin, Hinton, and Pérez-Baez credit BOL with changing archives both by instigating change in terminology—especially in language and nation names—but also in adding to richer metadata that includes the contributor names and relationships and information in the collections that reflect community interests and language uses. They also credit BOL with driving archives to digitize.[12] Based on years of working with heritage-language materials dating back hundreds of years, the Myaamia Center developed the Miami-Illinois Digital Archive: a hybrid database, search engine, and website that allows users to organize and easily access historic documents for reclamation use.[13] The National Breath of Life 2.0 at Miami University of Ohio worked with six researcher teams who already had BOL experience to test the broader application called Indigenous Language Digital Archive (ILDA).

I believe that BOL has had even more impact on building a respectful and continuous relationship between archives and communities. By including material culture and biological collections in BOL methods, language archives are more integrated with other collections, reflecting the seamlessness of language, culture, and the natural environment. This follows the philosophy of language found in most communities. In addition to changing metadata terminology, the BOL workshop *participants* become community *researchers*. Equal to any other learned researchers, they are considered experts on their communities' languages, knowledge for metadata on the resources, and access restrictions. Additionally, they provide instructions for the traditional care of collections of material culture. Responding to the needs of community researchers, whose interactions with legacy materials is intense and often powerfully emotional, archives have dedicated quiet or cleansing spaces for users. In spaces where fresh plant material and burning is generally prohibited, archives have suspended rules to accommodate the human side of research. Therefore, in many ways, the BOL approach for using archives for reclamation became a primary force for creating change in archives, especially in making archival spaces Indigenous spaces.

No archivist can work with BOL researchers and feel the same about the materials in their care. At one National Breath of Life in Washington, DC, two young language practitioners found one, and only one, short manuscript in their language. The translation gave a rather disconnected narrative, and it was immediately valuable for their efforts back home as a story and for the language contained within. But, instead of digging into the language, the researchers struggled with who the storyteller was and why he told that story. The contributor was far away from his home when he told this story to a linguist. Slowly, they could give a name and family reference to him. They began to see several meanings to the story beyond the translation provided to the linguist, a message for those who knew how to listen. And, like all good stories, it was rich in possible interpretations and connections to their own lives today. His voice reached across time and touched them. This narrative of agency is echoed in many of the chapters presented in this volume and experienced multiple times throughout language reclamation efforts. Yet BOL brings the life of manuscripts to the archival staff in a way that they experience themselves, and, for many, they can never look at the holdings in their care as just data or objects again.

BOL institutes typically give the researchers a homework assignment on reading a phonetic alphabet on the first night, and they come prepared to read a short phonetic passage in their language. During one BOL a young man from a sleeping-language community got up for his group and read a short prayer that had been taken down in phonetic transcription. This simple assignment was highly emotional for the other researchers on his team; it was the first time they had ever heard their language spoken. We all could feel the "breath of life" in the language and its speaker, and everyone in the room was changed by it. Legacy materials have life and a voice, a repurposing and a retranslating for every generation. The human connection with the materials as *living materials* and with each other is established through BOL moments like these.

According to Henke and Berez-Kroeker, we are just at the beginning of the next stage, where archives are constantly pushed to reexamine practices and to challenge underlying assumptions of history, use, and voice. Brian Carpenter exemplifies this when he states that the role of archivist has changed from knowledge holding to knowledge sharing and from reference requests to relationships.[14] Over the years linguists' roles reflect these same changes, from file cabinet collections to open archives, data analyzers to collaborative relationships. Originating communities have changed from nonuser to researchers and collaborators in the process from documentation to archiving. The current stage means open and continuous dialogue and collaboration between originating communities and archives. These massive changes in reorientation from a focus on manuscripts and data to users and relationships have occurred in just thirty years. Put in its historical context, this volume represents the vanguard of this change. Each section reveals pathways into how we reinterpret history, how we use collections in new ways as extensions of creativity, environmental stewardship, traditional lifeways, and wellness, and how we build and sustain relationships founded on reciprocity, inclusion, and empowerment.

There is still much work in these conversations for the future of language archives. An immediate task is reaching out to smaller archives and libraries with isolated-language collections. These institutions are generally not connected to these larger movements, nor do they always have staff with knowledge of how to contact, or even that they should contact, originating communities about their holdings. Indigenous- and non–Indigenous language archives could embark on a campaign to reach these sleeping collections and their caretakers. Some collections will always come to light purely by serendipitous means, but a concentrated effort to locate them will save individual community efforts much time and frustration. It will also help change the culture in more archives and libraries and provide a better overall inventory of language collections.

We can turn more approaches into policies, until codification is not required but natural. The APS Library's Center for Native American and Indigenous Research and their *Protocols for the Treatment of Indigenous Materials*, discussed in the preface of this volume and in many instances throughout, is a prime example of making reciprocity central to the mission.[15] The Ralph Rinzler Archives at the Smithsonian Center for Folklife and Cultural Heritage recently adopted the policy "Shared Stewardship of Collections."[16] The Mukurtu digital access tool of symbols easily denoting accessibility and use allows Indigenous communities to retain control over their digital cultural heritage while also sharing with the world.[17] Once a unique idea, it has been funded by the U.S. Institute of Museum and Library Services (IMLS) and NEH, and the system has been adopted by the U.S. Library of Congress for Native American with tribal nations for their holdings. Funders such as NSF-NEH, DEL, and ELDP now require letters of support from the originating communities and from all researchers, including community researchers. DELAMAN and Society for the Indigenous Languages of the Americas (SSILA) have both received awards for comprehensive language documentation collections that require, in addition to metadata and archiving, accessibility for the originating communities. The SSILA award is particularly geared toward communally and collaboratively created collections; it requires the collection be at least "impactful or potentially impactful for language learners, language maintenance, language teaching, and scholarly research."[18] Thus, the award assumes researchers engaged with community language and cultural documentation projects to be full participants in creating archival collections. More of these types of centers, policies, and recognitions are needed.

As this work represents, much of the conversation is still centered on non–Indigenous language archives and their building relationships with originating communities, or collaborations that interact with materials from these institutions. All archives have a lot to learn from the other direction: how Indigenous-language archives build relationships with noncommunity archives. While papers on non-Indigenous language archives often discuss hurdles in changing the culture of exclusiveness, ownership, and accessibility from within, there is too little published by Indigenous archivists on how Indigenous-language archives are removing internal roadblocks to collecting and accessibility, how they care for collections in an institutional setting, or how they negotiate issues of authority and authenticity. More work in these areas would help smaller or fledgling Indigenous archives, as well as contribute to the literature of all archives and their needs. In other words, we are in a period of indigenizing methodologies, but the next stage should be adopting Indigenous methodologies in creating, caring for, and accessing archival collections.

Language reclamation efforts invariably intersect with language archives and museum collections at some point, even for communities whose primary heritage-language resources are not housed in archives.

On the collections level, recognizing the agency of the creators or speakers of the collections, respecting the agency of the materials themselves, and continually reinterpreting history, lifeways, and knowledge systems are all vital components of language reclamation. In this manner the collections continue to be used in new and creative ways for new generations of speakers. On the human level, there is the growing reciprocity between the originating communities, researchers, and the caretakers. The archives and the staff themselves become part of the relational being of reclamation. And, in this way, on the institutional level, archives become part of the new landscape of the language. No longer just a place where materials are stored, they become powerful spaces of Indigenous knowledge.

NOTES

1. Leonard, "Framing Language Reclamation Programmes," 359; and De Korne and Leonard, "Reclaiming Languages," 5–14.
2. Smith, *Decolonizing Methodologies*.
3. Henke and Berez-Kroeker, "Brief History of Archiving," 411–57.
4. For a comprehensive yet highly readable look at twenty years of change in the field of language documentation and description, see McDonnell, Berez-Kroeker, and Holton, eds., "Special Issue 15."
5. For an overview of the early changes in methodology and theory in descriptive linguistics, see Rice, "Ethical Issues in Linguistic Fieldwork"; and Rice, "Documentary Linguistics and Community Relations," which provides an overview of how this has changed relationships with community. Another excellent overview from the community perspective can be found in Leonard, "Reflections on (De)Colonialism."
6. For a starting place on theory, practice, and perspectives of language revitalization, see Hinton, Huss, and Roche, eds., *Routledge Handbook of Language Revitalization*; Costa in *Revitalising Language in Provence* argues that language revitalization efforts are part of a global social process that seeks to redefine minority and majority classifications and relations.
7. Advocates for Indigenous California Language Survival, https://aicls.org/breath-of-life-institute/ (accessed August 21, 2020).
8. CoLang began as InField (2008, 2010). Links to all of the host CoLang pages and information about the workshops on arching can be found at the Linguistic Society of America website, www.linguisticsociety.org/content/colang-institute-collaborative-research (accessed August 21, 2020).
9. O'Neal, "Right to Know."

10. First Archivists Circle, Protocols for Native American Archival Materials, http://www2.nau.edu/libnap-p/protocols.html (accessed August 21, 2020), 2.
11. Digital Endangered Languages and Musics Archives Network, Constitution, http://www.delaman.org/constitution/ (accessed August 21, 2020).
12. Baldwin, Hinton, and Pérez-Baez, "Breath of Life Workshops."
13. Baldwin, Costa, and Troy, "Myaamiaataweenki eekincikoonihkiinki eeyoonki aaposaataweenki."
14. Carpenter, "From Reference Requests to Relationships."
15. American Philosophical Society Center for Native American and Indigenous Research, https://www.amphilsoc.org/library/cnair; and "Protocols for the Treatment of Indigenous Materials," https://www.amphilsoc.org/sites/default/files/2017-11/attachments/aps%20protocols.pdf (both accessed August 21, 2020).
16. Ralph Rinzler Archives, Smithsonian Center for Folklife and Cultural Heritage, Shared Stewardship, https://folklife-media.si.edu/docs/folklife/Shared-Stewardship.pdf (accessed August 21, 2020).
17. Mukurtu, https://mukurtu.org/ (accessed August 21, 2020).
18. Society for the Study of the Indigenous Languages of the Americas, Archiving Award, https://ssila.org/awards/archiving/ (accessed August 21, 2020). The DELAMAN award can be found at http://www.delaman.org/delaman-award/ (accessed August 21, 2020).

BIBLIOGRAPHY

Administration for Native Americans (ANA). Native Language Preservation Reference Guide for Establishing Archives and Repositories. 2016. https://www.acf.hhs.gov/ana/resource/1ana-native-language-preservation-a-reference-guide-for-establishing (accessed August 21, 2020).

American Philosophical Society (APS). Protocols for the Treatment of Indigenous Materials. *Proceedings of the American Philosophical Society* 15, no. 4 (2014): 411–20. https://www.amphilsoc.org/sites/default/files/2017-11/attachments/aps%20protocols.pdf.

Baldwin, Daryl, David J. Costa, and Douglas Troy. "Myaamiaataweenki eekincikoonihkiinki eeyoonki aaposaataweenki: A Miami Language Digital Tool for Language Reclamation." *Language Documentation and Conservation* 10 (2016): 394–410.

Baldwin, Daryl, Leanne Hinton, and Gabriela Pérez-Baez. "The Breath of Life Workshops and Institutes." In *The Routledge Handbook of Language Revitalization*, edited by Leanne Hinton, Leena Huss, and Gerald Roche, 188–96. New York: Routledge, 2018.

Carpenter, Brian. "From Reference Requests to Relationships: Stories from the American Philosophical Society." The Social Lives of Linguistic Legacy Materials Panel, American Anthropological Association Annual Meeting, Washington DC, November 22, 2017.

Costa, James. *Revitalising Language in Provence: A Critical Approach*. New York: Wiley, 2017.

De Korne, Haley, and Wesley Leonard. "Reclaiming Languages: Contesting and Decolonising 'Language Endangerment' from the Ground Up." *Language Documentation & Conservation* 14 (2017): 5–14.

First Archivists Circle. Protocols for Native American Archival Materials, 2007. https://www2.nau.edu/libnap-p/protocols.html (accessed August 21, 2020).

Henke, Ryan, and Andrea L. Berez-Kroeker. "A Brief History of Archiving in Language Documentation, with an Annotated Bibliography." *Language Documentation & Conservation* 10 (2016): 411–57. http://hdl.handle.net/10125/24714

Hinton, Leanne, Leena Huss, and Gerald Roche, eds. *The Routledge Handbook of Language Revitalization*. New York: Routledge, 2018.

Leonard, Wesley. "Framing Language Reclamation Programmes for Everybody's Empowerment." *Gender and Language* 6, no. 2 (2012): 339–67.

——— . "Reflections on (De)Colonialism in Language Documentation." In "Special Issue 15: Reflections on Language Documentation 20 Years after Himmelmann 1998." *Language Documentation and Conservation* (2018): 55–65.

McDonnell, Bradley, Andrea L. Berez-Kroeker, and Gary Holton, eds. "Special Issue 15: Reflections on Language Documentation 20 Years after Himmelmann 1998." *Language Documentation and Conservation*, 2018.

O'Neal, Jennifer R. "'The Right to Know': Decolonizing Native American Archives." *Journal of Western Archives* 6, no. 1 (2015): 1–17. http://digitalcommons.usu.edu/westernarchives/vol6/iss1/2.

Ralph Rinzler Archives. Shared Stewardship. Smithsonian Center for Folklife and Cultural Heritage. 2019. https://folklife-media.si.edu/docs/folklife/Shared-Stewardship.pdf (accessed August 21, 2020).

Rice, Keren. "Documentary Linguistics and Community Relations." *Language Documentation and Conservation* 5 (2011): 187–207.

——— . "Ethical Issues in Linguistic Fieldwork: An Overview." *Journal of Academic Ethics* 4 (2006): 123–55.

Smith, Linda Tuhiwai. *Decolonizing Methodologies: Research and Indigenous Peoples*. London: Zed, 1999.

CONTRIBUTORS

Jane Anderson is associate professor of anthropology and museum studies at New York University. She has a PhD in law from the Law School at University of New South Wales in Australia. Her work is focused on the philosophical and practical problems for intellectual property law and the protection of Indigenous and traditional knowledge resources and cultural heritage in support of Indigenous knowledge and data sovereignty. She is the co-founder (with Kim Christen, Washington State University) of Local Contexts, an initiative to support Native, First Nations, Aboriginal, Métis, Inuit, and Indigenous communities in the management of intellectual property and cultural heritage specifically within the digital environment (www.localcontexts.org).

Kayla Begay is a member of the Hoopa Valley Tribe and a board member of Advocates for Indigenous California Language Survival. An assistant professor in Native American studies at Humboldt State University, Begay received her PhD in linguistics from the University of California, Berkeley, focusing on description of California Dene languages and language revitalization.

Brian Carpenter is the curator of Native American materials at the American Philosophical Society (APS). Since 2008 he has worked with over 150 Indigenous communities to assist them in accessing and utilizing archival collections at the APS Library.

Jennifer Carpenter is a member of the Heiltsuk Nation; culture and heritage manager for the Heiltsuk Integrated Resource Management Department; and director of the Heiltsuk Cultural Education Centre, in Bella Bella, British Columbia. She has a BA in art history from Oberlin College (1966) and an MA in anthropology from University of British Columbia (1973).

Lisa Conathan is head of special collections at Williams College, overseeing the Chapin Library of Rare Books and the College Archives. Before joining Williams she worked at the Beinecke Rare Book and Manuscript Library at Yale University as an archivist and as the head of digital services. Conathan's research interests center on the creation and reuse of endangered language documentation, focusing on vernacular literacy and oral discourse in Native North America. She holds a PhD in linguistics from the University of California, Berkeley, and an MLS from the University of Maryland.

Regna Darnell is Distinguished University Professor of Anthropology and the founding director of First Nations Studies at the University of Western Ontario, where she also served on the core faculty of the Centre for the Study of Theory and Criticism. General editor of the Franz Boas Papers project, she is a fellow of the Royal Society of Canada, member of the American Philosophical Society, and holder of the Franz Boas Medal for distinguished service to the profession of the American Anthropological Association. She has published widely about symbolic, linguist, and humanistic anthropology; Indigenous languages and cultures; ethnographic theory; ecosystem health and public health; and the history of anthropology.

Jeffrey Davis is professor of sign language and linguistics at the University of Tennessee. For the past three decades he has been conducting archival research and ethnographic fieldwork to document historical and contemporary use of American Indian Sign Language, especially among Native communities of the historical Great Plains area in the United States and Canada.

James E. Francis Sr. is an accomplished historical researcher, photographer, filmmaker, and graphics artist. He serves on the board of directors for Four Directions Development Corporation, a Native American Community

Development Financial Institution. Francis serves on the Native American Advisory Committee for the Abbe Museum and the Native American Advisory Board for the Boston Children's Museum and is a lifetime member of the Maine Historical Society. He has served on the advisory board of the University of Maine's Hudson Museum in Orono, Maine; and the board of directors for the Bangor Museum and Center for History, where he served as chair of the collections committee. Francis has also served as chair of the Penobscot Nation's Cultural and Historic Preservation Committee. Recently he has returned to school to pursue an intermedia MFA degree from the University of Maine.

Kenneth Frank is the oldest son of Hamel Frank and Mary Johnson Frank. Born in Fort Yukon, Alaska, and raised in the village of Venetie, he is from the Ch'itsyaa clan. As a youth he learned subsistence hunting and fishing from his father and from his grandparents, Johnny and Sarah Frank, with whom he stayed for months at a time at Gold Camp, a remote cabin on the East Fork of the Chandalar River. After attending Indian boarding schools in Wrangell, Alaska, and Chilocco, Oklahoma, he served a two-year stint with the U.S. Army in Texas. In 1980 he moved to Arctic Village and married schoolteacher Caroline Tritt (another fluent speaker of Gwich'in). There they raised two daughters, Crystal and Tisheena. Today Frank is an Elder, a storyteller, a traditional drummer, and the lead singer for the Di'haii Gwich'in dancers. He is employed by the Effie Kokrines school in Fairbanks, where he teaches the Gwich'in language. Frank is frequently in demand for conducting youth workshops on teaching traditional games, making skin drums, and demonstrating traditional tools. In 2014 he was a recipient of the Oscar Kawagley Indigenous Scholar Award at the University of Alaska Fairbanks. He is the coeditor and a major contributor to the book *Dinjii Vadzaih Dhidlit: The Man Who Became a Caribou* (2019).

Richard A. Grounds is of Yuchi and Seminole heritage. He is executive director of the Yuchi Language Project based in Sapulpa, Oklahoma, and works with Yuchi Elders in creating new fluent speakers using immersion language methods. He is currently the chair of the Global Indigenous Languages Caucus and served as the expert for the North American Region at the Expert Meeting on Indigenous Languages held by the United Nations Permanent Forum on Indigenous Issues in 2016. After completing his PhD in the history of religions at Princeton Theological Seminary, he taught at St. Olaf College and in the Anthropology Department at the University of Tulsa.

Annie Guerin is a student in the University of British Columbia's First Nations Endangered Language program. She was born and raised in Vancouver, on Musqueam Territory, and is grateful to raise her four-year-old son, Callaloo, there. She is especially inspired to learn how best to support community-driven language recording programs and sound editing projects.

Sean P. Harvey is associate professor of history at Seton Hall University. His publications include *Native Tongues: Colonialism and Race from Encounter to the Reservation* (Harvard University Press, 2015) and "Native Views of Native Languages: Communication and Kinship in Eastern North America, ca. 1800–1830" (*William and Mary Quarterly*, October 2018). He is working on a book on Albert Gallatin.

Sara Snyder Hopkins is assistant professor of anthropology and sociology and the director of the Cherokee Language Program at Western Carolina University (WCU), where she teaches Cherokee language and linguistic anthropology courses. The WCU Cherokee Language Program is a long-standing language revitalization partner with the Eastern Band of Cherokee Indians.

Gwyneira Isaac (Oxford D.Phil. 2002) is curator of North American ethnology at the National Museum of Natural History at the Smithsonian Institution. Her research focuses on the dynamics of and intersections between culturally different knowledge systems. This includes her ongoing work in the Pueblos of Zuni and Hopi, exploring how museum collections are used for cultural revitalization efforts.

Michelle Kaczmarek is a PhD student at the University of British Columbia's iSchool (Library, Archival, and Information Studies). Using the lens of "information practices," Kaczmarek's work investigates the ties and tensions between aspirations and everyday practices, exploring how people redesign their relationships with information tools and technologies to work towards better futures.

Anne Keary researches the history of missionary-Indigenous relations. She is currently working with Niimíipuu Elders Bessie Scott and Florine Davis and linguist Harold Crook on a book tentatively titled *The Niimíipuu and the Written Word: Literacy, Colonialism, and the Making of a Mission Primer*. She completed her PhD at the University of California, Berkeley.

Gerry Lawson is a proud member of the Heiltsuk First Nation and manages the Oral History and Language Lab at the Museum of Anthropology at the University of British Columbia. He acts as the technology lead for the innovative UBC Indigitization Program and sits on the board of directors for the First Peoples' Cultural Council.

Kim Lawson is a Heiltsuk community member and has been a librarian at XWI7XWA Library at the University of British Columbia since 2006. She previously managed the Resource Centre for the Union of BC Indian Chiefs, where she initiated projects to digitally preserve at risk audio video materials in-house.

Adrianna Link is the head of scholarly programs at the American Philosophical Society. She received her PhD from the Department of History of Science and Technology at Johns Hopkins University, where she specialized in the history of twentieth-century American anthropology. She is currently preparing a book manuscript on the history of "urgent anthropology" at the Smithsonian Institution. In addition to her work at the APS, she also serves as a managing editor for the *History of Anthropology Review*.

Mary S. Linn is curator of cultural and linguistic revitalization at the Smithsonian Center for Folklife and Cultural Heritage. She founded the Native American Languages Collection at the Sam Noble Museum and is on the steering committee for the National Breath of Life Indigenous Archival Institute.

Diana E. Marsh is a museum anthropologist and postdoctoral fellow at the National Anthropological Archives, National Museum of Natural History, Smithsonian Institution. Marsh's work addresses how heritage institutions share knowledge with communities and the public. Her current research focuses on understanding and improving access to digitized ethnographic collections, especially for Native community researchers. From 2015 to 2017 she was an Andrew W. Mellon Postdoctoral Curatorial Fellow at the American Philosophical Society, where she curated exhibitions drawing on its collections (*Curious Revolutionaries: The Peales of Philadelphia*, April–December 2017; and *Gathering Voices: Thomas Jefferson and Native America*, April–December 2016). She completed her PhD in anthropology at the University of British Columbia in 2014, an M.Phil in social anthropology with a museums and heritage focus at the University of Cambridge in 2010, and a BFA in visual arts and photography at the Mason Gross School of the Arts of Rutgers University in 2009. Marsh's work has been published in *Journal of Material Culture, Museum Anthropology, Practicing Anthropology, Archivaria*, and *Archival Science*. Her book, *Extinct Monsters to Deep Time: Conflict, Compromise, and the Making of Smithsonian's Fossil Halls*, was recently released in Berghahn Books' Museum and Collections Series.

Cary Miller is Anishinaabe and descends from St. Croix and Leech Lake communities. She is associate professor in Native studies at the University of Manitoba, where she serves as department head and teaches courses in Indigenous history and governance. She received her PhD in history from the University of North Carolina, Chapel Hill.

Robert J. Miller is a professor at the Sandra Day O'Connor College of Law at Arizona State University and the faculty director of the Rosette LLP American Indian Economic Development Program. He was appointed in 2016 to the Navajo Nation Council of Economic Advisors. He was elected to the American Law Institute in 2012 and the American Philosophical Society in 2014 (which elected only 5,506 members between 1743 and 2014). He graduated in 1991 from Lewis and Clark Law School and clerked for Judge O'Scannlain of the U.S. Ninth Circuit Court of Appeals. Miller is a justice on the Grand Ronde Tribe Court of Appeals, the NW Inter-Tribal Court System, and is the interim chief justice of the Pascua Yaqui Tribe Court of Appeals. He has written dozens of books, book chapters, articles, and editorials on Indian law issues and spoken at conferences in over thirty states and in Australia, Canada, England, India, and New Zealand. He is the author or coauthor of four books: *Creating Private Sector Economies in Native America: Sustainable Development through Entrepreneurship* (Cambridge University Press, 2019); *Reservation "Capitalism:" Economic Development in Indian*

Country (Praeger, 2012); *Discovering Indigenous Lands: The Doctrine of Discovery in the English Colonies* (Oxford University Press, 2010); and *Native America, Discovered and Conquered: Thomas Jefferson, Lewis and Clark and Manifest Destiny* (Praeger, 2006). Miller is a citizen of the Eastern Shawnee Tribe of Oklahoma.

Craig Mishler first moved to Alaska in 1968 as a VISTA program volunteer. He began doing ethnographic field work in rural Alaska in 1972 and received his doctorate in folklore and anthropology from the University of Texas at Austin in 1981. He later made a career as an historian with the Alaska Department of Natural Resources and as a subsistence resource specialist with the Alaska Department of Fish and Game, Division of Subsistence. Most recently he was a research professor at the Alaska Native Language Center, University of Alaska, Fairbanks. Over the years he has worked extensively with the Gwich'in, Tanacross, and Kodiak Alutiiq people. Craig is the author, coauthor, translator, or editor of eight books, including *The Crooked Stovepipe: Athapaskan Indian Fiddling and Square Dancing in Northeast Alaska and Northwest Canada* (1993), *Neerihiinjìk: We Traveled from Place to Place: the Gwich'in Stories of Johnny and Sarah Frank* (2000), *The Blind Man and the Loon: the Story of a Tale* (2013), and (with Kenneth Frank) *Dinjii Vadzaih Dhidlit: The Man Who Became a Caribou* (2019).

Sarah Carmen Moritz is a PhD candidate in anthropology at McGill University, Montréal, Canada. Her research addresses human-fish relationships, Indigenous self-determination, and Interior Salish land, language, stewardship and livelihood issues. She is coauthor (leading author of one) of two books on environmental anthropology, Franz Boas, and Salish studies. She has written numerous peer-reviewed contributions on Indigenous language, land and legal revitalization, and collaborative action anthropological methods, especially regarding salmon and water.

Lisa P. Nathan is associate professor at the University of British Columbia's iSchool and served as the coordinator of the iSchool's First Nations Curriculum Concentration from 2010 to 2018. She teaches design-oriented courses related to information practice, information ethics, Indigenous information initiatives, and information policy. She holds a PhD from the Information School at the University of Washington.

Margaret Ann Noodin is Anishinaabe. She received an MFA in creative writing and a PhD in linguistics from the University of Minnesota. She is currently professor at the University of Wisconsin–Milwaukee, where she also serves as the director of the Electa Quinney Institute for American Indian Education.

Jennifer R. O'Neal (Confederated Tribes of Grand Ronde) is a professional historian and archivist who has led the development and implementation of best practices, frameworks, and protocols for Native American archives in nontribal repositories in the United States. Her research and teaching are dedicated to centering Indigenous traditional knowledge, decolonizing methodologies, applying Indigenous research methods, and implementing place-based education. She specializes in Native American history, political activism and social movements, with an emphasis on the intersections between sovereignty, self-determination, cultural heritage, and global Indigenous rights. She advocates for centering Indigenous priorities, perspectives, and knowledges into education, history, and archives. O'Neal currently serves as the university historian and archivist at the University of Oregon and affiliated faculty with Native Studies, Robert D. Clark Honors College, and the History Department. She previously served as the head archivist at the Smithsonian's National Museum of the American Indian in Washington, DC.

Bernard C. Perley is Maliseet from Tobique First Nation, New Brunswick, Canada. He is associate professor in the Department of Anthropology at the University of Wisconsin-Milwaukee, where he teaches courses in linguistic anthropology and American Indian studies. He received his PhD in Anthropology from Harvard University.

Abigail Shelton works at the Snite Museum of Art at the University of Notre Dame, overseeing a grant-funded digital collections project. Previously she served as the assistant to the librarian at the American Philosophical Society. She has graduate degrees in history and library science.

Michael Silverstein was Charles F. Grey Distinguished Service Professor of Anthropology, Linguistics, and Psychology, and director of the Center for the

Study of Communication and Society at the University of Chicago. He completed his undergraduate and graduate studies at Harvard University (BA, 1965, linguistics and romance languages; PhD, 1972, linguistics), and was elected to Phi Beta Kappa and Sigma Xi. He was a junior fellow of Harvard's Society of Fellows (1969–72 in anthropology and linguistics), and has held Guggenheim (1978) and MacArthur (1982) fellowships, as well as a wide variety of resident fellowships and visiting faculty appointments in the United States, Australia, Europe, and Japan. He is a fellow of the American Academy of Arts and Sciences (1991), a fellow of the American Association for the Advancement of Science (2011), and a resident member of the American Philosophical Society (2008). He received the 2014 Franz Boas Prize of the American Anthropological Association for "exemplary service to anthropology." Silverstein's research, writing, and teaching have ranged across language structure and function, the anthropology of language use, sociolinguistics, semiotics, language and cognition, language ideology, language history and prehistory, and the history of the social sciences.

Justin Spence is assistant professor of Native American Studies at the University of California, Davis. His research focuses on Native American languages and linguistics, especially Dene languages of California and Oregon, drawing on data from archival sources and original fieldwork with contemporary speech communities.

Patrick Spero is the librarian and director of the American Philosophical Society Library and Museum in Philadelphia. As a scholar of early American history, he specializes in the era of the American Revolution and has published over a dozen essays and reviews on the topic. He is the author of *Frontier Rebels: The Fight for Independence in the American West, 1765–1776* (Norton, 2018) and *Frontier Country: The Politics of War in Early Pennsylvania* (University of Pennsylvania Press, 2016) and the edited anthology *The American Revolution Reborn: New Perspectives for the Twenty-First Century* (University of Pennsylvania Press, 2016). Prior to his appointment at the American Philosophical Society, he taught at Williams College, where he served on the faculty of the History and Leadership Studies Department and received recognition for his integration of new technology in the classroom.

Mark Turin is associate professor in the Department of Anthropology and the Institute for Critical Indigenous Studies at the University of British Columbia in Vancouver. For over twenty years his regional focus has been the Himalayan region (particularly Nepal, northern India, and Bhutan), and, more recently, the Pacific Northwest.

Cheryl Tuttle is a member of the Yurok Tribe of Yurok/Karuk ancestry. An ITEPP graduate of Humboldt State University working in education since 1985, principal of Round Valley Elementary/Middle School, and director of Native studies for the Round Valley Unified School District, she has implemented and taught Wailaki since 2014.

Glenn M. Wasicuna is from Sioux Valley Dakota Nation in Manitoba. A fluent first-language speaker and writer of the Dakota language, he has twenty years of experience teaching Dakota language and developing curricula for K–12, postsecondary, and adult Dakota-language programs in the United States. His credentials include teaching certification from the South Dakota Department of Education with a K-12 Dakota-Lakota-Nakota endorsement, and completion of a course in Dakota language methods at Sisseton Wahpeton Tribal College. He has taught Dakota language and developed curricula for all four Dakota communities in Minnesota, as well as for Sisseton Wahpeton Tribal College, Gustavus Adolphus College, and Minnesota State University, Mankato. Wasicuna serves as a Dakota language and curriculum consultant with programs at the Flandreau Sioux Tribe in South Dakota, the Santee Sioux Tribe in Nebraska, the Spirit Lake Dakota Nation in North Dakota, the University of Minnesota, the Children's Museum of Southern Minnesota, and the Minnesota Historical Society.

Gwen N. Westerman lives in southern Minnesota, as did her Dakota ancestors. Her roots are deep in the landscape of the tallgrass prairie and reveal themselves in her art and writing through the languages and traditions of her family. Her essays and poetry have appeared in *Albany Government Law Review*, *Modern American Environmentalists*, *Sovereign Traces*, *New Poets of Native Nations*, *Poetry Magazine*, *Yellow Medicine Review*, *Water-Stone Review*, *A View from the Loft*, and *Natural Bridge*. An enrolled member of the Sisseton-Wahpeton Oyate and citizen of the Cherokee Nation, she is professor in English and director of the Humanities Program at Minnesota State University, Mankato. She is the author of *Follow the Blackbirds*, a poetry collection in Dakota and English, and coauthor of *Mni Sota Makoce: Land of the Dakota*, a history of Dakota land tenure in Minnesota. Neither of her parents spoke English before they were sent away to boarding schools in Oklahoma and South Dakota, so she knows the importance of the role language plays in who we are.

Bethany Wiggin is founding director of the Penn Program in Environmental Humanities (PPEH). She is associate professor of German and comparative literature and an affiliated faculty member in the English Department at the University of Pennsylvania. Her seminar on sustainability and utopianism is the first at the university to integrate the humanities and natural sciences. She also regularly teaches on topics including environmental humanities theory and practice, cultural and literary translation, and European and American literary and cultural history.

INDEX

Page numbers in italics indicate illustrations

Abbe Museum, 55
Abenaki Confederacy, 355
ACORNS project, 136
acoustic epistemology, 377, 388
Adelung, Frederick, 197–98
Administration of Native Americans (ANA), 33, 37
Adolph, Art, 320, 342n52
Advocates for Indigenous California Language Survival, 481
AkChin HimDak Ecomuseum, 446
Alaska Native Language Archive, University of Alaska, Fairbanks, 481
Alexander, Pete, 320–21, 322, 324
Algonquian languages, 99, 168, 198, 355
alphabets: for Dakota, 288–89; for Niimíipuu, 230–32; for Penobscot, 36–37; and "Uniform Orthography," 230, 271n12. *See also* writing systems
American Anthropological Association (AAA), 164
American Antiquarian Society (AAS), 204, 215–16n11

American Association for the Advancement of Science (AAAS), 170
American Board of Commissioners for Foreign Missions (ABCFM), 227, 232, 234; literacy campaign of, 228–30
American Indian boarding school system, 78, 172, 228
American Indian Sign Language (AISL): Boas study of, 158, 171; collections of material on, 158–59, 168–69, 174–75; documentation of, 176–79; early descriptions of, 164–66; as endangered, 156–57, 161; film dictionary of, 171–74; as full-fledged language, 166–68, 173–74; history of, 159; Mallery study of, 158, 169–70; Plains Indian variety of, 159–64; research on, 168–70; revitalization efforts for, 157, 175. *See also* Plains Indian Sign Language (PISL); sign language
American Museum of Natural History (AMNH), 2, 85

503

American Philosophical Society (APS): and Boas, 25, 480; Center for Native American and Indigenous Research (CNAIR), xiii, 13, 27, 88, 318, 339n17, 485; digitization of Native American collections by, 26–27, 53; and Du Ponceau, xii, 16, 25, 71, 191, 194, 207; first period at, 480; Franz Boas Papers at, xii, 25, 299; *Gathering Voices* exhibition at, xii, 189; Historical and Literary Committee of, 71, 189, 197, 200–201, 203; history of, xii, 2, 71; Indigenous communities using materials at, xiii; and intellectual property, 26, 27, 51–52; and Jefferson, xii, 2, 25, 69–70; mandate of, 378; Native American Advisory Board at, xiii, 18, 27; Native American collections of, xii–xiii, xv, 26–27, 33, 53, 71, 103, 115, 158, 164, 311; Native American Scholars Initiative, 27; "Protocols for the Treatment of Indigenous Materials," xiii, 27, 485; salvage paradigm of, 17, 200–201; sign language documentation at, 158, 164; Translating Across Time and Space symposium at, xi–xii, 2, 189, 462

American Revolution, 364, 367–68

American Sign Language (ASL), 19, 180n3; and AISL, 156, 166–67, 179n2

Anderson, Gary Clayton, 286

Andrews, Judith, 436, 453n3

animal stories: in *Numipuain Shapahitamanash Timash*, 239–41; of St'át'imc, 329–30. *See also* Coyote stories

Anishinaabemowin (Ojibwe) language, 359, 436, 438; translation from, 370–71; translations into, 352, 355, 356, 357

Anishinaabemowin (Ojibwe) people, 4, 307

anthropocentrism, 391–92

anthropology, 138, 170, 312, 446; collaborative, 435, 446–47; and cranial studies, 81–82; cultural, 8, 64; Deloria description of, 25, 26; four-field model of, 64; and "hunter-gatherers," 25, 63, 78–82; and intellectual property, 43; and language, 8–9, 157, 158; and salvage ethnography, 7, 17, 82–83, 105, 377, 434

Archambault, JoAllyn, 446

archives: agency in, xiv, xv; and accessibility, 12, 18, 46, 52, 86–87, 109–10, 201, 311, 318, 444, 449, 480–82; colonial heritage of, 32–33, 69–82, 194, 426, 480; and communities, xiv, 87–89, 111–16, 305–6, 483–84, 486; and copyright, 33–34, 46–48, 50–52; digital, 101, 317–18, 481–82, 485–86; Indigenizing of, 479–80; and language revitalization efforts, 18–19, 66, 311, 391, 449, 481–87; and museums, 47, 486–87; reciprocity as central to mission of, 485; terminology change in, 483; three periods of, 480–82; transformation of role of, xiv, 2, 18–19, 481–82, 484–85; of Wailaki language, 401–2, 419n14; of Yuchi language, 84–87. *See also* American Philosophical Society (APS); Smithsonian Institution

Archives of Traditional Music, Indiana University, 85

assimilation, 9, 189, 376; forced, 391, 431; linguistic and cultural, 180–81n7, 194, 198, 327, 430

Assiniboine (A'aniinen) people, 161, 167

Association of Tribal Archives, Libraries, and Museums (ATALM), 9, 482

Atapucha, 438, 440

Athabaskan languages, 79, 375, 400, 401, 404, 405, 415, 474; lexical units in, 407

audio recordings, 305; in Penobscot, 3, 39; in Tsaľálhmec, 336; in Wailaki, 401; in Yuchi, 67–69

Augustana College, Center for Western
  Studies, 299
Axtell, Horace, 227

backtranslating, 471–72
Balbi, Adrien: *L'Atlas ethnographique*, 210
Baldwin, Daryl, 482–83
Bancroft, George, 207
Barbour, James, 78
Barnett, Maxine Wildcat, 76
Basso, Keith, 122
BC Hydro, 314, 317
Beinecke Rare Book and Manuscript
  Library, 2, 27–28, 99–118; Cherokee
  collaborators of, 12–13, 28, 100, 110; and
  community-based transcription, 101–2,
  112–14; digitization of Cherokee material by, 28, 101; Kilpatrick Collection at,
  100–106; Mi'kmaw hieroglyphic texts
  at, 13, 27, 100, 117, 114–16
Bella Bella Community School, 127–28
Belt, Tom, 12, 113, 382, 383, 387, 388–89
Bible, 228–29, 380; Cherokee translation
  of, 230, 381, 383; Niimíipuu translation
  of, 247, 248; picture stories from, 232,
  273–74n26
Bigler, Joshephine Wildcat, 76
Binford, Lewis, 473
Black, Henrietta, 354, 372n5
Black, Samuel, 231
Blackfoot Confederacy (Niitsítapi), 161,
  167, 168
Blackfoot (Siksiká) people and language,
  161, 167, 168
Blood (Káínaa) people, 161, 167
Boas, Franz, 19, 63, 64, 305, 323, 341n45;
  "Americanist Tradition" of, 17–18; and
  APS, 25, 486; career of, 183n45; collaboration with native speakers bt, 16,
  311; four-field model of anthropology
of, 64; and Indian sign language, 158,
  171; papers of, xii, 18, 299, 318, 339n17;
  "Salish Notes" by, 326–27; salvage
  ethnography of, 7, 17, 82–83, 105; skulls
  provided by, 81
Bopp, Franz, 203
botanical terms, 441–43
Boudinot, Elias, 103, 200, 379, 396n2
Breath of Life (BOL) workshops, 2, 9, 400,
  416, 433, 481; collaborative methodology
  of, 482–84; for Wailaki, 403–5
Brinton, Daniel, 71
British Sign Language (BSL), 180n3
Brown, David, 203–4, 212
Brown, Jim, 68
Bryce, Cheryl, 310
Buck, Clayton, 442
Bureau of American Ethnology (BAE,
  originally Bureau of Ethnology), 79, 80,
  168, 169–70, 434

Cabeza de Vaca, Álvar Núñez, 163
Cahwee, Mose, 73
Campbell, Lyle, 162–63
Canadian National Railway (CN Rail), 314,
  317, 321
caribou, 15, 461–62, 472–74
Carter, Cecil, 227
Cash Cash, Phillip, 231, 241, 271n5, 277n71
Cass, Lewis, 78
Catherine the Great (Catherine II), 16, 69
Catholic prayers, 114–15
Center for Native American and Indigenous Research (CNAIR), 88, 318,
  339n17, 485; establishment of, xiii, 13,
  27; Translating Across Time and Space
  symposium of, xi–xii, 2, 189, 462
Champlain, Samuel de: *Les Voyages de la
  Nouvelle France*, 210
Charley, Karen, 443–44

Cherokee language, 27–28, 375, 379–80; Bible translated into, 230, 381, 383; community-based transcription of, 112–16; deciphering of texts in, 107–8; digitization of material in, 28, 101, 112; education programs in, 102, 114, 390–91; literacy in, 103; metaphors in, 377, 386–87; print culture in, 103; program at Western Caroline University, 390; syllabary of, 100, 105–6, 112–13, 381–82; translation of, 381–85; writing system of, 102–3, 117, 381–82

Cherokee Nation, 114, 213; and Christianity, 381–82; conception of music and sound in, 388–90; conception of translation in, 382–85; removal (Trail of Tears), 103, 382; and sensitive archival material, 109; use of English by, 102

Cherokee Singing Book, 11–12, 381, 385–87; Cherokee conceptualizations contained in, 385–86, 388–90; and language revitalization, 392–93; missionaries' purpose in preparing, 384; selected terms from, 394–96

Chickasaw language, 205

Chipeway (Chippewa) people and language, 156, 178, 192

Choctaw language, 84, 205

code talkers, Indigenous, 65–66

Collaborative Language Research Institute (COLANG), 482, 487n8

collecting practices: as colonial project, 32–33, 64, 69–82, 90, 194, 426, 480; Jefferson as promoter of, 6–7, 45, 46, 69–71, 80, 158, 433; and National Museum of Natural History, 434, 442; and salvage paradigm, 7, 17, 46, 64, 71–72, 77, 82–84, 91, 105, 200–201, 377, 378, 434; and Smithsonian, 103, 168–69, 175; by Yuchis, 25, 63, 69, 79–80, 83, 85, 91, 93;

collective memory, 358, 450–51

colonialism: and collection of Indigenous material, 32–33, 64, 69–82, 90, 194, 426, 480; and copyright, 43–48; intellectual, 82; neocolonialism, 359, 361; rationales for, 71–76; settler colonialism, 32–33, 43, 50, 52, 307.

commensuration, 383, 386

community collaboration: and archival collections, xiv, 87–89, 111–16, 305–6, 483–84, 486; and awareness of language endangerment, 481; and capacity building, 376; in evaluation of programs, 146–47, 148; in Hopi Pottery project, 443–45; and language revitalization, 2–3, 4, 8, 9, 143, 144–45, 149, 376, 377, 481, 483–84; with museums, 430–31, 435–45, 450; in *Papt ku Gwenis* project, 309, 316–17, 318; in Recovering Voices program, 432, 433, 443–45, 448, 451; in research, 53–54, 88–89, 142–43, 144–45, 150, 483; in transcription, 101–2, 112–16; in Wailaki program, 402–3

Community Research Program (CRP), and Recovering Voices, 432, 433, 448, 451; and Hopi Pottery project, 443–45

computers, 134, 149; databases, 40, 55, 128, 174, 449–50; and social media, 135–6, 141, 415. *See also* online data sharing

A Concise Dictionary of the Indian Tribes of North America (Leitich), 72

Confederacy of Cultural Education Centers, 146

copyright, 27, 33–34, 42, 51–52, 56; and colonialism, 43–48; definition of, 48–49; and language, 49–50; and public domain, 45; and sound technology, 49, 58n30; and sovereign immunity, 52

Corbiere, Alan, 436, 437
Corbiere, Mary Ann, and Recovering Voices, 436, 437
Corntassel, Jeff, 310
Coyote stories, 11, 276n56, 342n52; in *Numipuain Shapahitamanash Timash*, 237–39; and *Papt ku Gwenis*, 325–26, 348n52
cranial studies, 81–82
Crawford, James M., 86
creation stories: in *Numipuain Shapahitamanash Timash*, 243–45; and *Papt ku Gwenis*, 319
Creek people and language, 205, 210, 211–12
Crook, Harold, 227, 255
Crow (Apsaalooke) people, 161, 167
crowdsourcing, 112, 147, 148
cultural centers, 146, 402, 445–46, 485
cultural sensitivity, 108–11
Curtis, Edward, 46
Cyber PowWow, 140–41

Dakota Grammar with Texts and Ethnography (Riggs), 289
Dakota language: development of writing system for, 287–93; dictionary for, 293; orthography of, *193*; translation project from, 297–302
Dakota people: books about history of, 286; forced removal of, 13, 287, 292, 302; treaties with U.S., 291–93; and U.S.-Dakota War, 194, 285, 286, 293–94
Dakota Pipeline, 307, 369.
The Dakota Prisoner of War Letters, 297–98
Dakota prisoners: letters written by, 13, 192, 194, 296–302; mass hanging of, 295–96; relocation of, 296; trial and imprisonment of, 294–95
Dana, Carol, 35
Dana, Susie, 35–36

databases, 40, 55, 449–50; of botanical terms, 14, 442, 448; GRASAC knowledge-sharing, 436; Miami-Illinois Digital Archive, 449, 483; open-source, 128, 174
Davis, Florene, 227
Declaration of Independence, 366–67
Declaration of the Lillooet Tribe, 322, 324–25
decolonization, 21, 390; language revitalization as, 6–10, 22, 56, 376. *See also* colonialism
Deloria, Ella, 305
Deloria, Vine, Jr.: on anthropologists, 25, 26; on emotional provocation, 359, 360, 363, 370; on experiential history, 21, 350, 351; on textbook histories, 350
Dene. *See* Athabaskan languages
Densmore, Frances, 437
diffusionism, German, 323, 342n64
digital archiving, 40–42, 101, 110, 317–18, 449–50, 481–82, 485–86. *See also* online data sharing
digital divide, 125, 128, 129
Digital Endangered Languages and Musics Archives Network (DELAMAN), 482, 486
digital knowledge sharing, xiii, xviii, 18, 20, 302
digitization: and accessibility; 112, 116, 134–35, 140, 173, 298–300, 485–86; and collaboration, 13, 28, 41–42, 144; best practices for, 142–43; by American Philosophical Society, 26–27, 53; of Cherokee language texts, 28, 101, 112; of Dakota letters, 302; of Penobscot material, 40, 53, 54; technologies, 99–100, 138–39, 142, 415–16
Diidxazá language: dictionary for, 441–43; ethnobotanical database in, 448
Dishta, Joseph, 446
Documenting Endangered Languages (NEH program), 89

Driver, Myrtle, 387
Du Bois, W. E. B., 6
Dunbar, William, 158
Du Ponceau, Peter Stephen: and APS, xii, 16, 25, 71, 191, 207; biographical information, 200; correspondence network of, 189, 191, 197–98, 203–4, 213–14; and Gallatin, 209–12; and Heckewelder, 201–2; and Humboldt, 204, 207, 209–10; and James, 207, 208–9; letter to Jefferson by, 200, 201; and Lieber, 207–8; *Memoire sur le système grammatical*, 209; and Perez, 205–6; and Pickering, 202–3, 206–7; Prix Volney prize won by, 208; and Vater, 204, 205; and Von Hammer, 206

Eastern Band of Cherokee Indians, 102, 109, 396
Eastman, Charles, 286, 302n2
Educators for Social Justice Network, 370
effigy mounds, 359, 360
Eliot, John, 202, 228–29, 230
Ellis (Niimíipuu chief), 247–48
Endangered Languages Documentation Programme (ELDP), 482
evaluation: community-grounded, 146–47, 148; gap in, 136–38
Experiencing Native North America, 20, 351; experiential history in, 350, 351, 360–61, 371; installations, 353–54, 359–60; objectives of, 354; translations in, 355–58

fair use, 52
Film Dictionary of Indian Sign Language, 171–72
Feeling, Durbin, 110
Finney, Archie, 305
First Annual Intergenerational Hopi Pottery Festival, 444–45

First Nations and Endangered Languages Program, University of British Columbia, 128
The First Nations Principles of OCAP (ownership, control, access, possession), 21
First Nations Schools Association, 146
First People's Cultural Council, 135, 139
FirstVoices, 135, 139
fishing: and St'át'imc way of life, 310–11; Wanapum techniques of, 440–41
Folwell, William, 286
Fragnito, Skawennati Tricia, 140–41
Francis, Hartwell, 110–11, 113
Frank, Dan, 470–71
Frank, Robert, 465
Franklin, Benjamin, 2, 366, 372n10
Franz Boas Documentary Papers and Project, xii, 18, 299, 318, 339n17
Frasier, James Earle, 75–76
funding, 27, 39, 180n5, 298, 449, 486; for community language revitalization projects, 90–91, 92, 150; imbalances in, 89–90; models of sustainable, 144–45; for technology-based projects, 130, 481–82

Gallatin, Albert, 78, 210, 221n67; Du Ponceau exchange of letters and books with, 209–12; and Ridge, 212–13; *Synopsis of Indian Tribes*, 71
Gallaudet, Thomas H., 166
Gathering Voices exhibition, xii, 189
Gatschet, Albert, 79, 83–84
genocide, 22–23n4, 74, 77, 78; cultural, 63, 64
Geographical and Geological Survey of the Rocky Mountain Region, 79
Gilcrease Museum, 103
Goddard, Ives, 163, 412
Goddard, Pliny E., 378, 401, 407, 408, 409–10, 411

Goldfrank, Esther, 171
Goldtooth, Larson, 445
Great Lakes Research Alliance for the Study of Aboriginal Arts and Culture (GRASAC), 9, 435–38
Greene, David, 230, 278n13
Gwenis (salmon), 312–15, 335
"The Gwenis Lady That Turned into a Rock," 320–22, 324
Gwich'in language: documentation project on, 461–62; translation of, 464–72
Gwich'in people: and traditional knowledge, 15, 461–62, 472–74

Haas, Mary, 40, 43
habitat destruction, 438–39
Haida language, 135
Hallalhotsoot, 232, 233, 234, 244, 245, 246, 248–49
Hamelin, Augustin, Jr. (Kanapima), 208–9
Handbook of North American Indians (Smithsonian), 91
Hans Rausing Endangered Languages Project, 89, 91
Hardin, Margaret, 446
Harmon, Daniel Williams, 211
Harrington, John, 170, 171
Hawaiian language, 147, 230; revitalization programs in, 129–30
Hawkins, Benjamin, 204–5
Hays-Gilpin, Kelley, 445
Heckewelder, John G. E., 16, 71, 191, 201–2, 204–5, 210
Heiltsuk Nation, 19; Cultural Education Center, 127; language and culture initiatives by, 126–28
hieroglyphics: Mi'kmaw, 13, 27, 100, 114–16, 117
Historical and Literary Committee (HLC), 197, 203; formation of, 71, 189; salvage project of, 200–201; *Transactions* of, 201, 202, 204, 210
historical narratives, 236–37, 363; and identity, 362–63; and trauma, 35, 41, 50, 362–69, 371
Hopi: Cultural Preservation Office (HCPO), 443–44; Oral History Project (HPOHP), 427, 443–45; pottery, 14–15
Housty, Rory, 141
Hudson's Bay Company, 231, 272n17
Humboldt, Alexander von, 204, 207, 209–10
Humboldt State University: Cultural Resources Center at, 402
Hunt, George, 16–17, 19
Hupa language, 405, 408, 410–11, 412–13, 414
Hymes, Dell, 462

Indiana University, 85
Indian Primer (Eliot), 228–29, 230
Indian Sign Language. *See* American Indian Sign Language (AISL)
Indian Sign Language Council of 1930, 171–74
"Indigenous disappearance" narrative, 71–76, 191, 198, 212, 213, 378
Indigenous Language Digital Archive (ILDA), 449–50
Indigenous languages, and loss, 3, 28, 35, 40, 50, 78
Indigenous language suppression, 65–66, 125, 130, 172, 380
Institute of Museum and Library Services (IMLS), 485–86
intellectual property, 26, 33–34, 36, 57n17, 149; and colonialism, 43–48; Penobscot efforts for, 40, 42–43, 53–54. *See also* copyright
internet: indiginizing, 140–41; as medium, 132–33. *See also* online data sharing
Inuit-Nunavut people, 161

Ireland, Emmeline, 438, 440
Iroquois (Haudenosaunee), 162, 355, 367, 372n10; language of, 198, 210, 220n51
Ite Wakan Hdi Ota, Moses, 296–97

Jackson, Andrew, 84
James, Edwin, 207, 208–9, 219n45
Jefferson, Thomas, 76, 201; and APS, xii, 2, 25, 69–70; collection and documentation efforts of, 6–7, 45, 46, 69–71, 80, 158, 433; Du Ponceau letters to, 200, 201; and Lewis & Clark expedition, 77, 165; *Notes on the State of Virginia*, 69, 80; "Sign Language of the Indian Nations to the West of the Mississippi River," 164–65
John, Qwalqwalten Garry, 324
Johnson, Ron, 362
Jones, Evan, 382
Jones, William, 305
Journal of Voyages and Travels into the Interior (Harmon), 211

Kahe, Valerie, 443–44
Kauder, Christian, 115
Keetoowah Society, 104
Kendall, Daythal, 26
Keresan Pueblo, 161
Kilpatrick, Alan, 106, 107, 109, 382; *The Night Has a Naked Soul*, 108
Kilpatrick, Anna Gritts and Jack, 104–5, 106, 108, 110; *Notebook of a Cherokee Shaman*, 109
Kilpatrick, James J., 74–75
Kilpatrick Collection of Cherokee Manuscripts, 103–4; cataloging of, 100, 106; challenges to access of, 108–11; community-based transcription of, 101–2, 112–16; culturally sensitive nature of, 108–11; digitization of, 101, 112; diversity of material in, 103–4, 111; Mi'kmaw hieroglyphic texts in, 114–16; origins of, 104–6
kinship ties, 1–2, 289, 292
Kisima Inŋitchuŋa, 141
Klamath language, 79
K-Net, 132
Koyiyumtewa, Stewart, 443
Krauss, Michael, 88–89, 406
Kroeber, Albert, 158, 170
Kroeber, Alfred, 408
Kübler, G. F., 385
Kuratu, 438, 440
Kuwanwisiwma, Leigh, 443, 445

Lambertino, Lorenzo Tlacaelel, 404
language: academic analysis of, 86; anthropologists' view of, 8–9, 17, 306; changes to over time, 8, 438; and copyright, 49–50; and culture, 38, 54–55, 65, 418, 447–48, 450; and identity, 9–10, 65; Indian Sign Languages as, 166–68, 173–74; as living, 67–68, 306; loss of, 3, 28, 35, 40, 50, 74, 105, 310, 363, 371, 399, 432, 439; as more than itself, 7–8; and music, 387–88; ownership of, 5–6, 10, 49–50; and power relations, 194, 198–99, 213; suppression, 65–66, 125, 130, 172, 380; and worldview, 54, 377, 430
language *revitalization*: and authenticity, 417–18; best practices of, 136–37; and Breath of Life workshops, 2, 9, 400, 403–5, 416–17, 433, 481, 482–84; challenges of, 405–15; for Cherokee, 12–13, 390–91, 392–96; and collective memory, 358, 449–51; and community collaboration, 2–3, 4, 8, 9, 143, 144–45, 149, 376, 377, 481, 483–84; culture's ties to, 54–55, 65, 418, 447–48, 450; database use in, 14, 40, 55, 128, 174, 436, 442, 448, 449–50, 483; as decolonization,

6–10, 22, 56, 376; and digitization, 19, 40–42, 128, 131–32, 137, 148, 449–50; documentation's relation to, 49–50, 89–90; evaluation of, 136–38, 146–47, 148; funding for, 27, 39, 89–91, 92, 130, 144–45, 150, 180n5, 298, 449, 481–82, 486; for Hawaiian, 129–30; of Heiltsuk, 126–28; lexicalization strategies in, 411–14; and museums, 430—31, 435–45, 448–52; for Nimipuutímt, 227; notions of authenticity in, 400–01, 417–18; and oral history, 13–14; for Penobscot, 3–4, 26, 34–42, 54–56; as reclamation, 380–81, 400, 479–81, 483–87; and Recovering Voices program, 426, 429–30, 431–45, 448, 450–51, 452; role of archives in, 18–19, 66, 311, 391, 449, 481–97; for St'át'imc, 309–11, 338n2; technology use in, 4–5, 126–27, 130–32, 133–36, 138–39, 145, 146, 148; tools for, 19–20; for Tsal'álmec, 327–34; urgency of, 6, 7, 125, 180n7, 306, 349; for Wailaki, 375, 400, 402–3, 411–16; widespread nature of, 375–76; for Yuchi, 74–75, 76, 85–87

Láwa Gwenis Ceremony, 326–27
Le Clercq, Chrestien, 115
Leitch, Barbara, 72
Levitt, Martin, 26–27
Lewis and Clark expedition, 77, 158, 165–66, 230
Library of Congress, 486; Abraham Lincoln Papers at, 299; Penobscot collection at, 33, 55
Li Fang-Kuei, 378, 401–2, 408, 409–10
Lillooet Pictographs (Teit), 329–30, 332, 333
Lincoln, Abraham, 295, 303n20
Line of Proclamation, 365, 366, 373n11
lingua franca, 160, 161, 163–64
linguistics: changes in discipline of, 447; Enlightenment project of, 16; and Indigenous communities, 64–65, 88–89; value-neutral pretensions of, 82. *See also* salvage paradigm
Linguistics in a Colonial World (Errington), 65
Lipan Apache, 79–80
literacy, 103, 111; missionaries' efforts for, 228–30, 270–71n5, 380; and Niimíipuu, 230–32, 234–36, 245–49
Little Turtle, chief, 205
Local Contexts project, 55
Locke, John, 44
Long, Stephen H., 158, 166
Louisiana Purchase, 76
Lucio, Otto, 446

MacDougall, Pauleena, 35
Maillard, Pierre, 115
Makah Cultural and Research Center, 446
Malenfant, Jacques Julien Robert, 202
Maliseet language, 354–56; translations into, 307, 352, 357–58
Mallery, Garrick, 182–83n43; biographical information, 182n40, 183n45; and Indian sign language, 158, 169–70
Mandan-Hidasta (Moennitarri), 161, 167
manifest destiny, 73–74, 363
"The Man Who Became a Caribou," 471–72
Marias massacre (1870), 77
Maricopa people, 212
Mason, Lowell, 385
Massachusetts Historical Society, 215n11
master-apprenticeship programs, 147
McChesney, Lea, 443, 444
McCoy, Tim, 431, 453n3
Menominee people and language, 307, 355–56, 359
Merriam, C. Hart, 378, 401, 409–10, 419n14
Mesa Media, 444–45
metadata, 54–56, 112–13, 174, 480, 483, 486

INDEX 511

metaphors: of endangered language, 213, 448; as mode of expression, 10–11; in sign language, 174; social, 1, 310–11, 339n7; of sound, 12, 377, 386, 387–88; and translation, 15, 463–64
Miami-Illinois Digital Archive, 449, 483
Miami people and language, 205, 212
Michel, Gerald, 335
Mi'gmaq language group, 136
Migwan, Crystal, 436
Mi'kmaw hieroglyphics, 13, 27, 100, 117; described, 114–16
Milwaukee Indian Community School, 2, 354
Minnesota Historical Society (MNHS), 2, 298, 299
Minnesota History Center, 287, 298
missionaries: and Bible translations, 232, 273–74n26, 380; colonial project of, 234, 242–43, 377; conversion approaches of, 384; and Dakota, 288–90, 291–92, 297; and Indigenous animal stories, 238–40; linguistic knowledge emerging from, 11, 212; literacy efforts of, 228–30, 270–71n5, 380; modification of Indigenous languages by, 379–80; and Niimíipuu, 235–36, 246; publication of primers by, 227, 270n2; Western historical thinking instilled by, 230–31
mobile technologies, 133–36, 149
Mohawk: language, 198; Prayer of Thanks, 307–8
Mohegan language, 205
Mooney, James, 105, 384, 389; "The Sacred Formulas of the Cherokees," 108
Moore, Gordon, 132
Moreton-Robinson, Eileen, 43, 44
Mother Tongue Film Festival (MTFF), 431, 432–33
Mountain Chief (Nena-es-toko), 172

Mukurtu digital tool, 485
museums, 429–55; and collaborative revitalization efforts, 430–31, 435–45; collections of ethnographic objects by, 434–35; and cultural revitalization, 446; and intellectual property, 47; revitalization programs as necessity for, 448–52; tribal, 13. See also Smithsonian Institution
music, 385, 388–90
Music Modernization Act, 47, 58n30
Muskogean languages, 210, 211–12
Myaamia Center, 483

Nakoda-Lakȟóta (Tetonwan) people, 161, 167
Naokwegijig-Corbiere, Mary Ann, 436, 437
Nash, Phil Tajitsu, 440
Natchez language, 210–11, 212
National Anthropological Archives (NAA), 85, 158, 168, 175; and Recovering Voices project, 430, 431–32
National Archives, 174–75, 299
National Breath of Life Archival Institute for Indigenous Languages, 433
National Endowment for the Humanities (NEH), 27, 449, 486; Documenting Endangered Languages grants of, 89, 481–82; Scholarly Editions and Translation Program of, 298
National Museum of Natural History (NMNH), 3, 14, 175, 437, 439, 448; botany department at, 441, 453n19; collections, 434, 442; and Hopi pottery project, 444, 445; National Anthropological Archives of, 85, 158, 168, 175, 430, 431–32; Q?rius center at, 431; and Recovering Voices, 426, 429–30, 431–32, 450
National Museum of the American Indian (NMAI), 431–32

National Science Foundation, 461, 481–82
Native American Graves Protection and Repatriation Act (NAGPRA), 68, 92
Navajo, 161
Neerihíinìk: We Traveled from Place to Place, 463
neocolonialism, 359, 361. *See also* colonialism
Never Alone, 141. *See also* Kisima Inŋitchuŋa
New Kituwah Academy, 390–91
New-York Historical Society, 215n11
The Night Has a Naked Soul (Kilpatrick), 108
Niimíipuu (Nez Perce) people and language: and language revitalization, 227; and literacy, 230–32, 234–36, 245–49; and missionaries, 235–36, 246. *See also* *Numipuain Shapahitamanash Timash*
North American Languages Protection and Repatriation Act (NALPRA), 92–93
Northeastern State University (Oklahoma), 102
Northern Piegan or Peigan (Aapátohsipikáni) nation, 161, 167
No Wife, Andrew, 103–4
Numipuain Shapahitamanash Timash, 227–69; animals and animal stories in, 239–41; coyote stories in, 237–39; cross-cultural nature of, 191–92, 233–34; historical narrative in, 236–37; literacy lesson in, 234–36; making of, 232–34; morality tales in, 241–43; song of creation in, 243–45; translation into English of, 227; "Yehóova 'óykalanm hanyaw'aat," 243–44, 269
Numipuain Shapahitamanash Timash lessons: Himte'ke's V, 234–35, 251–52; Himte'ke's VI, 236, 253; Himte'ke's X, 237, 254–55; Himte'ke's XI, 237, 259; Himte'ke's XIII, 236, 258; Himte'ke's XIV, 236, 260; Himte'ke's XV, 235; Himte'ke's XVI, 235;

Himte'ke's XVII, 235; Himte'ke's XX, 239, 261; Himte'ke's XXI, 240, 256–57; Himte'ke's XXII, 239, 262; Himte'ke's XXIX, 241, 264–65; Himte'ke's XXX, 241, 263

Obama, Barack, 364
Office of Indian Affairs, 78
Ojibwe. *See* Anishinaabemowin (Ojibwe) language
Okiya, Wanmdi, 289, 290, 291, 300
Olbrecht, Frans, 105
O'Neal, Jennifer R., "The Right to Know," 482
Oneida (Onyota'a:ka) people and language, 161–62, 307, 355, 359
online data sharing, 29, 40, 110, 116, 125–26, 147, 416, 462–63, 469, 474; Google Drive, 462–63, 469, 474; Google Sheets, 147, 416
orthography. *See* alphabets; writing systems
ownership, control, and possession. *See* First Nations Principles of OCAP, 21

Papt ku Gwenis project, 306–7, 334–35, 336; as community effort, 309, 316–17, 318; and digital heritage repository, 317–18; and elders' stories, 318–26; methodology of, 312; as revitalization and decolonization, 309–11; and transformer myths, 319–22, 324, 341n5, 341n47; vision statement of, 315
Patrick, Aggie, 329
Penobscot language: alphabet in, 36–37; archival collections in, 33–34, 50–52; audio recordings in, 3, 39; Dana tapes in, 35–36, 37; dictionary for, 36, 37–38, 41, 57; digitization of material in, 40, 53, 54; Penobscot Nation as cultural authority of, 54; revitalization program for, 3–4, 26, 34–42, 54–56

Penobscot Nation: as authority for Penobscot language, 54; and copyright question, 26, 34, 36, 47–48, 51–52, 57n14; Collections Project, 54–56; Cultural and Historic Preservation Department of, 36, 41; intellectual property efforts of, 40, 42–43, 53–54; Tribal Council of, 48
Perez, Don Pedro, 205–6
Pérez-Baez, Gabriela, 14, 426, 441, 482–83
Peters, Desmond, Sr., 309, 314
Phillips, Ruth, 9, 436, 437
philology: Goddard definition of, 406; Heckewelder view of, 201–2; networks in, 197–214; racialized, 80, 199. *See also* linguistics
Philosophical Society of Washington, 170
Pickering, John, 202–3, 204, 206–7, 230
Pixem muta7 i7was, 334
Plains Indian Sign Language (PISL), 19, 122, 159–62; as full-fledged language, 173–74; lexical similarity studies of, 166–68. *See also* American Indian Sign Language (AISL)
Pond, Gideon, 287–88, 289
Pond, Samuel, 287–88, 288–89
Pontiac's Revolt, 365
Post, Lee, 472, 473
Potlatch Law, 17
Powell, John Wesley, 46, 71–72, 80, 434
Powell, Timothy, xiii, 26
power relations, 14, 52, 55, 122, 377; and language, 194, 198–99, 213
Prix Volney, 208
property law, 44, 46–47, 58n25. *See also* intellectual property
prophetic movement, 231, 273n22
Prosser, Morris, 318, 324, 337
"Protocols for the Treatment of Indigenous Materials" (APS), xiii, 27, 485

Quebec Act, 365–66
quillwork, 433, 436, 437, 438
Qwa7yán'ak (Elder Carl Alexander), 322, 324, 327, 335–36

Rafinesque, Constantine S., 208
Ralph Rinzler Archives, 485
Ramsey, Alexander, 294
Rand, Silas, 114
Rask, Rasmus, 205
reciprocity: of kinship, 291, 292, 293; of relationships, 15, 312, 326, 369, 444
Recovering Voices program, 426, 429–30, 448, 450, 453n3; and collaborative revitalization, 435–45, 452; Community Research Program of, 432, 433, 443–45, 448, 451; mission of, 432; origins of, 431–35; programmatic branches of, 432–33; value of objects shown by, 450–51
removal, 73, 211, 375; of Cherokees, 103, 382; of Dakota, 13, 287, 292, 302
Renville, Joseph, Sr., 288, 289
repatriation, concept of, 447, 444n30
reservations, 79, 83, 296, 402
Resource Network for Linguistic Diversity, 135
Ridge, John, 212–13
Riggs, Stephen Return, 288, 289, 291–93, 294
Roberts, Maggie, 466, 467, 469, 470–71
Rogers, Cornelius, 246, 274n31; and *Numipuain Shapahitamanash Timash*, 232, 233, 234, 241, 243, 244, 245
Rolland, Ann, 85
Round Valley High School (RVHS), 400, 402–3, 416, 418

Sacagawea, 165
sacred landscapes, 358–59, 360–61, 439
"Salish Notes" (Boas and Teit), 326–27

salvage paradigm, 46, 71–72, 77, 91, 377, 378, 436; of APS, 17, 200–201; of Boas and students, 7, 17, 64, 82–84, 105
Samper, Cristian, 431, 432
Sanderville, Richard, 172, 173
Sapir, Edward, 46, 480
Say, Thomas, 204–5
Schienke, Rachel, 299
Schoolcraft, Henry Rowe, 16, 71, 209, 433
Schoolcraft, Jane Johnston, 16
Scott, Bessie, 227
Scott, Hugh Lennox, 158, 171, 172–73, 184n50
Sequoyah (George Guess), 102–3, 381
Seton and Anderson Lakes, 309, 312–14, *316*
settler colonialism, 32–33, 43, 50, 52, 307. *See also* colonialism
Seven Years' War, 364–65, 372n10
Sibley, Henry, 294
Siebert, Frank, 3, 40, 41, 43, 46; biographical information, 35, 49; collection, 50–52; dictionary of, 38–39
sign language: history and origins of, 159, 162–63; as lingua franca, 160, 161, 163–64; misconceptions about, 175. *See also* American Indian Sign Language (AISL); American Sign Language (ASL); Plains Indian Sign Language (PISL)
Simms, Maxey, 85
Siouan languages, 168, 205, 220n51
situational fluency, 411–12
Smith, Asa Bowen, 246, 274nn30–31, 276–77n62, 277n65; and *Numipuain Shapahitamanash Timash*, 232–33, 234, 243, 244, 245
Smithsonian Institution, 2, 169; Arctic Studies Center of, 451; Bureau of American Ethnology of, 79, 80, 168, 169–70, 434; Center for Folklife and Cultural Heritage of, 485; collections of Native American items at, 103, 168–69, 175; Documenting Endangered Languages program of, 89; history of relationship with Native Americans, 433; Human Film Studies Archives, 168, 175; National Anthropological Archives of, 85, 158, 168, 175, 430, 431–32; National Museum of the American Indian of, 482; natural history collection of, 14; Transcription Center, 102. *See also* National Museum of Natural History (NMNH); Recovering Voices program
social media, 135–36, 415; Twitter, 136, 141
Social Sciences and Humanities Research Council (SSHRC) of Canada, 7, 19, 130, 137
Society for the Indigenous Languages of the Americas (SSILA), 486
Sonneck, Vera, 227
sound: Cherokee conceptions of, 385, 386–87, 388–90; metaphors of, 12, 377, 386, 387–88; technology, 49, 58n30. *See also* audio recordings
Southern Piegan or Montana Blackfeet (Aamsskáápipikani), 161, 167
Spalding, Eliza, 246
Spalding, Henry Harmon, 232, 246, 273–74n26
"Speaking the Language of Spiders" (Maskegon-Iskwewhe), 140
Species at Risk Act (SARA), 325, 343n74
Speck, Frank G., 40, 43, 46, 84–85
Spiess, Arthur, 473
Sqayt Culture Camp, 306–7, 328–30, 334, 338n2
Standingdeer, Jackson, 104
Standing Rock, 369. *See also* Dakota Pipeline
St'át'imc people, 306, 309, 336; elders' stories of, 318–26; Láwa Gwenis Ceremony of, 326–27; laws and social institutions of, 310–11

Sullivan-Clinton campaign, 367
Survey of Californian and Other Languages (now California Language Archive), 481

Tanner, John, 209
Tax, Sol, 312
Tea Party movement, 364
technology: archives' use of, 481–82; digital, 138–39, 142, 415–16; further research in use of, 147–49; and language revitalization, 4–5, 126–27, 130–32, 133–36, 138–39, 145, 146, 148; media, 133, 140; mobile, 133–36, 149; and platforms, 145, 146; pre-digital, 141–42; sound, 49, 58n30
Teit, James A., 306, 309, 311, 318, 326–27; *Lillooet Pictographs*, 332, 333; on Lillooet traditions, 329–30; political-activist support by, 322–23, 324–25; on transformer stories, 319–20
temporality, 349–51; Cherokee concepts of, 335–36
Terry, Willie, Sr., 316–17
This American Life, 296
Tip, John, 401, 403
Tobique First Nation, 360
Tolowa language, 404, 408, 410, 412, 414
Toulouse, Myna, 436, 437, 437, 438
Toulouse, Theodore, 436, 437, 437, 438
traditional knowledge (TK) label, 55–56. *See also* Mukurtu digital tool
traditional stories: of animals, 239–41, 323–24; and Gwich'in, 461–62; and Indigenous schooling, 393; of St'át'im elders, 318–26; transformer, 319–22, 324, 341n5, 341n47. *See also* Coyote stories
Transcribe@Yale, 99–100, 101, 102, 113–14, 117
transcription: community-based Cherokee, 101–2, 112–14; of Dakota, 299, 301, 302; of Wailaki, 401–2, 406, 408–11, 413, 415

Translating Across Time and Space symposium, xi–xii, 2, 189, 462
translation: from Anishinaabemowin, 370–71; into Anishinaabemowin, 352, 355, 356, 357; and backtranslation, 471–72; of Bible, 224, 381, 383; from Cherokee, 381–85; consultation with fluent speaker in, 470–72; and culturally based education, 390–96; culture and worldview embodied in, 8, 38, 352, 382–85, 391–93; from Dakota, 297–302; in *Experiencing Native North America*, 355–58; from Gwich'in, 463–72; into Maliseet, 307, 352, 357–58; and missionaries, 232, 273–74n26, 380; of *Numipuain Shapahitamanash Timash*, 227; poetry compared to, 462–63; as reparative, 121–22; of treaty language, 292–93; and verbal negotiation, 474–76; from Wailaki, 378
transliteration, 106, 108, 301; systems of, 112
treaties, 291–93
tribal heritage and preservation offices (THPOS), 435
Truth and Reconciliation Commission (Canada), 7
Tsal'álh people and language, 310, 324; children's story of, 327–34
Tukupe, 438, 440

U'mista Cultural Center, 446
"Uniform Orthography for the Indian Languages of North America," 230, 271n12
United Keetoowah Band, 102, 109
United States Constitution, 368, 373n15
United States–Dakota War, 194, 285, 286, 293–94
University of British Columbia (UBC), 2, 128
University of California, Berkeley, 400, 481
University of Iowa: DIY History site at, 102
University of Maine, 33, 53, 55

University of Massachusetts Amherst, 115, 117n17
University of Oklahoma, 103
University of Wisconsin-Milwaukee, 370
Upper St'át'imc language, 306. See also *Papt ku Gwenis* project; St'át'imc people
Upper St'át'imc Language Culture and Education Society (USLCES), 338n2

Valentine, Rand, 436
Vater, Johann S., 204, 205
Voegelin, Carl, 158, 170
Volkswagen Stiftung, 89
Von Hammer, Joseph, 206

Wabanaki Confederacy, 355
Wagner, Günther, 85, 95n42
Wailaki language: about, 375, 401; archival vocabulary lists and recordings in, 401–2, 419n14; collaborative revitalization efforts for, 415–16; and community involvement, 402–3; as "extinct," 375, 400, 403; high school teaching of, 400, 402–3, 416; morphological complexity of, 407–8; transcription practices in, 408–11; translation project in, 378
Waldayu Mobile, 134–35
Walker, Deward, 231, 273n22
Walk in Your Soul (Kilpatrick and Kilpatrick), 106
Walum Olam, 208
Wanapum Tribe, 440–41
Want, Rolinda, 404, 417
Warrington, Mary, 356
Washburn, k'asA Henry, 75, 87
Washington, George, 69, 367, 372n10

Wasicuna, Glenn M., *Mni Sota Makoce: The Land of the Dakota*, 291–92
Watkuweis, 272n16
Wauja people, 438–39
Webster, Noah, 229
West, LaMont, 158, 170
Western Carolina University, 110, 114, 375
Wet'suwet'en people, 369
White, Samuel, 205
Williams, Eleazer, 198, 212
Williamson, Thomas, 288, 289, 291, 296
Wisconsin Indian Education Association, 370
Worcester, Samuel, 11, 375, 379–80, 381, 383–84, 385
word borrowing, 412
Wounded Knee massacre (1890), 77
writing systems: Cherokee, 102–3, 117, 381–82; Dakota, 287–93. *See also* alphabets
Wyaco, Rose, 446
Wyena, Patrick, 442

Xaxlíp (Fountain), 320

Yale University. *See* Beinecke Rare Book and Manuscript Library
Yana Yahi, 77–78
Young, Lucy, 403
Yuchi language, 83–84, 86, 210–11 402, 403, 413; about, 66–67; archival collections of, 84–87; grammar on, 85, 95n49; recordings in, 67–69; revitalization efforts for, 74–75, 76, 85–87; vocabulary of, 85, 212; Yuchi Language Project, 76, 85
Yuchi people, 6, 25, 72–73

Zeisberger, David, 71
Zuni people, 439, 446

In the New Visions in Native American and Indigenous Studies series

Ojibwe Stories from the Upper Berens River: A. Irving Hallowell and Adam Bigmouth in Conversation
Edited and with an introduction by Jennifer S. H. Brown

Ute Land Religion in the American West, 1879–2009
Brandi Denison

Blood Will Tell: Native Americans and Assimilation Policy
Katherine Ellinghaus

Ecology and Ethnogenesis: An Environmental History of the Wind River Shoshones, 1000–1868
Adam R. Hodge

Of One Mind and Of One Government: The Rise and Fall of the Creek Nation in the Early Republic
Kevin Kokomoor

Invisible Reality: Storytellers, Storytakers, and the Supernatural World of the Blackfeet
Rosalyn R. LaPier

Indigenous Languages and the Promise of Archives
Edited by Adrianna Link, Abigail Shelton, and Patrick Spero

Life of the Indigenous Mind: Vine Deloria Jr. and the Birth of the Red Power Movement
David Martínez

All My Relatives: Exploring Lakota Ontology, Belief, and Ritual
David C. Posthumus

Standing Up to Colonial Power: The Lives of Henry Roe and Elizabeth Bender Cloud
Renya K. Ramirez

Walking to Magdalena: Personhood and Place in Tohono O'odham Songs, Sticks, and Stories
Seth Schermerhorn

To order or obtain more information on these or other University of Nebraska Press titles, visit nebraskapress.unl.edu.

www.ingramcontent.com/pod-product-compliance
Lightning Source LLC
Chambersburg PA
CBHW021812300426
44114CB00009BA/141